Auditing:
A Conceptual Approach

W. Thomas Porter, Jr.
University of Washington

John C. Burton
Columbia University

Wadsworth Publishing Company, Inc.
Belmont, California

L. C. Cat. Card No.: 70-133915

Printed in the United States of America

1 2 3 4 5 6 7 8 9 10—75 74 73 72 71

Preface

Auditing: A Conceptual Approach, a textbook that includes cases and readings, is designed for the first course in auditing at the college level. We have written this book with the particular intent of satisfying the needs of those interested in changes in auditing objectives and techniques. Our basic premise is that auditing is related to the information system of the organization audited and not only to its financial statements. The conventional audit report, therefore, should be only one of the outputs of the review of an information system.

Both authors of this book have themselves been practicing CPAs on the audit trail; both have had responsibilities in staff training and development for national public accounting firms; and both today consult with large public accounting firms. In the course of this work we have been confronted with a large number of auditors, some of whom perform audits of financial statements through the verification of account balances, while others perform creative evaluations of the information flows in the firm. It is our strong feeling that auditors of the latter class are performing a function far more valuable to their clients and to society.

Over the years, we have seen the accounting profession attract an increasing number of the creative type of auditor, and we are convinced that a significant trend exists toward this evaluative type of audit. The literature of auditing, however, and in particular the textbooks, are largely committed to the traditional approach. We feel that since the systems approach to auditing that we suggest in this book is the wave of the future and increasingly the practice of the present, it warrants more attention in the literature of the profession: Hence this book.

In the development of our ideas about the audit function, it will become clear that we are including a combination of current practice and hypotheses about the future development of those practices. We are writing about both what is and what may be, and this is something which the reader must bear in mind as he studies this book.

In writing the book we have tried to identify and distinguish between our reporting of the present and our extrapolations of trends into the future. Nevertheless, in our selection of material it is clear that our biases must show, and we have excluded a great deal of traditional auditing material from this volume because we feel that neither the auditor of today nor the auditor of the future will need it. For those who wish to expose their students to more of the conventional wisdom, and for those who wish to emphasize auditing material from current CPA examinations in auditing given by the AICPA, we recommend the use of supplemental material, from either articles or texts, to present this point of view. Our bibliography provides the reader with such references.

Our belief in a new order of priority in auditing dictated the organization of our book. In Section 1, we set the stage for our ideas by introducing the material on the nature of the professional practice and the historical development of the audit function. In Section 2, we present our basic analytical approach to auditing. Here we develop the conceptual framework for an audit and consider some of the tools which the auditor will need for gathering evidence in performing his function. In Section 3, we examine the methodology needed to perform an audit and trace these techniques through the firm's various data cycles. In Section 4, the final section, we discuss the auditor's reports on the information system, devoting one chapter to reporting in its current framework and a second to reporting as it may develop from the audit approach that we suggest.

Since there is a considerable amount of literature on the systems approach to management and auditing, it seems presumptuous to present only our own views. Accordingly, our text includes a number of articles and documents which we feel are an essential supplement. And because the practice of auditing that we suggest differs from the conventional approaches in many ways, we felt that it was also desirable to include a substantial amount of case material so that the implementation of our ideas could be discussed in a practical framework.

In summary, therefore, our attempt is dedicated to the training of today's outstanding auditor and tomorrow's only auditor. We hope that it will be but the first step in the development of a substantial body of literature and teaching materials aimed in this direction.

We would like to acknowledge our debt to those who reviewed the manuscript: Charles Lawrence, Purdue University; John H. Myers, Indiana University; Oswald Nielsen, Stanford University; John W. Soha, University of Oregon; Robert R. Sterling, the University of Kansas. Of course, we accept full responsibility for any errors or omissions.

Contents

1

Chapter 8   Gathering Evidence: Using the Computer   231

3

Chapter 9   Auditing the Information System   315

4

1

Chapter 1

The CPA
and His Environment

Without information a society's ability to harness scientific achievement would be enormously reduced. Society would be atomized and the efficiencies of specialization would be severely curtailed. Each community would have to reinvent the wheel many times. The waste of human effort in an informationless society would be very great.

It is clear, therefore, that society has a major stake in the development and maintenance of an effective system of information dissemination and retrieval in its broadest sense. This is true of course not only in pursuing economic efficiencies, but also in achieving the type of society in which we wish to live. The mere availability of information about activities tends to make them more effectively and honestly performed. It is no coincidence that dictatorship and freedom of the press have seldom existed together.

Information is a key element in the efficient functioning of economic society. This is true whether the society is centrally controlled or is pluralistic with many loci of economic power.

Information needed is of many sorts. The availability of goods and services must be described, as must the sources of demand for these services. Opportunities for employment must be communicated to the labor force. Forecasts of economic trends and evaluations of the effectiveness of resource use must also be developed. The list could go on indefinitely.

Role of Financial Information

Much of the information necessary to the effective operation of the economic segment of a society can be presented in terms of a common denominator: money. Such a common denominator allows the application of a single system of measurement to many diverse economic phenomena, enabling a comparison of the alternative uses of economic assets. Thus, while this conversion may occasionally lead to confusion between the monetary system and economic reality, a generally accepted medium of exchange translatable into a system of measurement makes financial information of great significance to the operation of an economy.

Within the business sector of the economy, where a significant portion of our wealth is ultimately being developed, financial information plays two particularly important roles. First, it provides the means by which choices can be made among the myriad demands for resources. This is true from both the manager's and the investor's viewpoints. Within a business entity, management must allocate a finite supply of resources to create the maximum amount of wealth. Financial information indicates to the investor in securities the areas where his funds may most profitably be committed. Not only will this help him to maximize his return, subject to whatever risk constraints he uses, but it will also serve to channel new investment funds into the parts of the economy where they can be most productively used.

The second principal function of financial information within the business economy is to provide a means of evaluating success in the use of economic resources. Within the firm, the corporate manager is able to measure the performance of his subordinates by examining their ability to add to the firm's wealth and by testing them against whatever other criteria he has established. Financial information makes it possible for investors and other interested parties to evaluate the stewardship of the managers of corporate assets, and in this fashion the society as a whole can determine whether or not its assets are being effectively invested by a corporation and effectively used. In addition, the canons of disclosure tend to protect society against unethical behavior and to some extent against the use of assets for purposes unacceptable to the public consensus.

The Functions of the Public Accountant

The public accountant is in the financial information business, and within this area he has three principal roles: to verify the accuracy of information, to report the results of his investigations, and to consult with management.

Perhaps the best-known function of the accountant is auditing.

Broadly speaking, auditing is undertaken to increase the reliability of information, where reliability may be defined as congruence between the message transmitted and the reality being described. Auditing may beneficially take place, therefore, whenever a review of information by a party other than the preparer increases the probability that it accurately reflects what it purports to. Though this objective relates auditing to information, it by no means limits its scope to financial information or, even more restrictively, to financial statements. In some cases, it is conceivable that the information to be audited may not be an explicit statement but perhaps an implicit representation by a management—such as that controls are adequate.

Given the objective, increasing the reliability of information, the following definition of auditing is suggested: Auditing is the examination of information by a third party other than the preparer or user, with the intent of establishing its reliability, and the reporting of the results of this examination with the expectation of increasing the usefulness of the information to the user.

Auditing Defined

Within the framework of this definition, many types of information may be audited by many different third parties. But the most common audit performed by the public accountant is of the financial statements of a business enterprise. This audit has for its end product a report on the fairness of these statements.

In this role, the public accountant evaluates one product of the financial-information system of the firm: the published financial statements. He then gives his professional opinion on whether or not they give a fair, adequate description of the company in the language conventionally used to describe such entities. This opinion is made public in the form of a report and lends the authority of the public accountant as an outside expert to the company's financial statements, thus increasing the reliability of the statements.

In order to evaluate financial statements the public accountant must combine three things: a thorough knowledge of the company and its operations, a complete familiarity with its information system, and an awareness of the principles of measurement and communication conventionally used to describe economic entities.

Since the public accountant must become well versed in the operations of the firm he is auditing, he must become an expert in the kind of information used by management as well as that data ultimately presented in financial statements to the public. This is because he must be able to evaluate the information system of the firm as a whole in order to determine its reliability for producing adequate measurements of the totality of firm activities.

The Management Consulting Function

Because the accountant must combine a thorough knowledge of the firm, a knowledge of its information system, and general competence in the area of understanding and using information, it is not surprising that he has regularly and increasingly been called upon to supply advice to management on the means of controlling the operations of the firm. Growing numbers of public accountants have been cast in the role of management consultants, primarily in the area that develops financial-information and control systems, but to some extent in much broader areas as well. While "management services" have always been a part of an audit, they have become increasingly significant in recent years; for the audit has ceased to relate primarily to the checking of numerical figures in a report and has become increasingly an evaluation of the firm's total system of internal control, with particular emphasis on its system of information flows.

Summary

As one looks to the future, it seems clear that the interdependent functions of evaluating financial statements and evaluating information systems will lead to increasing emphasis of and demand for the public accountant's services in the area of financial-information processing and use. As this trend continues it appears more than likely that the reporting function of the public accountant will be broadened somewhat to make available to the public the results of his audit in its fullest scope.

Introduction to Readings

In this chapter, the role of the CPA in the economic environment was introduced. Both the audit and consulting functions of the CPA are integral parts of the professional practice of accountancy, and the dual role of the CPA is being increasingly recognized by both the profession and the public.

An official description of the practice of certified public accountants, the first reading accompanying this chapter, was developed by the Planning Committee of the profession's national association, the American Institute of CPAs, and was approved by the governing body of that organization in 1967. It indicates the breadth of activity encompassed by the accounting profession today.

The common view of the CPA, however, has generally emphasized the audit function. This is where the CPA presents himself to the public as an expert in financial reporting and by attaching his imprimatur to a set of financial statements lends his reputation in support of their reliability. It is this role that puts the "public" into "certified public accountant."

The second article accompanying this chapter is probably the best-known summary of this role. It was written by Herman Bevis, then senior partner of Price Waterhouse & Co. It effectively develops the traditional view of the importance of the attest function and it indicates certain directions in which this function may expand.

American Institute
of Certified Public
Accountants

A Description of the Professional Practice of Certified Public Accountants

Certified Public Accountants practice in the broad field of accounting.

Accounting is a discipline which provides financial and other information essential to the efficient conduct and evaluation of the activities of any organization.

The information which accounting provides is essential for (1) effective planning, control and decision making by management, and (2)

Reprinted by permission from the American Institute of Certified Public Accountants. Copyrighted 1966.

Approved by Council at the meeting of October 1, 1966 as an official statement of policy of the American Institute of Certified Public Accountants.

discharging the accountability of organizations to investors, creditors, government agencies, taxing authorities, association members, contributors to welfare institutions, and others.

Accounting includes the development and analysis of data, the testing of their validity and relevance, and the interpretation and communication of the resulting information to intended users. The data may be expressed in monetary or other quantitative terms, or in symbolic or verbal forms.

Some of the data with which accounting is concerned are not precisely measurable, but necessarily involve assumptions and estimates as to the present effect of future events and other uncertainties. Accordingly, accounting requires not only technical knowledge and skill, but even more importantly, disciplined judgment, perception and objectivity.

Within this broad field of accounting, certified public accountants are the identified professional accountants. They provide leadership in accounting research and education. In the practice of public accounting CPAs bring competence of professional quality, independence, and a strong concern for the usefulness of the information and advice they provide, but they do not make management decisions.

The professional quality of their services is based upon the requirements for the CPA certificate—education, experience and examination—and upon the ethical and technical standards established and enforced by their profession.

CPAs have a distinctive role in examining financial statements submitted to investors, creditors and other interested parties, and in expressing independent opinions on the fairness of such statements. This distinctive role has inevitably encouraged a demand for the opinions of CPAs on a wide variety of other representations, such as compliance with rules and regulations of government agencies, sales statistics under lease and royalty agreements, and adherence to covenants in indentures.

The examination of financial statements requires CPAs to review many aspects of an organization's activities and procedures. Consequently they can advise clients of needed improvements in internal control, and make constructive suggestions on financial, tax and other operating matters.

In addition to furnishing advice in conjunction with their independent examinations of financial statements, CPAs are engaged to provide objective advice and consultation on various management problems. Many of these involve information and control systems and techniques, such as budgeting, cost control, profit planning, internal reporting, automatic data processing, and quantitative analysis. CPAs also assist in the development and implementation of programs approved by management.

Among the major management problems depending on the accounting function is compliance with tax requirements. An important part of the practice of CPAs includes tax planning and advice, preparation of tax returns, and representation of clients before government agencies.

CPAs also participate in conferences with government agencies such as the Securities and Exchange Commission, and with other interested parties, such as bankers.

Like other professional men, CPAs are often consulted on business, civic and other problems on which their judgment, experience, and professional standards permit them to provide helpful advice and assistance.

The complexities of an industrial society encourage a high degree of specialization in all professions. The accounting profession is no exception. Its scope is so wide and varied that many individual CPAs choose to specialize in particular types of service.

Although their activities may be diverse, all CPAs have demonstrated basic competence of professional quality in the discipline of accounting. It is this which unites them as members of one profession, and provides a foundation for extension of their services into new areas.

Herman W. Bevis

The CPA's Attest Function in Modern Society

The attest function results in the expression of an opinion by an independent expert that a communication of economic data by one party to another is fairly presented. Discharge of the function lends credibility to the representation and increases reliance upon it. The opinion implies (if it does not so state) that the data presented are appropriate for the purpose of the representation, that there is objective evidence underlying the data, and that the judgments exercised in interpreting the data are such as to justify the opinion.

What social need does the attest function fulfill in modern society? What is the attest function's probable and potential future course? What part does the CPA play in it now; what is his future role? Discussing these questions is the purpose of this paper. It may be well to set the stage for the discussion, however, by first defining some of the terms.

The text of this article was prepared by Mr. Bevis, but the material and ideas were developed in sessions of the long-range objectives committee of the American Institute. The committee, of which the author was chairman in 1961, then included Norton M. Bedford, Clifford V. Heimbucher, and Robert M. Trueblood, with John L. Carey serving as secretary.

"Economic data" consist of "material serving as a basis for discussion and inference pertaining to the management of the affairs of a government or community with reference to the source of its income, its expenditures, the development of its natural resources, etc."[1] The attest function is most frequently applied to data of individual political or economic units which, in the aggregate, make up a government or community. Economic data, which include economic activity and position, relate to resources—their source, nature, quantity, accumulation, allocation and exhaustion. The data can be expressed in various quantitative terms, including monetary. Although the attest function has in the past usually been utilized primarily in connection with monetary data, the subsequent discussion of its elements will indicate that there is no basis for an exclusive relationship. On the contrary, the function is applicable to economic data expressed in any quantitative terms.

The term "attest function" has been deliberately chosen for this discussion in preference to some such term as "independent audit function." One reason is that the latter

[1] See definitions of "data" and "economic" in Webster's New International Dictionary—Second Edition (Unabridged).

may still be interpreted by some laymen as applying to a process of meticulous detailed checking, searching for fraud, etc. Moreover, the term "attest function" (the root of which means to bear witness) seems particularly descriptive of the independent auditor's relationship to data communications. While in the minds of some the term may be narrowly associated with "truth" or "facts," as used here it is also considered applicable to expressions of judgment.

The CPA as a trained observer of economic activities, relationships and status is the most appropriate agent to discharge the attest function. His competence has been identified by a state authority. His position as independent auditor, which involves a peculiar responsibility to third parties, is not assumed by those in private employment. Other "auditors" (e.g., revenue agents, bank examiners, etc.) are affiliated with the users of data and their objectives and scope of activity are different from those involved in the discharge of the attest function. While the CPA's attest function is most frequently encountered in opinions on financial statements submitted to investors and creditors, as has already been indicated its use is not and should not be so confined.

The remainder of this paper is divided into three principal parts: first, a review of the present utilization of the attest function in this country and abroad and a catalog of some questions which arise from the review; second, a close look at the social purpose of communications of economic data and of the attest function related thereto, in the hope that these fundamentals will help answer some of the questions and point the way to the CPA's potential for future contributions to society; and, finally, an enumeration of some of the potential areas of expanded service and possible

areas of action by CPAs to accomplish their full social purpose.

The Use of the Attest Function Abroad

The writer has corresponded with associates in a small sample of countries abroad in an attempt to assess the degree to which the attest function has been locally developed elsewhere. By "locally developed" is meant the use of the function in connection with enterprises financed by capital generated within the country and managed by its citizens. Enterprises financed from another country, say the United States, are not necessarily dealt with, since the use of the function in connection with these enterprises would generally follow the custom in the U. S. The writer's observations resulting from a review of this correspondence are set out below.

The use of the attest function in other English-speaking countries—Australia, Canada and England—appears to be more extensive than in the U. S. It is applied to communications of financial data to investors by a greater variety of issuers because of statute or custom. Beyond that, it seems almost instinctive that reports from those handling other people's money be attested. Taxing authorities frequently call for the attested report to stockholders. There seems to be a widespread consensus as to appropriate standards for the measurement and communication of financial data.

Among Italy, France, the Netherlands, Switzerland and West Germany there are widespread differences in the manner and extent to which the attest function is both called upon and discharged. Statutory requirements for its use vary from all-inclusive to none. The dictates of custom show a wide range. In some cases, the independent auditor's opinion on financial statements is furnished to management but not used by the latter to add credibility (the end purpose of the attest function) in reports to investors. There is sometimes a disparity between statutory requirements for widespread application of the function, and the obviously inadequate qualifications required of those bearing the independent auditor designation or the clearly inadequate number of those who are unquestionably qualified. The consensus as to standards appropriate for communications of financial data seems to be far less clear than in the English-speaking countries.

The review of the attest function's role abroad suggests that the following are among the factors which have influenced its development and use:

Making for Greater Use	Making for Lesser Use
Widespread ownership of enterprises	Ownership concentrated in few hands, even for large enterprises
Highly industrialized society	Some industry, including a few large organizations, but most productive capacity resting in small units
Industry mostly privately owned, and mostly regulated by competition	Government participation greater through regulation and, sometimes, ownerships
Accounting standards for reporting to stockholders and creditors fairly well developed and applied	Little consensus as to accounting standards for reporting to stockholders and creditors

Since all of the factors enumerated above making for greater use are descriptive of conditions in the United States, it is pertinent to turn to that country.

Use of the Attest Function in the U.S.

The CPA's attest function, although widely employed in the United States, has an uneven usage. The following summary demonstrates this in connection with major types of communications of economic data:

Reports to stockholders. Attest function required for commercial and industrial companies in communications via the SEC and certain stock exchanges. Also required for electric, gas and certain other utilities but not for railroads and insurance companies (although used voluntarily by some of the latter).

Used unevenly by banks, to a fair extent by unlisted and unregulated widely owned companies and to a lesser extent by narrowly owned companies.

Reports to creditors. For long-term indebtedness: If registered with the SEC, the use of the attest function follows along the lines of reports to stockholders; its use in reports to bond trustees and institutional bondholders varies and is frequently confined to ratios, current asset levels and other selected data; it is rarely used for bond issuers which are governments or their instrumentalities.

For short-term indebtedness, such as to commercial bankers, the requirement for use appears to depend upon the policy of the institution and to vary from a rigid requirement of all borrowers, to borrower's option.

Reports to regulatory and supervisory authorities. Use of the attest function appears to vary by industries, or laws from which the authority derives, and the differences may derive partially from historical accident.

Reports to taxing authorities. The attest function is not legally required nor voluntarily used. (The CPA's participation in tax return preparation, and settlement of taxes, is presently more in the nature of advice and assistance rather than the discharge of the attest function.)

Reports by Governmental bodies to taxpayers. The attest function is used to a limited extent by municipalities and counties, and perhaps to a somewhat greater extent by Governmental authorities and instrumentalities.

Internal reports. The attest function is used to some extent by owner-managed companies, the degree appearing to vary proportionally to the size of the enterprise. For the large public companies, it is used in a few cases—mostly for subsidiaries or branches abroad or otherwise remote from the headquarters of the organization.

Considering the attest function's purpose and its significance to the user of financial and other economic data, the discrepancies in the above recital seem curious. This is particularly true in view of some of the trends which are in evidence.

As stated at the outset, the purpose of the attest function is to lend credibility to the representations of one party to another. The use of the function is increasing sharply. More and more of those handling other people's money are realizing that the attest function of CPAs may relieve them of responsibility which they would otherwise have to assume.[2]

The expansion of use of the attest function for small businesses is gaining impetus from the requirements of creditors.[3] There are signs that commercial credit grantors are now scrutinizing audited financial statements of prospective borrowers in addition to merely ascertaining their credit ratings. Credit agencies have been giving consideration to indicating in their reports whether or not financial data presented have been audited by CPAs and what kind of opinion has been issued. The emerging influence which the attest function is exerting in modern society seems clear. Yet its use is still uneven. Why?

Reasons for Uneven Use of the Function. Probably at least one or more of four causes explains the nonuse of the attest function where a useful purpose could be fulfilled:

1. The user of data believes he can satisfy himself sufficiently as to the data's credibility.
2. There is the mistaken impression that the attest function is being discharged.
3. Users may be ignorant as to the role and value of the function.
4. The user feels that the independent auditor either does not comprehend, or does not subscribe to, the accounting standards which he considers appropriate for the data he desires.

Under the first point, users undertaking the responsibility for satisfying themselves as to data's reliability and conformity to standards suitable to them include:

The owner-manager of an unaudited enterprise

The directors of an unaudited enterprise

Commercial lenders who consider that their intimate knowledge of the borrower's enterprise, and appraisal of the character of owners and management, are either more important than financial data or an assurance as to reliability of data, or both

Federal, state and local taxing authorities

Some Governmental regulatory or supervisory authorities

---

[2]John L. Carey, "The Next 50 Years," *The Ohio Certified Public Accountant*, Winter, 1959, pp. 7–14.

[3]Robert E. Witschey, "What's Ahead for the Accounting Profession," *Massachusetts CPA Review*, October 1959, pp. 22–35.

Each of these users, to the extent that he satisfies himself as to data he receives, does so only with regard to his own needs. Data suitable for his purposes are not necessarily appropriate or adequate for other purposes or for other groups of people.

Regarding the second point, many users of financial data, even some directors and members of management, believe that the attest function is being discharged in their enterprises by examiners from banking, insurance, public utility and other supervisory or regulatory authorities. This notion persists notwithstanding the disclaimers of the authorities themselves that their field of interest is narrower than that required to discharge the attest function for data directed to stockholders and other users. For example, whereas bank examiners primarily concern themselves with liquidity of assets looking toward the protection of depositors, the CPA reporting to stockholders is basically interested in a fair presentation of all financial data bearing on position and results.

Why have some users of data remained ignorant of the role and value of the attest function (point three above)? Perhaps, because of indifference, lack of education or complacency, they don't comprehend fully the part the CPA plays in the scheme of things. It is true that both the usefulness and the limitations of, say, conventional financial statements to investors can be best appreciated only with some knowledge of the techniques and judgments underlying them; this is also true in varying degree for communications of other economic data. With such knowledge, the importance of the attest function becomes clear. Whether the educational process is difficult or not, it assumes paramount importance if the CPA is to make his full contribution to society

in satisfying expanding needs for the attest function.

The fourth reason given above for nonuse of the attest function has to do with accounting standards. It seems probable that the fact that accounting standards can—and should—vary according to circumstances and needs of issuers and users of data has gradually become obscured. What seems to have disappeared from view even more is that review of the appropriateness of accounting standards is an integral part of the attest function.

The foregoing discussion suggests that it may be well to re-examine the nature and purposes of communications of economic data, and to dwell particularly on the role of standards in connection with them. Perhaps this exercise will give some guidance to the CPA in adapting to future calls on the attest function.

Why Are Economic Data Communicated?

A satisfactory system for communicating financial and other economic data is an essential condition for the accumulations of capital from widespread sources in single enterprises— i.e., for a successful industrial economy. Persons having an interest in resources are in various stages of remoteness from them and from the factors which affect them. The greater this remoteness, the greater the need for communication of data. Thus, the small-plot, one-crop farmer can obtain most of the economic data which he needs regarding his changing resources through his physical senses. The individual with extensive farming operations managed by others throughout the world needs many more communications of data. If the latter enterprise is owned by inactive investors, or borrows money, then the receipt of data by investor or creditor becomes even more important. In fact, without assurance of reliable economic data, the remote investor or creditor probably would not supply capital to the enterprise. (The extent of the remoteness also indicates the need for *internal* communication of data.)

The complexity of the resources involved and the events affecting them also evoke communication of economic data. The carnival medicine man needs little communication beyond the information furnished by his physical senses to assess the trend in his resources. On the other hand, the owner of a drug store stocking thousands of different items, and buying and selling on credit, needs a considerable amount of economic data before he can assess the trend in his resources—even if he handles every transaction personally. Thus, the necessity for measuring and communicating economic data can exist in complex situations even though the element of remoteness is absent.

The same elements of remoteness and complexity call for communications of data in connection with regulations, taxes and many other social functions.

The number of economic interrelationships among the units of a society multiplies the communications of economic data. In a primitive agrarian economy, these are few. At the other end of the scale is the highly industrialized United States with its combination of free enterprise, private capital, high rates of taxation, some degree of regulation or supervision over selected economic units, and a national policy of economic growth without severe fluctuations.

Within the United States, the communi-cations of economic data are enormous in scope and quantity. Besides investors and creditors, those to whom a large corporation might direct such communications would include: Governmental regulatory or supervisory authorities, Federal and state; taxing authorities, Federal, state and local; military, other Governmental and private customers where cost is a factor in determining price; courts, in a variety of issues where economic data are pertinent; legislative committees and commissions; suppliers and credit agencies; insurance companies for claims; public and industrial associations and agencies for economic statistics; royalty recipients; labor unions; employees; parties to legal contracts and covenants; and the general public. The small business communicates to fewer parties, of course, but the quantity still looms large to it. Every year the four million business organizations operated in this country create and communicate a vast quantity of economic data. Here are a few examples:

Over twelve million American investors are receiving reports from one or more of 5,000 publicly held companies. About two-thirds of these investors hold securities listed on the New York Stock Exchange.

In a recent year, over 990,000 corporate income tax returns were submitted to the Federal Government.

Under just *one* regulatory statute, the Securities Exchange Act of 1934, over 12,000 annual and other periodic reports were filed by issuers with the SEC in a recent year.

To repeat, satisfactory operation of a highly industrialized society, with its complex of interrelated units, requires the measurement and communication of an extraordinary scope and quantity of economic data.

Keys to Successful Data Communications. Before economic data can be communicated, they must be measured. The whole process of measurement and communication constitutes the accounting function. The end purpose of the function is to convey information to someone in such manner that he may utilize it in formulating judgments and making decisions. Naturally, all rules of basic communication apply.

In any successful communication, a meeting of minds must exist between issuer and user as to the meaning of terms. Before there can be a meeting of minds in the communication of financial and other economic data, these are among the conditions that must be satisfied:

1. The issuer and user of economic data must have an understanding as to standards for measurement and summarization.
2. The issuer must have the requisite knowledge and skills to carry out the antecedent steps leading up to, and to prepare, the communication.
3. There must be absence of bias in the communication (to the extent humanly feasible).
4. The communication must be intelligible to the user.

The importance of the last three conditions is patent; the matter of standards, being more complex, will be examined further. (It will be noted that all four conditions suggest a role for the attest function.)

Agreement on Accounting Standards. Whenever data regarding the quantity of and changes in resources are required for a continuing enterprise, conventions must be established to guide the measurement. Many of these conventions are mere assumptions as to the future and, being such (since the future cannot be accurately foretold), cannot be said to have precision. If periodic reports during an organization's existence (say, of net income) were not required, the assumptions would be unnecessary; the former being required, however, the assumptions are unavoidable. These are the accounting standards—underlying the measurement of economic data communicated—regarding which it is important that issuer and user have a meeting of minds.

There is sometimes a difference of objectives between the issuer and user of data which has a direct bearing upon standards chosen. Where this is known, the attest function cannot be fully discharged until issuer and user come into agreement. (However, the CPA may still be helpful either in isolating and identifying areas in which the two parties must come into agreement or in seeing that the issuer communicates sufficient information that the user may revise the data according to his own standards.) A few illustrations will demonstrate the point.

Income taxing authorities may well be inclined, from considerations of fiscal policy, toward standards for the measurement of annual net profit which result in the earliest possible reporting thereof for taxation. Issuers of data (taxpayers filing tax returns) may be inclined to the opposite. Taxable incomes may be increased or decreased, from considerations of social or economic policy, for all or selected groups of taxpayers, through the adoption by legislative or taxing authorities of standards for measuring net profits which achieve that end. Taxpayer issuers of data may or may not agree with the objectives or the standards suitable for reaching them. Where issuers and users of taxable income data differ as to important standards for their measurement, the standard is usually established by law as interpreted by the courts.

Standards are established under legal authority with judicial interpretation for the measurement of financial and other economic data communicated by utilities to regulating authorities. The regulatory objective is essentially to limit net profit to a fair return on invested capital. Both legislative and regulatory bodies are subjected to conflicting social, economic and political pressures from consumers, investors and managements. The choice among accounting standards for determing net profit or invested capital is sometimes strongly influenced by the dominant pressure. If the issuer of data—the utility—differs as to standards promulgated for his use, again the final authorities are the legislatures and the courts.

The supervisory authority of a banking or insurance institution has as his primary objective the protection of depositors or policyholders. Accounting standards which measure readily realizable assets at minimal amounts, and maximize liabilities, are the most suitable for the objective. The fact that the collateral effect of application of these standards might be distortion of, say, net profit reported to stockholders is outside the field of primary interest of the authority.

Some other important users of financial data, their principal objectives and the basis upon which they would judge the appropriateness of accounting standards, would include those in the following table.

One of the most important groups of users of financial data consists of long-term stockholders in public companies. The standards involved in the measurement and communication of data to this group assume great importance in the private enterprise system. The greatest

User	Objective	Standards Desired To Measure
Short-term creditor	Repayment of loan at maturity	Minimum prospective cash flow, or net assets readily realizable in cash, or both
Government purchasing nonstandard material	Allowance to supplier of specified rate of profit on contract costs and/or on capital employed	Minimum costs allocable to contract or capital associated with it
Purchaser of a business based upon equity or earnings	Lowest purchase price	Minimum equity or periodic earnings

interest of these users of data is the periodic net profit of their enterprise. The accounting standards appropriate for this purpose are essentially the same as those for measuring the extent to which each such privately owned unit has achieved the objective which society has established for it: to create resources in excess of those exhausted—to create economic values—which is another way of saying "to make a profit."

Long-term stockholders in publicly owned companies, unlike most of the other users of data, are largely inarticulate as to the standards most appropriate for their purposes. The role of enunciating these has largely fallen to the American Institute of Certified Public Accountants, acting formerly through its committee on accounting procedure and presently through the Accounting Principles Board.

It will be obvious that standards appropriate for measuring and communicating economic data to satisfy the needs of the long-term stockholder are not all necessarily the most appropriate to meet the needs of the income taxing authority, the regulatory or supervisory body, nor of the other data users which have been mentioned. A crying need exists to clarify the appropriate areas for the application of the many sets of standards which are in use today for the measurement and communication of financial and other economic data. This is also a condition precedent for full utilization of the CPA's attest function.

Proper Discharge of the Attest Function. It might be well at this point to recapitulate the principal conditions which must be met for the attest function to be effective. There must be:

1. Economic data measurable in quantitative terms (such as money, material, labor and time) for which a communication need exists.

2. Standards for measurement and summarization of economic data which are acceptable to the user and practicable of application by the issuer of such data. The attester must be able to satisfy himself that the standards are appropriate for the user's needs if the latter has not participated directly or through representatives in formulating them; if the user has so participated (as, say, in income taxation), the attester must be satisfied that issuer and user are in agreement.

3. Competent evidential matter supporting the economic data, on the nature and validity of which the attester must be able to pass judgment. By examination of such evidential matter, he must be able to satisfy himself as to whether or not established standards for measurement and communication of economic data have been properly applied or complied with. The attest responsibility includes ascertaining that there are no important distortions of data due to bias, ignorance or human error.

4. Agreement by the issuer to disclose all data and other information needed by the user to formulate his judgments and make decisions.

5. Readiness to accept a format for the communication which is comprehensible to the reasonably knowledgeable among the users.

6. Practicability of adequate timeliness in the communication to suit the user's purpose.

7. Independence, objectivity and reliability on the part of the attester.

8. Requisite knowledge and skills on the part of the attester in all important phases of the measurement, substantiation and communication processes which are involved. This includes the exercise of due professional care.

9. Familiarity, on the attester's part, with the purposes of the communication, including appreciation of the user's needs.

These conditions are being satisfied, and the attest function is being discharged, on a constantly widening scale.

Potential Future
of the Attest Function

The imaginations of many have ranged wide as to potential new areas in which the CPA's attest function would be valuable in that all requirements for its utilization exist. Here are some possible areas for the attest function which have been proposed:

1. Attestation of Federal income tax returns.[4]

---

[4]Robert E. Witschey, *The Journal of Accountancy, op. cit.*

2. Certification to business planning (prospective accounting). Since budgetary control already is oriented to the prospective view, it is suggested that this would be as excellent an avenue as any to commence auditing's new future in this field of business planning.[5]

3. The CPA could become a representative of the courts as referee in resolving issues in litigation turning on accounting questions.[6]

4. Congress has been considering independent audits of unlisted ("over-the-counter") companies.[7]

5. Various legislation or proposed legislation involving optional provisions for independent audits involve banks, credit unions, insurance companies, local Government units, labor unions, and trustees of charities, hospitals, nonprofit associations and educational institutions.[8]

6. Audits involving attestation to industrial and/or economic statistical compilations.[9]

7. Use of independent auditors by Government.

The last item merits some elaboration. All signs indicate that the Federal Government will spend, or control the expenditure of, a larger percentage of the gross national product in the years to come. This expansion will result in large measure from the challenge of communism, long-term foreign aid programs, housing, urban and rural redevelopment, education, unemployment benefits, public transportation, old-age security, etc.

Because of this amplified scope of activities, the Government is almost certain to require submission of financial data by an increasing number of private and quasi-private organizations for several basic purposes:

1. To develop acceptable cost data for purposes of Government defense procurement contracts and renegotiation.

2. To provide some protection for Government funds advanced to organizations in the form of loans, grants, insurance, etc.

3. To aid the Government in determining compliance with regulatory statutes (such as those affecting stock-issuing corporations, labor unions, etc.).

4. To afford a basis for the regulation of and/or the setting of rates to be charged by regulated companies (e.g., banks, gas, electric, transportation, insurance and communications companies).

Naturally, it is the public welfare which decides whether or not greater use should be made of the CPA's attest function by the Government. Several sound reasons exist for advocating the use of the function:

1. Regulated areas frequently involve private and quasi-private enterprises which historically have relied on independent auditors. Government "examinations" which ignore the auditor's work result in needless and costly duplication of effort.

2. The independent audit will often provide more useful and reliable information for regulatory purposes than the limited government "examination."

3. Since CPAs are geographically dispersed, substantial economies can be realized by using them at the site of regulated enterprises rather than dispatching Government examiners from a limited number of centers.

[5]Oswald Nielsen, "New Challenges in Accounting," *The Accounting Review*, October 1960, pp. 583–589.

[6]J. S. Seidman, "What is the Future of the Accounting Profession," *The Journal of Accountancy*, March 1959, pp. 29–36.

[7]John L. Carey, "The Next 50 Years," *The Ohio Certified Public Accountant*, Winter, 1959, pp. 7–14.

[8]*Ibid.*

[9]William A. Campfield, "Professional Accounting at the Crossroads," *The Illinois Certified Public Accountant*, Spring, 1961, pp. 1–6.

4. The CPA is not directly affected by the political problems confronting the Governmental agency staff.

5. More than twenty agencies of the Government already use independent auditors (REA and SBIC programs being the best examples).

Because of these and other factors, the accounting profession is entitled to encourage the greater utilization of independent auditors by the Government.[10]

Recently, there have been appearing in professional literature suggestions that the CPA will in due course be undertaking "management audits" and reporting thereon to third parties. These suggestions have coincided with observations by Berle and others as to the concentrations of economic power in the nonowner managers of public companies where the only protection against abuse of this power is a "public consensus." The thought is advanced that society has a growing desire that there be an "accounting" by these managements in nonfinancial as well as financial terms for the authority assumed and responsibilities undertaken—and that enlightened managements themselves would welcome this means of discharging the obligations which they have assumed.

It may well be that the future will see the CPA's services so utilized. However, any such challenges must be reviewed carefully against the conditions under which the attest function makes its contribution: a representation which is communicated; acceptable standards for the measurement and communication; relevant evidence available for examination by the independent auditor; etc. All these may come in the nonfinancial, noneconomic areas. They are not here yet.

Conclusions. The attest function in the United States and other highly industrialized nations of the free world serves an essential purpose in modern society by adding credibility to financial and other economic data via the measurement, substantiation and communication processes.

Discharge of the function in the U. S. is confined largely to the CPA, because of his professional knowledge, skills, stature and other qualifications—including the characteristics of independence, dependability and objectivity.

The social importance of the attest function and the changing economic environment strongly suggest the expansion of its use. To bring this about, it would seem important that these things be done:

1. Educate issuers and users of economic data as to the attest function's purpose, role and value. (This includes eradicating any mistaken impressions held regarding the functions being discharged.)

2. Inform the public and the CPA as to those areas in society where the attest function, although not presently performed, would fulfill a social need.

3. Cultivate judgment in selecting appropriate accounting standards for diverse economic units, issuers, users or purposes, and proper application of the standards chosen. (Included is the development of new or alternative accounting standards where needed.)

The responsibility for these projects lies squarely on the accounting profession.

---

[10]The American Institute as early as 1957 supported Federal legislation providing for independent audits of employee pension and welfare funds. (John L. Carey, "The CPA in a Changing World," *The Illinois Certified Public Accountant,* Winter, 1957–58, pp. 4–10.)

Chapter 2

Characteristics of
the Accounting Profession

Public accounting is one of the major professions that serve the public in the United States. The characteristics of a profession are generally considered to be as follows:[1]

What is a Profession?

1. a body of specialized knowledge;
2. a recognized formal educational process for acquiring the requisite specialized knowledge;
3. a standard of professional qualifications governing admission to the profession;
4. a standard of conduct governing the relationships of the practitioner with clients, colleagues, and the public;
5. recognition of status;
6. an acceptance of the social responsibility inherent in an occupation endowed with public interest;
7. an organization devoted to the advancement of the social obligations of the group.

As was indicated in the first chapter, public accounting is primarily concerned with financial information. Accountants work in many different areas of the financial-information world and there is no narrowly defined

---

[1]Report of the Commission on Standards of Education and Experience for Certified Public Accountants, University of Michigan, 1956.

body of facts that can be sharply outlined to define the bounds of knowledge expected of practitioners. Recent attempts at definition of the body of knowledge that CPAs must possess have all stretched the boundaries of professional requirements beyond those previously contemplated.

The uniform test for accredited entrance into the profession, the CPA examination, tests a candidate in the areas of business law, accounting theory, auditing, and in the ability to do specific accounting problems. The accounting problems and the theory examinations today require a knowledge of tax law. In recent years there has been considerable feeling that questions that relate to the accountant's consulting function and to the information-systems expertise he must develop should be included in the examination, but to date relatively little has been done on this score.

In 1963 the Carnegie Corporation of New York and the American Institute of Certified Public Accountants jointly sponsored a study undertaken by a commission that included an attorney, a banker, a stock exchange official, two college deans, two professors, and five practicing CPAs. This commission was to ascertain what is the common body of knowledge that is required for entrance into the public accounting profession. Research was conducted among practicing accountants, financial executives and educators by interview and questionnaire. The summary of their report is reproduced at the end of this chapter. It can easily be seen that little of this body of knowledge is tested by the CPA examination, which still emphasizes that knowledge which has traditionally been unique to the professional accountant.

The means by which candidates for entrance into the profession should acquire and demonstrate competence have changed significantly over the years and are still the subject of lively debate. Traditionally, an accountant became qualified by gaining experience as an apprentice under the tutelage of a practicing accountant. In England, this is still the principal way in which accountants are trained. In the United States, however, it has been increasingly felt that academic training should supplant apprenticeship as the means of acquiring initial technical competence. In some of the areas of knowledge outlined by the Common Body Commission, this is clearly the only practical available means.

More and more states, therefore, have been including academic credentials among the evidence a candidate must present to gain professional accreditation. While a minority of states still require no more than a high school diploma, the bachelor's degree is more frequently required before a candidate can sit for the CPA examination. As for the future, it has been suggested that ultimately a graduate degree may be necessary for entrance into the profession.

The role of experience in professional accreditation has been decreasing, but there is considerable disagreement within the profession as to whether it should be eliminated altogether. Some feel that to acquire a body of knowledge experience is not required, while others argue that a professional designation should mean more than knowledge of a certain set of facts and should include practical experience in the profession prior to accreditation.

In the spring of 1969, the governing body (Council) of the AICPA (American Institute of Certified Public Accountants) approved the report of a committee on education and experience requirements for CPAs, chaired by Elmer Beamer; the report recommended the elimination of the experience requirement for a candidate who has completed at least five years of college study. This action showed the institute's desire to move the CPA's professional accreditation toward the approach of the legal profession, in which the bar examination is generally taken immediately on graduation from law school. It seems likely, therefore, that the trend toward de-emphasizing experience as a basis for professional accreditation will continue.

Professional Organization

An additional characteristic of a profession is the existence of a professional organization which can encourage the development of knowledge in the field, accredit members, and create standards of conduct and performance which adequately protect the public who rely on the members of the profession. In public accounting a number of different groups fulfill this function. The national professional organization of accountants is the American Institute of Certified Public Accountants (AICPA). This is a group to which a large majority of practicing CPAs belong. Membership is granted to all accredited CPAs who apply, with no significant additional qualifications. Through its committees and full-time administrative officers, the institute works to improve the technical standards of the profession in all aspects, including accounting principles, auditing standards, and tax and consulting practice. It prepares the uniform CPA examination that is now given in all of the fifty-three jurisdictions in the United States and its territories, and grades the examination for substantially all of these jurisdictions. The institute has disciplinary authority over its members and may expel them from membership for failure to meet professional or technical standards. However, this power is infrequently used, and the institute makes little formal effort to police the practice of accountancy in the United States.

While the AICPA is the largest organization and has the greatest influence on the development of accounting standards and practices in the United States, the CPA designation is a license granted by each of the fifty-three jurisdictions to practice as a CPA within the state and, accordingly, at the state level there has grown up an additional set of professional organizations and a group of regulatory authorities.

The professional organizations are normally the state societies of CPAs, and they perform on a local level many of the same functions that are performed by the AICPA on a national level. The state societies have their own committee structures, professional meetings, and administrative apparatuses. On a number of occasions in recent years attempts have been made to combine membership in the AICPA and in the state societies by a variety of techniques, but attempts to enforce joint membership have generally met with failure.

The regulatory bodies are the State Boards of Accountancy. These boards are charged with the regulatory authority under state accountancy legislation. It is their responsibility to grant the CPA certificate and to revoke it when necessary, and their activities are normally concentrated in this area. In fulfilling this function, the various boards have adopted a wide variety of rules in regard to the education and experience required for the certificate. They do not generally participate in professional research or leadership in other respects.

The variety of standards resulting from this three-tiered organization of the accounting profession has often led to agitation for a national CPA licensing act and for a more integrated profession. These efforts have failed to date, because of both the unwillingness of the states to surrender their authority, and the apprehension of many CPAs that the establishment of a national certificate would centralize regulatory power to the detriment of the profession.

Professional Standards

Professional standards in the accounting profession can be divided into standards of conduct and technical standards. The former relate to the behavior of members of the profession while the latter concern the technical aspects of the conduct of an engagement.

Standards of conduct are primarily defined in the AICPA's Code of Professional Ethics and the corollary rules of professional conduct established by the state societies. Technical standards derive primarily from the statements of the various AICPA technical committees. As should be clear, the two types of standards cannot be completely divorced, since standards of conduct may require the implementation of technical standards.

In any profession that encourages the public to rely upon a professional designation, it is essential that recognized standards of personal conduct be established for the orderly conduct of professional activities which validate that reliance and protect the public from the unscrupulous. In auditing, the AICPA has developed a Code of Professional Ethics, reproduced at the end of this chapter, which serves as a national basis for ethical standards. The code is administered by the Committee on Professional Ethics of the AICPA, which has issued formal opinions interpreting the code from time to time as well as responding informally to a large number of requests by practitioners for interpretation. Violations of the Code of Professional Ethics calling for disciplinary actions against members are handled by the Trial Board of the institute, normally with the advice of the Committee on Professional Ethics.

Most state societies have adopted similar codes, although in some circumstances they are either more or less restrictive than that of the AICPA. In the many states where regulatory laws limit the practice of accountancy to licensed practitioners, these rules of professional conduct are legally enforced, and violation may result in the revocation of the right to practice. The Code of Ethics of the institute is currently under revision in an attempt to express its canons in a more positive fashion, but the basic content is unlikely to be substantially changed.

The social rationale of a professional code of ethics is the protection of the public. The existence of a body of knowledge beyond the competence of most interested parties, and the reliance of the public on qualified practitioners to apply this body of knowledge, require disciplines above those offered by the common law and the marketplace. At the same time, these higher ethical standards may supplant and render inappropriate the more normal forces of economic society, such as the profit motive and antitrust legislation.

The Code of Ethics, therefore, can be divided into, on the one hand, those sections which deal with the high technical and professional standards which must be maintained and, on the other hand, those which deal with constraints on normal business practice that is not acceptable behavior in a professional environment.

The first two articles of the Code of Ethics primarily relate to the standards which must be maintained. The first article sets forth the requirements of independence, which are discussed more fully below, and identifies the confidential relationship that exists between accountant and client.

The confidential-relationship section enables a client to rely on the accountant not to disclose his affairs or to make his working papers available to any outside party without the client's consent. For many years, accountants have attempted to extend this confidential relationship to the point of legal privilege, which would exempt the accountant from being required to disclose communications between himself and his client even under subpoena in a court of law. To date, this effort has been largely unsuccessful, and accountants in most states may therefore be subpoenaed and forced to submit work papers and testify to a client's detriment in court under penalty of contempt proceedings for refusal to do so.

The absence of legal privilege has had the effect of constraining communication between client and accountant, and it must be considered in deciding what should be included in working papers. There are certainly some cases where the depth and adequacy of an audit has been damaged as a result. At the same time, it must be recognized that accountants are not advocates with the sole duty of representing a client as in the case with lawyers, who are granted legal privilege. Accountants have a public responsibility as well as a duty to clients, and the denial of legal privilege may be more consistent with this view of their role and function.

The second article covers technical standards which define the responsibilities of a public accountant in reporting on his activities, and the limits that exist on the way he will report and what he can report on.

The first section of this article requires that an accountant not offer an opinion of financial statements unless they have been examined by himself or an employee. The section does permit an accountant to rely in part on the examination of other CPAs "whose independence and professional reputation he has ascertained to his satisfaction." This section therefore prohibits reliance on management's representations without investigation. The extent to which other accounting firms can be relied upon is not spelled out and practice varies in this matter.

The second and third sections relate to reporting practices and require that after obtaining sufficient information to warrant expression of an opinion, a public accountant disclose, in accordance with generally accepted accounting principles, all material facts necessary to make the financial statements not misleading. These sections also require clear disclosure of what opinion, if any, the auditor is giving on the statements and, where statements are being presented without an opinion, that on each page disclosure be made that the financial statements were not audited.

The fourth section forbids the public accountant to allow his name to be associated with any forecast in a way which makes it appear that he vouches for the accuracy of the forecast. This section has effectively prevented accountants from reporting on forecasts in any way and as such is the subject of considerable controversy. As more and more users of financial data are seeking reliable forecasts of the future, it seems doubtful that auditors should be prevented from fulfilling this need, not by making forecasts but by increasing their reliability through defined review procedures and then association of their name with the statements. It is clear that today's audited financial statements include any implicit and explicit forecasts, and there seems no reason for the ethical prohibition of an expanded role for the professional accountant in the forecasting field.

The remaining parts of the Code of Ethics deal primarily with constraints on the auditor's business practice in the interests of the orderly conduct of professional activities. These are justified as being necessary to maintain professionalism and to avoid business practices that would encourage short-run economic interest at the expense of the social function of practitioners. There are those few, however, who argue that these canons of ethics serve primarily to perpetuate the status quo and make entrance into the profession more difficult, thus reducing the dynamism of public accounting. Also, some have expressed concern about whether some provisions of the Code of Ethics were in violation of the antitrust laws; advice by AICPA attorneys that the section prohibiting competitive bidding exposed the code to antitrust attack led the AICPA in 1966 to try, unsuccessfully, to eliminate the section, and subsequently to announce that the Ethics Committee would not attempt to enforce it.

Whatever the reason, under these articles members of the AICPA are prohibited from advertising or soliciting business, from paying commissions to nonmembers for work referred, from accepting an engagement on a contingent-fee basis, or from making a competitive bid for an engagement. Additionally, relations between members are proscribed and limits are placed on the performance of other business activities that are inconsistent with those of the public accountant.

Prior to 1969, the code also prohibited the practice of public accounting in corporate form. During that year, however, the Institute removed that absolute prohibition, and made possible the incorporation of a practice if the corporation conformed to the characteristics spelled out by resolutions of the AICPA Council. These included constraints on name and business purpose, and limited ownership of shares to qualified CPAs. This step made it possible for CPAs to gain the tax advantages of a corporation under the professional incorporation statutes which have been enacted in all but a few states.

The American Institute has a number of committees working in the various areas of professional accounting. There is a Committee on Auditing

Standards of Technical Performance

Procedure, a Committee on Tax Practice, a Committee on Management Services, the Accounting Principles Board, and several others. These committees have from time to time issued statements setting forth standards of technical performance in the various areas. The best known of these, of course, is the Accounting Principles Board, which operates in the area of defining accounting principles. Its pronouncements on these technical standards of measurement are authoritative, and, under the Code of Ethics of the AICPA, any deviation from these principles must be disclosed by CPAs in the auditor's report on financial statements. The accounting principles defined by the board are still not codified and there is considerable dispute about whether or not a single codification should exist. In recent years, however, the board has been far more aggressive in advocating its own opinions rather than simply serving as a codifier of existing practice, and, largely as a result its prescribed technical accounting standards have represented a significant advance in many respects.

The Committee on Auditing Procedure has issued a series of statements on auditing procedure, including one that defines generally accepted auditing standards. These standards will be discussed in greater detail in subsequent chapters.

The Committee on Federal Taxation has issued a number of statements on responsibilities in tax practice that have started to set forth what a CPA should do in reviewing data in returns which he signs.

The Problem of Independence

In both the Code of Ethics and in generally accepted Auditing Standards (described in Chapter 6 below), the troublesome concept of independence is mentioned. Since the purpose of auditing is to increase the reliability of information through impartial review, the auditor must be sufficiently independent of the auditee so that those who use the audit reports can be confident of their impartiality. Without independence, reliability is not increased.

On the other hand, complete independence is not consistent with good auditing. Ultimate independence could be defined as the absence of any relationship. The detailed knowledge of a business and its information system that an auditor needs arise from experience with the firm and its officers over a period of time. The nature of an audit does not accommodate a review without reference to the people who make a company operate. Yet whenever relationships with people are established, independence is no longer complete. What must be sought, therefore, is sufficient independence to permit the auditor to express an impartial professional judgment about the information system of the firm and its output, thus fulfilling his public responsibility.

Even with this more limited objective, however, the problem remains to define sufficient independence. The basic difficulty is that the cost of the audit service is borne by the entity being audited; thus an economic relationship between auditor and auditee is established. It must be recognized that public accounting firms are in the business of selling service and thus, even in connection with an audit, the CPA is aware of the fact that he is serving his clients and not solely performing a public function. When a CPA is used extensively for consulting activities as well, this problem becomes more difficult.

On a strictly economic basis it is possible to assure impartiality by making the costs of bias greater than any economic benefits that may be derived therefrom. It is clear to all national public accounting firms today that any short-run economic benefits to be derived from a compromise in auditing procedures or accounting principles would be overwhelmed by the short- and long-run economic costs from loss of reputation and future clients resulting from any discovered compromise with principle. Beyond the purely economic basis of impartiality, however, is the accountant's recognition that as a professional he must not simply serve his client but must also bear greater public responsibility, which he can only fulfill by "calling them as he sees them" in reporting on financial statements.

The efforts of the AICPA and the Securities and Exchange Commission to assure impartiality have placed substantial emphasis on the appearance of independence. An auditor may not express an opinion on financial statements if he serves as an officer or director of the corporation or if he or any of his partners owns stock in the corporation or has any direct financial interest in its operation. This prohibition was introduced into the Code of Ethics in a recent revision but most large firms have applied this rule for many years. This rule is consistent with the SEC's requirements for independence on the part of auditors who are expressing opinions on financial statements included in registration statements filed with the SEC.

Therefore, neither the fee relationship between the auditor and his client nor the performance of consulting services for the client seems likely to significantly damage the impartiality of the auditor as a third party. It is very doubtful that the spin-off of management-consulting practices from the public accounting firms would improve audits. In fact, the elimination of consulting or its complete segregation from the audit activity would deny the auditor significant information which should help him in the course of his audit. In addition, in today's competitive recruitment environment, the management-consulting activity of CPAs is one of the most attractive recruitment devices of the profession and its elimination would lower the calibre of personnel entering the profession, which would in turn reduce the quality of auditing.

While it is entirely appropriate that impartiality be sought from the CPA, auditing is not likely to be improved by more radical curtailment of the CPA's consulting practice, as the advocates of such curtailment claim. The AICPA has explicitly endorsed the point of view that consulting and auditing are compatible, and despite the obvious bias of the source, a consideration of all effects seems to support this finding.

Accountants' Legal Liabilities

While an impartial professional approach is necessary in the public interest, it is also necessary because of the potential legal liabilities which confront auditors in the course of their professional engagements. Auditors are responsible for the work which they do and the reports which they issue, and this responsibility can be enforced at law when necessary. In recent years there have been an increasing number of lawsuits against CPAs, both under common law and under the Securities Act, and while comparatively few judgments have been won against auditors, the cost of liability insurance has risen alarmingly and the risk of lawsuit has clearly increased.

In general, under common law the accountant is liable to his client for negligent performance of his duties, and liable to third parties and the general public solely in the event of fraud. This distinction is based on the legal concept of privity of contract, by which it has been held that the auditor has no relationship with third parties. Under this concept, if strictly interpreted, liability to third parties would exist only if the auditor knew that what he was reporting on was incorrect but still fraudulently gave his opinion on the financial statements without mentioning the material error.

In practice, these rules have been amended considerably by court decisions. In situations where the auditor knew that the financial statements were to be used for some specified purpose with a specified third party, courts have suggested that the auditor can be held responsible for negligence. Similarly, a landmark case in the area (Ultramares Corp. vs. Touche) indicated that it was possible for negligence to be so gross as to constitute fraud. It has been suggested by some legal writers that as time passes the legal responsibility of the auditor under common law will be increased.

The largest number of recent cases affecting the accountant's legal liability, however, has been brought under the securities laws. The Securities Act of 1933 and the Securities Exchange Act of 1934 include provisions that hold the accountants liable as experts to third parties who rely upon their representation in the purchase of securities. This liability would exist even in case of negligence without fraud. Recent years have brought a rash of lawsuits under these provisions, many of which are still pending. In one case a partner of a large public accounting firm was convicted in criminal court for the failure to insist on adequate disclosure in a registration statement. In other cases there have been substantial settlements of civil liability suits. These various cases have created an understandable sense of nervousness within the accounting profession. This has had both good and bad effects. On the one hand, increased quality control has been instituted, which should improve the uniformity of auditing and reporting standards. On the other hand, there has been a tendency on the part of auditors to narrow the definition of their task in order to avoid liability. If followed to a substantial extent this tendency could have the effect of sharply limiting the growth and usefulness of the accounting profession.

The extent of the accountant's legal liability is clearly a book in which the last chapter has not been written, but it is an area of intense interest to the profession and one which will undoubtedly affect its development in the future.

This chapter has developed the implications derived from the status of public accounting as a profession. One of the first of these is the requirement that a definable body of knowledge exist with which professionals can be expected to be familiar. The first reading which follows is the summary of a report on the common body of knowledge which should be required of the CPA when he begins his professional career. While this report does not have "official" status, it has been extensively discussed within the profession and it does represent the best judgment of an informed group of men from accounting, education, business and law who made up the commission.

A second requirement of professional status is the existence of an ethical code to guide the activities of practitioners. This is an area to which the accounting profession has devoted a great deal of time and attention in developing, amending, and enforcing a prescribed code of ethics. Any student of the accounting profession must be familiar with the Code of Ethics of the American Institute of CPAs which is therefore included as the second reading to this chapter. This version includes 1969 amendments approved by the membership. At the time of this writing, a Committee of the AICPA is attempting to rewrite the code so as to emphasize the positive attributes of ethics as opposed to the current "thou shalt not" approach. The conclusion of this effort seems some years in the future.

Even with a common body of knowledge and a code of ethics, there are times when the discipline of the law must be brought to bear on the practitioners of a profession. This phenomenon has been discussed in the chapter above, but due to the significant impact of legal liabilities on the

Introduction to Readings

practice of public accounting today, a more extensive treatment seemed desirable. The third reading, a comprehensive article by Professors Taussig and Reiling, deals with this area and includes a discussion of the principal cases which have recently indicated significant changes in the accountants' exposure. The failure of traditional defenses and the tendency of the courts to reject concurrence with minimum professional standards as a total defense are highly significant developments which are having and will have a major effect on the accounting profession.

Robert H. Roy
James H. MacNeill

The Common
Body of Knowledge

The conclusions of this study, describing our recommendations for the common body of knowledge for beginning CPAs, are grouped in major categories as follows: Accounting, The Humanities, Economics and Behavioral Science, Law, Mathematics, Statistics, Probability, and The Functional Fields of Business.

Accounting

Accounting, by its nature, operates within a broad socio-economic environment and, consequently, the knowledge required of the CPA cannot be sharply compartmentalized. The description of the common body of knowledge is characterized by an interdisciplinary flavor, and it is difficult to discuss one area without relating to other areas of knowledge.

Although previously referred to, it is essential to reiterate here that we place great emphasis upon conceptual knowledge; that is, that the

Excerpts from *Horizons for a Profession*, American Institute of Certified Public Accountants, 1967.

beginning CPA not only know, but that he *understand.*

Functions of Accounting. It is our opinion that the beginning CPA cannot perform his role intelligently without a thorough knowledge of the functions of accounting. He must know who utilizes its products, the nature of the decisions to be made and, specifically, how accounting can facilitate this process. In short, the CPA must understand accounting as an integral part of the decision-making process.

Our recommendations concerning taxes are that the beginning CPA need not be a tax expert, but he should at least understand the nature of the various taxes, upon whom they are imposed, the tax base, the general range of rates, and any important characteristics or peculiarities. And, while this same broad conceptual approach is recommended for all important taxes, its materiality and wide applicability prompts us to suggest that the beginning CPA have a more detailed knowledge of the federal income tax.

Concepts of Accounting. We do not believe that the beginning CPA should be an expert theorist, but we do feel he should possess a good knowledge of accounting theory; viz., the various approaches to asset measurement, the recognition of liabilities, and the concepts that comprise periodic income measurement. He should know what is meant by the expression "generally accepted accounting principles," the principles themselves, their applicability, their limitations, and the conflicts involving them. Furthermore, his knowledge of accounting theory should not be limited to those principles and practices which are generally accepted.

Since communication is an intrinsic part of the accounting process, the CPA must know how to present data in such form as to be readily understandable and of maximum utility. He must also be concerned with the characteristics of information systems that tend to minimize the time elapsing between initial input and useful communication.

The beginning CPA must be familiar with the ways in which accounting information is made reliable. The principle of objectivity must be known, as well as its applications and limitations. The CPA should also understand how the employment of statistical inference can improve reliability through sampling techniques. And, inseparable from the audit scope itself, the concept of internal control and the many ways it may be achieved should be an integral part of his knowledge.

The auditor must be qualified through his technical competence, his independence and his personal standards. The beginning CPA must know the codes of professional ethics, not just as a collection of rules but as a philosophy of professional behavior.

Audit methodology is not a set of programs that can be committed to memory, but it is a body of ideas that must be comprehended so that the auditor can create his own audit program as the need arises.

Application of Accounting Concepts. We have stated that the common body of knowledge must be conceptual; before dealing with asset measurement, one must understand service; he must also be familiar with the kinds of assets he can expect to encounter, their characteristics and their problem areas. For example, collectibility is a factor that is uppermost in the valuation of receivables, whereas alternative cost flow is a key factor of inventory presentation. Both receivables and inventories share the general characteristics of all assets, but each evokes problems peculiar to its own nature. Similarly, each of the many classes of liabilities and equity involves special considerations which must be understood by the beginning certified public accountant.

The kinds of formal organization which CPAs encounter also possess certain general characteristics which are unique to each class. The concept of limited liability is essential to the corporate form. Since the partnership is conceptually quite different from the corporation, the CPA must be familiar with those features which distinguish partnerships from other forms of organization.

Above, brief reference was made to inventories and their costing procedures. But in the case of manufactured inventories, costing becomes vastly more complex, embracing the field of cost accounting. The beginning CPA should have knowledge of the application of accounting concepts to production; he should be familiar with such things as cost allocations, cost centers, burden distribution and standard costs. His knowledge should embrace not only the procedures themselves, but also their basic concepts, rationale and limitations.

Methods and Techniques Available to the CPA. As in any profession, accounting employs numerous methodologies to carry out its functions. While there is no need to be a skilled bookkeeper, machine operator or mathematician, the beginning CPA must understand the nature, uses and limitations of the methods and techniques that are available to him. These range from the basic debit-credit structure itself to complex data processing equipment and include the various quantitative techniques.

The computer Our recommendations for the common body of knowledge with respect to computers are as follows:

1. That beginning CPAs be required to have basic knowledge of at least one computer system
2. That they have knowledge of at least one computer language (e.g., COBOL)
3. That they possess the ability to chart or diagram an information system of modest complexity
4. That they have the ability to design an information system, prepare a program for it and carry their work through the stages of debugging and testing.

Also desirable is additional knowledge of such concepts as reliability and redundancy, and

of computer capabilities for simulation, real time operation, and shared time use.

The substance of these recommendations is that tomorrow's beginning CPA shall have computer capability and fluency to the extent possible with but limited experience.

The Humanities

This part of the common body of knowledge for beginning CPAs concerns man himself, his history, the philosophies by which he lives, the languages by which he communicates and the arts which give expression to his passion for creativity. For most of these we can give no more than a very general recommendation, for we cannot say that knowledge of literature, art, music, or of a foreign language is *required* of a CPA. We can, however, having so often emphasized the qualities of true professionals, say that the humanities are the hallmarks of cultivated men and women, and we can express the strong hope that beginning CPAs will of their own volition pursue culture as it is exemplified in these areas of learning. A CPA who can listen to music with discernment as well as enjoyment, or one who reads for style and cadence as well as content, or who appreciates the art of drama or painting is likely not only to have a livelier intellect but also to be a better practitioner.

Logic and Ethics. More specifically, CPAs do need to be concerned with two areas of philosophy: logic and ethics. We do not intend to specify that requisite knowledge of these must be the product of exposure to college courses—although that would be desirable—but we do say that beginning CPAs must have sufficient knowledge of logic to demonstrate capability. Certainly, nearly everything done in future professional practice will be bound by the tenets of logic, for which understanding will be essential.

Ethics, while more elusive to impart and ascertain, is comparably fundamental. If there were no ethical foundation to the profession, there would in fact be no profession. Beginning CPAs, we believe, should *know* these ethical precepts, not in the manner of dogma or catechism but in full understanding of their significance to their own futures, as well as to the future of their profession.

Written and Spoken English. In one area germane to the humanities we have been specific. Whatever a CPA may do in behalf of his clients, the end results must always be communicated, usually in writing, sometimes orally. However communicated, it is essential that there be clarity and specificity, unblemished by incoherence, disunity or ambiguity, untarnished by grammatical, syntactical or rhetorical errors. We have sought to recognize this essential role of written and spoken English by declaring that those who cannot perform above a minimum threshold should be denied admission to the profession.

We further recommend that examiners at various levels of candidates' progress eschew the familiar rationale that they are grading accounting, or economics, or history, or psychology, and *not* English, by making it their practice to judge English on *every* such occasion and informing candidates when they are found deficient. For the guidance of examiners we have

proposed in our report three decision rules which give consideration both to technical proficiency and to writing skills.

Economics

It is important, as part of the common body of knowledge for beginning CPAs, to have appreciation of the social sciences simply as a matter of desirable cultivation for a professional man. Beyond this general recommendation, however, are two areas of social science, knowledge of which may be stated as professionally necessary. These are economics and those aspects of social science which are concerned with the behavior of formal organizations.

The raw materials of accounting are economic events and the products of accounting are used to make decisions and to formulate policies operative in the world of economics. The beginning CPA therefore must have extensive knowledge of this essential subject.

Micro-Economics. Of the two broad divisions of the subject, micro- and macro-economics, we believe more extensive knowledge of micro-economics to be desirable, this being the domain of the individual organization, where economic events are translated into dollars, where there is concern with such matters as value, prices, competition, investment, financial position, income.

Knowledge of micro-economics should encompass the nature of economic forces which affect the firm: the relationship of price to demand, the behavior of costs, cost concepts (marginal, opportunity, etc.), productivity, the role of government in the regulation of business. Some familiarity with antitrust measures, public utility regulation, prohibitions of price discrimination and restrictions on the movement of international capital, as mechanisms of government regulations, should also be understood.

Macro-Economics. Knowledge of micro-economics can provide the CPA with the tools of analysis he uses in his day-to-day work; knowledge of macro-economics, pertaining to the economy as a whole, can provide him with perspective. We regard such knowledge as comparably desirable, not only as intellectual background but also for essential understanding. As the organizations served by CPAs grow increasingly large, diverse and international in the scope of their activities, and as government policies increasingly seek to control the economy, CPAs must increasingly become participants in the formulation of those policies, as well as advisers to those affected by them. Understanding of such matters as monetary theory, resource allocation, business cycles, international finance, national income and its measurement, labor economics and economic planning therefore become significant parts of the CPA's intellectual armament. Comparably, the institutions which comprise the economy, the nature and interactions of government, industry, unions, financial institutions, and the like, become germane to the professional practice of accounting.

Behavioral Science

CPAs are advisers to the formal organizations of their clients, and they themselves function as members of formal organizations. Research on the behavior of the individuals and groups who comprise formal organizations is being carried on very actively and one may anticipate that significant results are just over the horizon. Based upon a combination of anticipated and realized results, we recommend that the beginning CPA be required to have knowledge of the fundamentals of psychology and sociology, these to provide a foundation capable of absorbing the future results expected from research in behavioral science.

To those who may regard this as a weak rationale for requiring knowledge, another argument may be offered. Exposure to instruction in business and industrial management has long been a requirement for those preparing to be CPAs. While we do not discount or derogate knowledge pertaining to ownership, location, purchasing, storekeeping, compensation, and the like, we do believe knowledge of the fundamentals of individual and group behavior to be relatively more desirable. Furthermore, we believe this to be so whether behavioral research yields applicable breakthroughs in the future or not.

An added reason for this conclusion is provided by the fact that behavioral research already has yielded applicable insights of significant value. Knowledge that local autonomy yields better organization performance than does tight central control does not prescribe what an executive should do nor tell him how to do it but it does tell him something of transcendent importance about motivation, which— granted adequate understanding—he may use to great advantage. In the same way behavioral research studies of communication, decision-making, innovation, conflict, leadership, authority, learning, perception and creativity are providing knowledge which cannot be categorically prescribed or, like a poultice, applied but which can be understood and used to great advantage.

Law

We recommend that the beginning CPA be charged with possession of a good knowledge of business law; that is, that he be familiar with the relationships between the parties, the concepts involved, and the special terminology employed. To a lesser degree, but in a philosophical way, we believe he should have a general knowledge of the role of law in society.

These conclusions are based upon our observations of the wide scope of financial activities in which CPAs are engaged and on the nature of accounting itself. In determining the very existence and measurement of assets and liabilities, CPAs must deal with property rights, written contracts of many kinds, commercial paper, and a wide variety of other legal relationships. His involvement with taxes, security issues, corporations, estates, etc., further strengthens our conclusions.

The beginning CPA's knowledge should include an understanding of: enforceability of contracts—the rights, obligations and remedies of the parties; negotiability of instruments; the nature, varieties and evidence of title to property; the implications of the legal distinctions between the corporation and the partnership; the jurisdictions of the more widely applicable administrative laws and the CPA's obligations under them. And because of his special status, the beginning CPA should have an even more extensive knowledge of his own rights and duties under the law, including his liability to his client and to third parties.

We emphasize that our recommendations should not be construed as meaning that the beginning CPA, or even the seasoned veteran, should be a legal expert. In law, as in every other area of knowledge to which accounting relates, the CPA must be able to recognize a problem, and further, must know when it is necessary to consult with a specialist.

Mathematics, Statistics, Probability

A rationale for the organization and conduct of this study could be based upon those prospects for change which in days to come are likely to affect the practices of certified public accountants. In no other areas of knowledge can change be predicted with as great certainty or in as significant degree as in the disciplines germane to mathematics. Changes in the behavioral sciences remain largely prospective; the impact of mathematics, statistics, and probability upon the world of formal organizations—and hence upon the practices of CPAs— already is present.

Our warrant for recommendations which go beyond those to be inferred from the results of the card deck experiment derives from both evidence and prediction:

1. CPAs increasingly are confronted with problems of sampling, both in the installation of financial information systems for their clients and in the conduct of their audits. As these practices grow, empirical, judgmental samples will no longer suffice; understanding of sampling theory will be required.

2. CPAs increasingly are confronted with mathematically derived decision rules in the systems of their clients' organizations. To conduct audits in such situations, understanding will, to say the least, be necessary.

3. CPAs themselves increasingly are engaged in the performance of services for their clients which utilize quantitative methodologies.

4. Information and control systems often are encountered by CPAs in performance of the audit function and in providing advisory services. A measure of mathematical sophistication is necessary in many such situations.

5. It appears probable that accounting itself, at both operational and instructional levels, increasingly will make use of symbolic notation.

As in every other part of this report, we place much higher value upon conceptual understanding than procedural skills. Accountants, by and large, deal with discrete rather than continuous phenomena;[1] one might say therefore that finite mathematics is to be valued above calculus. While we agree with this, we once again argue that topical knowledge is secondary; the important thing is that tomorrow's CPAs have the same feeling for, understanding of and facility with the symbols of arithmetic. It matters little whether this facility derives from algebra or calculus, new math or old, topology or geometry; the important thing is the achievement of an enhanced *rapport* between the disciplines of mathematics and the disciplines of accounting on the part of tomorrow's CPAs.

The substance of this recommendation does *not* require that the beginning CPA be a mathematician, statistician or probabilist, not at all. It does ask that the beginning CPA be trained to conceptualize, to think in symbols, just as he has always thought in numbers, just as a Frenchman thinks in French. As stated elsewhere, the beginning CPA must be *literate* in mathematics, however he need not be *literary*.

Mathematics, statistics, and probability all depend upon the abstractions of symbolic notation and this demands the conjunction of suitable aptitudes and requisite motivation.

Since correlations between aptitudes for mathematics and other disciplines are lower than between aptitudes for other fields (e.g., an individual with aptitude for history is likely to be apt in other discursive subjects as well; he may also be facile in mathematics but this is less likely), it may be that some change will be needed in the talents of those seeking to enter the profession. But since accounting itself is quantitative, there seems little reason to be fearful on this score, especially since enhanced requirements seem always to attract more talented recruits.

Despite good aptitudes, motivations are not infrequently dampened by excessively abstract presentation; we therefore strongly recommend copious and meaningful exemplification to reinforce learning.

A syllabus prepared by the Committee on Undergraduate Program in Mathematics[2] is appended to the report on the Common Body of Knowledge. While we believe this syllabus

---

[1]"*Continuous* means that the variable can assume any numerical value within a particular range. For instance, a dimensional measure can be divided into fractional parts of any size. . . . Weight, length and time are common examples of continuous variables. . . .

"*Discrete* variables, in contrast, change in definite increments and cannot assume a numerical value between the increments. Money, for example, is discrete in the sense that you can pay a man only to the nearest cent. People are discrete in the sense that they can only be counted as integers; i.e., whole numbers."

Clifford H. Springer, Robert E. Herlehy and Robert I. Beggs, *Basic Mathematics*. Volume I of the Mathematics for Management Series, Richard D. Irwin, Inc., 1965, p. 32.

[2]"Tentative Recommendations for the Undergraduate Mathematics Program of Students in the Biological, Management and Social Sciences," Mathematical Association of America, January 1964.

to be the best of its kind in existence, we do not propose slavish adoption but remain more concerned with conceptual understanding.

The common body of knowledge that is presented here calls for substantially *more* knowledge of mathematics, statistics, and probability than hitherto has been needed by beginning CPAs. But in the days to come we think it likely that our recommendations may be *less* than needed for professional practice. These proposals therefore must be regarded over time as minimal. What we recommend is not intended as a static inventory of knowledge but as a foundation upon which a beginning CPA can build.

The Functional Fields of Business

Finance. Since finance is by its nature identified with the functions of accounting itself, one cannot understand accounting without a knowledge of finance. We conceive of the body of financial knowledge in two broad classes: evaluation of capital needs and sources, and the financial environment.

As to the former, we believe the beginning CPA should be capable of making financial projections: he should understand and know how to develop the various ratios, turnovers, and use other analytical tools. Furthermore, he should understand the factors involved in, and know how to determine the cost of, alternative sources of capital.

Since financial institutions comprise a large portion of the environment in which he will work, the beginning CPA should have a fair knowledge of the functions and operations of the more widespread kinds of institutions,

including those of government. His knowledge should also include the terminology of finance.

Production. CPAs are engaged frequently by clients who are themselves engaged in manufacturing and from this circumstance it follows that some knowledge of production is necessary. Again emphasizing conceptual understanding, we recommend that beginning CPAs have a good grasp of the two basic production procedures: the continuity of process manufacturing on the one hand and the interrupted sequences of jobbing production on the other.

Also relevant is the relationship between cost accounting systems and the production processes which they often parallel, not infrequently becoming realistic accounting models of the factory itself. Understanding of this plus adequate acquaintence with the terminology of accounting related to production (e.g., relevant cost, incremental cost, sunk cost, production center, etc.) become proper parts of the common body of knowledge. So also does knowledge of cost-volume relationships, often assumed to be simple, more often found to be complex as a consequence of cost discontinuities which make both computations and predictions difficult. The beginning CPA should have a firm grasp of this important area, including coverage of those methods related to concepts of economic lot size.

Decisions on capital investment are often intertwined with considerations such as these, and this of course is an area in which CPAs have served clients for a long time. Knowledge of how to compare present and prospective production procedures; how to make breakeven analyses; how to take account of such matters as opportunity costs, sunk costs, cash position, and relevant taxes; and how to predict the elusive costs of transition and prevent or minimize the now-familiar phenomenon of cost overrun; all these are part of the necessary intellectual equipment of certified public accountants.

Marketing. Our recommendation with respect to marketing's place in the common body of knowledge for beginning CPAs is best described as an orientation. The key roles played by sales management, product planning, physical distribution, and the like, should be understood sufficiently so that these vital functions are served by the information system. The nature of the decisions to be made and the kinds of data needed to facilitate these decisions should be known to the beginning CPA.

Of the marketing environment, the retailing-wholesaling system, we suggest only minimal knowledge.

Elsewhere, our recommendations include knowledge of human behavior. With this, the beginning CPA will have a general appreciation of the human factors involved in the marketing function: consumer behavior, sales personnel incentive and advertising psychology.

Personnel Relations. Management of the many individuals who comprise formal organizations is a major concern of every executive, and knowledge in this area is important to CPAs, both as members of their own firms and for understanding of the client organiza-

tions they serve. We believe, however, that requisite knowledge for beginning CPAs is best given a sound foundation through the behavioral sciences.

Business Management. Analogously, we have said that knowledge of this functional field of business can also best be acquired through the behavioral sciences. But we have recognized that the beginning CPA himself often becomes a business manager, as an executive of his own firm. In this capacity he must be concerned with capital requirements and means for financing the firm's operations, with setting and collecting fees, with attracting and retaining clients and with accounting for the firm's affairs. We have not recommended these as necessary for beginning CPAs but have pointed them out as important.

Conclusion

As a conclusion, we reaffirm our consistent position: To perform the services which are within reach, and which the public will come to expect, requires the efforts of a professional.

The beginning CPA must therefore have a conceptual grasp of accounting, its interdisciplinary aspects, the environment in which it functions, and of those bodies of knowledge which are ancillary to its central purpose. Finally, he must be prepared to grow with changing conditions and ideas. These are the horizons we have tried to portray.

The reliance of the public and the business community on sound financial reporting and advice on business affairs imposes on the accounting profession an obligation to maintain high standards of technical competence, morality and integrity. To this end, a member or associate of the American Institute of Certified Public Accountants shall at all times maintain independence of thought and action, hold the affairs of his clients in strict confidence, strive continuously to improve his professional skills, observe generally accepted auditing standards, promote sound and informative financial reporting, uphold the dignity and honor of the accounting profession, and maintain high standards of personal conduct.

In further recognition of the public interest and his obligations to the profession, a member or associate agrees to comply with the following rules of ethical conduct, the enumeration of which should not be construed as a denial of the existence of other standards of conduct not specifically mentioned:

Article 1: Relations with Clients and Public

1.01. Neither a member or associate, nor a firm of which he is a partner, shall express an opinion on financial statements of any enterprise unless he and his firm are in fact independent with respect to such enterprise.

Independence is not susceptible of precise definition, but is an expression of the professional integrity of the individual. A member or associate, before expressing his opinion on financial statements, has the responsibility of assessing his relationships with an enterprise to determine whether, in the circumstances, he might expect his opinion to be considered independent, objective and unbiased by one who had knowledge of all the facts.

A member or associate will be considered not independent, for example, with respect to any enterprise if he, or one of his partners, (a) during the period of his professional engagement or at the time of expressing his opinion, had, or was committed to acquire, any direct financial interest or material indirect financial interest in the enterprise, or (b) during the period of his professional engagement, at the time of expressing his opinion or during the period covered by the financial statements, was connected with the enterprise as a promoter, underwriter, voting trustee, director, officer or key employee. In cases where a member or associate ceases to be the independent accountant for an enterprise and is subsequently called upon to re-express a previously expressed opinion on financial statements, the phrase "at the time of expressing his opinion" refers only to the time at which the member or associate first expressed his opinion on the financial statements in question. The word "director" is not intended to apply to a connection in such a capacity with a charitable, religious, civic or other similar type of nonprofit organization when the duties performed in such a capacity are such as to make it clear that the member or associate can express an independent opinion on the financial statements. The example cited in this paragraph, of circumstances under which a member or associate will be considered not independent, is not intended to be all-inclusive.

1.02. A member or associate shall not commit an act discreditable to the profession.

1.03. A member or associate shall not violate the confidential relationship between himself and his client.

1.04. Professional service shall not be rendered or offered for a fee which shall be contingent upon the findings or results of such service. This rule does not apply to cases involving Federal, state, or other taxes, in which the findings are those of the tax authorities and not those of the accountant. Fees to be fixed by courts or other public authorities, which are therefore of an indeterminate amount at the time when an engagement is undertaken, are not regarded as contingent fees within the meaning of this rule.

Article 2: Technical Standards

2.01. A member or associate shall not express his opinion on financial statements unless they have been examined by him, or by a member or employee of his firm, on a basis consistent with the requirements of Rule 2.02.

In obtaining sufficient information to warrant expression of an opinion he may utilize, in part, to the extent appropriate in the circumstances, the reports or other evidence of auditing work performed by another certified public accountant, or firm of public accountants, at least one of whom is a certified public accountant, who is authorized to practice in a state or territory of the United States or the District of Columbia, and whose independence and professional reputation he has ascertained to his satisfaction.

A member or associate may also utilize, in part, to the extent appropriate in the circumstances, the work of public accountants in other countries, but the member or associate so doing must satisfy himself that the person or firm is qualified and independent, that such work is performed in accordance with generally accepted auditing standards, as prevailing in the United States, and that financial statements are prepared in accordance with generally accepted accounting principles, as prevailing in the United States, or are accompanied by the information necessary to bring the statements into accord with such principles.

2.02.   In expressing an opinion on representations in financial statements which he has examined, a member or associate may be held guilty of an act discreditable to the profession if:

a.   he fails to disclose a material fact known to him which is not disclosed in the financial statements but disclosure of which is necessary to make the financial statements not misleading; or

b.   he fails to report any material misstatement known to him to appear in the financial statement; or

c.   he is materially negligent in the conduct of his examination or in making his report thereon; or

d.   he fails to acquire sufficient information to warrant expression of an opinion, or his exceptions are sufficiently material to negative the expression of an opinion; or

e.   he fails to direct attention to any material departure from generally accepted accounting principles or to disclose any material omission of generally accepted auditing procedure applicable in the circumstances.

2.03.   A member or associate shall not permit his name to be associated with statements purporting to show financial position or results of operations in such a manner as to imply that he is acting as an independent public accountant unless he shall:

a.   express an unqualified opinion; or

b.   express a qualified opinion; or

c.   express an adverse opinion; or

d.   disclaim an opinion on the statements taken as a whole and indicate clearly his reasons therefor; or

e.   when unaudited financial statements are presented on his stationery without his comments, disclose prominently on each page of financial statements that they were not audited.

2.04.   A member or associate shall not permit his name to be used in conjunction with any forecast of the results of future transactions in a manner which may lead to the belief that the member or associate vouches for the accuracy of the forecast.

Article 3:
Promotional Practices

3.01.   A member or associate shall not advertise his professional attainments or services.

Publication in a newspaper, magazine or similar medium of an announcement or what is technically known as a card is prohibited.

A listing in a directory is restricted to the name, title, address and telephone number of the person or firm, and it shall not appear in a box, or other form of display or in a type or style which differentiates it from other listings in the same directory. Listing of the same name in more than one place in a classified directory is prohibited.

3.02.   A member or associate shall not endeavor, directly or indirectly, to obtain clients by solicitation.

3.03. A member or associate shall not make a competitive bid for a professional engagement. Competitive bidding for public accounting services is not in the public interest, is a form of solicitation, and is unprofessional.

3.04. Commissions, brokerage, or other participation in the fees or profits of professional work shall not be allowed or paid directly or indirectly by a member or associate to any individual or firm not regularly engaged or employed in the practice of public accounting as a principal occupation.

Commissions, brokerage, or other participation in the fees, charges or profits of work recommended or turned over to any individual or firm not regularly engaged or employed in the practice of public accounting as a principal occupation, as incident to services for clients, shall not be accepted directly or indirectly by a member or associate.

Article 4:
Operating Practices

4.01. A firm or partnership, all the individual members of which are members of the Institute, may describe itself as "Members of the American Institute of Certified Public Accountants," but a firm or partnership, not all the individual members of which are members of the Institute, or an individual practicing under a style denoting a partnership when in fact there be no partner or partners, or a corporation, or an individual or individuals practicing under a style denoting a corporate organization shall not use the designation "Members of

the American Institute of Certified Public Accountants."

4.02. A member or associate shall not practice in the name of another unless he is in partnership with him or in his employ, nor shall he allow any person to practice in his name who is not in partnership with him or in his employ.

This rule shall not prevent a partnership or its successors from continuing to practice under a firm name which consists of or includes the name or names of one or more former partners, nor shall it prevent the continuation of a partnership name for a reasonable period of time by the remaining partner practicing as a sole proprietor after the withdrawal or death of one or more partners.

4.03. A member or associate in his practice of public accounting shall not permit an employee to perform for the member's or associate's clients any services which the member or associate himself or his firm is not permitted to perform.

4.04. A member or associate shall not engage in any business or occupation conjointly with that of a public accountant, which is incompatible or inconsistent therewith.

4.05. A member or associate engaged in an occupation in which he renders services of a type performed by public accountants, or renders other professional services, must observe the by-laws and Code of Professional Ethics of the Institute in the conduct of that occupation.

4.06. A member or associate may offer services of type performed by public accountants only in the form of either a proprietorship, or a partnership, or a professional corporation or association whose characteristics conform to resolutions of Council.

Article 5: Relations with Fellow Members

5.01. A member or associate shall not encroach upon the practice of another public accountant. A member or associate may furnish service to those who request it.

5.02. A member or associate who receives an engagement for services by referral from another member or associate shall not discuss or accept an extension of his services beyond the specific engagement without first consulting with the referring member or associate.

5.03. Direct or indirect offer of employment shall not be made by a member or associate to an employee of another public accountant without first informing such accountant. This rule shall not be construed so as to inhibit negotiations with anyone who of his own initiative or in response to public advertisement shall apply to a member or associate for employment.

Henry B. Reiling
Russell A. Taussig

Recent Liability Cases—Implications For Accountants

For the accounting profession, the late 1960's was a time of prosperity and a time of peril. Each year accountants posted new highs in billings and earnings, but at the same time they were reportedly subjected to an unprece-

dented number of lawsuits. A staff reporter for the Wall Street Journal opined that nearly 100 law suits were pending against auditors in late 1966.[1] More recently an associate editor of *Fortune* reported that as many claims for damages were filed against accountants in the

Reprinted by permission from *The Journal of Accounting*, Copyrited 1970 by the American Institute of Certified Public Accountants.

[1]Berton, "CPAs Under Fire," *Wall Street Journal*, Nov. 15, 1966, at 13.

twelve months of 1968 as in the previous twelve years.[2] While some are skeptical that the volume of cases is so dramatically high,[3] it seems clear to the authors that there has been a meaningful increase in volume of suits filed,[4] that these suits have frequently involved the profession's more prestigeous firms and that four cases surfaced which were particularly qualified to capture the profession's attention: *BarChris, Continental Vending, Yale Express and Westec.*

Many readers are familiar with these cases. Those who are not may refer to Appendix A, which summarizes the facts, issues and rulings as developed to the date of this article. Litigation is far from over. Indeed, *Yale* and *Westec* have yet to go to trial; nevertheless, enough is known at this time to make a tentative assessment of their characteristics and their potential implications for the public accounting profession. It must be kept in mind, however, that allegations are not synonymous with findings after trial and lower court conclusions can be overturned on appeal. Subsequent developments may affect the tentative conclusions of this article.

In the authors' opinion these cases collectively have the following three significant characteristics:

---

a.   Recent and pending interpretations of federal securities laws appear likely to give plaintiffs not in a contractual relationship with accountants easier access to accountants than was heretofore the case under common law.

b.   Judges and juries composed generally of laymen, not experts in the field of accounting, are beginning to render decisions interpreting accounting principles as well as auditing procedures.

c.   The responsibilities of officers, directors and other professionals for financial statements appearing in prospectuses and related documents have received judicial comment for practically the first time; the result is a new awareness of responsibilities and risks and a related request for accountants to expand their attest function.

These characteristics raise at least five long-range planning questions for the accounting profession:

1.   Must fee structures be adjusted to reflect the greater potential liability which appears to be emerging from recent lawsuits against public accountants?

2.   What are the dangers in allowing courts to assume leadership in the pronouncement of accounting principles?

3.   How can the accounting profession properly restrict its legal hazards?

4.   Should accountants extend their attest function to financial information not now included in certified statements, and certify interim financial statements that are presently unaudited?

5.   What are the advantages and pitfalls for accountants in accepting a new role regarding financial statements?

As background for the consideration of these questions let us examine the features of

[2]A. Louis, "The Accountants Are Changing the Rules," *Fortune*, June 15, 1968, at 177.

[3]An attorney particularly competent in the area of accountants' liability has expressed this view privately to the authors. On the other hand Mr. Berton informed the authors that his conclusion in the *Wall Street Journal* represented a middle ground of estimates solicited in approximately 200 interviews with members of leading accounting firms, accounting organizations and their attorneys.

[4]It should be noted that accounting is not the only profession experiencing a flurry of litigation. There is a rash of malpractice suits pending against doctors, lawyers, architects and investment bankers. "Professional Liability and Malpractice," *Federation Insurance Council Quarterly*, Summer 1967, at 8.

recent cases of particular significance to accountants.

Impact of Recent Cases upon Relationship of Accountants to Society

Circumvention of Common Law Defenses. Three recent cases, *BarChris, Yale Express* and *Westec* include as plaintiffs third parties who are not in a contractual relationship with the auditor. Until recently, third party actions against accountants generally failed due to the limited scope of legal doctrines available to the plaintiffs. The plaintiffs either had to espouse common law negligence or deceit doctrines, or they had to assert statutory rights available under the Securities Act of 1933 or the Securities Exchange Act of 1934. The common law alternative brought them face to face with *Ultramares Corp. v. Touche, Niven & Co.*[5] or the formidable task of proving fraud;[6] the securities law alternative forced them to assume the uncertainty and risk of pioneering in the interpretation of the statutes.

Judge Cardozo in *Ultramares* held that an accountant was ordinarily liable for negligent misrepresentation solely to the person who retained him, or to the person who was known to be the primary beneficiary of the information. The Court went on to say, however, that an accountant could be held liable by a broader group if his conduct was fraudulent or so grossly negligent as to amount to fraud. A few subsequent cases have imposed liability on this constructive fraud theory, but these cases have been inconsequential. *Ultramares* has been widely followed for more than three decades, and it has effectively blocked negligence actions by third parties under common law. However, the vitality of the common law privity doctrine is once again being tested. Security holders represented by the trustee in bankruptcy are using common law negligence as an alternative theory for recovery in *Westec*. Today the prospects for a successful attack against accountants by security holders are better than in the past; there is evidence that the utility of the privity defense for accountants has begun to deteriorate.[7]

Westec itself may not pose any direct threat to privity. This will become clear only as the facts are developed at trial. Nevertheless, the case is a potentially important barometer of judicial attitude toward privity and the tone of any comment on privity even in dictum must be watched with care and with Holmes' prediction theory of the law[8] clearly in mind. Should the pressures on privity from dictum and articles continue to mount,[9] and the authors antici-

---

[5]255 New York 170, 174 N.E. 441 (1931).

[6]The conditions under which misrepresentations are fraudulent are sent forth in note 51 *infra*.

[7]A very good discussion of the English and American cases and articles questioning the privity defense is summarized by District Judge Pettine in Rusch Factors Inc. v. Levin 284 F. Supp. 85, 90–93 (1967). Expressing considerable doubt regarding the wisdom of the privity defense in negligence action involving accountants, the Court nevertheless had to stop short of a holding on the subject since the plaintiff in Rusch Factors came within the exception to privity available to those whose use is the very end and aim of the audit.

[8]Mr. Justice Holmes defined law as "[t]he *prophecies* of what the courts will do in fact. . . ." [Emphasis added.] Address by Oliver Wendell Holmes, Jr., then a Justice of the Supreme Judicial Court of Massachusetts, Dedication of the new hall of the Boston University School of Law, Jan. 8, 1897, published as "The Path of the Law," 10 *Harv. L. Rev.* 457, 461 (1897). Thus law is a prediction. And precedent constitutes a major but not the only basis for that prediction. See *Id* at 457 and 467.

[9]Accountants accustomed to taking the privity defense

pate that they will, the probability of an adverse decision on the doctrine will at some point become sufficiently great that professional practices of individuals and firms should reflect the increased liability risks in advance of any actual adverse holding.

Recent developments also imply an expansion in the legal hazards facing accountants under statutory law. Since passage in 1933 and 1934, the federal securities law has represented a potentially effective way for litigants to reach accountants when blocked at common law by *Ultramares* or the difficulty of proving fraud. Indeed, aside from the attractiveness of the federal securities laws the potential means for circumventing common law doctrines, it contains several ancillary features which enhance its usefulness as an alternative legal weapon.[10] However, the securities laws have evolved slowly in areas governing the relationship between accountants and the investing public,[11] and its potential aid to investors has not yet

been fully realized. This situation may be changing.

In *BarChris* plaintiffs finally used Section 11 of the 1933 Act[12] against accountants, and in *Yale Express* and *Westec* plaintiffs are testing the utility of Rule 10b-5 promulgated under the 1934 Act[13] as a means of reaching accountants.[14] The outcome of these cases and the accompanying legal rationales will probably do much to encourage or discourage other plaintiffs and define the legal environment for accountants during the 1970's.

Although the accountants were held liable for non-fraudulent conduct to third parties not in privity with them, *BarChris* produced no unexpected legal theories or statutory interpretations directly affecting accountants; it was clear from reading Section 11 that a privity relationship was not a prerequisite to recovery and it was also clear that conduct short of fraud would support a recovery. Nevertheless, *BarChris* is likely to have legal significance for

---

for granted should also reflect on the fact that it has recently been virtually eliminated from its formerly entrenched position in the product liability area. See Prosser, "The Fall of the Citadel (Strict Liability to the Consumer)," 50 Minn. L. Rev. 791 (1966). There are of course many socially significant distinctions between that area and the accountants' liability area, one of the more significant of which is the personal injury often attending defective products in contrast to the financial injury that can attend incorrect financial statements. The point is that privity is under attack generally and the mere citation of precedent may no longer be adequate. Accountants' continued insulation from third party negligence claims will in the authors' opinion turn on the marshalling of the social justification for that insulation.

[10]For example, the 1933 and 1934 Acts reduce the problem of quantifying the amount of damage sustained, and the additional problem of establishing a causal connection between the allegedly improper conduct and the damage.

[11]For example, prior to 1954 the total number of suits brought under the civil sections of the 1933 Act against defendants of all classes totaled only 38, an average of less than 2 per year. *L. Loss, Securities Regulation*, 989 (Supp. 1955).

[12]Sec. 11 of the Securities Act of 1933 at issue in *Bar-Chris* provides for a civil action for damages against accountants caused by their material errors in a registration statement. The statutory language of Section 11 makes it clear that privity is not needed for a successful suit under that section.

[13]The courts have interpreted Rule 10b-5 to permit a civil action for damages caused by fraud and misleading statements made in conjunction with the purchase or sale of securities. This provision reaches conduct which Sec. 11 and Sec. 18 do not.

[14]The following two additional provisions though less important than Section 11 and Rule 10b-5 are also involved in one or more of the four cases treated in this article:

Sec. 18 of the Securities Exchange Act of 1934. In essence it provides for a civil action for damages against any person who makes or causes a fraudulent statement to be made in statements filed with the exchanges or SEC.

Sec. 17 of the Securities Act of 1933. This provision is used to secure criminal indictments and injunctions. It is a general antifraud provision, making unlawful any form of fraud, untruth, or omission of a material fact associated with the sale of securities. This provision has not yet produced any case law of special significance to accountants.

accountants. It is the first important case decided under Section 11 and it involved a major firm. The authors anticipate that it may alert potential litigants to a previously little used statutory provision, and similar cases will soon follow.

In the authors' opinion the legal environment surrounding Rule 10b-5 is alive with the prospects for an extension of legal doctrines which would increase accountants' risks. The march of cases under the frequently interpreted Rule 10b-5 has steadily enlarged the list of potential plaintiffs and defendants. This expansion has occurred along with the erosion of the privity defense, a common law concept which was judicially appended at an early date to the Rule. The question today is whether the erosion of privity is sufficiently advanced and the absence of direct personal gain sufficiently unimportant so that accountants can be reached. Although *Westec* and *Yale Express* are still in the pre-trial stage, they both involve 10b-5 and are capable of defining the relationship between accountants and the Rule.[15]

Accounting Principles. Current cases differ from the past not only with respect to legal theories used but also with respect to allegations of accounting errors. Plaintiffs increasingly allege violations of generally accepted accounting principles, a marked depar-

ture from such classic cases as *Ultramares, Supra,* and *McKesson and Robbins,*[16] whose decisions were based largely on auditing deficiencies. Judges and juries not only are finding deficiencies in the way auditors examine financial records, but also are making statements on accounting principles and the way in which they should be applied.

In *Bar Chris* the Court rules that profits on a sale-leaseback should have been eliminated; however, the AICPA statements on accounting principles at the time of the transaction were silent as to the need for eliminating such profits. Publication of APB Opinion 5 resolved the question concerning the accounting for sale-leasebacks. Opinion 5 of 1964 clearly provides that " . . . the sale and the leaseback usually cannot be accounted for as independent transactions. Neither the sale price nor the annual rental can be objectively evaluated independently of the other. Consequently, material gains or losses . . . should be amortized over the life of the lease. . . . " However, APB Opinion 5 did not exist in 1960 when *Bar Chris* entered into the sale and leaseback of its bowling alleys. The applicable section of ARB 43 simply provided that: ". . . in the year in which the transaction originates, there should be disclosure of the principal details of any important sale-and-lease transaction."

Let us reexamine the *Bar Chris* sale-leaseback transaction in the light of then existing accounting principles to answer the claims of some commentators that the relevant principles were sufficiently defined before the case was brought to trial. One might advance several reasons to explain why BarChris should have eliminated the profit in its consolidated statements on its sale of a bowling alley to a finance

[15]Indeed, Judge Tyler in *Yale Express* denied the accountants' motion to dismiss certain parts of the complaint which were premised on 10b-5, though he did so without prejudice to renewal of the motion at trial. Judge Tyler's stress upon the importance of the questions involved and his stress upon the Court's need for further factual and legal development of those questions suggests further important comment will be forthcoming from *Yale Express.* The importance of the case is underlined by the fact that the SEC is participating as *amicus curiae.*

[16]McKesson & Robbins, Inc., SEC Accounting Series Release No. 19 (1940).

factor after the alley was leased back by a subsidiary. One might argue that an arm's length transaction was lacking and the auditor could therefore not attest to the amount of profit on the transfer. One might also claim that management could time the recognition of profit to suit its private needs. Moreover, BarChris still had the use of the property after the sale-leaseback, and to recognize profit portrayed legal form not economic substance. Furthermore, one might argue that recognition of profit violated the ancient principle of conservatism: "recognize all losses, but anticipate no gains." Finally, the overriding doctrine of fairness might be invoked; one might argue profit should be eliminated so that financial statements would fairly present the financial position and results of operations for BarChris.

But the doctrine of fairness is necessarily egocentric. He who espouses it presumes to know the one and only correct interpretation of a given transaction. Unfortunately, fairness, like beauty, lies in the eyes of the beholder. What appears fair to one often appears unfair to another. No one denies the propriety of fairness, but accountants need more explicit guidelines.

A similar comment applies to conservatism. Understatement of earnings can be just as harmful as overstatement. An investor can suffer economic injury from selling a stock on understated earnings as well as he can from buying on overstated earnings. The doctrine of conservatism, a disappearing one,[17] by itself is not sufficient to dictate non-recognition of gain on a sale-leaseback.

It appears that ambiguity as to the definition of the accounting entity existed at the time BarChris entered into its sale-and-lease-back transaction. Furthermore, in reviewing the pros and cons for eliminating the profit on the BarChris sale-leaseback, it becomes apparent that reasonable doubt existed as to what was required in accordance with the generally accepted accounting principles circa 1960. In fact, the issuance of Opinion 5 would have been unnecessary if the principles regarding sale-leaseback transactions were unambiguous. In rebuttal, one might contend that the principles always existed; and that the opinions were mere codifications of existing practice. This argument runs contrary to fact, however, for the APB opinions frequently have changed previous accounting methods, as they did with respect to earnings and losses on unconsolidated subsidiaries. It appears to the authors that generally accepted accounting principles for sale-leasebacks were not clearly stated at the time of the *BarChris* audit, and because of this uncertainty, the Court, perhaps inadvertently, prescribed a method of accounting it considered proper under the circumstances.

Westec is another case in which the Court is asked to consider accounting principles, and to rule on the way in which financial statements should have been prepared.[18] The complaint of Westec's trustee in bankruptcy charges, among other things, that reported earnings for 1964 and 1965 were inflated by the Company's improper accounting for several acquisitions. The plaintiff claims five acquisitions accounted for as a pooling did not meet the established criteria. The handling of these is also attacked on grounds that it was improper to consolidate earnings of companies acquired after the close

---

[17]Maurice Moonitz, "The Basic Postulates of Accounting," *Accounting Research Study No. 1*, (American Institute of CPAs, 1961) at 46–47.

[18]The description of Westec is based on the original complaint of August 23, 1968 filed in U.S. District Court (Houston). It must be remembered that all of the comments concerning Westec are based only on allegations. The case had not gone to trial as of February 1, 1970.

of the financial period but before release of the period's audit report.[19]

The allegations concerning the acquisition of Seacat-Zapata Offshore Co. illustrate the difficult questions the Court may have to face. Westec's negotiations for Seacat allegedly produced a tentative agreement whereby Westec would acquire Seacat's assets other than $1.5 million cash in exchange for $9.5 million in stock; and Westec would subsequently lease the assets to Zapata, a company which owned 50 percent of Seacat. The auditors, when asked if pooling could be used, said no. In their opinion the lease of assets prevented pooling since the surviving entity failed the continuity-of-business test. Seacat would have changed from an operating to a leasing company. Although, in the authors' opinion this interpretation is questionable, management was convinced and allegedly asked the auditors for help in revising the terms of the acquisition.

The complaint charges that the auditors then suggested the substitution of a "work contract" for the lease, which in their opinion would permit pooling. According to the terms of the contract, Westec retained legal ownership of the properties and Zapata operated them, receiving as its fee a percentage of profits which rose as profits increased. It was anticipated that the work contract would produce the same cash flow to both parties as the lease, though it was not a lease[20] and therefore would not prevent pooling. The suggestion was imple-

mented and the auditors approved the use of pooling in the annual reports.

The Seacat aspect of Westec raises three basic accounting questions. Did the work contract differ sufficiently from the original lease to justify pooling? Did the auditors lose their independence by the depth of their involvement? Was it proper to include in the audited statements an acquisition made subsequent to the accounting period in question? In the authors' opinion answers to the first two questions are not available in the accounting literature to date.[21] Nevertheless, the Court must make its rulings, and rulings necessarily rendered in the absence of clear guidelines are fraught with risk for the accountants.

The Court in *BarChris* was confronted with accounting alternatives and, as a byproduct of its decision, a preferred treatment for sale-leasebacks was identified. Alternatives are present in *Westec* and the possibility exists that it will have a similar consequence. This raises the serious question of whether, as a practical matter, judges and juries can avoid selecting amongst alternatives. A related important question is whether accounting guidelines which emerge from the judicial process will be as well conceived as those resulting from the careful method of review and public exposure developed over the years by the AICPA.

Disclosure of Privileged Information.
The plaintiffs in *Yale Express* are asking the

---

[19]The complaint alleges that three acquisitions were consummated on March 26, 1965, the date of the 1964 audit report; it is further alleged that the 1965 audit report was held open until April 28, 1966 to enable three additional acquisitions to be effected for the purpose of inflating 1965 earnings.

[20]Should the level of operations have deviated from that which was expected, the work contract would have produced a cash flow higher or lower than the lease.

[21]The Accounting Principles Board has promulgated a statement on this matter. American Institute of Certified Public Accountants, *Accounting Principles*, current text, Sec. 1091.13 (1969). Consequently, if the plaintiff is seriously going to urge that retroactive inclusion was wrong, it appears he must argue that the Accounting Principles Board erred in creating the principle, or argue that the Westec situation represented an exception to the principle.

Court to decide whether independent accountants, who have expressed an opinion on financial statements in a 10-K, must disclose to the public material errors and omissions from those statements which they have discovered during the course of a subsequent management services engagement.[22] The accountants' dilemma arose from the dual responsibilities it assumed. Judge Tyler observed in *Yale Express* that as auditor of the 10-K financial statements its responsibility

> is not only to the client who pays his fee, but also also to investors, creditors and others who may rely on the financial statements which he certifies. . . . The public accountant must report fairly on the facts as he finds them whether favorable or unfavorable to his client. His duty is to safeguard the public interest, not that of his client. (In the Matter of Touche, Nivin, Bailey and Smart, 237 S.E.C. 629, 670–671 (1957)) [footnotes omitted][23].

On the other hand in performing the subsequent special study the accountant's "primary obligations, under normal circumstances, were to its client and not the public."[24] The unique question posed in *Yale Express* is whether the duty to the investing public terminated once the financial statements were certified or alternatively whether a duty to the investing public existed after the certification, which duty dominated the obligation to the client.

The Court deferred until after the trial the question of whether a dominant post-certification duty to investors was imposed by one or more of the following: common law deceit doctrines; Section 18 (a) of the Securities Exchange Act of 1934; and Rule 10b-5. In its ultimate resolution of this question the Court must reconcile the needs of investors for unfavorable financial information against the possible benefits to companies from preserving a confidential relationship between consultants and clients. Should this question eventually go against the accountants, it seems reasonable to anticipate that for companies with less than normal financial strength accountants and clients may find it undesirable to have audits and special studies performed by the same firm.

The Threat of Criminal Action. *Continental Vending* adds the threat of criminal action to the legal hazards of accountancy. In this case, criminal action was instituted against the auditors by the U. S. Attorney for the Southern District of New York. Significantly, criminal actions against accountants, particularly major firms, have been infrequent in the past.[25] Instead, incidents of alleged wrong doing and substandard accounting practices have been resolved by administrative proceedings within the SEC[26] or in civil suits brought by the injured parties.

[22]The Committee on Auditing Procedure of the American Institute of Certified Public Accountants recently issued Statement on Auditing Procedure No. 41 (October, 1969), "Subsequent Discovery of Facts Existing at the Date of the Auditor's Report." The statement establishes procedures to be followed by the auditor who, subsequent to the date of his report upon audited financial statements, becomes aware that facts may have existed at that date which might have affected his report had he then been aware of such facts.

[23]Fischer v. Kletz, 266 F. Supp. 180, 184 (S.D.N.Y. 1967).

[24]*Id.*

[25]Diligent research has uncovered no other criminal prosecution where the motive of personal gain was so lacking and the argument for conformity with generally accepted accounting principles so strong.

[26]The SEC brings disciplinary or "disbarment" proceedings against accountants under Rule 2 of its Rules of

The severity of the government's decision to pursue a criminal charge—particularly since the accountants were not alleged to have benefited directly from their wrongdoing—leads one to speculate as to its motivation. Perhaps an analogy to the antitrust area is valid. When the government sustains a judgement against a company for an antitrust violation, that judgement can be used to establish a *prima facie* case by a private party allegedly injured by the violation.[27] Considerable help is given to the private litigant. A violation of the law is tentatively established, substantially reducing the risk of an unsuccessful suit. The prospect of a criminal suit as well as a civil suit makes a company more willing to acquiesce to a consent decree or some other settlement short of prolonged litigation. Perhaps the government is attempting to facilitate civil suits by resorting to criminal action. The criminal judgement would not have *prima facie* civil power;[28] but evidence would have been gathered, and much of the rationale for a civil case would have been developed. Alternatively, where civil suit has already been instituted, as in *Continental*, the threat of criminal action might encourage prompt settlement.[29]

Expanded Responsibilities. Last but not least significant of the characteristics of the cases under review is that they result in a pressure for expansion of the auditors' responsibilities. Two forces may cause this expansion. Section 11 of the 1933 Act[30] has been interpreted to impose a broad responsibility for financial information upon underwriters and signatories of the registration statement. Consequently, they are asking auditors to attest to new financial data. Also, for the first time a court has articulated the responsibilities of independent accountants in S-1 reviews.

The demand for an expansion of the audit function is an outgrowth of the "due diligence" defense in *BarChris*.[31] At issue was that defense as embodied in Section 11(b). The statute

Practice. Those rules provide in part as follows: "(e) Suspension and Disbarment. The Commission may deny temporarily or permanently, the privilege of appearing or practicing before it in any way to any person who is found by the Commission after notice of any opportunity for hearing in the matter
1. not to possess the requisite qualifications to represent others, or
2. to be lacking in character or integrity or to have engaged in unethical or improper professional conduct." 17 Code Fed. Reg. Sec. 201.2.

[27] 15 U.S.C. Sec. 15 (1964).

[28] The successful securities law plaintiff cannot recover treble damages as could his counterpart in the antitrust area. See Globus v. Law Research Service, Inc., 418 Fed. 1276 (ad. Cir. 1969).

[29] The prospect of criminal action is particularly threatening to accountants because of its potential impact on

their professional lives. AICPA by-laws 7.3.1, as amended February 20, 1969, specify that membership shall be terminated without a hearing if there is filed with the Secretary of the Institute a judgment for conviction of a crime defined as a felony under the law of the convicting jurisdiction. The Trial Board of the Institute according to Section 7.4 of the by-laws may expel a member if he has been convicted of a criminal offense which tends to discredit the profession. More significantly, state boards have the power to revoke a CPA's license to practice. However, it has been held that revocation was too severe a penalty where the improper conduct consisted of preparing and issuing certified statements in which the corporate client's liabilities were deliberately understated when the CPA's professional conduct had previously been unobjectionable and his motivation had been solely to give the corporation a chance to stay in business. Shander v. Allen, 28 A.D.2d 1150, 284 N.Y.S.2d 142 (1967).

[30] The most significant prior case discussing Section 11 is Shonts v. Hirlman, 28 F. Supp. 478 (S.D. Cal. 1939). Although the accountants escaped liability in that early decision, it has been roundly criticized by Professor Loss because of ". . . the surprising low accounting standards which seemed to satisfy the court . . . " *L. Loss, Securities Regulation*, 1020 (Supp. 1955).

[31] The so-called "due diligence" defense is embodied in the following provisions of Section 11 of the Securities Act of 1933: Section 11(b) of the Act provides that ". . . no person, other than the issuer, shall be liable . . . who shall sustain the burden of proof . . . (3) that (A) as regards any part of the registration statement not purporting to be

indicates that underwriters and signatories generally must make a reasonable and good faith investigation according to a *prudent man standard*; however, if they make statements in good faith on the authority of an expert, a *lesser standard* is operative with regard to the expertised statements. They must then merely have no reasonable grounds for believing the statements to be incorrect. Applying these standards the Court even held new outside directors to be liable since their investigations consisted only of questions put to officers and tenured directors, individuals who were not experts. Accordingly, directors (on their own initiative and at the request of underwriters) are asking independent accountants (experts within the meaning of Section 11) to expertise a larger portion of the information filed with the SEC, such as sales backlog and plant capacity.

The Court in *BarChris* also discussed the particular responsibility of the accountants in an S-1 review.[32] The question arose because the accountants tried to establish the due diligence defense; and, therefore, had to prove that when the registration statement became effective they had, based on a reasonable investigation, reason to believe and did believe that the expertised statements, i.e., the audited annual statements, were not misleading. The Court observed that the objective of an S-1 review is "to ascertain whether any material change has occurred in the company's financial position which should be disclosed in order to prevent the balance sheet figures from being misleading."[33] Although the Court ruled that the scope of the S-1 program as written conformed to generally accepted auditing standards, it found that the program was not properly executed.[34] It failed because some of the steps in the program were not taken, because an inadequate amount of time (20½ hours) was spent on the job, and because the in-charge accountant was too satisfied with what the Court styled "glib answers."

Part of the program required that the auditors "inquire as to changes in material contracts." Although the in-charge accountant asked the controller about uncompleted contracts and secured a list of them, he did not

---

made on the authority of any expert . . . he had, after reasonable investigation, reasonable ground to believe and did believe, at the time such part of the registration statement became effective, that the statements therein were true and that there was no omission to state a material fact required to be stated therein or necessary to make the statements therein not misleading; . . . and (C) as regards any part of the registration statement purporting to be made on the authority of an expert (other than himself) . . . he had no reasonable ground to believe and did not believe, at the time such part of the registration statement became effective, that the statements therein were untrue or that there was an omission to state a material fact required to be stated therein or necessary to make the statements therein not misleading. . . ."

Section 11 (c) defines "reasonable investigation" as follows: "In determining, for the purpose of paragraph (3) of subsection (b) of this section, what constitutes reasonable investigation and reasonable ground for belief, the standard of reasonableness shall be that required of a prudent man in the management of his own property."

[32]An accountant carries out an S-1 review to discharge an obligation which arises by implication from the language of Section 11. Since the section makes the accountant responsible for his opinion upon the audited financial statements as of the effective date of the registration statements, and since the effective date will not occur until sometime after the accountant has completed his audit and issued his opinion, he must satisfy himself as of the effective date, that the audited financial statements still fairly present the financial position and results of operations as of the end of the audited period.

[33]Escott v. BarChris Construction Corp., 283 F. Supp., 643, 701 (S.D.N.Y. 1968).

[34]This improper execution denied the accountants the due diligence defense: "[t]here had been a material change for the worse in BarChris's financial position. That change was sufficiently serious so that the failure to disclose it made the 1960 figures misleading. Berardi did not discover it. As far as results were concerned, his S-1 review was useless." *Id.* at 702.

actually examine each contract. The Court ruled this inquiry to be inadequate since in the Court's opinion the absence of prices from some examined contracts should have prompted further investigation. The Court's ruling illustrates the grave danger to the accounting profession of undefined standards. The Court in *Bar Chris* has in fact enunciated new and higher procedures for S-1 reviews, than would be considered acceptable practice by many accountants. Although the Court stated that the auditors should not be held to standards higher than those recognized in their profession, the standards were undefined and the Court filled the void.

Implications for the Profession

Let us turn now from the characteristics of the recent cases to a consideration of their implications.

1. Insurance. Accountants have realized for some time that increased legal hazards require greater liability coverage. Through the efforts of leaders in the profession higher limits have been obtained, but the uninsured exposure is still staggering. For example, the market value of a major conglomerate's common stock declined more than $250 million in the year from July 1, 1968, to June 30, 1969. The mind boggles at the thought of a class suit by the company's stockholders against its auditors alleging the drop was the consequence of negligent or fraudulent auditing. The need for increased liability insurance is obvious.

To the extent that coverage is not available, accountants must either absorb the loss or pass it on as part of their cost of business. The authors believe that miscreants should bear the brunt of loss when liability is the consequence of fraud. However, the recent civil cases fall short of fraud; they do not involve false statements deliberately made with the intent to deceive. The authors are of the opinion that in such cases it is practical and reasonable for accountants to pass on the costs of an evolving and increasingly demanding standard of professional conduct—especially when, as in several current cases, the standard extant at the time of the engagement was at best vague. Indeed, as the courts broaden the reach of federal securities law they are in effect forcing accountants, and others, to assure investors against damage sustained as a result of reliance upon incorrect financial data, a type of information which is inherently imprecise. The authors believe that because of considerations of social advantage, the losses due to the ordinary claims under the securities law should be spread as widely as possible throughout the economy. This spreading of the risk can most conveniently be implemented by accountants' liability insurance, the cost of which ultimately is diffused through the entities of the economy and their participants.[35]

2. Reference of Accounting Issues to a Master. One implication of the phenomenon whereby judges and juries are shaping ac-

[35]A similar argument was made by Judge Traynor of the California Supreme Court in a famous concurring opinion in a case involving product-liability:

"The cost of an injury and the loss of time or health may be an overwhelming misfortune to the person injured, and a needless one, for the risk of injury can be insured by the manufacturer and distributed among the public as a cost of doing business." Escola v. Coca-Cola Bottling Co., 24 Cal.2d 453, 462, 150 P.2d 436, 441 (1944).

counting practice is that defendants may wish to give new consideration to the advisability of urging the Court to refer accounting questions to a special master.[36] It seems reasonable that a master learned in accounting would handle accounting questions more capably than a lay judge or jury.

The Federal Rules of Civil Procedures permit the District Courts to appoint a special master and to refer matters to him.[37] The judge has considerable discretion over the scope of the reference. For example, the master may be directed to report only on a particular issue, or he may be directed to receive and report on evidence only.

Judicial discretion over the use of a master as opposed to the scope of the reference is more limited. In a jury trial a judge is authorized to refer questions to a master only when they are complicated. In a trial without a jury the master may be used only when some exceptional condition requires it. Thus, although a master cannot be used at the whim of the litigants or of the court, the option generally is available since many cases involving accounting issues would qualify as "complicated" or represent "exceptional circumstances."

Reference of accounting issues to a master both solves and creates problems. Difficult questions receive the sophisticated consideration they deserve; but selection of the master becomes a point of contention among plaintiffs, defendants, and judge. In addition, reference to a master generally delays the case and adds to its cost. On balance, the procedure would seem to have particular merit in cases where the accounting questions are particularly numerous and/or difficult.[38]

3. Probability Approach.

Since cases increasingly concern accounting principles as well as auditing procedures, accountants should warn the readers of financial statements regarding the probabilistic nature of their contents. Section 11 of the Securities and Exchange Act refers to "material facts." Unfortunately, accounting statements are still prepared as though their contents were indeed "facts" capable of being measured exactly to the penny. Small wonder the auditors in *BarChris* were sued partly because they failed to require the establishment of a proper allowance for doubtful accounts.

Auditors should not express an opinion on financial statements without qualification as to the level of confidence for the estimated amounts in those statements. Financial reporting would be greatly improved if a Bayesian probability approach[39] were applied to the financial statements. Confidence limits should be published for the principal items along with their expected values. For example, earnings per share should be reported as $4.02 with the probability that they are between $3.90 and

---

[36] *Fed. R. Civ. P.* 53.

[37] Although the Federal Rules of Civil Procedure govern only procedure in federal courts, they are crucial because of diversity of citizenship and size of claims in cases against accountants qualify them for consideration by a federal civil court.

[38] An example of the use of a special master where accounting questions are involved is 601 West 26 Corp. v. Solitron Devices, Inc., CCH Fed. Sec. Law Rep., paragraph 92,611 (S.D.N.Y. Jan., 1970). There the special master supervised the taking of 401 pages of minutes which produced findings on 14 accounting questions. The questions ranged from whether the accountants had subordinated their judgment to that of the client to the determination of whether earnings were artificially inflated or otherwise misrepresented. The District Court disposed of the case—vindicating the accountants—based on the findings and conclusions of law of the special master.

[39] See R. Schlaifer, *Probability and Statistics for Business Decisions* (1959).

$4.14 at the 95 percent level of confidence. Many lawsuits would be avoided if auditors would simply indicate that they are not certifying to deterministic facts, but rather are expressing an opinion on estimates from a probability distribution. A caveat should be included in the auditor's opinion putting the reader on notice of the stochastic nature of the quantities covered by the report.

4. **Marginal Companies.** One characteristic common to all of the cases in this article is that they involve businesses which have failed. Clearly, as a matter of self protection, an auditor must perform a more extensive investigation when he suspects financial difficulties. Unfortunately, evidence of business failure may be more apparent in retrospect than at the time of an audit. Nevertheless, the current cases indicate the wisdom of expanding an audit program for a company with declining earnings or weak credit.

The accountant's dilemma in this area has implications for society at large. If it becomes commonplace for stockholders to sue the auditors of every failing company, those firms least able to pay will be hindered by above average audit costs. Additional barriers to competition will be introduced because the cost of raising money and doing business will be higher for marginal companies.

5. **Extension of Attest Function.** As a result of *BarChris* directors, underwriters, and their attorneys recognize that for them to secure maximum protection under the "due diligence" defense of Section 11(b), discussed *supra* at 13, as much of the prospectus as possible must be covered by an opinion of independent accountants. This recognition has prompted them to pressure accountants to expand in several ways the scope of their work as it related to registration statements. Counsel for some underwriters, accepting the accountant's premise that he should only attest to "financial data" have in effect argued that the term "financial" has evolved and today encompasses more data than in the past. For example, in one instance independent accountants were asked to attest to the total floor space in a plant. In another, they were asked to attest to the amount of unfilled orders. Nevertheless, auditors typically have been unwilling to expand their attest function to cover data in the text of the prospectus and new types of data sought to be added to the annual financial statements via footnotes.

In addition, underwriters are asking independent accountants to expand the scope of their investigation of events subsequent to the date of the certified balance sheet. This request is a consequence of the underwriters' increased awareness of the due diligence defense at issue in *BarChris*. It will be recalled that maximum protection under the defense is available to the underwriter if at the time the registration statement becomes effective he had no reasonable ground to believe the expertised portions of the registration statements (audited financial statements, for example) were misleading. In order to satisfy these statutory requirements, the underwriter, aware that accountants conduct S-1 reviews to maximize their own due diligence protection,[40] typically secures from the company's independent auditors, "comfort letters" which contain comments on financial developments during the stub period. These comments are secured either by requesting them from the accountants who provide them as an accommodation, or by requiring in their underwriting agreement that the comments be provided.

In the authors' opinion *BarChris* suggests that standards for S-1 reviews need to be re-examined and made more specific, despite the fact that the Court stated that "accountants should not be held to a standard higher than that recognized in their profession" and the additional fact that the Court stated that it did not hold them to a higher standard. In the authors' opinion the S-1 review program prepared by the auditors in *BarChris* would have been acceptable to many accountants; and it appears that at least some accountants are out of touch with the standards as perceived by the Courts.

Since S-1 reviews and inquiries for comfort letters are generally done at the same time, the authors suggest that the profession reexamine its posture regarding those letters when it reconsiders S-1 reviews. Two basic options are available regarding comfort letters. Accountants can restrict the rendering of them, or they can increase the scope of the work for their preparation. Accountants, generally, have tended to resist an expansion of comfort letters. They prefer that the letters continue to refer only to changes in capitalization and to material adverse changes in financial position which occur subsequent to the latest financial statements in the registration statement. Furthermore, they traditionally state that an examination for the stub period has not been made, and that an opinion is disclaimed. They generally state explicitly that the procedures followed by the accountant would not necessarily disclose adverse changes in either financial position or results of operations and the assurances given are negative, couched in language such as ". . . nothing came to our attention which caused us to believe that the accounting infor-

mation requires any material adjustment for a fair presentation . . ."[41]

Anticipating that some reconsideration of S-1 reviews and comfort letters will be forthcoming, the authors suggest that the profession go far beyond the most pessimistic reading of *BarChris* and consider several radical changes in stub period practice. They believe that the expression of opinions on "adverse changes" should be discontinued since it is impossible for the accountants to determine whether a change was in fact "adverse."[42] They recommend that all unaudited statements be audited and that the auditor attest to such other data contained in the registration statement as is capable of being measured. A complete examination for the stub period, though it would take more time than the present review, could generally be accomplished during the interval between the registration and effective date of the prospectus.[43] The updating of information supplied on initial filing would be accomplished by an amendment. The incremental cost of this work would vary depending upon the length of the stub period; assuming for purposes of illustration that a company went into registration three months after the close of its fiscal period, the authors estimate that in most cases the cost would run between 20 and 40 percent of the annual examination. If as a practical matter the audit can be carried to within a few days of

---

[40]The reasons for conducting an S-1 review were discussed *supra* at note 32.

[41]*Statements on Auditing Procedure*, No. 35, at 23.

[42]For example, an increase in research and development expense with a consequent decrease in income might be beneficial for the company in the long run.

[43]Although Section 8(a) of the Securities Act of 1933 provides that the registration statement becomes effective 20 days after filing unless the SEC accelerates the effective date or determines that the statement is incomplete or inaccurate, almost invariably the registrant files a delaying amendment which postpones the effective date substantially. The average time difference between registration and effectiveness was 65 days during 1969.

the effective date of the registration statement, the underwriters will have more due diligence protection, prospectus readers will have more useful information, and the accountants will have avoided the difficult problem of articulating detailed standards for the statutorily implied S-1 review.

6. **Accounting Principles.** The courts, through their judges and juries, are affecting accounting principles as well as auditing standards. For example, the Court enunciated a basis for reporting a sale-leaseback in *BarChris*. These developments challenge the method developed by the AICPA over the years whereby it issued statements on accounting principles only after comprehensive research, publication of exposure drafts, and extended deliberation by the Accounting Principles Board. The courts are in a difficult position and may, inadvertently or otherwise, bypass this careful procedure unless the Institute accelerates its publication schedule.

The authors believe that the development of accounting principles by judges and juries as a by-product of their disposition of a series of cases will not result in the most desirable formulation of guidelines for financial reporting. Present litigation typically involves unusual circumstances, which could prejudice a decision on general principles. For instance, in *Westec* officers of the company have been found guilty on a number of criminal counts, including improper security transactions. The moral taint from these convictions might affect the Court's regard for the defendants and might prejudice its ruling on whether a pooling of interest fairly presented acquisitions by Westec. The authors believe that accounting procedures should be generalized from the experience of going concerns run by ethical managers, not failing companies run by wrongdoers.

The recent cases on accountants' liability highlight the pressing need for a massive expansion in accounting research. The SEC no longer stands alone in pushing the AICPA to narrow the differences in accounting principles. Judges and juries not expert in financial reporting are wrestling with highly complex accounting problems, and there is little reason to hope that they will do any better than the APB in developing viable accounting standards.

The AICPA expended $353,000 on research in 1968,[44] an increase of 64 percent over 1966; but an amount which constituted less than one-tenth of one percent of the reputed annual gross billings of the Big Eight firms. These figures do not reflect the enormous donation of time and labor to the Board by the individual members and their firms; however, the authors hypothesize that a massive increase in the AICPA research budget with a comparable increase in either donated or paid professional time would be of prime importance in combatting the increasing number of liability cases. In addition, government sponsored research, possibly in the form of support by a National Social Science Foundation, would be helpful.

Some critics of financial reporting take the position that further research and increased output by the APB is less necessary than the creation of an authoritative panel to choose between conflicting accounting procedures. Leonard Spacek's 1958 recommendation for an accounting court was a suggestion in that direction.[45] It will be remembered that Spacek

---

[44]American Institute of Certified Public Accountants, "Annual Report," *The CPA*, November 1968, at 13; *Fortune, supra* note 2, at 178.

[45]Leonard Spacek, "The Need for an Accounting Court," *Accounting Review*, July 1958, at 368.

recommended that the AICPA established a professional tribunal, which was not to be a court of law; hence its discussions would not affect the laws nor the administration of the laws by regulatory bodies. One reason why the proposal for an accounting court has languished is that the financial community has never been convinced of the wisdom of putting the supreme rule–making authority on accounting in the hands of three judges, however learned they might be. This skepticism regarding a professional accounting court seems equally applicable to our nation's civil courts.

An interesting parallel exists between the formulation of accounting principles and the development of common law. It is desirable that law be equitable, yet it is also essential that particular principles of law be certain and the outcome of litigation involving them predictable. In some situations considerations of equity are inconsequential or competing considerations cancel each other. In such a case it is more important that *some* rule be adopted, rather than that any particular rule be adopted. For example, in contract law it is important that the act for accepting an offer be certain. It makes little difference whether that act be the mailing of a letter by the offeree, or its delivery to the offeror. Some research in accounting might usefully determine the sensitivity of the user to alternative methods of financial reporting. Where it is found that one method of accounting is not better than another, the APB should stipulate the rule in accordance with the principle of certainty discussed above. Eliminat-

ing the options available to management for choosing between accounting principles will facilitate intra-industry comparisons. It also will reduce the financial credibility gap that invites litigation under legal doctrines emerging from the cases under review.

The authors believe that by accepting responsibility for the principles underlying financial statements, that CPAs will renew the stress on "Public" in Certified Public Accountant. The march of recent cases indicates that the courts believe independent accountants should accept a greater responsibility. The profession should respond to the challenge.

Summary

Recent litigation has been characterized by a successful effort on the part of plaintiffs to reach accountants in heretofore untested situations. Occasionally where auditing standards and accounting principles were unclear, the Courts, though stating that they adhere to generally accepted accounting principles, have selected those which appear to them most reasonable. This expansion of the law and articulation of accounting principles when combined with requests for broader attestation makes it incumbent upon accountants to consider a positive approach to the new problems and opportunities facing the profession. The suggestions presented in this article constitute the thinking of the authors on how this might best be done.

BarChris Construction Corp.
(Escott v. BarChris Construction Corp.)[46]

Plaintiffs: Purchasers of 5½% convertible subordinated 15 year debentures.

Defendants: The defendants can be subdivided into three groups: (1) those who signed the registration statement, including officer-directors; the controller, not a director; outside directors, including the company attorney, and another who was a partner of the lead underwriter; (2) the underwriters, consisting of 8 investment banking firms led by Drexel & Co.; (3) BarChris' auditors, Peat, Marwick, Mitchell & Co.

Court: U.S. District Court, Southern District of New York (Manhattan). District Judge McLean. By agreement of the parties, Judge McLean, rather than a jury, decided the questions of fact.

Factual Summary:

1. *Re: Certified financial statements as of December 31, 1960.* The Court concluded that earnings had been overstated by 14%, a figure not deemed material given that the securities involved were B rated convertible debentures and that the reported earnings per share on the underlying common would still have nearly doubled compared to the preceding year ($.33 to $.65).

The Court also concluded the current ratio was overstated 16%, a figure deemed material.

The Court gives little insight into why a 16% overstatement of working capital is material whereas a 14% overstatement of eps is not.[47] Possibly it hinges on the intentional nature of the overstatement. An officer of Bar-Chris persuaded a factor to temporarily release $147,000 of an unconsolidated subsidiaries' funds, being held as security to the subsidiary; $145,000 of this temporarily available money was then transferred to BarChris and was accounted for by a debit to Cash and credit to the noncurrent asset Investment in Non-Consolidated Subsidiary.

The overstatement of earnings was caused primarily by:

a. Overstatement of the percentage of completion on some contracts.

b. The recording of a loan to BarChris as a sale.

c. The recording of a sale-leaseback to a factor

---

[46]283 F. Supp. 643 (S.D.N.Y. 1968).

[47]A feature of the financial statements not discussed in the opinion tends to rationalize these conclusions. The effect of the balance sheet error was to exacerbate BarChris's violation of the 2:1 test of current ration used by the financial community. In contrast, as the Court observed, earnings increased dramatically even without this overstatement. The authors conclude that it is worse to minimize violation of a financial standard than it is to overstate the dramatic amount by which a standard has been exceeded.

as a sale: a bowling alley sold to Talcott (a factor) who leased it to a consolidated subsidiary of BarChris treated as a sale by BarChris in its consolidated statements.

d. The recording of a sale-leaseback to a customer as a sale: a subsidiary leased property to an operator but treated the transaction as a sale.

The overstatement of the current ratio was caused primarily by:

a. Overstatement of cash by $145,000 transferred from an unconsolidated subsidiary. This cash was received by the subsidiary as a short-term loan from a finance factor. It was not disclosed that the subsidiary had to repay this money 25 days after acquiring it.

b. Reserve for bad debts was understated by $50,000.

c. Accounts receivable contained $150,000 due from a consolidated subsidiary.

d. All reserves held by a factor were treated as current despite the fact that some of them would in the normal course of events not be released within one year.

e. Regarding footnotes, contingent liabilities were understated by $375,795 and a direct liability of $325,000 should have been included in the recorded liabilities on the balance sheet.

Plaintiffs unsuccessfully questioned other items. These included:

a. The theoretical justification for the percentage of completion method of reporting sales.

b. The absence of a reserve for contingent liabilities.

2. *Re: Unaudited income statement for first quarter 1961.* Sales were overstated by the inclusion of two intercompany transactions.

3. *Re: Unaudited backlog as of March 31, 1961.* Backlog was overstated by $4,490,000 due to the inclusion of transactions for which BarChris had no enforceable contracts.

4. *Re: Unaudited contingent liabilities as of April 30, 1961.* Contingent liabilities were understated by $618,853, and a direct liability of $314,166 was omitted.

5. *Re: Text of prospectus.* Inaccuracies in the prospectus included the following:

a. It was incorrectly implied that there were no outstanding loans from officers (they amounted to $386,615).

b. It failed to indicate that substantial sums would be expended to pay prior debts incurred as a result of alley construction already undertaken.

c. It gave the incorrect impression that BarChris' problems with customers' credit and performance were minimal.

d. It failed to mention that BarChris was operating alleys as well as constructing them.

Legal Doctrines and Statutes Relied Upon by Plaintiffs. Section 11, Securities Act of 1933. A registration statement filed with the SEC allegedly contained material false statements and material omissions.

Status: The Court found that the registration statement contained false statements of material facts. It was decided that no defendant established his "due diligence" defense with regard to all the material errors although several established that defense with regard to some of them. The Court reserved decision on such defense as causation, estoppel, waiver, release, and the statute of limitations. The Court also reserved judgment on the claims of some defendants against other defendants; these included the underwriters' claims against Peat, Marwick based on its comfort letter. The case has since been settled.

Continental Vending Machine Corp.
(United States v. Simon)[48]

Plaintiffs: United States through the U.S. Attorney's Office for the Southern District of New York.

Defendants: Carol Simon, a senior partner of Lybrand, Ross Brothers & Montgomery, partner in charge of the Continental Vending Machine Corp. audit; Robert Kaiser, partner; Melvin Fishman, audit manager.

Court: U.S. Court of Appeals for the Second Circuit. Circuit Judges Waterman, Friendly and Smith. Opinion by Circuit Judge Friendly.

Factual Summary: The appellate court upheld the criminal conviction of defendants for certifying to misleading financial statements of Continental at September 30, 1962. The case turned on the reporting of loans by Continental Vending to its affiliate, Valley Commercial Corp.

Harold Roth, president of Continental, dominated both Continental and Valley. He owned about 25 percent of Continental which was listed on the American Exchange. He supervised day-to-day operations of Valley, which were conducted from an office on Continental's premises. Roth from 1958–62 borrowed large amounts of money from Continental for his personal stock market dealings, much of which he repaid by the end of each fiscal year. Instead of borrowing directly, he had Continental lend to Valley; Roth then borrowed from Valley.

At September 30, 1962, the receivable from Valley resulting from Roth's borrowing amounted to approximately $3.5 million; and during the 1962 audit Roth informed the auditors that Valley was unable to repay Continental since he was unable to repay Valley. Conse-

quently Roth agreed to post adequate collateral. However 80% of the collateral Roth produced consisted of holdings in Continental; moreover, the total had a value of only $2.9 million on February 15, 1963, the date of the opinion on the 1962 statements. Nevertheless, the auditors attested to a Continental footnote which stated, in effect, that the $3.5 million receivable from Valley, less the balance payable to Valley, was collateralized by marketable securities of an amount greater than the difference between the receivable and payable.

Actually, the reporting of the Valley receivable and its pledged security was complicated by the fact that Valley was used for transactions other than Roth's personal borrowings from Continental. From time to time, Continental secured financing by issuing negotiable notes to Valley which in turn discounted them at banks and transferred the discounted amounts to Continental. At September 30, 1962, these notes amounted to about $1.0 million. The $1.0 million notes payable to Valley could not be offset against the $3.5 million receivable from Valley since the holder of the notes payable (the bank) differed from the debtor on the accounts receivable (Valley and ultimately Roth). Nevertheless, the footnote to the September 30, 1962 statements indicated that the payable was deducted from the receivable in figuring the adequacy of the collateral.

The pertinent sections of the September 30, 1962 Continental balance sheet and related footnotes are as follows:

Assets
Current Assets:
  . . . .
    Accounts and notes receivable:
      . . . .
        Valley Commercial Corp.,
          affiliate (Note 2) $2,143,335

---

[48]   F.2d   (2d. Cir. 1969).

Noncurrent accounts and notes receivable:
Valley Commercial Corp.,
    affiliate (Note 2)   1,400,000
. . . .

Liabilities
Current liabilities:
. . . .
Long-term debt,
    portion due within one year   8,203,788
. . . .
Long-term debt (Note 7)
. . . .
Valley Commercial Corp.,
    affiliate (Note 2)   486,130
. . . .

Notes to Consolidated Financial Statements
2. The amount receivable from Valley Commercial Corp. (an affiliated company of which Mr. Harold Roth is an officer, director and stockholder) bears interest at 12% a year. Such amount, less the balance of the notes payable to that company, is secured by the assignment to the Company of Valley's equity in certain marketable securities. As of February 16, 1963, the amount of such equity at current market quotations exceeded the net amount receivable.
7. . . . . The amounts of long-term debt, including the portion due within one year, on which interest is payable currently or has been discounted in advance, are as follows:
. . . .
Valley Commercial Corp.,
    affiliate $1,029,475
Legal Doctrines and Statutes Relied upon by Prosecution: The indictment charged defendants with conspiring and adopting a scheme to violate federal criminal statutes prohibiting one or more of the following: 1) the filing of false statements with a governmental agency (18 U.S.C. Section 1001); 2) the use of the mails to perpetuate a fraud (18 U.S.C. Section 1341);

and 3) the filing of false statements with the SEC (Section 32 of the Securities Exchange Act of 1934, 15 U.S.C. Section 78ff.). The appellate court stated that the Government's burden "was not to show that defendants were wicked men with designs on anyone's purse, which they obviously were not, but rather that they had certified a statement knowing it to be false."
Status: The three accountants were found guilty by a jury in June, 1968 after an earlier trial ended in a hung jury. Simon was fined $7,000. Kaiser and Fishman were fined $5,000 each. The Second Circuit upheld the conviction and the Supreme Court declined to review the case.

In related cases the defendants were Harold Roth, president of Continental; David Roth, his brother; and Clair Gans, his administrative assistant. Harold Roth entered a plea of "guilty," and was put on probation for three years after serving six months of an 18 month term. The case against David Roth and Gans had not gone to trial at December 1, 1969. In November, 1967, Lybrand settled a civil suit against it for $1,960,936.

Westec Corp.
(*Carpenter v. Hall*)[49]

Plaintiff: Trustee of Westec Corporation. The trustee either directly or indirectly represents the interest of 1) Westec Corp., 2) the Fraud Claimants Fund for Creditors Class Six as set forth in the Trustee's Amended Plan of Reorganization, 3) a class of people consisting in part of all persons who sustained a loss as a result of any purchase of or loan against Westec common stock between September 2, 1964 and August 5, 1966.

---

[49]Complaint, C.A. No. 68-H-738 (S.D. Tex. filed August 23, 1968).

Defendants: There are 93 defendants. These include: James W. Williams, formerly Board Chairman of Westec; E. M. Hall, Jr., formerly president of Westec; numerous business associates of Williams and Hall and the companies with which these associates were affiliated; the American Stock Exchange specialists handling Westec trading; a variety of brokerage houses and their employees; and Ernst & Ernst, together with Clarence T. Isensee and Newman T. Halverson (Partners), and John F. Maurer (Audit Manager).

Court: U.S. District Court, Southern District of Texas (Houston).

Factual Summary: The bulk of the 32 page complaint alleges that various defendants joined in or abetted an unlawful conspiracy to misuse the corporate funds of Westec and associated companies; and/or to victimize the company, its shareholders and the investing public through manipulating the company's stock. Several defendants are singled out for different or additional allegations. The complaint directed at Ernest & Ernest alleges:

1. The auditors made a superficial examination in 1964 which failed to detect (a) that the sale of a plant had not been completed ($90,000 profit), and (b) that the sale of a warehouse ($150,000 profit) made to a company controlled by one of the conspirators was fictitious.

2. The auditors' 1965 examination was inadequate in that it failed to discover (a) that the $1.3 million sale of a production payment by an acquired company was reported as 1965 income although the sale occurred prior to the non-pooling acquisition of the company; and (b) a fictitious sale of oil properties was superseded by a non-arm's length sale of the properties at an inflated price.

3. The pooling of interest approach to the accounting for six acquisitions was improperly applied. The audit report was held open until March 26, 1965, the date when three of the six contested poolings were acquired, so that the prior year's earnings of such acquisitions could be included in the consolidated reports. The plaintiff alleges that earnings of six acquired companies for periods prior to acquisition should not be combined with the parent company. It is also claimed that five of the six acquisitions failed to meet established criteria for pooling.

4. Ernst & Ernst were so involved in the structuring of acquisitions that they lost their status as independent accountants.

5. The auditors deliberately concealed the material impact (23%) of the three pooling acquisitions upon the 1964 earnings. They should have disclosed that the five 1965 poolings produced net earnings of $5 million, whereas reported 1965 earnings were only $4.8 million for the company as a whole.

Legal Doctrines and Statutes Relied Upon by Plaintiff: The accountants are charged with: 1) common law negligence for breaching contractual and fiduciary duties to Westec requiring professional care; and 2) engaging in fraudulent acts proscribed by the Securities Act of 1933 and the Securities Exchange Act of 1934.

Status: In pre-trial stage at December 1, 1969.

Yale Express
(Fisher v. Kletz)[50]

Plaintiffs: Stockholders and debenture holders of Yale Express Systems, Inc. (Yale).

Defendants: Peat, Marwick, Mitchell & Co. (Peat), numerous officers and directors of Yale and underwriters for Yale debentures.

---

[50]266 F. Supp. 180 (S.D.N.Y. 1967).

Court: U.S. District Court, Southern District of New York (Manhattan). Judge Tyler.

Factual Summary: Plaintiffs claim damages from errors and omissions in three sets of financial statements, namely: (1) the unaudited statements appearing in the prospectus for an August 20, 1963 debenture offering; (2) the audited statements for the year ending December 31, 1963; and (3) unaudited interim statements issued during 1964. These statements were distributed to the public and filed with the SEC and stock exchanges. The consolidated earnings for 1963, the interim earnings for 1964 and year-end assets, particularly receivables, appear to have been overstated.

In early 1964, Peat undertook several management service studies for Yale; thus Peat changed its relationship to Yale from that of "independent public accountant" with statutory duties under the 1934 Act to that of management consultant. In this new capacity Peat discovered that figures in the 1963 annual report were substantially false and misleading. The litigants differ on when this discovery was made; Peat contends discovery occurred after the report was filed while plaintiffs contend discovery occurred before the SEC and others received the annual report. Peat did not disclose its findings to the SEC or public until May 1965, when the results of its management studies were released.

Legal Doctrines and Statues Relied Upon by Plaintiffs; Procedural Settings: In what is so far the major opinion in the case, Peat moved to dismiss those parts of the complaint dealing with the 1963 annual report and the 1964 interim reports. This procedural setting required the Court to view the facts in the light most favorable to the plaintiffs and to deny the motion if there was any viable legal theory for sustaining the plaintiffs. Plaintiffs opposed the motion regarding the 1963 reports by arguing that the failure to disclose the inaccuracies as soon as discovered violated common law deceit doctrines,[51] and Section 18(a) of the Securities Exchange Act of 1934 Rule 10b-5[52] promulgated by the SEC pursuant to Section 10(b) of the Securities Exchange Act of 1934. With regard to the 1964 interim statements, plaintiffs argued that the failure to disclose the findings of its studies constituted a violation of Rule 10b-5. The motion to dismiss was denied.

Status: The case was in the pre-trial stages as of December 1, 1969.

---

[51]The Restatement of Torts identifies the elements of deceit involving business transactions as follows:

Sec. 525—Liability for Fradulent Misrepresentation.
One who fradulently makes a misrepresentation of fact, opinion, intention or law for the purpose of inducing another to act or refrain from acting in reliance thereon on a business transaction is liable to the other for the harm caused to him by his justifiable reliance upon the misrepresentation.

Sec. 526—Conditions Under Which Misrepresentation is Fradulent.
A Misrepresentation in a business transaction is fradulent if the maker
a. knows or believes the matter to be otherwise than as represented or
b. knows that he has not the confidence in its existence or non-existence asserted by his statement of knowledge or belief or
c. knows that he has not the basis for his knowledge or belief professed by his assertion.

[52]Rule 10b-5 provides as follows: It shall be unlawful for any person, directly or indirectly, by the use of any means or instrumentality of interstate commerce, or of the mails, or of any facility of any national securities exchange,
a. to employ any device, scheme, or artifice to defraud,
b. to make any untrue statement of a material fact or to omit to state a material fact necessary in order to make the statements made, in the light of the circumstances under which they were made, not misleading, or
c. to engage in any act, practice, or course of business which operates or would operate as a fraud or deceit upon any person,
in connection with the purchase or sale of any security.

1. Discuss the underlying reasons for the accounting profession's adopting a code of professional ethics.

2. The CPAs' code of professional ethics prohibits the direct or indirect offer of employment by a CPA to an employee of another CPA without first informing the other CPA.

  a. What are the justifications for this rule?

  b. What action, if any, may the employee of a CPA take should he learn that another CPA firm has an open position for which he would like to apply?

3. What is meant by "independence" as applied to the CPA's function of auditing and expressing opinions on financial statements? Discuss.

4. The Wallydrag Company is indebted to a CPA for unpaid fees and has offered to issue to him unsecured interest-bearing notes. Would the CPA's acceptance of these notes have any bearing upon his independence in his relations with the Wallydrag Company? Discuss.

5. The Rocky Hill Corporation was formed on October 1, 1964 and its fiscal year will end on September 30, 1965. You audited the corporation's opening balance sheet and rendered an unqualified opinion on it.

A month after rendering your report you are offered the position of secretary of the Company because of the need for a complete set of officers and for convenience in signing various documents. You will have no financial interest in the Company through stock ownership or otherwise, will receive no salary, will not keep the books, and will not have any influence on its financial matters other than occasional advice on income tax matters and similar advice normally given a client by a CPA.

  a. Assume that you accept the offer but plan to resign the position prior to conducting your annual audit with the intention of again assuming the office after rendering an opinion on the statements. Can you render an independent opinion on the financial statements? Discuss.

  b. Assume that you accept the offer on a temporary basis until the Corporation has gotten under way and can employ a secretary. In any event you would permanently resign the position before conducting your annual audit. Can you render an independent opinion on the financial statements? Discuss.

6. During 1966 your client, Nuesel Corporation, requested that you conduct a feasibility study to advise management of the best way the Corporation can utilize electronic data

---

From AICPA Uniform CPA Examinations.

processing equipment and which computer, if any, best meets the Corporation's requirements. You are technically competent in this area and accept the engagement. Upon completion of your study the Corporation accepts your suggestions and installs the computer and related equipment that you recommended.

a. Discuss the effect the acceptance of this management services engagement would have upon your independence in expressing an opinion on the financial statements of the Nuesel Corporation.

b. Instead of accepting the engagement, assume that you recommend Ike Mackey, of the CPA firm of Brown and Mackey, who is qualified in specialized services. Upon completion of the engagement your client requests that Mackey's partner, John Brown, perform services in other areas. Should Brown accept the engagement? Discuss.

c. A local printer of data processing forms customarily offers a commission for recommending him as supplier. The client is aware of the commission offer and suggests that Mackey accept it. Would it be proper for Mackey to accept the commission with the client's approval? Discuss.

7. Your CPA firm decided to form a partnership with Fred Reitz, a non-CPA management consultant, which would result in a "mixed partnership" of a CPA and a non-CPA.

Under what circumstances, if any, would it be ethically proper for a CPA to form a "mixed partnership"? Discuss.

8. Alex Pratt, a retired partner of your CPA firm, has just been appointed to the board of directors of Palmer Corporation, your firm's client. Pratt is also a member of your firm's income tax committee which meets monthly to discuss income tax problems of the partnership's clients. The partnership pays Pratt $100 for each committee meeting he attends and a monthly retirement benefit of $1,000.

Discuss the effect of Pratt's appointment on the board of directors of Palmer Corporation on your partnership's independence in expressing an opinion on the Palmer Corporation's financial statements.

Chapter 3

Evolution of
Auditing Objectives

The primary objective of an audit examination by an independent auditor today is the expression of an opinion on the fairness with which the financial statements prepared by his client present the financial position and results of operations of the client company in accordance with principles generally accepted by the accounting profession. In a society where ownership and management are generally separated, this independent and impartial professional review of the reports of management adds reliability to the statements and hence performs a significant function for the owners.

Auditor's Report

The expression of an opinion on the fairness of financial statements usually takes the form of the standard "short-form" report. This report describes the scope of the audit undertaken and then expresses an opinion on the financial statements. The various forms of this report will be considered in Section 4.

The first line of the auditor's standard short-form report indicates that the financial statements are those of the client organization. The client therefore has the ultimate responsibility for the representations made in these statements and for the manner in which they are presented. The responsibility of management for these financial statements is very clearly indicated in the AICPA publication *Auditing Standards and Procedures*, which states:

Management has a responsibility for adopting sound accounting policies, for maintaining an adequate and effective system of accounts, for the safeguarding of assets, and for devising a system of internal control that will, among other things, help assure the production of proper financial statements. . . . Accordingly, the fairness of the representations made through financial statements is an implicit and integral part of management responsibility. . . . [The auditor's] responsibility for the statements he has examined is confined to the expression of his opinion on them. Financial statements remain the representation of the management.[1]

Since the financial statements are the responsibility of management, the independent auditor can only express his opinion on them; he cannot make changes in the statement, although he can and does propose changes where he believes the accounting treatment and disclosure should be different from that made by the client. If the client is unwilling to follow the auditor's recommendations, the auditor will probably find it necessary to modify his auditor's report to point out anything which might be important to a third party reading the statements.

The Audit Examination

The auditor obtains data to support his opinion by critically and systematically evaluating the client's system of accounting and internal control, reviewing selected financial and accounting transactions processed by the system, and determining the reasonableness of the individual balances reported on the financial statements. The examination is conducted in accordance with generally accepted auditing standards, which will be discussed in a subsequent chapter, and includes various auditing procedures used in gathering evidence about the system of accounting, the transaction buildup, and the reasonableness of the accounts represented.

Almost all audit examinations are performed by testing various records used by the client and gaining confirmation of these records by observing the various assets and by corresponding with third parties about the existence and valuation of certain accounts such as receivables, inventory, liabilities, cash. The concept of testing, or sampling, is important in auditing, and a more detailed examination of the sampling process used by auditors will be made in subsequent chapters. As a result of the audit examination, the auditor is normally able to give an opinion on the financial statements that fulfills his specific audit objective.

[1] AICPA, *Auditing Standards and Procedures*, p. 9-10

The current status of auditing objectives and the auditor's report is the result of an evolutionary process. The accounting profession has developed dramatically over a relatively short period of time. Unlike law and medicine, which were organized professions before the Middle Ages, accountancy as a profession can be traced back only to the nineteenth-century British Isles. It is true that the bookkeeping techniques of the accountant were known in fifthteenth century Italy, but the characteristics of accounting as we know it today were not then present even in vestigial form.

As has often proved the case in the history of accounting, much of the initial stimulus for the profession arose out of economic disaster. The speculative fervor of eighteenth century England culminated, in 1720, in the South Sea Bubble, which gave rise to a public uproar that in turn led to investigation requiring the talents of accountants. For the century that followed, it became increasingly common to call upon outsiders skilled in record-keeping to investigate bankruptcies, settle disputes over accounts, and to some extent maintain the records of merchants.

By the middle of the nineteenth century, the use of accountants had developed to the point where a group of Scottish accountants could petition the crown for a royal warrant of incorporation in 1854 in the following terms:

> That the profession of Accountants, to which the Petitioners belong, is of longstanding and great respectability, and has of late grown into very considerable importance: That the business of Accountants, as practiced in Edinburgh, is varied and extensive, embracing all matters of account, and requiring for its proper execution, not merely thorough knowledge of these departments of business which fall within the province of the Actuary, but an intimate acquaintance with the law of Scotland, and more especially with those branches of it which have relation to the law of merchant, to insolvency and bankruptcy, and to all rights connected with property: That in the extrication of those numerous suits before the Court of Sessions, which involve directly and indirectly matters of accounting, an accountant is almost invariably employed by the court to aid in eliciting the trust: That such investigations are manifestly quite unsuited to such a tribunal as a Jury, yet cannot be prosecuted by the court itself without professional assistance on which it may rely, and the accountant, to whom in any case of this description a remit is made by the court, performs in substance all the more material functions which the Petitioners understand to be performed in England by the Masters in Chancery: That Accountants are also largely employed in Judicial Remits in cases which are peculiar to the practice of Scotland, as for instance, in Ranking and Sales, in process of Court and Reckoning, Multiple poinding, and others of a similar description: That they are also most commonly selected to be Trustees on

Sequestrated Estates, and under Voluntary Trusts, and in these capacities they have duties to perform, not only of the highest responsibility, and involving large pecuniary interests, but which require, in those who undertake them, great experience in business, very considerable knowledge of law, and other qualifications which can only be attained by a liberal education: That in these circumstances, the Petitioners were induced to form themselves into a Society called the Institute of Accountants of Edinburgh, with a view to unite into one body those at present practicing the profession, and to promote the objects which, as members of the same profession, they entertain in common; and that the Petitioners conceive that it would tend to secure in the members of their profession the qualifications which are essential to the proper performance of its duties, and would consequently conduce much to the benefit of the public if the Petitioners who form the present body of practicing accountants in Edinburgh were united into a body corporate and politic, having a common seal, with power to make rules and by-laws for the qualification and admission of members, and otherwise.[2]

No English society was chartered until 1870, and the Institute of Chartered Accountants in England and Wales received its charter in 1880.

The growth of the public accounting profession in Britain was hastened in the nineteenth century by a series of acts that necessitated the performance of this function. The Companies Act of 1862 required the appointment of inspectors who would examine the corporate records and report their opinion on them to the Board of Trade. The Bankruptcy Act of 1869 also created work for accountants. By the end of the nineteenth century, the accounting profession was firmly established in the British Isles.

The development of public accounting in the United States was less rapid and sprung from its British antecedents. A large majority of nineteenth-century accountants were trained in the British Isles and originally came to the United States at the request of British investors who wished to have their interests protected. While many of these chartered accountants came only for a particular engagement and returned to the mother country as fast as possible, others remained and formed the nucleus of the American profession. Large British firms such as Price Waterhouse and Co. and Barrow Wade Guthrie opened American offices.

In 1887, the first national organization of accountants, the American Association of Public Accountants, was formed, and in 1896 the first legal recognition was given to the profession with the passage of the first CPA law in New York State. By 1921, all the states had passed CPA legislation.

---

[2]Richard Brown, *A History of Accounting and Accountants*, p. 208.

Many factors contributed to the growth of accounting during the first thirty years of the twentieth century. This was a period of rapid industrial growth and the accounting profession grew in part simply because the economy grew. Additionally, the growth of public-securities markets and the increasing practice of publishing annual reports, encouraged by the New York Stock Exchange, led to use of auditors to add reliability to these reports. In the case of new securities offering, investment bankers were urging that financial statements disclosed to the public be audited. During this period, the Federal Reserve Board began requiring audited financial statements to support applications for the discount of commercial paper and in 1917 the Board, in cooperation with the American Institute of Accountants, published *Approved Methods for the Preparation of Balance Sheet Statements*, outlining the nature of a balance-sheet audit. Finally, the passage of the income-tax (sixteenth) amendment of the Constitution paved the way for the imposition of a tax based on income, which enormously increased the demand for accounting services—both in the preparation of returns and in setting up the record-keeping systems necessary to produce the required data.

In 1929, the stock market crash presaged the termination of economic growth for ten years, but legislation and other action resulting from the debacle made this another decade of growth for public accounting. Recognition by the stock exchange that public confidence in securities markets and business reports had been severely shaken led to conferences with the American Institute of Accountants and an ultimate announcement in January 1933 that all companies requesting listing for securities on the exchange would have to submit statements audited by an independent public accountant.

Later in the year, the Securities Act of 1933 substantially increased both the business and the responsibilities of auditors by requiring that all new issues of securities would have to be registered with the Federal Trade Commission, and that the registration statement would have to include financial statements audited by an independent public accountant. As discussed in the previous chapter, the act also redefined the liabilities of any auditor whose name was included in the registration statement.

The Securities and Exchange Act of 1934 set up the Securities and Exchange Commission with broad regulatory power over the form and content of financial statements. In addition, it required audited financial statements for all listed companies and thus further increased the demand for auditing services. Since its creation, the SEC has played a significant role in the development of accounting and auditing. It has worked closely with and encouraged the organized accounting profession in defining

Early Twentieth Century

accounting principles and auditing standards, and through its releases and decisions it has established guidelines to be followed by reporting entities and their auditors.

Post World War II

As growth in industrial activity resumed during the war and in the twenty-five years which followed, the profession has once again grown with the economy, but at a much greater pace than the economy as a whole. Perhaps the most significant cause of this greater pace has been the expansion of services offered by public accounting firms. The growth in data-processing technology has led to a tremendous demand for services in this area. Additionally, as periodic reviewers of financial information, auditors are in an excellent position to identify areas of a client's operations that could be improved. Finally, business managements have tended to seek the services of outside experts to evaluate and suggest changes in operating methods. All of these factors have led to the tremendous growth of the consulting function performed by public accounting firms. It has been estimated that in the case of several of the large national firms of CPAs, management-consulting billings are in excess of 20 percent of gross fees, and this share is growing. This development, together with the more than average increase in auditing and tax advisory work, has made the accounting profession one of the most dramatic growth areas in the economy.

Historical Development of the Audit Function

As the public accounting profession has grown and developed, its best-known function—auditing—has also changed dramatically, both in objectives and in the techniques used.

In the early days of public accounting, the audit function was primarily a police function: Its objective was to detect fraud and error. One of the earliest textbooks on the subject, *Dicksee's Auditing*, outlines the objective of an audit as follows:

The object of an audit may be said to be threefold:
1. The detection of fraud.
2. The detection of technical errors.
3. The detection of errors of principle.

On account of its intrinsic importance the detection of fraud is clearly entitled to be considered an "object" in itself, although it will be obvious that it can only be concealed by the commission of a technical error, or of an error of principle. It will be appropriate, therefore, to combine the search after fraud with search for technical and fundamental errors; but it can never be too strongly insisted that the auditor *may* find fraud concealed under *any* item that he is called upon to verify. His research for fraud should therefore be unwearying and constant.[3]

The means for achievement of such an objective was a detailed analysis of transactions. While Dicksee mentioned the concept of internal check, and pointed out that when a good system of internal check existed, "a detailed audit is frequently not necessary in its entirety," the emphasis in that and other texts of the day was on careful examination of all details. The auditor's knowledge of bookkeeping was his paramount skill. Two of the required questions in the first CPA examination in New York in 1896 are indicative of this emphasis:

1. State what is necessary in auditing case payments, and how to prevent the reproduction and passing of vouchers a second time.

2. In an audit stipulating for the examination of all vouchers of every description, what would be proper vouchers for the following: purchases, returned purchases, sales, returned sales, cash receipts, cash payments, journal entries?[4]

With the passage of time and the growth of enterprises to the size that made significantly improved internal systems of control economical, a detailed audit of transactions became impractical and the objectives of the audit function changed significantly. By the 1920s the auditor's report on financial statements became an end product rather than merely an evidence of absence of fraud. At this time, the balance sheet was the preeminent statement and the auditor's report emphasized it accordingly. During this period, auditing procedures still related primarily to recorded transactions, although there was increasing recognition that when record-keeping systems were adequate limited tests of details could represent an adequate audit. In practice, however, auditing procedures still required a great deal of detailed checking work. Although the examination of supporting detail was somewhat reduced, accounts were still analyzed in detail and transactions scheduled in the working papers.

Auditing procedures in this era tended to emphasize account balances

---

[3]Lawrence R. Dicksee, *Auditing, A Practical Manual for Auditors*, London Gee & Co., 1907, p. 7.

[4]James D. Edwards, *History of Public Accounting in the United States*, MSU Business Studies, 1960.

and the verification thereof at the balance-sheet date. Relatively little auditing was performed on income-statement accounts, since it was felt that proof of beginning and ending balance-sheet figures proved the income statement. Since reporting practices of the day provided only the most abbreviated income statement, if indeed any was presented, this audit emphasis on the balance sheet is not surprising.

In the 1930s, audit procedures were extended to include verification outside the books of the client as a regular and required procedure. The McKesson-Robbins fraud was primarily responsible for the inclusion of physical observation of inventories in generally accepted auditing procedures. The confirmation of accounts receivable with debtors, which had been a common practice, was also enshrined in the list of necessary audit procedures in this era. Both of these additions, however, related to the continued verification of balances. Both steps were initially performed at year-end to develop evidence supporting the specific year-end figure in the financial statements. Whenever this was impossible, observation or confirmation was undertaken as nearly as possible to the balance-sheet date, and these balances were then carefully reconciled to the balance-sheet figure.

In the 1940s and 1950s, two significant changes occurred in the audit approach. First, emphasis of financial-statement users shifted more and more to the income statement and away from the balance sheet, and the auditor's objective moved accordingly. As more detailed information was given in the income account and analysts and investors paid more attention to earnings per share, the auditor devoted more of his audit effort to these areas. Even when his programs were still written in terms of balance-sheet options, he was urged to think of the implications for income measurement of any unusual items arising in connection with his audit. Such concepts as materiality were more generally considered in relation to net income rather than to balance-sheet captions. Thus could be observed the beginning of the trend toward the audit of continuing income flows rather than of periodic balances.

The second major change that occurred in auditing during this period was the increasing emphasis on the review of internal control as the key to the audit, and the broadening of the auditor's definition of internal control. As a corollary of this change, concepts of sampling came to be more frequently used and the time-honored pursuit of fraud ceased to be a significant audit objective. The Committee of Auditing Procedure of the AICPA dealt with this subject as follows:

. . .the ordinary examination directed to the expression of an opinion on financial statements is not primarily or specifically designed, and cannot be relied upon, to disclose defalcations and other similar irregularities, although their discovery may result.[5]

Auditing textbooks during this period began to emphasize the limitations on detailed auditing procedures that were possible if good controls existed, and devoted more time to the review of internal control. The definition of internal control was significantly broadened. Whereas the old-time auditor thought of control primarily in terms of bookkeeping and cash-handling mechanics (Is the check signer different from the bank reconciler?, etc.), the new definition encompassed the problems of managerial control over the totality of the business and its operations. The Committee on Auditing Procedure offered the following definition:

> Internal control comprises the plan of organization and all of the coordinate methods and measures adopted within a business to safeguard its assets, check the accuracy and reliability of its accounting data, promote operational efficiency, and encourage adherence to prescribed managerial policies. . . . A "system" of internal control extends beyond those matters which relate directly to the functions of the accounting and financial departments.[6]

An increasing part of the audit was devoted to this system of internal control, both in understanding the existing system and in executing tests of it. Where tests of controls indicated a reliable system, detailed verification of balances was virtually eliminated. It became possible for auditors to express an opinion on financial statements within ten days of the end of the fiscal year.

Under this system, large parts of what had previously been balance tests could be executed at interim dates and this became part of the auditor's test of transactions in the internal control review. No longer did the auditor have to spend New Year's Day climbing oil tanks in freezing weather. Now he could observe inventory at any time during the year as part of his internal-control review. If the system proved to be satisfactory, he could accept the year-end data produced by the system as reliable without further physical tests. Divisions and subsidiaries needed to be visited solely at interim dates.

Even though the primary objective of the audit has not changed in

---

[5]AICPA, *Auditing Standards and Precedures*

[6]*Ibid.*

recent years, this change in audit approach has resulted in a significant evolution of auditing procedures. What the emphasis on internal-control review has brought about, however, is the development of additional audit objectives. In his evaluation of internal control, the auditor is placed in a position enabling him to suggest improvements/in the client's accounting system and controls, as well as to offer ideas for improving financial planning, tax planning, and clerical efficiency. The development of such suggestions is a significant additional audit objective. At the end of each audit, the auditor normally summarizes these suggestions in a "management letter" which is submitted to the client.

During the 1960s these trends accelerated, and at the beginning of the 1970s such is the nature of the auditor's task that no longer can rendering an opinion on financial statements clearly be appropriately identified as the auditor's preeminent objective. These developments will be considered in the following chapter.

Yale Express

Richard J. Whalen

Case

In the conventional tale of business chicanery it usually comes to light that an insider has lined his pockets by practicing deceit on outsiders, as witness the famous cases of McKesson & Robbins' phantom inventory, Billy Sol Estes' restless ammonia tanks, and De Angelis' invisible salad oil. But there is a rarer kind of decep-

Reprinted from the November issue of *Fortune* Magazine by special permission; ©1965 Time Inc.

This case originally appeared as an article in the magazine, under the title "The Big Skid at Yale Express."

tion in which insiders are essentially self-deceived and become their own principal victims. This is what seems to have happened at Yale Express System, whose story deserves a place among the classic misadventures of American business.

Late in 1964, Yale, a New York–based trucker and freight forwarder, reported nine months' net earnings of $904,000, a figure somewhat disappointing to the creditors and stockholders. It indicated that Yale, after a year and a half, still was not enjoying the promised high return on its very ambitious acquisition of Republic Carloading & Distributing Co., a leading freight forwarder twice as large as the parent company. But the figure was routinely accepted as fact by some observers who could, and certainly should, have taken the trouble to look behind it. If they had, they would have found that the "profit" was pure fiction, and that Yale was out of control and headed for bankruptcy.

Unfortunately, no outsiders, except the auditors, Peat, Marwick, Mitchell & Co.—who played a central but ambiguous and embarrassing role in the drama—looked closely at what was going on inside Yale until it was much too late. Yale's distress was disclosed early last March, when the company announced that its interim reports of profits during the previous year were incorrect "in the light of errors discovered in the 1964 accounts." Instead of the anticipated year-end profit, which the senior lenders had privately been told might be as much as $1,800,000, Yale announced that it would suffer a *loss* estimated at $3,300,000. This was merely the first shock. Next came the stunning disclosure that the $1,140,000 profit shown in the *audited* 1963 financial statement was also incorrect. The figure had been restated, and it now was a loss estimated at $1,200,000 (later revised to $1,880,000).

Only the barest hint of what had happened was contained in Yale's March announcement. In addition to citing accounting "errors," the company said that the 1964 accounts included substantial payments to the railroads for freight moved in 1963, "the liability for which was not recorded in the 1963 accounts because the documentary evidence supporting these payments was withheld from the public

auditor." Despite this suggestion of fraud, the company went on to say that it had found no evidence of "direct personal gain" on the part of any directors, officers, or employees. Nor, apparently, has anyone since, although an army of lawyers and accountants has been searching.

For a young, middling-sized company, Yale had acquired an impressive array of financial backers and sponsors, who were now severely embarrassed. Chief among the creditor banks was First National City, which had $10 million in loans outstanding; however, its liability as the lead bank was only $6 million, because Marine Midland was a 40 percent participant in loans to Yale. Among the long-term lenders were Massachusetts Mutual Life Insurance Co. ($2,600,000) and Aetna Life Insurance Co. ($700,000). Late in the summer of 1963 a syndicate headed by Eastman Dillon, Union Securities & Co., and Hemphill, Noyes & Co. had underwritten Yale's $6,500,000 issue of convertible debentures and $5,500,000 worth of common stock. After the windows stopped rattling and silence fell, all eyes turned toward Peat, Marwick, the nation's largest public accounting firm, which had certified the 1963 financial statement. What was the explanation for the bombshell just exploded?

Though under intense pressure from the anxious leaders, Peat, Marwick proceeded cautiously and its report did not appear until May. Its audit set the net loss for 1964 at $2,850,000, but the focus of Peat, Marwick's concern, understandably, was the restatement of the previously audited 1963 figures. The loss for 1963 was finally fixed at the $1,880,000 figure. More interesting than that figure, however, was the way it was arrived at. The auditors made a series of massive adjustments, which included charging against 1963 some

$2,630,000 in additional transportation costs and other expenses and $827,000 in additional loss, injury, and damage claims. Most staggering of all, Peat, Marwick wrote off $1,325,000 in accounts receivable, which had been carried as assets, but which the company had never collected.

All told, the swing from Yale's reported pretax profits for 1963 and nine months of 1964 to the final audited losses was on the order of $11 million, an almost incredible amount for a company with annual revenues of only about $84 million. Roughly a third of this swing reflected accounting changes, the rest operating losses. Eye-popping hindsight thus reveals that Yale had been in deep trouble for more than a year; the mystery is how it went undetected.

Late last May, after the failure of desperate efforts at refinancing, Yale sought reorganization under Chapter X of the Bankruptcy Act. Much reduced in size, the company has been under the control of a court-appointed trustee, New York's former Senator Kenneth Keating, now counsel to the Manhattan law firm of Royall, Koegel & Rogers. Under a highly unusual contract arrangement, Denver Chicago Trucking Co. has spent more than three frustrating months trying to run Yale Express. Should Yale be reorganized, it is certain that it will not remain the two-sided trucking and freight-forwarding company it is now. It was the attempt to merge these unlike businesses, springing from mistaken assumptions and wrong judgments, that put unbearable weight on Yale's inadequate management and produced the company's downfall.

Yet the company did not fall simply because of mismanagement. It was nudged and fumbled with by outsiders who went about business as usual under most unusual circumstances. Wherever legal responsibility may finally be fixed, if it is fixed at all, there is blame enough to share around among almost all of those concerned with managing, financing, and overseeing the company. Stock and debenture holders have filed suits against Yale's officers and directors, and against the underwriters and auditors as well. What may emerge from this litigation, among other things, is a definition of the auditor's responsibility in the circumstances that prevailed at Yale.

Audits are based on testing, sampling, and reliance on internal controls. Such controls as existed at Yale were wholly inadequate, and Peat, Marwick, which had audited the account since 1959, should have realized this well before the company slipped into chaos. However, Peat, Marwick properly insists that the auditor's present function does not embrace ensuring anyone against fraud or the consequences of bad judgment. Some of the victimized outsiders, notably First National City, initially acted on mistaken beliefs and later accepted plausible-sounding excuses when danger signals appeared. Last May, when the creditors were urging that Denver Chicago be retained without delay to manage Yale, Federal District Judge Harold R. Tyler observed that their concern was somewhat belated, and tartly inquired: "Why wasn't something done long ago like this, if it is so obviously necessary now?"

As for the possibility of fraud, the information withheld from the auditors, it has been learned, falls into three categories: accounts payable, intercompany accounts, and unapplied credits. This is not the sort of paper that one stuffs in a bag and skips off with to Brazil. It is, however, the sort of paper that can jeopardize things men may value above money—power, prestige, vainglorious illusions. Plaintiffs' lawyers will attempt to draw out the details of an enormously complicated story. What can now be seen in broad, dramatic outline is a situation founded on false hopes, which men tried to shore up in the belief that it was righting itself, when all the while everything was crumbling.

Ironically, when Yale confessed itself on the ragged edge of bankruptcy last spring, it was almost two years to the day since the company's greatest moment. With the acquisition of Republic Carloading in May, 1963, Yale seemed to be leading the transportation industry, and lenders and investors were swinging aboard for a profitable ride. Everyone—not least himself—had supreme confidence in the young man at the wheel, the son of Yale's founder, its hard-driving president, Gerald W. Eskow.

The View from Seventh Avenue

Something of Gerry Eskow's personality is revealed in a small incident that occurred only a few hours after Yale had gone into bankruptcy. Eskow, his wife, and a few friends were sitting disconsolately in one of his favorite restaurants, a place overstuffed in maroon plush only a few steps off Seventh Avenue, in the heart of Manhattan's garment center. Eskow ordered roast beef, but the waiter said there was none.

"That's the second bad thing that's happened to me today," he quipped. The gloom lifted and everyone laughed.

This flash of gallows humor epitomizes his ebullience. He is extremely personable and succeeds so well in making people like him that even stunned former friends at First National City Bank still find personally kind things to say about him. His engaging manner once was combined with boundless egotism, and even sophisticated judges of executive talent came away convinced that Eskow was a man behind whom millions of dollars could be safely ventured.

Though now only forty-two, Eskow is a graduate of the old school of trucking, which, until quite recently, was the only school. Trucking is a young, fast-growing industry, typified by very small companies. The executive among them who has never driven a truck is still something of a rarity. Eskow began in the business at the age of fourteen in 1938, when his father, Benjamin, started Yale with a few hundred dollars and a rented truck. Although Gerry took a few evening courses in transportation at New York University, his training was almost entirely practical. What he learned was a specialized kind of trucking, founded on his father's previous experience as a soft-goods retailer. Yale took as its customers the neglected small shippers, principally retailers and garment manufacturers, and promised through such innovations as late pickups and night and weekend deliveries to move goods when they were needed. Thus Eskow's choice of a restaurant on that sad evening last May was no accident: he contemplated the wreckage around Yale from the small world where it had started, one remote from the alien environment of Park Avenue banks and prestigious old law firms where the company had overreached itself.

The Customer Comes before Costs

In the original role Ben Eskow defined, Yale grew steadily, establishing itself as a short-haul trucker specializing in carrying less than truckload freight to points along the east coast within 500 miles of New York. His oft-quoted credo emphasized service: "We must ever consider the needs of our customer—not the cost to Yale." It was Yale's boast that it could profitably carry freight other truckers regarded as too expensive to handle. This depended, in the early years, on Ben's cost-cutting tricks and, later, on Gerry's introduction of up-to-date technology. By the time the elder Eskow moved up to the chairmanship and Gerry assumed the presidency in 1960, Yale was using closed-circuit TV to monitor loading platforms, two-way radio to link driver and dispatcher, and transceivers to move punched cards over leased telephone lines. Boldly wading into the sea of paper that perennially threatens to engulf the industry, Eskow threw away multicarbon forms and introduced the three-part waybill prepared by a tabulating machine. His pioneering spirit was widely applauded, and I.B.M. invited him, as a prize customer, to address a seminar of transportation executives.

It would later develop that many of his innovations were ill advised and unworkable; that the latest electronic data-processing equipment overtaxed the capabilities of his billing and accounting personnel; that many of the discarded pieces of paper were indispensable; that Yale, in short, had gone too far, too fast. But between 1955 and 1961, Eskow earned considerable respect as Yale raced ahead: its revenues in this period grew 235 percent (vs. 30 percent for the industry as a whole) and its 94 percent operating ratio put it among the top-ranking truckers in the region. In the summer of 1960, Yale had made its first public offering of stock and had been listed on the American Stock Exchange. However, in spite of the switch to public ownership, Yale remained very much a family concern: the Eskows retained 61 percent of the stock and only the family and their close advisers sat on the board. With very little debt, except for equipment loans, and solidly profitable, Yale seemed a secure base for Gerry Eskow's far-ranging ambitions.

A Piggyback Ride for a Philosophy

These ambitions centered on the mating of truck and rail transportation, "piggybacking," which Eskow believed had unlimited potential. In 1959, Yale had acquired a small company, American Freight Forwarding, for only $250,-000, and had seen its revenues grow more than sevenfold in just two years. Eskow believed that the same service-oriented philosophy that had built Yale could be carried over to freight forwarding. And so, in the fall of 1961, addressing the New York Society of Security Analysts, Eskow made it a point to chide a larger competitor, Morris Forgash's U.S. Freight, for perhaps becoming "too big and cumbersome to be able to provide the personal service that we are able to provide." While Forgash hired owner-operators to truck his freight, Eskow declared, American used its own and Yale's fleet of 1,200 vehicles.

As it turned out, Forgash, who pioneered piggybacking, knew very well what he was doing. (See "Freight Goes Forward with

Forgash," FORTUNE, July, 1962.) Essentially, a forwarder is a broker who purchases transportation and provides as little service as possible to preserve his narrow margins. This Eskow would learn only painfully. At the time, dazzled by the soaring revenues of American Freight Forwarding, which he described to the analysts as "our brightest star," he did not realize—his accounting system did not reveal it—that its "profits" probably were losses subsidized by Yale's trucking operations.

Eskow's mistaken assumptions about freight forwarding laid the groundwork for trouble, and so did his misjudgment of a newcomer to Yale. This was Fred H. Mackensen, who joined the company as administrative vice president in October, 1961. Mackensen was a principal author of Yale's swift and mysterious collapse, but on his arrival he seemed to be precisely the kind of professional manager the company needed. Gerry Eskow needed him not only for his presumed financial competence, but also for the apparent ease with which he moved in the wide business world. The chairman's letter in the annual report summed up the winning impression Mackensen had made, welcoming "the addition of this talented, experienced executive to our management group."

If those at Yale misjudged Mackensen, they were not alone. He came highly recommended by the transportation department of First National City Bank, which knew Mackensen as the man who had cleaned up a messy situation in the Boston freight-bills clearinghouse, and who had done a creditable job trying to save an even worse situation in the New York clearinghouse. The New York clearinghouse eventually went into bankruptcy, but no one blamed the late-arriving Mackensen.

Of Mackensen's earlier career, not many details were known. He had worked for trucking companies in Detroit, Denver, and Salt Lake City, and afterward ran an avocado ranch that he owned in California. His gift for creating favorable impressions made thorough investigation of his background seem unnecessary. This was unfortunate, because the background contained odd twists and turns. For instance, in the mid-1950's, Mackensen, who was then employed by Ringsby Truck Lines in Denver, negotiated on behalf of Ringsby for the purchase of M. & M. Fast Freight of Salt Lake City; for some reason he was abruptly dismissed by Ringsby's chief competitors, Pacific Intermountain Express. No one bothered to investigate the facts underlying this intriguing chain of events. No one at Yale or the bank knew about it. All that Eskow knew was that Mackensen, in Eskow's idiom, appeared to be "a very heavy guy."

Mackensen at once swung his weight convincingly. He led Eskow away from Marine Midland Trust Co., where Yale had been financing new equipment under chattel mortgages, and took him to First National City, which made available $5,200,000 in revolving credit. (Marine Midland, when it learned of the impending switch, asked to be allowed to participate, and First National City agreed. Marine Midland, thanks to its enterprise, thus ironically retained its place among Yale's creditors.) Mackensen's early coup confirmed Eskow's decision to assign to him all financial responsibility. Within a year, the banks were joined by Massachusetts Mutual Life Insurance, which provided Yale with an additional $3-million loan. This package represented an unusual commitment to a trucking company, but one that reflected the lenders' judgment that Yale had come of age. Eskow recently had hired a public-relations firm, which issued a glowing release quoting an unnamed official at First National City: "Yale Express System, Inc., has a good earnings record, good equity base, and is an extremely well-managed company."

It was early in 1963 that Eskow, with Mackensen urging him on, lost interest in merely building American Freight Forwarding and began looking for quick growth through a major acquisition. Mackensen told him that Republic Carloading was available. When it turned out that the Southern Railway wanted $8 million for its 80 percent interest in Republic, Eskow hesitated, but Mackensen assured him that First National City liked the idea and would provide interim financing. At the last minute, however, the price suddenly climbed above $13 million: the founders and chief officers of Republic, William R. Mote and Theodore R. Bartels, had retained a one-fifth interest, on which they had set a price of more than $4 million. Unless Yale paid it, the deal was off.

As Eskow remembers it, he again hesitated, and was prepared to walk away, but was persuaded that Republic still was a bargain. He has described First National City as "the catalyst in the Republic acquisition from the very beginning." This rather exaggerates Eskow's sense of caution; once the cash was in sight, he needed little convincing. There seemed to be valid reasons for enthusiasm. An investment banker, noting that U.S. Freight's stock sold for twenty times earnings, counseled that Republic would be cheap at $17 million. Everyone agreed—it then seemed unarguable— that Yale would be able to feed business to Republic, which operated in one of Yale's heaviest originating and terminating areas.

Once Eskow was assured by the bank that the necessary $12-million loan would be forth-coming, the deal was closed. Within four months Yale began repaying the bank with the proceeds of its issue of debentures and 400,000 shares of common stock. Almost effortlessly, Eskow had leaped from the presidency of a $29-million regional trucking company to the head of a nationwide transportation empire with a volume of more than $80 million.

"It's Very Hard To Motivate Millionaires"

What Yale had done, of course, was to shift its operations heavily toward freight forwarding, a fact that disconcerted Eskow not at all. But there were crucial differences between running the new and larger business and running the old one. Republic was not an operating company in the sense that Yale was; its tangible assets were valued at only $4 million. Yale had paid nearly $9 million for Republic's ICC certificate authorizing it to serve all fifty states. This was one of only five such certificates, and therefore a sound asset— if properly used. Fashioned by Mote and Bartels, Republic was basically a sales-organization that had been a consistent, but hardly robust, profit maker: in 1962 it had net earnings of just under $1 million on a $55-million volume. Although Mote and Bartels stayed on, they now were bound only by short-term contracts, rather than by the stake of ownership. In view of the millions they had just pocketed, their zeal to manage vigorously was open to question. "I learned," Eskow recalls, "that it's very hard to motivate millionaires." His efforts to do so resulted first in coolness and later in open hostility between the managements of Yale and Republic.

In the beginning, however, it seemed that the expected large economies and profits would follow almost automatically from the fact that two companies had been joined. With the lower piggyback rates that Eskow hoped Yale would qualify for, he figured that "we would save a million dollars a year—just by using a different bill of lading." Other economies were expected to result from consolidation of terminals, from the use of Yale labor, from the use of Yale trucks for pickup and delivery, and—this rings especially ironic—from what was described to the underwriters as Yale's "scientific approach to paper," symbolized by its two I.B.M. 1401 computers and the 1410 (with RAMAC features) on order.

Also nourishing Eskow's optimism was the prospect of uniting Yale and Republic, then scattered in several Manhattan buildings, under the roof of the new terminal and headquarters being constructed on the West Side. The building had been planned and the foundations poured before Republic was acquired, but Eskow simply added four stories and rearranged the structure's 475,000 square feet. In every respect, from its haphazard design to its executive-suite grandeur, the building expressed Eskow and rose as his monument. It was to be completed in March, 1964, but Yale did not actually move in until the following December, a delay that proved fatal to many of Eskow's hopes. Neither Yale nor its creditors are now clear about what the building was supposed to cost, or what it actually did cost— the best guess at the latter figure is between $7 million and $8 million. At any rate, Yale, under its mortgage-financing arrangement, was forced to put up one-third of these spiraling costs in cash.

But in the period immediately following the acquisition, euphoria prevailed. Within six weeks the board gave its mood concrete expression and, assuming that the merger had doubled profits, voted to double the quarterly dividend to 15 cents. Thus Yale's management committed itself to producing at least the pre-merger level of profits, under pain of otherwise perhaps being forced to reduce the dividend and make embarrassing explanations.

Mating Antelopes and Giraffes

The first move toward physical consolidation of Yale and Republic was dictated by necessity. Yale had been compelled to move out of its old building, which was being demolished to make way for the new one; and so Eskow decided to put operations together— temporarily, he believed—in grotesquely inefficient rented railroad sheds along the Hudson River. Every pound of freight had to be lifted or lowered by hand. Amid wild confusion, freight was moved in iron-wheeled carts so heavy that, even when empty, two men had to push them. Drivers delicately maneuvered forty-foot trailers into platform spaces designed for horses and wagons. But the worst disadvantage, incredibly enough, was apparent from the beginning: Yale's chief landlord, the New York Central Railroad, did *not* offer the reduced piggyback rates on which the company had been counting so heavily.

Unfortunately, the "temporary" disorder and high costs continued month after month, as the completion date of the new building slipped. At the same time the railroads, aiming a blow at their trucking competitors, introduced new rules that upset the established economies of freight forwarding. Forwarders were faced with the urgent necessity of refiguring their costs and devising new operating formulas. However, the chaotic consolidation of Yale and Republic in New York had destroyed the bases on which each had measured its business. Traditionally, Yale had calculated costs and profits on the basis of revenues, Republic on the basis of tonnage moved. Now everything had been thrown together and, as Eskow recalls, "I found that all the meaningful yardsticks were gone." In addition, there was the deeper confusion arising from Eskow's determination to impose Yale's operating philosophy on Republic, an effort that, in retrospect, strikes an industry observer as a futile attempt "to mate antelopes and giraffes." Under Yale's "antelope" philosophy of swift service, piggyback trailers sometimes went off to their destinations half empty, an inefficiency that had grim consequences. Republic's largest single expense, running to more than 70 percent of revenues, was purchased transportation. If Republic's load factor dropped as little as 10 percent, the swing in profits could be as much as $3,850,000 in a year.

Cost controls in both companies were inadequate. Hence even when trailers moved fully loaded, it was often with marginally profitable freight. Many of Yale's trucks also rolled at a loss, a fact that went undetected. The company's competitors in New York succeeded in luring away some of Yale's most desirable traffic, for shippers were afraid to rely too heavily on the merged Yale and Republic when both could be crippled by a strike. Sales campaigns rebuilt Yale's volume, but much of it was low-rated freight other truckers didn't want. In one instance, Yale carried a truckload of inflated basketballs from upstate New York to Tennessee, handling the shipment (a costly half-dozen times en route) for total revenues of $400 versus actual costs of $800.

Late in 1963, Eskow, underestimating the magnitude of the problems and assuming they would all be solved with the move to the new building, remained publicly optimistic. But, aware that the old formulas were no longer valid, he gave Mackensen the assignment of devising new profit-and-loss yardsticks for the combined operations.

At the same time, plans were made to combine the accounting systems of the merged companies. As with so much else, the accounting procedures of Yale and Republic were incompatible—and so, unfortunately, were the chief accounting personnel of the two companies, who were jockeying for position and scarcely speaking to each other. Competent enough to perform routine functions for the separate companies, they were unable to cope with change, and certainly not with the radical change that Mackensen had in mind. Furthermore, the basic data with which they worked was suspect; the vaunted "scientific" EDP system at Yale was badly programed and almost nightmarishly erratic.

Historically, Yale picked up both its revenues and its costs—principally depreciation, payroll, and maintenance—very quickly, and kept its books on a semi-cash basis. After twenty days it cut off and drew a balance, picking up late-arriving bills in subsequent periods. This was a very liberal form of accounting, but did not significantly affect the financial statements of what was essentially an overnight trucker. Republic, in contrast, was extremely conservative and, as befitted a freight forwarder, kept its books on a full-accrual basis—that is, full reserves were set up against anticipated expenses, which consisted mostly of transportation bills that often arrived months after freight had been moved.

In spite of the apparent differences between them, Mackensen decided to put Republic on essentially the same semi-cash accounting basis as Yale. He reasoned that the merger had speeded up Republic's transactions, and that the old accrual formulas failed to take into account many presumed economies, with the result that Republic was needlessly over-accruing. In November, 1963, Republic began to switch to the fast cut off. Up to this point Yale Express had been in trouble; now it started to go out of control.

Errors, Oversights, and Overstated Profits

Mackensen discussed the switch with Robert Conroy, the Peat, Marwick partner in charge of the audit, and later paid a call on John Peoples, who headed the firm's department on professional practices. When Mackensen proposed adopting the fast cutoff used by most truckers, which would have the result of drastically reducing the accruals for transportation costs, Peoples remembers that he disagreed. He argued that if Republic needed these before the merger, it surely needed them now. He recalls that he cautioned—prophetically, as it turned out—that putting Republic's accounting on the fast cutoff would not provide "the right answers" in 1964.

The annual audit would be made on the basis of accrual accounting; bills applicable to 1963 received in the early months of 1964 would be accrued at year-end. As Peoples saw it, in the next period, with a fast cutoff, expenses would be understated as they would no longer include the bills received after the end of

the period. If Yale's income were steady, the system might yield reasonably accurate figures in the middle months, when bills omitted earlier would be included, offsetting omissions at the end of the period; but, in fact, Yale's income fluctuated sharply. In the final months the pleasing first-quarter effects of the fast cutoff would be painfully reversed: in addition to the earlier bills that would have accumulated, late-arriving bills would be held and applied after the end of the year, greatly reducing earnings. People foresaw that Yale would "take a bath" at year-end. The fourth quarter, traditionally Yale's best, could become its worst.

Despite this warning, Mackensen kept Republic on the fast cutoff. He also took into Yale's income $575,000 from a Republic reserve for duplicate claims—that is, for refunds of customers' overpayments. Meanwhile, the first of a series of accounting "errors" occurred: one of Yale's accountants "forgot" to set up a $750,000 reserve for interline payments—that is, payments Yale would owe to other carriers hauling its freight. The effect of taking in the $575,000 Republic reserve and neglecting to set up the $750,000 Yale reserve was to overstate Yale Express' pre-tax income for 1963 by $1,325,000.

The formal consolidation of the Yale and Republic accounting departments began in January. However, while both were in the same building, they were on separate floors. The disorder was compounded by the fact that Republic, acting on plans made before the merger, had just installed a magnetic-tape system, while Yale was using punch cards. Communications were further impaired by the jealousy between the departments.

When, in February, a newspaper inquired about Yale's 1963 earnings, Eskow replied that the audit was in progress and promised an estimate. He asked Mackensen to give him a figure, telling him to make it "conservative." Eskow was thinking in terms of pre-tax earnings of $6 million or $7 million, but Mackensen soon laid before him a figure that seemed incredible: $3 million. Then, when Peat, Marwick's figure came through, Eskow hit the ceiling. Peat, Marwick had fixed pre-tax earnings at less than $2 million.

"What happened to the million dollars?" roared Eskow.

The answer was that, among other adjustments, the auditors had insisted that Yale set up the reserve for payments to other carriers, and had adjusted income downward by nearly $1 million. However, Peat, Marwick did not take exception to the $575,000 Republic reserve contained in Yale's income. Peat, Marwick (prepared the 1963 audit) on what it believed was a full accrual basis, keeping Yale's books open through February and entering invoices attributable to the previous year. But clearly, in view of the enormous adjustments subsequently made in restating the 1963 results, millions of dollars of accounts payable either were temporarily lost and went unrecorded; or were not found by the auditors; or were deliberately withheld from the auditors. Following the audit, Yale resumed fast-cutoff accounting.

The Great Volume Illusion

If the reported 1963 net profit of $1,140,000 fell far below Eskow's expectations, the first-quarter 1964 results also must have seemed disappointing. This was usually a slow period, but the loss in the trucking business (Yale Transport) was higher than in the previous year. Republic's earnings appeared to offset this loss, and combined net earnings of $164,000 were reported to the banks and the press. However, this "profit" was illusory; it contained a $790,000 error. Actually, Republic, too, had lost money.

Amid the confusion of closing and opening the books while the two accounting departments were being combined, an accrual had been reserved *twice* instead of once. The technical explanation of this "double reversal of an accrual" is tedious and unnecessary; the net effect is what matters. It was to overstate first-quarter earnings by $790,000 and to understate accounts payable by the same amount.

Even though Eskow had not yet learned of this error, he was worried by the "missing" million dollars in the 1963 earnings that he positively *knew* existed. Suspecting theft or fraud, he called in Peat, Marwick to make an investigation, but no evidence was turned up. So obstinate was the optimism of Yale's management, recalls one of the auditors, that "they would rather believe that someone was stealing than to imagine that they weren't operating the company right."

Thus, in April, Peat, Marwick began a series of special studies that expanded fantastically throughout the year, finally involving nearly 8,000 man-hours and a bill of $97,500. According to the auditors, few of the studies were ever completed, for often when they produced evidence of inefficiency or mismanagement the assignment was changed. Mackensen, described by former associates as autocratic and overbearing, resented the intrusion of these outsiders.

Mainly, Yale was trying to get some clear idea of its operating costs. By the old standards, which no longer applied, Yale was still making healthy profits, and its volume was still high. But Conroy of Peat, Marwick believes that "Yale and Republic often were handling the same freight over and over; and if by the time they got through with it it was still in one piece, they were just lucky." Huge piles of misdirected and lost freight accumulated, on which Yale was forced to pay claims. In just two years its claim ratio jumped from 1 percent of revenues (the industry average) to 3 percent. Adequate intercompany accounting might have deflated the great volume illusion, but incompetence and intercompany cold war made the accounting woefully inadequate.

Even more serious in its consequences was Eskow's mistaken assumption that the company's accounting was still on full accrual. By the late spring of 1964 he was beginning to mistrust Mackensen's figures, not for the valid reason that the latter's formulas were wildly wrong, but rather because the profits he expected and had promised publicly were not showing up. Eskow finally called in Conroy and told him: "I don't want these surprises." Conroy replied that in order to get an accurate account of the company's operations it would be necessary to reconstruct every transaction from the beginning of the year—a tremendous task. Eskow told him to go ahead. A force of college accounting students were hired by Yale and put to work under Peat, Marwick's direction. Although Peat, Marwick believed it had made adequate tests of the 1963 payables in its audit, the reconstruction project was set up to catch not only 1964 payables but stray 1963 payables as well. Slowly, as countless old bills came filtering in, Peat, Marwick was building up to a very rude surprise of its own.

When Is a Doubt Dishonest?

While the college boys breasted their way backward through a sea of paper, trying to determine where Yale had been months earlier, the company moved blindly ahead under the momentum of its mistakes. But the past had already begun to overtake it. According to Gerry Eskow's brother Burton, himself a Yale director, he met his father on the morning of Yale's annual meeting in May, 1964, in a corridor of the New York Hilton Hotel. Mackensen had just told the elder Eskow of the $790,000 double reversal. Burton noted that his father appeared stunned ("Dad's eyes were glassy"). To avoid upsetting Gerry Eskow, who was shortly to explain to the stockholders why Yale's 1963 earnings had been disappointing, it was decided not to tell him the news until later.

After the stockholders' meeting several members of the board met informally to discuss the apparent error and spent most of the afternoon questioning Mackensen and Republic's accounting people. According to Eskow, no clear explanation of the error emerged; furthermore, Mackensen emphasized the possibility that it might be a false alarm. Though unfounded, this possibility was comforting because the board, even if it could not grasp how the error had occured, was acutely conscious of its potential consequences: it would mean reducing reported income for the first quarter by $790,000. There is no record of who attended this rump caucus, but the directors present at the annual meeting that morning, in addition to the three Eskows and Mackensen, were Mote and Bartels and Michael G. Kletz, an investment banker and family friend. There were two absentees: Stanley Steingut, who had just been elected to the board, and D. Frederick Barton, managing partner of Eastman, Dillon, who had become a director in December. Barton carried another impressive title: member of the board of governors of the New York Stock Exchange. Yale had been listed on the Big Board only five months earlier.

Five days later the board met again, this time officially and with all members present. According to the minutes of the meeting, the board discussed Yale's first-quarter financial results. Mackensen also announced that Peat, Marwick was then engaged in "special studies for the verification of certain matters for management." Evidently the directors were not unduly alarmed by what they learned from all this discussion, for no action was taken, then or subsequently, on the $790,000 error. It was carried in Yale's income for the rest of the year. Eskow insists that it "hung in suspense," an unresolved mystery.

The most generous interpretation of this assertion is that the company apparently decided to give itself every benefit of the doubt. A dramatic turnaround in Yale's fortunes would make it possible to correct the error without serious embarrassment. However, this inaction had the effect of falsifying Yale's financial statements. At some point a doubt that has this effect ceases to be honest.

A Moment of Truth—Almost

By early July the auditors had seen enough of Yale's internal turmoil to become apprehensive. It was still several months before preliminary work would begin on the 1964 audit, but when Peat, Marwick learned that Yale intended to release a six-month financial statement showing net earnings of $430,000, it raised an objection.

Precisely what form this objection took will not be established until Peat, Marwick testifies in court. The firm is now willing to make only this guarded comment: "We suggested that, in the absence of an audit, the most conservative figures should be put out. Management chose to disregard this." By one account, Conroy told Yale's management that it had not made a profit in the first six months of 1964, but instead had suffered a substantial loss. Eskow denies "categorically" ever receiving Conroy's warning—it may be questioned whether any such warning was really necessary—and he, too, will tell his story on the witness stand.

Eskow asserts that, whatever Peat, Marwick told him, he countered with an offer to issue any figure the auditors would provide. This could not have been a serious offer, unless Eskow was unaware that the auditors' figures were tentative and incomplete. As a result of the tediously slow process of reconstruction, the company's first-quarter performance was coming into focus, but it was much too early to know for certain about the second quarter. Nor was it the auditor's function to provide such an interim figure. Yale finally issued the statement provided to Eskow by Mackensen, showing earnings of 20 cents per share, and the board voted the second quarterly 15-cent dividend.

About this time Conroy reportedly discussed the Yale situation with Peat, Marwick's senior partners. Peat, Marwick says that it never considered the possibility of resigning the Yale account. As a general rule, Peat, Marwick believes that it is justified in keeping its clients in the absence of demonstrable fraud. The firm also feels that the confidential relationship had been made known to the New York Stock Exchange or the creditors. Everything could await the yearend audit. What might have been a moment of truth was rationalized into little more than a difference of opinion.

Looking for Two Cardboard Boxes

Of course, the creditors were by no means completely in the dark. They received quarterly profit-and-loss statements and balance sheets from Yale's management. In addition, there were frequent personal contacts, some of a semisocial nature: Robert Graham, vice president in charge of First National City's transportation department, lived not far from Mackensen in Greenwich, Connecticut, and they and their wives occasionally dined together. The relationship between Yale's management and the banks appeared to be excellent in every respect. Yet the creditors heard nothing to alarm them.

It may be wondered whether Yale's figures did not speak for themselves. According to the company's report filed with the ICC, Yale's pre-tax figures for the first six months of 1964, as compared with the same period in the previous year, looked this way:

Republic Carloading	1964	$709,000
	1963	$829,000
Yale Transport	1964	($174,000)
	1963	$474,000

These figures, which, incidentally, were *not* filed on the full-accrual basis required by the ICC, represented the best face Yale's management could put on the company's perform-

ance. The 1964 income for Republic contained the uncorrected $790,000 error. The senior creditors received essentially the same figures as the ICC; they also had a great deal more detailed information from the company.

Yet the banks saw nothing worrisome in the reports they received. Yale's volume was holding up, cash flow appeared healthy, and the company seemed to be comfortably meeting the debt-equity ratio and other financial tests set forth in the loan agreements. (Actually Yale, if the facts had been known, was in default.) In April and again in July, First National City and Marine Midland extended additional credit to Yale; all told, Yale raised more than $5 million in new money during 1964.

Much of it went into the new terminal building, the rising cost of which, in Eskow's words, was "like putty, always changing." As one completion date after another passed, he authorized work at night and on weekends—anything to bring its expected economies within reach. A terrible cash squeeze was slowly building up, as the 1964 audit would later reveal. In 1964, with a net loss of $2,850,000 and depreciation of only $1,900,000, Yale had a *negative* cash flow of $950,000. In addition, it paid out $811,000 in dividends. But the effects were not perceptible outside the company, and Yale's credit remained good. Of the ease with which the floundering Yale borrowed, Eskow, referring to Mackensen, says wryly: "Money was no problem. I had my fat friend with the mustache and the little black bag who'd go to the bank and get a million."

As accounts payable piled up, Yale had to pay certain bills or its freight would be embargoed. Someone contrived to pay them in a way that disguised the worsening cash shortage and so did not impair the company's standing with the creditors. This was discovered early in August when Donald Palmer, who had been recommended by Peat, Marwick, joined the company as controller, replacing Norman Goldwasser, who left shortly afterward. Learning that a bank reconciliation had not been made for five months, Palmer promptly made one—and saw that checks amounting to $438,000 had been drawn, but not entered on Yale's books, which, of course, had the effect of overstating the cash balance by this amount. As Palmer recalls it, he asked Goldwasser for the unrecorded vouchers covering the $438,000. On the third insistent request, Goldwasser excused himself and disappeared toward the elevators. A few minutes later he returned carrying two cardboard boxes containing vouchers, and canceled checks that referred to 1963 payables.

Not long afterward Mackensen approached First National City with a request for still another increase in Yale's indebtedness. As a matter of course, the bank asked for certain information, including an "aging" of accounts receivable. Palmer had an "aging" prepared, and was appalled to discover that those receivables deemed over-age amounted to 24 percent, or nearly $2 million. The banks never saw the "aging" figure because Mackensen withdrew his request for additional funds. The massive accumulation of uncollected receivables struck Palmer as amazing. Yale was having difficulty paying its bills—checks were being written but not issued—but Yale was not collecting badly needed money. Pathetically enough, it *could* not: the EDP billing system was hopelessly fouled up, and, thanks to Eskow's streamlining, Yale lacked the backup carbons to prove some of its claims. An artificial revenue shrinkage thus tightened the company's very real cash squeeze.

From mid-August on, Yale, in effect, had parallel accounting operations: one reporting to Mackensen that worked by day, the other headed by Palmer, in collaboration with Conroy, that toiled by night. Both submitted their results to Eskow. Mackensen's figures, though inaccurate, were offered with a great show of definiteness; Palmer's, based on the continuing Peat, Marwick reconstruction, were tentative. Eskow took Mackensen's figures and released them to the creditors, the ICC, and the public. On this basis, Yale reported nine months' net earnings of $904,000 and declared the regular dividend.

The Snowball of Debt Descends

Not until pending suits are tried will the full story of the final months of 1964 at Yale be known. All through that year Eskow clung to his hopes. Those who knew the worst kept silent. Appearances were kept up—e.g., the regular quarterly dividend was declared, and paid in January. But the gigantic snowball of accounts payable that had pursued the company throughout the year, steadily gathering size and momentum, ultimately caught up. Finally, and largely by chance, First National City learned of the true internal situation.

In mid-December, long after the event could have any good effect, Yale had moved into the new terminal building, and in January it was making final arrangements on the mortgage financing. At the closing session, someone pointedly asked Mackensen what Yale's 1964 net earnings would be; he replied that earlier forecasts ranging up to $1,800,000 were no longer quite accurate. There would have to be some onetime adjustments—rather large ones, he conceded. That night Disque D. Deane, of Longstreet Corp., who had been present at the meeting, telephoned his friend Bob Graham at home and passed on the alarming word. "It came like a bolt out of the blue," Graham recalls. The next evening Deane, Mackensen, and Graham had dinner together at the New York Athletic Club. Mackensen repeated what he had said the previous day and promised to furnish work sheets "explaining" the adjustments.

On his arrival at the Yale office the following morning, Mackensen told Eskow: "The bank is mad at you."

Eskow looked up, surprised. "Why *me*?"

The bank's confidence in Mackensen collapsed when the work sheets he produced proved to be incomprehensible. Eskow was summoned and he delivered a further jolt, informing the bank for the first time that Peat, Marwick had been at work inside Yale for several months. Two days later the auditors met with Graham and his associates at First National City's Park Avenue headquarters. The auditors said they could not estimate prospective earnings because the 1964 audit was only in its early stages. However, they said operating data indicated the situation was improving. A few days later, before a meeting of the senior lenders, Peat, Marwick repeated this report with the same optimistic overtones. In view of what the auditors knew firsthand of Yale's condition, their optimism can be explained only on the ground that Peat, Marwick itself had no idea just how bad the situation actually was.

The Great Moneymaking Machine

At one of their early meetings, the bankers recall, Eskow bravely insisted that it would take only some priming to start "this great moneymaking machine going again." The senior creditors didn't know how much it *would* take, but they no longer wanted Eskow at the controls. Eskow, however, resisted attempts to remove him.

Then came the stunning disclosure to the creditors by Peat, Marwick that Yale might very well show a loss for 1964. And a worse revelation, particularly for Peat, Marwick, soon followed. Bone-weary from the ordeal of the past several months, Conroy asked to be relieved of the Yale account, and was replaced by Walter Hanson, who is expected to be elected Peat, Marwick's senior partner this month. Very reluctantly, with a mixture of horror and disbelief, Hanson came to realize that Yale's audited figures for 1963 would have to be reopened. "It was like pulling on what you thought was the tail of a pussycat," he recalls. "You pulled and pulled and out came a tiger."

While the audit was in progress Yale was running out of cash, but the creditors could not advance additional money without reliable figures. By early March, Eskow, unable to resist the mounting pressures, stepped down. But before doing so he issued the statement publicly disclosing Yale's estimated losses for 1963 and 1964.

The Unanswered Question is: "Why?"

The last months before Yale sought refuge under Chapter X are, in the minds of all those who lived through them, an emotion-charged blur of frantic days and sleepless nights. Voting control of the company passed from the Eskows to the creditors, but Gerry Eskow remained as a vice president and began working almost around the clock to repair the damage that had been done under his administration. He yielded the presidency to John Oberdorf, a Republic vice president, who was clearly not a miracle worker, but the only man available to the now panicky creditors. Mote and Bartels, who had quit, returned at the creditors' request but later quit again. "Courage money" flowed into the company: $500,-000 from Lazard Freres for an option on a million shares of Yale stock; $1,500,000 from a sale-leaseback deal with an American Export Isbrandtsen subsidiary; and $750,000 from the banks. But this money flowed right out again, most of it gushing out at the rate of $150,000 daily during a sixteen-day period in early May, when Yale either had to pay bills at once or stop functioning.

Looking backward, all the obvious reasons for Yale's long skid come into view. The merger was ill-considered, and the management of the consolidated company was inept and haphazard. Also important were less obvious factors, such as the willingness of senior lenders to rely entirely on appearances and explanations. Perhaps nothing more can be done in the high-volume, keenly competitive lending business, but this raises questions about the possibility of more Yale Expresses. As for the performance of the auditors, it would seem that the application of "generally accepted auditing standards" failed Peat, Marwick. Ordinary precautions, routinely taken, simply did not work in extraordinary circumstances.

But the obvious is insufficient. The question persists: *Why?* In addition to Gerry Eskow, the explanation will be sought from Fred Mackensen, who was fired in March and has since returned to the trucking business in California. So far as anyone can determine, Mackensen gained nothing in the debacle and may have lost money: in February, First National City severed its last tie with him by selling 20,000 shares of Yale stock—his entire holding—that he had pledged as security for a loan. Perhaps the real explanation is more subtle. For a time, both Mackensen and Eskow may have achieved something for which each ached inwardly; and while they dreamed of rising above themselves, a nightmare overtook Yale Express.

Yale Express Case

Discussion Questions

1. What auditing issues are raised by this case?

2. What was the auditor's responsibility in the Yale Express situation?

3. Was the auditor's responsibility fulfilled?

4. How differently might the auditors have handled the special circumstances that prevailed at Yale such as:
   a. Cost control weaknesses.
   b. Competence of financial and accounting management.
   c. Incompatibility of accounting systems between Yale and Republic.
   d. Yale's reporting of first six months' earnings in 1964.
   e. Data-processing system.

Chapter 4

Auditing Objectives:
Today and Tomorrow

The decade of the 1960s was one of enormous improvement in information technology. The growth of data-processing equipment has made possible the design and implementation of systems with much greater capability and reliability than ever before. Substantial additional information can be developed and processed within such systems, and sophisticated new controls have been developed to assure the reliability of the system outputs.

These changes have had a significant impact on auditors. Many of the internal controls to which the auditor of the past had become comfortably accustomed have been made obsolete by the new technology. The visible trail that could be followed through journals and ledgers disappeared as pen and ink were replaced by electronic impulses.

These have been troubling developments for many trained in the traditional disciplines, and the auditor has not always been in the forefront of response to them. Nevertheless, if the function of the auditor is to be adequately fulfilled in a changing world, prompt response is essential.

During the 1960s, therefore, the auditor has had to deal increasingly with what can be called an information system rather than a set of books. The output of the system is used not only for public financial reporting but for the myriad needs of the management for decision-making and control information. The sum of data in the system is no longer confined to internal accounting only, but includes nonfinancial data on personnel, sales, and inventory quantities, and other information relating to the firm's operations, both in the past and as expected in the future; the system contains as well data from outside the firm about competitors, customers, and the economic environment within which the firm operates.

Basically, an information system may be defined as a group of information flows designed to relate necessary inputs to stored information and desired decisional outputs. This obviously implies the need to determine the information requirements for a given business decision-making process and to develop a flow of information to link the information requirements with the data sources. Thus, to design information systems it is necessary to identify and evaluate existing information flows and where appropriate to design new information flows. The methodology would necessarily include (1) specifying the requirements for information in each decision-making activity or in each business-problem area, (2) listing sources of data available or that could be available in satisfying these requirements, and (3) matching requirements for information with sources of data by use of selective management-science tools and techniques.

A concept introduced by the computer to auditing is that of system control—as contrasted with individual control—in the recording, processing, and summarizing of data. In manual processing of accounting information, each individual involved in the processing flow exercises a certain amount of control over documents for valid transaction codes, unreasonable amounts, arithmetic errors, and other improper data. In manual systems, then, the internal control is largely achieved by individual review and cross-check. In an EDP (electronic data processing) system, however, control is systems oriented rather than people oriented (because the transactions are either entered into the processing flow in machine-readable form or are converted to machine-readable form early in the processing system). The transactions are then processed without human intervention or human review under the control of programs. These programs, internally stored in computer memories, constitute the systems, and much of the control is embodied in them in the form of program checks.

Such a transfer of activities previously performed by many people to one "person" is not a surrender of internal control. In fact, the kind of control attributed to separation and specialization of clerical functions is strengthened in an electronic system because of (1) the computer's uniformity in the execution of policies and procedures, and (2) the difficulty of making changes in detailed and complex programmed instructions.

While it must be noted that a substantial lag exists between equipment capability and system design and implementation, it seems apparent that tomorrow's auditor will have to deal nearly exclusively with computer-processed information built around the operating needs of the business.

The computer is one of the most important technological developments of the twentieth century. The increased capability and reliability of information systems is largely due to its influence. New controls are now both possible and necessary in the absence of visible records associated with the processing of data.

The Computer

The computer has caused significant changes in business information systems, expanding both scope and operation. The first computer data processing systems tended merely to computerize existing clerical functions. Soon, however, systems embracing larger areas of the business and incorporating decision-oriented analytical techniques not practicable in clerical systems began to be implemented. Thus, although many computer data processing systems merely automate the prior manual processes, the trend is plainly toward higher level information systems. The auditor, therefore, frequently faces not only a computer but new system concepts as well.[1]

The activities undertaken by business to utilize the computer in processing data and accounting information all affect the auditor in the auditing process. Examination of audit objectives, standards, and procedures and their relationship to the concepts of existence and evaluation leads to the conclusion that the computer's role significantly affects auditing techniques.

The use of the computer in evaluating the quality of the data-processing system and in determining the quality of information generated by the system appears to provide the auditor with the opportunity to perform a more selective and penetrating audit of activities and procedures involving a large volume of transactions.

Through a proper review of the client's EDP system and the use of well-designed test data, the auditor may gain a better knowledge of the client's procedures and controls. By developing computer audit programs that employ auditing by exception, the auditor can cover a greater area of business activity, both financial and operational, and can utilize human resources in analyzing and evaluating problem areas in the client's operation. Such an approach enhances the auditor's ability to provide optimum service to his clients.

---

[1]Gordon B. Davis, "The Auditor and the Computer," *The Journal of Accountancy*, March 1968, pp. 44-47.

Management-Services Activities

Because of the developments taking place in information systems and computerized data processing, and because of the need for assistance from outsiders by professional managers dealing with the problems of complex social organizations, the management-services activities of professional accounting firms have grown in recent years to the point where the management-services function covers a broad range of business operations.

In addition to such accounting-related services as cost accounting, budgeting, profitability accounting, and responsibility accounting, management services also include such management-engineering activities as work measurement, work flow study, work simplification, and systems and procedures studies that involve the analysis and design of systems that provide data and information for management purposes. Such systems-work may include evaluation of the feasibility of using a computer, and if a computer is required, an analysis of alternative equipment configurations that might be appropriate for a particular system. Management services may also involve the application of quantitative methods simulation, critical path methods, inventory-management techniques, line balancing, waiting line methods, etc.

As a result of involvement in management services, accounting firms have developed a viewpoint and a competence in areas of management-information systems other than purely traditional accounting systems, and have assumed concern with the evaluation of information required by management to deal with a range of business problems broader than those of accounting and finance alone.

Professional Management Viewpoint

Auditing is also affected by a uniquely American process that has developed a growing number of professional managers. Formally educated in university schools of business, kept abreast of new management techniques in programs of continuing education, and participating in a group decision-making process characterizing corporate activity, these managers look with more favor upon the collateral services of the auditor, in many instances, than upon those services necessary only to attest to the fairness of financial statements. As two authors put it:

> In general, it is the presence of these (collateral) services which makes the audit an economical package from management's point of view.[2]

[2]Skinner and Anderson, *Analytical Auditing*, London: Sir Isaac Pitman & Sons, 1966, p. 8.

In addition to the increasing number of people in client organizations who are professionally educated in management, we have witnessed an increasing number of M.B.A. students with a professional management viewpoint entering public accounting. Several accounting firms have accelerated their recruiting efforts at leading graduate schools of business, and have designed special training programs to attract M.B.A.s who do not have significant accounting backgrounds.

As a result of our society's approach to management education, auditors are confronting, in many client organizations, managers who expect more from the auditors; in addition, auditing firms are attracting many students who are suggesting an approach to auditing which provides creative contributions to the solution of the problems confronting clients and readers of management reports.

Relationship of These Developments to Auditing

The traditional audit has historically been concerned with satisfying regulatory and custodial requirements and emphasizing accounting controls. This service has been and still is of great significance and value to our business community in maintaining the creditability of financial reports and the free flow of funds in our capital markets.

However, with the advent of information-system technology, there has grown a need for an evaluation of the adequacy of management information as well as its accuracy. In addition to the need to audit the financial records of an organization, there has evolved a need to audit the tools of management to determine the relevance of information being provided for strategic planning, management control, and the operating activities of the organization.

Recently, more and more professional managers have seen the need for someone who is capable of performing independent analysis, and of comprehending and contributing to the totality of plans and operations with which a management must deal. For example, William Campfield indicates that such an audit is "an informed and constructive analysis, evaluation, and series of recommendations regarding the broad spectrum of plans, processes, people, and problems of an economic entity."[3] Cyert and Churchill[4] indicate that "a management audit may be defined as an audit which results in a statement of opinion by a CPA with regard to the performance of the management function." They go on to discuss

[3] *Journal of Accountancy*, July 1967, p. 42.

[4] *Journal of Accountancy*, February 1966, p. 39.

the results of their experimentation with students in the use of a management game. In this experimentation, some students took the role of auditors and examined "the methods and procedures (or lack thereof) by which the decisions were made and. . .they evaluated the methodology against the existing body of knowledge relevant to these areas."

As Cyert and Churchill pointed out, "the auditors were subject to the same standards of objective evidence and evaluation criteria for their judgments in the management audits as in the financial audit. Instead of generally accepted accounting principles, the auditors used accepted principles of management. In making their evaluation the auditors raised a number of questions. For example: (1) Do sales and production have established procedures for coordinating their activities and do they follow them? (2) Are sales forecasts prepared, updated, and used? (3) Does the firm prepare capital budgeting studies prior to making major investments? (4) Does the firm establish goals and consistent internal procedures pertaining to these goals?[5]

Dodwell,[6] writing on the subject of operational auditing, states:

the operational auditing concept is the bridge and at times the catalyst between a basic traditional financial audit and a management services approach to a client's problems. . . . the extension of the basic audit to include the appraisal and establishment of administrative and operational controls. . . .

Buckley,[7] in discussing the management audit, suggests:

At the root of the management audit concept is the belief that a systematic evaluation of an organization (or of its components, plans, objectives, information and control systems, operating structure, and/or utilization of human and physical resources) is a fruitful, and perhaps even indispensable, exercise. Implicit assumptions of the system include an emphasis on the importance of nonfiscal as well as fiscal data in management decisions; a concept of the organization as a person-oriented and directed system; and the notion that a countervailing influence is needed to curb abuse on the "management by exception" strategy. Management auditors subscribe to the philosophy that the gray areas of marginal efficiency are more critical to the success of business operations in the long run than are problems of the acute and recognizable variety.

[5]*Journal of Accountancy*, July 1967, p. 41.

[6]*Journal of Accountancy*, June 1966.

[7]*California Management Review*, Fall 1966, p. 47.

Carey[8] suggests that there should be two objectives of an audit:

(1) to support a professional opinion on financial statements for external reporting purposes; and (2) to support a report to management on the effectiveness of the information system for internal planning, control, and decision-making purposes.

The implications of these suggested approaches are great. The auditor must build his audit around the various operating systems of a business: marketing, production, procurement, personnel, and cash management. He must develop an understanding of the information needs of each of these systems in order to evaluate the adequacy of management and accounting controls. He must also have a comprehensive grasp of data-processing technology so that he can satisfy himself that the system is programmed to produce reliable data from the inputs which he can test and examine.

As we indicated in Chapter 3, auditors have to a large extent shifted their emphasis away from sole concern with an analysis of balance-sheet accounts to an approach which enables them also to offer timely suggestions for strengthening the client's operating systems and management controls. Management-control questionnaires have been developed and are increasingly being used. A sample of such a questionnaire follows this chapter as an Appendix. Operational audits have been performed on a selective basis. Increased use of analytical techniques and computers in auditing has helped to free the auditor from many of the routine procedures and allows him to devote more time to assisting clients in solving problems that confront them.

Audit of Systems

All of these developments suggest an evolutionary process away from the primary audit objective of rendering an opinion on the fairness of the financial representations of management. We have already seen an auditor's opinion on the fairness of representations of management other than those reflected in financial statements. For example, in the past few years we have witnessed an auditing firm render an opinion on the reasonableness of the cost savings reported by the Department of Defense as a result of its Cost Reduction Program. We have seen an opinion (see Figure 1) on the effectiveness of a time-shared computer system in providing reliable

[8] *The CPA Plans for the Future*, AICPA, 1965, p. 196.

TOUCHE, ROSS, BAILEY & SMART

80 Pine Street
New York, 10005
January 15, 1965

Mr. Charles W. Adams, President
Keydata Corporation
575 Technology Square
Cambridge, Massachusetts

Dear Mr. Adams:

At your request we have made a review of the Keydata organization and system, as defined in your document No. KD 3, dated December 29, 1964. This letter summarizes our findings: accompanying it is a report containing detailed comments.

Our review comprised a complete systems analysis and included an evaluation of the following requirements which are both unique and essential to an on-line real-time data processing system which is to be time-shared by multiple customers:

1. The equipment used must have the capability of handling transactions on-line and in real-time.

2. The programming must be done by personnel who are highly experienced and qualified in time-shared computing technology.

3. Maximum security must be provided for individual customer's programs and information.

4. Procedures must include protection of all information in the system in the event of equipment malfunction or human error.

In our opinion the Keydata organization and system, as defined, met all of these requirements and the system is an excellent example of controlled data processing. All aspects of the system have been well designed, reflecting the previous experience and capabilities of your personnel in the programming and operation of real-time systems as well as the soundness of the approach you have taken. When coupled with a customer's normal internal control procedures, the system provides an outstanding degree of control over both the accounting functions and the operating elements of a business. The Keydata system makes a practical and effective time-shared management information system now available to the central business community.

Very truly yours,
TOUCHE, ROSS, BAILEY & SMART

Figure 1. Example of auditor's opinion on effectiveness of an information system.

information to users of the system. We look for additional examples of attest to representations of management about existing systems or potential systems.

Another move away from the attestation of traditional financial statements may come in attesting to business plans and budgets. Increasing interest in this area has been evidenced by analysts and bankers, and this will be discussed further in the reporting section of this book.

As is suggested in the reading at the end of this chapter, the auditor may also be involved in attesting to the effectiveness of management performance beyond that implicitly provided by historical results reported in conformity with generally accepted accounting principles.

Suggested Audit Objective

After evaluating the evolution of auditing and the developments in the profession, we suggest that the audit examination have as its objective: *to develop an understanding of the information requirements of a firm, and to evaluate the adequacy of the firm's information systems in meeting these requirements.* We feel that by virtue of such an objective, not only would management's stewardship function or accountability as reflected in financial statements be evaluated, but so would the adequacy of management information for planning, control, and decision-making purposes as well, making the audit a much more productive activity.

Application of this approach requires that the traditional audit function and the consulting function of the public accountant grow together. Evaluation of controls will require the diagnostic approach of the information consultant, even if no specific consulting engagement is requested by the client. Finally, a report on the fairness of financial statements will be only one of the outputs of the audit, rather than its major end product. Once the information system has been reviewed, an evaluation furnished to the client, and perhaps made available to outside parties, should be a principal result. In addition, other outputs of the information system may be reported on with relatively little additional work.

The remaining sections of this book will be devoted to a discussion of the audit approach, methodology, and reporting process required to achieve our stated audit objective.

Introduction to Readings

In this chapter, it is suggested that audit objectives are changing in response to changing needs and information technology. The traditional audit of financial statements and account balances is giving way to an audit relating to the information system of the firm and its adequacy in meeting the information requirements of the enterprise. This new approach has many implications and leads to significantly expanded auditing opportunities and problems.

The three readings which accompany this chapter explore some of these implications. The first is a paper by one of the authors dealing with the need for some form of management audits and developing criteria for such audits and audit reports. The second is a speech given by Joseph Roth, partner in Price Waterhouse & Co., and then chairman of the Committee on Auditing Procedure of the AICPA. Mr. Roth considers both the present fulfillment of the attest function and its expansion into new areas. He considers the practical implications of audit reports on controls, management systems, and forecast. The final article is an attempt to develop a theoretical framework for the audit of management. Professors Langerderfer and Robertson make a pioneering effort in a difficult area and while they identify their structure as tentative, it is a worthwhile starting point for the development of a theory.

Appendix

MANAGEMENT CONTROLS QUESTIONNAIRE
BASIC INFORMATION

GENERAL — MS 101

Client: Number:_____ S.I.C._____Code _____

Partner contact: _____Reviewed (date): _____

Prepared by: _____ Date: _____

MS review by: _____Date: _____

Action taken: _____

(1) Management letter prepared by: _____
     Date:_____

(2) MS personnel participate in preparation of management letter?
     Yes_____No _____

(3) MS work discussed with client? Yes_____No_____

(4) MS proposal submitted to client? Yes_____No_____ Written_____
     Oral_____
     Remarks: _____

Client personnel consulted in connection with this questionnaire:

Name   *Title*

_____   _____

Type of organization: _____Corporation _____Partnership _____Proprietorship _____Other. If Other, specify: _____

Trade customers: _____Manufacturers _____Service Trades _____Retail Merchants _____Wholesalers _____General Public _____Other (specify): _____

Principal products or services: _____

Principal channel of sales: _____Outside Salesmen _____Brokers or Agents _____Catalog Order _____Direct Mail _____Walk-in _____Other
    If Other, specify:_____

Number of employees: _____Administrative _____Sales _____Manufacturing _____Service _____Accounting _____Total

Number of clerical employees, all departments:_____

Has overtime been substantial during past year? _____Yes _____No. In what department(s)? _____

Is the business seasonal?_____Yes _____No. If yes, explain: _____

Principal office machines or equipment in use: (Specify model or type where possible—data processing, posting, mail, pegboard, duplicating, copying, sorting, filing, etc.) _____

Approximate number of trade accounts receivable: _____. Accounts payable?_____

Approximate number of items in inventory: Finished goods_____ Raw materials_____

Brief description of method of accounting: _____

Receivables billed on a cycle basis?_____Yes _____No
    Window envelopes used?_____Yes _____No

Collection policy appears: _____Too loose _____Too tight

Do controls of cash include a system of cash forecasting? _____Yes _____No

Are temporary excess funds invested? _____Yes _____No

When was the last insurance survey made? Date:_____
    By whom? _____. Were coverage deficiencies noted in audit of prepaid insurance? _____Yes _____No. Are safety or prevention programs in effect to reduce premium cost? _____Yes _____No

Is maximum advantage taken of cash discounts? _____Yes _____No

Turnover: Accounts receivable_____. (Net sales divided by year-end balances.) Inventory_____. (Cost of sales divided by year-end balances.) Compute hi and lo turnover, if business is seasonal:

	High Balance	Low Balance
Accounts receivable	_____times	_____times
Inventory	_____times	_____times

If the client maintains perpetual inventory records, take a random sample (at least 10 items) of usage. Divide *quantity* balance on hand by the *quantity* used or sold in the preceding 12 months. Carry to two decimals and convert to day's supply on hand by multiplying by 365. (Describe results in Comments Section following.)

Result: #1	Item #2	Day's Supply	Item	Day's Supply

What is bad debt write-off experience? (% of net sales)

    5th year prior to this review   _____%

    3rd year prior to this review   _____%

    This year   _____%

Who, in general, may initiate purchase requisitions? _____

Comments

(As requested. Also describe briefly the payroll, receivables and payables systems)_____

_____

_____

Complete the following:

                                         Yes   No

I   *Organization*

    a.   Are organization charts in use?   _____ _____

    b.   Are they up to date?   _____ _____

    c.   Are management policy and operating procedure

        manuals in use?   _____ _____

    d.   Are job descriptions prepared and used?   _____ _____

II *Budget*

    a.   Is a formal system used?   _____ _____

    b.   Does it include:

        1.   All divisions and departments?   _____ _____

        2.   Forecasting cash and budgeting capital

           expenditures?   _____ _____

        3.   Timely comparisons to actual results?   _____ _____

        4.   Responsible explanations of variances? _____ _____

        5.   Is it a motivation system for corrective action? _____ _____

III	*Office Management*		Yes	No

III *Office Management*　　　　　　　　　　Yes　　No

    a. Does office layout provide for efficient work flow? _____ _____

    b. Is a good system of forms control in effect? _____ _____

    c. Is there a written records retention program? _____ _____

    d. Is there an office procedures manual? _____ _____

    e. Has a clerical work measurement program been introduced? _____ _____

    f. Does office machinery appear best suited for the job? _____ _____

IV *Management Reports*

    a. Are internal reports to management issued quickly? _____ _____

    b. Are there apparent duplications in reports? _____ _____

    c. Is "responsibility reporting" in effect? _____ _____

    d. Is "management by exception" a company practice and are reports prepared on this basis? _____ _____

V *Cost Accounting*

    a. Is a cost accounting system used? _____ _____

    b. Does it provide for performance measurement? _____ _____

    c. Does it tie into the general ledger? _____ _____

    d. Are standards and overhead rates up to date? _____ _____

    e. Are cost centers clearly defined? _____ _____

    f. Are cost variances analyzed and reported? (as to performance, price, usage, etc.) _____ _____

    g. Does system provide adequate information for compilation of break-even data and analysis of profit-volume relationship? _____ _____

VI *General Accounting*

    a. Are accounting manuals used? _____ _____

    b. Does chart of accounts provide for the accumulation of adequate financial and cost information? _____ _____

    c. Are "fast closing" techniques utilized? _____ _____

VII *Purchasing*

    a. Is there evidence that adequate procurement control is concentrated in the purchasing department? _____ _____

    b. Is there evidence of too much concentration of control resulting in production delays or other inefficiencies? _____ _____

    c. Is competitive bidding a continual practice? _____ _____

    d. Are purchases made from budgets, production schedules or automatic reorder points in formalized economic lots? _____ _____

    e. Do purchasing department files and records appear adequate? _____ _____

    f. Are materials purchased to clients' specifications? _____ _____

VIII *Personnel Practices*

    a. Do they include:
      1. A formal selection process including a testing program? _____ _____
      2. A job classification and evaluation program? _____ _____
      3. A training program (including management development)? _____ _____
      4. An employee handbook? _____ _____
      5. Meaningful reports? _____ _____
      6. Incentive compensation systems for personnel in:
        (A) Sales? _____ _____
        (B) Production? _____ _____
        (C) Office? _____ _____
        (D) Supervisory classifications? _____ _____

    b. Are any of the following in force or under consideration:
      1. Pension Plan? _____ _____
      2. Profit-sharing? _____ _____
      3. Deferred compensation? _____ _____

    c. Are estate planning programs established for principal officers and directors? _____ _____
      1. Do they have wills? _____ _____

IX *Operating Performance*

a.

	Sales	Gross Profit %of Sales	Operating expense	Net income (pre tax) % of sales
Fifth year prior to this review	_____	_____	_____	_____
Third year prior	_____	_____	_____	_____
This review	_____	_____	_____	_____

b. Select the appropriate business classification
(S.I.C. Code) from D & B Key Ratios and show
below: (Use D & B definitions.)

	Selected Industry Median	Client
Current assets to current debt	_____	_____ times
Net profits (after taxes) to net sales	_____ %	_____ %
Net profits to tangible net worth	_____ %	_____ %
Net sales to tangible net worth	_____	_____ times
Collection period	_____	_____ days
Net sales to inventory	_____	_____ times
Current debt to tangible net worth	_____ %	_____ %
Total debt to tangible net worth	_____ %	_____ %
Inventory to net working capital	_____ %	_____ %

John C. Burton

Management Auditing

In the coming decade, it seems very likely that there will be increasing demand for information about corporate performance. In part, this will manifest itself in additional requirements for disclosure of historical financial data. In addition, however, there may well be demand for some impartial evaluation of management performance beyond that implicitly provided by historical results reported in conformity with generally accepted accounting principles.

This demand may come from several sources. Investment analysts today recognize that the evaluation of management is of crucial importance and, at the same time, extremely difficult for any outsider. They may require managements to submit more data on this subject. Similarly, stockholders—particularly those who control large holdings in trust for others—may want more assurance that their capital is being effectively used. Finally,

there is an increasing tendency for the public to feel that corporate management has the responsibility of using assets under its control effectively as a service to society as well as to its own stockholders. Several different groups might argue for some appraisal of management beyond conventional financial statements.

If some auditor in the future is to be asked to attest not only to financial results but also to the effectiveness of management's stewardship, it is important to consider what the nature of the "management audit" will be and how this auditor is to be qualified. Although there has been some writing on this subject, to date there has been no attempt to construct a total framework for the management audit.

In developing such a framework, four areas must be examined. First, the criteria for a management audit must be considered. Second, standards of managerial performance must be developed if the evaluation of management stewardship is to have meaning. Third, a method of reporting must be established so that the auditor can have a structured means

Reprinted by permission from *The Journal of Accountancy*, May 1968, pp. 41-46. Copyrighted 1968 by the American Institute of Certified Public Accountants.

of disclosing the results of his examination. Finally, it will be necessary to develop management auditing procedures and standards of documentation to support the report given.

Turning first to the criteria underlying the management audit, it seems that three premises may be established:

1. The audit must deal with the objective and the measurable.

2. It must deal with the present and the past and not with the future.

3. It must produce a result which is understandable and usable by the various interested publics.

The first of these criteria has always created problems for the advocate of management auditing. This is because the accountant has traditionally thought of measurability and objectivity in terms of countability and the ability to recount. It seems clear, however, that measurement need not imply the tally clerk's precision and that objectivity does not require that an identical answer always be derived from the same data. Objective is defined as detached, impersonal and unprejudiced. This definition can surely be met by a trained auditor exercising professional judgement on the effectiveness of managerial stewardship. Two separate auditors might emerge from an audit with slightly different results, but the variation should not exceed that attributable to normal sampling errors if due professional care is used.

The second criterion for a management audit indicates that the auditor must examine that which exists and has existed rather than that which it is hoped will develop. Almost by definition an audit cannot be a forecast and, accordingly, it is clear that a management audit will not supplant the investor's task of forecasting the relative success or failure of enterprises. Rather, it will improve data so that the marketplace will be better informed and the analyst will be able to make a more reasoned forecast based upon his own expectations of movements within the economy.

The elimination of forecasting from the audit function, however, does not mean that the future will be totally ignored. Management's present outlook is primarily future-oriented and, therefore, in evaluating the management of the present, the future must be implicitly considered. What the auditor must do, therefore, is to measure and evaluate whether or not management is currently performing its future-oriented function appropriately. This implies an audit of procedures, which is clearly part of the management audit.

At the same time, part of the auditing procedure must concern itself with the past since the results of past decisions may be the best means of estimating future results. The second part of the management audit, therefore, will be reporting on and evaluation of the results of the past.

Finally, the management audit must produce a result which is understandable and usable by the interested publics. The users of the audit must know what has been done and be aware of the significance of it. It has been charged by some that the auditor of today has failed in this respect even in regard to the financial audit, and it is most important that a similar failing does not occur if an expansion of the audit function takes place. This implies reporting needs, which will be discussed later.

Development of Performance Standards

If the first two criteria for a management audit are to be met, one prerequisite is the development of standards of managerial performance that can be expressed in specific terms. These standards are needed to evaluate both procedures and results. In the procedural area, the principal objective normally sought by the management of a firm is effective managerial control over the operations of the business. In order to achieve this control, management conventionally sets up a series of procedures. While it is true that procedures alone do not create control, it still appears plausible to evaluate the effectiveness of management control through the appraisal of the existence and use of the control procedures which the firm has established.

A first approach to the development of a control measure might be to identify the various areas of managerial control within the firm. One possible classification would be as follows:

1. Organization control
   a. Chart of organization
   b. Job descriptions
   c. Procedure manuals
   d. Stated corporate objectives

2. Planning and information systems
   a. Long-range planning—strategic and operational
   b. Operating budgets
   c. Cost accounting systems
   d. Cost controls

3. Asset management
   a. Liquid asset control
   b. Credit and receivable control
   c. Inventory control
   d. Capital budgeting system

4. Marketing system
   a. Product planning
   b. Market research
   c. Sales forecasting
   d. Sales analysis

5. Production system
   a. Production planning
   b. Quality control
   c. Labor relations
   d. Purchasing and procurement

Within each of these areas, it may be possible to identify the various procedures which are most significant in improving the quality of managerial control.

Relative "quality points" might then be assigned reflecting the existence and effective use of these procedures in each area and, by totaling these quality points, an overall index of the quality of control procedures might be developed which would serve as a basis for comparison among firms.

Considerable research is needed in determining what these quality points should be, and it may be that no quantitative evaluation of this sort is possible. Nevertheless, the evaluation of the adequacy of procedures and controls within each of these areas, even if performed on a nonquantitative basis, may be of significance in the evaluation of the management of the firm.

Beyond procedural standards, it is necessary to develop financial standards to evaluate the performance of the firm. Some bench marks are needed to supplement conventional net income which is the figure commonly used today. These might include the development of additional absolute figures, such as income exclusive of holding gains and charges related to future activities (like most research expenses), though the major financial standards will be relative ones. Reported achievements must be related to the industry and economic environment in which the firm operates, to the prior performance of the firm and to the prior plans of the corporation.

As an example of the type of approach that could be used, the following are possible measures of relative success:

1. Ratio of operating return on sales earned by the company compared to the return earned by the industry

2. Ratio of operating return on long-term capital earned by the company compared to the return earned by the industry

3. Comparative variability in return compared to average industry variability

In addition to standards for annual or periodic corporate data, financial standards might also encompass the comparison of results with expectations on a major project basis. There seems to be an increasing tendency today for firms to control operations not only by the calendar period but by major projects of a strategic nature. As information systems are improved, it is likely that the interpretation of corporate results will require an analysis of projects as well as of periods. In this way, past strategic decisions of the management can be evaluated as evidence develops relating to their success. While this will not be definitive evidence of the effectiveness of current strategic planning, it may be of some help to the investor to see the varying major decisions of corporate

management identified and their results reported on as well as having successes and failures combined into a single net income figure.

Reporting on the Management Audit

The third principal problem associated with the development of the management auditing framework is the establishment of the method of reporting to be used in connection with the audit performed. First, the recipient of the report must be identified. It is conceivable that management might seek a management audit from independent auditors and wish to be the only party receiving the auditor's report. Similarly, the directors might commission the audit and wish the report to be made solely to them. If the management audit develops to meet the needs mentioned above, however, the report must ultimately be available to stockholders and to the public.

The format of such a report will require considerable thought. It seems obvious that the report will bear little similarity to the standard short-form auditor's report which is predominant today. It is impractical to expect the auditor to report simply that the management is following "generally accepted standards of management" and leave it at that. Such a report would tend to become a formality as indeed reports following this approximate wording seem to have become in certain European countries. What will be needed, therefore, is a longer and less standard statement.

It is premature to suggest the exact appearance of this report, but one approach might be to include three basic sections: first, a scope section where the auditor would describe the nature of his examination; second, a section in which the auditor evaluated the past performance of the company, perhaps including a variety of measures of performance in both absolute and comparative terms; and finally, a section in which the auditor evaluated the current management procedures of the corporation, perhaps including a "management control score." In all, a management audit report might take two or three pages in an annual report to stockholders.

Supplementing this report, there might be made available to management and to the directors a more detailed discussion of corporation. The auditor might also complete a management questionnaire which would be submitted to the directors and perhaps made available to the public through filing with the Securities and Exchange Commission.

Management Auditing Procedures

The final part of the management audit framework that must be developed is the determination of the auditing procedures associated with this audit and the documentation which is necessary to support the auditor's opinion. Today's auditing procedures provide a reasonable starting point. In connection with his examination of financial statements, today's auditor must develop a thorough understanding of the business enterprise. A major part of the audit today is the review of internal control and, in the expansion of the audit function, this is the area to which the greatest attention will have to be paid.

The current review of internal control normally focuses upon accounting controls.

Under management auditing, however, the review of management controls will take on an enormously greater importance. This review today is normally performed on an occasional but not an intensive basis. The auditor generally has an organization chart in his working papers, but he does not spend a great deal of time on the planning side of the business. His analysis of the financial information system is more geared to satisfying himself about its reliability than to determining whether it produces appropriate information for the management of the firm. In a management audit, this emphasis will be changed. The auditor will look to see whether management is getting information relevant to the decisions and actions which it must take. This will require a much more intensive analysis of information needs and the efficiency of the existing system in meeting them. In the marketing and production areas particularly it is likely that the auditor will have to develop increased familiarity with the information needed to make decisions, including that which is not part of the conventional books of account. The auditor will not have to decide whether management is making the *right* strategic and operative decisions but rather whether management has available to it and is using the relevant information and techniques necessary to evaluate rationally the various alternatives that exist.

The procedures associated with the management audit, therefore, will include a substantial increase in the amount of time spent in evaluating internal control. They will include increasing reliance upon interviews with corporate managers, and they will require a study of the information system of the firm with new objectives in mind.

The second part of the management audit will require the auditor to undertake a financial analysis of the company in order to compare its results with the appropriate financial standards of performance. In the connection, the auditor must consider the operating results of the various parts of the firm. He must select those data which are most significant in the evaluation of corporate performance and array them in an understandable fashion so that the investor and the outside analyst can use such data for their purposes. In this connection, data will have to be accumulated about the company and its environment from the accounting and other records of the firm and from outside industry and government sources.

The increased scope of the management audit will create problems of audit documentation, although the changes in this area will not be as great as the changes in reporting on the audit. Presumably, the working papers of the auditor will include copies of the procedural manual of the firm and sample copies of the varying reports used by management to run the business, together with interview data indicating the extent to which formal procedures are actually used. There will be flowcharts of the information system, a description of the corporate planning process, and a record of the varying interviews and tests undertaken during the audit.

To support the financial analysis, there will be a compilation of the firm's operating data, a description of industry and government data sources and a record of calculations made. In addition, there might be a questionnaire designed to elicit from management the most significant facts for performance evaluation.

While the volume of documentation may not be great, there will be a need for an increased number of memorandums outlining in a reasoned manner the various judgments made in connection with the audit, and the logic supporting them. There will be relatively few schedules supplying arithmetic support, since the final judgments will not be verifiable by counting in the way an inventory may be checked today.

Implications for the Public Accounting Profession

In this discussion, it has been tacitly assumed that the management audit would develop out of today's financial audit. Certainly the CPA has a reasonable claim to be the most qualified management auditor. His current function requires that he be thoroughly familiar with the business of his client. He has traditionally given business advice, and in recent years his management consulting function has been growing rapidly. On the other hand, this function would require major changes in the reporting philosophy moving away from the increasingly standardized reports which are being given to the public today. There will be significant implications in the areas of competence, independence and legal liability which must be considered carefully before deciding whether management auditing should represent a major part of the activity of the public accounting profession.

If the measurement function of the public accountant is to be dramatically expanded, it is essential that the profession recruit and develop a cadre of people with competence in this form of measurement. This will require an increasing number of specialties within the profession and it will require a significant upgrading in the quality of personnel recruited. The public accounting firm will need specialists in production and marketing as well as financial information specialists in order to perform the management audit.

In part, this competence is currently being developed in management consulting divisions of the larger firms. The development of management auditing will put tremendous demands on these divisions since the skills they possess will initially be in short supply within the firm. This will require increasing integration between the audit function and the consulting function in firms since a management auditing engagement requires many of the people who are now used primarily in consulting work.

An additional implication which must be considered is the perennial problem of independence. The management auditor will start with fewer rules than govern the performance of the conventional financial audit. In the absence of generally accepted principles and standards, the auditor will have to feel his way. He will have to measure in an area where there is little precision. Given the increasing difficulty of measurement and the lack of fixed standards, the importance of independence of outlook becomes of increasing significance. The faith of the public in the integrity and ability of the auditor must be very great as the element of professional judgment in measurement becomes more significant.

The problem of independence will be particularly acute in the consulting area. If an auditor is to evaluate and report specifically on the procedures of a firm, is he barred from making recommendations for improvements? If he has suggested procedures which have been adopted, can he then independently review them? On the other hand, can one audit procedures without at least implicitly recommending changes, except in the unusual case where perfection has been achieved? These are questions which will certainly become increasingly heard with the development of management audits, and no simple solutions are apparent.

The third implication that must be considered in connection with the management audit is that of the auditor's legal liability. As the management audit grows in stature and investors and other parties put increasing reliance upon this report of the public accountant, the potential for damage claims increases. The degree of responsibility which an auditor takes in his management attestation must be spelled out. Since errors in judgment can be increasingly costly, it must be clear that the auditor is not guaranteeing the future in his attestation. Rather he must be charged with the responsibility of justifying a professional opinion on the adequacy of current management procedures and past management performance. This, it would seem, presents no insurmountable difficulty if audit documentation has been properly prepared.

A Forecast

Despite these problems, the existence of the need for the attestation of corporate performance makes it likely that the management audit in some form will come to be. While it appears that the public accounting profession is in the best position to serve this function, if the profession declines to expand its attest function beyond what it currently undertakes, then some other professional or governmental group might well perform the task required.

The management audit will not develop overnight. Rather it is more likely that it will come from an evolution perhaps already under way. Two examples of this trend are the use of auditors in preacquisition investigations and the engagement of CPAs to attest to the existence of controls against conflict of interest situations arising in a corporation. The next step might well be the evolution of the internal control letter to management into the expression of an opinion on efficiency. From this point it would not be difficult to develop a routine for reporting on managerial effectiveness to directors.

Once such a trend starts, it is likely that it will grow since most outside boards feel somewhat vulnerable in the absence of significant external review of corporate management's activity.

Once managements and directors begin receiving regular opinions on the efficiency of management performance, it will not be long before principal creditors will demand such opinions as well. There is already evidence that some creditors feel such information should be made available to them. Once creditors have this information, it would not be surprising to see the managements of one or two corporations begin to publish such attestations in the annual report to stockholders and at that

point pressure on other managers to do likewise would no doubt grow. Thus, the evolution of the management audit might well take place without the force of law ever being invoked.

An alternative means of meeting the information need implied by the management audit would be by act of law. Congress might require that an independent appraisal of management be performed either by an independent auditor or by a government agency. Such an act might require regular filing of management audit reports so that such information would be available to investors and potential investors.

Whatever the route, however, it seems logical to assume that this need for additional information about the performance of management will be met and in the not-too-distant future. It is incumbent upon the public accounting profession to prepare itself to meet this demand.

Joseph L. Roth

What's Ahead for the Auditors?

Since I am nearing the completion of my term as chairman of the committee on auditing procedure, I might be able to furnish some guidance for its next chairman. After giving some thought to the many problems facing the

Reprinted by permission from *The Journal of Accountancy*, August 1969. Copyrighted 1969 by the American Institute of Certified Public Accountants.

committee, I may really be furnishing a list of things to do for several future chairman.

To establish a background for my comments, I'll mention briefly some of the important matters of auditing and reporting to which the committee on auditing procedure has been, and still is, devoting considerable amounts of time and effort. In this way, I can give you some idea of what remains to be finished, what is on the waiting list and what might be coming up in the future.

Background

The role of the CPA has adjusted over the years to the changing environment in which the profession has found itself. Our present era is no exception to the general rule of change. The financial community—credit grantors, financial analysts, financial writers and others who utilize financial information—is making more and more demands on the profession. Intermixed with and almost inseparable from the clamor for eliminating alternative accounting principles and establishing more rigid accounting practices are appeals for more preciseness in financial reporting and more clarification of the responsibility of the auditor for the reported results. These pressures on what we have come to accept as our role in auditing cannot be ignored.

More specifically, it is only natural that a profession react immediately to any widely publicized events which might somehow cast a reflection on its image or pose a serious threat to its established relationship with the society it serves. As the body of the Institute which establishes standards for the profession in the field of auditing, the committee on auditing procedure is constantly alert to any occurrence involving members of the profession which receives the attention of the press. It is prompt to take steps to investigate all of the circumstances and to consider the implications they may have for changes in our procedures and the possible impact of the events

on the profession. In fact, the committee originated with the investigation of the circumstances of the McKesson and Robbins affair. This investigation resulted in its first official pronouncement. More recently, responding to the publicity over the "Great Salad Oil Swindle," the committee conducted a study on the controls and auditing procedures in connection with goods held by warehouses. This, too, resulted in an official report of the committee. Several of the matters now on our agenda resulted from highly publicized events. Attention to these has required such a substantial portion of the committee's time that it has been diverted from a number of other important matters requiring its attention.

In addition to responding to these day-to-day—or, more correctly, year-to-year—problems, the committee is responsible for establishing standards and providing guidelines for the observance of those standards. Statement on Auditing Procedure No. 33 went far in placing the established standards in proper perspective and in relating them to the many guidelines which had been set forth in its previous official pronouncements. Other statements are expected to provide further clarifications of the standards and to provide guidance in specific areas as, for example, Statement No. 38 did with respect to unaudited statements. Above and beyond its response to day-to-day problems and the need to amplify the present literature, the committee must also stand ready to establish standards for any expansion of the role of the auditor as might develop in response to public demand. There are a number of important matters which fall within these three broad categories of responsibility which I expect the committee will have to face in the future.

Publicized Events

Dealing first with events which have received wide publicity, there are three which have already received considerable attention from the committee.

The first of them is the decision in the case referred to as *Fischer* v. *Kletz* which is the litigation resulting from the financial difficulties of Yale Express System, Inc. After considerable deliberation on the questions raised by this decision and with close collaboration with legal counsel the committee now has under consideration a draft statement which may be exposed shortly. It suggests the steps an independent auditor might take when he discovers information subsequent to issuing his report which would have materially affected his opinion on the financial statements had he been aware of the information before issuing the report.

Another matter the committee has under study is the possible effect on the profession of the much publicized decision in the *Bar Chris* case. This decision has implications concerning the adequacy of the procedures an auditor follows with respect to events occurring subsequent to the balance sheet date which may have a bearing on the audited financial statements. As a side issue, the decision has also caused us to focus on the form and content of "comfort letters" which are usually required, under the provisions of underwriting agreements, to be provided by the independent auditors in connection with public offerings of securities.

Third, the committee is considering the circumstances relating to the *Continental Vending* case in which the independent auditors were charged in a criminal action. While this matter is still under appeal, the committee must determine whether additional guidelines for the profession are needed in the very specific areas involved in this case.

In addition to these legal cases there are several other widely publicized ones in which CPA firms are involved, but which have not yet reached decisions. There are also numerous cases involving smaller firms of CPAs which have not received wide publicity. Many of these are in connection with unaudited statements. The cumulative effect of all these court cases will naturally have some effect on the legal concepts of the independent auditor's responsibilities. Some of our former concepts of legal liability associated with our examinations of financial statements on which we have relied may be changed. As cases occur, the committee must identify those areas of our practice where standards of procedure have not been adequately established and be ready to provide guidelines for the profession. Establishing our own standards might avoid having them established by unwise case law. In the course of this, however, the committee should be extremely careful that it does not imprudently establish such precise procedures, rather than broad guidelines, that needless legal difficulties are created.

Better Understanding of the Auditor's Role

A better understanding of the independent auditor's role by the users of our reports and by the public generally might go far toward reducing the number of cases taken to court and resultant unfortunate legal decisions. One means of attaining better understanding could possibly be a clearer explanation of the scope and purpose of our audit in our short-form report. A revision of the short-form report aimed at making it more understandable is, I think, much needed. While it may not be the most urgent of our present projects, the committee should continue its attempts to draft a report which will more clearly set forth the nature of our examination and the intended meaning of the opinion we express.

Amplifications of Present Literature

There are a great number of other auditing and reporting problems which need the committee's attention. Some of these, like the revision of the short-form report, are on the active agenda of the committee. Others should have high priority for getting on it. Some are needed to provide clarification of our present official literature on auditing. Examples of these are, briefly:

1. Reliance on the report of other auditors and the extent of such reliance. Our present literature in this area is quite cryptic and needs considerable amplifying.

2. Proper reporting procedures when the auditor lacks independence. Some direction is required to provide clarification of our present rules of ethics.

3. Guidelines for determining at what point a "disclaimer" of opinion may be needed rather than a "subject to" opinion and where an "adverse" opinion is required rather than an "exception."

4. Rules governing the use, rather I should say the prohibition of the use, of "negative assurance" language.

Other problems are broader in scope and may be more challenging. Some I will mention are:

1. The relationship between the auditor's evaluation of the effectiveness of internal controls and the extent of his auditing procedures.

2. The effect of the computer on internal accounting controls and guidance not only for establishing adequate controls but also for the auditor's evaluation of their effectiveness.

3. Development of the theory of continuous auditing. This involves the concept that all auditing procedures are but a chain of continuing tests of reliability of the accounting records and controls which need not all be accomplished with respect to the period under review. Acceptance of this concept could even lead to enabling the auditor to express an opinion on any interim statements.

4. The development of computer audit tapes for use by independent auditors. These could radically change the methods by which auditors perform their examination even if they do not change basic audit objectives.

There are many other subjects which have been suggested from time to time, but I feel those I have mentioned are among the most urgent.

Expanded Scope

Now, how about the problems which may need to be faced in meeting the demands associated with the changing environment? If the court cases to which I referred earlier result in any appreciable increase in auditors' legal responsibility, particularly if the present concepts of materiality are affected, the scope and extent of auditing procedures will have to be reappraised. In addition, what *Forbes Magazine* called the "growing credibility gap" in corporate financial reporting is creating demands for less flexibility and more preciseness in financial statements. This will also have to be taken into account in any such reappraisal.

The public is also demanding more and more financial information, such as ten-year summaries of earnings, profits by product lines and a vast amount of other statistical data. Will not these demands result in expanding the independent auditor's role to include his attesting to all such additional information—possibly with even more preciseness than is now expected? There are sufficient reasons to expect that the auditor's role will be affected by the rising demands for more and more accountability by corporate managements and greater and greater preciseness of the accounting. The profession must be ready to meet this challenge, and the committee will have to provide the leadership.

Reporting on Internal Controls

Another challenge which I think must be met soon is the recurring suggestion by bankers and other credit grantors that CPAs report on the adequacy of their clients' internal controls.

The suggestion rises rather logically from the realization that the degree of comfort a credit grantor has during the year—that is, in between his receipt of the year-end audited financial statement—depends considerably on the reliability of the company's internal controls. At present there are no established criteria for determining the relative adequacy of internal controls nor any standards for reporting publicly on their adequacy. Some instances of reporting publicly on the adequacy of controls have already occurred. Therefore, it seems that the needed action by the committee is urgent.

Going a step beyond this is the matter of management controls. Over the last 20 years, CPAs have expanded their service to clients beyond audits of financial statements and the traditional tax work. Many CPA firms' management advisory groups now provide a wide variety of services, such as feasibility studies, system design, cost control, production and inventory controls, budget systems and organization structure.

It seems to me not only possible but even probable that, possessing the competence to assist clients in establishing effective management controls and reliable information systems where needed, independent auditors may be expected to report on their own evaluation of the effectiveness of the information system of clients whose financial statements they audit. In other words, we may even be expected to go beyond just reporting on the internal accounting controls, as I have suggested, to reporting on management controls and the information system generally. Objective assurance of the effectiveness of the system by which management makes its major decision in the running of the business would be most useful to credit grantors and potential investors. How quickly this expansion of the auditor's role may develop is difficult to predict, but the profession should be ready to equip itself with standards and guidelines for such reporting if the demand does arise.

Another possible area for expansion of the auditor's role may be with forecasts of expected profits. The public demand for more accountability by management may lead inevitably but reluctantly, I expect, to the practice of furnishing profit forecasts for future periods. Certainly this information would be extremely useful to credit grantors, investors, potential investors and other users of financial reports. To a considerable degree, any interest these users may have in present and past performance is only to provide a means of guessing at future earnings prospects. Wouldn't it be better to have management's well-considered plans? While managements now generally refrain from predicting future results or releasing information about their budgeted earnings, a more sophisticated generation of investing public may demand this additional data. Corporate officials may be faced with the alternatives of furnishing it, reluctantly, or admitting that they do not have sufficient confidence in their plans for future periods to commit themselves publicly to them.

If the practice of furnishing forecasts does develop, is it not likely that the "growing credibility gap" will cause the users to expect the independent auditors to report on the fairness of them? Our Code of Professional Ethics now prohibits members from associating their names with forecasts of future results in a way which might lead to the belief that they are vouching for their accuracy. This has caused CPAs generally to avoid associating themselves with budgets of future earnings. On the other hand, the Council of the Institute of Chartered Accountants in England and Wales has recently issued a statement for the guidance of their members who may be asked to

review and report on profit forecasts. It provides suggestions for the procedures to be considered by the accountant in making such a review and what matters should be included in his report. I am certain that the profession in this country can perform this added service if it becomes necessary. Again standards must be established and suggestions for procedures provided.

Conclusion

In summary, I expect that the audit function will come under more and more scrutiny and our procedures will have to be more specifically described and better understood. This means further amplification of our literature to provide guidelines for meeting adequately our established auditing standards. It also means clearer and more understandable reporting practices. There is also the possibility that added responsibility may require an extension of the scope and extent of auditing procedures to provide additional audit satisfaction.

Beyond this, I expect an expansion of the independent auditor's role to cover such things as reporting not only on our evaluation of the client's internal accounting controls but possibly all management controls and, beyond that, on forecasts of future earnings. To the extent that our role may be expanded, it follows necessarily that additional responsibility will result. The profession has always stood ready to assume the additional responsibility which has attached to the increased services for which our clients and the investing public have expressed a need. I am sure we are ready to meet any additional responsibility that the future holds in store for us.

Harold Q. Langenderfer
Jack C. Robertson

A Theoretical Structure for Independent Audits of Management

Current events have shown that there is a widespread interest on the part of stockholders, creditors, and other members of the financial community in the problem of assessing the management of a firm within a broader framework than that offered by audited financial statements alone. Additional information about management and managerial activities appears to be in demand. A potential approach for satisfying this demand is through management auditing, which has often been described as the *art* of assessing management. The assessment process itself has been called a "management audit."

In general, discussions of management auditing have produced more emotion than logic up to the present time for two reasons. First, there is no general agreement as to the precise meaning of the term *management audit*, and secondly, there exists no explicit theory of *management auditing* in the context of an independent audit function.

Reprinted by permission from *The Accounting Review*, October 1969.

These two aspects of the topic make a study of management auditing one of the more troublesome, yet one of the more interesting areas of current accounting and auditing thought. In this paper, the authors explore briefly the definitional problem and the matter of a rationale for management auditing, and then propose in some detail a theoretical structure for extending the audit function to include independent audits of management.

A Matter of Terminology

In order for a theory of management auditing to be meaningful, a clear statement of the context of the term *management audit* is necessary. The term has been used in several different ways by persons of varying professional interests. Consequently, there is no specific meaning for the term.

Management consultants have referred to *management auditing* in the context of organizational evaluation for the purpose of defining and explaining problem areas.[1] This usage is similar to that employed by some Certified Public Accountants with reference to management services engagements.[2] Internal auditors frequently refer to their internal audits, or operational audits, as *management audits*.[3] The distinguishing feature of these uses of the term is that in each case of audit engagement is in the nature of an audit *for* management. *Independence* is not considered to be particularly relevant to such audit examinations as these.

In contrast, other definitions of *management auditing* have been framed in the context of *independent attestations* of management for the benefit of third parties. The American Institute of Management (AIM) has a program for conducting a management audit by which management's overall performance may be systematically examined, analyzed, and appraised. AIM professes the ability to make not only a complete evaluation of a firm, both objectively and subjectively, but also the ability to render an authoritative judgment on the efficacy of management itself.[4] This is a form of attestation, but some

serious questions can be raised about the methodology employed.[5]

Churchill and Cyert have offered a definition that parallels the AIM concept of management audit: "The management audit is defined as an audit which results in a statement of opinion by a CPA with regard to the performance of the management function."[6] This definition leaves much to be desired in the way of precision, but it has captured the essence of attestation—an expert opinion. Churchill and Cyert contemplate an independent examination of the information system, management control, and management procedures in the course of a management audit, using as standards some "accepted principles of management."[7] In this context, the audit is more in the nature of an audit *of* management.

Consequently, the theory presented in this paper perceives of management auditing in the context of *independent audits of management*, a use of terms that is intended to connote the *attestation* context of management auditing. *Attestation* is defined as the process by which credibility is attributed to the representations of one party to another through the offices of a third party—the attestor. Solomon has placed the attest function on firm ground by stating the following: "Attestation as such has a social meaning. . . because it has a fundamental utility."[8] This notion of the utility of attestation arises out of

---

[1]Richard I. Levin, "A Management Audit for Purchasing," *Journal of Purchasing*, February, 1968, pp. 60, 68.

[2]Arthur E. Witte, "Management Auditing: The Present State of the Art," *Journal of Accountancy*, 124 (August, 1967), p. 55. John L. Carey, "The Integrated Accounting Service," *Journal of Accountancy*, 120 (November, 1965), p. 62. John L. Carey, *The CPA Plans for the Future*. (American Institute of Certified Public Accountants, 1965), pp. 194-213.

[3]William L. Campfield, "Trends in Auditing Management Plans and Operations," *Journal of Accountancy*, 124 (July, 1967), pp. 42, 43, 45-46, Warren B. Coburn, "An Approach to Management Auditing." *NAA Bulletin*, 47 (March, 1966), p. 60.

[4]Jackson Martindell, *The Appraisal of Management: For Executives and Investors*. 1st ed. (Harper, 1960), pp. 3-4.

[5]Daniel Seligman, "Mr. Martindell's Curious Institute." *Fortune*, (November, 1956), p. 252.

[6]N.C. Churchill, and R. M. Cyert. "An Experiment in Management Auditing." *Journal of Accountancy*, 121 (February, 1966), p. 39.

[7]*Ibid.*, p. 41.

[8]Ezra Solomon, "Accounting in the Next Decade." *Journal of Accountancy*, 119 (January, 1965), pp. 22-26.

the complex economic environment which generates requirements for information about the operations of a firm. Such information is required by a multitude of persons, both internal and external to a particular firm, for the purpose of making informed decisions with respect to the firm.

Rationale for the Study of Management Auditing

The foregoing comments concerning information requirements of decision-makers interested in a firm provide the initial elements of a rationale for the study of management auditing. In addition, many accounts and auditors have recognized this same need for information within a framework that looks toward an extension of the traditional financial attest function. Their comments have dealt with information disclosures by management which extend beyond the traditional financial statements to other financial and non-financial data.[9]

In a recent study, Mautz surveyed the information needs of persons concerned with the operations of diversified business entities.[10] The responses of investors and in-

vestment advisors indicated that *managerial ability* ranked high among the factors to be considered heavily in reaching decisions about a firm. Of the seven reported indicators of managerial ability, four are perceived as explicit financial measures (return on common equity, ratio of net income before interest to invested capital, financial condition, and net income), and three others (growth of company, reputation of key personnel, and market performance of stock) are perceived as essentially non-financial in many respects. From the point of view of this paper, the most interesting aspect of the Mautz data is that the decision-oriented respondents reported that they relied less heavily upon the financial statements (presumably audited) than upon other sources (e.g. interviews, other publications) to assess the *managerial ability* factor.[11]

In other words, even though one might observe that the managerial factor is most often perceived in the light of financial measures, the Mautz data indicate that non-financial measures of management ability are consulted more often: Either the non-financial information tends to be weighted more heavily, or else decision-makers must go to several sources in order to gather information for an assessment of the managerial ability in a firm. Both of these inferences lead one to believe that a comprehensive attestation of managerial ability and related information would be well received by investors and investment advisors.

Toward a Theoretical Structure

To articulate a complete theory of management auditing is beyond the scope of this

---

[9]A representative sample of such references is as follows: (a) Robert W. Clarke. "Extension of the CPA's Attest Function in Corporate Annual Reports," *The Accounting Review*, 43 (October, 1968), pp. 769-776. (b) Herman W. Bevis, "The CPA's Attest Function in Modern Society," *Journal of Accountancy*, (February, 1962), pp. 28-35. (c) R. K. Mautz and Hussein A. Sharaf. *The Philosophy of Auditing* (American Accounting Association, 1961), pp. 192, 200.

[10]R. K. Mautz, *Financial Reporting by Diversified Companies*. (Financial Executives Research Foundation, 1968).

[11]*Ibid.*, p. 104.

short article; therefore, this paper presents only a skeleton of a theoretical structure. Fortunately the theory-building process does not have to state from scratch. Mautz and Sharaf, in their monograph, *The Philosophy of Auditing*, have presented what appears to be an acceptable statement of financial auditing concepts and postulates along with a rigorous philosophical rationale to support their theoretical assertations.[12] Even though the *Philosophy of Auditing* is general in nature and places emphasis on the processes of the financial audit, one would be remiss in disregarding this work as a basis for making further statements about auditing theory. However, because of its emphasis on financial auditing, the theoretical foundation presented by Mautz and Sharaf should be viewed only as a tentative set of building blocks for a theory of independent audits of management.

The theoretical structure for independent management audits rests upon the broad conceptual basis of independent attestation. In a more specific context, the process of management auditing is concerned with the examination of the efficacy of the processes which are examinable. Implicit in this specific context is the need to evaluate the supportive elements (*i.e., contributory* system) of decision processes which contribute to the achievement of enterprise goals. This examination of the management processes constitutes, then, the basis for an independent attestation concerning management's representations with respect to its operations and its goals.

Since this theory of management auditing is constructed on a basis parallel to the existing theory and practice of financial auditing, the

notion of "management representations" has a particular definitional meaning. *Management representations* is a term used herein to refer to two classes of data: (1) the information that management presently chooses to disclose to the public in widely disseminated reports with regard to its decisions with respect to investments, policy, organization structure, personnel, marketing, production, and expectations of future conditions, and (2) the information that management may not choose to disclose for a variety of reasons. The second category is included in order to close loopholes left in the first category. The analogy to financial statements in the context of financial auditing should be clear.

Before presenting the core of a management audit theory in the following two sections, one vital warning must be raised. Throughout this article, the authors have drawn upon the knowledge and research of accountants and auditors, almost to the exclusion of other professionals. Indeed, auditing is almost the exclusive domain of accountants. Even so, the authors must insist that the following statement of theory *does not advocate* that management auditing necessarily should be performed by Certified Public Accountants. This warning is emphasized because of a desire to eliminate the biases that may accompany lines of traditional auditing thought, and because it *may* be that an entirely new breed of auditing professionals will be required for the task. For the time being, the matter of who should perform such audits is an open question.

Concepts and Postulates

Fortunately, the concepts and postulates that constitute the core of auditing theory

---

[12]R. K. Mautz, and Hussein Sharaf. *The Philosophy of Auditing*. Monograph No. 6 (American Accounting Association, 1961).

(both financial and management auditing) are amenable to a diagrammatic representation. Within the broad structure of the theory, two distinct categories of concepts are revealed. For convenience, these two categories are designated as the *pre-postulate* concepts and the *post-postulate* concepts. Fugure 1 presents both sets of concepts in relation to a systemàtic theory of auditing.

The pre-postulate concepts are broad philosophical matters that underlie the specification of postulates in all auditing theory. These important aspects of the theory were the subjects of intensive examination in *The Philosophy of Auditing*. The post-postulate concepts may be perceived as being of a lesser order in the theoretical hierarchy, but they are no less important to the theory in a systematic sense (*i.e.*, from broad concept to operational procedures); and it may be noted that further extension of the structure in Figure 1 would reveal *procedures* and *rules* relevant to execution of the attest function in both areas of audit concern. (No such extension is presented here.)

A review of the post-postulate concepts of financial auditing discloses ideas and objects that are quite familiar in an independent auditing context. However, the post-postulate concepts of management auditing, while familiar in the general context of management, have no clear or specific meaning in the context of independent audits of management. The hypotheses presented in comparative form, Table 1, are offered as a means of attributing theoretical meaning to these terms in order to move one step closer to an operational theory of management auditing. (See Table 1.)

These postulates now constitute the core of a theory of management auditing. Some brief commentary on each of them would appear to be in order.

The Hypotheses of Management Auditing

At this stage of theory-building, these hypotheses are extremely tentative since most of them have never been tested, much less even discussed, in an auditing context. Empirical research involving these hypotheses is the most pressing requirement for future development of the theory. However, at this point some further elaboration on the eight brief statements may be useful for clarification purposes.

1. Management representations and the bases for decisions are verifiable. The following general explanations offered by Mautz and Sharaf with respect to the financial auditing postulates are equally applicable to the theory of management audit, *viz.*, "If we release this assumption (of verifiability), we do away with the very subject of auditing."[13] Furthermore, they explain that *verifiability* implies that "there must be something that auditors do to give them a basis for expressing an opinion on the reliability of the financial statements they examine."[14] From this single postulate may be identified at least three ancillary concepts—evidence, verification, procedure, and management representations. Along with the concept of evidence, the relevance of probability theory in examination procedures must be recognized because of the inherent non-deterministic nature of many forms of evidential matter.

The management audit hypothesis parallels its predecessor postulate in order to establish the major pre-postulate concept of evidence. In a management audit, concern

[13]*Ibid.*, p. 43.
[14]*Ibid.*

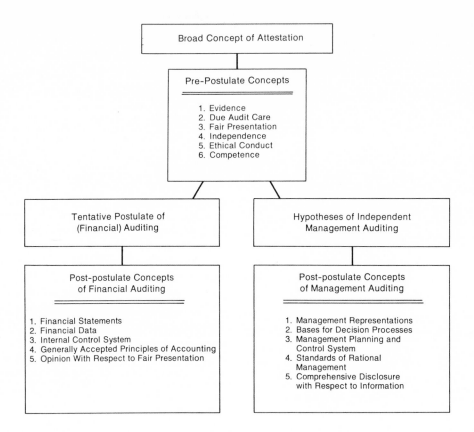

Figure 1. A structural representation of auditing theory.

lies with *management representations* (the first important post-postulate concept) which may be conceived broadly as being a larger set of data than the previously expressed limitation to financial data. The term *bases for decisions* has been inserted to infer reference to the decision-making processes with more emphasis on the process than on the decision solution itself. This emphasis produces the second post-postulate concept—decision bases— in a framework of decision theory, though the concept is treated in an admittedly brief

fashion herein. Specific descriptions of *management representations* and *decision bases* may come to mind easily; yet, there exists no generally accepted complete statement of either concept.

2. *There is no necessary conflict of interest between the auditor and the management of the enterprise under audit.* The hypothesis is exactly the same as its counterpart financial auditing postulate, and it is similar to hypothesis Number 7 in one important respect: Both

Table 1. Comparison: Financial Auditing Postulates and Management Auditing Hypotheses

Tentative Postulates of (Financial) Auditing*	Hypotheses of Independent Management Auditing
1. Financial statements and financial data are verifiable.	1. Management representations and the bases for decisions are verifiable.
2. There is no necessary conflict of interest between the auditor and the management of the enterprise under audit.	2. There is no necessary conflict of interest between the auditor and the management of the enterprise under audit.
3. The financial statements and other information submitted for verification are free from collusive and other unusual irregularities.	3. The management representations and other data relevant to the management system submitted for verification are free from collusive and other unusual manipulations.
4. The existence of a satisfactory system of internal control eliminates the probability of irregularities.	4. The existence of a satisfactory system of management control eliminates the probability that management representations and information upon which managerial decisions are based are subject to unusual manipulations in their promulgation to either internal or external recipients.
5. Consistent application of generally accepted principles of accounting results in the fair presentation of financial position and the results of operations.	5. Consistent awareness of, and adherence to, the standards of rational management contribute significantly to the efficacy of the management system for achieving organizational goals.
6. In the absence of clear evidence to the contrary what was held true in the past for the enterprise under examination will hold true in the future.	6a. In the absence of clear evidence to the contrary it is presumed that the internal management system is relatively resistant to change and will function in the future as it did in the immediate past.
	6b. In the absence of clear evidence to the contrary it is presumed that the external environmental variables that affect the firm will *not* necessarily hold for the future as they did for the past.
7. When examining financial data for the purpose of expressing an independent opinion thereon, the auditor acts exclusively in the capacity of an auditor.	7. When examining management representations for the purpose of presenting a comprehensive disclosure thereof, the auditor acts exclusively in the capacity of auditor.
8. The professional status of the independent auditor imposes commensurate professional obligations.	8. The fact that internal and external parties to the firm will rely upon the disclosures made by the independent auditor imposes commensurate obligations upon him.

*R. K. Mautz, and Hussein Sharaf. *The Philosophy of Auditing.* Monograph No. 6 (American Accounting Association, 1961), p. 42.

refer implicitly to states of mind and of conduct of two groups of individuals. In the case of hypothesis Number 2, the reference is to both auditors and management, and for hypothesis Number 7 the reference is solely to the auditor group.

Mautz and Sharaf explain *interest* for audit theory purposes as follows:"Management is concerned with the progress and prosperity of the enterprise it directs; auditors perform a service which is intended to benefit the various interests (*i.e.*, 'interest groups') in the enterprise by providing some degree of assurance as to the reliability of the financial data essential to various important decisions. Surely these are compatible purposes."[15] The postulate assumes only no necessary conflict, not the impossibility of conflict of interests. From this assumption Mautz and Sharaf then deduce certain "corollary propositions" dealing with "rational" actions of management concerning safeguarding and use of assets.[16] The theory of management auditing finds such corollary propositions highly important. What Mautz and Sharaf

[15]*Ibid.*, p. 44
[16]*Ibid.*, p. 45.

accept on the basis of deductive logic for financial auditing happen to be of the nature of fundamental standards for the theory of management auditing. Further elaboration on this point is found in the discussion of hypothesis Number 5.

3. *The management representations and other data relevant to the management system submitted for verification are free from collusive and other unusual manipulations.* Again, this management audit hypothesis is parallel to its financial audit counterpart with the only difference being in the subject matter of the audit examination. Mautz and Sharaf offer a variation on the method of "proof by contradiction" to explain their postulate (as they do for postulate Number 2, as well): If the assumption is made that such statements *do* contain unusual irregularities, then the auditor would have to greatly expand the extent of his examination, possibly making it prohibitively expensive. Also, auditor and management would be in conflict (Number 2), and presumably the interests of neither would be served.

This postulate raises the important questions of due audit care and auditor's responsibility for discovering errors. These topics are discussed extensively in many sources, including Mautz and Sharaf (pp. 111-158), so further discussion is not offered here.

4. *The existence of a satisfactory system of management control eliminates the probability that management representations and information upon which managerial decisions are based are subject to unusual manipulations in their promulgation to either internal or external recipients.* Management control—the third post-postulate concept—is a parallel to

the traditional concept of internal control, except that management control is much broader and includes the elements sometimes termed "administrative controls,"[17] which are concerned with policy, planning, and long-range forms of the means by which entities provide for effective and efficient adaptive activity commensurate with enterprise goals. A more specific definition is as follows: Management control is the process of applying management directive action to the functions of an enterprise, where action is based on judgments arising from the evaluation of data provided by the several *contributory systems* of the management system.[18]

By this last definition, *management control* implies: (1) process rather than structure, (2) executive action, (3) contributory systems, and (4) data generated by the contributory systems. The existence of a satisfactory system of management control would imply that management acts rationally—a conclusion that is deducted from hypotheses 2 and 5. Most important of all, the existence of such a system implies that *data* is generated. Whether or not the sum of the data parts equals the whole of the total system's data, and likewise whether the sum of the contributory systems equals the total system of management control, is a matter for empirical investigation. The outcome of such research would certainly have a bearing on the procedures of management audit.

In the previous discussion it is noted that an assessment of the contributory systems

---

[17]Committee of Auditing Procedure, *Internal Control.* (American Institute of CPA's, 1949.)

[18]Louis Fried has presented an interesting treatment on the relation of contributory systems to overall management control in "Executive Controls," *Management Services.* (May-June, 1968) pp. 17-26.

constitutes an implicit (and large) part of the examination context for the management attestation concept. It may also be noted that the concept of management control with contributory system elements is a highly important notion for the theory of management auditing. Hypothesis Number 4 explicitly assumes that the existence of a satisfactory system eliminates the *probability* of unusual manipulations but does not necessarily eliminate the *possibility* of such irregularities, which is the same position as that taken by Mautz and Sharaf with respect to internal control.[19]

5. *Consistent awareness of, and adherence to, the standards of rational management contribute significantly to the efficacy of the management system for achieving organizational goals.* This hypothesis, containing the fourth post-postulate concept—standards of rational management—is perhaps the most critical one of all, because standards are the means by which the auditor may judge with minimal bias the effectiveness of the management system. For the financial auditing process, auditors adopt the standards of generally accepted accounting principles. Mautz and Sharaf state that they accept the financial audit postulate with reservations, because of the sharp differences of opinion on the standards. Their stated reasons for accepting the generally accepted accounting principles as standards, despite their reservations are: (1) the principles of accounting already have great force; (2) they can be expected to gather strength as research continues; and (3) release of this assumption would deprive auditors of any standard of fairness whatever.[20]

With a little thought and a few changes in phraseology, these same reasons could be related to standards of rational management. After all, such principles or standards are what management science is all about, and few would deny that great strides are being made in this field of inquiry. Even so, the theory cannot contend that the standards of rational management exist, or if they exist, that they are known. Still, it must be recognized that the standards relate primarily to the matter of expressing an *objective opinion*, or at least one that contains minimal bias. Lacking an existing set of codified standards, the theory of management auditing may be varied to provide not for an *opinion on fair presentation* but instead for a *statement of comprehensive disclosure* of management representations. This last notion is discussed more fully under hypothesis Number 7.

6a. *In the absence of clear evidence to the contrary it is presumed that the internal management system is relatively resistant to change and will function in the future as it did in the immediate past.* Mautz and Sharaf explain that the parallel financial auditing postulate embodies the continuity or going concern concept of accounting. They go on to say that "acceptance of the postulate places important limits on the extent of an auditor's responsibilities and provides a basis for deducing the future and to have his work judged on the basis of hindsight."[21]

For the management auditing hypothesis, a similar pair of statements can be made about the internal management system. This limitation of internal aspects creates an outer boundary of the firm, where management interacts with the external environment. Thus

[19]Mautz and Sharaf, *op. cit.*, p. 47.

[20]*Ibid.*, pp. 47-48.

[21]*Ibid.*, pp. 48-49.

hypothesis 6a takes an *internal* viewpoint for the firm, and hypothesis 6b takes a view of looking *from* the firm *toward* the external environment.

The going-concern concept (6a) of management auditing, then, considers a number of behavioral variables and, in effect, "holds them constant" for examination purposes. A large body of references with respect to such variables is available in the theoretical and empirical studies of organizational behavior, managerial psychology, social psychology, and bureaucratic structure and behavior. These resources are certainly relevant for management auditing. As for the management auditor's responsibilities, acceptance of hypothesis 6a limits his obligation to predict change or to predict future interaction of the many human and mechanical components of an enterprise beyond the limits of the management system that exists at the time of audit.

6b. *In the absence of clear evidence to the contrary it is presumed that the external environmental variables that affect the firm will not necessarily hold for the future as they did for the past.* The essence of this hypothesis is an explicit recognition of the very reality of imperfect knowledge about the future. All manner of forces impinge on the firm, and there seldom exists much certainty about the timing or magnitude of their occurrence. The most significant thing that the theory can say about such forces is that the enterprise typically *reacts* to them. Most treatments of the theory of the firm, from the economic to the behavioral, describe the firm as an adaptive mechanism that acts through its decision-making, action-taking capabilities in order to meet environmental demands. This last description embodies the dynamic aspects of a management system, management control, and rational standards of management that have been implicit in previous hypotheses.

Thus, one might conclude that part of the assessment of contributory systems and of management control would require the auditor to deal with the system's ability to receive signals from the environment and to *react* to them. Evaluation in this respect will likely be a severe problem; yet a great deal is already known about effective organizational structure and about other visible means of facilitating adaptive behavior, and research in these areas is currently progressing at a rapid pace. More will be added on this and other evaluation questions under the heading of hypothesis Number 7.

7. *When examining management representations for the purpose of presenting a comprehensive disclosure thereof, the auditor acts exclusively in the capacity of auditor.* Two implications of this hypothesis deserve commentary. First, as for the auditor acting exclusively in the capacity of auditor, the implication is that he retains independence in fact and in appearance. Independence, in fact, is a "state of mind" and there is no *a priori* reason that such independence cannot be achieved for the management audit in the same manner that independence is obtained in the financial audit. The same type of statement can be made with respect to independence in appearance, even though such an assertion may give accountants cause to reflect. The important thing to remember, however, is that the management audit is conceived of as a third-party attest function and *not* as a management consultation service. Any questions concerning the auditor's independence in the management audit function

should be approachable in exactly the same manner as these questions are approached for the financial audit function.

The second implication deals with the manner of reporting the findings of a management audit examination. Hypothesis Number 7 departs significantly from its counterpart in financial auditing theory, in that the management auditors may not logically express an *opinion* in the classical accounting sense of fair presentation. First of all, a cohesive set of standards has not been generally agreed upon, and secondly, there is a real question as to whether or not there are persons competent (and confident) enough to express such an opinion. Furthermore, there is that nagging question of what to do about the evaluation of uncertainty, *i.e.*, future events and how the enterprise may be expected to react to them (see hypothesis 6a and 6b). It should be noted that the theory thus far expressed has carefully avoided the use of the word *measurement* and has instead referred primarily to *evaluation*. Such care is not by accident, because notice has been taken of the following distinction between the two: evaluation refers to the subjective assessment of things past, present, and future, while measurement means the assignment of numbers to things past and present. The point to be made is that in an evaluative manner of assessment, an opinion in the classical accountancy sense, would appear to be impossible.

These severe restrictions on opinion-rendering force the acceptance of a less deterministic mode of reporting, which finds expression as a *statement of comprehensive disclosure* (the fifth post-postulate concept). But this circumstance is a happy one! It patiently prevents any sort of "short form" rubber stamp, and instead requires a careful, analytical disclosure of management representations.

In a stronger approach to reporting, the audited management representations might be transmitted in the form of an assessment, rather than as mere disclosures without assessment. The present state of the art, however, constrains the content of a management audit report to the weaker notion of careful, analytical disclosure. Nevertheless, in the process of reporting, the auditor may be able to reveal the many uncertainties that beset an enterprise, accompanied with a statement of how a management system is constituted to meet the environment. Possibly, the management system is constituted to meet the environment. Possibly, the management might be required to make a statement of how it *expects* to meet future events.

The audit report would thus contain many of the characteristics of information while avoiding some, if not all, of the characteristics of mere *data* that are typically issued under the guise of information. Perhaps these comments are an unwarranted indictment of traditional "certified statements," for no conclusive evidence has ever been produced to reveal that traditional statements are, in fact, a shadow of what they purport to be. Still, there does exist extensive evidence to support the assertation that such informational releases by business enterprises could, and should, transmit more useful information than is the case now. This last idea is the major *raison d'etre* for management audit disclosures.

8. *The fact that internal and external parties to the firm will rely upon the disclosures made by the independent auditor imposes commensurate obligations upon him.* Management auditing can as yet lay no claim to

professionalism as the practitioners of financial auditing are able to do. With respect to financial audit theory, this postulate reflects recognition of the auditor's institutionalized professional responsibility to society, to his client, and to fellow auditors.[22] But even though management audit theory at this time cannot call upon an established body of professional rules of ethics and rules of conduct, the management auditor is not released from such obligations. The essential concept for the auditor, be he of the management or of the financial variety, is one of service rendered to the best of available ability. Perhaps in the future the word "professional" can be inserted in the management audit hypothesis, and management auditing can be placed in a recognized professional standing alongside financial auditing.

Conclusion

The theory designed and explained here is admittedly tentative. As was noted earlier, there is a great need for empirical research to confirm or disprove all of the management auditing hypotheses. If grounds for rejection of one or more of the statements can be found,

---

[22]*Ibid.*, p. 50.

then perhaps another, better one can be put in its place. Only thus may the theory, and consequently the practice, and management auditing be improved. Further research should also be directed toward clarifying the component concepts of the theory. Mautz and Sharaf offer a comprehensive study of what have been termed the pre-postulate concepts, but the post-postulate concepts presented in this paper still retain many of the characteristics of undefined terms, and these are vital elements of the theory. Thus the topics of management representations, decision systems, management control, standards of rational management, and comprehensive disclosure remain as potentially fruitful areas for investigation. At the very least, existing knowledge of these concepts could be integrated more fully into the management audit concept.

Management auditing, as long as it carries the name of auditing, should be perceived in the general context of attestation, just as financial auditing is accepted in that context. The other uses of the term to connote consultation services, internal auditing, and investment advice should be discouraged. Only with general agreement and acceptance of terminology and theory can practice move forward to achieve the benefits that can accrue by extending the attest function to include independent audits of management.

2

Chapter 5

Auditing Concepts

For an attempt to relate the auditing objectives that we have suggested to the auditing tasks required, we would find it useful to structure the discussion in terms of the major phases of an audit examination: the evaluation of the system, and the evaluation of the system's output. For in order to conduct the audit examination we contemplate, the auditor has to obtain sufficient evidential matter to:

1. Determine that a *system* does exist to provide reliable and relevant data for planning and control;
2. Determine that this system does produce *outputs*—i.e., plans, budgets, forecasts, financial statements, control reports—which are reliable, relevant, and understandable by the user.

The key to carrying out these two broad tasks is the evaluation of the client's information system. This evaluation is important to an assessment of those areas in the system where deficiencies exist and where improvements could be made; to establishment of the reliability of the accounting records; and to determination of the amount and type of testing of the client's records necessary to support an opinion on the system and the output produced by the system.

The influence of the information system on the quality of the system's output—records, balances, reports, financial statements, plans—has been documented by authors with a variety of viewpoints.

The Committee on Auditing Procedures of the AICPA indicates:

A function of internal control, from the viewpoint of the independent auditor, is to provide assurance that errors and irregularities may be discovered with reasonable promptness, thus assuring the reliability with integrity of the financial records. The independent auditor's review of the system . . . assists him in determining other auditing procedures appropriate to the formulation of an opinion on the fairness of financial statements.[1]

Discussing systems in general, others have suggested that all systems have the elements of input, transformation, and output. The inputs can be identified and the transformation process can be defined. The more we know about the data to be transformed and the transformation process itself, the more we can predict about the form, substance, structure, accuracy, and reliability of the output.

To obtain "sufficient evidential matter" to form an audit opinion on the system, the auditor performs certain specific procedures using a variety of techniques. It is not our intention to list for example, specific audit procedures for such applications as sales-receivables and inventory, but rather to classify the specific auditing procedures into some fundamental audit tasks common to most audit applications.[2]

Evaluate the System in Existence

In evaluating an information system, or internal control system, or any system, the auditor is concerned with an analysis of the structure and design of the system itself, rather than an intensive examination of the documents and records produced by that system. In such an approach, any examination of transactions and records is primarily designed to confirm the existence of procedures and their effectiveness and to further an understanding of the nature and elements of the system.

In the review and evaluation of systems, the auditor should go through a process basically similar to that which the systems analyst goes through in designing and implementing systems; the difference will lie chiefly in objectives and procedural emphasis. In his article "Management Services and

---

[1] AICPA, *Auditing Standards and Procedures*, p. 32.

[2] There are several texts available which discuss specific auditing procedures. For example, see Stettler, *Systems Based Independent Audits*. In addition, most CPA firms have internal guides for audit procedures in specific areas.

The authors are indebted to Gregory M. Boni, Partner in Touche, Ross, Bailey & Smart, who initially formulated many of the audit tasks discussed in this text.

Management Audits by Professional Accountants," Buckley cites the differences and similarities between the analyst and the auditor:

> In discussing the performance of extended services by professional accountants, it is perhaps useful to distinguish two areas of practice: management services and management audits. The line between these practices may be narrow, but there is a significant theoretical difference.
>
> Essentially, management services denote activities that provide assistance to management, while management audits describe activities related to the appraisal of management.
>
> Of course, there are also many similarities. For example, both types of analysis extend beyond fiscal data and take account of whatever environmental factor bears on the task at hand. Similarly, the qualities of independence, objectivity, competence, and adherence to professional standards are applied in both instances. And in both programs an exerted effort is made to use scientific methods of research, where these are appropriate, and to avoid conclusions based on insufficient or biased information.[3]

To evaluate the system, the auditor performs these tasks:

1. Defining the system supposed to be in existence;
2. Testing the system to confirm the accuracy of his definition and the completeness and effectiveness of the system defined;
3. Evaluating strengths and weaknesses of the system so as to determine:
    a. additional audit procedures required in areas where weaknesses exist;
    b. recommendations for improving the system in light of the information requirements of the client.

To initially understand the structure, elements, and properties of the system, the analyst-auditor must define the system he wishes to evaluate. In systems definition, it is important to specify the purpose and restrictions of the system under analysis. Classical methods including flow diagrams and matrix representations have been used in systems definition. Such methods are designed to define a system in sufficient detail and with enough analytical efficiency to provide the auditor with a working description of the system's structure and components. The description must

Systems Definition

---

[3]*California Management Review*, Fall 1966, p. 45.

be able to specify what the system is doing and what output will occur given the stated inputs.

In system terms, the transformation process, or conversion operation, that converts input to output is sometimes thought of as a "black box" that represents a grouping of procedures. The analyst may group the procedures because he does not choose to deal in any further detail with the individual or because he is unable to penetrate the "black box" quandary. For example, the "black box" concept has been very relevant to the auditor's review of computerized accounting systems. Many systems in which the computer is used as a high-speed calculator and which provide the traditional audit trail require no penetration of the computer by the auditor. Other systems currently being developed are characterized by integrated data processing and multiple file updating; an understanding of these systems requires a knowledge of the transformation process within the computer. Typical of such a system is one which automatically performs all of the following steps based on the entry of a sales order:

1. finished-goods inventory reduced (and perhaps a reorder that triggers a purchase or a production-order process leading eventually to payment from materials, labor, etc.);
2. order priced;
3. billing prepared;
4. accounts receivable updated;
5. sales analysis updated;
6. sales analysis compared with sales forecast, forecast revisions made if necessary;
7. order costed;
8. cost of sales updated.

Obviously, such a system, with a single input triggering a number of data-processing activities and initiating the updating of all records associated with the transaction, is more difficult to understand and more complex to evaluate and review for audit purposes than is a traditional system.

Because he is usually reviewing a system that has been defined and described and for which systems documentation is available, the auditor usually begins his evaluation of the system by reviewing procedural documentation, making inquiries of responsible systems personnel, and observing the system in operation. Such a process should give the auditor a provisional definition and description of the system. Further analysis is required to gain assurance that the provisional definition is reasonably good, or definitely bad, and to note specific strengths and weaknesses in the system.

To confirm his definition of the system and to determine the effectiveness of the system's elements, the auditor must introduce tests or diagnostic procedures. Specifically, the reasons for testing are to answer these questions:

Testing the System

1. How does the system operate?
2. Does it work as defined by the client?
3. Can it be improved?[4]

The objective of testing the system is to provide some evidence that the system in operation corresponds to the auditor's definition of the system and to determine whether the procedures which are supposed to be in effect are, in fact, in effect. The objective is not to determine if the procedures are in effect and functioning an acceptable percentage of the time. Given such an objective, a limited number of tests of each type of significant transaction in the system will suffice. Because of the somewhat contradictory objectives of testing expressed in auditing discussions, a few specific points should be made in support of limited testing.

First, although the auditor is limiting his tests, he is not limiting his testing to a small portion of the system being reviewed. Although the auditor is testing only a few transactions in total, he is testing a few transactions of each type that is processed in a different manner. For example, in a sales-order processing, the sales orders selected for testing would include orders from each different branch, from each different class of customer, for each different type of product, and each different pricing arrangement.

Second, at this point in his systems analysis, the auditor is not trying to make any valid statistical inferences about the population of all transactions of a given type. He is not trying to prove that errors never occur, but merely to establish what the system in operation is.

---

[4]From the viewpoint of the systems analyst, there are other reasons for testing. For a general discussion of systems testing, see Van Court Hare's *Systems Analysis: A Diagnostic Approach*, New York: John Wiley & Sons, 1967, pp. 237-241.

Had he wanted to prove by his examination of sales invoices, for instance, that pricing errors were less than 1 per cent, he would have had to examine several hundred.

Fifty or one hundred would not be enough to establish a reasonable confidence concerning a 1 percent frequency. Therefore, there would be little point in his testing thirty, fifty, or even one hundred invoices; such samples would be generally too little to establish the frequency of occasional errors, yet too much merely to establish the nature of the system in force. Since, at this point, he is only attempting to establish the latter, a minimum test is all that is required. A test of one transaction might, of course, happen to be an unusual case. Even the results of a pair of transactions might, by chance, be misconstrued. But if four or five selected randomly are examined and all correspond to the system as described to him, then this constitutes reasonable prima-facie evidence of the system in operation.[5]

Third, because he is trying to make his understanding of the system and its evaluation ". . . a basis for reliance thereon and for the determination of the resultant extent of tests to which auditing procedures are to be restricted," the auditor's investigation, requiring extended testing, should be conducted *after* the system has been evaluated. For example, in analyzing the sales-order system, the auditor, after introducing a limited number of tests, determines that a check of the credit limit is not made before the order is filled and shipped. This is a weakness, and no additional testing of this particular procedure of the system will indicate otherwise. When a procedure is obviously weak, the repeated rechecking of its details is of little value in determining *what the system is and what its strengths and weaknesses are.* After he understands what the system is and has evaluated its strengths and weaknesses, he may decide to do additional testing in areas where the system is not effective or does not exist. But in this testing, his objective is not to understand and place reliance upon the system but to make evaluations *based* on his tests. Here statistical sampling may be very important.

Referring to our example above, we have determined that there is no procedure for credit checking; accordingly, we cannot rely on the "system" and must perform other tests to determine the extent to which such a weakness affects the shipments of orders to customers who may be potentially or in fact unable to pay for the order shipped. Tests may be per-

---

[5]Skinner and Anderson, *op. cit.*, p. 15.

formed on accounts receivable by statistical sampling to give us assurance that the allowance for doubtful accounts is sufficient to provide for potential losses due to this weakness in the system.

Another important phase of the audit is the determination that the outputs of the system are reliable, relevant, and understandable by the user. To evaluate, for example, the account descriptions and balances reflected in the client's published financial statements, the auditor must perform the following tasks:

Evaluating the Output of the System

1. external (outside of the records) confirmation[6] of balances through contact or correspondence with debtors or creditors;
2. search for the quality attributes of assets and liabilities recorded;
3. comparison of balances with transactions for the key to unrecorded amounts or to ascertain the reasonableness of the amount of the remaining balance;
4. making of inferences about the existence of an item from the logical relationship of certain transactions and computations;
5. determination that appropriate generally accepted accounting principles have been accurately and consistently applied.

Many areas in an audit examination require the auditor to go outside the records and make physical contact with items—i.e., cash, inventory, property—represented in the accounts, conduct correspondence with debtors or creditors in the case of receivables and liabilities, and conduct correspondence with a depository such as a bank or warehouse.

External Confirmation of Balances

Such a task includes selecting a sample, interpreting the significance of the results obtained, and from the sample results, making a conclusion about the universe sampled. The sample may be selected on a random basis, or by some specific criteria such as dollar value, or according to a statistical-sampling plan. We will discuss sampling and its relationship to this task in a subsequent chapter.

---

[6]Confirmation here is used in the broad sense of "added knowledge" rather than a specific sense related to accurate receivable work.

A very important task involved in obtaining evidential matter is the search for quality attributes of assets and liabilities. Attributes such as size, obsolescence, customer payment patterns, restrictions, and liens may require that certain assets and liabilities be described or disclosed in representations of management differently than in the records at the time of the search. The search for these quality attributes involves observations and inquiries; testing and trend analysis of accounts, records, and variance reports; comparison of accounts and balances with yardsticks such as bills of material, period of use, systems specifications, and credit standards. The auditor also examines authoritative documents such as contracts and minutes to support management representations and to determine the adequacy of disclosure.

Inventory is an area which provides a good example of a search for quality attributes. In inventory analysis, the auditor is concerned, among other things, with slow-moving items as a clue to obsolete and excess quantities requiring possible valuation other than that shown in the financial records. To find evidence of obsolete or excess quantities, the auditor may search inventory files to determine those items of inventory over a certain dollar amount and (1) for which returns and allowances are over a certain percentage of the balance on hand; or (2) for which no sales have been made in the last few months; or (3) for which the balance on hand bears a certain relationship to maximum stock quantities, reorder quantities, sales this year or last, and future requirements; or (4) for which some combination of the above criteria exists.

In the area of accounts receivable, records often contain information such as credit limit, credit history, sales history, delinquency history, and payment pattern. The auditor could search these records to determine all accounts in excess of credit limit; all accounts with balances delinquent for a certain number of days; all accounts with balances that bear a certain percentage relationship to sales this year; all accounts with unusual credits subsequent to the balance-sheet date; and all accounts that have significantly increased in amount in the last few months.

The search for such quality attributes may be assisted by use of computerized techniques which will be discussed in a subsequent chapter in the book.

The task of comparing balances with transactions is primarily concerned with finding unrecorded amounts or with determining the reasonableness of the balance amount remaining. To perform this task, the auditor will usually review transactions recorded subsequent to the balance-sheet date and review the activity during the year on certain accounts. The review of transactions subsequent to year-end is based on the assumption that all amounts eventually will be reflected in the accounts, either through payment or other means. The auditor's review of activity during the year is based on the assumption that much business activity is repetitive and somewhat constant in amount from one month to another or from one quarter to another. A review of transactions in selected accounts should be a major procedure in determining the reasonableness of the account balances at year-end.

Obviously, comparison of balances against transactions is important in an area such as purchases-accounts payable and sales-receivables.

An important audit task is to make inferences about the existence of an asset or equity item from the logical relationship of certain transactions and computations. For example, the examination of insurance policies and premiums paid gives the auditor information about the nature and value of the asset insured. Capital assets and accumulated depreciation can be related to depreciation expense for the period.

Developments in integrated-system design should assist the auditor in this task. For example, it appears feasible and beneficial to design a bonds-payable record to show the amount of the bond outstanding, the original amount of the bond, maturity dates and amounts, date and amount of payments, rate of interest, and interest paid for a particular period and/or during the life of the bonds. By analyzing the bonds-payable file, the auditor would be able to determine not only that interest payments were made on bonds outstanding but that these interest payments were computed correctly.

Inferences from Logical Relations

In evaluating the published financial statements as one major system output, the auditor must not only determine that the output is reliable but also that the amounts represented have been consistently valued in accordance with generally accepted accounting principles. The auditor must perform audit tasks to satisfy himself that this has been done; several are involved:

1. to determine the accounting principles followed;
2. to challenge the appropriateness of the valuation method used;

Determination that Appropriate Accounting Principles have been Applied

3. to check the accuracy with which the appropriate valuation method has been applied;
4. to check the consistency of the generally accepted accounting principles and of the methods used in applying them.

Accounting Principles.   Today the differences and discussions in the accounting profession about accounting principles make systematizing "generally accepted accounting principles" a very difficult task, to say the least. Because of the wide range of alternative practices—all equally in accord with "generally" accepted principles—the auditor has to draw upon his knowledge and experience to develop constructively useful solutions, and to judge the applicability and effectiveness of the principles applied by the firm in the accounts and statements he reviews.

Appropriateness of the Valuation Method.   Whether to challenge the appropriateness of the valuation method being used is largely judgmental and is normally inherent in the process of collecting and evaluating evidential matter. Auditors are constantly on the alert for quality aspects or attributes requiring different disposition—that is, obsolete and surplus inventory items, or old and potential loss accounts receivable. If the auditor ascertains that the method of valuation used for these unusual items is unacceptable, he must determine the materiality of the resulting difference between this valuation and an acceptable method of valuation of assets. An immaterial difference would not require the auditor to take exception to the fairness of the financial statements.

Accurate Application of the Appropriate Valuation Method.   An accurate application of the appropriate valuation method involves (1) the selection of the sources appropriate for the accounting principles or method followed—that is, recent purchase invoices when pricing inventory on the FIFO basis; (2) the selection of the correct amount from the sources; and (3) an accurate arithmetic operation.

To illustrate this task, assume that the client maintains his inventory records on magnetic tape and prices the inventory at standard cost. To establish the reasonableness of the final inventory, the auditor, once he has determined the method of valuation, will make sufficient tests to assure himself that the methods the client represents as being in use were actually used. Included will be a test of final inventory prices against the client's book of standard prices and a test of a representative number of source documents and work papers to determine the currency of the standards being used. In addition, the auditor is interested in determining that arithmetic calculations involved in compiling the final inventory are accurate.

By processing the inventory file, a computer audit program could test the standard unit prices for selected items against prices taken from the book of standards and loaded into the computer's memory. In addition, the program could have the computer test the extensions for selected items and also foot the entire file. The computer program could also test the consistency of pricing for like items.

Consistency. One of the audit standards of reporting requires that the client's financial representations have been valued in accordance with generally accepted accounting principles "consistently observed in the current period in relation to the preceding report." Thus one of the auditor's tasks in relation to valuation is checking the consistency of the generally accepted accounting principles and of the methods used in applying them.

Evaluation of Other Outputs

The above discussion has developed an example of the auditor's approach in evaluating account descriptions and balances in published financial statements, one of the significant outputs of the system and the one with which auditors have been traditionally most concerned.

The many other outputs of the system are also of importance to the auditor, although his published attestation may not include them. In an audit of an information system the reliability, relevance, and understandability of internal management reports, plans, budgets, physical data, control charts, and many other outputs must also be considered. In such cases, no body of generally accepted principles may be available, but the basic information concepts of relevance, verifiability, freedom from bias, quantifiability, and economic feasibility still apply. These concepts will be discussed more fully in Chapter 9.

Summary   In this chapter we have analyzed, in a conceptual way, the fundamental tasks necessary to render an opinion on the adequacy of the information system for planning and control. We have developed the concept that the key to carrying out audit tasks is the evaluation of the system. We have shown the relationship of the evaluation of the system to the evaluation of output produced by the system. For one of the major outputs of the system—published financial statements—we have discussed specific tasks for obtaining evidence.

Chapter 6

Auditing Standards and the Nature of Evidence

The preceding chapters have described the evolution of the audit function over many years to the point where today, we believe, the appropriate audit approach and objective is to develop an understanding of the firm's information requirements with the audit objective of evaluating the adequacy of the firm's information system to meet those requirements.

In the last chapter, we discussed in a conceptual way our approach to auditing. Now we turn to the problems of implementing the audit whose objective we have described. In this chapter we deal with auditing standards as a basis background for the audit of systems rather than statements. In following chapters, we consider the specific methodological problems of auditing within the framework of this developing approach.

Basic Changes in Traditional Audit Approach

This evolving audit objective implies a number of significant changes in the traditional audit approach. First, since an information system represents a continuous entity and not a discrete one, the auditor must direct his attention to the flows of information through the various operating data cycles of the enterprise rather than to the balances at a point in time.

Additionally, the auditor is no longer primarily concerned with establishing the reliability of financial-statement data, nor is the reporting of this data the principal objective of auditing methodology. While some clients may still want only the opinion of the auditor on financial statements, a good audit of that client will still require an evaluation of his information system, even if no explicit report is to be rendered thereon. A report on financial statements is only one of the possible end products of such an audit.

One more implication of this developing approach to auditing is its effect on the nature and organization of public accounting practice. Inevitably, this approach will bring closely together the evaluative aspects of the consulting function and the evaluative aspects of the audit function. The auditor will need training in the consulting approach, and a number of what have in the past been considered consulting engagements will be done routinely during an audit. While there will still be a separate consulting function to achieve particular designated tasks, the developing audit approach will bring the audit and the management-services functions together in the accounting firm.

How Is an Audit Accomplished?

Given the audit objective—to evaluate the ability of the firm's information system to meet its information requirements—we must turn our attention to the means of its achievement. Clearly, if the auditor is to understand the other information requirements of the business, he must be aware that the basic requirement is the production of financial statements in accordance with generally accepted accounting principles for external reporting purposes. This, however, is only one of the requirements of the system, which must also be geared toward decision making and control tasks of the management.

To understand the current information system, the auditor must ascertain what information is being processed, how it is being processed, and the reliability of the output. It is in this area that a substantial amount of audit time will be spent.

Finally, the evaluation of the system must be undertaken. This would include the evaluation of the financial statements of the enterprise. If the auditor is convinced by his studies that the information system does not produce reliable data, he may have to perform additional tests in order to evaluate a specific output on which he is asked to report. Thus, if the information system is not adequate to meet the reliability requirements of financial statements for outside parties, the auditor may have to evaluate the specific statements through additional procedures aimed at the verification of particular figures.

It is clear that for the performance of such an audit, standards are needed—both of approach and of evaluation. Standards of approach govern the way in which the necessary understanding of the firm and its information system is developed, while standards of evaluation govern making the judgment about the adequacy of the firm's information system and its various outputs.

Within the framework of generally accepted auditing standards, the Committee on Auditing Procedure of the AICPA has developed a group of standards that govern approach. The first set they suggest, general standards dealing with the characteristics and the approach of the auditor in very broad terms, are as follows:

Standards of Approach

1. The examination is to be performed by a person or persons having adequate technical training and proficiency as an auditor.
2. In all matters relating to the assignment an independence in mental attitude is to be maintained by the auditor or auditors.
3. Due professional care is to be exercised in the performance of the examination and the preparation of the report.

It seems clear that these standards are appropriate to any audit, although the means for their implementation must change as the audit objective changes. Clearly, for example, the technical training and proficiency required of one who is performing an evaluation of an information system is significantly different from the qualifications required to examine details in support of account balances. The auditor must increasingly be trained in diagnostic skills and information- and data-processing technology, as well as have a firm educational basis in other areas. The Common Body of Knowledge Study described in Chapter 2 demonstrates the way in which the profession is moving in this direction.

The independence standard has been discussed above in Chapter 2, as have the practical implications of due professional care. Due care is both a legal term supported by case law and a term which relates to the general attitude of the auditor in performance of the examination.

The second generally accepted group of auditing standards, standards of field work, are perhaps more helpful in developing more specifically the way in which an audit of an information system should take place. These standards are set forth as follows:

1. The work is to be adequately planned, and assistants, if any, are to be properly supervised.
2. There is to be a proper study and evaluation of the existing internal control as a basis for reliance thereon and for the determination of the tests to which auditing procedures are to be restricted.
3. Sufficient competent evidential matter is to be obtained through inspection, observation, inquiries, and confirmations to afford a reasonable basis for an opinion regarding the financial statements under examination.

These standards, although originally designed within the framework of the traditional audit objective of rendering an opinion on financial statements, still provide useful guidelines as to the way in which an audit should be undertaken. They will accordingly be discussed in greater detail.

The Planning Standard

In any auditing engagement the planning function is clearly very important. Planning must begin as soon as an audit engagement is accepted. At this stage the auditor must begin to determine how he can gather the necessary data for achieving audit objectives. This clearly means that he must develop a general approach that will help him in determining the appropriate introductory questions to ask. As answers are obtained, a plan of the specifics of the particular engagement must be drawn up. The planning function will include an estimate of the scope of the engagement, an understanding of the basic business operations of the client, and the ways in which these operations can be more completely grasped. It requires development of personnel budgets, timing schedules, and the selection of individuals to perform the specific tasks which will be required.

Many firms today require the preparation of a formal audit plan before any audit work is undertaken. The audit plan includes a great deal of raw data about the business, such as its organization structure; the importance of its various subsidiaries, divisions, and plants; a description of the business or businesses carried on; a discussion of the client personnel with whom the auditor must deal; recent financial information; data on plans for public financing; and the like. It will also include a description of the reports which the auditor is asked to render at the conclusion of his audit, and planning data related to the audit, such as the audit personnel scheduled for the engagement. The audit plan therefore represents a strategic preview of the engagement.

After the audit plan has been completed, the specific steps to be undertaken in gathering evidence are generally described in several audit programs which will be followed by the various men working on different parts of the engagement. These programs are important both in that they enable the more experienced auditor to apply his knowledge to a variety of situations and in that they supply a means of quality control over the engagement.

The audit programs are an integral part of audit workpapers and are generally initialed by the auditor on completing the various steps and then reviewed by the audit supervisor at the completion of the job. As such, the programs serve as evidence that due professional care has been exercised and that adequate planning has been undertaken.

Despite their importance, audit programs are sometimes misused. This occurs when they are considered as a list of mechanical steps to be completed rather than as a plan for the systematic gathering of evidence. As in the case of any plan, the effective implementer uses the plan as a guide which may be changed as information becomes available.

When the audit plan and audit programs are drawn up prior to an initial audit of a client, there are substantial uncertainties that must be filled in as additional information is gathered while auditing work is being done. In the case of a continuing engagement, the plan for a particular year's work can normally be spelled out with considerably more assurance.

It seems likely that as the orientation of the auditor becomes directed increasingly toward the client's information system and its adequacy and decreasingly to a specific set of financial statements, the purely annual basis of an audit engagement is likely to be modified. Even today, where the legal formality of separate annual audits is maintained most large companies are continually under audit by their independent CPAs, and it is probable that in the future auditors will be employed to perform a continuing audit of the information system rather than a periodic audit of the financial statements. A report on the financial statements will be able to emerge from this continuing information review.

The Internal-Control Standard

In the audit oriented toward the firm's information system, a review of all aspects of internal control will constitute virtually all of the audit work. Additional work will be necessary only where the information system does not produce data needed for a particular report by the auditor. What must be done, therefore, is to develop a means by which the traditional scope of the review of internal control is expanded and appropriate evidence is developed with which to measure the adequacy of the firm's information system. The details of this approach are the basis of the chapters that follow in Section 3.

The Evidence Standard

The third standard of field work requires that the auditor obtain "sufficient competent evidential matter." This leads us to a discussion of the kind of evidence which must be gathered and evaluated if a rational opinion, based on a systematic process is to be formed on the adequacy of the client's information system and the system's output. Within the framework of the audit objective that we suggest, the primary gathering of evidence must relate to both the nature of the business and the nature of the information system that is used to manage the business.

Sources of Evidence

There are numerous sources to which the auditor may turn in obtaining evidence about the nature of the business, the information system used therein, and the system's output.

Mautz and Sharaf suggest these types of audit evidence:

1. Physical examination by the auditor of the thing represented in the accounts.
2. Statements by independent third parties:
   Written.
   Oral.
3. Authoritative documents:
   Prepared outside the enterprise under examination.
   Prepared inside the enterprise under examination.
4. Statements by officers and employees of the company under examination:
   Formal.
   Informal.
5. Calculations performed by the auditor.
6. Satisfactory internal control procedures.
7. Subsequent actions by the company under examination and others.

8. Subsidiary or detail records with no significant indications of irregularity.
9. Interrelationships with other data.[1]

We have shown the relationship of the phases of the audit, the fundamental audit tasks discussed in the previous chapter, and the types of audit evidence in Table 1, page 164.

Interviews with officers and employees of the business are usually the first step in gathering evidence. The systems auditor spends a great deal of time in questioning management about its perception of the business, its objectives, and the ways it is going about the achievement of these objectives. These questions may start on a fairly broad philosophical level and then move down into a detailed analysis of the procedures used in the various operating segments of the business. While interviews with top management are normally a first step, throughout the audit engagement interviews with operating personnel at all levels are a principal source of evidence about the company and its systems.

A second source of evidence about the company and its systems are the various summaries of financial information that are used in operations. The auditor should start by achieving a familiarity with the basic financial statements of the business and should then spend a good deal of his time examining both the financial information available to managers and how it is used. In the interviewing process, he should ask questions about the data most frequently used and most important to the individual managers who are running the business. Examples of the various financial statements and operating reports should be included in the work papers together with a description of their use. In addition, the actual data in the reports should serve to give the auditor trained in financial analysis an opportunity to understand the economic results of different parts of the entity.

A third source of evidence would be company policy statements, procedures manuals, and systems documentation. The auditor should review the written statements of management in regard to its plans and methods of operation in order to understand the nature of the business enterprise. In addition, procedures manuals which spell out the flow of data and the classifications by which they are accumulated are a valuable tool for understanding the details of the information system.

Fourth, the auditor obtains evidence by observing all the operating systems of a business: marketing, procurement, production, personnel,

---

[1] Mautz and Sharaf, *The Philosophy of Auditing*, p. 86.

and cash management. In each of these areas the auditor should spend a certain amount of time simply watching what goes on. Of great utility in this respect are several audit procedures in common use today that were originally designed to aid in the audit of balances. The prime example is the observation of physical inventories, which was originally a step taken to enable the auditor to verify an inventory balance on the financial statements. Today the observation of physical inventories is primarily valuable because it gets the auditor away from the accounting system of the business and into its operating end. In connection with the observation of physical inventories, he normally has the opportunity to observe the production process in operation and to talk informally with operating personnel in the nonfinancial areas of the business. Thus, even an audit procedure that has been traditionally associated with balance-sheet audits is today primarily systems oriented and will be increasingly so in the future. The observation of operations, however, should not be limited to physical inventories. The auditor should spend some time observing the distribution system in operation and watching the purchasing agents, personnel administrators, and cash managers as they perform their daily tasks. The technique of following a member of middle management in each of these areas for a period of time can be an important source of evidence for the auditor, since items will inevitably come up which are not considered in a formal interview.

Fifth, other documents are also a source of audit evidence. The auditor should be aware of the various types of documentation that exist for each of the various transactions which the business enters into. Insurance policies, customer correspondence, warranties, and a host of other documents may provide useful insights into the operations of the firm and its information system.

Finally, statements by third parties often are an important part of the evidence needed to understand the firm and its systems. These can be either statements specifically requested by auditors, such as the confirmation of various events, or statements not generated by specific audit requests. The auditor preparing to undertake an engagement or to become part of a continuing audit should obtain published data on the company. A Dun and Bradstreet report, for example, would be significant evidence. Similarly, the auditor should seek out the data about the company's expectations developed by investment analysts and other third parties. A comprehensive analysis of a firm prepared by an investment banker might be one of the most useful sources of evidence about the nature of the business. Additionally, various statements requiring examination may be part of the legal record. The proceedings of regulatory agencies often include substantial data about a company subject to its jurisdiction, and this source should certainly be explored. Finally, in addition to written statements by third parties, a good deal of evidence about a firm may be obtained through informal interviews with outsiders. The auditor may find much value in interviews with the firm's banker or with investment analysts responsible for following a particular industry, particularly in the case of a technical industry, in which analysts with technical backgrounds are involved in the review of its investment potential.

As this evidence is gathered from various sources, a record should be made of it in the working papers of the engagement—the auditor's record of his examination. As a record, the papers serve four principal purposes. First, they are a means by which the audit staff communicates its findings to the audit supervisors and partners. Second, they are a means by which the audit supervisors maintain control of the audit work already done and yet to be done. Third, they serve as a data bank for information needed in the preparation of reports, and for other purposes. And fourth, they provide the auditor with legal evidence for the work which he performed.

Audit Working Papers

Of these purposes perhaps the most important is to supply communication. Partners and audit supervisors cannot do all of the work required in an audit of a large corporation, but they must be aware of the work that has been done and the various problems which have arisen in connection with that work. They must also be able to absorb the relevant information developed by the audit so that they can evaluate the client's information system and determine the kind of opinion to be expressed in their reports. The working papers enable the staff to advise the audit supervisors of what has been accomplished and to focus their attention on the most important areas requiring decisions. While any critical problems that arise will be discussed immediately with supervisors and partners, most ideas and discoveries which are developed as a result of audit work are presented when that particular part of the audit is completed.

Any set of working papers, therefore, should start with a summary prepared by the man in charge of that part of the engagement which the papers cover. This summary should briefly describe the most important items covered in the working papers and it should highlight those items which require decisions, including recommendations where appropriate and references to the facts which must be considered in making decisions. Decisions made at a supervisory level should be recorded immediately in the working papers and the reasoning supporting those decisions outlined.

In a large engagement, the preparation of working papers will include a process of summarization at various levels. Each part of an examination will be summarized by a staff assistant and these summaries will then be reviewed and in turn summarized by a senior accountant in charge of auditing a subsidiary or division. As the various parts of the audit of a large enterprise are brought together, a more comprehensive summary may be prepared for the attention of the partner who has the final responsibility for the entire engagement. In this fashion the senior partner on the engagement can see in the minimum time the crucial elements that have emerged from the audit and can devote his attention to those areas where he feels he can most productively make decisions or recommendations.

The second major purpose for working papers is to maintain control over the audit. The first standard of field work requires the proper supervision of assistants, and working papers help to achieve this. Initially, the audit supervisor will include instructions, plans, and programs in the papers he turns over to the staff assistants who will be performing various tasks. These will become a part of the working papers, and once the tests and other audit steps have been completed the assistant will note the results in the papers. He will also include whatever schedules and analyses he believes are required to support the figures which he is reviewing. He will then submit his working papers to the audit supervisor for review.

The essence of the auditor's control over the engagement is the process of working-paper review by successive levels of supervisors in an audit. The reviewer is expected to deal with the specific issues that the staff assistant has outlined for him in the summary, and to examine carefully the remainder of the papers to see whether or not audit work was adequately done and whether there are additional questions which were not immediately apparent but do require consideration. If the working papers do not indicate that a satisfactory audit was performed the supervisor must return them to the staff assistant for the performance of additional auditing procedures. While many questions may have been raised by the staff assistant in the course of his work and hence the supervisor may know a number of the issues to be disclosed in the papers, the final review nonetheless requires him to focus his attention on the entire area under audit and to take responsibility for the adequacy of the work done.

In order to produce all relevant information, the working papers for a particular part of the engagement may have to rely upon steps performed in another part—either steps normally performed or steps specifically required to complete or validate information developed elsewhere in the audit. For example, certain sales transactions with subsidiaries may have to be compared with the subsidiaries' records, while certain liabilities may be confirmed by banks in connection with cash work which require tracing to

Tennessee Technological University

OPERATING RECEIPT

B.I. _____

S. S. NO. _____ 415-96-7785 _____

RECEIVED OF ___ Munday ___ Judy _____ DATE __ 3-18-81

LAST   FIRST   MIDDLE

F D	FUNCTION	SUB. ACCT.	OBJECT	AMOUNT
	ACCOUNT NUMBER			
	01 00401			

ticket

Total Received

How Paid

Cash ___ Check ___✓___ Other ___

PAYER

SIGNED - FOR BUSINESS MANAGER

RECEIPT NUMBER

351549

the audit tests of notes and accounts payable. Such items are generally summarized in the front of a set of working papers on a single list so that the reviewer can see what work is still required in the area.

Finally, the audit supervisor will use information in the working papers to control the amount of time spent on the engagement. Most working-paper segments include a time budget and record of time spent, and the supervisor must consider not only the adequacy of the audit procedures, but the amount of time spent thereon in determining whether or not a satisfactory job has been done by the auditor in charge of a particular segment.

The third purpose of the working papers is to serve as a data bank, in which information required for reports of all sorts is accumulated. Additionally, the working papers will include information about the history of the company and its procedures for use in future audits. In deciding what information to include in his working papers, therefore, the auditor must keep in mind the various kinds of reports which will be issued at the end of the audit and the types of information that may be required on a continuing basis from year to year.

In order to save audit time, the auditor generally can have client personnel prepare a large number of the schedules required for data-bank purposes. The auditor can then perform whatever verification he feels necessary and put them in his working papers. Often machine copies of client reports will serve this purpose. While auditors traditionally did a great deal of work analyzing individual accounts and reconciling balances at different points in time, today this analytical work is generally considered unnecessary; but to the extent that analyses are needed to explain unusual transactions, or are needed for particular reports, they can be prepared by the client.

Data on company procedures are also generally included in the working papers, normally by use of various flowcharting techniques which will be discussed in a later chapter. Company procedures manuals and other materials may also be included.

In order to fulfill all of their purposes, it is imperative that working papers be appropriately indexed so that information can be retrieved from them with a minimum of time. This requires both an initial systematic indexing system as the working papers are prepared and a summary index in the front of the working papers at the completion of the engagement. If information cannot be readily obtained from the working papers, it is clear they are not fulfilling their purpose.

Finally, working papers serve the auditor as legal evidence of the work which he has performed. While this should not be considered

Table 1. Types of evidence

Phases of Audit	Fundamental Tasks	Physical Examination and Observation	Statements by Independent Third Parties	Authoritative Documents
Evaluation of system in existence	Defining system	X		
Evaluation of outputs produced by system to determine that they are reliable, relevant and understandable by the user	Testing system	X	X	X
	External confirmation of records	X	X	X
	Search for quality attributes	X	X	X
	Comparison of records (balances) with transactions			
	Inferences from logical relationships between records			
	Determine accounting principles followed			
	Challenge appropriateness of valuation method			
	Check accuracy of application of valuation method			
	Check consistency of accounting principles			

their primary purpose, it is one of the considerations to be made in determining the form and content of the papers being prepared. On some occasions it will be necessary for an auditor to defend his work in a court of law, and in such situations his working papers will be a principal source of evidence that his work did meet professional standards.

Working papers are the property of the auditor, but they are subject to subpoena in civil and criminal cases. The auditor, therefore, must be aware that the entire set of working papers may be obtained by someone whose interests are not at one with the accountant or his client, and care must therefore be taken not to leave any loose ends of an audit in the working papers of the engagement. The final review of working papers on an engagement, for example, should include the determination that all items listed as requiring attention have been considered and dealt with in some satisfactory way.

Perhaps the most important thing that working papers should include is memoranda outlining the reasoning behind the audit steps undertaken and the various auditing and accounting decisions which were made in

Statements by Officers and Employees	Calculations	Systems and Internal-Control Procedures	Subsequent Actions	Subsidiary or Detail Records	Interrelationships with Other Data
X		X			
	X			X	X
X					
X			X		X
	X		X	X	
					X
X	X				
	X				
	X	X		X	
	X	X			X

the course of the engagement. Where a problem has been considered and a professional judgment made, there is less likelihood of liability than where the working papers bear no evidence that a particular difficulty was uncovered or considered in the course of the work performed.

A set of audit working papers that adequately fulfill the purposes of communication, control, and data accumulation outlined above will normally also serve as adequate evidence that professional standards have been maintained. The possibility of legal liability, therefore, should merely add a small dimension of additional care rather than a predominant factor in the determination of the content and use of working papers.

Standards of Evaluation

Once evidence has been gathered about the operations of the firm and about the information system describing these operations, it is necessary to develop standards of evaluation to determine whether or not the information system of the firm is meeting the information requirements of management and outside parties. The very objective of the audit as we have defined it makes such standards necessary.

One of the most difficult parts of systems auditing, however, is the development of such standards. In today's world the auditor and systems analyst have not developed any explicit standards for adequacy of information. In fact, the auditor who has been working with internal control for many years has not developed explicit standards about what constitutes adequate internal control; generally accepted auditing standards require that the internal control be evaluated and, as a result of this, evaluation testing procedures developed, but there have been no accepted standards developed as to the means of evaluation or the measurement of adequacy.

There have been some attempts by various parties to develop an index of control through the use of questionnaires of various sorts. For example, Gene Brown developed in 1961 what he called "a scientific approach to auditing" in which he assigned relative control value to the various questions on an internal-control questionnaire and suggested that these values, although subjectively developed, could serve as the basis for determining the extent of audit samples necessary in reviewing various areas. A few public accounting firms have attempted by this and other systems to quantify control evaluations but with little success to date. Most such efforts have been subsequently abandoned.

The American Institute of Management developed a management auditing program and questionnaire in which they assigned weights to various management functions; their analysts, on reviewing the corporation, subjectively assigned points in each area on the basis of management success. The end result of such a management audit is a management score, but the subjective aspects of the evaluation procedure and the weighting of relative factors in importance have prevented this system from achieving general acceptance. Any quantitative system based upon the subjective assignment of weights and points will be open to the criticism of others whose evaluation of relative importance and relative success may differ.

In the final analysis, it may have to be recognized that the evaluative function of the auditor will remain an area where the management-services approach, offering a judgment or recommendation, must take precedence over the audit approach aimed at determining "truth."

It seems likely that no ultimate truth exists in the area of systems evaluation. Auditing probably must remain in the area of the social sciences rather than the physical sciences: Whereas in the physical sciences a reality does exist susceptible to exact methods of description that yield statements that are verifiable, in the social sciences tools are not yet enough developed to make such description possible. In auditing as in social science the concepts of relative strength will continue to be paramount.

Today's auditor, employing the systems approach, must therefore, still accept the role of informed and experienced judgment. He can be trained in procedures, but he cannot assume that there is only a single set of procedures that will produce the adequate information for the management of a business. The outsider using the opinion of the auditor as an expert's judgment must accept it within this limitation.

Problems of Auditing Standards

1. The preparation of working papers is an integral part of a CPA's examination of financial statements. On a recurring engagement a CPA reviews his audit programs and working papers from his prior examination while planning his current examination to determine their usefulness for the current engagement.

Required:

a. 1. What are the purposes or functions of audit working papers?
   2. What records may be included in audit working papers?

b. What factors affect the CPA's judgment of the type and content of the working papers for a particular engagement?

c. To comply with generally accepted auditing standards a CPA includes certain evidence in his working papers, for example, "evidence that the engagement was planned and work of assistants was supervised and reviewed." What other evidence should a CPA include in audit working papers to comply with generally accepted auditing standards?

d. How can a CPA make the most effective use of the preceding year's audit programs and working papers in a recurring examination?

e. What advice should a CPA give a client

From Uniform CPA Examinations.

about discontinuing the use of records needed in an examination and how should a CPA complete his examination when he finds that records reviewed by him in prior examinations have been discontinued by the client?

2. You have been assigned by your firm to complete the examination of the 1967 financial statements of Carter Manufacturing Corporation because the senior accountant and his inexperienced assistant who began the engagement were hospitalized because of an accident. The engagement is about one-half completed. Your auditor's report must be delivered in three weeks as agreed when your firm accepted the engagement. You estimate that by utilizing the client's staff to the greatest possible extent you can complete the engagement in five weeks. Your firm cannot assign an assistant to you.

The working papers show the status of work on the examination as follows:

a. *Completed*—Cash, fixed assets, depreciation, mortgage payable and stockholders' equity.
b. *Completed except as noted later*—Inventories, accounts payable, tests of purchase transactions, and payrolls.

c. *Nothing done*—Trade accounts receivable, inventory receiving cutoff and price testing, accrued expenses payable, unrecorded liability test, tests of sales transactions, payroll deductions test and observation of payroll check distribution, other expenses, analytic review of operations, vouching of December purchase transactions, auditor's report, internal control investigation, internal control letter, minutes, preparation of tax returns, procedural recommendations for management, subsequent events, supervision and review.

Your review discloses that the assistant's working papers are incomplete and were not reviewed by the senior accountant. For example, the inventory working papers present incomplete explanations and no cross-referencing.

Required:

What field work standards have been violated by the senior accountant who preceded you on this assignment? Explain why you feel the work standards you list have been violated.

Chapter 7

Gathering Evidence: Flowcharting and Sampling

Audit evidence is obtained through the application of a number of techniques basic to an examination of a corporate information system; these auditing procedures are mentioned in the report of the independent accountant. Many of these techniques for gathering evidence are simply common-sense approaches and do not require any great technical skill to apply, although the judgment of the experienced auditor may be of great use in deciding how and for what purpose they will be used.

Techniques for Gathering Evidence

It is clear, for example, that one of the most-used techniques for gathering evidence is simply inquiry, usually directed to the employees of the client but sometimes also to outsiders. Inquiry is used throughout an audit as the source of basic data about the company's system in actual operation and as the principal means by which an auditor obtains answers to the many questions which inevitably arise during an audit.

The most effective use of inquiry requires the establishment of comfortable human relationships with client personnel. The auditor must be aware of the various responses to being audited, ranging from annoyance at the time required and dislike of having work reviewed by an outsider, to an interested encouragement of any new ideas and suggestions an auditor might develop. With experience, the auditor learns the need to ask questions which give the impression of being directed to obtaining information for use in assisting the party being questioned rather than for the purpose of finding error. Once mutual confidence has been established, the task of gathering information through inquiry can be much more effectively performed.

169

Inquiry is usually made of outsiders by correspondence, rarely by personal contact. Normally directed to outsiders who have dealt with the client in a variety of ways, such external inquiry is intended to implicitly or explicitly confirm the information gathered directly from the client or shown on his records. Confirmation requests may be directed to banks, customers, creditors, attorneys, and other parties as the occasion warrants. In most cases, confirmation of specific balances is requested, although in some cases the inquiries are more general and seek either data on possible unrecorded transactions or opinions on legal matters.

In addition to inquiry, there are many other techniques for gathering evidence, some requiring the auditor to be present as corporate activities take place; among them is the physical examination of assets such as inventory and productive facilities. And a useful technique in the process of understanding the basic nature of the client's activities is the observation of the firm's production and marketing activities. An auditor who confines himself to the books can seldom develop an effective overview of the information system of the firm and the needs which it must fulfill.

The techniques above provide some evidence for the auditor in his overview of the client's information system. Additional evidence must be obtained by a group of techniques applied to the client's books and records. These techniques include examination of source documents supporting the entries on the books, the tracing and verification of bookkeeping procedures, the review of computations, the scanning of accounts and journals for unusual transactions, and the comparison of various sources of information for consistency.

Flow Charting and Sampling

So far we have been describing methods of gathering audit evidence, but for handling this evidence, once gathered, there are two important techniques, flowcharting and statistical sampling. Flowcharting is the method whereby we accumulate evidence in its most readily useable form; and by statistical sampling we maximize the reliability of the results derived from the evidence.

Flowcharting is a technique for recording and analyzing the evidence gained from inquiries about a system, observation of activities, and examination of transactions and documents flowing through the system.

The gathering techniques listed above clearly cannot be applied to the totality of a firm's assets and records. Not only would such a procedure be prohibitively costly, but it is not needed to form reliable judgments about the system being audited. To apply most of these techniques, therefore, a selection process is needed to choose the items to be examined, counted, confirmed, computed, traced to the books, or inquired about.

The selection process requires a sampling system. Statistical theory has shown that characteristics present in a sample drawn from a series of items called a population reflect the characteristics of the population. Although the probability of congruence between the characteristics of the sample and the population increases as the sample size is increased, it can be mathematically demonstrated that a relatively small sample properly drawn has a relatively high probability of reflecting the characteristics of a population with considerable accuracy. The concept of sampling will be more extensively treated in a subsequent part of this chapter.

The techniques of selection, computation, scanning, and listing are also aided by the use of a computer. It is quite evident that the computer presents a powerful tool to the auditor, processing data at electronic speeds in accordance with auditor's criteria. A detailed discussion of the ways in which the computer can be used in auditing will be included in the next chapter.

The System Flow Chart

Systems review is initially concerned with an analysis of the structure and design of the system itself rather than with an intensive examination of documents and records it produces. In such an approach, any examination of transactions and records is primarily designed to confirm the existence of procedures and their effectiveness and to further an understanding of the nature and elements of the system. To initially understand the structure, elements, and properties of the system, the analyst-auditor must define the system he wishes to evaluate.

Probably the most accurate and comprehensive way to record the procedures in existence is the flow chart. The flow chart is designed to define a system in sufficient detail and with enough analytical efficiency to provide the auditor with a working description of the system's structure and components. Given the stated inputs, the description must be able to specify what output will occur.

The flow chart has several advantages over a narrative description of a system. First, it is much easier to use in describing a system of any size and complexity. When narrative descriptions are used in large systems, it is difficult to absorb the amount of detail, to relate and integrate mentally the various parts of the system, and to record changes in the system. Second, the flow chart is more efficient than the narrative description in analyzing the system. The charts clearly show what is taking place and provide an easy means of spotting weaknesses in the system or areas where improvements could be made. An article by Robert Rennie describing flowcharting techniques in greater detail follows this chapter.

The Sampling Process

Sampling has been widely accepted as the basis for the opinion the auditor expresses. The sampling operation is used, and the need to select a sample arises, only insofar as the auditor needs to project his test findings as a generalization of the state of affairs in the universe, or entire field, of documents or entries. This point is an important one since there are audit areas where statistical inference may not be important and where statistical sampling is not applicable. Carmichael, in the third reading at the end of this chapter, points out that there are three types of audit tests, classified in terms of their usually recognized objectives:

1. Those which provide the auditor with *prima facie* evidence of the existence and implementation of a system of internal control through observation and inquiry, and testing—usually of selected items from their inception through ultimate disposition.
2. Tests of items in quantities sufficient to obtain assurance that the functioning of the system of internal control is as planned and that the results of an examination of a portion of data are representative of the whole. These tests usually have the dual purpose of procedural tests and tests of *bona fides*.
3. Examination of especially significant items as to which the auditor may feel it necessary to require substantial assurance based on external evidence or detailed verification procedures.

These three types of tests will be referred to, respectively, as:

1. Single-purpose tests
2. Dual-purpose tests
3. Tests of *bona fides*.

It is submitted that the adequacy of the size of the sample of transactions is dependent upon the type of test, which, in turn, is dependent upon the objective of the auditor.

Testing Systems

Testing is important to determining the existence of a system. Limited tests will suffice, since the objective of the testing—a single-purpose test—is to confirm the auditor's understanding of the system and to determine whether the control procedures supposed to be in effect are, in fact, in effect. It is not the auditor's objective to draw statistical inferences about whether these procedures function an acceptable percentage of the time.

This type of test, to determine the existence of system procedures and controls, is sometimes referred to as a "walkthrough" or a "sample of one." In this test, the auditor selects a typical transaction and follows it from the beginning to the end of the system, making inquiries of those who process it and verifying that it is being processed in accordance with the auditor's understanding of the system and that it properly appears in system outputs. For example, if a sales and receivables system were being tested by this technique, the auditor might start with the receipt of a customer order, check the credit evaluation and approval, the shipping and billing process, accounts-receivable updating, sales reporting, and cash receipt and application.

Additional Tests

The walkthrough approach to testing the system should suffice to indicate that a system does exist and what its strengths and weaknesses are. After the auditor understands what the system is and has evaluated its strengths and weaknesses, he may decide to do additional testing of transactions or tests of output produced by the system. But in this testing, his objective is not to understand the system and place reliance thereon but to make evaluations *based* on his tests. Here statistical sampling may be very important.

Statistical Sampling and Auditing

In auditing practice, the auditor uses his judgment to determine sample size, the selection of the items or accounts for the sample, and the inference made about the universe from the sample results. For using judgment samples, auditors have developed certain criteria, which may be summarized:

1. The sample or group of documents selected for examination must be representative or typical of the entire mass from which they are drawn. Judicious selection, however, may be used as the basis for drawing the samples. The auditor may introduce into the sample selection process known circumstances which he regards as important to the final conclusion. For example, if the auditor knows that several large accounts exist in a file of receivables being confirmed these large accounts would usually be in the confirmation sample.

2. The size of the sample varies inversely with the quality of the internal control system. Thus, the required sample in a weak system of control would be relatively larger than the sample required in systems having strong internal control.

3. The examination of documents included in the sample must be exhaustive to increase the probability that proper inference about the universe may be made from the sample selected.

4. Risk is involved in sampling. No matter how the sample is selected, there is some probability that an improper conclusion will result from examination of sample evidence. Sample sizes vary inversely with the degree of risk assumed.

5. Samples are not designed for the detection of fraud. Samples are selected to enable the auditor to examine sufficient evidence to express an opinion on the reasonableness of financial statements.[1]

The above criteria for sampling are both explicit and sound in terms of audit philosophy. Also, the judgment samples embodying these criteria may be as accurate as statistical—that is, randomly chosen—samples in describing the universe of documents from which they are drawn. However, the use of judgment samples does not provide objective criteria by which to measure the effectiveness or adequacy of particular sampling plans. Statistical sampling, on the other hand, is a methodology based on the laws of probability, and the sample result can be evaluated according to precision and reliability measurements based on widely accepted and mathematically provable statistical principles.

The Statistical-Sampling Approach

The statistical-sampling approach has three characteristics:

1. A method for selecting a random sample.

2. A method of measuring the accuracy (precision and reliability) of sample estimates and the risks attached to an inference made from the sample.

3. A method of adjusting sample sizes to provide any desired level of accuracy for sample estimates or any desired level of risk for sample conclusions.

[1]R. J. Monteverde and R. M. Trueblood, "Statistical Sampling Methods in Auditing Practice—An Evaluation," *Quarterly Review* (Touche, Ross, Bailey & Smart), November 1955, pp. 3–4.

Table 1. Random Numbers

15	62	38	72	92	03	76	09	30	75	77	80	04	24	54	67	60	10	79	25	21	60	03	48	14
77	81	15	14	67	55	24	22	20	55	36	93	67	69	37	72	22	43	46	32	56	15	75	25	12
18	87	05	09	96	45	14	72	41	46	12	67	46	72	02	59	06	17	49	12	73	28	23	52	48
08	58	53	63	66	13	07	04	48	71	39	07	46	96	40	20	86	79	11	81	74	11	15	23	17
16	07	79	57	61	42	19	68	15	12	60	21	59	12	07	04	99	88	22	39	75	16	69	13	84
54	13	05	46	17	05	51	24	53	57	46	51	14	39	17	21	39	89	07	35	47	87	44	36	62
95	27	23	17	39	80	24	44	48	93	75	94	77	09	23	48	75	91	69	03	55	51	09	74	47
22	39	44	74	86	25	95	28	63	90	41	19	48	46	72	51	12	97	39	83	35	83	23	17	29
69	95	21	30	11	98	81	38	00	53	41	40	04	16	78	67	29	83	41	18	30	90	44	37	64
75	75	63	97	12	11	57	05	86	52	82	72	47	72	14	37	72	69	75	48	72	21	52	51	81
08	74	79	30	80	70	11	66	79	25	88	01	94	52	31	38	57	98	71	62	12	56	61	01	54
04	88	45	98	60	90	92	74	77	87	40	18	65	87	37	08	68	62	39	52	84	74	90	63	18
97	35	74	05	75	42	13	49	48	38	74	19	06	42	60	20	79	90	81	77	18	51	71	27	27
53	09	93	28	29	80	19	68	30	45	94	49	49	71	21	93	93	71	30	34	52	65	83	40	13
26	36	68	48	09	37	69	26	22	80	23	34	10	45	70	83	51	07	37	44	62	96	74	42	64
49	16	57	15	79	56	63	22	94	28	11	39	69	55	38	53	06	97	20	42	09	14	90	43	48
03	51	79	78	74	75	23	73	75	98	47	85	07	26	02	61	28	01	22	16	14	12	15	67	22
21	88	87	28	48	23	44	03	03	80	53	89	07	87	93	30	17	84	17	74	16	53	31	39	01
56	41	73	33	41	59	16	59	50	98	24	24	87	06	75	99	52	09	88	05	86	25	43	50	94
72	39	19	70	17	01	04	01	22	33	04	84	63	27	65	84	39	45	55	31	95	88	93	90	37
97	28	25	81	49	71	69	22	04	51	56	46	56	15	10	69	59	99	50	29	33	50	16	93	09
18	87	02	72	08	74	52	16	03	82	20	19	66	23	62	37	51	04	89	31	32	19	59	85	57
53	40	11	75	45	13	56	85	31	37	09	17	71	96	79	39	50	79	27	62	71	14	95	53	03
60	49	03	41	56	78	33	77	28	92	21	90	10	62	01	97	06	45	01	19	95	12	24	18	52
09	16	12	75	04	39	69	95	00	48	26	85	28	73	08	65	92	10	66	75	62	61	27	82	57
64	20	19	87	54	88	15	12	54	24	06	99	57	07	28	51	34	54	98	50	70	88	02	86	48
31	28	07	58	77	03	98	26	76	09	10	44	57	61	28	60	29	85	70	79	80	29	19	98	92
80	04	28	47	76	35	73	67	78	28	09	39	88	63	74	41	26	92	42	33	06	80	06	33	84
24	60	22	51	19	34	54	08	24	73	86	72	11	44	69	76	90	81	17	85	57	47	35	16	84
59	16	11	26	29	18	97	78	44	43	58	92	78	70	80	09	65	32	68	26	65	73	90	50	46
58	54	29	98	27	40	51	92	07	13	58	41	59	56	94	16	32	51	42	54	77	37	13	85	19
20	18	34	22	73	57	40	67	17	28	63	57	74	36	18	65	55	25	50	68	35	90	00	03	38
53	90	46	56	19	50	58	33	84	53	14	74	17	40	73	86	11	04	02	04	02	28	49	62	36
97	16	93	94	65	70	95	95	83	20	91	42	57	95	63	00	86	29	02	53	02	27	86	70	95
72	55	71	70	92	04	22	53	19	29	67	29	13	56	70	45	73	45	05	04	32	43	30	93	41
99	19	72	58	35	49	09	26	00	74	25	42	94	52	02	83	31	85	65	66	31	97	67	52	15
48	21	49	72	97	79	19	64	81	82	78	92	51	96	31	28	79	13	20	82	34	81	39	46	86
52	37	68	15	53	22	98	30	16	31	83	24	87	69	29	24	85	44	25	50	75	62	83	95	41
97	50	52	53	52	26	78	22	68	69	57	79	42	40	89	55	81	75	24	52	51	32	79	97	05
36	05	09	16	11	71	01	63	17	60	11	65	19	43	07	44	86	19	58	92	23	71	32	96	19
20	79	70	09	30	81	14	53	80	93	71	94	10	18	14	89	69	76	53	25	27	36	65	65	05
13	07	89	72	08	00	37	75	14	94	83	85	06	72	65	07	47	30	17	11	16	02	63	97	30
94	26	82	37	43	34	23	00	14	50	98	85	41	17	71	69	20	15	98	82	79	69	68	50	31
13	55	88	38	43	75	37	43	83	85	53	74	54	62	99	68	93	74	43	95	06	26	79	78	87
02	44	24	97	71	97	93	12	70	89	42	52	33	24	91	05	87	53	15	77	49	92	83	97	80
34	90	96	63	54	22	84	36	38	99	85	36	25	03	27	49	24	72	10	50	95	14	18	26	64
13	67	06	34	98	04	20	80	12	54	01	18	54	20	76	92	10	47	04	65	54	45	82	42	90
18	75	55	82	66	34	77	27	71	79	67	65	85	92	63	14	43	83	13	74	12	48	68	87	22
91	25	52	57	15	21	54	40	05	50	67	51	66	45	69	84	72	74	32	30	17	70	40	90	24
76	24	00	14	92	14	29	12	17	73	77	46	44	24	30	48	50	36	30	24	93	08	01	39	37

Taken from *Statistical Tables and Formulas*, by A. Hald, New York: John Wiley & Sons, Inc., 1952.

Each of these characteristics will now be discussed in terms of estimation sampling, the most common of sampling techniques used in auditing.[2]

---

[2]There are several books on statistical sampling, accounting, and auditing to which the reader should refer for a detailed coverage of the concepts discussed in this chapter. These books include: R. Cyert, and H. J. Davidson, *Statistical Sampling for Accounting Information* (Englewood Cliffs, N. J.: Prentice-Hall, Inc., 1962) and Herbert Arkin, *Handbook of Sampling for Auditing and Accounting*, New York: McGraw-Hill Book Company, Inc., 1963.

Selection of a Random Sample

Random sample selection is a method whereby every item in the universe being sampled has an equal chance of being selected. There are several ways by which random selection can be performed. A table of random numbers, such as that in Table 1, offers a solution to the selection problem. The order of these random numbers is itself generated by a random method. To use the random-number table, we pick any point in the table as a starting point. Then using a systematic pattern, we select sufficient numbers to obtain the desired sample size. For example, if we wanted to calculate the estimated average value of the normally distributed universe of 100 vouchers shown in Table 2, we might randomly select a sample of ten vouchers to calculate the estimate. If we started at the upper left-hand corner of Table 1 and proceeded down the column of two-digit numbers, we would select vouchers 15, 77, 18, 08, 16, 54, 95, 22, 69, 75 in our random sample. Of course, the estimates of the average value of the ten vouchers would be $20.21, as calculated in Table 3.

Random sampling always results in more "representative" samples than samples judgmentally selected. A random sample, however, will not necessarily give a more accurate estimate of a universe characteristic than any specific judgment sample. Random sampling is more likely to yield a better estimate and, more importantly, random sampling enables measurement of the accuracy of sample results. Judgment sampling, as we have said, does not allow the measurement of sample accuracy.

Measuring the Accuracy of Sample Results

In statistics the term "accuracy" is used to mean the reproducibility of estimates made from samples: the degree to which successive statistics computed from successive samples tend to resemble one another. In measuring the accuracy of a sample estimate, the concepts of precision and reliability, both based on probability considerations, are important.

In order to evaluate sample estimates in terms of probabilities, the estimates must be in terms of intervals, rather than specific values. The procedure used is to compute an interval called a confidence interval. The degree of confidence that this interval includes the true value is numerically equal to the percentage of such intervals—if many were to be computed by the same procedure—that may be expected to include that value. The hypothetical repetitive process here is the sampling, followed by the computation of the confidence interval.

We know that many actual distributions of data are "normal," or bell-shaped. For example, if we were to plot the values of the vouchers in Table 2 on a graph, we would have a discrete distribution which would

Table 2. Hypothetical Universe of 100 Vouchers

Voucher Number	Amount	Voucher Number	Amount	Voucher Number	Amount	Voucher Number	Amount
00	$ 1.65	25	$16.01	50	$12.52	75	$19.28
01	11.87	26	21.06	51	14.54	76	17.94
02	11.18	27	23.38	52	15.12	77	19.93
03	11.32	28	16.32	53	20.57	78	15.98
04	10.16	29	21.54	54	18.36	79	22.50
05	4.15	30	3.65	55	21.27	80	13.98
06	12.35	31	17.69	56	23.57	81	16.36
07	7.89	32	27.14	57	24.40	82	24.27
08	12.74	33	21.60	58	25.08	83	24.52
09	6.86	34	25.30	59	17.48	84	27.20
10	5.08	35	22.34	60	8.95	85	18.77
11	21.18	36	19.88	61	26.89	86	19.33
12	21.90	37	21.84	62	18.59	87	24.05
13	19.98	38	25.00	63	26.68	88	18.27
14	23.23	39	22.28	64	18.70	89	24.40
15	23.60	40	13.18	65	27.58	90	13.69
16	19.04	41	18.85	66	18.86	91	31.01
17	23.33	42	21.04	67	26.96	92	32.08
18	22.06	43	20.56	68	24.45	93	27.63
19	17.84	44	25.38	69	16.76	94	29.41
20	11.74	45	24.20	70	11.90	95	33.68
21	16.64	46	22.26	71	22.04	96	31.96
22	16.63	47	23.85	72	24.62	97	28.36
23	24.25	48	18.50	73	25.78	98	33.41
24	21.76	49	19.97	74	16.01	99	28.40

Total Value of 100 Vouchers: $1,995.34

Average Value of 100 Vouchers: $19.95

Taken with permission from "Statistical Sampling," by H. Justin Davidson, *The Quarterly* (Touche, Ross, Bailey & Smart), Vol. 8, no. 3, September 1962.

Table 3. Random Sample

Voucher	Amount
15	$ 23.60
77	19.93
18	22.06
08	12.74
16	19.04
54	18.36
95	33.68
22	16.63
69	16.76
75	19.28
	$202.08
Average:	$ 20.21

approximate the smooth curve shown in Figure 1. The normal distribution is extremely important in statistics, since it can be easily manipulated mathematically. The ease of mathematical manipulation is due to the fact that the shape of the normal distribution is completely defined by two quantities: the arithmetic mean and the standard deviation. Of course, the arithmetic mean is the sum of the values of the observations divided by the number of observations summed, and is expressed as $\bar{x} = (\Sigma x / n)$ and for theoretical distribution as $\mu = \Sigma \times P(x)$. The standard deviation is a sort of average of the deviations of the individual observations about their arithmetic mean and may be expressed as $\sigma = \sqrt{[\Sigma(x - \bar{x})^2 / n]}$ and for theoretical distributions as $\sigma = \sqrt{\Sigma(x - \mu)^2 \ P(x)}$.

The arithmetic mean and standard deviation define the shape of the normal distribution, since the equation for the normal distribution is:

$$y = \frac{1}{\sigma\sqrt{2\pi}} e^{-\frac{1}{2} \frac{(x - \mu)^2}{\sigma^2}}$$

where π and e are constants that we need not bother about. By use of this equation, tables have been compiled showing the area under the normal curve and the percentage of observations contained within any given distance measured from the arithmetic mean. A few of the more important of these areas are shown in Table 4.

The normal distribution has another remarkable property, stated in the so-called central-limit theorem. This law states that the distribution of sample estimates based on the mean and computed from random samples of a given size tend to follow the normal distribution.

What precisely does this law mean? Suppose we are sampling any particular universe with a specific sampling procedure. Suppose, also, that we repeat this sampling process many times, obtaining an estimate from each sample. If we then plot these many sample estimates in relative-frequency distribution form, we shall find that the sample estimates follow the normal distribution.

Figure 1.   Normal Distribution Curve.

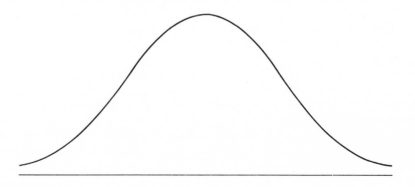

Table 4. Areas under Normal Curve

Distance from Arithmetic Mean $(x - \mu)$ in Terms of Standard Deviation (o) on Both Sides of the Mean $\dfrac{x - \mu}{o}$	Area under Normal Curve between u and x on Both Sides of μ
+1.00	63.26%
+1.65	90.00
+1.96	95.00
+2.58	99.00
+3.00	99.73

In addition, the standard deviation of the distribution of sample means is related to the standard deviation of the population being sampled, and can be calculated. Actually, the mathematical relationship is that the standard deviation of the distribution of sample arithmetic means—also called the *standard error of the arithmetic mean*— varies directly with the standard deviation of the parent population (σ) and inversely with the square root of the size of the sample (n). Its symbol is $o\bar{x}$ and the formula is:

$$o\bar{x} = \frac{\sigma}{\sqrt{n}}$$

Of course, in actually estimating the mean of the population, the auditor takes only one sample. He computes the arithmetic mean of the sample and finds the confidence interval by first deciding upon the confidence coefficient or reliability. If he decides to use 95 percent, his confidence interval will extend 1.96 $o\bar{x}$ on either side of the sample mean.

$$\text{Confidence limits} = \bar{x} \pm Z_r o\bar{x}$$

where Z_r is 1.96 when we seek to compute the 95 percent confidence interval. The symbol Z refers to the normal distribution and Z_r is the specific numerical value of Z associated with a particular confidence coefficient or reliability. Z_r is the number of standard deviations required on either side of the mean of a normal distribution for the required level of reliability r.

When the auditor has computed the confidence interval, he does not know whether it includes the true mean. He does know that if he were to repeat the procedure many times, he would obtain many intervals, and in the long run 95 percent of the intervals would encompass the true mean and 5 percent would not. He hopes that his one interval is one of the 95 percent and he acts as if it were. He knows that he may be wrong, but his is a calculated risk.

To illustrate, previously we selected ten vouchers randomly from a universe of 100 vouchers and calculated the mean of the sample to be $20.21. Suppose that the sample is drawn from a normal parent population known to have a standard deviation of $6.17. We can estimate the mean or average value of the 100 vouchers by computing a confidence interval based on the reliability of 95 percent.

We start by computing confidence limits using the formula:

$$\text{Confidence limits} = \bar{x} \pm Z_r \sigma \bar{x}$$

In this formula Zr is 1.96 since reliability has been specified to be 95 percent. Also, $\sigma \bar{x}$, the standard error of the arithmetic mean, is equal to $\sigma / \sqrt{n}$. Thus:

$$\text{Confidence limits} = \$20.21 \pm (1.96)\frac{(\$6.17)}{\sqrt{10}}$$

$$= \$20.21 \pm (1.96)(\$1.95)$$

$$= \$20.21 \pm \$3.83$$

$$\text{Confidence interval} = \$16.38 \text{ to } \$24.04$$

Thus the auditor can say that there is a 95 percent chance of the interval $16.38 to $24.04 containing the true value being estimated, or in this case, the average value of the 100 vouchers. Precision, in this example, is ± $3.83 or the interval about the sample mean. In this example, we did not specify any precision requirements.

Suppose the auditor was to specify a precision of $1.00. In this case the confidence interval would be $19.21 to $21.21 and we would compute the reliability as 39 percent or .51 standard deviation on both sides of the mean computed as follows:

$$Z_r \sigma \bar{x} = \text{Precision (one-half the confidence interval)}$$

$$Z_r \sigma \bar{x} = \$1.00, \text{ and since } \sigma \bar{x} = \$1.95 \text{ (as previously computed), then}$$

$$Z_r = \frac{1.00}{1.95} = .51 \text{ standard deviations on both sides of the mean.}$$

Going to a table of areas under the normal curve, we find that .51 standard deviations on each side of the mean include 19.5 percent of the area under the normal curve or 39 percent on both sides of the mean (see shaded area in Figure 2).

Figure 2. Normal curve showing area under curve .51 standard deviations on both sides of mean. .

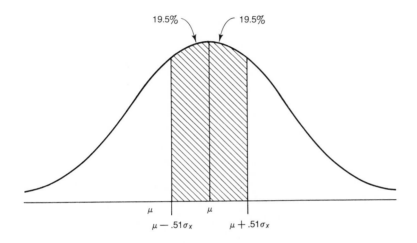

Similarly, if the required precision were ± $6.00, the reliability would be 99.8 percent Z_r = $6.00/$1.95 = 3.09 standard deviations on both sides of the mean). Thus, it can be noted that, for a given sample: (1) reliability increases as precision decreases or, conversely, (2) precision increases as reliability decreases. Thus, the accuracy of a sample estimate is measured by the interrelated statistical concepts of precision and reliability, both of which are calculated by using the sample data itself. In speaking of statistical accuracy, the terms precision and reliability must always be used together. Specifying the precision of an estimate does not mean anything unless the reliability is specified, and vice versa.

Controlling Sample Accuracy

Statistical sampling enables control of sample accuracy by adjustment of the sample size. The fact that control of sample accuracy is afforded by control of sample size can be seen by considering the formula for the population standard deviation:

$$\sigma\bar{x} = \frac{\sigma x}{\sqrt{n}}$$

This formula indicates the relationship of the standard error of the mean and the standard deviation of the population. In sampling practice, we generally do not know the value of the population standard deviation, and instead we must estimate it from the sample. This estimation can be expressed as:

$$S_{\bar{x}} = \frac{S_x}{\sqrt{n}}$$

We also know from the discussion of sample accuracy that the distribution of sample estimates, and therefore the precision and reliability, reflects the value of the standard error. From the equation $S_{\bar{x}} = S_x/\sqrt{n}$ we find that control of sample size is the primary means of controlling the value of the standard error. For as the sample size, n, increases, the value of the standard error, $S_{\bar{x}}$, decreases and vice versa. Thus, we can conclude that control of sample accuracy is afforded by control of sample size.

We can further express the relationship of the standard error, sample accuracy, and sample size by further considering the equation for precision of the sample estimate:

$$\text{Precision (P)} = Z_r \sigma\bar{x}$$

Substituting $S_{\bar{x}}$ for $\sigma\bar{x}$, we get

$$P = Z_r\, S_{\bar{x}}$$

where

P = the precision of the sample estimate (one-half the confidence interval);

Zr = the number of standard deviations necessary for the required level of reliability;

Sx = estimated value of the standard error of the mean.

We can relate this formula to sample size by substituting the expression for the estimated standard error, $S_{\bar{x}}$:

$$P = Z_r \ S_{\bar{x}}$$

$$= Z_r \ \frac{S_x}{\sqrt{n}}$$

With a specified sample accuracy, we can determine sample size as follows:

$$\sqrt{n} = Z_r \ S_x$$

$$n = \frac{(Z_r \ S_x)^2}{P^2}$$

Using the universe of 100 vouchers and estimating the population standard deviation to be $6.00, we can determine the required sample size to obtain a precision of $2.00 and reliability of 95 percent:

$$n = \frac{(1.96 \times \$6.00)^2}{(\$2.00)^2} = \frac{137}{4} = 34$$

To summarize, as the sample size increases:

1. Reliability increases if precision is held constant.
2. Precision increases if reliability is held constant.
3. Both precision and reliability increase.

Sampling Techniques

There are three basic sampling techniques: (1) estimation sampling, (2) acceptance sampling, and (3) discovery sampling. The technique to be used is determined by the objective of the audit procedure. The objective of an audit procedure must be explicit if statistical procedures are to be used.

Estimation Sampling

Estimation sampling is the most widely used sampling technique in auditing. This technique, as illustrated in our sample of vouchers, provides the auditor with an estimate of the frequency of an event in the universe or an estimate of an average or total value.

If the sample is used as a means of determining the frequency of occurrence of some kind of transaction or event, the approach is known as attributes sampling. Examples of attributes categories include the incidences of error versus correctness, missing documentation versus documentation that is present, improperly completed invoices versus properly completed invoices. Attributes sampling, then, is designed to answer how many, and the result of such a sampling operation is commonly expressed as the percent of the type of event specified.

Variables sampling, on the other hand, is designed to answer how much. Each observation, instead of being counted as a member of a certain category, provides a value which is totalled or averaged for the sample. Variables sampling would be used to estimate the dollar value of an inventory file, the average or total dollar value of errors of a certain type, or the total dollar value of certain expenses.

Acceptance Sampling

Acceptance sampling is a technique used to determine the effectiveness of internal controls or to verify the quality of clerical work. Generally speaking, it is more useful for the control of error than for the auditor's test purposes. When acceptance sampling is used, a sample of a given size is drawn by random sampling methods. The universe examined is considered acceptable if not more than that number of errors are found. Conversely, if more than that number are found, the universe is rejected as unacceptable.

This sampling technique provides only an accept or reject decision and provides no information as to how good or bad the universe is. This technique requires a precise advance decision as to the rate of error for which rejection is necessary. Such an advance decision is often difficult if not impossible for the auditor, since the rate of error existent must be considered in relation to other auditing techniques and procedures, some of which may not be accomplished at the time the decision is to be made.

Discovery sampling can be used when the auditor is interested in disclosing an irregularity which may be evidence of a fraud or flagrant violation of the system. With such a testing objective, the auditor must assure himself that if such situations do exist he will be reasonably sure of disclosing evidence to this effect in his test. The type of evidence required need be only one example of the irregularity. The one example would then be sufficient evidence to precipitate a broader test or detailed examination.

Discovery Sampling

The question to be answered in such a sampling situation is how big a sample will be required to give reasonable probability of disclosure. Tables, similar to those in Table 5, have been constructed through the use of probability theory, to show the sample size required to provide any degree of assurance that the sample will include at least one occurrence of the event sought, provided it occurs in the field with some minimum frequency or rate. Of course, such tables cannot be used with anything but random samples.

Each of these three techniques requires the auditor to use his best judgment as to: (1) the objective of the sampling process, (2) the required accuracy of the sample estimates, and (3) the variance existing in the universe. Once these factors are determined, it is necessary to calculate the number of items to be selected and to select the individual units to make up the sample. The computation of the appropriate sample size will depend on the sampling technique used. Appropriate sampling tables[3] are available, thus making unnecessary the computing of sample sizes in the majority of cases.

---

[3]Some of these tables are: R. G. Brown and L. L. Vance, *Sampling Tables for Estimating Error Rates or Other Proportions* Berkeley: University of California , 1961 H. F. Dodge and H. G. Roming, *Sampling Inspection Tables*, second edition New York: John Wiley & Sons, Inc., 1959 A. Hald, *Statistical Tables and Formulas* New York: John Wiley & Sons, Inc., 1952 Rand Corporation, *A Million Random Digits* Glencoe, Ill.: The Free Press, 1955.

Table 5. Probabilities of Including at Least One Occurrence in a Sample

For Random Samples Only

When Sample Size Is:	When Occurrence Rate is:						
	.05%	.1%	.5%	1%	2%	5%	10%
	Probability of Finding at Least One Occurrence Is:						
Field Size is 3,000							
10	0.5%	1.0%	4.9%	9.6%	18.3%	40.2%	65.2%
100	5.0	5.7	39.3	64.0	87.2	99.5	100.0
200	9.8	18.7	64.6	87.5	98.5	100.0	100.0
400	19.3	34.9	88.4	98.7	100.0	100.0	100.0
600	28.4	48.8	96.5	99.9	100.0	100.0	100.0
800	37.2	60.6	99.1	100.0	100.0	100.0	100.0
1,000	45.6	70.4	99.8	100.0	100.0	100.0	100.0
Field Size is 10,000							
100	4.9%	9.6%	39.6%	63.6%	86.9%		
200	9.6	18.3	63.7	86.9	98.3		
500	22.6	40.1	92.4	99.4	100.0		
1,000	41.0	65.1	99.5	100.0	100.0		
Field Size is 15,000							
100	4.9%	9.6%	39.5%	63.5%	86.8%		
200	9.6	18.2	63.4	86.8	98.3		
500	22.4	39.9	92.2	99.4	100.0		
1,000	40.4	64.5	64.5	100.0	100.0		
Field Size is 40,000							
100	4.9%	9.5%	39.5%	63.4%	86.8%		
200	9.6	18.2	63.4	86.7	98.3		
500	22.2	39.6	92.0	99.4	100.0		
1,000	39.7	63.7	99.4	100.0	100.0		
Field Size is 100,000							
100	4.9%	9.5%	39.4%	63.4%	86.8%		
200	9.5	18.2	63.3	86.7	98.2		
500	22.2	39.5	91.9	99.3	100.0		
1,000	39.5	63.4	99.3	100.0	100.0		

For a more detailed table, see Appendix J in Herbert Arkin, *Handbook of Sampling for Auditing and Accounting*, pp. 525–553.

Introduction to Readings

Systems review is initially concerned with an analysis of the structure and design of the system. The analysis of the system must be recorded in some way. The flow chart is an accurate and comprehensive way to record the procedures in existence, to highlight any system deficiencies, and to facilitate future reference to the system. The first article in the readings illustrates and explains the use of flow charts as an aid to analysis of the client's system and to recording findings in systematic fashion. It is recommended that the student work some flowcharting exercises to understand the advantages and disadvantages of flowcharting and some of the conventions and techniques of preparing flow charts. There are two flowcharting exercises in the problem material at the end of the chapter.

Many articles and, indeed, several books have been written on statistical sampling in auditing. We have selected two articles to complement and expand upon the material on statistical sampling in the chapter. Stettler's article, "Some Observations on Statistical Sampling in Auditing," has been selected because the author points out: (1) the limited usefulness of acceptance sampling and discovery sampling in making tests of transactions and (2) the nature and purpose of limited tests in evaluating internal control. Carmichael's article was written in response to Stettler's article and presents a different view of the usefulness of various sampling techniques. In our opinion, the major contribution of Carmichael's article is the classification of audit tests and the relationship between types of audit tests and techniques of estimation sampling, acceptance sampling, and discovery sampling.

Flow Charts
for Audit Purposes

Robert M. Rennie

Introduction

A fundamental requirement for the auditor in expressing a competent opinion of the credibility and fairness of financial statements is that he has sufficient knowledge—particularly from the point of view of internal control—of the accounting system which produced the information used in the statements. It is therefore essential, particularly because of the continuing nature of most audit engagements, that this knowledge of the system be recorded in such a way as to facilitate future reference and to highlight any system deficiencies.

The purpose of this article is to illustrate and explain the use of flow charts as an aid in the determination and evaluation of a client's accounting system, and as a means of recording

these findings in an orderly, concise and comprehensive manner. It should be clearly understood that flow charts and their related narratives are only a part, though an important one, of the information we must have in our files with respect to a client's accounting procedures and internal controls. They are not intended to be an elaborate or detailed systems study; their prime purpose is to assist the auditor in evaluating the client's accounting system as a means of producing satisfactory information for financial statement purposes.

The flow chart techniques used in this outline are not elaborate. Using six basic symbols, a simple but effective method is demonstrated of flow charting two major segments of an accounting system in a medium sized manufacturing company. The accounting procedures which are illustrated are not intended to be ideal but are used only as a means of showing how flow charts may be developed on an audit assignment. The following sections indicate some of the advantages and disadvantages of flow charts for audit purposes as well as outlining how the techniques may be applied.

Reprinted by permission from *The Quarterly* (Touche, Ross, Bailey & Smart), March 1965.

Authors' note: Since the preparation of this article, the United States of America Standards Institute (USASI) approved and published, in June 1966, a set of standard flow chart symbols. This standard set of symbols is provided as a supplement to this article.

Advantages

There are a number of advantages in the preparation of flow charts and they include the following:

Comprehensive Survey — Highlight Weaknesses. In order to prepare proper flow charts a *comprehensive survey* of the accounting functions must be made. The fact that information is incomplete or piecemeal is usually more evident when it is being recorded on flow charts rather than by some other means —for example in complete narrative form. In addition, because of their graphic nature, flow charts tend to indicate and highlight more clearly weaknesses or deficiencies in accounting systems and systems of internal control. This is one of the prime functions of flow charts for audit purposes and is sufficient in itself to justify their use.

Understand System. It enables the system to be more quickly understood by the members of the audit staff; the information is presented in a concise graphic manner which may be understood with minimum difficulty. This is particularly important where for various reasons members of the audit staff are being rotated. For larger clients it is often the most desirable way of acquiring an overall grasp of accounting procedures and the system of internal control.

Creates Interest. It creates more interest and enthusiasm on the part of the audit staff because they can better appreciate the functioning of the system and hence the reasons for our tests.

Recommendations for Improvements. It produces more valuable and more realistic recommendations to clients on internal controls and system efficiency because of the increased awareness by the audit staff of accounting systems and document flow.

Better Use of Audit Time. It emphasizes more forcibly those areas of the accounts which require more attention and therefore assists in a better budgeting and use of audit time.

Reduces Interference with Client's Staff. It fosters client's goodwill because new audit staff usually require less time for system orientation, and interference with client's staff is kept to a minimum.

Reduces Test Checking. It can result in a reduction in the volume of test checking. This may be achieved by (a) indicating certain areas where the internal controls are satisfactory and the volume of test checking could be reasonably reduced; or (b) by suggesting certain areas where it would be more appropriate to test in depth a lesser number of transactions instead of checking a greater volume in a superficial manner.

Disadvantages

In spite of the number of advantages which flow charts have for audit purposes, they do have several disadvantages:

Unusual Transactions Overlooked.
Flow charts are usually concerned with the normal type of transactions. Unusual transactions which are also of interest to the auditor may be overlooked. This is perhaps the most serious disadvantage that flow charts have from an audit point of view and it must be guarded against. One of the safeguards is an effective test of transactions which is designed to expose any unusual conditions which may exist and which are unacceptable deviations from normal procedures. However, there may be acceptable deviations from a procedure which are not practical to flow chart. These deviations should be indicated in a supplementary narrative to the flow chart as described in the following sections of this article. Such a record is necessary to prevent these acceptable deviations from being overlooked by the auditor in his review of the system in subsequent years.

Difficulties in Preparation.
Some auditors because of lack of familiarity or training in preparation of charts may not produce neat and intelligible flow charts in a reasonable length of time. This could be a serious shortcoming which would defeat the purpose of preparing flow charts. However, some brief instruction and subsequent practice in using the simple techniques described in this article should reduce this disadvantage to a minimum.

Changes in System.
Minor changes in the client's system may occasion the complete redrafting of certain of the charts. However, the same condition applies regardless of the method the auditor employs to record his review of the client's accounting procedures. In some cases involving a completely narrative type of system description, it could require a complete rewriting of a narrative with considerably more time involved.

The advantages, therefore, under normal circumstances far outweigh the disadvantages of using flow charts for audit purposes.

When To Use Flow Charts

The decision to use flow charts must rest with the partner in charge of the audit. Very small clients operating mainly on a cash basis would not normally require flow charts. Usually a brief narrative description would provide the necessary information. However, where a client has a number of accounting procedures requiring the use of various forms in each procedure, then the use of flow charts is recommended. In a medium-sized trading or manufacturing company the auditor should have on file flow charts for at least the following eight general areas. In the larger companies it may be necessary to have two or more flow charts in a particular area.

Sales
Accounts receivable

Receipts
Purchases
Payables
Payments
Payrolls
Inventory control

Generally speaking, the larger the client in terms of accounting paper flow and diversification of accounting procedures the more appropriate and useful are flow charts.

In summary, it is essential that we have adequate information in our files which outlines the client's accounting procedures and our opinion on the internal control. If this information is lacking the audit files are deficient, and flow charts are recommended to correct the deficiency.

Preparation of Charts

There are two stages in flow charting a client's accounting system. These are:

a. A preliminary survey
b. The preparation of the charts and supplementary narratives

Preliminary Survey. As the description implies, the preliminary survey involves the selection of a particular accounting procedure (for example, sales), determining the type of transaction involved in the procedure and then investigating and documenting the forms and methods which are used to record and account for the transactions. This may be achieved by the selection of a number of transactions—for example sales orders—and tracing them through the client's accounting system and obtaining any explanations necessary from the employees actually performing the work.

It is usually helpful to obtain blank copies of the forms in question, making whatever notes are necessary on the respective forms as to approvals, routing and other significant information. It is also helpful to draw very rough flow charts to show where documents are routed and where the internal control check points are. (An example of an internal control checkpoint is the balancing of subsidiary ledgers with control accounts.) The determination of internal control check points and whether or not they appear to be working, as evidenced by the test samples being used, is *extremely important*. Careful notes should be made in this area. An internal control questionnaire should be very useful during the preliminary survey.

The time required to complete a preliminary survey is dependent almost entirely on the size and complexity of the client's accounting procedures but it should be continued until the auditor is satisfied that he has sufficiently accurate information to prepare his flow charts and have a reasonable idea of the system of internal control.

Up to this point the auditor's approach to a system review for audit purposes is the same for any audit whether or not flow charts are used to document the results of the review.

Drawing Flow Charts. The flow charts which are presented for illustration in this article are divided into two main parts:

1. The chart
2. The supporting narrative

The preparation of the charts, using the information obtained in the preliminary survey, is relatively simple. However, the following points should be kept in mind:

1. The standard set of symbols used in the illustration should be used for sake of uniformity by our offices when charting non-EDP systems.

2. The arrangements of the departmental columns on the chart should be such that the direction of flow on the chart is from left to right as much as possible.

3. The description of the form should appear only once at the point of origin.

4. Avoid charting those copies of a form which are used for non-accounting purposes. These may be mentioned briefly in the narrative and the destination indicated.

5. The disposition of all forms on the chart *must be indicated*—at any stage a form can be either (1) filed or (2) used in another operation. This must be indicated in each and every case.

6. The consecutive number reference of each form on the flow chart should if possible follow the actual sequence of the form in the system. For example, a weekly payroll would precede the payroll summary and this should be indicated by the numerical sequence.

7. When a document originates in a department it should appear, where possible, in the departmental column above other documents coming into the department.

8. Where possible the operation to be performed should be indicated in the operation symbol. If the operation is lengthy, a numerical cross-reference to the supporting narrative may be made in the operation symbol and the narrative would then outline the procedure.

9. Do not crowd the chart—use enough space. If necessary a second sheet may be added to complete the flow charting of the procedure in question. The rough flow chart prepared in the preliminary survey will provide some idea of how much information is required on various portions of the chart.

10. If two flow lines for different forms intercept, the lines causing the interception should be broken by means of a half loop.

11. Every chart should have a title, showing the client's name and procedure as well as the person preparing the chart and the date it was prepared.

12. Use an eraser freely. You may find you erase more often than you write—even after long experience.

13. Use chart paper and template.

Supplementary Narrative. The supplementary narrative to the flow chart will, like the chart, be developed out of the information gathered during the preliminary survey of the system. This narrative is intended to supplement and *must not duplicate* information that is evident on the chart. The narrative should show for example the approvals required on various documents, the reasons for sending certain documents to a particular department (unless this is self evident) and any other information which cannot practically be placed on the chart but is essential for understanding the accounting system and the features of internal control.

In addition, the narrative should also show any exceptions which cannot be charted. For example, the chart may show that a reconciliation of certain information must be prepared at a particular point. If the items do not reconcile, the narrative should indicate what adjustment steps are necessary—the narrative should show particularly the name of the individual who investigates and approves the adjustment.

It is recommended that a concise outline of the major features of internal control in the accounting procedures be indicated in the narrative outline as well as any weaknesses which have been detected in the system review. This information on internal control is essential since it is the logical and necessary outcome of the system review and it supports our audit program.

If possible an estimate of the volume of paper processed per period (weeks, months, etc.) should be indicated for the respective accounting forms. This is significant for our audit test work as well as for possible suggestions for improving the system.

In summary then the following points should be observed when preparing a narrative supplement to a flow chart:

1. Be concise.
2. *Do not duplicate* information which is evident on the flow chart.

3. Deal with matters that are concerned primarily with the accounting system and the system of internal control.
4. Highlight the major features of internal control.
5. Outline any major weaknesses detected.
6. If possible estimate the volume of the respective forms—per period.

Conclusion

Flow charts are a simple and effective technique for recording in a clear, concise manner information which is essential for an efficient and productive audit. Their use is strongly recommended—

1. for the increased efficiency they can promote in our work,
2. as a means of highlighting weaknesses and deficiencies in a client's accounting system and
3. for the savings in time and money they can produce for us and our clients.

Appendix

Standard Flow Chart Symbols

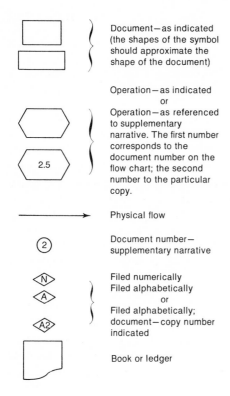

Document—as indicated (the shapes of the symbol should approximate the shape of the document)

Operation—as indicated
or
Operation—as referenced to supplementary narrative. The first number corresponds to the document number on the flow chart; the second number to the particular copy.

Physical flow

Document number—supplementary narrative

Filed numerically
Filed alphabetically
or
Filed alphabetically; document—copy number indicated

Book or ledger

Client: ABC Company Limited
Procedure: Weekly factory payroll
Chart No.: I
ACCOUNTING PROCEDURES
AND INTERNAL CONTROL

Accounting Procedures

Document Number
1. *Employment and rate authorization slip.*
All forms have rate authorized by personnel manager. Rate changes are by means of an approved rate change slip prepared in triplicate by personnel department; routing similar to original slip—300 employees—changes 10 per month.
2. *Deduction slips.*
Both copies signed by employee. Changes effected by new forms which are signed by employee (as above).
3. *Job time tickets.*
Prepared by employees daily for each job, including indirect labor. All tickets approved by shift foreman. This includes the approval of any overtime. On Friday of each week, factory cost clerks sort all tickets by employee number, review all tickets for foremen approval and general completeness. Tickets are batched and a duplicate adding machine tape is prepared of hours shown on time tickets; the original tape is sent with the batch to the time keeping department; duplicate tape is kept by factory cost clerk. Any differences in hours are investigated by time keeping department with factory superintendent who must approve any adjustments. Tickets are sorted after reconciliation into job number order—400 direct labor; 60 indirect labor tickets per week.

4. *Employee time cards.*

All factory employees are required to punch a time card. All punch clocks are at main door under surveillance of time keeper—300 per week.

5. *Time reconciliation report.*

Approved after completion by cost accountant.

6. *Labor distribution summary.*

Approved by factory superintendent; used for standard journal entry 15. (Debit work in process and indirect labor, credit payroll clearing.)

7. *Weekly payroll.*

Payroll sheets are reviewed and initialled by department foremen. A payroll accounting machine is used to prepare the payroll and this also produces the payroll checks and the payroll summary.

8. *Payroll summary.*

Prepared simultaneously with weekly payroll. Both copies are approved by the comptroller and the factory superintendent.

9. *Payroll voucher.*

Payroll voucher is approved by secretary-treasurer and is the basis for making a bank transfer from the general fund to payroll bank account. (Debit payroll clearing, credit withholding taxes, deductions, etc., general bank account.)

10. *Payroll checks.*

Payroll checks are prepared simultaneousl' with weekly payroll sheets and are signed by secretary-treasurer and comptroller. Checks are drawn on an imprest payroll bank account and are distributed on Wednesday of the week following the pay week. Checks are delivered by payroll accountant to the shift foremen on Wednesday morning and afternoon. Pay is distributed by shift foremen accompanied by a general accounting department employee. Unclaimed wages are returned to the payroll accounting department and after three days are deposited in payroll bank account—300 checks distributed per week.

Internal Control

Main Features. Internal control is satisfactory and the following are the main features:

1. There is a clear separation of duties between employees preparing payroll (payroll department), timekeeping (factory and timekeeping department) and distribution (foremen and general accounting staff). Occasional pay-offs are made on a surprise basis by the chief accountant on positive identification.

2. There is an internal check between two independent departments on hours and dollars—

Hours—time reconciliation summary for job time tickets in the factory and clock cards in timekeeping department.

Dollars—payroll clearing account in general ledger which records clearing entries from the cost department (labor distribution summary—journal entry 15) and accounts payable department (payroll voucher).

3. Authorizations are required for all rate changes, additions and separations.

4. Approvals are required for overtime (foremen)—payroll sheets examined and ini-

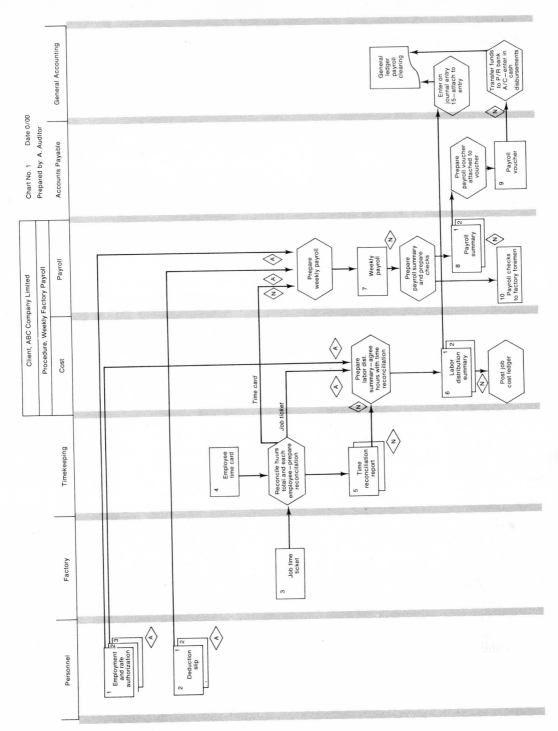

Figure 1. Weekly factory payroll procedures chart.

tialed (foremen)—and payroll summary is approved by comptroller and factory superintendent.

5. Time clocks are in use.

6. Employees paid by pre-numbered checks drawn on an imprest bank account which is reconciled monthly by an employee (general accounting clerk) unrelated to the payroll function. This clerk picks up checks and bank statements directly from bank. Reconciliation is reviewed and initialed by chief accountant.

7. Proper control is exercised over unclaimed wages, deductions from payrolls, old outstanding checks and blank checks.

8. All clerical work checked.

Weaknesses Noted in System. Our payroll examination has disclosed the following weaknesses (which have been reported to the client) and our audit procedures have been designed with these weaknesses in mind:

1. Missing approvals on labor distribution summaries and payroll summaries.

2. Several instances of unexplained differences between clock card hours and job ticket hours.

3. Missing foremen approvals on payroll sheets.

4. Delays in investigation of differences in general ledger clearing account.

Prepared by: A. Auditor
Date: October, 1964

Client: ABC Company Limited
Procedure: Sales (credit)
Chart No.: II
ACCOUNTING PROCEDURES
AND INTERNAL CONTROL

Accounting Procedures

Document Number

1. *Customer's order.*

The customer's mail request is attached to the original order. All customer's orders prenumbered and numbers are accounted for. Acceptance of order is indicated by department managers initialing form—volume 800 per week.

2. *Sales invoice and shipping set.*

Copy Number

Operation

2.1 Order acknowledgement—after acceptance.

2.2 Approved by the manager sales department as authorization for finished goods department to send goods to shipping department. Posted to material quantity control Kardex in finished goods department.

2.3 Approved for quantity and type of material by inventory control manager in finished goods department; sent with material to shipping department; shipping department must have this approved form before material is shipped.

2.4 Inventory turnover report.

2.5 Held as control over customer's orders awaiting shipment—regular follow up is made of orders delayed more than three days in absence of special instructions.

2.6 On receipt and comparison of completed shipping report document 3.1, copy 5 is sent to customer; and copy 6 with shipping report attached is entered on weekly billing summary and then sent to accounts receivable department for customer account posting.

2.7 Packing slip copy—held pending receipt of goods with copy 3—compared with copy 3 and packed with material—sent to customer.

2.8   File copy for sales order department.

All clerical operations are checked and the numbers of all sales invoice sets are accounted for in sales order department. Customer's order, shipping report and sales invoice numbers are correlated and numerically cross referenced. Billing department checks quantities, prices, extensions and terms before mailing invoice to customer. Billing department also accounts for the numerical sequence of sales invoice numbers. Delays longer than three days in receiving shipping report from shipping department are investigated by the billing department manager. Differences between quantities shipped (per shipping report) and customer's invoice are also investigated by billing department manager who must have sales manager's approval of any adjustments. Special terms or discounts must be authorized in writing by credit department with a copy to the billing department. Standard terms are 2% 10 days net 30 days—volume 800 per week.

3.   *Shipping report.*

The material to be shipped together with document 2.3 approved by the inventory control manager is received from the finished goods department. Document 27 is removed from pending file and agreed for quantity and type of material with form 2.3 and prenumbered shipping report is then prepared.

Copy Number

Operation

3.1   Local delivery—sent with goods to customer for signature as acknowledging receipt; returned by trucker to shipping department.

Out-of-town—copy of bill of lading attached by shipping department.

Attached and routed with document.

All numbers are accounted for. Any undue delays in receiving material for shipment (file of open packing slips document 2.7) are investigated by head shipper. Any differences in quantities or types of goods are investigated by head shipper. Differences require approval of both sales order and billing managers—volume 750 per week.

4.   *Billing summary—weekly.*

Summary approved by billing department manager.

5.   *Cost of Sales summary-weekly.*

Approved by cost accountant.

Internal Control

Main Features.   Internal control is satisfactory and the following are the main features:

1.   Approval of credit terms; approval and acceptance for quantity and type of merchandise.

2.   Department originating invoices is divorced from custodianship and record keeping.

3.   Goods are released only on receipt of approved orders (sales department approval to finished goods; finished goods department approval to shipping).

4.   Internal check points correlate sales order, sales invoice and shipping report.

5.   Independent accounting control over accounts receivable and inventory.

6.   All major documents prenumbered, cross referenced and numbers accounted for.

7.   Proper approval of all adjustments.

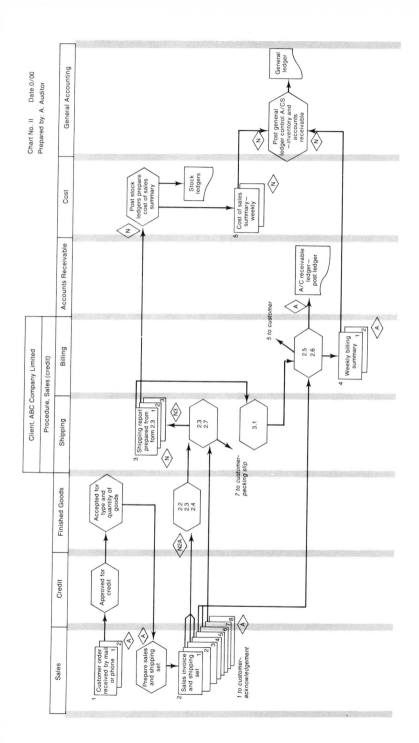

Figure 2. Sales–credit procedures chart.

Weaknesses Disclosed in the System.

A few minor weaknesses have been disclosed by our examination but they are isolated, infrequent, relatively unimportant and have been corrected. Our sales audit program therefore may be kept to a minimum.

Prepared by: A. Auditor
Date: October 1964.

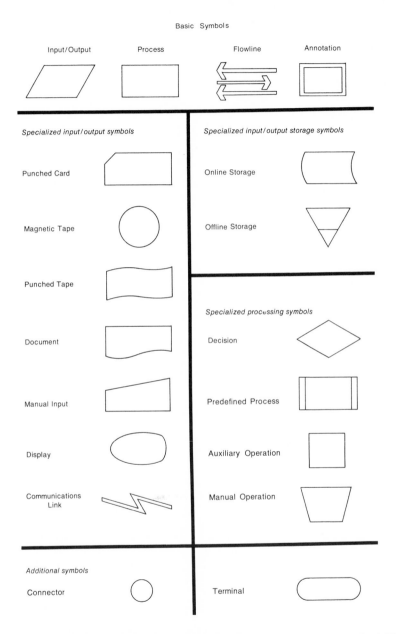

Summary of standard flowchart symbols (American National Standards Institute).

Basic Symbols

| Input/Output | Process | Flowline | Annotation |

Specialized input/output symbols

Punched Card

Magnetic Tape

Punched Tape

Document

Manual Input

Display

Communications Link

Specialized input/output storage symbols

Online Storage

Offline Storage

Specialized processing symbols

Decision

Predefined Process

Auxiliary Operation

Manual Operation

Additional symbols

Connector

Terminal

Source: Section 5, "Summary of Flowchart Symbols," from USA Standard X3.5–1966, *Flow Chart Symbols for Information Processing*, p. 9.

Basic   Symbols

Symbol	Description and Use

Connected to flowchart where meaningful

Annotation Symbol — *For added comments*

Console Switch Should be Off

Test SW 1

Flowline Symbol — *To show flow of work. Normal flow is from right to left and from top to bottom. Arrowheads must be used if flow direction is not normal. Otherwise, arrowheads are optional.*

Process Symbol — *Represents an operation or group of operations*

Compute Payroll Tax

Card to Tape Conversion

Basic Input/Output Symbol — *Represents the input of information for processing or the output (recording) of processed information*

Read Payroll Data

Print Reports

Specialized input/output symbols

Symbol	Description and Use

Punched Card Symbol — *Represents input/output using any kind of punched card*

Commission Data

Magnetic Tape Symbol — *Input/output using magnetic tape*

Transactions

Master File

Update Master File

Up-dated Master File

Punched Tape Symbol — *Input/output using punched paper tape*

Sales

Paper Tape to Magnetic Tape Conversion

Sales

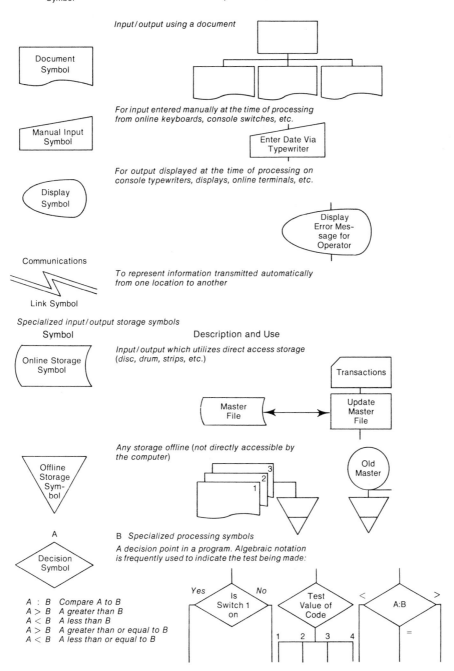

Symbol | Description and Use

Document Symbol

Input/output using a document

Manual Input Symbol

For input entered manually at the time of processing from online keyboards, console switches, etc.

Enter Date Via Typewriter

Display Symbol

For output displayed at the time of processing on console typewriters, displays, online terminals, etc.

Display Error Message for Operator

Communications

To represent information transmitted automatically from one location to another

Link Symbol

Specialized input/output storage symbols

Symbol | Description and Use

Online Storage Symbol

Input/output which utilizes direct access storage (disc, drum, strips, etc.)

Transactions

Master File ◄──────► Update Master File

Offline Storage Symbol

Any storage offline (not directly accessible by the computer)

3
2
1

Old Master

A

Decision Symbol

B *Specialized processing symbols*

A decision point in a program. Algebraic notation is frequently used to indicate the test being made:

A : B   Compare A to B
A > B   A greater than B
A < B   A less than B
A > B   A greater than or equal to B
A < B   A less than or equal to B

Yes / No
Is Switch 1 on

Test Value of Code
1 2 3 4

< / >
A:B
=

Symbol	Description and Use

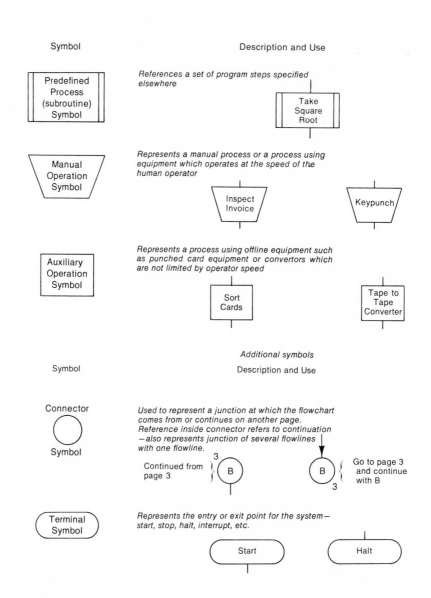

Predefined Process (subroutine) Symbol — *References a set of program steps specified elsewhere* — Take Square Root

Manual Operation Symbol — *Represents a manual process or a process using equipment which operates at the speed of the human operator* — Inspect Invoice — Keypunch

Auxiliary Operation Symbol — *Represents a process using offline equipment such as punched card equipment or convertors which are not limited by operator speed* — Sort Cards — Tape to Tape Converter

Additional symbols

Symbol	Description and Use

Connector Symbol — *Used to represent a junction at which the flowchart comes from or continues on another page. Reference inside connector refers to continuation —also represents junction of several flowlines with one flowline.* — Continued from page 3 } B (3) — B } Go to page 3 and continue with B (3)

Terminal Symbol — *Represents the entry or exit point for the system— start, stop, halt, interrupt, etc.* — Start — Halt

Some Observations on Statistical Sampling in Auditing

Howard F. Stettler

The professional literature refers most frequently to three types of statistical sampling: acceptance sampling, discovery sampling and estimation sampling. The first two types can be effectively used only in sampling for what statisticians commonly refer to as "attributes." In auditing applications, these attributes will be whether a document has been processed correctly or incorrectly, or whether a transaction has been recorded correctly or incorrectly. Tests of transactions to arrive at a conclusion concerning compliance with a client's plan of internal control represent the most common application of sampling for attributes. The client's records are "accepted" if the number of defectives (errors) disclosed in the test does not exceed the number specified by the sampling plan—usually zero defectives, if the sample size is kept to a minimum.

Sampling for variables can be best handled by the use of statistical estimation, the variables typically being such items as the

Reprinted by permission from *The Journal of Accountancy*, April 1966. Copyrighted 1966 by the American Institute of Certified Public Accountants.

amounts of individual accounts receivable or the cost extensions for goods in inventory. A sample of the variables is "blown up" to arrive at an estimate of the total dollars represented by the class of items being sampled. Statistical estimation can also be utilized in attribute sampling to develop an indication of the proportion of defectives in the population.

A Caveat about Sampling Results

Sampling is intended to reveal information about a population of items by examining only a portion of the items in the population. A common assumption is that sampling yields positive information about the population, when in fact it can only yield negative conclusions. Thus a sample will *not* reveal the exact percentage of defective vouchers in a population consisting of all vouchers prepared during a year's time. (Assume that a defective voucher is being defined as one not containing the initials of a person who is expected to determine that prices on the supporting vendor's invoices agree with those on the related purchase order. A voucher could be defective for other reasons as well.) What the sample *will* do, if the number of defectives disclosed by the sample is equal to or less than the number specified by an acceptance sampling table, is tell the auditor that he can accept the population, with a stated amount of confidence, as *not having more* than a stated percentage of such defectives.

For example, the auditor may seek 95% confidence that the percentage of defective vouchers in the population does not exceed 2%. The sampling table in "A Simple Tool to Assist the Auditor in Statistical Interpretation of Test Checks," by the author in the January 1954 *Journal of Accountancy* (page 57), specifies a sample of 150 items with no defectives in the sample to give the results specified. Note, however, that the sample of 150 with zero defectives provides no basis for concluding that the population as a whole contains zero defectives, which would be a positive conclusion about the population. Instead, the only statement that can be made about the population (and the statement is a very useful one) is the negative conclusion that the sample affords 95% confidence that the percentage of defectives in the population *does not exceed* 2%.

The difference between defects appearing in the sample and the maximum percentage specified in arriving at the sample size is the *precision* of the estimate. The precision of the estimate can be improved by increasing the size of the sample. If the sample is increased to 300, with no defectives appearing in the sample, the precision changes from 2% to 1% with 95% confidence. Hence there is then 95% confidence

that the defectives in the population do not exceed 1%, a more precise statement about what the population is not.

The approach just discussed may be referred to as a "one-sided" test, for it is concerned only with the single question of confidence that the population contains no *more* than a stated percentage of defectives. To accept the population on the stated basis, the sample must reveal no defectives or, for larger sample sizes, only a very limited number of defectives. Such a sample is likely to be obtained only if the population is substantially better than the specified maximum percentage of defectives. A sample of 200 revealing 4 defectives (2%) suggests a probable error rate of about 2%, but the caveat still applies that a sample offers no basis for a precise statement about what the population *is*. What the sample does offer is a basis for saying something about what the population *is not*. Based on the same table previously referred to, we can have 97% confidence that the error rate does not exceed 5%. We can also have 95% confidence that the error rate is not less than 1%, for we would only rarely obtain samples of 200 containing as many as 4 defectives from a population containing less than 1% defectives. Here we are in effect using our sample in a two-sided test, giving further indication of what the population *is not*: it is *no better* than 1% (95% confidence) and it is *no worse* than 5% (97% confidence). Thus in sampling we must disregard the urging of the once-popular song to "accentuate the positive; eliminate the negative" and, instead, place all our emphasis on the negative.

The same observations apply to conclusions based on estimation sampling. Assume the following facts:

10,000 individual accounts receivable

$25 standard deviation of the population of accounts receivable balances

625 accounts selected for positive confirmation

$98 mean of confirmed balances for 625 accounts

Based on the $98 mean calculated from the sample of 625 accounts, it would appear reasonable to estimate the total accounts receivable at 10,000 x $98 or $980,000. Actually, however, given the facts as stated above, the only appropriate statement to be made is the negative one that, with 95% confidence, the total of the receivables is not less than $960,000 and not more than $1 million.[1]

Precision is again a factor in the results, and in this case would be stated as $20,000 of the total calculated from the sample mean. A larger sample size would give better precision (less than $20,000) or greater confidence based on the same precision of $20,000; a smaller sample size would give less precision (more than $20,000), or less confidence based on the same precision.

Discovery Sampling: a Delusion

Discovery sampling has been presented as a means of discovering at least one defective item in a population if defective items are present in excess of some stated percentage, thus giving the opportunity for the auditor to see an example of any serious breakdown of internal control or any evidence of fraud. A likely first impression on encountering the term is that discovery sampling holds the answer to discovering the "needle in the haystack"; i.e.,

the rare item in a population. The point that is easily overlooked is that the defective is likely to appear in a given size sample only if the defectives in the population exceed some stated percentage. Hence, what is "discovered" if a defective appears in the sample is not a rare item but rather an indication that the population may contain a percentage of defectives in excess of what the auditor is willing to tolerate: the maximum percentage that the auditor specified in order to determine the size of the sample to be taken, based on a confidence level that must also be specified.

On further examination, discovery sampling turns out to be little more than a different way of looking at the results of an acceptance sampling plan such as has already been discussed. Thus, with a sample of 150 specified to give 95% confidence that the percentage of defectives in the population does not exceed 2%, the presence of one or more defectives in the sample indicates that the population cannot be accepted, and the auditor has achieved the specified result of finding at least one of the defectives because the population may have more than 2% defectives.

---

[1] Standard deviation of sample means:

$$\frac{\text{Standard deviation of population}}{\sqrt{\text{Sample size}}}$$

Standard deviation of sample means:

$$\frac{25}{\sqrt{625}} = \frac{25}{25} = 1.00$$

Two standard deviations of the sample means would encompass 95% (approximately) of all sample means.

Hence, from a population whose mean is 96, only 2½% of samples of 625 would exceed a mean of 98, and for a population whose mean is 100, only 2½% of the samples of 625 would be less than a mean of 98, or 95% confidence that a sample mean of 98 came from a population whose mean was no less than 96 and no greater than 100.

Limited Usefulness
of Acceptance Sampling

Present day auditing relies heavily on a client's system of internal control to produce figures that fairly reflect the client's financial position and results of operations. The final figures are independently tested by such procedures as accounts receivable confirmation or inventory test counts. For very large clients with good internal control, the extent of receivable confirmation or inventory count tests in relation to the population being sampled suggests that the purpose may not be to provide information directly about the reasonableness of the total being tested, but rather to ascertain the efficacy of the client's internal control. By implication, auditors thereby place almost complete reliance on the client's system of internal control to produce acceptable figures when the verification of balances is limited to samples of nominal size.

It is commonly assumed that tests of transactions must be made to give assurance of compliance with the stated plan of internal control, and acceptance sampling is generally proposed as an effective means of satisfying the auditor of compliance with the client's internal control. Two objections can be raised, however, to such use of acceptance sampling.

First, it is extremely difficult, if not impossible, to set a meaningful maximum for the percentage of defectives that can be tolerated in the population being sampled. For example, at what point would it be assumed that material differences might exist in resulting figures for inventory, cost of sales and accounts payable if some vouchers are not initialed to show that receiving report quantities agree with the quantities invoiced and paid for? Would it be missing initials on 10% of the vouchers, or 40%, or even 100%?

The answer would have to depend largely on other internal controls present in the system: primarily, internal control over the year-end physical inventory and the maintenance of a book perpetual inventory. If the year-end physical inventory has been accurately taken, and if the difference between the book inventory and physical inventory is a reasonable figure, then even complete absence of initials evidencing the comparison of receiving report quantities and invoice quantities would seem to have had little effect on the client's figures. Consequently, there seems to be little or no reason to test the stated internal control over purchases and disbursements, or any other internal controls related to that area.

A better approach than testing transactions to ascertain compliance with internal controls is to ascertain what controls exist to give assurance that the basic internal controls are being followed. The development of differences between book and physical inventory figures is one such control. Others are the review and approval of invoices by a person who checks to see that all other required initials have been inscribed, tests by an internal audit staff, the existence of procedures manuals and written job descriptions that spell out each employee's responsibilities, and personnel selection and review procedures that assure a competent employee work force. In a computer-based system there may be many additional programed controls to test the validity and accuracy of input to the system and the appropriate processing within the computer.

Utopia at Last, or the Magic Sample of One

Given that a client's internal control looks good on paper, and that there is an indication of adequate controls over the controls, the auditor will still wish to know that he is not dealing with an imaginary empire that exists only on paper. Here it becomes necessary to ascertain that there are real ledgers, journals, documents, assets, and liabilities and that the procedures described to the auditor are actual procedures that are in effect. And it is here that the "magic sample of one" comes into its own. Even Noah had to obtain two of each kind, but one of each kind of transaction should be adequate for the auditor when the added support of good control over internal control is present!

What the proposal of a sample of one boils down to is that what is sometimes referred to as a "walkthrough" of one of each kind of transaction should suffice for the test of transactions. The walkthrough of a transaction involves following it from beginning to end, to show that each step in the procedures stated by the client as being in effect is actually being followed. For purchasing procedures the walkthrough would begin with the creation of the purchase order and extend through the writing and mailing of the check for payment to the reconciliation of the bank account against which the check was drawn. Other types of disbursements should similarly be subjected to walkthroughs, such as the reimbursement of petty cash funds, the payment for services such as utilities, and the payment for the acquisition of plant assets subject to capital budget appropriations and finance committee authorization.

Another way to look at such walkthroughs has been suggested by Gregory M. Boni of Touche, Ross, Bailey & Smart in a seminar on auditing EDP systems recently conducted by his firm for a group of college professors. Boni considers the walkthrough not as a test of the operation of a client's system, but rather as a means of assuring that effective communication with clear understanding has taken place between the auditor and the client's employees being questioned about company procedures. Thus, if the auditor asks whether prices on a vendor's invoice are compared with prices on the related purchase order, the auditor may be more certain that the employee understood his question and that the auditor understood the answer if follow-up of a selected transaction shows that (a) the audit block placed on the invoice contains a statement, "Prices charged agree with purchase order," (b) the employee's initials appear in the box that follows the statement, and (c) the related purchase order is attached to the invoice. Failure of the employee to make the stated comparison in every instance, or failure of the employee to detect existing discrepancies, need not concern the auditor if other controls exist to give assurance that the work was actually performed as prescribed.

Similar questions must be asked of a computer system, with the auditor taking a variety of samples of one by means of a "test deck" of hypothetical situations and asking how such input containing known exceptions is actually processed by the computer. The questions are "asked" by processing the test deck under the client's existing computer program (the equivalent of the employee who is questioned when manual procedures are involved) to see whether the program contains the necessary steps to recognize and report out such exceptions as an invalid account number, an employee's pay amount that would exceed a stated maximum, or a customer order that should be rejected because the customer's credit limit would be exceeded or because payments on past purchases are delinquent. The important point here is that a sample of one is taken of each different situation that the computer program is supposed to recognize and treat as an exception; each sample of one in effect "asks" the computer program what it actually does in the specified situation, in support of what an analysis of the client's program flow chart shows is supposed to be done.

If the test of one of each type of situation shows that the auditor's "question" was understood and the stated program check was actually incorporated in the program and functioning, the auditor relies on other controls, such as records of program changes during the year, to satisfy himself that the stated checking was being done throughout the year. The auditor also has the results of his balances verification work to further indicate whether the system was functioning effectively throughout the year.

Sampling when Internal Control Is Deficient

If tests of transactions are based on statistical measures, presumably the following guideline set down by the AICPA committee on statistical sampling applies: "Since samples taken for this purpose (to test compliance with internal control) are intended to provide a basis for relying on compliance with internal control procedures, the committee believes they should be evaluated at a reliability level the auditor considers reasonable in the light of factors other than the procedures themselves."[2] The committee does not identify the other factors, but second-level internal control over the internal control of the procedures being tested would seem to be one such factor. If such overall controls are good, reliability can apparently be set below the 90% to 95% range customarily used, and perhaps even 50% reliability would be reasonable in a test of transactions, thereby reducing sample size.

By contrast, it is my contention that the auditor may properly ignore the question of sample reliability when adequate controls over internal control are present, reducing reliability practically to zero, so that only one of each type of item need be tested. On the other hand, if internal control is deficient, the auditor's modification of his examination should not be in the direction of increasing sample size for his tests of transactions to achieve increased reliability for his conclusions about compliance with the system of internal control. The sample of one of each type of transaction should suffice to indicate that the system such as it is, is operative, and a larger sample that would disclose the extent of compliance helps very little in assessing the fairness or propriety of the account balances produced by the system.

It is in the tests of the balances themselves against verifiable supporting evidence that the auditor must expand his sample to achieve increased reliability. Also, if internal control borders on the nonexistent, then the tests of balances may have to be supplemented by tests

[2]"Relationship of Statistical Sampling to Generally Accepted Auditing Standards," a special report by the AICPA committee on statistical sampling, *The Journal of Accountancy*, July 1964, p. 56.

of the transactions that developed those balances to gain additional evidence of the credibility of the balances. In that case, the tests of transactions are not made to ascertain compliance with internal controls, but to gain direct support of the validity of the balances themselves.

Estimation Sampling for Tests of Balances

The preceding discussion brings us to the conclusion that estimation sampling is perhaps the only statistical sampling approach that is valid and useful for auditing purposes. The application of estimation sampling to tests of account balances is not, however, the normal type of application for this form of sampling. Ordinarily under estimation sampling little is known about the population being sampled and the sample is "blown up" to arrive at an estimate of the total variables in the population. The design of the sample affords some stated confidence that the estimate is accurate within a range of precision specified in the design of the sample.

An auditor, however, usually has a control balance or other total previously determined by the client that indicates what the total of the population is supposed to be. The sampling approach may then be considered as a test of the hypothesis that the sample taken could in fact have come from a population whose total is as represented by the client.

The statement has been made earlier that the auditor seeks to determine not what a population is, but what it is not. In applying estimation sampling under this concept, the objective is not to estimate the total of the population, but rather to gain a certain amount of assurance that the total of the population is no less than some figure that is not materially less than the client's total, and no more than a larger figure that is not materially greater than the client's total. Clearly this approach to estimation sampling requires the auditor to come to grips with the very elusive question of what is a material difference. Unlike the usual case, where the auditor evaluates a given difference and decides whether the difference is or is not material, here he must carry the matter of materiality to its extremes, and state rather precisely and in advance the maximum difference that would not be material in the given situation.

An Application of Estimation Sampling

Here we may return to the example of estimation sampling given earlier dealing with accounts receivable. Note that if account balances are being sampled on the basis of confirmation results, there is no need to prove a trial balance as would be true in the usual auditing application, an important saving of the auditor's time.

We will assume that the client's control account for receivables has a balance of $1 million, that we have counted, or estimated by a test count, the number of ledger cards to be 10,000, and that further we have made the necessary estimate of the standard deviation of the population,[3] and have found it to be $25.

---

[3] A simple way to estimate the standard deviation is to select 49 balances at random, divide these into seven groups each containing seven items, calculate the dollar range between the highest and lowest balance for each group, calculate the mean of these seven ranges and divide the mean by 2.704.

To calculate the size of the sample to be taken, we must specify the confidence desired from our sample, which we will assume to be 95%—a reasonable confidence level for most audit samples. Finally, we must set the minimum and maximum amounts by which the receivable total might differ from $1 million without the difference being material; i.e., without having to insist that the client change the $1 million figure in the financial statements or, alternatively, to insist that the client agree to a qualification or disclaimer of opinion. We will set the extremes at $900,000 and $1,100,-000, or $1,000,000 ± $100,000.

In proceeding to the next step, we must recognize that if repeated samples of a given size are taken from a population, the means of those samples if plotted will form a normal curve, and the sample means will be evenly distributed on either side of the true mean of the population. The standard deviation of the curve of the sample means will vary inversely with the size of the samples taken, because as larger samples are taken the effect of extreme values appearing in a sample is submerged, and there will be less variability in sample means from one sample to the next.

The relationship of sample size, standard deviation of the population and standard deviation of the sample means is expressed by the formula given earlier, which can be transposed to read:

$$\frac{\text{sample}}{\text{size}} = \frac{(\text{standard deviation of the population})^2}{(\text{standard deviation of sample means})^2}$$

All that is necessary, then, to compute sample size is to set the standard deviation we seek for the sample means.

Here, let us consider the significance of possible sample means of $95 and $105, and let us assume that the sample size is such that

if the true value of our population is actually $1 million, 95% of our sample means would fall within the range of $95 and $105. There would then be some possibility, although slight, that we might draw a sample with a mean of $95. Actually, however, we do not in fact know that the true value of the population is $1 million, but even if the true value of the population were only $900,000 there would be an equally slight likelihood of drawing a sample with a mean of $95 from such a population as from a population of $1 million. The same reasoning applies to the possible sample mean of $105, and an equally slight likelihood of the sample being drawn from a population of $1 million or $1,-100,000. What has just been said may be shown graphically as in Figure 1.

We are seeking a sample size such that if repeated samples were drawn, the curves would appear as shown if the populations from which the samples were drawn were $900,000, $1 million and $1,100,000, with corresponding population means of $90, $100, and $110. The curves have been specified as containing 95% of all sample means within ± $5 of the true mean of the population, which turns out to be approximately two standard deviations. That being so, the value of one standard deviation must be $2.50, and this value can be substituted in the preceding formula, giving a sample size of 100.

Thus, when the sample of 100 is drawn, if the mean of that sample lies between $95 and $105, the auditor can state with 95% confidence that the true value of the accounts receivable is not less than $900,000 and not greater than $1,100,000. The reader should note that in the original example given earlier a sample of 625 accounts was stated to give precision of ± $20,-000; by contrast, if precision requirements are relaxed to ± $100,000 as above, the sample size is reduced to 100 accounts.

Summary

The major contentions that have been set forth are:

1. There is little justification for using either acceptance sampling or discovery sampling in making tests of transactions.

2. A sample of one of each type of transaction should constitute an adequate test of transactions.

3. When internal control is too weak to permit acceptance of account balances at face value as having been appropriately determined, tests of balances must be expanded to give increased reliability as a partial substitute for internal control.

4. A properly designed estimation sampling test of an account balance does not reveal what the balance is, but only a stated confidence in what the balance is not.

Figure 1. Distribution of sample means in repeated samples from populations with means of $90, $100, and $110.

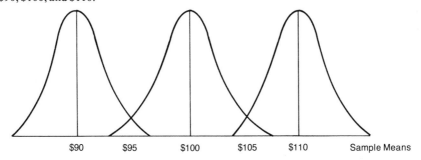

Tests of Transactions—
Statistical
and Otherwise

D. R. Carmichael

Statistical sampling is gaining increased acceptance as an audit tool. While much atten-

tion has been devoted to the characteristics of statistical sampling, sufficient attention has not been given to an integration of the characteristics of audit tests and statistical tests. In a previous article published in *The Journal of*

Reprinted by permission from *The Journal of Accountacy*, February 1968, Copyrighted 1968 by the American Institute of Certified Public Accountants.

Accountancy,[1] for example, Howard F. Stettler explained the meaning and relative merits of three approaches to statistical sampling: acceptance sampling, discovery sampling and estimation sampling. Although he presented a lucid explanation of these three sampling approaches, his explanation of "tests of transactions" was not equally clear. In fact, there was inadequate recognition of the different types of tests made by auditors. His conclusions appear valid for one type of test, but not for all.

Types of Audit Tests

There are three types of audit tests, classified in terms of their usually recognized objectives:

1. Those which provide the auditor with *prima facie* evidence of the existence and implementation of a system of internal control through observation and inquiry, and testing —usually of selected items from their inception through ultimate disposition.
2. Tests of items in quantities sufficient to obtain assurance that the functioning of the system of internal control is as planned and that the results of an examination of a portion of data are representative of the whole. These tests usually have the dual purpose of procedural tests and tests of *bona fides.*
3. Examination of especially significant items as to which the auditor may feel it necessary to require substantial assurance based on

external evidence or detailed verification procedures.[2]

These three types of tests will be referred to, respectively, as:

1. Single-purpose tests
2. Dual-purpose tests
3. Tests of *bona fides.*

It is submitted that the adequacy of the size of the sample of transactions is dependent upon the type of test, which, in turn, is dependent upon the objective of the auditor. Before the reasoning underlying this contention can be explained, the exact nature of each type of test should be clarified.

Single-purpose tests are audit tests designed solely to determine the existence of internal control procedures. The single-purpose test of transactions is frequently referred to as a "walkthrough." Such tests take the form of:

. . . following typical transactions through from cradle to grave or, if one prefers, from grave to cradle. That is, in the first section, a few sales orders would be selected, traced to other copies of these same documents along the way, checked to shipping records, thence to corresponding sales invoices, their various copies, and ultimately to the sales journal and accounts receivable ledger. All along the way the auditor should discuss with each employee involved what his procedures are

[1]Howard F. Stettler, "Some Observations on Statistical Sampling in Auditing," *The Journal of Accountancy,* Vol. 121, April 1966, pp. 55–60.

[2]Francis J. Schaefer, "Statistical Sampling—An Audit Tool," *The New York Certified Public Accountant,* Vol. 33 (November 1963), p. 777. For a similar analysis of types of audit tests see Charles T. Steele, "An Auditor Samples Statistics," *The Journal of Accountancy,* Vol. 114, Sept. 1962, p. 52.

with these documents, where he received and sends them, and what his approvals mean.[3]

A test of *bona fides* involves the direct verification of the balance of a specific account, usually by examination of evidence external to the internal control system. The comparison of the quantity of cash on hand, determined by a physical count, with the balance in the cash account is an example of a test of *bona fides*. This type of test is primarily applicable to the verification of assets and liabilities. However, a few revenue and expense accounts can be supported in this manner; e.g., verification of dividends by reference to independent reporting services.

Dual-purpose tests have characteristics of both single-purpose tests and tests of *bona fides*. They are tests which serve the dual purpose of providing assurance as to the effective functioning of the internal control system and of providing a degree of assurance as to the *bona fides* of the transactions supporting an account balance.

The three types of tests can be viewed as a continuum. Tests designed solely to determine the existence of internal control procedures—single-purpose tests—and tests designed solely to determine the integrity of the account balances—tests of *bona fides*—are the polar positions on the continuum of audit tests. Dual-purpose tests lie all along the continuum between the two polar positions. In fact, most of the auditor's tests are in the dual-purpose range.

Whether dual-purpose tests will lie closer to single-purpose tests or closer to tests of *bona fides* will depend on the intent of the auditor. The auditor may consider the tests to be ex-

aminations of internal control, although they are generally associated with determining the validity of account balances, or vice versa. The form of a test may resemble a test of *bona fides*, but the primary purpose may be to test internal control; e.g., interim confirmation of a sample of accounts receivable. Conversely, although the form of a given test may resemble a test of transactions, the purpose may be to add to the validity of an account balance when there is an internal control weakness; e.g., the tracing of book receipts to bank deposits as shown by the cutoff bank statement at year-end.

Since a test of transactions may be either a single-purpose test or a dual-purpose test, Professor Stettler's conclusion that "a sample of one of each type of transaction should constitute an adequate test of transactions"[4] must be examined with respect to both types of tests.

Sample Size for Single-Purpose Tests

Single-purpose tests are used only in the review of internal control. By reviewing the procedure manual, chart of accounts and systems department memorandums, and by discussing the system with the controller or chief accountant, the auditor can gather the preliminary information on internal control. This inquiry, however, is not sufficient to establish the existence of internal control procedures. Procedure manuals may be out of date or lacking in necessary detail; in addition, officials may be unaware of modifications of procedures

---

[3]R. J. Anderson, "Analytical Auditing," *The Canadian Chartered Accountant*, Vol. 83, November 1963, p. 323.

[4]Stettler, *op. cit.*, p. 60.

made by operating personnel. It is at this point that single-purpose tests of transactions are necessary.

In applying single-purpose tests of transactions, the auditor traces each type of transaction from initiation to ultimate disposition. He discusses the procedures with the employee who performs them; he examines all documents on or related to the transaction he is tracing; and he notes any deviations from standard company procedure and any weaknesses in the procedures in effect.

The objective of this single-purpose test of transactions is to determine whether the internal control procedures which are supposed to be in effect are, in fact, in effect. The objective is not to determine if these procedures are in effect and functioning an acceptable percentage of the time.

Given the objective of single-purpose tests of transactions, Professor Stettler's conclusion is sound. A limited test of transactions will suffice because the auditor's objective does not include making valid statistical inferences about the population of all transactions of a given type.

The suggestion that single-purpose tests of transactions should be restricted to one of each type has merit. It cautions the auditor to avoid over-testing. A sample of 20 or 30 would generally be too small to establish the extent of compliance with procedures but would be far more than would be necessary to establish the existence of procedures.

The applicability of Professor Stettler's conclusion to dual-purpose tests of transactions is a separate issue. There are several differences between the two types of tests which must be made clear.

Sample Size for Dual-Purpose Tests

One difference between dual-purpose tests and single-purpose tests is their timing. Dual-purpose tests follow single-purpose tests. The extent of dual-purpose tests is usually based on the apparent weaknesses in the internal control system which was diagnosed on the basis of the single-purpose tests.

In addition, single-purpose tests of transactions differ from dual-purpose tests of transactions in their inclusiveness and direction. Dual-purpose tests of transactions are generally less inclusive. The example cited in the explanation of a walkthrough proceeds from inception, sales order, to final disposition, sales journal and accounts receivable ledger. Emphasis is placed on the auditor's concern with all the documents and procedures along the path of the transaction. A dual-purpose test of transactions will, however, usually focus on the compliance with a specific procedure where an internal control weakness was found to be present. Shipping records, for example, may be traced to the accounts receivable ledger to assure the validity of the inference that an acceptable percentage of the orders shipped were billed. The direction of dual-purpose tests of transactions will be selected to meet a specific objective, rather than as a matter of the auditor's preference, as in single-purpose tests. If, for example, there is a system weakness which could create an understatement of sales, the auditor would trace a sample of sales orders to the sales journal. If the weakness permitted an overstatement, transactions would be traced backward from the sales journal.

Dual-purpose tests are not used solely as a follow up of weaknesses. A possibility of error in the auditor's judgment in evaluating internal control always exists. As a defense against this fallibility, dual-purpose tests are frequently applied on a rotating basis each year in areas where the control system seems satisfactory. This cyclical application of dual-purpose tests is usually planned to cover all key areas of the system over a three- or four-year period in a continuing engagement.[5] Application of dual-purpose tests would be more extensive in an initial examination.

In summary, dual-purpose tests of transactions are used by the auditor for investigation of internal control weaknesses established by single-purpose tests of transactions and for reinforcing the auditor's conclusions on the reliance to be placed on the internal control system. They provide assurance as to the effective functioning of the internal control system as well as to the *bona fides* of an account balance. For this purpose, a sample size sufficient to support statistically valid inferences would seem to be required.

Necessity of Dual-Purpose Tests

Professor Stettler seems to advocate the elimination of dual-purpose tests when he states:

. . . The sample of one of each type of transaction should suffice to indicate that the system,

such as it is, is operative, and a larger sample that would disclose the extent of compliance helps very little in assessing the fairness or propriety of the account balances produced by the system.

It is in the tests of the balances themselves against verifiable supporting evidence that the auditor must expand his sample to achieve increased reliability.[6]

The audit would then proceed from single-purpose tests to tests of *bona fides*. A judgment of the validity of this contention involves two related issues: (1) the availability of tests of *bona fides* and (2) the auditor's reliance on the internal control system.

The auditor must express an opinion on the fairness of presentation of the financial statements as a whole. His opinion includes the fair presentation of the individual components of the income statement. Tests of *bona fides*, by the verification of net assets at the beginning and end of the year, could establish the fair presentation of net income, but the fair presentation of the individual components could not be verified in this manner. Tests of *bona fides* usually provide assurance that revenues and expenses are fairly presented, because the auditor determines that the internal control procedures which relate net assets with revenue and expense flows are functioning an acceptable percentage of the time; this relationship is ascertained, in part, by dual-purpose tests of transactions.

This argument is not meant to reject Professor Stettler's advocacy of second-level internal control;[7] his point is well taken. The

---

[5]This is essentially the viewpoint expressed by Tietjen in his advocacy of rotation of audit procedures. See A. Carl Tietjen, "A Suggested Change in Examination Approach," *The Journal of Accountancy*, Vol. 101, April 1956, pp. 47–49.

[6]Stettler, *op. cit.*, p. 58.

[7]*Ibid.*

auditor is not concerned with each and every internal control procedure. The "control points" must be determined. If an omission of a procedure or an error in the application of a procedure would be detected at a later point in the system, then the auditor is not concerned with adherence to that specific procedure. Once the second-level controls are determined, however, the auditor must still establish that these controls are functioning an acceptable percentage of the time.

The above argument is intended to state the case for dual-purpose tests of transactions. The relationship between types of audit tests and sampling approaches remains to be considered.

Sampling Approaches and Audit Tests

This relationship—between types of tests and sampling approaches—must clearly identify the sample unit involved. The sample unit is the individual item which is chosen for testing and may be either quantitative or qualitative in nature.

A quantitative sample unit can be immediately observed in numerical form. In the audit of accounts receivable, for example, the actual dollar amounts of the account balances are quantitative sample units. These quantitative sample units are often referred to as variables.

Some observations, however, only provide information concerning the existing quality of an item. An observation may be that an account requires investigation, that a credit to an account has been properly approved, or that a sales transaction has been recorded in the correct period. Frequently these qualities are referred to as attributes. Each observation is tallied against a particular category and numerical data, necessary for statistical operations, emerge when the number in each classification is counted and expressed as a ratio of the total number of observations; e.g., the percent of accounts requiring investigation.

Estimation sampling is the only statistical sampling approach which can be used to test for attributes or variables. Acceptance sampling and discovery sampling are confined to testing for attributes.

Explanation of the Three Approaches

For those unfamiliar with sampling terminology, a brief explanation of these sampling methods is offered.

The object of the estimation sampling approach is to make a quantitative estimate of a characteristic of the population being sampled within specified precision limits and with a specified level of confidence. Precision is a statistical term for the maximum probable difference between the sample estimate and the true, but unknown, population characteristic and is usually stated as a plus and minus range around the sample estimate. The confidence level is a number between 0 and 1 which measures the degree of confidence attached to the sample estimate and precision limits.

In an examination of 200 vouchers, for example, in which the auditor discovers eight procedural errors, the sample estimate of the procedural error rate is 4%. If precision has been specified as 2% and the confidence level has been specified as .95, the auditor can state that he has 95% confidence that the procedural error rate is not less than 2% and not more than 6%.

The object of acceptance sampling is to determine whether to accept or reject a group of items (the population) on the basis of the information provided by the sample. The auditor specifies a maximum acceptable error rate and the desired confidence level. By referring to an acceptance sampling table, the auditor can determine the number of errors which can be disclosed by the sample without "rejecting" the population.[8]

Assume, for example, that in an examination of vouchers for procedural error the maximum acceptable error rate is specified as 4% and the specified confidence level is .95, for a population of 1,250 vouchers. Assume, further, that an acceptance sampling table indicates an acceptance number of seven for a sample size of 120. If the auditor selects a sample of 120 vouchers and the sample contains seven or fewer procedural errors, the auditor can state that he has 95% confidence that the procedural error rate does not exceed 4%.

The discovery sampling approach is a means of selecting a sample and achieving a specified confidence that at least one error will be disclosed by the sample if errors exist in a specified proportion in the population. There are tables available which indicate the probability (confidence level) of finding at least one example of an event if the total number of events in the population are at various levels.[9] The auditor must specify the maximum allowable occurrence of errors and the confidence level desired. Reference to an appropriate table for the population involved will indicate the required sample size. If the sample does not disclose any errors, the auditor may conclude that the true error level does not exceed the specified maximum allowable error rate.

Since Professor Stettler considers only single-purpose tests and tests of *bona fides*, the polar positions on the continuum of audit tests, his argument leads him to the conclusion that "estimation sampling is perhaps the only statistical sampling approach that is valid and useful for auditing purposes."[10] Because a single-purpose test requires the observation of only one transaction, statistical sampling is not necessary. Since estimation sampling is the only sampling approach available to test variables, a test of *bona fides*, which involves verification of the dollar balance of a specific account, must use the estimation sampling approach.

Professor Stettler's conclusion ignores the relationship between sampling approaches and dual-purpose tests. He does not seem to notice that even the audit test chosen for his example, confirmation of accounts receivable, is frequently a dual-purpose test.

Considering the Test's Objective

In a study to investigate the applicability of statistical sampling techniques to the con-

---

[8]For example: Harold F. Dodge and Harry G. Romig, *Sampling Inspection Tables*, John Wiley & Sons, Inc., New York City, 1944.

[9]See the table illustrated in: Herbert Arkin, "Discovery Sampling in Auditing," *The Journal of Accountancy*, Vol. 111, Feb. 1961, p. 53.

[10]Stettler, *op. cit.*, p. 59.

firmation of accounts receivable, Professor John Neter concluded that this audit procedure had two purposes:[11] (1) "evaluating the effectiveness of internal controls and procedures" and (2) "evaluating the integrity of the account balances." His conclusion that "only one of these [purposes] would be used in some instances; in other cases, both would be employed simultaneously"[12] seems to support the contention that the objective of the test, rather than its form, determines the position of the test on the continuum of audit tests. Professor Neter's study involved two industrial companies and a public utility. Although the test of *bona fides* was emphasized for the industrial companies, the evaluation of internal control effectiveness was far more important for the public utility. He cautioned that "a sample size adequate for one purpose may not be adequate for another."[13] Professor Neter's study would seem to indicate that conclusions as to sampling approach should not be made without first considering the objective of the test.

Conclusion

While, as Professor Stettler explained, estimation sampling seems to be the most useful method for applying tests of *bona fides*, another sampling approach may be more appropriate for dual-purpose tests.

If the primary objective of the dual-purpose test is to evaluate the integrity of an account balance, the concern with a dollar amount, variable, would dictate the use of estimation sampling. On the other hand, if the primary objective is to evaluate the effectiveness of internal controls and procedures, the principal concern with an existing quality, attribute (e.g., that a confirmation reply indicates an account requires investigation), would allow the use of any of the three sampling approaches. Either estimation sampling, acceptance sampling or discovery sampling may be used in sampling for attributes.

Sample sizes required for acceptance sampling and discovery sampling are relatively small when compared to those required for estimation sampling. On the other hand, estimation sampling can be used to estimate error rates, while the other approaches only provide information that the rate of error is higher or lower than a previously specified tolerable error rate.

The main point is that conclusions drawn about the adequacy of sample size of audit tests are directly related to the type of audit test. The conclusions that a severely restricted sample is adequate for single-purpose tests and that estimation sampling is most useful for tests of *bona fides* do not necessarily have a bearing on dual-purpose tests. Since the primary objective of dual-purpose tests is frequently to determine that internal control procedures are functioning an acceptable percentage of the time, acceptance sampling may be most suitable. This conclusion is, at this time, tentative, but any refutation should be directed to dual-purpose tests, rather than single-purpose tests or tests of *bona fides*. No matter what sampling approach is chosen for dual-purpose tests of transactions, the sample size must be large enough to support statistically valid inferences.

---

[11]John Neter, "Applicability of Statistical Sampling Techniques to the Confirmation of Accounts Receivable," *The Accounting Review*, Vol. 31, January 1956, p. 82.

[12]*Ibid.*, p. 84.

[13]*Ibid.*, p. 87.

Problems
in Flowcharting

1. Prepare a flow chart from the following information:

Sales Department prepares six-part sales invoice form from customer's order and files order alphabetically by customer. Part 2 is sent to Credit Department as credit slip for approval; remaining parts are held until credit is approved. After credit approval, credit slip is returned to Sales and filed with customer's order. Parts 1 (sales invoice) and 3 (ledger) are then sent to Billing; part 4 is sent to Shipping as a packing slip; part 5 is sent to the warehouse as a stock request; and part 6 is sent to the customer to acknowledge the order.

The warehouse releases the goods and sends stock request with the goods to Shipping. In Shipping the goods are compared with the description on the stock request and units shipped are noted on this request. Shipping takes the packing slip from the files and sends it with the goods to the customer. The stock request is sent to Billing.

Billing enters shipped items, marked on stock request, on sales invoice and ledger copy, makes extensions and checks them, compares prices to price list, and runs tape of amounts on ledger

copy. Stock request is filed numerically; numerical sequence is accounted for at this time. Sales invoice is sent to customer. Ledger copy is sent to Accounting, where it is placed in the open invoice file. Tape is also sent to Accounting, where it is posted to the Sales Control Account in the general ledger and discarded at the end of the month. The open invoice file is balanced monthly to the general ledger sales control.

2. Prepare a flow chart from the following information, which describes a purchasing and cash disbursements system for RST, Inc.

Purchasing Department prepares a four-part purchase order from a verbal request by the plant superintendent or one of the foremen. Parts 1 and 2 are sent to the vendor. Part 4 is sent to the Receiving Department for use as a receiving report. Part 3 is filed as a control and follow-up copy for open orders.

Goods received are indicated on the appropriate receiving report (part 4). The receiver is then sent to Purchasing where it is filed with part 3 of the purchase order and held until the vendor's invoice is received. (No perpetual inventory records are maintained.)

When the vendor's invoice is received, purchase order copies 3 and 4 are pulled from the file and checked against the invoice. The clerical accuracy (including prices) is checked and the invoice is assigned a number and recorded in the invoice register. The account distribution code is written on the invoice. Part 3 of the purchase order is filed numerically. The invoice and part 4 of the purchase order are sent to the accounts payable clerk.

The accounts payable clerk files the invoice and copy 4 of the purchase order by due date. When the invoices are due, the clerk pulls the invoices and purchase orders and prepares checks and check copies (copies show account distribution). From the checks, the clerk prepares an adding machine tape of the cash amounts. He then forwards the invoices, purchase orders, checks, check copies, and tape to a clerk in the General Accounting Department.

General accounting clerk posts (by hand) the check copy amounts to the cash disbursements book. The tape forwarded from the accounts payable clerk is compared with the totals in the cash disbursements book, and if they agree, the tape is discarded. The clerk then forwards the invoices, purchase orders, checks, and check copies to the Treasurer for his signature.

The Treasurer reviews the support, signs the checks, and returns all items to the general accounting clerk.

The general accounting clerk protects the checks and mails them to the vendors, files the check copies by number, stamps the invoices "paid," and forwards the invoices and attached receivers to the purchasing department.

Problems in Statistical Sampling

1. Your client's inventory has an estimated value of $50,000. Using random sampling techniques, you determine that the standard deviation is $1,000.

a. Calculate the absolute precision of the sample estimate at 68.26 percent, 89.9 percent, and 95 percent reliability respectively.

b. The client asks you for a letter stating that, based on the sample, the minimum estimate of the inventory value is $49,000 with a reliability of 95 percent. What alternatives do you have?

c. What is the likelihood that the value of the inventory is less than $48,000 or more than $52,000? Discuss fully.

2. A random sample of 100 delinquent charge accounts at the Sell-All Department Store has yielded the following calculations:

$$\sum_{j=1}^{j=100} x_j = \$9,450.00$$

$$\sum_{j=1}^{j=100} (x_j)^2 = 1,067,661$$

a. Management has asked you to estimate confidence limits for the average size of delinquent accounts with no more than two chances in 100 of being wrong. What is your estimate?

b. What is the probability that the average size of the delinquent accounts might be as high as $105.00?

3. A manufacturer of a seasonal product wants to estimate the average number of units in dealers' inventories at the end of the season. The manufacturer has 2,500 dealers, and a random sample of 25 of these dealers shows that:

$$\sum_{j=1}^{j=25} x_j = 250$$

$$\sum_{j=1}^{j=25} (x_j)^2 = 3,100$$

Write a letter to management summarizing:

a. The accuracy indicated by this sample

b. The sample size required to bring this precision within ±1 unit with a reliability of 95 percent.

4. In the examination of a particular account, the auditor must test certain items within a finite population to form an opinion of the reliability of the account as a whole. In a judgment sample the auditor commonly tests most of the large dollar-amount items and a smaller proportion of lesser dollar-amount items. A random stratified sample makes the same type of selection, but is said to be superior to the judgment sample.

Required:

a. For each of the following define the terms and explain how the selection process could be applied to a test of accounts receivable:

    1. A judgment sample.
    2. A stratum in a finite population.
    3. A systematic random stratified sample.

b. Explain why a random stratified sample is superior to a judgment sample.

5. You are now conducting your third annual audit of the financial statements of Elite Corporation for the year ended December 31, 1966. You decide to employ unrestricted random number statistical sampling techniques in testing the effectiveness of the Company's internal control procedures relating to sales invoices, which are all serially numbered. In prior years, after selecting one representative

---

Questions 4 through 6 are adapted from Uniform CPA Examination.

two-week period during the year, you tested all invoices issued during that period and resolved all of the errors which were found to your satisfaction.

Required:

a. Explain the statistical procedures you would use to determine the size of the sample of sales invoices to be examined.

b. Once the sample size has been determined, how would you select the individual invoices to be included in the sample? Explain.

c. Would the use of statistical sampling procedures improve the examination of sales invoices as compared with the selection procedure used in prior years? Discuss.

d. Assume that the Company issued 50,000 sales invoices during the year and the auditor specified a confidence level of 95 percent with a precision range of plus or minus 2 percent.

   1. Does this mean that the auditor would be willing to accept the reliability of the sales invoice data if errors are found on no more than four sales invoices out of every ninety-five invoices examined? Discuss.

   2. If the auditor specified a precision range of plus or minus 1 percent, would the confidence level be higher or lower than 95 percent assuming that the size of the sample remains constant? Why?

    6. The Cowslip Milk Company's principal activity is buying milk from dairy farmers, processing the milk and delivering the milk to retail customers. You are engaged in auditing the retail accounts receivable of the Company and determine the following:

1. The Company has 50 retail routes; each route consists of 100 to 200 accounts, the number that can be serviced by a driver in a day.

2. The driver enters cash collections from the day's deliveries to each customer directly on a statement form in record books maintained for each route. Mail remittances are posted in the route record books by office personnel. At the end of the month the statements are priced, extended and footed. Photocopies of the statements are prepared and left in the customers' milk boxes with the next milk delivery.

3. The statements are reviewed by the office manager, who prepares a list for each route of accounts with 90-day balances or older. The list is used for intensive collection action.

4. The audit program used in prior audits for the selection of retail accounts receivable for confirmation stated: "Select two accounts from each route, one to be chosen by opening the route book at random and the other as the third item on each list of 90-day or older accounts."

   Your review of the accounts receivable leads you to conclude that statistical sampling techniques may be applied to their examination.

Required:

a. Give the reasons why the audit procedure previously used for selection of accounts receivable for confirmation (as given in #4 above) would not produce a valid statistical sample.

b. What are the audit objectives or purposes in selecting 90-day accounts for confirmation? Can the application of statistical sampling techniques help in attaining these objectives or purposes? Discuss.

c. Assume that the Company has 10,000 accounts receivable and that your statistical sampling disclosed 6 errors in a sample of 200 accounts. Is it reasonable to assume that 300 accounts in the entire population are in error? Explain.

The Wheelox Corporation: Part A

Case

This is a description of an accounts-receivable system in a medium-sized manufacturing company.

All orders are transmitted from various branches to the home office over the teletypewriter system, and a paper tape is prepared for the orders received. As the paper tape is created, sales orders are generated at the home office. Seven copies are created, with distribution to division sales, branch office, customer acknowledgment, shipping and stores, district sales, delivery receipt, packing list. The paper tape is then converted to magnetic tape. This tape is then sorted to create an open file in order-number sequence. The open-order file is then processed to generate a printed daily orders-entered register, an updated open-order file, an inventory control tape file, and punched cards for the day's orders.

The home office does the invoicing of all shipments. Invoices are prepared by computer program B-OID, which processes the open order and shipment cards. The source document for keypunching the shipment cards is the shipping and stores copy of the order. On this document, shipping personnel indicate the pieces or pounds shipped, the heat number, shipping method, freight information, and special charges. This information is in addition to the standard information already printed on this copy of the standard order forms (item number, quantity ordered, unit price, customer, and branch information). The documents arrive at random from all possible shipping points and are edited by a member of the Control Group concerned with invoicing. After editing, they are sent to be keypunched once a day, with no batch or control totals being utilized. After keypunching and key-verification, they are transferred to the machine operator (again with no batch control) for processing. They are sorted in mill-order-number sequence and merged with the open-order file, from which an invoice is prepared. Output in machine-readable form for subsequent processing is:

1. Magnetic tape file for stock items, sales analysis, and perpetual inventory updating.
2. Punched cards to be used for production item sales analysis.
3. Punched cards to be used for indicating the day's billings on the daily status report and to be used for updating the customer accounts-receivable magnetic tape file.
4. An updated open-order magnetic tape file.

The daily status report is prepared by processing punched cards indicating the day's billings (see item 3 immediately above) and punched cards indicating the day's orders entered (from order-entry program described previously). The daily status report indicates—by product—orders entered today, month-to-date, and last month-to-date; billings today, month-to-date, and last month-to-date; backlog today and a month ago. The report also shows total orders entered, total billings, and total backlog. The total orders entered today can be compared to the total orders per the daily orders-entered register resulting from the processing of orders. The total billings for the day can be compared with total billings shown on the daily cash receipts—sales register, the output of subsequent processing in the receivable cycle.

In addition to the daily status report, a monthly status report is prepared, presenting information shown on the month's daily status reports.

Six copies of the invoice are prepared, with distribution as follows:

Three copies to the customer. The original also includes a payment identity coupon. This coupon is to be torn off and returned by the customer with his remittance. The coupon is processed by the cashier as indicated in the cash-receipts section of this program and is used as the source document for keypunching cash-receipts punched cards to be used in updating the accounts-receivable magnetic tape file and in preparing the daily cash receipts-sales register.

One copy each goes to the Control Group, salesman, and branch from which the sale originated.

In addition to the computer output described above, a punched card referred to as the "invoice control card" is also punched out by the computer. This card is distributed to the Control Group for review and follow-up, and indicates:

1. The total number of shipment punched cards read by the computer.
2. The total number of billings punched cards punched by the computer and invoices prepared.
3. The total number of shipments cards read but not invoiced because there is no order in the open-order file.
4. The total number of consignment shipments (interbranch sales) for which no invoices are prepared.

5. The total number of invoices for partial shipments.
6. The total number of invoices written.
7. The total dollar amount of open orders in the open-order magnetic tape file.

The company does not print out, at periodic intervals, the open-order magnetic tape file so that visible review can be made by the Control Group for unusual delays in shipping and invoicing, and for back orders.

All credit memorandums for returned material are initiated by the Control Group or the branches upon receipt of a returned material receiving report. Branches forward their credit memorandums, approved by the branch manager, to the home office for approval. All credit memorandums, originated by the Control Group and in excess of $1,000, must be approved by the comptroller and divisional vice president before they can be posted to accounts receivable. All other credit memorandums must be approved by the general ledger bookkeeper and the inventory supervisor.

Miscellaneous credits also originate in the Control Group to correct invoicing errors. These are processed the same as material-returned credits.

The accounts-receivable file is maintained on magnetic tape. This file is processed by several computer programs, the purpose of these programs being:

1. To prepare a daily sales-cash receipts register with a deposit slip (Program D-01D).
2. To prepare a daily exception report for subsequent analysis and action by the accounts-receivable supervisor in the Control Group (D-13D).

3. To prepare an aged trial balance weekly and at the end of the month for review by the accounts-receivable supervisor in the Control Group and other interested management personnel (D-13W).
4. To prepare monthly statements for customers who desire them (D-15M).
5. To prepare a monthly overdue-accounts list (D-06M and D-07M).

Preparation of Daily Sales-Cash Receipts Register with Deposit Slip

The daily sales-cash receipts register with deposit slip is prepared by computer processing of punched-card input consisting of cash receipts, credits issued, sundry cash receipts, and billings.

All cash is under the control of the treasurer, and all collections are received at the home office. The company maintains four general checking accounts and various branch and divisional general and/or payroll accounts that are handled on an imprest basis.

All mail, except pieces addressed to specific individuals, is opened in the mailroom. No listing is prepared before the checks are forwarded to the cashier who tapes the amounts received.

The cash receipts cards are keypunched from the payment identity coupons sent in by the customer with his remittance or by a payment identity coupon originated by the accounts-receivable supervisor in the Control Group for those customers not sending the payment identity coupons. Source documents for keypunching credits issued and sundry cash receipts cards originate with the general ledger bookkeeper. Billings cards are prepared as output from the computer processing of invoices.

In addition, punched cards are prepared for new accounts, charges in customer accounts (that is, new credit limit, new customer number, name, address) and other cancellations, increases, or decreases. Other activity input consists of month-to-date cards showing sales by division, sales tax by taxing body, and sundry cash receipts by account. These cards are used in printing monthly totals for posting to the general ledger. Also processed are orders entered cards, the output from order-entry processing are processed.

After the above activity and change cards are sorted, they are processed by the computer against the master accounts-receivable magnetic tape files. There are two master tapes. One, the basic record, contains the total account balance, the amount on order by product line, credit limit, credit history, delinquency history, and sales history. The other master tape is the item record and shows the detail supporting the basic record account balance.

This computer processing of the punched-card input and the master tapes produces the following machine-readable output for subsequent processing and visible output for distribution:

1. Machine-readable output.
   a. Updated accounts-receivable master tapes.
   b. Updated month-to-date cards.
   c. Exception report cards used to prepare a daily exception report for review and follow-up by the Control Group.

2. Visible output.
   a. Daily sales-cash receipts register. This register is prepared in customer-number sequence and shows, for each customer having transactions that day, the cash receipts and/or billing information. Cash receipts information includes gross amount of the billing, discount amount, and amount paid. The billing information includes invoice number, gross amount of the billing, and the amount applicable to material, transportation, and sales tax. Also shown are the balance in the customer's account after the transactions are posted, the grand totals for cash receipts and billings, total sundry cash receipts, the total balance of all accounts receivable, and the number of invoices processed during the day.
   b. Cash deposit slip. This slip is actually a part of the daily sales-cash receipts register and lists all cash receipts processed by the computer. This slip is prepared in duplicate and returned to the cashier for agreement with her remittance adding-machine tape and for deposit in the bank.

The Control Group compares the total billings printed in the daily sales-cash receipts to total billings shown on the Daily status report and on the invoice control card.

Preparation of Daily Exception Report

An exception report is prepared daily as the result of the computer processing of exception report cards. These cards are produced as the result of programmed controls in the computer program that cause the accounts-receivable transactions to be posted to the accounts-receivable magnetic tape files.

Exception report cards may be classified as (1) exceptions to operational policies, (2) information only, and (3) errors in input data.

The exception codes and an explanation of the codes are:

A. Order received today over credit limit. A credit limit check is not made until the order is received, processed for shipment, and posted to the accounts-receivable basic-record magnetic tape. The computer program then compares the total of the customer balance and orders entered with the amount of the credit limit on the customer records.

B. Order received today—from new customer.

C. Order received today—no credit limit in basic record.

D. Order received today—from delinquent account.

E. Account opened today.

F. Inactive account (no sales last three years).

G. Account closed today.

H. Account with credit balance.

I. Item Coded—"do not age."

J. Item delinquent today.

K. Delinquent item—paid today.

L. No "special terms effective date" in record.

M. 01 (Subcode). Cash discount not taken but allowable because it is within five-day grace period.
02. Cash discount taken but should be disallowed.
03. Cash discount not taken but allowable because the discount is less than $1.00.

P. Unassigned payment in item record. When customer remits payment without payment identity coupon and the payment cannot be identified by some other means.

Q. Unassigned credit in item record. All credits except those for the same amount as an invoice or group of invoices are processed unassigned until payment is received for the remaining amount due in the invoices for which the credit(s) apply.

R. Difference in amount between basic record balance and total of items in item record.

S. Special terms items in file.

T. Confirmation of change. Change is printed out (that is, address, credit limit).

U. Customer number change—record deleted. When customer number change requires a change in the order of customers on a sequential file, it is impossible to back up on tape and insert the customer where it belongs on the file. So when a customer is to be deleted, cards are punched up to show all information for that customer. The "customer number change" information indicates what is punched on the cards.

V. Customer number change—record inserted. On the following day, the punched cards resulting from the "customer number change—record deleted" process are processed and inserted on the master record and a print-out of the information inserted results in the exception report for comparison against information deleted from the master record.

W. Answer to query. Exception report shows what is in a customer's records.

X. Error card. Card shows, by code, the type of error in the punched-card input and information on the card that is not processed because of the error. Several of these errors relate to program checks for proper date, proper sequence of customer number and transaction code, and valid transaction codes.

Preparation of Aged Trial Balance and Monthly Statements

The aged trial balance is prepared weekly and at the end of the month by computer processing of the accounts-receivable master magnetic tape files. The aged trial balance lists, in customer number sequence, all invoices, credit and debit memos, and contra (application of company purchases against a delinquent customer's balance) by date number and amount; the aged trial balance ages the amount according to 30-60-90 and over categories. This tape includes only information on customers whose basic record is coded to show they desire statements. This tape is then processed by the computer to prepare monthly statements.

As the result of the aged trial balance processing program, the computer prepares an "overdue accounts" magnetic tape used to prepare an overdue accounts list that shows all overdue accounts by branch office.

Requirement:

Prepare a system flowchart of the Wheelox Corporation system, using the ASA flowcharting symbols.

Chapter 8

Gathering Evidence: Using the Computer

The audit use of the computer in evaluating the data-processing system and its output affords the auditor the opportunity to perform a more selective and penetrating audit of activities and procedures involving a large volume of transactions.

The evaluation of a system rests first on the review of the system to obtain a knowledge of how it is reported to operate and on testing the system to accumulate evidence which demonstrates how it actually does operate. In reviewing a data-processing system, the auditor should review various documents such as systems flow charts and programming documentation to gain an understanding of the system and the controls designed into the system. In EDP systems, the auditor is likely to encounter new controls, some made necessary by the automation of processing and some which substitute for those controls which in manual systems were based on human judgment and the division of duties. Many of the controls in data-processing systems may be embodied in the computer programs and may perform functions previously performed by humans in manual processing. Obviously, in order to properly evaluate and test the computer data-processing system the auditor needs to understand the nature of these controls.[1]

---

[1] For a detailed discussion of controls in EDP systems, see Davis, *Auditing and EDP*, Chapters 2-7.

To assist in the review of the data-processing systems and the internal controls, questionnaires are sometimes very useful in obtaining information on the system. The second reading at the end of this chapter is a questionnaire developed by the AICPA for evaluating internal controls in electronic data processing.

Having obtained information on the system, the auditor must next obtain evidence of the existence and effectiveness of the client's processing procedures and controls. This is done by making tests of the performances and control procedures. The nature and availability of evidence and the types of tests to be performed depend somewhat upon the complexity of the system design and upon the audit trail found in the electronic system being audited.

The sample-of-one approach, discussed in the previous chapter, is particularly suited to the understanding and testing of computerized systems. To confirm the auditor's understanding of what goes on in the "black box" and to determine whether or not computer programs and their related controls operate as described, the auditor can use test data. The test-data approach involves the preparation of test data that are processed under auditor control by the client's computer programs. Test data consist of transactions illustrating all the valid and invalid conditions which the auditor wishes to test. Only one transaction of each type need be tested, since a given program consistently processes all transactions of a particular type in exactly the same way. In effect, the auditor allows the EDP system to audit itself by presenting the system with test transactions that the system cannot distinguish from operating transactions. The auditor then evaluates the results to determine that the test transactions actually did get processed in the manner described to him in his review of the system. The auditor should be aware of the limitations and practical difficulties in implementing the test approach. The approach is most probably applicable when:

1. A significant part of the system of internal control is embodied in the computer program.

2. There are gaps in the audit trail, making it difficult or impractical to output or to verify calculations. This situation is possible in simple applications as well as in complex integrated systems.

3. The volume of records is so large that it may be more economical and more effective to use test data methods (and related procedures) instead of manual testing methods.[2]

[2]Davis, *Auditing and EDP*, p. 161.

The second reading at the end of this chapter discusses the development of test data.

This study illustrates the use of test data in evaluating a real-time system of labor recording. The EDP system reviewed and tested by auditors in this case study consists of an automated system that records labor transactions and processes payroll in a major plant for a large manufacturer. This case study illustrates many of the points discussed above on the review and testing of internal control in an EDP system.

Automatic time-recording devices are located throughout the shop areas. For the 11,600 employees covered by this system, these devices have completely replaced the human timekeepers and manually prepared time cards. Data from the system flows through the company's payroll and job-order cost accounting and control records. Basic timekeeping tools are (1) the plastic employee badge, prepunched with identifying information, and (2) the job card, prepunched with the charge number and other information about a particular job.

The badge is permanently assigned to each employee. The job cards follow the parts or assemblies to be worked on. Exceptions are indirect-labor and other special cards, which are located in racks adjacent to the time recorders. Clock-in on reporting for work requires only insertion of the badge and one or more job cards, and depression of other keys.

All time recorders are linked electrically to a central control box, a master clock, and an in-line key punch that creates a punched card for each entry. The cards are converted to magnetic tape for passing through computer processes. The first of these, a match against an employee identification master tape, begins one half-hour after the beginning of each shift.

Within an hour after shift start, an exception report has been prepared for distribution to shop foremen. The report indicates absences, tardy clock-in, preshift overtime, and failure to check in on a job. Each exception must be approved by the shop foreman. Transactions accepted for the remainder of the shift are "posted" to a random-access file arranged by employee. Transactions rejected must be analyzed or corrected for reentry into the processing cycle.

All labor transactions for the day read out onto another magnetic tape that goes through a series of further computer processes:

1. Preparation of final report to shop foremen. Again prepared for exceptions only, this shows overtime, early clock-out, and other items for approval by foremen.

2. Daily report that balances job time by employee with time between clock-in and clock-out.

3. Daily labor tape prepared after process 2.

4. Matching of job transactions against a random-access file of job numbers. This processing involves application of labor standards on certain jobs, accumulation of time by classification, and preparation of output tapes for numerous reports. These include daily reports of actual and budgeted time to certain shops, summary management reports by type of labor, and job status reports.

5. Entry of the daily labor tape from process 3 above into a larger computer for the payroll process.

Audit Approach   In pre-EDP days, an auditor was able to begin with either a payroll report or a labor-distribution report and to trace individual time charges back through the system to underlying time cards or other source documents. When the labor transaction is initiated mechanically, this is obviously impossible.

To evaluate this labor-recording and payroll system, the auditors decided upon a two-phase review:

1. Testing of actual transactions from their initiation through to final reports; the transactions were selected according to the normal testing of labor charges and employees' payroll records and paychecks.

2. Testing of the labor-recording and payroll system in normal operations by use of simulated, but realistic, transactions designed to test not only routine processing but also the various exception procedures.

Emphasis was placed on the second phase because it enabled many facets of the operation to be tested with only a small number of transactions. In designing the simulated transactions, the auditors made a thorough review of the client's system flow charts and documentation describing the programmed controls. Also, inquiries were made of responsible persons about the various control points designed in the system.

1. Employee clocks in on time, works normally for full shift.
2. Employee checks in on job without clocking in.
3. Employee clocks in but fails to record a job transaction.
4. Employee is absent.
5. Employee is tardy.
6. Employee is tardy but within three-minute "grace period" allowed.
7. Employee leaves before shift ends.
8. Employee leaves early but returns.
9. Night-shift employee clocks in on day shift.
10. Employee works overtime into next shift.
11. Employee is loaned to a different shop.
12. Employee charges jobs improperly (for example, direct as indirect time).
13. Employee uses Transactor keys improperly when checking in on job.

Since the auditors desired to perform the test under normal operating conditions, using actual shop locations and job cards, the only simulated items necessary were a group of employee badges. The employee information was entered into the master records to agree with the badges.

Using the transactions outlined above, the test was carried out in two shops during normal working hours. Both day and night shifts were used. Data-processing supervisors were made aware of the general nature of the test but not of the specific types of transactions being tested. Shop foremen were not informed until after they had questioned the simulated transactions that appeared as exceptions on attendance reports.

All transactions were traced through to reports that emerged from the data-processing system on the same day and the following day. These included preliminary and final attendance-exception reports, exception reports of erroneous job transactions, and the daily balance report of proper job and attendance transactions.

With two exceptions, the auditors identified every simulated transaction as being processed properly, and concluded that the system was functioning as it had been described to them. The two exceptions were system discrepancies.

The auditors made extended tests on a subsequent day to determine the reasons for these discrepancies. The first discrepancy resulted in the rejection of certain apparently proper transactions as exceptions. This happened because the client had previously made a change in "leave early" cards but had failed to collect all the superseded cards from the rack in the shop.

The second discrepancy was the result of a programming error. The program instructions said, in effect, "If the next to last employee in the processing cycle is an exception, do not process the last employee." Since the simulated employee master records used by the auditor were the last on the master file and since the simulated transaction for the next to last employee was an exception, the transactions for the last employee were not processed.

Tests of Payroll Processing

To test payroll processing, the auditors again designed simulated transactions to be processed with simulated employee-payroll master records by the client's computer payroll programs. Payroll is processed by applying pay rates, included in the permanent portion of the employees' master-payroll records, to the labor-hour transactions accumulated in the variable portion of the employees' master records. The labor is accumulated by employee for biweekly payroll processing and by job for weekly accounting distribution reports. The fixed portion of the master record includes, in addition to the pay rate, data such as name, social-security number, number of tax exemptions, budget sections, year-to-date amounts, and vacation and sick-leave hours. The variable portion contains earnings and deduction data resulting from payroll transactions processed. The variable section, of course, is cleared at the end of each payroll period.

In developing the transactions, the auditors first reviewed the client's flow charts and other documentation that described the input formats, programmed controls, output, and exception reporting for all transactions processed by the computer payroll programs. They then reviewed the tests designed by the company's programmers to test the payroll programs. Many of the company's tests were selected by the auditors for inclusion in their tests. The auditors also formulated additional tests. All test transactions to be processed were then keypunched and listed in transaction-number sequence. The nature and objective of each test was described on this transaction listing as an aid in review and in subsequent debugging of the test processing. The listing was, of course, included in the work papers. One hundred ninety-six transactions were included in the test data, several examples being:

1. Employee is hired on same day as terminated.
2. Employee has rate change greater than programmed limit.
3. Employee charges labor hours while on vacation.

4. Employee is not entitled to bonus, charges bonus hours.
5. Employee requests vacation hours exceeding vacation-hours balance in master record.
6. Employee charges labor hours exceeding the programmed limit.
7. Terminated employee charges labor hours.
8. Terminated employee requests cash advance.
9. Employee has accumulated year-to-date earnings and FICA tax at taxable limit prior to processing of valid labor hours.
10. Employee requests tax exemptions exceeding programmed limit.
11. Valid employee charges normal labor hours.

The auditors requested, on a surprise basis, the client's computer programs from the EDP librarian. The reel serial numbers of the program tapes were then traced to the proper documentation in the EDP library. The auditors had previously reviewed the client's organization controls and EDP library procedures (physically and organizationally, the EDP library and programming activities were segregated). This review assured the auditors that the client's regular computer programs were being obtained. The auditors then controlled the programs and the test data, observed the processing of the test data, and obtained the processing results.

Again, the results of processing proved highly satisfactory and enabled the auditor to properly evaluate the adequacy of the data-processing and internal-control systems. The processing of the test data did disclose a few areas where programming changes would result in strengthened internal control. These program changes were largely concerned with input validity checks and reasonableness tests on incoming data. The tests also indicated that some documentation and some of the client's test data were no longer current.

As mentioned previously, the audit program also included some conventional tests of labor charges and employees' payroll records. The procedures included (1) reconciling payrolls paid with distributed labor, (2) tracing labor distribution from accounting entries to weekly and daily reports, and (3) tracing information from actual employee master records selected randomly to evidence supporting pay rates, exemptions, and all deductions.

Use of Computer in Evaluating System Output

In the previous chapter we mentioned several techniques of gathering evidence. A computer program can be of great assistance in performing some of these techniques since a computer program can be used for any computational or comparison task for which quantitative criteria can be established. Examples of these types of tasks in auditing are:

1. examining records for quality: completeness, consistency, validity of conditions, etc.;
2. selecting and printing audit samples;
3. testing calculations and making computations;
4. summarizing data and performing analyses useful to the auditor;
5. comparing the same data maintained in separate files for correctness and consistency;
6. comparing audit data with company records.

A common characteristic of these applications is the fact that the auditor can define clearly and precisely what is to be computed, compared, summed, printed, etc.

Examining Records for Quality

In the normal course of the audit, the auditor will observe any sloppy record keeping, incompleteness, and other conditions affecting the quality of the visible records. If the auditor obtains a complete printout for use in manual evaluation methods, the records can be tested for evidence of unsatisfactory record keeping. If the records are in machine-readable form, the auditor has the option of using the computer for testing the records. The auditor using the computer writes a program in order to examine the records for completeness. For example, the customer-file records might be examined to determine the number of records in which there is no credit limit specified. The records can also be tested for consistency between different items in valid conditions—e.g., account balances exceeding credit limit in unreasonable amounts; more than ten dependents for payroll deduction on a man's payroll record.

Selecting and Printing Audit Samples

A computer can be programmed to select audit samples through the use of either random numbers or statistical sampling techniques. Or the sample selection may be programmed to use multiple criteria such as random samples of items under a certain dollar amount, plus all items having certain characteristics such as high dollar values. The sample selected in this way can be used for conventional audit tests such as confirmation, price test of inventory items, physical observation, etc.

The computer can be used to perform audit computations that will test the accuracy of client computations and will perform quantitative analyses necessary to evaluate the reasonableness of management representations. The computer's speed and low cost per computation means that it takes only a small amount of extra time and expense to perform the test on all records rather than on a sample.

Testing Calculations and Making Computations

In order for the auditor to perform an analysis and summary, he frequently needs to have the client's data summarized in different ways. Examples are aging of accounts receivable, and preparation of annual usage of parts and inventory to compare with demand forecasts.

Summarizing Data and Performing Analyses Useful to the Auditor

Where there are two or more separate records having data fields which should be the same, the computer can be used to test for consistency. For example, the pay rates on the payroll master tape may be compared with the pay rates used in computing the payroll as a transaction tape.

Comparing the Same Data Maintained in Separate Files for Correctness and Consistency

Audit data such as inventory-test counts can be compared to the inventory records by using computer programs. This requires that the audit data be converted to machine-readable records. Other examples of this use are tracing cash receipts to accounts-receivable records or comparing inventory costs with the master-file cost data.

Comparing Audit Data with Company Records

Three approaches have been used in obtaining suitable computer programs for use in the evaluation and testing of records:

1. Programs written by the client.
2. Programs written by or under supervision of the auditor.
3. Generalized audit programs.

Obtaining an Audit Program

Programs Written by Client

Much analysis desired by the auditor is sometimes useful to the client. Therefore, the client will frequently write computer programs for his own use or will prepare the program for the computer installation if the auditor requests the analysis and there is also internal use for it. Examples are programs to age accounts receivable, analyze inventory turnover and obsolescence, review open-order files, etc. Obviously, to use such programs in his audit work the auditor will need to test the client's programs to have assurance of their proper functioning. The extent of testing would depend, of course, on the reliance the auditor can place on the installation's control over programs and operations. As a general rule, the auditor should, at the minimum, obtain a copy of the run book for the application, review the documentation for the run, and be present when the program is run.

Writing an Audit Program

Since a computer-audit program is written in the same way as any other computer program and since the programming process is explained very well in other literature, the steps involved in preparing a computer program to perform audit activities will not be discussed in any detail. There are four basic phases to developing computer audit programs: (1) determining audit objectives and procedures; (2) developing systems flow charts; (3) developing program flow charts; (4) coding, assembling, and testing programs. The extent to which the auditor can or should perform each of these tasks depends upon many factors such as the auditor's knowledge of EDP and competence in developing computer programs, the complexity of the programs being developed, the source language being used, and the availability of client programming assistance.

Case Study

This case study illustrates the use of a computer program that was written to aid in the performance of year-end audit procedures for finished-stock inventories in a medium-sized manufacturing company, and the discussion will be confined to audit testing and evaluating the inventory records.

After reviewing and evaluating the system of internal control within the data-processing area and after testing the client's computer programs for finished-stock inventory, the auditors determined that the system of internal control was adequate.

The company was a specialty-metals manufacturer with two divisions, steel and tungsten. The steel division manufactured hot and cold finished specialty steels which were distributed in the form of bars, rods, flats, and rounds. The products of the tungsten division included metal-cutting and mining tools, tips, and dies.

Aggregate finished-goods inventories of the two divisions totalled about 11,000 items, representing about 18 percent of total assets. These items were warehoused at the principal manufacturing plant and at eight sales offices throughout the United States. There was no physical product deterioration, but slow movement and obsolescence presented a continuing audit problem.

For financial reporting purposes, inventories were stated at the lower of cost or market (current replacement cost) on a last-in first-out (LIFO) basis. For internal data-processing purposes, detail inventories were initially accumulated using variable standard costs, which approximated first-in first-out (FIFO) costs. The standard costs were revised annually. At year-end, the inventory was adjusted to full-absorption LIFO cost. The detail inventories were priced and accumulated at both the old and the new standard prices, so as to reveal the amount of the pricing adjustment and to facilitate calculation of the current year's price index for the steel-division LIFO calculation. The LIFO reserve for the tungsten division was calculated only on the tungsten content. Fixed costs were added to the inventories (valued at variable cost) to make reporting on a "full absorption" basis possible in accordance with generally accepted accounting principles.

In both divisions, all inventories other than the two finished-goods inventories were physically counted at or near year-end; the latter were cycle-counted throughout the year, that is, various classes of inventory were counted at various times throughout the year to effect the counting of all classes once a year.

The computer system consisted of a medium-scale business-oriented configuration and a teletypewriter order-entry network. The perpetual finished-stock records, maintained on magnetic tape, contained the following information:

1. *General information*: item code, description, standard cost, gram weight per piece, date of stock authorization.

2. *Procurement information*: order date and order number for all procurements; supplier code for purchased procurements.

3. *Inventory status and transaction information*: actual and available inventory quantities; unshipped quantity (material available); back-order quantity (no material available); interdepartment transfers, receipts, and scrapping for the current month; date and quantity of the most recent physical adjustment.

4. *Inventory control and sales information*: lead-time; set-up and order costs; reorder-point quantity; economic order quantity; maximum stock; inventory on order; sales forecast; designations of discontinued, "slow-moving," and "dead" items; date of last sale; largest sale in current and preceding year; gross sales (amount and quantity) for the month and year to date.

Two inventory files were maintained: the perpetual inventory and the historic inventory. At the end of each month the historic inventory file was updated from the month-end perpetual inventory file. Month-end analysis resulted in various reports—of obsolete and dead stock, warehouse overstocks, activity analysis, distribution, and so on.

The Computer Programs

Two computer audit programs (INV-01 and INV-02) were developed to utilize the client's computer for the accumulation and pricing of finished-goods inventories. The audit system is shown in Figure 1. Program INV-01 was used to process the client's year-end perpetual inventory files (at both new and old standard costs) and the year-end historic inventory file. Each item selected by the program was assigned a code that identified the reason for its selection. This program performed the following tasks:

1. Reviewed and reported on an exceptional basis all items on the inventory files, as follows:

    a. items in files with no new or old standard cost (exception codes 1 and 2);

    b. items for which the standard cost did not change (exception code 3);

    c. items for which the standard cost increased or decreased by more than 30 percent (exception codes 4 and 5);

    d. items appearing in new or old standard-cost file, but not in both (exception codes 6 and 7);

e. tungsten items with no gram weight (exception code 8);

f. items stocked at invalid or fictitious locations (exception code 9);

g. items with procurements outstanding classified as discontinued (exception code 10);

h. items with procurements outstanding, for which procurements plus actual inventory exceed both the preceding six months' sales and the current back order (exception code 11);

Figure 1. Systems flowchart for audit routine.

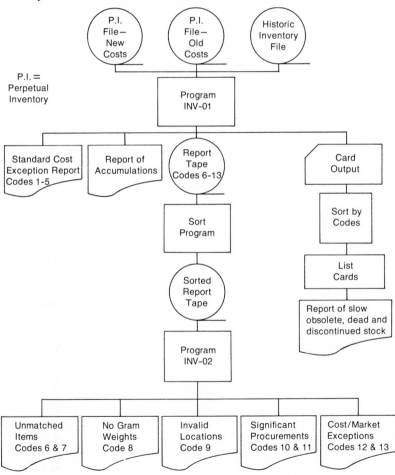

i. items for which the unit cost exceeds the unit market value (exception code 12);

j. items for which there have been no sales in the current year (exception code 13).

2. Accumulated and reported the following data:

a. number of items or records on the file;

b. total gram weight of tungsten products;

c. value of items classified as discontinued; the preceding twelve months' cost of sales of these items;

d. value of inventory in excess of the preceding twelve months' sales; cost of the twelve months' sales of these items;

e. market value and cost value of the inventory by major product category;

f. value of "slow-moving" and "dead" stocks; value by location of inventory with no physical adjustments in the current year.

A Standard Cost Exception Report was made from this processing. It contained items with exception codes 1 through 5, indicating item code, description, exception code, inventory quantity, and old and new standard costs where available. A listing of the various accumulations performed during the processing was also printed out.

The machine-readable output from program INV-01 included a magnetic tape containing the data on items with exception codes 6 through 13. This data included item code, description, exception code, and inventory quantity. Inventory value, location, procurement quantity, procurement cost, cost of preceding six months' sales, and unit market value were also included where applicable. The tape was sorted according to exception code; the client's sort program was used for this procedure but the sort control cards used were those maintained by the auditor. Audit computer INV-02 was then used to process the sorted tape and to prepare reports of unmatched items, tungsten items with no gram weights, invalid locations, significant procurements, and cost value in excess of market value.

During the INV-01 processing, cards were also punched for items for which there was no new standard cost and which conformed to the conditions listed below. These conditions relate to slow, dead, obsolete, missing, discontinued, and unauthorized stock. In each card a code was punched identifying the reason for its selection. These codes were used in sorting the cards:

1. no inventory cycle counts made during the current year;

2. item "dead" at a particular location;

3. item "slow-moving" at a particular location;

4. item discontinued;

5. inventory quantity greater than the preceding twelve months' sales quantity;

6. no "date stock authorized" in the record.

The punched-card output was sorted and the client's card-to-print utility program was then used to process the punched-card output and to list the items.

Generalized Audit Programs

It has become apparent to auditors involved in computerized systems that there are many audit functions that fundamentally change very little from client to client. This is not really a very novel observation. Indeed, public accounting firms issue to all audit personnel guides to the preparation of audit programs. The guides suggest an outline of procedures to be employed in audit examinations and to be included in the individual audit programs prepared for each client.

The idea of generalized computer programs is also not a novel one. Equipment manufacturers and other organizations involved in supplying computer programs to clients have been involved in developing generalized programs, or software, for a number of years. These programs perform activities related both to the operation of the computer system (systems programs) and to the manipulation and processing of data used in the management of the business (applications programs). Systems programs such as assembly routines, utility routines, compilers, and applications programs such as payroll, inventory control, and demand-deposit accounting find widespread use in many computer installations today. The availability of such programs is a great aid to personnel trying to use the computer in that these programs make unnecessary the development of systems flow charts, programming flow charts, source-language instruction, and the assembling and testing of programs. If developed, designed, and tested properly, generalized programs are available for use in any function designed to be performed by the computer, with a minimum of preparation on the part of the user.

Until recently, generalized computer-audit programs have been used to a limited extent. One approach has been the use of a program applicable to all clients in an industry; the best example is the brokerage audit, in which generalized audit programs have been used to perform standard audit procedures having to do with confirmation, margin computations, etc. The client's files are transferred to a standard format on magnetic tape; the data file in standard form is processed by an audit program used for all clients. The conversion program is unique for each client having a different computer; the client's computer is used only if it fits the model and configuration specifications for which the audit processing program was written. It should be noted that even though two computer systems are not program compatible, they are probably data compatible if the data is put on magnetic tape.

The second approach is a generalized set of audit routines which can be useful for a variety of audit and management purposes and used on a restricted set of compatible computers meeting specified configuration requirements. These routines can be used in a wide variety of records and applications without any need for writing special programs for each type of application processed.[3]

A good example of this approach is the Auditape system, the primary component of which is a series of audit routines written in machine language that are executed by virtue of specification cards developed by the auditor. In addition, the system includes an instruction sheet for computer operations, specification sheets, and an operating manual. The operating manual includes a general discussion of the Auditape System, excerpts of which follow:

> The Auditape is in machine language, ready for immediate use, and includes several programs or what might be better referred to as routines to perform specific operations and a monitor routine to control the selection of these several operating routines.
>
> The instruction sheet for the computer operator includes all explanations necessary for operation of the equipment. The person using the Auditape system need not be concerned with any actions taken by the computer operator unless the application is being made for an audit purpose that requires control against possible manipulation of data by intervention of the operator.

---

[3]In addition to the generalized approach discussed here, there are several other generalized routines available:

Audassist	Alexander Grant & Co.
Auditpak	Lybrand, Ross Bros. & Montgomery
Auditronics	Ernst & Ernst
CARS	Computer Audit Systems, Inc.
Strata	Touche, Ross & Co.

The specification sheets are the means by which the person using the Auditape system adapts it to his purpose and to the input records available for each application. The specification sheets are used as a source document from which specification cards are key punched and read into the computer memory and combined with instructions read from the auditape to complete the program for the particular routine being processed.

The routines, other than the monitor routine, comprising the auditape are:

1. Edit routine, including the subtotal subroutine and an include-exclude subroutine.
2. Print/punch routine
3. Summarize routine
4. Mathematical routine
5. Audit sample routine

Edit Routine

The principal problem in developing the Auditape system, or any set of generalized programs, arises from the wide variety in the format of the computer records to be processed. This variety occurs not only in the records used by different companies for similar applications, but also for different applications by any one company. . . . In the absence of a generalized program, a separate program is required for each specific record format to be processed, even though the basic operation to be performed by each of the specific programs might be the same.

This problem is solved in the Auditape system by use of the Edit Routine, which causes selected data to be read from any specified position in the input record regardless of its format and written in any specified field on an output tape in the Auditape record format. This output tape then becomes the input for any of the other routines in the system.

The Subtotal or Include/Exclude Subroutine can be processed simultaneously with the Edit Routine at the option of the person using the Auditape system. These subroutines can be used for special analyses and other purposes by providing subtotals of input data in certain specified classifications and by including or excluding input data based on certain specified criteria.

Print/Punch Routine

Aside from control totals and processing messages, the results from each of the other routines are written on an output tape in the Auditape record format. With any of these tapes as input, the Print/Punch Routine can be used to provide printed or punched card output or both. This routine also includes options to permit the fields in the Auditape record to be printed out in any desired order, and to print appropriate descriptive headings over each column of data.

Summarize Routine

The Summarize Routine can be used to summarize details of records by some identifying characteristic such as customer number or inventory part number.

Mathematical Routine

The Mathematical Routine performs addition, subtraction, multiplication, or division of amounts in any two quantitative fields in the Auditape record, or of amounts in one of such fields and a specified constant amount.

Audit Sample Routine

The Audit Sample Routine computes the approximate optimum sample size required to obtain the statistical precision and reliability specified for a particular sample and selects the items to be included in the sample.

Use of Generalized Programs: an Illustration

To compare the use of a generalized program with the use of programs written by or under the supervision of the auditor, one of the authors used Auditape in an accounts-receivable audit application for which special computer-audit programs had previously been written to perform certain audit procedures. Included in these specialized audit programs were accounts-receivable year-end procedures in a medium-sized manufacturing company. The auditor's objectives were (1) to determine the validity of the client's year-end accounts-receivable amount and (2) to evaluate the collectibility of the accounts.

Trade accounts receivable, in the aggregate, totalled approximately $2,500,000 and consisted of over 6,000 accounts, approximately 5 percent of which represented about 80 percent of the total dollar value. The accounts receivable were on two magnetic-tape files, one being the basic record file containing data records for each customer (as shown in Table 1), the other being the item record file containing the details—i.e., invoices, unidentified cash payments—which supported the basic record account balance (see Table 2 for item record of unpaid invoices).

Audit Procedures

In performing the year-end audit procedures for the accounts-receivable files, the auditor developed certain computer programs using the client's accounts-receivable basic record file and the item record file.

Table 1. Accounts Receivable Basic Record

Data Field	Number of Characters	Data Field	Number of Characters
Customer number	7	Highest delinquency	
Current A/R balance	9	Number of items	3
Amount on order		Amount	9
Steel	9	Date	4
Tungsten	9	Date last sale	6
Sundry	9	Sales history (material amount only)	
Credit Limit		(By-product line—steel, tungsten, sundry)	
Amount	7	3rd prior year	9
Date limit established	6	2d prior year	9
Credit history		1st prior year	9
Date account opened	6	This year to date	9
Highest credit extended	9	This month	9
Date highest credit extended	6	Potential	9
Original credit limit	9	Profit at standard—year to date	9
Date original credit limit established	6	Payment history	
Previous credit limit	9	Payment ratings (company establishes	
Date previous credit limit established	4	payment ratings 0-9 based on payments	
Number of months of previous credit limit	2	for each quarter):	
Number of items currently delinquent	3	3rd prior year—by quarter	4
Amount currently delinquent	9	2d prior year—by quarter	4
Delinquency history		1st prior year—by quarter	4
Months reporting	2	This year—by quarter	4
Months delinquent	2	Dollars paid this quarter	
Consecutive months delinquent	2	By discount date	9
Last month delinquent	4	By due date	9
		Customer name and address	136

Table 2. A/R Item Record for Unpaid Invoices

Data Field	Number of Characters
Item record code	1
Customer number	7
Date	5
Invoice number	12
Gross amount of invoice	9
Net amount of invoice	9
Cash discount	7

These files were then processed with the computer/audit programs as shown in Figure 2. The procedures performed by the three programs were:

1. Select for positive confirmation, and print on the circularization report, accounts with:

   a. balance ≥ $5,000 (type Code 1);

   b. balance ≥ $1,000 but ≤ $5,000 and with any portion of the account 30 or more days delinquent (type Code 2);

c. balance $\geq$ $1,000 and with sales this year five-hundred percent $\geq$ last year's sales or $\leq$ 20 percent of last year's sales (type Code 3).

2. Randomly select for negative confirmation, and print on the circularization report, 10 percent of the remaining accounts (type Code 0).

3. Age all accounts.

4. Select and print on the exception report all accounts:

   a. over credit limit (type Code 4);

   b. whose basic record balance is not in agreement with the total amount of all items in its item record (type Code 5);

   c. with credit balance $\geq$ $500 (type Code 6).

Figure 2. Systems flowchart computer-audit programs.

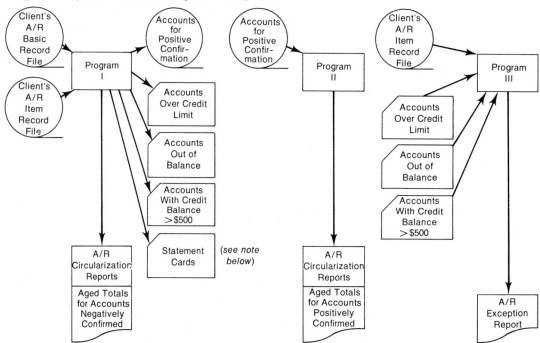

5. Accumulate and print on the circularization report:

    a. number of accounts in basic record file;

    b. aged totals of all accounts in basic record file;

    c. number of items in item record file;

    d. total balance of all items in item record file;

    e. total balance of all accounts with credit balances;

    f. number of accounts selected for negative confirmation and aged totals for these accounts;

    g. number of accounts selected for positive confirmation and aged totals for these accounts.

Developing Computer/Audit Programs

After formulating the audit procedures for the accounts-receivable work and the systems flow charts, the auditor prepared program flow charts and designed output records to include the required audit information.

Of the three programs shown on the system flow charts, (see Figure 2) Program I includes most of the processing logic and decision criteria. Programs II and III merely print the machine-readable output of Program I.

The primary output from the computer processing is the accounts-receivable circulation report (see Table 3). The report was set up in working-paper form ready for the auditor's analysis. The digit under the "T" column in the report corresponds to the type of confirmation request— that is, 1 represents a positive confirmation request. File totals are printed at the end of the report for comparison with file totals shown on the client's aged trial balance.

The Auditape System Applied

In using the Auditape system to perform the audit procedures enumerated above, the auditor completed the relevant specification sheets required to use the system. There were 38 separate computer runs required to perform the necessary audit procedures. Many of these runs were necessary to get the data into the Auditape record format for performing the audit procedures.

Table 3.   Accounts-Receivable Circularization Sept. 30, 19XX

Number	Name and Address	T	S	Balances	Difference	No Reply	Explanation and Disposition
0333500	Ace Inc. 2105 Winspear Ave. Madison, Ill.	1	0	7,280.31 937.41	Balance 30 Days 60 Days 90 Days		
0350000	Acme Company 7055 Best Rd. Lansing 4, Mich.	1	0	12,408.47 2,463.94	Balance 30 Days 60 Days 90 Days		
0514000	Adder Co. Yakima, Wash.	1	0	33,347.91 23,180.43	Balance 30 Days 60 Days 90 Days		
1161000	Boom Tools 12360 Aspen Lane Boulder, Colo.	1	0	6,037.19 3,022.76	Balance 30 Days 60 Days 90 Days		
1466000	Crisp Forging Mfg. Lowell, Mass.	1	0	34,246.84 23,082.57	Balance 30 Days 60 Days 90 Days		
2511000	Dunhill Supply 4890 South Canton St. Canton, Ohio	1	0	5,772.28 2,236.99	Balance 30 Days 60 Days 90 Days		
2620075	Earth-Movers Inc. Puyallup, Wash.	1	0	11,784.47 7,121.74	Balance 30 Days 60 Days 90 Days		
2646000	Esther Tools College Lane Williams, Pa.	1	0	7,234.73 255.96	Balance 30 Days 60 Days 90 Days		
3170000	First Supply 6360 Division Rd. Battle Creek, Mich.	1	0	8,098.33 75.20	Balance 30 Days 60 Days 90 Days		
3262310	Gunn Forging Barnesville, Ind.	1	0	6,738.26 3,212.17	Balance 30 Days 60 Days 90 Days		

Page total   10 Accounts: Balance 132,948.79; 30 DAYS 65,589.17; 60 DAYS; 90 DAYS

From the analysis it was concluded that the Auditape system could perform all of the significant procedures included in the specialized program.

As to a comparison of time requirements of both approaches, the analysis indicated:

	Specialized Programs	Auditape
Analysis of problem (including flowcharting, input-output design)	150.0 hrs.	30-50.0 hrs. (estimated)
Programming (including coding, key-punching, assembly and testing)	70.0 hrs.	
Completion and key-punching of specification sheets		12.0 hrs. (estimated 2 hrs. for key-punching)
Run time	0.5 hrs.	2.5 hrs.
	220.5 hrs.	44.5—64.5 hrs.

One footnote to the above time analysis should be added. The actual time for the analysis of the program originally was 230 hours; this reflected some developmental and learning time. Discounting this time, it is more realistic to think in terms of 150 hours, which I have shown above, for the analysis of the problem. Approximately 100 to 120 of the 150 hours would be required for flowcharting and input-output design and would be unnecessary when using the Auditape system; hence the 30 to 50 hours for analysis under Auditape.

It is reasonable to state that there will be considerable activity in the area of generalized audit programs in the future by CPA firms and software companies.

Introduction to Readings

Many methods and measures for achieving control objectives are affected by electronic data processing. Traditional functions and departments in the organization have been broken up and rearranged as information flows through new channels in the corporate structure. Systems of authorizing and recording business transactions formerly used people for processing and reviewing data, but these systems are becoming heavily dependent on automated techniques and controls in EDP-dominated situations. Obviously the auditor needs to understand the nature of these controls in order to properly evaluate and test the computer data processing system, to challenge traditional methods of control, and to minimize the cost of achieving control.

The first reading, "Plugging the Leaks in Computer Security," presents some control concepts for EDP systems and the role of auditors in evaluating EDP controls and procedures. The second reading is a questionnaire developed by the AICPA to assist auditors in the review of data processing systems and internal controls. The main purpose of including the questionnaire is to illustrate the types of controls the auditor should review in EDP systems and the level of understanding of electronic data processing required to perform a control review.

The third article presents a method of testing computerized systems—the test-data approach. This approach involves the preparation of computer-readable data processed under auditor control to test the client's computer programs. The use of test data and use of computer audit programs are the two techniques of using the computer in auditing.

Plugging the Leaks
in Computer Security

Joseph J. Wasserman

Foreword. Computers are not supposed to make mistakes, but the humans who instruct them often do. And the results can be disastrous unless management has developed controls for spotting and correcting mistakes early. As the new generation of computer systems becomes increasingly complex, the people who run them need to develop a corresponding sophistication. In particular, top management should be aware of the importance of new control and auditing concepts. In this article, the author describes some of these concepts and shows how a company can use them. One

starting point is to develop a top-level executive whose prime responsibility is to formulate a comprehensive computer control policy and made sure that operating personnel understand it, especially the company's internal auditors, who must adapt conventional control practices to meet the needs of the new EDP system. Most of the new techniques he describes are designed to control unintentional human errors, since these are the cause of most malfunctions in computer systems. However, fraud and natural disaster also pose serious threats, and a secure system must have adequate safeguards against these dangers, too.

Many companies are working to develop new business applications for electronic data processing (EDP). All too often this effort is not accompanied by a proportional effort to develop computer control systems which will protect the company's assets from misuse or error. Yet the importance of effective computer control is increasing, for a number of reasons:

The growing size and complexity of EDP systems, which make errors more costly and more difficult to detect.

The sophistication of third-generation hardware, where original documents may exist only in the form of magnetic records within the computer, placed there directly from remote terminals. (This development presents many new problems, such as security of data, and it increases the number of sources where incorrect inputs can be generated.)

The growing reliance of management on information generated by computer systems, not only for financial data but also in such areas as marketing, production, engineering, and forecasting.

A continuing shortage of skilled computer personnel, which leads to rapid turnover and the hiring of marginal workers.

When management does think of computer control systems, it tends to focus mainly on fraud, and there have been some widely publicized cases of this. But the real problem for most companies is not fraud but ordinary human error, which can cost a company millions of dollars without criminal intent on anyone's part. Computer security thus involves a review of every possible source of control breakdown—a highly demanding, but not impossible, job.

New Control Concepts

One factor that has made the job more difficult is lack of awareness by many executives of new control concepts required for computer systems. EDP systems are so new that few top executives have had much first-hand experience with them. While computer manufacturers do attempt to give executives an understanding of computer capabilities, the introduction is often quite general, and the need for controls is not sufficiently emphasized.

Because of this basic misunderstanding about EDP systems, many companies have eliminated traditional controls for checking human calculations—"the computer doesn't make mistakes." But computers are programmed and operated by humans, who still do make mistakes. Therefore, traditional control techniques still can be important and should be evaluated in terms of their usefulness to EDP systems. In addition, new control concepts must be devised to use the powerful capabilities of the computer. Although top management has the primary task of formulating a basic control policy, *all* employees connected with an EDP system have a responsibility to ensure that data processing is adequately controlled.

One slowly developing trend that fosters this approach is the strategic placement of a qualified top-level executive whose primary responsibility is to direct the corporate computer efforts. With this technical know-how available on the executive level, the company has taken a positive step toward establishing an up-to-date control philosophy. The company can then establish meaningful procedures to protect computer programs and data against

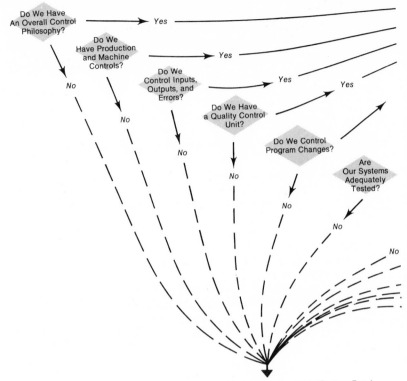

Figure 1. Steps toward a secure computer system.

error, malice, fraud, disaster, or system break-downs.

In this article, we will analyze these potential problem areas and show how a combination of good judgment and machine capabilities can control them. Figure 1 summarizes the problems and the primary elements in an adequate control system.

Getting off to Good Start

Testing is vital to the success of a system and, therefore, is worth careful scrutiny. In particular, the last test phase, where all elements of a new installation are tested as a unit, indicates whether the system is reliable.

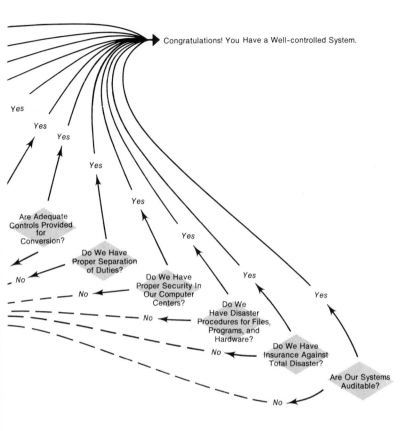

Congratulations! You Have a Well-controlled System.

Yes

Yes

Yes

Yes

Yes

Yes

Yes

Yes

Yes

Are Adequate
Controls Provided
for
Conversion?

Do We Have
Proper Separation
of Duties?

Do We Have
Proper Security In
Our Computer
Centers?

Do We
Have Disaster
Procedures for Files,
Programs, and
Hardware?

Do We Have
Insurance Against
Total Disaster?

Are Our Systems
Auditable?

No

No

No

No

No

Here the best method is to run the new and old systems in parallel, comparing results where possible. For example:

Parallel testing was successfully applied to a telephone company operation involving rating and billing of toll messages. When the new system was considered ready for use, the design

staff extracted 300,000 toll messages that were prepared for processing by the old system. The 300,000 messages were adjusted so they could be entered as inputs to the new system.

The results of processing these messages through both systems were compared by the computer to determine whether the new system was capable of rating, filing, and billing the toll messages correctly. Any toll messages that created exceptions not encountered in the old system were traced by the systems design staff to discover the cause of discrepancy, and corrective action was taken before the new system was introduced.

If a parallel test is not feasible, the operation of the new system may be checked by a test deck consisting of fictitious transactions especially designed to test the system's logic. The test deck should be as complete as possible, since minor oversights can cause major losses. In one instance, an organization that pays benefits to large numbers of people neglected to include a test case to ensure that a check on the termination data for benefits was part of the computer program. As a result, many millions of dollars were paid out to persons whose benefit periods had expired.

Canvassing of Data. Finally, during the changeover to the new system, a careful check should be made to ensure that all data are converted as requested. This may sound elementary, but it is very important. For instance, one major corporation, when making a changeover, failed to convert all the data from its old system; and this failure cost the company nearly $3 million.

The controls also should ensure that data are converted only once, or a company may find itself duplicating asset records or billing its customers several times for the same item.

A final check should be made to ensure that the data going into the new system have been verified and are as complete and error-free as is economically feasible. Control totals

of items such as dollars and units based on the old system should be checked as the records are converted. One way of doing this is to write, *prior to conversion*, computer programs that will edit individual records for missing data and invalid codes; this step amounts to "scrubbing" (i.e., cleaning) the data in the old system. For example, prior to converting to a new payroll system, the employee records from the old system should be checked to ensure that significant data, such as tax codes and social security numbers, are present and valid. The problems of converting to a new system are great enough without adding the burden of erroneous data.

Quality Control

As part of a plan for monitoring an EDP system, a quality control unit should be established to sample the accuracy of data both before and after computer processing (see Figure 2). Such quality control units were common in the precomputer era, when it was possible to follow the flow of data by checking documents as they were processed manually. The era of large-volume computer input and output makes quality control even more important.

The degree of training needed for the quality control unit depends on the sophistication of the system. The unit's major function is to spot data that are obviously unrealistic. For example, if the number of errors is increasing, the quality of incoming data should be scrutinized more carefully at its source to determine the cause(s) of error. This type of control and analysis will detect minor problems before they become major and will in-

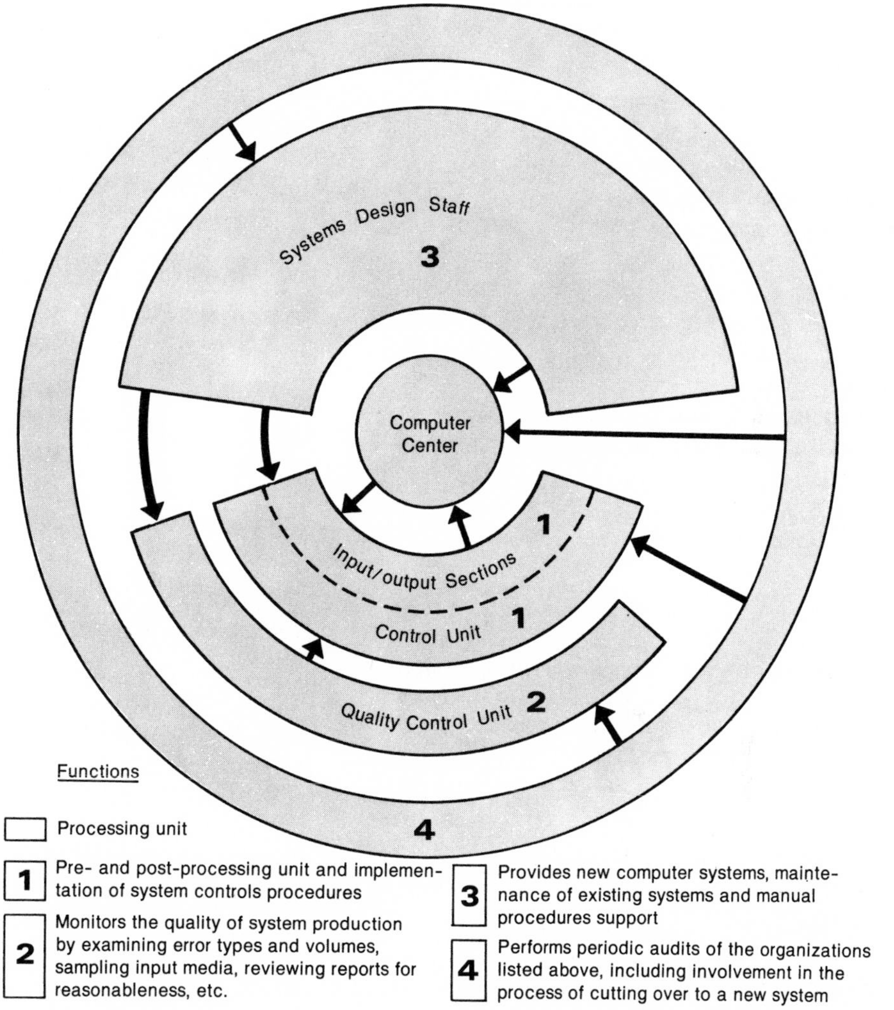
Systems Design Staff
3
Computer Center
Input/output Sections
1
Control Unit 1
Quality Control Unit 2
4
Functions
Processing unit
1 Pre- and post-processing unit and implementation of system controls procedures
2 Monitors the quality of system production by examining error types and volumes, sampling input media, reviewing reports for reasonableness, etc.
3 Provides new computer systems, maintenance of existing systems and manual procedures support
4 Performs periodic audits of the organizations listed above, including involvement in the process of cutting over to a new system

Note: Each of the above functions should have a person(s) designated responsible for organizational control standards and coordination of standards with other organizations.

Figure 2. Relationships among control groups.

dicate where the system needs to be reinforced through additional training or improved controls.

Input, Output and Errors. As part of the control unit, an input section (see Figure 2) should maintain positive controls over all transactions it receives and, wherever possible, should identify them by type, source, and date. Once such controls are established, they should be part of an interlocking system of control totals which serve to assure that data accounted for as input are not subsequently lost or distorted.

As for controlling the accuracy of a system's output, care must be taken to ensure that machine controls cannot be overridden because of human error. To illustrate:

Although it possessed an apparently foolproof system, one company came close to a disastrous loss of records stored on a master computer tape because of an operator's mistake. The tape was updated daily by adding the latest day's results to the master file. A computer operator once mistakenly used the previous day's master tape, which was kept as a backup. The computer program recognized that the wrong tape had been mounted and printed out a message saying so, but the operator ignored the message and pushed the restart button. The fact that one day's results were missing from the master file was not discovered until 20 days later, and reconstructing the master file was extremely costly.

When the serious consequences of such an error were recognized, the internal auditors requested the systems design staff to change the program so that the master file could be processed only if the proper tape were mounted.

Output controls over receipt and distribution of data will ensure reasonableness, timeliness, and completeness of computerized results. Output data should be balanced against machine-generated control totals when practical.

While some errors in an EDP system are inevitable, the manner in which they are corrected and reentered may determine the success or failure of the system. Even when the fact that errors are being made is noted, system designers often neglect manual and machine methods of correcting the mistakes. A good control system should provide a built-in method of error analysis, including information on the type, quantity, value, and age of errors, so that the source can be determined and corrective action taken.

In the case of systems that process large volumes of data and, as a consequence, are subject to a significant number of mistakes, management should consider maintaining a master file of detected errors that provides a positive control of errors, records their magnitude, quantity, source, and age. Statistics from this file will provide management with a computerized indication of error trends, which can then be countered by appropriate controls.

Other Checks and Safeguards. There should be written instructions for all machine operations. These instructions should be kept complete, current, and understandable; and computer room managers should ensure that their operations personnel are following the procedures outlined. The best control system is no better than the performance of the people who run the computer operation, so records of the performance of both men and machines should be kept. Supervisors should also periodically review operator interventions, machine halts, and other occurrences indicating unusual conditions. Records of machine performance, preventive maintenance periods, and schedules of operation should, of course, be kept current. All this falls in the category of what are often called "production and machine controls."

The EDP library deserves more attention than it usually gets. Many companies fail to realize the size of their investment in programs and data files for an EDP system. The loss of a production or program tape can be very costly, so careful controls should be established to ensure that tapes are removed from the library only when needed, that only authorized personnel have access to the library, that all tapes are clearly labeled, and that records of tape use are kept.

Library controls should also include maintenance of backup tapes (usually referred to as "grandfather," "father," and "son," depending on how far back they go). Such backup data can restore current data files in case the latest tapes are damaged or destroyed.

The problem of maintaining backup files is more complicated for the newer random-access computer systems, in which outdated information is erased as new data are processed. However, magnetic tape can duplicate the various files contained on storage devices (such as disks, drums, and data cells) so that the system can be restored to its most current status in case of hardware or program failure.

Program Changes. In view of the possibility of major losses resulting from minor program changes, management should limit the number of people who are authorized to change operating programs or internally stored program data. The slightest change can have extraordinary effects. For instance:

> At Cape Kennedy a space launching failed recently because, during a program change, a computer symbol equivalent to a comma was inadvertently omitted from the program. The omission sent the rocket so far off course that it had to be destroyed.

In Company operations, the possibility of fraud through unauthorized program changes is obvious. To illustrate:

> In one bank, a programmer altered a savings account program to transfer the "round off" fractions of cents in the interest calculation to an account he maintained under a fictitious name; he was able to withdraw large sums of money before his scheme was detected.

Yet as far as *internal* security is concerned losses from fraud are dwarfed by losses from honest mistakes resulting from unauthorized program changes. The likelihood of loss from mistakes can be substantially reduced if programs are changed only by those persons having the proper authority.

An adequate security system should make clear the type of information to be made available to each employee. Classified information, such as data relating to customer credit, shareholders, payroll, marketing, and manufacturing processes, must be categorized by appropriate security levels.

Today, setting up a security program is complicated by the growing use of remote terminals. It is not uncommon for a company to have its computer in one center, data transmission points in several different cities or states, and assembly of final reports in still another location. When employees hundreds of miles away are in direct contact with the computer files, there must be controls to ensure that the files are not changed from remote locations without authorization, and that classified or sensitive data are available only to authorized personnel in those locations. For instance:

The number of remote terminals through which computer files can be changed should be limited.

Identification codes for each terminal and authorization codes should be used for the limited number of employees who are authorized to operate remote equipment. The computer should be programmed to check the validity of the codes before it accepts or gives information. Since personnel turnover is high, identification codes should be changed frequently.

The adequacy of controls themselves should be checked. One way is to have supervisors try to gain access to a remote terminal without authorization. If they can use the terminal without being challenged, so can others.

External Security

While fraud tends to be overpublicized as a problem of internal security, just the opposite seems to be the case in matters of security against outsiders. Yet knowledge about computer systems is widespread enough that numerous persons outside the company may use a system's weaknesses for their own pro-fit. A striking illustration of how this calls for controls occurred when banks introduced computerized accounting systems:

In these systems each customer had his account number preprinted in magnetic ink on his deposit slips and checks. A supply of the preprinted deposit slips was sent to all bank customers, and blank deposit slips were made available at the bank. Several cases of fraud came to light in which customers defrauded the bank by interspersing their magnetically coded deposit slips with the blank deposit slips provided at the bank. An unsuspecting customer using the defrauder's deposit slip would have his deposit credited to the defrauder's account, because the computer would apply the deposit to the account number that was magnetically inscribed on the deposit slip. After calling the bank to find out the balance in his account, the defrauder would withdraw his supposed funds. Many thousands of dollars were stolen until a system of controls was developed.

This simple but ingenious fraud is typical of the new challenges to security systems that EDP advances create. Even the concentration of vital records, programs, and equipment in a single location—an obvious security problem produced by having a centralized EDP operation—often goes unnoticed by management.

Guarding the System. There is every reason to keep unauthorized personnel and visitors out of the computer room. Yet many companies view their computer installations as showplaces, welcoming visitors with relatively little supervision and failing to provide even minimum security precautions. These companies apparently have not considered the possible losses from damaged files or lost programs and the consequences of having equipment out of service.

Protection from Disaster. The EDP system control plans should include protection against disruptions ranging up to major disasters.

One of the most obvious protective measures—and hence one that is often overlooked— is simple observance of fire prevention rules. There should be well-established and frequently practiced procedures for protecting files, programs, and hardware against fire hazards. As far as is possible, duplicates of all vital files, programs, and related documentation should be maintained in another location. Provision should be made for emergency use of backup equipment and even temporary manual processing of critical data.

Most companies are aware of the risks inherent in fire, flood, or natural disaster, but other potential hazards may not be so obvious. To illustrate:

Lack of a complete set of backup files caused a serious problem for one company. An employee, who was cleaning the interior of a magnetic drum cabinet, attached his magnetic flashlight to the frame of the unit. The magnet destroyed a portion of the data on the drum, a portion which the company did not ordinarily duplicate. The company lost six days of computer time reconstructing the lost data. In addition to the need for backup files and programs, this situation points out the need for proper training of personnel who maintain computer equipment.

Equipment or program failure is a continual problem. With high-speed EDP systems, the possibility of losing, duplicating, or misprocessing transactions because of these failures is great. "Recovery/restart" is the term applied to the programs and procedures used by a computer system to isolate and correct failures and to continue processing after a failure has occurred. These procedures may range from a simple rerun of the job being processed to a very elaborate and complex system involving programs designed specifically for this function.

Adequate Insurance. Increasing investments in program development, computer hardware (if owned), and stored data make it important for management to evaluate a company's insurance coverage. Is there enough insurance to avert substantial *financial* loss in the event of an EDP system disaster from causes such as fire, natural disaster, and vandalism? Recent unrest on college campuses has accounted for three serious situations involving computer centers:

In Montreal, Canada, at Sir George Williams University, students set fire to the computer center, causing an estimated $1 million damage to computer equipment.

At Brandeis and Northwestern Universities, militant students occupied the computer centers. In both of the latter situations the students held the computer as a hostage, so to speak, and were not destructive.

A number of insurance companies offer EDP policies. In calculating the amount of coverage needed, the insurance and data processing managers should determine the cost of reconstructing files (both revenue producing and administrative data) in case they are destroyed, and of carrying on normal business while this is done.[1] The added cost of using backup equipment should also be taken into account.

Control of/by People

In data processing, one employee can perform functions that were previously assigned to several business units. Unless there are proper controls, such as those mentioned, knowledgeable but unscrupulous employees can manipulate programs for their own benefit, and incompetent employees can cause lasting damage by making errors. If duties are properly separated, the possibility of such damage is minimized, since each employee will have only a limited role in the entire system's operation.

However, management has tended to overlook separation of duties because of the rapid growth in computer use and the general shortage of personnel. Separation of duties may also be overlooked when a reduction in EDP staff or a combining of functions is carried out as a means of cost saving with the new system. These factors often make management dependent on a handful of experienced EDP people who "grew up with the system" and have a monopoly on operating know-how. This increases the vulnerability of records and makes it difficult to assess individual performance and pinpoint weak spots in the EDP system.

Only one person or operating group should be responsible for an operation at any one time. Ideally, this means drawing lines between the employees who authorize a trans-action and produce the input, those who process the data, and those who use the output for reports or for other management purposes. The same controls should cover scheduling, manual and machine operations, maintenance of programs, and related functions. For example, programmers should not have access to the entire library of programs, if only to guard against the possibility of malicious damage.

An equally important control measure is rotation of employees within the EDP group. This has a twofold value:

1. It prevents an employee or group of employees from so dominating one area of operations that losses from fraud or error are not detected.

2. The high rate of turnover among computer personnel makes it prudent to avoid relying on any individual. Every employee should be replaceable by someone with a working knowledge of the position.

New Role for Auditors. The advent of computers caught the audit world unprepared. Most executives still envisioned the auditor doing the traditional finance-oriented audit; a few managements had their auditors take a look at the new computer world, but the auditors lacked the knowledge and know-how they needed to master it. Thus there was a scarcity of auditors grounded in computer system principles and equipped to effectively deal with computerized operations.

In the Bell System, an executive decision was made in 1959 to utilize the internal auditing staff as an important new influence on the development of future computer-control

---

[1]See Haig G. Neville, re: "Danger Ahead! Safeguard Your Computer," (Letters to the Editor) *Harvard Business Review*, May–June 1969, p. 40.

systems. Bell realized that computer processing imposed new control requirements, new areas of audit interest, and the elimination of some traditional audit concerns. In order to establish an effective EDP audit function, management selected a staff of EDP auditors who had a good grasp of auditing principles and sufficient aptitude and knowledge of the EDP field, and it gave them the following objectives:

1. Develop new computerized audit techniques and have them built into the system wherever possible.

2. Develop control requirements and techniques, and emphasize to the systems design staff the need for an adequate control system.

3. Evaluate the effectiveness of the control system while it is still in the design process.

4. Evaluate all other areas, such as system testing and conversion, where controls are essential.

In general, the EDP auditor was not to assume responsibility for the development of a control system but was to evaluate the procedures and facilities being designed. This was an important point, for management saw that if the auditor did design control systems, he would lose his objectivity and, in effect, end up auditing himself. Similarly, he was not to be responsible for enforcing control procedures, but only for evaluating the effectiveness of these controls. The EDP auditor thus became a "devil's advocate" on behalf of top management.

The new approach to EDP auditing was called "preconversion auditing." It provided management with an independent control appraisal of future computer systems.

In an approach like the preconversion audit, management is called on to mediate between the systems design and auditing viewpoints. If there is a difference of opinion on a control question, it is up to management to listen to both points of view and make a decision by weighing the cost of controls against the degree of risk involved.

Making the System Auditable. It is the auditor's responsibility to ensure that computer systems are auditable when they become operational. He should be continually on the alert for possible effects that the proposed new system will have on internal controls, and should develop audit requirements accordingly. It has become increasingly difficult to audit using conventional techniques, because hard-copy printouts are being substantially curtailed and very often source documents are not in a readily usable sequence. More often than not, information required by the auditor is no longer readily available without additional costly computer runs, and computer time is becoming more and more difficult to obtain. For these reasons, it is essential for him to make his audit requirements known to the systems people at the earliest possible time.

It seems clear that the EDP auditor should attempt to make optimum use of computer technology as an audit tool. He should attempt to have audit techniques and routines built into the computer system, where it is feasible and economical to do so. In this manner, much of the auditing work can be performed as a by-product of the regular operation at little or no extra cost.

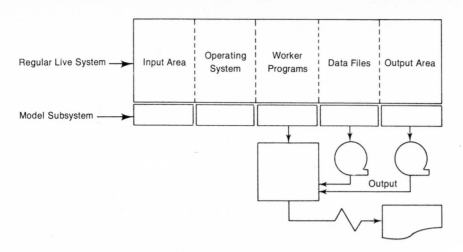

Figure 3. Testing the main system with a mini-company. This schematic diagram of a third generation computer system has been broken down into five basic components. The known results of processing the mini-company data are stored in magnetic form. The results of each day's test transactions are verified by using a comparison program that is one of the worker programs. Only exceptions are reported.

The Mini-Company Test. As indicated earlier, the test deck is one useful method of checking a new computer system. The method is popular among auditors. A refined and more sophisticated method is what I call the "mini-company" test. A mini-company can be defined as a means of passing fictitious test transactions through a computer system simultaneously with live data, without adversely affecting the live files or outputs. In other words, it is a small subsystem of the regular system. A separate set of outputs, including statistics and reports, are produced for the mini-company. This not only ensures that the test material does not interfere with any outputs concerning the real company, but also enables the auditor to check that statistics and reports are being prepared correctly (see Figure 3).

Let us see how the mini-company concept might be applied to a hypothetical payroll system:

Suppose the computerized payroll system of the hypothetical company has a master tape file that contains a record for each employee in the company. Each pay period, a payroll computation program is run which has as its input the current master file and transactions consisting of employee time allocation (hours worked, absence, vacation days, and so forth) during the pay period. The program produces three output tape files: (a) an updated master file, (b) a payroll register and check file, and (c) a reports file.

To define the mini-company, a fictitious Department 9999 is established. It of course consists of fictitious employees. Records must be established for the employees on the live master file. Once the master records are established, fictitious transactions will be prepared to be applied to these records. The fictitious master records and associated transactions constitute the mini-company base and must be designed to test as much of the payroll system's program

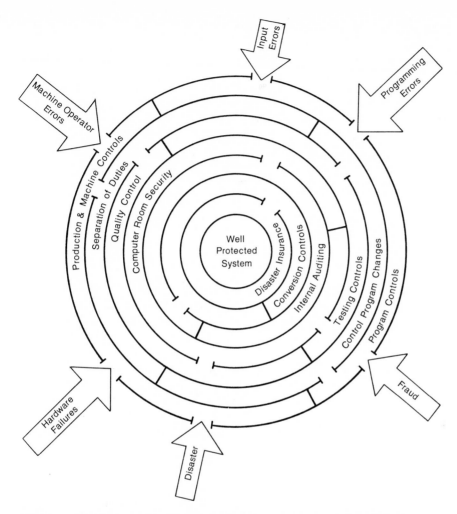

Figure 4. The control maze. The attack arrows have as their objectives destruction of the "Well-Protected System." If the system is properly controlled, each of the factors represented by an arrow will be interrupted and negated by applicable control elements as it attempts to penetrate the control maze.

logic as possible. Mini-company transactions are entered into the payroll computation and run right along with live transactions.

The mini-company data are separated from the live data in a subsequent computer run.

Then the live data or "output files," as they are called, are processed in the normal manner, with checks printed and scheduled reports made. Similarly the mini-company data are processed to produce a payroll register, checks, and reports. The results produced by computer processing of the mini-company's input are compared with results previously calculated outside the computer to determine if any irregularities in controls or processing have occurred.

This concept is particularly advantageous because it permits continuous testing of the system on a live basis. Auditors will utilize the mini-company for periodic system reviews, and a quality control group can use the continuous-testing capabilities to great advantage in meeting its daily responsibilities for monitoring the quality of system production.

Other Auditing Techniques. In addition to the mini-company, other special audit programs can be developed. Briefly, here are some special programs which can be used by the auditor on either an off-line or on-line basis:

Comparison—matches two duplicate files contained on magnetic tape, cards, or disks; determines if they are identical; and identifies any unmatched records. (This type of program has been used in the Bell System to verify rating tables for toll messages. In one instance tape files containing tables of approximately 35,000 rating points were compared in approximately ten minutes using second-generation computer hardware. The advantages of the comparison program are its ability to perform 100% verification and identify for the auditor any exceptions for more detailed review.)

Sampling—samples records in a file on a random basis.

Extraction—extracts specific records from the file.

Compilation—checks mathematical computations made by the computer, such as adding or subtracting related fields of data or multiplying a data field by a constant. (This type of program is particularly useful in verifying the proper application of formulas in computer runs. For example, if employee group insurance deductions are developed in a payroll system by multiplying annual salary by a fixed rate, the compilation program can make these calculations independent of the regular programs. The comparison program just outlined can then be used to determine if the results of the compilation program and the regular payroll runs are in agreement.)

Systems that are auditable also should meet the requirements of public accountants and various government agencies. For example:

Certified public accountants need the ability to audit computerized records of assets, liabilities, expenses, and income for yearly financial statements.

Internal Revenue Service auditors want to check on how transactions are handled, whether expenses are correct, and whether all income is stated properly.

Department of Defense contract auditors want to check that expenses are properly allocated to government contracts.

Conclusion

The establishment of a well-controlled and auditable computer system no longer should be the impossible dream of the executive. Management might picture a computer control system as a control maze (see Figure 4). Each control function should complement another function, so that a breakdown in one area is corrected by controls in another area. Most losses through error or fraud can be prevented by such interlocking controls.

No one group should bear complete responsibility for protecting the computer system. The need for controls should be instilled in the entire organization, starting with top management and extending to all personnel.

Questionnaire
for Evaluation of
Internal Control in
Electronic Data Processing

This appendix* contains a model questionnaire for obtaining information on internal control in an electric data processing installation.

The questionnaire is divided into two major parts:

1. Questions relating to the operation of the electronic data processing installation.

2. Questions relating to an individual data processing application.

*Appendix E from the AICPA's Auditing and EDP. Reprinted by permission from the American Institute of Certified Public Accountants, Copyrighted 1968.

This division reflects the fact that the organization, the policies and the procedures of the installation provide an environment in which individual applications are run. This environment must be understood before the controls associated with individual applications can be evaluated.

The review of a computer processing application should be carried out in the context of the entire processing cycle, including both computer and non-computer processing and controls. The firm's internal review questionnaire (or other method used to obtain information) should cover the non-computer procedures and controls; the application questionnaire is structured to provide only the added questions related to computer processing.

The number of questions to be included in a review questionnaire depends somewhat on how broadly the auditor views his audit assignment—whether he looks at items affecting operational efficiency as well as items directly affecting the audit. The control significance of the response to a particular question often, however, depends on the characteristics of the system being evaluated and the total picture of internal control. Each question in the model is coded A, B or C according to its general control significance. This code is only an indicator to aid the auditor; he must evaluate the significance in each particular case.

Code	In General, Question Relates to:
A	Control element which may affect the auditor's evaluation of internal control
B	Control element which tends to affect data processing safeguards but is, however, not likely to affect audit procedures
C	Element affecting operational effectiveness or efficiency

. . . All yes-or-no questions are worded so that "yes" is a favorable response and "no" indicates that further investigation or evaluation is required. The auditor may also wish to expand and clarify his answers by adding comments.

Part I. Questionnaire for Operation of the Electronic Data Processing Installation

1. *Background*

1–1. Where is the computer located? _____

1–2. Give a brief description of equipment _____
_____

   a. Manufacturer and model number of computer (this can be obtained from a copy of the manufacturer's invoice) _____

   b. Internal memory size _____

   c. File storage devices
   Magnetic tape (no. units ____) ☐
   Disk (no. drives ____) ☐
   Other (describe) ☐
   _____
   _____

   d. Input/output devices
   Card reader ☐
   Card punch ☐
   Printer ☐
   Other (list) ☐
   _____
   _____

1–3. Applications
   Cash ☐
   Receivables ☐
   Inventory ☐
   Property, plant and equipment ☐
   Payables ☐
   Sales ☐
   Payroll ☐
   Cost and expenses ☐

Other (list major ones below)   ☐

_____

_____

_____

2. *Organization*

2–1. Prepare or obtain an organization chart of the EDP organization. Determine position titles, job descriptions and names of persons in these positions.

2–2. Is there a segregation of duties such that:

a. The functions and duties of system design and programming are separate from computer operation?   ☐ ☐ A

b. Programmers do not operate the computer for regular processing runs?   ☐ ☐ A

c. Computer operators are restricted from access to data and program information not necessary for performing their assigned task?   ☐ ☐ B

d. The employees in data processing are separated from all duties relating to the initiation of transactions and initiation of requests for changes to the master files?   ☐ ☐ A

2–3. Are the operators assigned to individual application runs rotated periodically?   ☐ ☐ A

2–4. Are the computer operators required to take vacations?   ☐ ☐ B

2–5. Is supervision of operators sufficient to verify operator's adherence to prescribed operating procedures?   ☐ ☐ B

3. *The Control Function*

3–1. Is there a person or group charged with responsibility for the control function in the data processing department? Obtain description of duties. These duties will normally include:

a. Control over receipt of input data and recording of control information?   ☐ ☐

b. Reconciliation of control information (batch control with computer control totals, run-to-run controls, etc.)?   ☐ ☐

c. Control over distribution of output?   ☐ ☐

d. Control over errors to ensure that they are reported, corrected and reprocessed?   ☐ ☐

e. Review of console logs, error listings and other evidence of error detection and control?   ☐ ☐

3–2. Is the person or group responsible for control over processing by the data processing department independent from the person or group responsible for the operation of the equipment?   ☐ ☐ A

3–3. If there is an internal auditing group, does it perform EDP control activities related to:

a. Review or audit?   ☐ ☐ A

b. Day-to-day control activities?   ☐ ☐ A

If "yes" note the nature and extent of these activities.

3–4. Are master file changes or changes in program data factors authorized in writing by initiating departments? ☐ ☐ A

3–5. Are departments that initiate changes in master file data or program data factors furnished with notices or a register showing changes actually made? (Examples of such changes are changes in pay rates, selling prices, credit limits and commission tables.) ☐ ☐ A

4. *Control over the Console*

4–1. Are provisions adequate to prevent unauthorized entry of program changes and/or data through the console? The following questions reflect the types of controls which may be used.

  a. Are adequate machine operation logs being maintained? For each run, these should include information covering the run identification, operator, start and stop time, error halts and delays, and details of reruns. Idle time, down time, program testing, etc., should also be logged. ☐ ☐ B

  b. Is there an independent examination of computer logs to check the operator performance and machine efficiency? If "yes," ☐ ☐ B
    1. How often ——————
    2. By whom ——————
    3. How carried out ————
    ——————————
    ——————————
    ——————————

  c. If the computer has a typewriter console, is there an independent examination of the console printouts to detect operator problems and unauthorized intervention? ☐ ☐ B
    1. How often ——————
    2. By whom ——————
    3. How performed ————
    ——————————
    ——————————
    ——————————

5. *Management Practices*

5–1. Is there a written plan for future changes to be made to the system? ☐ ☐ C

5–2. Is approval for each application supported by a study of cost and benefit? ☐ ☐ C

5–3. Is a schedule of implementation prepared showing actual versus planned progress? ☐ ☐ C

5–4. Is there a systems and procedures manual for the activities of the installation? ☐ ☐ C

6. *Documentation*

6–1. Is a run manual prepared for each computer run? ☐ ☐ C

6–2. Are operator instructions prepared for each run? ☐ ☐ C

6–3. Are documentation practices adequate? ☐ ☐ C

Does the normal documentation for an application include the following?

	Yes	No
Problem Statement	☐	☐
System flowchart	☐	☐
Record layouts	☐	☐

Program flowcharts ☐ ☐
Program listing ☐ ☐
Test data ☐ ☐
Operator instructions ☐ ☐
Summary of controls ☐ ☐
Approval and change record ☐ ☐

6-4. Is there supervisory review of documentation to ensure that it is adequate? ☐ ☐ B

6-5. Is documentation kept up to date? ☐ ☐ C

7. *Program Revisions*

7-1. Is each program revision authorized by a request for change properly approved by management or supervisory personnel? ☐ ☐ B
a. Who authorizes? _____
b. How evidenced? _____

7-2. Are program changes, together with their effective dates, documented in a manner which preserves an accurate chronological record of the system? ☐ ☐ C

7-3. Are program revisions tested in the same manner as new programs? ☐ ☐ B

8. *Hardware Controls*

Unless there is evidence of hardware-based processing difficulties, the auditor can usually rely on the hardware. No review is ordinarily required for audit purposes.

9. *Control over Input and Output Data*

Although the control over input and output data must be exercised for each application, general questions regarding these controls may be used to ascertain policy regarding the use of control procedures.

9-1. Are initiating departments required to establish independent control over data submitted for processing (through the use of batch totals, document counts, or otherwise)? ☐ ☐ A

9-2. Is a schedule maintained of the reports and documents to be produced by the EDP system? ☐ ☐ B

9-3. Are output reports and documents reviewed before distribution to ascertain the reasonableness of the output? ☐ ☐ A

9-4. Are there adequate procedures for control over the distribution of reports? ☐ ☐ B

10. *Programmed Control over Processing*

Programmed controls must be evaluated in terms of each application.

11. *Controlling Error Investigations*

11-1. Are all error corrections reviewed and approved by persons who are independent of the data processing department? ☐ ☐ A

11-2. Are records maintained of errors occurring in the EDP system? ☐ ☐ C

11-3. Are these error records periodically reviewed by someone independent of data processing? ☐ ☐ C

12. *Physical Safeguards over Files*

12-1. Are important computer programs, essential documentation, records and files kept in fire-proof storage? ☐ ☐ C

12–2. Are copies of important programs, essential documentation, records and files stored in off-premises locations? □ □ C

13. *Procedural Controls for Safeguarding Files*

13–1. Are external labels used on all files? □ □ B

13–2. Are internal labels used on all magnetic tape files? □ □ B

13–3. Are file header labels checked by programs using the files? □ □ B

13–4. Are file protection rings used on all magnetic tape files to be preserved? □ □ B

13–5. Is the responsibility for issuing and storing magnetic tape or portable disk packs assigned to a tape librarian, either as a full-time or part-time duty? □ □ C

14. *Capability for File Reconstruction*

14–1. Are there provisions for the use of alternative facilities in the event of fire or other lengthy interruption? □ □ C

14–2. Is there adequate data processing insurance (other than fire coverage)? □ □ B

14–3. Are data processing personnel covered by fidelity insurance? □ □ B

Part II. Questionnaire for Individual Applications

The questions in this section are expected to supplement an internal review questionnaire or any other information-obtaining method. They should enable the auditor to obtain information on whether or not various control techniques have been used in the computer processing phase of a particular application.

The questionnaire is organized around the following control points:

1. Adequacy of control over input data
   a. Verification of correctness of input data
   b. Control over transmittal of data for processing
   c. Validity tests and other tests of input data

2. Adequacy of control over processing
   a. Control for completeness of processing
   b. Checks for correctness of processing
   c. Handling of rejects
   d. Management trail or audit trail

3. Adequacy of control over programs and data files
   a. Documentation
   b. Control over changes to master files
   c. Back-up procedures

The questions are numbered from 101 to distinguish them from questions in the general questionnaire. In cases where a control can be implemented by two or more methods, the related question is followed by a check-list of common control procedures. For each application (or run) related to the audit, the auditor should obtain information sufficient for answering all the relevant questions.

A data processing control review sheet may be used as a means of describing the input, processing and output controls for a particular application (see Figure 1, page 275). It may be used in place of or in addition to questions 101 and 102.

101. *Control over Input and Output for an Application*

Run No. and Run Name	Description of Control Field or Control Item	Type of Control	CONTROLS ESTABLISHED BY				CONTROLS VERIFIED BY			
			Department Sending Data	Data Processing Department Control Section	Computer Program	Preceding Run (run-to-run)	COMPUTER PROGRAM		Data Processing Department Control Section	User or Other Outside Department
							Control Information Output	Exception Output Only		

Data Processing Control Review Sheet

Prepared by _____ Date _____

Application _____

Reviewed by _____ Date _____

Figure 1. Sample questionnaire for processing control review.

101–1. Are there adequate controls over the creation of data and its conversion to machine-readable form? ☐ ☐ A

a. Procedural controls ☐

b. Mechanical or visual verification ☐

c. Check digit ☐

101–2. Is there adequate control over transmittal and input of data to detect loss or nonprocessing? Note data field controlled. ☐ ☐ A

Field

a. Financial control totals _____

b. Hash control totals _____

c. Document counts _____

d. Sequential numbering of input documents _____

e. Other _____

101–3. Are the input control totals and run-to-run control totals for each application checked by someone other than the equipment operator? ☐ ☐ A

By whom? _____

101–4. If data transmission is used, are controls adequate to determine that transmission is correct and no messages are lost? ☐ ☐ B

a. Message counts ☐

b. Character counts ☐

c. Dual transmission ☐

d. Other _____

101–5. Is input data adequately tested for validity, correctness and sequence? ☐ ☐ B

Note: Questions may have to be applied to each important data field of the input being reviewed by the auditor.

Fields Tested

a. Validity tests:
    1. Valid code _____
    2. Valid character _____
    3. Valid field _____
    4. Valid transaction _____
    5. Valid combinations _____
    6. Missing data _____
b. Sequence _____
c. Limit _____
d. Reasonableness _____
e. Other _____

101–6. Is control over distribution of output adequate? Describe. ☐ ☐ B

101–7. Describe the control function, if any, for evaluating quality of output.

102. *Programmed Control over Processing*

102–1. Are control totals used to check for completeness of processing? These may include trailer file labels, run-to-run totals, etc. ☐ ☐ B

102–2. Are programmed controls used to test processing of significant items? ☐ ☐ B

Item applied to

a. Limit and reasonableness test _____
b. Crossfooting test _____

102–3. Does the program check for improper switch settings (if sense switches are used?) ☐ ☐ C

103. *Control over Handling of Errors*

103–1. Does the program provide an adequate console printout of control information (switch settings, control violations, operator intervention, etc.)? ☐ ☐ B

103–2. When a program is interrupted, are there adequate provisions for re-start? ☐ ☐ C

103–3. Are there adequate controls over the process of identifying, correcting and reprocessing data rejected by the program? ☐ ☐ B

103–4. Inquire into handling of un-matched transactions (no master record corresponding to transaction record). Is it adequate? ☐ ☐ A
a. Reject and note on error log ☐
b. Reject and write on suspense record ☐
c. Other _____

104. *Control over Program and Data Files*

104–1. Is there adequate up-to-date documentation for the application? ☐ ☐ C

Yes No

a. Application summary ☐ ☐
b. Run manuals ☐ ☐
c. Operator instructions ☐ ☐

104–2. Is test data documented and kept up to date? ☐ ☐ C

104–3. Are controls over master file changes adequate? ☐ ☐ B

Yes No

a. Written request for change from outside data processing ☐ ☐
b. Register of all changes reviewed by initiating department ☐ ☐
c. Supervisory or other review of changes ☐ ☐

104–4. Are there adequate provisions for periodically checking master file contents?   ☐ ☐ B

Yes No

a. Periodic printout and review   ☐ ☐
b. Periodic test against physical count   ☐ ☐
c. Other _____

104–5. Are the back-up and reconstruction provisions adequate?   ☐ ☐ B
Describe _____

105. *Management or Audit Trail*

105–1. Do the records or references provide the means to adequately:
a. Trace any transaction forward to a final total?   ☐ ☐ A

b. Trace any transaction back to the original source document or input?   ☐ ☐ A
c. Trace any final total back to the component transactions?   ☐ ☐ A

105–2. When ledgers (general or subsidiary) are maintained on computer media, does the system of processing provide:
a. An historical record of activity in the accounts?   ☐ ☐ B
b. A periodic trial balance of the accounts?   ☐ ☐ B

105–3. Are source documents retained for an adequate period of time in a manner which allows identification with related output records and documents?   ☐ ☐ C

W. Thomas Porter

Evaluating
Internal Controls
in EDP Systems

The evaluation of the system of internal control is a point of departure in auditing. Such an evaluation serves as a gauge of the quality of

Reprinted by permission from *The Journal of Accountancy*, August 1964. Copyrighted 1964 by the American Institute of Certified Public Accountants.

the system. It also gives the auditor the foundation upon which he will construct his examination and build his conclusions. The importance of and increased emphasis on the evaluation of internal control are clearly revealed by a review of auditing literature. R. K. Mautz and H. A. Sharaf wrote:

Because the extent and effectiveness of internal control is so important in audit programming and performance, a prudent practitioner will tend to give this phase of the examination a full measure of emphasis. At best, internal control is a rather amorphous subject and difficult to comprehend and reduce to satisfactory work paper notes. Yet no part of the examination is more important than his review and evaluation of internal control. Also, there is no area in which he can be of more real assistance to his client than by scrupulously examining and reporting on the client's control procedures.[1]

Although internal control does not lend itself to any simple set of rules by which it can be evaluated, it has historically been evaluated by the auditor through:

I. Observation, inquiries, and review of manuals and charts to determine whether:

1. The formal and informal organization of the company clearly establishes and specifically prescribes a functional segregation of duties between people responsible for

   a. Authorization of transaction

   b. Recording and processing of the transaction

   c. Custody of the assets involved in the transaction

2. The financial and accounting procedures are sufficient to assure that

a. Transactions are reviewed sufficiently to establish the propriety and accuracy of their recording.

b. Data processing flow permits detection and‹ correction of errors in operating and financial data and reduces such errors to the level permitted by management.

c. Reports are required and prepared to reflect the responsibility for the authorization, performance, and review of financial and accounting transactions.

II. The selection of actual transactions to determine whether the purported policies, procedures and controls are operating as described.

The effect of electronic data processing on the evaluation of the system of internal control largely centers on point II above, the testing of the system. In any system, EDP or otherwise, a review of the organizational aspects, procedural controls, and administrative practices is necessary to establish the extent of the audit examination and to make constructive suggestions about improving the system. But obviously, EDP affects the nature of such a review. The importance of systems development and programming practices and documentation, input-output controls, programmed controls, tape library procedures, and computer operating controls require the auditor to observe different activities, ask different questions, and review different manuals and documents than he would in his review of a non-EDP system.

[1] R. K. Mautz and H. A. Sharaf, *The Philosophy of Auditing*, American Accounting Association, Madison, Wisconsin, 1961, p. 146.

Testing the System

Conventionally, the auditor has selected actual accounting transactions that have been previously processed by the client to test the system. Typically, this approach calls for the tracing of a "representative" number of transactions from the recording of the source documents through whatever intermediate records might exist to the output reports or records produced. Such an approach is taken without any regard to the manner in which the output was actually developed. It is based on the logic that if the source data or system input can be proven correct and if the results of the system accurately reflect these source data, then the output must be correct and the manner in which the system processed the data is inconsequential.

In an EDP-dominated situation, such an approach has been called the "around the computer" approach to testing the system. This approach is the one which, in the majority of EDP installations, has been taken by auditors. Auditors have been using this "around the computer" approach because:

1. It is a familiar method.

2. It does not require technical knowledge of the EDP equipment.

3. The relatively unchanged audit trail conditions encountered in the EDP installations have not required a different approach.

An often unstated but perhaps more significant reason for the auditor's use of the "around the computer" approach is the auditor's unwillingness to come to grips with EDP.

The other approach to the testing of the system is the "through the computer" approach, which follows the concept that, if the controls and procedures incorporated in computer programs are effective and if a proper control of computer operations is employed, then proper processing of proven and acceptable input is bound to result in acceptable output. Such an approach is entirely dependent upon the consistency of processing operations found in computer operations.

In addition to an over-all review of the EDP system, this approach obviously requires an explicit knowledge of input and master file record layout, a fairly comprehensive knowledge of computer operations and built-in and programmed controls, and a thorough understanding of the development and use of "test decks."

Test Decks. In my opinion, often the conventional audit approach of testing the system by selecting actual transactions previously processed by the client is incomplete and inexact. In some cases, the transactions selected do not include the unusual ones requiring exception handling. In addition, the auditor, even with "representative" tests, can never be certain that the individuals carrying out the system actually do what they say they do or are supposed to do.

But with the advent of electronic systems, the operations research concepts of "models" and "simulation" appear applicable in the auditor's testing approach. The "model" is the client's computer program:

. . . complete and accurate in all respects, not subject to the deviations caused by human idiosyncrasies or human temptation . . . containing in very specific language the exact instructions as to what the machine is to do. You can tell just what happened to a transaction.[2]

"Simulation" can be performed by the auditor by experimenting and testing the procedural model. The auditor can feed it all sorts of good and bad transactions to see how the EDP system reacts. These simulated transactions are commonly referred to as "test decks." The test deck is developed by preparing machine-readable data (i.e., punched cards, magnetic tape) designed to simulate every feasible type of transaction and to test specific program controls. These transactions are processed using the existing computer program, and the results of the computer processing are compared with predetermined results. Obviously, the purpose of the test deck technique is to determine for the auditor exactly how a specific processing system will react to particular types of transactions.

In effect, the auditor allows the automatic data processing system to audit itself by merely presenting the system with a set of test problems or situations which the system cannot distinguish from normal processing activity, and then ascertaining how these test cases are handled. Since no . . . programming is required to implement a test of this type the procedure is a relatively inexpensive one from the standpoint of operating costs, and the results obtained are both effectively presented and irrefutable.[3]

While it is true that the computer operating costs to process test decks are rather minimal, it is also true that the development of test decks can be a complex and time-consuming project, and the auditor should be cognizant of the problems involved.

Before discussing the development of test decks, it is important to make two points clear. First, some writers fail to differentiate between test decks and computer audit programs and, as a result, such writing discusses the use of "test programs" in auditing. Test decks, as defined above, are used to evaluate the *quality* of the data processing *system* in use. Computer audit programs are used to determine the *quality* of *information* generated by the system. Such programs, to be sure, can perform detailed tests and computations. They are more often designed to elicit, from current master files, exception reports or sample selections based on criteria specified and programmed by the auditor. Such information is then used by the auditor in his evaluation of the evidence supporting the reasonableness and adequacy of disclosure of the accounts descriptions, balances, and footnotes in the financial statements under examination. Secondly, some writers and speakers have often mentioned another technique of auditing computer records—the review of computer programs. There are several reasons why this method is not very satisfactory:

[2]A. B. Toan, Jr., "The Auditor and EDP," *Journal of Accountancy*, June 1960, p. 44.

[3]Department of United States Air Force, *Guide for Auditing Automatic Data Processing Systems*, Government Printing Office, Washington, D.C., 1961, pp. 8-14 and 8-15.

1. It requires a higher level of programming skill than that required to write the original program. To go through a program which may contain thousands of instructions, complex logic, and numerous switches is an exceedingly difficult job. Even if the auditing profession had enough persons competent to make such an evaluation, it would be too costly.

2. It would not guarantee that the program reviewed is the most current version. Because of the numerous minor changes made over a period of time in the ordinary course of computer operations, the auditor would have to repeat the detailed review periodically, or control program changes, neither of which is very practical.

3. It would not guarantee that the program reviewed is the regular production program being used by the client. The auditor must have assurance that the program he is evaluating is the one which is being used to process transactions and produce financial information.

In my opinion, the only practical answer to evaluating the performance of a computer is utilization of test decks, not reviews of programs. However, a review of the client's documentation used to develop the applicable program is desirable in developing the test deck. Such documents include flow charts, block diagrams, input and output media, exception reports, and narrative descriptions of the procedures and controls in the system.

A review of these documents must be sufficient to give the auditor a complete knowledge of the procedural controls, both manual and programmed, in the EDP system so that the transactions included in the test-deck check the existence and effectiveness of these controls.

In addition, this review must enable the auditor to determine whether the client's controls are adequate or necessary to achieve the client's control objectives.

In developing and using the successful test deck, there are several important factors which the auditor must take into consideration:

1. He must decide upon the exact point in the system where the test data are to be entered.

2. He must determine the types of transactions to be included in the test deck.

3. He must obtain the master records to process against the test transactions and to compute the predetermined results for comparison with the output resulting from the test processing.

4. He must carefully consider the effects that the processing of the test transactions will have on the results of the system produced under normal operating conditions.

5. He must obtain the client's regular processing programs and assure himself that the program is used to process the test data.

6. He must make whatever arrangements are necessary to get the test data prepared and processed and to get the output in the desired form.

Where the Tests Are To Be Entered in the System. Before developing the test deck, the auditor must first decide the point at which he wishes to enter the test data. If the operations and controls in the preparation of input are to be included in the test, the test-deck data must be fed into the input portion of the system as basic source documentation. If only computer operations are being tested, the data may be introduced into the computer operations in the form of punched cards or magnetic tape records.

Determining the Types of Transactions. The inherent advantage of the test deck over the selection of actual transactions is that the auditor may include every type—normal or abnormal—of conceivable transaction in his tests with relative ease. And theoretically, a sample of one for each type of transaction is as statistically sound as a large number because of the uniformity involved in the processing of data.

There are several methods which may be used to construct a simulated transaction deck, all of which require a review of systems and program documentation to gain a complete knowledge of the procedural controls in the EDP system. Although the auditor can prepare entirely imaginary transactions, it may be expedient to select transactions from the client's actual data or from the test data used by the client's programmer to check out the computer program. For example, the programmer's test deck was used in developing the auditor's test deck to evaluate payroll processing in a large manufacturer. Many of the programmer's tests were applicable from an audit standpoint and were readily included in the auditor's test deck. The review of the client's test data also uncovered some outdated tests and areas in the program which were not tested at all. The client's data processing management felt such a review was highly informative and beneficial to operations.

Selection of the client's input data or test data usually will not include all the possible variables, and additional transactions must be created. The determination of possible variables to be tested may be made by analyzing the input record layout. By analyzing the fields of data included on the input record, all combinations of data can be determined. In this connection, several observations should be made:

1. It is not necessary that all possible combinations within all fields be set out as separate problems. Distinction should be made between variables which merely represent identification data (i.e., account numbers, social security numbers) and those which involve alternate handling. In the case of the former, only a limited number of possibilities need to be included to test the identification routines in the program. To illustrate, Table 1, below, shows the fields and their description for a rate charge input card used in a payroll system of the large manufacturer mentioned earlier. The transaction will change an employee's hourly rate and pay code. The transaction is program edited for validity of dates, alpha name, old pay code and rate and whether the new rate is equal to the old rate. In addition, any new rate greater than $10 is excepted. The tests included in the test deck for this transaction were:

a. Valid rate change with all other fields valid

b. Rate change greater than $10

c. Valid rate change, old rate wrong

d. Valid rate change, old rate equal to new rate

e. Valid rate change, alpha name wrong

To test sequence checking and identification comparison routines, a card with a valid transaction number or employee number and containing valid information could be placed out of sequence in the test deck. Additional tests for sequence checking and identification comparison would not be necessary.

Table 1. Rate Change Card Format

Card Field	Description
4-12	Social security number
13-14	Transaction code (03)
16	Division
18-22	New hourly rate
24-29	Rate change date
30	New payroll code
31-34	First four characters of last name (alpha name)
48-52	Old hourly rate
75	Old payroll code

2. It is necessary to include at least two of each type of variable requiring alternative handling in order to test the existence and effectiveness of programmed controls. For example, in the above illustration, all rates equal to or less than $10 are handled by one processing routine; all rates greater than $10 are handled by an exception routine.

3. The tests should include transactions which determine the processing and handling of the following general conditions:

a. Out of sequence conditions

b. Out of limits conditions

c. Routines arising from a major decision point where alternative processing takes place as a result of the comparison of transaction records with master records; i.e., where the transactions identification number can be greater, equal to, or less than the identification number on the master record

d. Units of measure differences

e. Incomplete or missing input information

f. Wrong tape files

g. Numeric characters in fields where alphabetic characters belong and vice versa

h. Characters in certain fields which exceed prescribed length (an overflow condition)

i. Illogical conditions in fields where programmed consistency checks test the logical relationship in the same field

j. Conditions where transaction codes or amounts do not match the codes or amounts established in tables stored in internal memory

Obviously all these conditions cannot be tested with each type of transaction, but the majority of them, if not all, may be tested in processing all transactions included in the test deck.

One of the problems involved in developing a test deck is the difficulty of reviewing its substantive aspects. Apart from a detailed review, which is impractical and time consuming for the audit manager or partner, it is very difficult for the reviewer to get a general idea as to the scope and "rightness" of a test deck. For audit review purposes, it may be useful to construct a matrix during the development of

Table 2.

Type of Condition Tested	Test Transaction Number					
a	0	1	2	3	4	n
b						
c						
d						
e						
f						
g						
h						
i						
j						

the test data which would indicate the types of conditions tested by each transaction. Such a matrix is shown in Table 2 above. Another device which is helpful in review and which is necessary for the audit workpapers is a transaction listing of the test deck. Such a listing indicates, in code sequence, the information punched or recorded on the transaction input record. This information can be sorted and listed by tabulating equipment. The listing should include a narrative description of the type of test, the objective, and what output will result from the test.

Obtaining the Master Records. The auditor must obtain the master records in machine-readable form against which the test transactions are to be processed and in visible form to compute the predetermined results for comparison with output resulting from the test deck processing.

With sequential processing, there is usually not much of a problem in obtaining the master records in machine-readable form since the master file is not written over or destroyed in processing the test transactions. There is a problem in random processing since the master records maintained on random access equipment are written over or destroyed by processing transactions. To protect the client's

master records, the test deck can be run immediately after the random access file "dump."[4] After the "dump," the master records are on both the random access master files and on magnetic tape. The test data can then be processed against the tape files as discussed above. In such a situation, the client's computer would have to be altered slightly to have the computer "read" and "write" tape rather than "read" and "write" random access files. In situations where the auditor must or wishes to run his test transactions between the "dump" cycles, the random access files may be protected by physically locking the files to prevent writing on them and altering the program so that the "write random access file" instruction becomes "write tape."

In some installations such as the large manufacturer referred to previously, test master records are used, against which the test data are processed by the company's programmers in testing the system. These masters, although comparatively few in number, represent actual masters. The advantage of these test masters is the ease with which they can be used and changed to reflect certain conditions necessary for testing, and the ease with which they can be printed out for visible review. For example, the manufacturer uses twenty-four test master records, in punched card form, as a test model payroll master file. These twenty-four records are used instead of the 20,000-employee master record file to avoid time in selecting and printing actual master records. The use of test masters is based on the premise that the computer cannot tell the difference

---

[4]A file "dump" refers to the transfer or writing of the contents of the random access files on magnetic tapes, at realistic intervals, to provide the ability to reconstruct the file in the event the original file is accidentally damaged or destroyed.

between the processing of a test master record and an actual master record. A variation of the use of client's test master records is the creation, by the auditor, of "dummy" master records for use in testing the system. Such was the case in the test of an automated labor recording system in this large manufacturer.[5]

Although actual master records may be readily obtained in machine-readable form in many systems, it is difficult to get the same records in printed form without advance planning. One method is to time the tests so they are processed with the output master file used to prepare a printed report such as the accounts receivable aged trial balance or an inventory report. Another method is to have an inquiry program prepared which will print out selected master records from the master file to be used in processing the test transactions. Most installations have the ability to inquire into any file, and the auditor may, with a little planning, have his file-searching needs met by a routine procedure.

The Need to Carefully Consider the Effects Test Transactions Will Have on the Results of the System. Obviously, the auditor does not want to have his test transactions affect the results produced under normal operating conditions. Accordingly, he must carefully consider what effects the processing of the test data will have on the results of the system. For example, the output tape resulting from the processing of test data should be clearly labeled so as to prevent improper use and subsequent incorrect processing of operating data.

---

[5]R. M. Benjamin, "Auditing Automatic Source Recording," *The Quarterly*, Touche, Ross, Bailey & Smart, September 1963.

Any tests that are processed along with actual transactions must be carefully controlled so as to preclude undesired results from taking place. For example, in a test to determine that the open order file was reviewed periodically for unusual items in a medium-sized steel manufacturer, a valid order was transmitted by the auditor from a sales branch location and the shipping copy was destroyed. This order had to be controlled by the auditor to prevent shipping of the order and to insure subsequent removal from the open order file.

Obtaining and Controlling the Client's Regular Processing Program. One of the important procedures of testing a company's EDP system is obtaining assurance that the program being tested is the one the company actually uses to process data. Basically there are two ways in which this can be achieved:

1. If the data processing organizational and administrative controls are adequate, the program can be requested, on a surprise basis, from the program librarian and duplicated for the auditor's control and use in processing test data. As a further measure, the auditor may request that test data previously processed with the auditor's copy of the program be processed with the client's operating program and then compare the end results. This method has the added advantage of checking any computer operator intervention.

2. The auditor may request, on a surprise basis, that the operating program be left in the computer at the completion of processing operating data so that he may process his test data with it. This method has an advantage over the method above in that it

usually ensures a current version of the program. In many installations and particularly in earlier stages of conversion, program changes are made frequently. These continuing program changes may make it quite difficult for the auditor to review and check all significant changes in order to be satisfied with the operations performed by the program.

As a general rule, the auditor should observe the running of the test data with the computer program. In many installations, this may not be practical because of the "graveyard shift" scheduling of test data processing. The adequacy of the controls in the EDP department, however, should be the dictating factor here rather than the time of day, or night.

Arranging To Get Test Data Prepared and Processed. In addition to obtaining master records and the client's regular processing program, the auditor must carefully design test data, obtain the necessary key punching equipment and/or personnel, and obtain computer time from authorized personnel in order to get the test data prepared and processed, and to get the output in the desired form. Most of these arrangements are procedural and involve advanced planning with systems and computer operations people.

The design of test data is not procedural in nature but is something that the auditor will find worthy of his careful consideration. Essentially the test deck should be so designed as to limit the amount of work required of the auditor to review the results of the test. The use of special codings or distinctive names which allow invalid test transactions to be easily identified, sorted out of valid tests, and listed on separate output listings are devices which can be employed to make the auditor's job of interpreting and evaluating the test results more simple and less time consuming.

In some installations where the audit trail has been drastically altered, it is pure nonsense to argue for alternative methods of testing and evaluating the system. The only practical approach is auditing "through the computer" with the use of a well-conceived test deck. In some installations where the audit trail has not been altered with the use of EDP equipment, the "around the computer" approach may seem to be a valid alternative. But even in these electronic systems, the benefits accruing to the auditor using the "through the computer" approach appear to outweigh the problems and additional considerations involved in using such an approach. These benefits are:

1. Better knowledge of the client's system of procedures and controls—many computer installations are integrated management information systems providing operating, as well as financial, information. A review and evaluation of such a system will necessarily provide the auditor with a more complete understanding of the client's "total" system of data processing and controls than normally obtained by auditing "around the computer."

2. Better letters of recommendations—a detailed review of the computer system along with the design and use of effective tests will enable the auditor to evaluate the client's input-output controls, built-in machine controls, programmed controls, and operating controls. Such an evaluation will result in more informative and constructive

letters of recommendations and, hence, increased service to clients.

3. More representative tests—through the use of well-designed test decks, the auditor is able to evaluate the system's ability to handle all types of transactions, both normal and abnormal. The kind of transactions included in the test deck is limited only by the auditor's imagination, rather than by the practical limitations of time and cost involved in obtaining the same types of transactions from a sample of actual transactions. This point is emphasized by an audit manager in writing about the use of the computer in the audit testing of an automated labor recording system: ". . . The number of unusual conditions which were tested with a few simple prearranged plans would have required thousands upon thousands of transaction selections had random sampling or any other conventional testing procedures been used."[6]

4. Continuous auditing more readily achieved—one of the objectives of auditing in recent years has been the smoothing of the work flow in an annual audit examination. This has been achieved to some extent by spreading the examination between the "interim" period and the "year-end" period. Since the test deck is designed around a series of business transactions that do not change in nature from day to day, its usefulness can survive minor and perhaps major changes in the computer program. As a result, the auditor can make more frequent tests and obtain "readings" of the client's activities at different operating periods during the year without expending more time, if as

---

[6]*Ibid.*, p. 11.

much, than previously spent in testing the system.

The use of EDP equipment in no way lessens the auditor's requirement for evaluating the system of internal control; in my opinion, it makes the evaluation increasingly important to the audit examination and to the concept of service to the client. The auditor must recognize the importance of electronic procedures and the significance of the work performed within the EDP equipment. Accordingly, he must resist the temptation of assuming that, if the input to the machine system is adequately reviewed and controlled and the output can be checked back to source documents, he can then be unconcerned with what went on within the machine system itself.

At present, rarely will exclusive use of either of the two approaches discussed above be applicable to an electronic accounting system. The unusually large volume of data handled by EDP systems makes the "around the computer" approach impractical except in unusual circumstances. On the other hand, the inconsistency of processing found in all but the most sophisticated "total" systems renders the "through the computer" approach ineffective except in equally unusual circumstances. Experience has shown that the most effective method of auditing electronic systems will generally be some combination of these two approaches. Accordingly, the auditor can still use conventional techniques in evaluating and testing the system of internal control to some extent. But to a large extent a fresh approach to the problem combined with the effective use of the computer is necessary.

1. The eight following items contain examples of internal control deficiencies observed by a CPA in his client's computer data processing system. For each of these conditions or situations, select from the list of control features or procedures given the one which, if properly utilized, would have been most useful in either preventing the error or in ensuring its immediate detection and prompt correction.

a. The master file for inventory did not seem right. The file was printed out and many errors were found. The best control procedure would be

   i. Trailer label control totals.

   ii. A periodic test against physical count.

   iii. A parity check.

   iv. Limit tests.

From Uniform CPA Examinations.

b. The master payroll file on magnetic tape was inadvertently written on by another processing run. The best control procedure would be a

   i. File protection ring.

   ii. File destruction date on header label.

   iii. Control figure.

   iv. Trailer label check.

c. A weekly payroll check was issued to an hourly employee based on 98 hours worked instead of 38 hours. The time card was slightly illegible and the number looked somewhat like 98. The best control procedure would be

   i. A hash total.

   ii. A code check.

   iii. Desk checking.

   iv. A limit test.

d. In preparing payroll checks the computer omitted 24 of a total of 2,408 checks which should have been processed. The error was not detected until the foremen distributed the checks. The best control procedure would be

   i.   A parity check.

   ii.   A module N check.

   iii.   Control totals.

   iv.   Desk checking.

e. The magnetic tape containing accounts receivable transactions could not be located. A data processing supervisor said that it could have been put among the scratch tapes available for use in processing. The best control procedure would be a

   i.   Header label.

   ii.   Trailer label.

   iii.   External label.

   iv.   File protection ring.

f. A sales transaction document was coded with an invalid customer account code (7 digits rather than 8). The error was not detected until the updating run when it was found that there was no such account to which the transaction could be posted. The best control procedure would be

   i.   Parity checks.

   ii.   Keypunch verification.

   iii.   A hash total check.

   iv.   A check digit.

g. The operator, in mounting the magnetic tape containing the cash receipts for the processing run to update accounts receivable, mounted the receipts tape from the preceding rather than the current day. The error was not detected until after the processing run was completed. The best control procedure would be a

   i.   Header label check.

   ii.   Trailer label check.

   iii.   Parity check.

   iv.   Hash total check.

h. An expense report was prepared by the cost center. One executive questioned one of the amounts and asked for the source documents which support the total. Data processing was not able to routinely do so. The best control procedure would be

   i.   An error listing.

   ii.   An audit trail.

   iii.   Transmittal control.

   iv.   Documentation.

2. The audit of the financial statements of a client that utilizes the services of a computer for accounting functions compels the CPA to understand the operation of his client's electronic data processing (EDP) system.

Required:

a. The first requirement of an effective system of internal control is a satisfactory plan of organization. List the characteristics of a satisfactory plan of organization for an EDP department, including the relationship between the department and the rest of the organization.

b. An effective system of internal control also requires a sound system of records control of operations and transactions (source data and its flow) and of classification of data within the accounts. For an EDP system, these controls include input controls, processing controls, and output controls. List the characteristics of a satisfactory system of input controls. (Confine your comments to a batch-controlled system employing punched cards and to the steps that occur prior to the processing of the input cards in the computer.)

3. The independent auditor must evaluate a client's system of internal control to determine the extent to which various auditing procedures must be employed. A client who uses a computer should provide the CPA with a flowchart of the information processing system so the CPA can evaluate the control features in the system. Shown opposite is a simplified flowchart, such as a client might provide. Unfortunately the client had only partially completed the flowchart when it was requested by you.

Required:

a. Complete the flowchart below.

b. Describe what each item in the flowchart indicates. When complete, your description should provide an explanation of the processing of the data involved. Your description should be in the following order:

1. "Orders from Salesmen" to "Run No. 5."

2. "From Mailroom" to "Run No. 5."

3. "Run No. 5" through the remainder of the chart.

Flow Chart

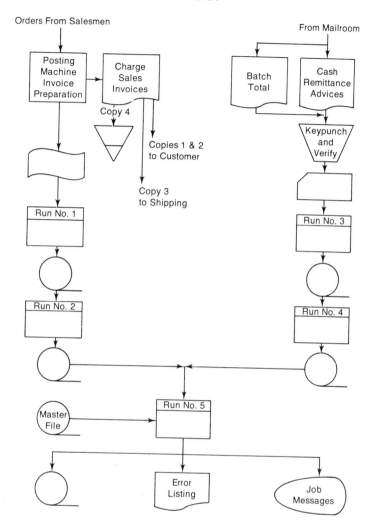

Airdraft, Inc.

This case describes an automated system of labor recording and payroll processing in a major division of Airdraft, Inc., a large manufacturer.

Labor-Recording and Payroll System

Automatic time-recording devices ("Transactors") are located throughout the shop areas. For the 11,600 employees covered by this system, these devices have completely replaced the human timekeepers and manually prepared time cards. Data from the system flows through to the company's payroll and job-order cost-accounting and control records. Basic timekeeping tools are (1) the plastic employee badge, prepunched with identifying information, and (2) the job card, prepunched with the charge number and other information about a particular job.

The badge is permanently assigned to each employee. The job cards follow the parts or assemblies to be worked on. Exceptions are indirect labor and other special cards, which are located in racks adjacent to the Transactor. Clock-in on reporting for work requires only insertion of the badge into the Transactor, and depression of certain keys. Check-in on a job requires insertion of the badge and one or more job cards, and depression of other keys.

All Transactors are linked electrically to a central control box, a master clock, and an in-line key punch that creates a punched card for each entry. The cards are converted to magnetic tape for passing through computer processes. The first of these, a match against an employee-identification master tape, begins one-half hour after the beginning of each shift.

Within an hour after shift start, an exception report has been prepared for distribution to shop foremen. This report indicates absences, tardy clock-in, preshift overtime, and failure to check in on a job. Each exception must be approved by the shop foreman. Transactions accepted in this first processing routine plus transactions accepted for the remainder of the shift are "posted" to a random-access file arranged by employee. Transactions rejected must be analyzed and corrected for reentry into the processing cycle.

All labor transactions for the day are read out onto another magnetic tape that goes through a series of further computer processes:

1. Preparation of final report to shop foremen. Again prepared for exceptions only, this shows overtime, early clock-out, and other items for approval by foremen.

2. Daily report that balances job time by employee with time between clock-in and clock-out.

3. Daily labor tape prepared after process 2.

4. Matching of job transactions against a random-access file of job numbers. This processing involves application of labor standards on certain jobs, accumulation of time by classification, and preparation of output tapes for numerous reports. These reports include daily reports of actual and budgeted time to certain shops, summary management reports by type of labor, and job status reports.

5. Entry of the daily labor tape from 3, above, into another larger computer for the payroll process.

Payroll is processed by applying pay rates, included in the permanent portion of the employees' master payroll records, to the labor hour transactions accumulated in the variable portion of the employees' master records. The labor is accumulated by employee for bi-weekly payroll processing and by job for weekly accounting distribution reports. The fixed portion of the master record includes, in addition to the pay rate, data such as name, social security number, number of tax exemptions, budget sections, year-to-date amounts, and vacation and sick leave hours. The variable portion contains earnings and deduction data resulting from payroll transactions processed. The variable section, of course, is cleared at the end of each payroll period.

Required:

1. What specific steps would you use in evaluating this system?

2. What tests would you use in evaluating the existence and effectiveness of computer processing, programmed controls, and exception procedures?

Keydata System

Case

This case describes the Keydata system, which is based on the concept of time-sharing a large-scale computer on-line in real-time among many remote users. You have been asked to evaluate the effectiveness of the system to provide the following requirements, both unique and essential to an on-line real-time data-processing system that is to be time-shared by multiple customers.

1. The equipment used must have the capability of handling transactions on-line and in real-time.

2. The programming must be done by personnel who are highly experienced and qualified in time-shared computer technology.

3. Maximum security must be provided for individual customer's programs and information.

4. Procedures must include protection of all information in the system in the event of equipment malfunction or human error.

The description of the system includes selections on information flow, the operating system, file organization, security, journalizing, control and verification, management information system capabilities, the equipment configuration, and operations.

Contents

I. Information Flow

Basic to the Keydata system is the concept of time-sharing a large-scale computer on-line in real-time among many remote users.

"Time-sharing" is a relative term. Two men, one of whom uses a computer during the morning and the other during the afternoon, actually time-share the computer. This definition is much too loose, however, to be applied to the Keydata system; for in the system, time-sharing means the ability both to store many individual programs within a computer and to switch from one program to another the moment that the latter program is required by a user.

Through time-sharing, Keydata gives to each of its subscribers the impression as well as the benefits of having his own computer. That this is possible is the result of the operating-speed imbalance between internal computer functions and external functions such as reading punched cards or printing a line of information, and more particularly the manual keying of data. For instance, keying a quantity and stock number takes at least two seconds and usually an average of several when allowance is made for handling documents, etc. On a high-speed printer the results could be printed in a fraction of a second but to no avail — a slower printer could keep pace. The Keydata system, for example, performs the file lookup, internal calculating, and information updating required for one line on a typical invoice in only a small fraction of a second. Thus dozens, even hundreds of lines can be processed internally by the computer in the same time as is required to print one line. Moreover, many facilities in effect waste computer time and therefore money by forcing the machine to remain idle while waiting for a single printer to finish one line before the next can be processed. The Keydata system is capable of processing data and printing results for many Keydata Stations at the same time.

A Keydata Station (KDS) has all the outward appearances of a typewriter. It has a keyboard and a printing element housed in one unit. An operator "types" information just as she would on a typewriter. The difference between the two, though, is that in a KDS, keying does not cause printing; it sends the information directly to the Keydata computer. The computer then determines what information should be printed and transmits it to the printer part of the KDS.

The connection between these stations and the computer is over private telephone lines, thus allowing a KDS to be located anywhere within a reasonable distance from the Keydata Computer Center, the maximum distance being limited entirely by how much a subscriber is willing to pay if long-distance communication is required. From this direct connection the term "on-line" is derived, while "real-time" stems from the fact that the computer is programmed to process instantaneously any incoming message.

The private telephone line from each KDS is physically connected to a communications interface. As information is keyed at the station, it is transmitted over the phone line into the interface one character at a time. The computer continually scans the interface area and transfers each character as it comes in to an area within the computer allocated to receiving the next message from the given KDS. A complete scan is made 120 times each second to insure that every incoming character of data is properly recorded by the system. When an operator completes a message (for instance, after keying the quantity and item number) she presses the key marked "end of message." When the computer recognizes the incoming character as an "end of message" character, it knows that it is time to execute the program for this subscriber. The appropriate program is then transferred from a high-speed drum into the central processing unit and is executed.

The program for a particular customer will select whatever stored information it needs from the working storage assigned to the KDS and from the appropriate subscriber's file, process the information, return updated information to the file, generate and record a journal entry of all necessary information about the transaction, determine what information should be printed on the KDS, and place this information in a special output area so that it can be transmitted back to the KDS. This entire procedure is executed so rapidly (the computer having the ability to perform 300,000 instructions per second) that there is no perceptible delay between the end of the operator's keying and the beginning of the actual printing, even when many users happen to reach this point in their processing at the same instant.

The full-duplex telephone lines used in the Keydata system, which allow information to flow in two directions at the same time, give several important characteristics to the system. First, any field can be right- or left-justified regardless of the number of digits actually keyed. The printing format is determined by the computer, not the keyboard. Second, the operator who realizes before finishing a "message" that she has made a mistake may correct it very easily by pressing any one of a several keys which "erase" individual characters or the entire message (much as on a conventional adding machine). Since nothing has yet been printed, no corrections need be made to the printed copy. Third, the information entered by the operator can be verified for accuracy before it prints. In the event of an error during invoicing, for example, a code number prints in a tear-off portion of the invoice identifying the error. The operator then need merely reenter the information correctly and, since no erroneous information was allowed to print, proceed normally, without the necessity of redoing that portion of the invoice already completed correctly. And last, an operator can be keying information at the same time the computer is causing other information to be printed on the same KDS. For example, one line of an invoice can be printing and the operator can be entering the quantity and item number for the next line. No time delays are encountered waiting for the printing of description, price, and extension before entering more information.

II. KOP-3

There are two levels of programming in the Keydata system. The first has already been mentioned, that is, the program necessary to process a particular subscriber's job. The second level is the operating system, referred to as KOP-3, which is required to monitor and control all the individual functions of the system: the scanning and operation of the communications interface, the transferring of information from the interface to the computer, the selection and transfer of appropriate customer programs from drum storage to central processor, the scheduling of each task to be performed, and other functions not yet discussed. KOP-3 is an abbreviation for the third generation of the Keydata On-Line Processor. Both KOP-1 and its successor, KOP-2, were used successfully and routinely by Keydata on a smaller installation continously over a period of 18 months starting in July 1963. Hence the basic concepts and techniques employed by KOP-3 have all been proven in actual operation.

III. File Organization

Any on-line in real-time system must provide randomly accessible storage for whatever data in each subscriber's files needs to be referred to during on-line processing. In the Keydata system, actively used records are stored on a large magnetic drum and less active ones on a magnetic disc file resembling a jukebox. Space on each of these units will be allocated to the records comprising each individual file. In addition to the space actually in use for these files, an expansion area will be left available to accommodate any new items a subscriber may wish to enter during actual operation. To minimize the space required (and thereby the cost to the subscriber) all records will be variable in length and binary compression will be applied to all numerical fields.

Addressing of an individual item will be done through a randomizing technique; that is, the number used by the customer and entered into his KDS will be converted by the computer to a new number which will tell exactly where that item is stored within the disc or drum file. While in some cases it may be recommended that a subscriber renumber his files, this technique permits the continued use of almost any numbering scheme the subscriber may be presently employing if he feels that this would be advantageous to his operation. This applies as well to numeric, alphabetic, or mixed coding structures. The randomizing technique also eliminates any problems caused by two subscribers using the same codes since it considers not only the code entered but also the KDS from which it emanated. The same code number entered by two different subscribers would therefore result in two clearly distinct addresses being determined within the computer.

IV. Security

A major problem encountered in a time-shared system is the security of file information and programs. This problem exists, of course, in any computerized system and may represent even more of a menace in some conventional approaches than it does in an on-line facility. The additional area of vulnerability encountered in a multi-user environment is that of protecting data from another subscriber to the same facility. The Keydata system does, in fact, provide absolute security to its subscribers against interference or unauthorized use of any data by others. To explore further the nature of this security, each problem area is discussed below in some detail.

In order to begin operation, it is necessary for the KDS operator to key in a preestablished code identifying herself and the procedure she wishes to apply (for example, preparing invoices, credit memos, cash receipts, etc.). The procedure number includes the identity of the KDS itself as well as a check digit to insure accurate entry. To identify herself, the operator must key in a "password" for that procedure (a password being any series of numbers, chosen by the subscriber, which gives him protection at least as good as a combination lock gives a safe). This combined identification and checking procedure insures that no one, not even if he knew a particular password, could have access to information from a KDS located at another place than in the office of the subscriber. Accident and intent are effectively blocked by this method.

One subscriber may use many passwords. If a particular procedure is of a confidential nature, such as an executive payroll, the password is given only to personnel who have been authorized to perform that procedure. Effective protection has thus been provided not only against another KDS having access to a subscriber's information, but also against the performance of a particular procedure by unauthorized personnel within the organization. The password is also used to protect information stored in the computer from unauthorized exposure and altering. An entire record or any item of information in it may be protected against alteration or even examination of any individual type of data in a subscriber's file except when the operator has established, through a password, that she is authorized to be privy to the data in question.

One other area of concern in the use of a time-shared system is the possible destruction of one program by another. In the Keydata system this cannot be done, because in KOP-3 the operator has no way whatever of addressing parts of the computer memory, and the programs can neither address one another nor modify themselves. Instead, they must keep track of variables in the working storage block assigned to the KDS being served at the time. This, incidentally, has been the approach taken in many military systems where the destruction of a program due to data errors or hardware failures could be disastrous.

V. Journalizing

All activity processed by the Keydata system is recorded on magnetic tape at the time it occurs. These journal records are of two basic types. The first is a verbatim reproduction of the input information, the primary use of which is reconstruction. Hence, if files become inaccurate, they can be totally reconstructed. The second type of journal record reflects actions taken by the computer. Containing data derived from input messages, file records, and the logic table, these records provide all necessary information for verifying that the files are in balance and for preparing off-line reports as needed.

Each record contains both a KDS number and a unique sequence number which establishes the chronological sequence of activity and can be readily used to determine the exact time and date of occurrences. Journal records reflecting computer activities resulting from a given input message will have the same sequence number as the journal record created for the input message.

This journal tape plays an important role in the overall design of the Keydata system in that it provides a completely detailed, machine-readable history of every transaction processed. From this tape there can now be prepared, with no further manual transcription, any historical or statistical report desired by subscribers. A company's accountant or auditor will find this feature extremely beneficial in designing additional controls or audit trails to satisfy his particular requirements. In Sections VI and IX, other uses of the journal tape in these specific areas are discussed.

In Section VIII is an explanation of the automatic checking devices built into Keydata's equipment to preclude, among other things, the erroneous or unreadable transcription of information onto magnetic tape. Because of the many uses made of this journal tape, however, even greater protection has been given to it. As each piece of information is being recorded onto the journal tape, it will also be recorded in a reserved portion of the disc file. Periodically, a second tape will be mounted and this information transferred from the disc to the second tape, thereby producing two identical journal tapes that record in detail every transaction processed by the Keydata system.

VI. Control and Verification

One of the outstanding characteristics of the Keydata system is the exceptional thoroughness and immediacy of control and verification which can be easily maintained over every function. Consider, for example, a typical invoicing procedure.

Under normal conditions, a KDS operator will enter a customer number followed by a series of quantity and item-number messages. To insure accuracy of input wherever possible, all identification numbers (account number, item number, etc.) are expanded by a digit which is the result of a mathematical formula applied to the original number. This is called a check digit. The identification number together with its check digit now becomes a unique number that cannot be inadvertently altered into another valid identification by any single transposition, substitution, or deletion of a character in keying the number. This causes the system to reject any such errors rather than post data to a wrong account or item as might occur if check digits were not used.

When the Keydata system receives this unique identification, it immediately checks to determine whether there is such an item or customer on file. If not, it may then put the number through the check digit formula so that it can inform the operator whether there was a keying error or a valid number for which no file entry has been set up as yet.

The value of check digits has been well established, of course, over many years of use in conventional data-processing installations. The Keydata system, however, gives immediate rejection of such data when entered incorrectly and it carries the use of check digits one step further as well: Identification numbers generated by the system (for example, the invoice number on an invoice) are assigned and printed under computer control. As this is done, the computer assigns check digits to these identification numbers. During cash-receipts posting, for instance, when an invoice number reenters the system, its accuracy can be immediately verified through the use of the check digit. Any reentered number which originally printed on a KDS can now carry a check digit. Format checks, such as that the correct number of digits is in a field or that a particular number is within certain limits, can also be made at this time. And data can, of course, be verified where necessary by having a second operator key the same data through the same or a different KDS at any time prior to the actual processing, the results of the first keying being compared automatically with the data entered at the time of processing.

Another proven technique of input control is the use of batch totals (that is, the total of all quantity amounts in a group of invoices). Prior to entering orders into a conventional data-processing system, a clerk would total the quantity amounts by adding machine. In most systems the orders are then converted into some machine-readable form, such as punched cards, and run through an accounting machine or computer which adds the quantity amounts in the cards and prints out a total. The operator then checks this total against the adding machine tape. If an error exists, the operator must first locate the order on which the error was made, then find the source document, make the correction, rerun the cards, and re-check the control totals.

Such batch totals are provided, of course, by Keydata; but the system goes a little further toward improving accuracy and operational ease. The KDS operator can be required to key in the amount of the control total as well as the individual items, allowing the computer to indicate automatically the existence of an error and thus eliminate the need for visual comparison. Further, due to its on-line nature, the KDS facilitates the use of smaller batches, making the correction of errors quicker and easier. In fact, Keydata recommends the use of a batch total for each individual invoice if the number of items is sufficient to give it validity.

When an operator calls for an invoice to be totaled, the batch control check is made immediately before the invoice is totaled. In case of an error, no time is lost in locating the source document, since it is still in front of the operator. Further, for some errors, such as the omission of an entire item, the operator merely keys in the information omitted. The computer processes it, and then, if the control checks, proceeds to total and finish printing the invoice. Back orders and out-of-stock conditions have no effect on the accuracy of the control furnished by the Keydata system. Batch total controls may be applied to quantity, dollars, or any item best suited to the particular procedure.

Visual verification can be performed with ease. As the operator keys information, the actual invoice is being printed in front of her; hence she can check the output against the source document from which she is working. Because all printed information comes from the computer and not from the keyboard, this visual check is even more valuable in that it allows the operator to verify not only that she keyed accurately but also that the computer received the information correctly.

As each invoice is processed, three levels of control are employed to insure the accuracy of the computer system itself. The individual items controlled will vary with the subscriber and the procedure involved, and they can be easily specified. The illustrations below, however, are based on three levels, using only dollars billed and inventory piece counts.

First, the dollars billed and the total pieces allocated will be added to a single control total for this Keydata subscriber. At the end of the day or any period of time, these totals will show total dollars billed for that day and total inventory pieces allocated. If the subscriber desires, he may easily add a manual control at this point by taking from the invoices prepared on his KDS an adding-machine-tape total on dollars and/or item quantities. The totals maintained within the computer are available for inquiry at any time and can be used not only as a control but also as a source of information for determining the daily progress of business.

The second level of control is in the random-access file. One subscriber will, of course, have many individual customer and item records in his random-access file. The dollar amount of each invoice will be added to the accounts-receivable outstanding field in the appropriate customer record. At the end of a specified period of time, the individual totals from the random-access records are totaled. Balancing these totals to the user-control totals guarantees that the pertinent disc files have been correctly updated.

It is difficult to visualize a situation where an item could be invoiced correctly, posted to the correct subscriber's file, and then posted by error to another customer record within the subscriber's file. To prevent this, however, the individual customer totals on the disc records will be verified periodically against similar totals on the journal tape. The time at which this check will be made will vary from one procedure to another. In the example given, the comparison will be made at statement and stock-status writing time. If an error does exist, the journal tape which contains a record of each individual invoice will be run against the disc file. The error will then be identified and corrections can be easily made.

The third level of control concerns the journal tape. At the end of each day it is sorted into transaction-within-user sequence, and all invoice amounts and inventory item quantities are totaled for each subscriber and proved against the user control totals.

Should discrepancies occur in the three totals, the journal-tape items for the subscriber involved will be run against the disc file. During this run the location of any dollar error will be identified by customer number and a listing of all invoices written that day to that customer. (In most cases there will be only one invoice.) Because of the three control totals, the corrections required should be obvious; but if there is any doubt, a quick and efficient check can be made by invoice number on the office copies of the few invoices involved.

These control totals will be automatically carried through all off-line reports. Moreover, in most cases they will be designed to match general ledger accounts. Where this is done, the subscriber will have available accurate and highly-controlled figures which can be transcribed directly to his general ledger statement.

With any data-processing system, changes must periodically be made to information stored in the system. For example, the selling price of an item will change, and this must be entered into the system. Such changes must obviously be closely maintained. In the Key-data system, two controls are imposed on this type of activity. First, as previously mentioned, password restrictions may be placed on certain changes; that is, only those who know the required code number or password will be able to enter changes through the KDS. Second, as each change is entered, a journal record will be created. This will contain the number of the KDS, the operator's initials, the type of change, the new information, the old information, the time and date of the change, and a sequence number. All this information is printed on the KDS at the time the change is entered so that it may be immediately verified. At the end of the month, a report will be prepared for each Keydata subscriber showing all changes made. Because it is written in sequence number, he can quickly ascertain that all changes have been reported, review the changes for accuracy, and have a quick reference to show the time at which questionable changes were made as well as the operator who made them.

VII. Management Information System

The Keydata system, because of its random-access characteristics, makes available to its subscribers a true management information system. Such a system must have several features. First, it maintains accurate values of such things as inventory levels and accounts-receivable balances, current to the last transaction processed, and this information is immediately available upon inquiry. The Keydata system provides random-access storage for information which a subscriber wishes to maintain with up-to-the-minute currency and permits inquiry into any of these records; by entering an inquiry code and an identification number, an operator can cause all the information desired to be printed on her KDS.

A management-information system must also perform certain management decision-making functions and be able to report instantaneously when any controllable items are out of balance. A simple example of this ability is the manner in which the KDS checks inventory levels after each transaction to determine if a reorder condition exists, or a customer's credit level after or before each invoice is prepared to determine if the cus-

tomer has exceeded his credit limit. In either case the KDS automatically types out an exception notice on an auxiliary printer, giving all the information required to take immediate corrective action.

The degree to which any data-processing system meets the requirements of a management-information system is determined by the immediacy with which information is entered into the former system and by the ease and immediacy with which questions or inquiries can be asked and exception notices prepared. The Keydata system acquires information at the earliest possible moment on a transaction-by-transaction basis. Further, the auxiliary printer provides a continuous means of answering inquiries and printing out exception notices the moment they occur, with no disruption to the procedure being performed.

VIII. Configuration

While the features of the Keydata system discussed above are dependent on the design of the KOP-3 system and related procedures rather than on the equipment which performs the actions called for, the system could not function properly if the hardware were unreliable. Toward that end, Keydata Corporation has selected for its first computer center a large, efficient, and reliable computer of very recent design, the Digital Equipment Corporation PDP-6. This computer is described briefly below.

The arithmetic processor of the PDP-6 has a repertoire of 363 instructions that operate completely asynchronously, communicating with all memory and input/output devices through special memory and I/O busses. When in user mode, each program is assigned a specific area of memory; any unauthorized memory reference or request for an input/output device will generate a program trap resulting in an automatic return to executive mode. The system includes 49,152 (48K) words of memory consisting of three two-microsecond memory modules of 16,384 words each. Each word contains one parity bit and 36 data bits; parity is checked during each memory reference before the information bits are transferred to the processor. A priority interrupt occurs if parity is incorrect.

An input/output processor controls the high-speed transfer of data from the drum directly to and from memory without utilizing the central processor. This processor signals conditions of data missed, late memory cycle, or any attempt to reference nonexistent memory. The one-million-word high-speed magnetic drum is capable of transferring a 36-bit word to the processor every 4.12 microseconds. Longitudinal parity is checked at the completion of each 16-word sector.

Mass storage is provided by a random-access disc file of about 33 million characters with an access time which ranges from a minimum of 52 to a maximum of 325 milliseconds. Each sector transferred is checked for longitudinal parity. (In addition to the built-in parity check, KOP-3 is designed so that all data written on the disc is reread and compared with core storage.)

Magnetic tapes, card and tape readers, and a line printer function as peripheral devices to the on-line system. Normal input/output to the system is provided by a full duplex data-communications system capable of handling five- or eight-level 100-word-per-minute teletype equipment.

Initially, Keydata Stations will be Model 28, Model 33, or Model 35 Teletypewriters with keyboards connected by a telephone line to the computer and with a second line being used to connect the computer to the printer of the same Teletypewriter. Since the keyboard and printer are not mechanically connected, each character keyed will be transmitted to the computer and not appear on the printer until retransmitted by the computer. One of the features of full duplex operation not previously discussed is the ability to assign any desired significance to individual keys and even varying configurations to a subscriber's keyboard. Since each character can be evaluated and translated within the computer before the print character is sent, great flexibility can be achieved.

Many Keydata stations will be equipped with a Model 28 auxiliary printer. This unit will be parallelled with the main KDS printer by means of a switch actuated by the computer to permit selected data to be printed on either print unit. This feature will enable a subscriber to receive error messages, out-of-stock conditions, and inquiry replies on the auxiliary printer while a finished form is being prepared on the KDS.

IX. Operations

Conventional computer centers must be concerned with the control and protection of customer source records as well as magnetic and card files. In the Keydata system, however, these records are processed and maintained by the subscriber and Keydata's operational security problem is reduced to the protection of magnetic files.

Physical control of the Keydata center will be accomplished by a control officer on duty at all times during which the center is operating. He will be fully responsible for the security of the center and must identify each person entering and leaving it, record in a log the person's name, company affiliation, reason for entering, the information delivered or removed, if any, and the time the person entered and left.

The control officer is thus responsible for all punched cards delivered to the center, magnetic tapes stored therein, and reports that are to be delivered to subscribers. He will insure that all manual controls and procedures for both files and equipment are understood and enforced. He will also maintain all manual computer room logs and journals and record any exception to the normal procedure.

One or more computer operators are assigned to each shift; they are responsible for normal duties such as loading the tape drives, line printer, and card reader; performing routine maintenance procedures; monitoring switchboard connections and console error messages; and loading and unloading the on-line system at the end of the day.

In addition to the control officer and computer operators, support personnel perform such tasks as operating local KDS's keypunches, and verifiers, as well as other functions related to the normal operation of a computer center.

All personnel in Keydata who are in a position to have access to subscriber information are required to be bonded.

During normal operations, the on-line system will require certain tapes, cards, etc. The computer console teletype unit will provide the means by which the operator and the computer communicate. The printed output of this unit serves as a permanent daily log, providing a hard copy of system statistics, error conditions detected on any KDS, and computer operator actions. The console unit will be equipped with distinctive two-part paper with each page prenumbered. The computer control officer will be responsible for keeping the historical log up to date and insuring that no page is misplaced.

The console will consist of three teletype units (connected in series) located in three areas within the computer room; two remote consoles will also be located in the offices of Keydata Corporation senior executives. Units thus connected in series result in three or more identical copies of the log. This procedure guards against the possibility of accidental destruction of the log. Further, a malfunction of one unit will not result in a loss of the logging capability.

At frequent intervals a system statistic message will be produced which includes, among other things, the date, time of day, journal transaction number of the item, and the cumulative number of messages processed for the day.

Since some subscribers, especially engineering users, many require only part-time service, a switchboard will be installed in the computer center. Incoming lines from part-time subscribers and wires loading to a number of computer communication interface channels will be connected to the switchboard so that any part-time subscriber may be connected to any interface not already in use when he needs service.

The computer operator will be responsible for physically moving the jack; the control officer will verify the move and enter the jack number and interface number in his log book. When the connection is completed, the operator will record both the interface and KDS numbers on the console teletype. When the identification code from the KDS is received, the system will verify the connection with the information keyed in by the operator and type out either proper verification or an error message. The control officer will verify the system typeout and record the completed entry in his journal. The subscriber will then be allowed to begin processing data.

To insure maximum control during loading and unloading of the system, control of file-tape selection and of the integration of file tapes and journal tapes is accomplished by numbering the file tape internally and externally. The operator wishing to load a particular file tape must enter this number in the console keyboard to successfully load the file tape. During the process of file loading, the new journal tape is numbered and this number entered at the end of the file tape after the files have been successfully loaded. This will assist in the recovery procedures necessary to reload the file tape and process all subsequent journal tape transactions into the files.

When each file is unloaded, a summation is run on the items specified by the file description. This sum, when added to the cumulative changes in the file-control field in working storage, should equal the original grand total of these items. In the unlikely event that the two tallies do not match, an analysis will be performed using the original file-input tape and the journal tape to determine the exact error. A printed listing (primarily for internal use) is made to reflect for each subscriber the results of the check, the file length, the number of new records added, the number of records deleted, and the entire contents of each deleted record. This printout is prepared by the subscriber and maintained in a log by the control officer. After the file has been written onto magnetic tape, a count of the number of words is recorded on the tape, and the tape is then read backwards to check against parity errors or otherwise unreadable records.

When the system has been unloaded, the magnetic tape will be given to the control officer on duty. He will secure this tape in a file cabinet provided solely for this purpose. The only ones authorized access to this cabinet will be the control officers (and two senior Keydata executives).

At loading time on the following working day, after the magnetic tape file is reloaded onto the drum and disc file, it will be read back and the control totals and item counts compared against the totals recorded during off-loading. Printed listings are produced of the number of records in the file, total file length, and any changes made to the file at loading time. When the system has been loaded, the load tape is returned to the control officer who later that day stores it in the vault of the Harvard Trust Company, located next door to Keydata in Technology Square.

In the unlikely event of a failure of any unit of the system, where the status of the file would be questionable, a single recovery procedure is possible, since the on-line file has been unloaded every 24 to 72 hours, kept on magnetic tape, and loaded the next time the system is put on-line. Reconstruction can now be accomplished by utilizing the off-loaded files and the journal tape (which reflect every transaction that occurred since the files were on-loaded), reprocessing the journal as the input data. This, of course, will be accomplished in a relatively short time since no input or output message need be processed for any KDS Station. Since the system has a power failure interrupt, restarting after a power failure is essentially automatic and reconstruction is not required.

Keydata will provide a courier service for its subscribers. All information transmitted or received at the Keydata center will be assigned a log number and entered in a correspondence log. This log will include a control number, the subscriber's name and address, the time it was picked up, and the name of the Keydata employee receiving the information. All information leaving the center will be placed in a properly addressed sealed envelope. An outgoing control number will be assigned and a log entry indicating the control number, the name and address of the subscriber, the time and date it was mailed or delivered, and, if the latter, a signature of an authorized representative of the subscriber. It will be the responsibility of the control officer to insure that all information transmitted to or received from the Keydata center has been properly recorded in the correspondence log.

Required:

1. What applications seem best suited for the system described?
2. a. What control problems may exist in such a system?
   b. What control procedures exist to minimize control problems?
3. How would you determine the effectiveness of the processing routines, control procedures, and safeguarding of files? Be specific.

The Wheelox Corporation: Part B

Case

The Wheelox Corporation: Part A described the order invoicing of a cash-receivable updating system of the Wheelox Corporation. Accounts-receivable files are outputs of that system. As part of your audit task, you wish to evaluate these accounts-receivable files. The accounts receivable are on two magnetic tape files. One is the basic record file that contains data records for each customer as shown in Table 1 attached. The other tape is the item record file and contains the details—i.e., unpaid invoices—supporting the basic record account balance. See Table 2 for item record of unpaid invoices.

Required:

1. Determine audit objectives and audit procedures to accomplish your objectives.
2. Determine procedures that can be computerized.
3. Develop your audit output requirements.
4. Develop program flow charts indicating the major processing steps included in your computer audit programs.

Table 1. Accounts Receivable Basic Record Description

Data Field	Number of Characters
Customer number	7
Current A/R balance	9
Amount on order —	
Steel	9
Tungsten	9
Sundry	
Credit limit —	
Amount	7
Date limit established	6
Credit history —	
Date account opened	6
Highest credit extended	9
Date highest credit extended	6
Original credit limit	9
Date original credit limit established	6
Previous credit limit	9
Date previous credit limit established	4
Number of months of previous credit limit	2
Number of items currently delinquent	3
Amount currently delinquent	9
Delinquency history —	
Months reporting	2
Months delinquent	2
Consecutive months delinquent	2
Last month delinquent	4
Highest delinquency —	
Number of items	3
Amount	9
Date	4
Date last sale	6
Sales history (material amount only) —	
(By product line — steel, tungsten, sundry)	
3rd prior year	9
2d prior year	9
1st prior year	9
This year to date	9
This month	9
Potential	9
Profit at standard — year to date	9
Payment history —	
Payment ratings (company establishes payment ratings 0–9 based on payments for each quarter):	
3rd prior year — by quarter	4
2d prior year — by quarter	4
1st prior year — by quarter	4
This year — by quarter	4
Dollars paid this quarter:	
By discount date	9
By due date	9
Customer name and address	136

Table 2. Accounts Receivable Item Record for Unpaid Invoices

Data Field	Number of Characters
Item record code	1
Customer number	7
Date	5
Invoice number	12
Gross amount of invoice	9
Net amount of invoice	9
Cash discount	7

You have been engaged to perform a general audit of Daisy Corporation, a manufacturing concern, for the year ended June 30, 19X0. The physical inventory, which you observed, was taken at an interim date and the client's perpetual inventory tape has been adjusted for inventory differences. Each record on the tape represents a perpetual inventory record including, among other things, quantity and unit cost, but not extended value.

The inventory records are fixed-length, 81-character records with ten records to a block and are contained on 1 reel of magnetic tape. The record format and a description of the fields are shown in Table 1.

You have decided to use the computer in assisting you in the audit of the inventory records.

Required:

1. List the audit procedures you would use in the audit of inventory.

Adapted by permission from a copyrighted case of Haskins & Sells.

2. How could you use the computer to assist you in performing the procedures? Be specific.
3. With your knowledge of generalized audit programs, what routines would be used or developed for performing your audit procedures?

Table 1. Tape Record Format

Field Numbers	Descriptions	Positions
1	Region code	1–2
2	Hold control	3
3	Buyer	4
4	Stock number (First three numbers designate product line)	5–16
5	Warehouse stored	17
6	Bulk pack	18–21
7	E.O.Q. (Economic Order Quantity)	22–24
8	M.O.P. (Minimum Order Point)	25
9	Lead time	26–27
10	Unit of issue (ea.)	28–29
11	Date (Julian)* of last issue	30–32
12	Total hold	33–38
13	Future quantity	39–43
14	Back order	44–48
15	Unit cost (xxx.xx)	49–54
16	Due in	55–60
17	On hand quantity	61–66
18	Unit selling price (xxx.xx)	67–71
19	Contingency	72–73
20	Demand forecast	74–79
21	Card code	80
22	Record mark	81

*Under the Julian dating system, January 1 is day number 001; February 1 is day number 032, etc.

Oxwheel Company

The Oxwheel Company has a large general mail-order business with annual sales of about a hundred million dollars. Most of the sales are made on a monthly payment plan basis. At December 31, there were approximately $1,500,000. Very few customers' balances exceed $1,000. The company's general office maintains the accounts-receivable records. The large volume of transactions processed by the company has necessitated extensive segregation of duties and frequent balancing of data during processing. Accordingly, the company's internal accounting controls are considered to be very good.

A complete record of each customer's account is stored on magnetic tape and includes those in the right column.

All source documents are in the form of cards or are converted to cards. Daily, all of the transactions in account sequence are read into the computer and processed against the customer master tape. Each account is updated and analyzed to determine whether the transactions just processed have created a condition that should be brought to the atten-

Description	Positions Required on Tape Record
Type of account	1
Customer account number	9
Customer name and address	60
Credit limit	1
Status code	1
Number of transactions this month	2
Current month's charges	6
Current month's payments	6
Current month's credits	6
Balance	6
Aged balance over 30 days	6
Aged balance over 60 days	6
Aged balance over 90 days	6
Aged balance over 120 days	6
Year account opened	2
Year last active	2
Total purchases this year to date	6
Total returns this year to date	6
Number of months active	2
Number of months over 90-day category	2
Total purchases last year	6
Total returns last year	6
Number of months active last year	2
Number of months over 90-day category last year	2
Highest balance owed	6

tion of the authorization or collection sections. Notification cards are automatically punched and forwarded to these groups to alert them to such conditions as accounts over credit limits, unusual buildups, and payments by delinquent accounts.

During the order-filling, collection, and credit processes, totals are generated to control all input transactions entering the data processing system. The computer operation accumulates totals of all input that must agree with the predetermined totals developed outside the system.

A control record is kept on tape for each cycle. As the accounts are updated, the day's transactions are accumulated and added to the starting control figure for each cycle. The new control figures are balanced with the sum of all the individual accounts in the cycle (accumulated as each account is processed). In addition, a detailed transaction and cycle-control report is prepared, providing an audit trail in customer-account-number sequence. Figure 1 is a flow chart of the updating, analysis, and control activities.

Required:

1. List the audit procedures you would use in the audit of the accounts-receivable processing described above.
2. How could computer audit programs be developed to perform some of your procedures?
3. Prepare a program flow chart for the audit procedures you would have in the computer audit program(s).

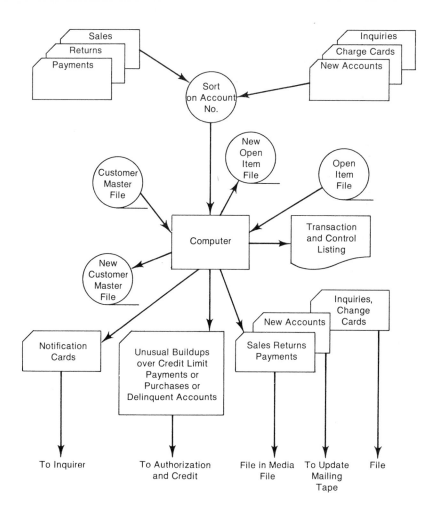

Figure 1. Flow chart of updating, analysis, and control activities.

3

Chapter 9

Auditing the
Information System

In Chapter 4, we introduced the idea that the auditor's objective should be the evaluation of the firm's information system. To fulfill this objective, the auditor must understand the concepts of relevance and reliability and the methodology for evaluating the adequacy of the system to produce relevant, reliable, and useful output.

To usefully discuss the concept of relevance in an information-systems context, we must first define the terms "data" and "information." Data can be defined as raw material; any information system requires data, or input. Every organization must collect data about events or transactions that take place both in the environment in which the business operates, and within the organization. What data must be collected, how it is collected, whether it is to be reported and if so to whom, are all questions that must be answered by anyone designing the information system. Obviously there is a need in each organization for systematic collection of data to provide the basic information necessary for operating the business activities of the firm.

The collected data must then be transformed into "relevant" data— that is, information. Relevant data bear upon or are useful to the action they are designed to facilitate or the result they are intended to produce. One

Relevance

author has summarized the difference between data and information as follows:

> . . . The distinction between data and information (is) predicated on this difference: *data* were materials to be used inferentially but had not been evaluated for their worth to a specified individual in a particular situation, whereas information was inferentially intended material evaluated for a particular problem, for a specified individual, at a specific time, and for the explicit purpose of achieving a definite goal. Thus what constitutes information for one individual in a specific instance may not do so for another or even for the same individual at a different time or for a different problem. Useful information for one manager may well turn out to be sheer nonsense for another. Not only is the particular organizational level important but also the intended functional area. A production manager, for example, is typically unconcerned with sales analysis by product, territory, customer, etc. while the one in charge of inventory control is little concerned with the conventional accounting reports that affect him only indirectly. To recapitulate, in the definition adopted above, information concerns *selected data*—data selected with respect to problem, user, time, place, and function (reduction of uncertainty).[1]

Determining the Relevance of Data

To determine the relevance of the data processed, the auditor must take an approach which emphasizes information flows and the adequacy of information systems to facilitate management functions. The audit approach we envision reviews systems and evaluates the manner in which they are functioning, rather than assisting management to cope with individual events. The primary focus should be on how decisions are made and the system or flow of information necessary to promote effective decision making. This means that questions must be asked to determine if relevant information was available and was brought to bear on decisions, if modern techniques of decision analysis were used, if the decisions made were promptly and efficiently implemented, and if there was adequate feedback to enable management to review the results of their decisions.

To review and evaluate the firm's information systems, the auditor should use procedures designed to thoroughly acquaint him with the nature of the business being audited, should gain an overall understanding of its existing information systems, and should identify the client's business problems. For such an approach, analysis must be made of the decisions required of individuals in their functions, of the information necessary for these decisions, and of the adequacy of the present or potential data supply to meet these information requirements.

[1] Peter P. Schoderbek, ed., *Management Systems: A Book of Readings*, p. 44.

Such an approach should include both a review of organization charts policy manuals, and job descriptions, and inquiries with people responsible for the principal activities of the company such as marketing, research and development, production, personnel, and finance. Inquiries should be made in such a way as to elicit responses that are both comprehensive and specific. For example, one management consulting group has prepared the following set of questions to be addressed to various managers in performing an initial, overall review of information requirements:

1. What are your major functions?
2. What specific kinds of decisions are you faced with in the performance of these functions?
3. What information do you require in order to make these decisions?
4. Is all this information presently available to you in the form you need and on a timely basis?
5. If not, how do you compensate for this lack of information?
6. Are there, in fact, instances when decisions must be made although adequate or appropriate information is not available? Explain.
7. In what areas within your functional responsibilities are such decisions being made?
8. What are the three problems that you consider to be most critical to your operations?
9. What are the major "information blocks" with which you are faced?
10. If you had unlimited authority and resources, what actions would you take to relieve these problems and to correct present unfavorable conditions?

Such a review should suggest the primary information requirements for various management functions. The auditor, however, will have to use his professional judgment to interpret the results of his review. Managers are not aware of all the factors which may be relevant to their decisions. The alert auditor can often perceive areas of information deficiency or data excess that operating managers have not noticed. This is particularly the case in situations where various functions cross with imperfect flow of data among them.

It is difficult to predict the results of this review of information requirements since the needs of different corporations in different industries vary greatly and to a large extent are dependent upon the individual circumstances of their case. In general, however, in a typical manufacturing company information needs for various functional areas of the business might approximate the following:

Marketing management needs information about customer characteristics and profiles; competitive actions; advertising effectiveness; and sales by product, by salesmen, by distribution channel.

Logistics or operations management needs information about the physical flow of materials through the organization and the major activities of procurement, production, and distribution related to producing and distributing the goods desired by the customer.

Information is needed for inventory control, production planning and control, and transportation.

All activities in any organization require resources—people and money—and personnel information and financial information are required for resource planning, allocation, and control.

Data Cycles

To provide relevant data, or information, for the management functions being reviewed, several basic data-collecting and processing cycles must be designed by the firm to record and transform the data into information.

1. A *procurement data cycle* concerned with the data about the acquisition of equipment and materials necessary in the production or fabrication process that results in goods and services required by the consumer.[2]

2. A *production data cycle* concerned with a flow of data about production requirements and production scheduling.

3. A *marketing data cycle* concerned with the flow of data about customers, acquisition of orders, status of customer orders and their filling, including shipping and billing.

These three constitute the major data cycles and, in a broad sense, encompass the two other cycles we will discuss. However, the other two—(1) cash and (2) personnel—are so important in the operation of any organization that we shall treat them separately.

4. The *cash data cycle* is concerned with providing data about the availability of and requirements for cash, and obviously relates to those aspects of the above data cycles involving cash disbursements and cash receipts.

---

[2]Consumer in the broad sense: any entity such as an individual or organization outside the firm, department or individual within the firm, having a demand for the goods or services.

5. The *personnel data cycle* is concerned with providing data for determining job workload and requirements, evaluating job performance and talents available for filling specific jobs and for promotions, designing training programs, and determining obligations to the employee for services rendered.

All these data cycles must be reviewed by the auditor for several reasons. Much of the data used in developing management plans and generating control reports comes from these operating systems. Moreover, since these data cycles focus upon individual transactions which must be recorded, classified, and processed in a highly structured system, most of the management-science techniques involving optimization models and programmed decision rules have been adaptable to these data cycles, and their application has resulted in substantial benefits to organizations using them.

The review of the client's data cycles should be accomplished by:

1. Reviewing existing policy manuals or written procedural instructions.
2. Seeking out the people who are responsible for the activity under study and inquiring about the procedures in existence.
3. Selecting individual events representative of the major categories of transactions and tracing the handling of each event throughout its cycle.

The first two steps are designed to gain an understanding of the client's data-processing cycles and to provide data to the auditor for recording in his working papers the procedures in existence; as we discussed in Chapter 7, the most accurate and comprehensive way to record the procedures in existence is the flowchart. The third step enumerated above, the selection of individual transactions, is designed to establish the existence of system procedures and to confirm the understanding of the system the auditor has obtained through discussions with responsible executives and managers and through review of systems documentation. The objective of this individual-transaction testing is not to determine if the procedures are in effect and functioning an acceptable percentage of the time. A limited test of the transactions in each cycle will suffice because the auditor's objective for the data-cycle review does not include making valid statistical inferences about the population of all transactions of a given type.

The next five chapters discuss the audit procedures involved in the review and evaluation of the procurements, production, marketing, cash and personnel cycles.

Reliability

Information systems must provide output that is not only relevant but reliable. Reliability is that attribute which allows users of the information produced to have a high degree of confidence in it. A system is reliable when it produces similar information or results from examining, recording, measuring, and processing similar evidence, data, or records. Reliability emphasizes the need for internal controls in the system to detect erroneous data, and to prevent processing errors from exceeding the system's acceptable error levels. Since erroneous data tends to create suspicions and resentments that may extend to the entire information system, errors may undermine the general usefulness of the information produced.

To determine the reliability of information, the auditor must evaluate the client's system of internal control; he should be guided about the principles and characteristics of internal control by pronouncements of the AICPA, which has defined internal control as comprising "the plan of organization and all of the coordinate methods and measures adopted within a business to safeguard its assets, check the accuracy and reliability of its accounting data, promote operational efficiency, and encourage adherence to prescribed managerial policies."[3]

Systems of internal control have been increasingly relied upon by business in the past several years. As business organizations have increased in size and complexity, owners and managers have found it impossible to have personal knowledge of the day-to-day operations of a business. As a result, they have come to rely on information provided by others; they need a system that provides information that is reliable and accurate.

The objectives of internal control in a system are: (1) assurance that the assets of the business are safeguarded, (2) assurance that information supplied by others is reliable, (3) assurance that operations are being performed efficiently, and (4) assurance that management policies are being followed. A system of internal control that is designed to accomplish these objectives has certain elements or characteristics which may be enumerated as follows:

1. An organizational plan that provides a segregation of responsibility for authorizing transactions, for recording transactions, and for custody of assets.
2. A system of record keeping which establishes control of assets, liabilities, revenues, and expenses.
3. Established procedures to be followed in the performance of responsibilities.
4. Personnel qualified for their responsibilities.

---

[3]AICPA, *Auditing Standards and Procedures*, p. 27.

Although the shape of an organizational structure in any particular company results from a variety of influences, one principle of organization is universally applicable: the establishment of clear lines of authority and responsibility. To achieve adequate control, functions should be divided in such a way that responsibility for initiating and authorizing a transaction is separated from responsibility for its recording, which in turn is separated from responsibility for the custody of the resulting assets. In addition to safeguarding assets, such a division of responsibility provides for the efficiencies derived from specialization, makes possible a cross-check that promotes accuracy without duplication or wasted effort, and enhances the effectiveness of a management reporting system.

The processing of an incoming order provides a good example of the separation of duties. After the receipt of the order from the customer, salesman, or some other source, the sales-order department initially records data about it and begins processing the order. Before release to the shipping department for filling or to the production department for production of the item ordered, there is normally a credit approval in the treasurer's office. The customer and the sales-order department serve as controls over the accuracy of the order filling by the shipping department. In addition, periodic review of the open-order file would reveal unusual delays in shipments or errors that may creep into the process. Knowledge that such a review is taking place would give the sales-order department, shipping department, and accounts-receivable and billing personnel an incentive to carry out their work with some care. After the item is shipped to the customer, an invoice is prepared and is used for posting data to accounts-receivable records. The receivable would be reduced upon the treasurer's deposit of the customer's remittance.

As data processing has been made electronic, its processes and procedures have become centralized. The concentration of data processing in one department necessitates proper control of the processing center itself. In order to achieve satisfactory internal control, the basic separation discussed previously—of those people who authorize a transaction from the people that have custody of the asset required, and from those people who record the accountability for the asset—must be maintained in EDP systems.

Although nothing in EDP is inconsistent with this requirement, the means for authorization and the nature of the authorization may have changed. To maintain the continued integrity of the system in which the authorization and recording functions are embodied in the program itself, it is necessary to separate the systems-planning and programming functions from the machine-operating function. For example, if under automated inventory management the computer prints out a purchase order because an inventory item has fallen below a certain balance, this may on the surface appear to be elimination of a separate authorization. The authorization, however, originates with the operating people and is passed along to systems designers and programmers for consideration of factors that will result in a purchase order.

Authorizing and Recording Transactions

Once management has determined its objectives and formulated a plan of organization with an appropriate segregation and delegation of functional responsibilities, it must have an adequate system to insure that the duties delegated are handled in a satisfactory manner. Such a system provides proper authorization, approval, or review of all transactions with the record of such authorization serving to establish full accountability for all actions taken. This record of authorization is usually a source document. The system must also provide for accurate and efficient processing of the transactions and their summarization in accordance with the operating responsibilities and information needs of the individuals involved in making operating decisions. Basically, any system of authorizing and recording transactions has three levels: (1) the recording level, (2) the data-processing level, (3) the reporting level.

Normally, basic records such as the source document, the journal, and the ledger are used to record, process, classify, and summarize data in order to provide the type of information management desires. The processing is usually performed by people instead of machines, and the accuracy and propriety of the processing is insured by a segregation of duties and by human review and inspection of the documents and records.

Using our previous example of order processing, page 321, we must design a system to get the goods or services specified by the customer to him at a price agreed upon by the contractual agreement entered into and within the time constraints imposed by the customer-service policies of the company. The design of such a system must reflect a thorough analysis of the information requirements of the various levels of management concerned in some way with the customer's order. Obviously, there is a need for such information about the individual order as customer name, address, quantity ordered, price, etc., to satisfy some very basic questions about how much of what is to be sent where. This in turn is input for summary reports on salesman performance and for order-analysis reports related to product, territory, customer, etc. After the origination of the order and generation of information to relevant operating people in shipping (if the order can be filled from existing inventory) or production (if the order has to be produced) there is information required as to the status of the order in relation to promised delivery date. After shipment, there is a need for information to remove the order from the open-order file, to generate an invoice to the customer, and to update the customer's accounts-receivable balance. Since in conventional accounting terms the invoice is used as evidence of the sale, there must be a means of summarizing invoices to generate sales statistics for accountability, performance measurement, and planning purposes.

Sound Practices of Administration

To implement a system of internal control having appropriate segregation of duties and procedures for authorizing and processing transactions, an organization must develop sound administrative practices. Such practices might include organization charts, written job descriptions, systems and procedures manuals, and flow charts. Operating reports are required to show whether the company's various segments are operating according to plan and how well the responsibilities of operating managers have been discharged.

Personnel

Obviously, to implement a good plan of organization, a system of authorization, and record-keeping procedures, and to develop and implement sound administrative practices, it is necessary to have competent people. As business becomes more complex, there is an increasing need for qualified people who have both the managerial and technical capabilities to develop effective and efficient systems of internal control and management information. The acquisition and development of such capabilities is an integral part of the control system of a corporation.

Review of Internal Control and the Reliability of Information

It will be remembered from Chapter 6 that the second audit standard of field work states: "There is to be a proper study and evaluation of existing internal control as a basis for reliance thereon and for the determination of the result and extent of the tests to which auditing procedures are to be restricted."

This standard can be satisfied by reviewing internal control as part of the review of relevant information and of the data cycles producing such information. In conducting his analysis of internal control and of the reliability of data as part of a broader systems review, the auditor should make inquiries of responsible personnel involved in the design and operation of the internal-control system, should observe the system in operation, should review internal audit reports, if any, and existing documentation of accounting and data-processing policies and procedures, and should select and trace test transactions that are designed primarily to confirm the understanding of the internal controls in the system that he has obtained by the above methods, and to obtain evidence as to the accuracy and reliability of the data processed.

Summary

We have discussed the methodology of auditing the information system and determining the adequacy of the system to produce relevant, reliable, and useful output. We examined the attributes of relevance and reliability. We have introduced the thought that the review of internal control should be included as part of the broader systems review in order to examine the relevance of management information as well as its accuracy. The next five chapters examine the auditor's approach to reviewing the primary data cycles in the information system.

Introduction to Readings

We have introduced the idea that the auditor's objective should be the evaluation of the firm's information system. To implement this objective the auditor must apply the methodology of auditing the information system in an ongoing situation. He needs a place to begin. The two articles that follow have been selected because they do provide observations on the practical application of information-system audits.

Witte, in the first article, suggests that the internal-control review is the best starting point for extending the attest function. The internal-control review can be followed by a management-control review to identify management practices and policies that require improvement and further detailed study.

Dodwell, in the second article, suggests that there must be a bridge between the traditional basic audit, concerned with satisfying regulatory and custodial requirements and accounting controls, and a management-services approach to a client's problem. He defines this bridge as operational auditing and discusses the methodology of performing an operational audit. He suggests an evolutionary rather than revolutionary approach to implementation because of the cost of retraining and refocusing the auditor's traditional objectives.

Management Auditing: the Present State of the Art

Arthur E. Witte

It was only a few years ago that our firm operated a nice, peaceful accounting and auditing practice catering to the needs of a few loyal and conservative clients. Then the Russians shot off the first Sputnik, the computer became common in business, the treadmill was speeded up and we have been racing madly ever since to keep up.

As part of the process of running to keep up, we sought out a good CPA friend of ours, Marvin L. Stone of Denver, Colorado, when we were both attending the annual meeting of the American Institute of CPAs in Philadelphia in 1960. We discussed the problems of meeting the new challenges and concluded that an audit of our management policies and methods by an outsider would be of benefit. We exchanged some correspondence on the subject and developed the idea of a reciprocal management audit. This was done in 1961 and repeated again in 1964.

The engagement was written up for *The*

Reprinted by permission from *The Journal of Accountancy*, August 1967. Copyrighted 1967 by the American Institute of Certified Public Accountants.

Journal of Accountancy and appeared in the July 1962 issue ("CPA Services for the CPA," p. 31). It covered many aspects of accounting office operation.

No matter how detached one thinks he is, self-objectivity is never completely possible and the shock of the exposure of long-held prejudices can be traumatic. It took our organization a long time to recover. In fact, we made a complete reversal in certain underlying concepts and overall objectives of the firm.

It is as a result of this performance as auditor and auditee that we think we now have sufficient humility to discuss the subject of management audits.

There is another reason, however. The clientele of our firm consists primarily of smaller, usually family-held companies. The relationship of the CPA in these situations is quite different from that of the large publicly owned company to its CPA firm.

The smaller business frequently does not have the sophisticated financial and administrative skills available to it because the founder may have been sales- or production-oriented.

In these cases, the need may be filled by the CPA. This process is referred to in the profession as "hand holding." It has many of the ingredients of operational auditing, but it is usually done on an informal basis and takes place as problems are identified by the client or the CPA.

The trouble with this method of operation is that it tends to stunt the growth of the CPA firm because, with each partner having only two hands, there is a limit to how many hands the firm can hold.

One of the changes in firm concepts which arose out of the management audit by Marvin Stone was the adoption of a growth philosophy. Since this was incompatible with the "hand holding" concept, it was necessary to compromise by the development of standardized forms and codified procedures designed to fragment the operation of "hand holding" so that it could be delegated and to formalize it so that it could be taught. This had some interesting and unpredicted effects on the firm's recruitment and training problems which will be discussed briefly later.

It is in this manner that the management audit is evolving in our firm and, we assume, in other firms serving the small business community.

Before going into this process in more detail, it would be useful as background to see how the audit or attest function has developed historically.

Development of the Attest Function

Originally, attestation dealt with completed commercial endeavors. The classic example of this type was the formation of a company to sponsor a ship's voyage. The financial information consisted of the investment of cash at the start of the venture, the receipts and expenditures during the voyage and the payout at the end. The audit was a cash audit and the statement was a cash statement. The time period was the voyage or venture time.

As business operations became more continuous, the nature of the required information changed. It was necessary to have periodic reports before a final liquidation of the business occurred. Thus the annual audit evolved. It still consisted primarily of "counting" but the counting procedures were extended beyond cash to include merchandise, equipment, receivables, liabilities, etc.

Thus, financial reports became balance sheets with income statements serving as bridges between successive position reports. The auditing further became the audit of the total balance sheet and any procedural tests performed were done in connection with attesting to the balance sheet.

As business evolved, big companies became essentially self-perpetuating and continuous beyond the lifetime of the founder. The emphasis shifted from periodic inventory-takings as represented by the balance sheet to continuous reports. The balance sheet now became the bridge between successive income statements. Where, previously, the value of the company was established by reference to the balance sheet, the report of income is now primarily used in determining value.

With the shift in emphasis, the role of the auditor has been changed, too. Auditing of procedures has assumed primacy over auditing of the balance sheet items. This is where we stand now, although the essential concern of the auditor is still almost exclusively with the figures rather than the processes.

Since the continuous profitability of a business is dependent upon the decision-making process and decision-making is based upon the information systems, it is logical to assume that the next step for the auditor will be the attestation of these processes. The profession is moving inexorably in this direction. Where does it stand now in the use of operational or management audits?

There has been very little published on the practical application of management audits, and the best I can offer is to describe what progress our own firm has made and assume that other firms, as well, are working in the same direction.

Internal Control Review

Most firms have found, and we are no exception, that the best place to begin a review of operations is with the check of internal control which is required in connection with the audit.

In the process of this review, the accountant collects a substantial amount of data on the business operation and many of the forms in use. He questions the top executives and others in the company and completes a voluminous file of working papers for review by the partner-in-charge preparatory to deciding on audit extensions or limitations and to writing the report.

In the year of the first audit by the firm, this work takes a considerable part of the total audit time. In subsequent years, it is necessary only to follow up on previous recommendations and test the system to determine whether there have been any other changes.

This gives the firm the opportunity to extend its audit function into other areas without substantially increasing the overall time. Con-

sequently, in the second year the firm recommends that the client have a management control review.

Management Control Review

The management control review is a management audit. The emphasis is on the location of problem areas. Its purpose is to identify the management practices or policies requiring improvement and further organize detailed study. The solution of the problems and their implementation are not part of this process. They are thought of as the second and third steps and they are performed either by the company's management, the audit staff, the management services department of the firm, outside consultants or any workable combination. It is the accounting firm's responsibility to recommend the one best qualified to solve the problem at the lowest possible cost to the client.

As in the case of the internal control review, the basis of the investigation is a questionnaire. It is used as an interview tool for developing information on the client's management controls. The senior accountant, audit supervisor or audit manager collects the data, interviews the client and his executives, and completes the questionnaire. In his working papers he makes notes as to weaknesses, impressions, recommendations, conclusions and suggestions for discussion. He reviews his findings with the partner-in-charge and the contents of the report are agreed upon. The report is completed in draft form and the recommendations approved by the management controls department.

The purpose of the final report is to serve as the agenda for a conference with the client. After this conference, the responsibility is the client's, although the firm will continue to follow up its recommendations.

Without going into the details, it may be informative to indicate the major management areas covered by the review. The reason for auditing them will be obvious.

1. *General information, objectives and policies.* The auditor prepares, in summary form, a three-year statement of income, preferably on a marginal income basis separating variable and fixed expenses to determine the trend of profit margins and overhead payroll and expenses. He calculates the return on investment, working capital and current ratio and other turnover figures and ratios to give him an overview of the financial trends of the business in the past three years. If industry or competitors' statistics are available, they are inserted for comparison.

The auditor then ascertains what the long-range goals of the business are and whether they are in writing and have been communicated to the executives. He determines the concept of the business and whether any major changes are contemplated. This study will help him to understand and evaluate the rest of the data he must accumulate.

2. *Organization and personnel.* One part of the study calls for an organization chart showing the areas of responsibility and lines of authority. It covers the policies with regard to recruitment and training of executives and the maintenance of operating manuals. It will uncover existence of one-man rule or "dynasties" within the organization.

Other questions expose problems of morale, turnover, overtime, promotion and advancement policies, wage and salary evaluation and union problems. They also cover the available fringe benefits and employee plans.

3. *Financial management.* Here we leave the conceptual areas and move to the matters of financial management. Are operating budgets and cash forecasts prepared? How are they developed and used? What about cash management? Are there periodic excess funds? How are they invested? Does the company have a credit line? How is it used? Are purchase discounts lost? Why?

Insurance is studied with the emphasis on the control procedures rather than the coverage. Who handles the insurance? How is the agent selected? When was the last survey made? Are there any loss or accident prevention programs? Are there any procedures for determining new hazards? What policy records are kept?

There are questions on the cost controls. What cost system is in use? Are cost records tied into financial records? How often are labor and overhead rates revised? Are they current?

4. *Marketing.* What are the channels of distribution, the territories, the extent of coverage? What is the discount structure, the commission structure? How are they determined? How is advertising planned, budgeted, its effectiveness measured? What is the system of credit and collection followup? How are selling prices determined?

5. *Systems and procedures.* The systems and procedures are also reviewed. The auditor determines the policies and procedures with regard to requisitions, order quantities, competitive bidding, the maintenance of inventory records, problems of excess stock or stock-outs, obsolete and slow-moving items, make-or-buy

decisions, and production planning and scheduling.

He investigates the basic office equipment and procedures for reducing and distributing the work load, fast-closing techniques for timely reports, and internal verification, editing and error tracing.

The remaining questions deal with payroll costs and distribution, plant and office facilities and equipment, accounting systems and procedures, reports, forms and record maintenance and destruction.

By the time his questionnaire and the related report are completed, the auditor, the partner-in-charge and the management controls department have a fairly comprehensive idea of the operations of the business and the effectiveness of the management.

One might think that after this kind of review the firm would leave the client alone. In serving the smaller business, however, we must remember that the CPA wears many hats, not the least of which is that of a tax planner and adviser. In shifting from the hand holding process described earlier, it is necessary to substitute still another management audit, which the firm has named the tax control review.

Tax Control Review

The tax control review is performed in connection with the third-year audit of the client. This is not to say that obvious tax problems are not handled as they are uncovered but a systematic, in-depth review is not conducted earlier unless specifically requested by the client.

The procedure is identical to that used in the management control review except for the involvement of the tax department in lieu of the management controls department.

The emphasis shifts somewhat because in a closely held company the owner-operators want to be sure that they are benefiting from all that the tax laws permit. Hence, a portion of the review deals with the personal income of the owners, their estate and gift programs, life insurance, personal contributions, retirement plans, age, status and occupation of the children and plans for succession of the business.

The balance of the review and the portion that we are interested in here is concerned with the preservation of the after-tax income dollar and the maximization of employee incentives through nontaxable fringe benefits. It is divided into separate sections for tax accounting methods, sales, excise and miscellaneous taxes, and executives' compensation and benefits.

1. *Tax accounting methods.* The section on tax accounting methods goes through the balance sheet accounts and many income and expense items.

In connection with accounts receivable and sales, the auditor finds out about the bad debt method, whether there are any guaranteed sales, consignment sales, installment sales on long-term contract and how they are treated for tax purposes.

Inventories are studies to determine valuation methods, whether supplies of various categories are included, handling of obsolescence—all from a tax rather than an audit point of view.

The tax accounting for property and equipment reveals capitalization policies and depreciation methods. The handling of leased equipment, tools, dies, molds, patterns, etc., is reviewed from the standpoint of maximum tax benefit.

The questionnaire goes into the handling of investments, officer loans, intercompany loans, excess of idle funds indicating a possible Section 531 problem. Accruals are studied to determine the method of handling vacation pay, property taxes and warrantee of guarantee liabilities.

Expense accounts are reviewed to determine maintenance and repair policies, officers' compensation methods, contribution policies, travel and entertainment expense handling, and the existence of any quasi-personal expense to determine the adequacy of the documentation for tax purposes.

2. *Sales, excise and miscellaneous taxes.* The review of sales, excise, payroll and other taxes is conducted in the same vein—that is, from the point of view of control and minimization of cost.

3. *Executives' compensation and benefits.* The tax laws permit a number of benefits for company executives which are deductible by the company but are either tax-deferred or tax-free to executives. A long checklist is completed to be sure that consideration has been given to these benefits.

These three studies, the internal control review, the management control review and the tax control review, constitute a management audit. They range from the broadly conceptual to the basic nuts and bolts. They cover the points of view of the auditor, the manager and the tax man—that is, asset preservation, profit maximization and tax minimization.

The only step remaining is the *explicit* expression of an opinion on the management performance. Actually, an opinion is implicit in the firm's recommendations and it is not difficult to foresee that, when interested outsiders require such an audit, an opinion by the auditor will naturally follow. Considering the present state of the art, in our judgment it is not a matter of whether an opinion will ultimately be required or not, but how soon.

A Profile of the New Auditor

The really big question that comes to mind is: "What kind of man is going to do this work?" Since the profession began moving in this new direction, it has discovered what a truly specialized accounting graduate the universities were turning out. The typical accounting major was, and to a great extent still is, manufactured by the university to be a good junior accountant and to pass the CPA examination. Lacking in broad business and economic concepts, weak in communication skills and unaware of the interrelationships of the other social and behavioral sciences, this graduate is not presently prepared for the new challenge.

What the profession needs now is the graduate with the ability to think, to wade through irrelevant detail and concentrate on the important information, to express himself clearly and to grasp what others say and write. The technical knowledge can be transmitted on the job. If the schools teach key ideas and basic principles, a much broader range of subjects can be covered in a four-year curriculum. This idea is very well developed in an article in the July 1966 *Accounting Review* by Herbert J. Weiser, entitled "Accounting Education—Present and Future."

Many practicing accountants and university professors are cognizant of the problem and gradually something is being done about it. In the meantime, what are we to do?

In our firm we have met the problem by simply reversing roles with the universities. If they are going to teach the mechanics, then we must teach the broader concepts; this is what we have done to develop the kind of auditor our firm will need in the future.

The firm's basic training plan is an intensive three-year program which we call our professional development program. The accountant is not permitted to specialize but is given a broad general background in auditing, taxes and management controls. The emphasis is on planning and control and is designed to turn out a well-rounded senior accountant at the end of three years.

His next two years are devoted to our executive development program. The accountant still does not specialize. Using outside lecturers, seminars conducted by the partners and outside reading, the subjects become even more conceptual and philosophical to give him the broader view he will need. A few of the subjects covered are as follows: motivation and productivity; communication; the art of teaching; conceptual foundations of business; strategy and tactics in business; buying and selling businesses; stimulating business growth; the art of negotiation.

Although a number of management texts are required as outside reading for these sessions, there are others designed to broaden the accountant's view: *The True Believer* by Eric Hoffer, to teach mass motivation; *Manhood of Humanity* by Alfred Korzybski, to explain why everyone must teach; *The Way of Zen* by Alan Watts, for lessons in communication; *The Art of Teaching* by Gilbert Highet, to teach teaching.

At this point, the accountant is permitted to specialize if he wants, but even now the firm is working on adding a third year to the executive development program which would be a refresher course in the other social sciences.

This course is still on the drawing boards, but we are considering sessions on history, economics, psychology, sociology, philosophy and anthropology and using as texts the works of some of the newer and more controversial thinkers in these fields—Robert Theobald, Eric Berne, Marshall McLuhan, R. Buckminster Fuller, etc.

The obvious point of all this is that at present the entire educational process for the undergraduate is upside down. Apparently there is no way today to get an education as a generalist in a formal school. R. Buckminster Fuller refers to this as Whitehead's Dilemma. Alfred North Whitehead was the first to notice this tendency shortly after he came here from England in the early part of this century—the tendency, that is, for the best minds to be turned into specialists by the universities.

We find our firm inverting the training process in order to complement the inverted educational process. In this fashion we will be able to staff the firm in accordance with its coming needs. Other firms are trying to compensate in other ways. They have experimented with hiring liberal arts graduates and giving them intensive training in accounting subjects, perhaps on the theory that it is easier to make an accountant out of a bright person than a bright person out of an accountant.

Conclusion

We have reviewed the present state of the management audit in our firm and have given consideration to what qualities and qualifications the new auditor should have.

Thinking back over 20 years in this profession and remembering the businessmen I have known, I find that accounting and business are not as much fun since things have become so scientific. The change in the auditor's function is coming about now that the concept of long-range planning has been injected into business operations as a requirement. This kind of planning does away with the opportunistic and buccaneering businessman we used to know who flew by the seat of his pants, with no instruments, in an open cockpit with goggles and a long silk scarf whipping in the wind behind him.

There is no turning back, but, to put it another way, as *The New Yorker* said in its eulogy for Winston Churchill, "the last long cavalry charge is over and," in many ways, "we live in a lesser time."

Operational Auditing: a Part of the Basic Audit

Joseph W. Dodwell

As American business and industry continue to respond to explosive economic and technological change with increasing size, diversity and complexity, new links have had to be forged in the constantly lengthening chain of delegated administrative and operational authority and control.

Under the impact of rapid growth, competition and more critical profit margins, top management has had to delegate primary and secondary authority over wider areas of operations—first through middle management and then subdivided through progressively lower levels of operating personnel. The advent of the specialist has produced yet another level of delegated authority.

Reprinted by permission from *The Journal of Accountancy*, June 1966. Copyrighted 1966 by the American Institute of Certified Public Accountants.

Each new delegation thus establishes another operational link, the integrity of which determines the efficiency and profitability of the whole. In addition to size per se, wider geographic distribution of operating units has placed added emphasis on the need for more sophisticated and significant control techniques.

Shared or delegated authority and responsibility may provide the appearance, if not the substance, of control. Far too often, however, management has failed to provide adequate reporting systems to appraise the existence and adequacy of administrative and operational controls established either by those delegating authority or, less frequently, by those to whom it is delegated.

Such controls are essential to the support of management's operating plans, programs and policies. Without their continuing objective appraisal, however, an information vacuum is often created between top management and those to whom authority has been delegated for the profitable realization of the organization's objectives.

It is in this growing, increasingly critical area that the accounting profession has the opportunity to broaden its scope and service to the business community. This occurs at a time when management and clients are looking to the profession for assistance in assessing and solving problems in functional and operational areas. The extension of the basic audit to include the appraisal and establishment of administrative and operational controls is part of the logical evolution in the conceptual change in the accountant's role in assisting business management.

The traditional basic audit, historically concerned with satisfying regulatory and custodial requirements and accounting controls, will continue to be of the greatest significance and value. At the same time, it often appears that management is more aware, or at least more perceptive, than the accounting profession in recognizing the values inherent in quantitative and qualitative analysis which can be offered to the broader areas of management's responsibilities.

Some firms have sought to meet this problem by enlarging the range of the general service (or general practice) partner and staff in two or three of the basic skills offered by the public accounting profession today: auditing, tax and management services.

This "integrated" audit brings to bear all three basic audit skills offered by a firm on each audit for all clients.

The operational audit concept, with its concern for operational controls, is the bridge and at times the catalyst between a basic tradi-

tional financial audit and a management services approach to a client's problem. It is a necessary ingredient in fully implementing the integrated audit.

The concept of operational auditing, when conveyed to partners and staff by the use of manuals and training seminars, develops the ability to recognize readily and almost intuitively the probable underlying operating causes for indicated adverse surface symptoms. It permits the evaluation of breakdowns in operational controls in one functional area and their effect on the conditions and situations in other functional areas.

Conceptually, operational audit manuals are structured to provide significant background information with respect to the operations of each major functional area of a business.

Specific functional operational audit programs in each major functional area provide the auditor with a guide to the kinds of controls, conditions and circumstances that he is apt to find. They also provide specific questions to highlight significant control elements. In this overall approach, the auditor concerns himself with a review and appraisal of the adequacy of operational controls.

Orientation and training seminars put the subject in focus by emphasizing that the primary objective of operational auditing is to identify those areas in which cost reduction, operating improvements or increased profitability can be achieved by the initiation or modification of administrative and operational controls or policy directives or by related corrective action.

The ability to view the business as a whole enables the auditor to make constructive suggestions and recommendations to a client for improving the overall profitability of the enterprise.

Thus, the successful implementation of operational auditing can represent a substantial contribution to client relationships.

It is noteworthy that the extension of the scope of the traditional financial audit to a review of administrative or operating controls is consistent with the definition of internal control by the American Institute of Certified Public Accountants. This definition refers to two types of controls: accounting and administrative.

Accounting controls comprise the plan of organization and all methods and procedures that are concerned mainly with, and relate directly to, safeguarding of assets and the reliability of the financial records. They generally include such controls as the systems of authorization and approval, separation of duties concerned with record-keeping and accounting reports from those concerned with operations or asset custody, physical controls over assets and internal auditing.

Administrative controls comprise the plan of organization and all methods and procedures that are concerned mainly with operational efficiency and adherence to managerial policies and usually relate only indirectly to the financial records. They generally include such controls as statistical analyses, time and motion studies, performance reports, employee training programs and quality controls.[1]

Operational auditing consists of the reviews and evaluation of two major elements of management:

1. Corporate Policy
   Determination of the existence, adequacy and comprehension of policy, and the significance of its directives as control elements in major functional areas
   Assessment of the effects of the absence of

policy, or recommendations for adoption or modification of formalized directives.

2. Administrative Controls
   Determination of the existence and adequacy of administrative or operational controls as such, and as support to the profit objectives of management; the degree of compliance in major functional areas; and the co-ordination of operating controls with corporate policy directives
   Assessment of the effects of the absence of administrative or operational controls in significant areas and recommendations for adoption or modification of such controls.

The nature and function of administrative or operational controls, therefore, are fundamental to effective management control.

They represent procedures, routines and other mandatory requirements or specific guidelines indicating how, and by what means, operating authority should be exercised or channeled. They may also take the form of documents or reports which act as controls per se, or which are designed to measure the effectiveness with which other operational controls function. From a functional standpoint, they are the means of implementing corporate policy objectives.

Conversely, the absence of vital policy directives or effective operational controls in significant functional areas can have a substantial adverse effect on overall profitability.

On initiating an operational audit, the auditor develops significant background data on the client which includes historical profits, return on investment, major product classes, number of products in the line, usual channels of distribution, unusual trade characteristics in the marketing area, production control and inventory policy. Information should also be developed on market conditions, approximate

---

[1]*Auditing Standards and Procedures*, American Institute of CPAs, 1963, p. 28.

annual sales volume, gross assets and the influence of "custom" orders or defense contracts on overall planning and operations.

These data can be supplemented by inspections of plants and other facilities to appraise physical conditions and to spot clues to possible problem areas. The auditor can also apply financial analysis techniques to operating statistics which may also suggest problem areas or conditions influencing an unfavorable return on investment or adverse operating statistics.

Preliminary Survey— the "Big Picture" Approach

The actual methodology of the operational audit involves two steps: The first is the *preliminary survey* which consists of limited testing in functional areas to isolate critical problem areas. On the basis of this survey, decisions can be made on the functional areas to be audited in depth to determine the causes of significant adverse indications. The second is the *depth audit* which penetrates the selected functional areas.

The preliminary survey includes the use of programmed interviews in each major functional area keyed to operational audit manuals and programs and the employment of sophisticated interview techniques. Emphasis in this approach can be given any problem area suggested by the physical tour of plants, warehouses, administrative offices, or by the financial analysis work. A limited examination of documents, records, reports or a review of methods and procedural testing may lend additional supporting evidence to the preliminary findings.

Operational audit manuals and programs for *each* functional area of a business should be followed so that the major problems, if any, of the client may be identified and given priority of attention in a subsequent depth audit. In this way, circumstances not known to the auditor can be discovered, isolated and evaluated as to the relative significance in the overall situation.

In conducting the preliminary as well as the depth audit, assumptions should not be made by the auditor that, because of some prior knowledge, he is necessarily aware of the client's major operating problem. For example, the auditor may know that the client has a marketing problem due to excessive delivery delays to customers and failure to meet delivery commitments. Unless the auditor were to review, on an operational audit basis, the production control department, he may never arrive at the basic causative factors producing the market problem. It may be that the client has poor productive inventory management and frequent productive inventory stock outs that result in production interruptions. This, in turn, would affect delivery commitments because of interruptions in the fabrication cycle. There may be excessive absenteeism in the plant, frequent turnover of personnel or the facilities may not be adequate to produce the volume required in the given time cycle. These are just a few of the factors that may be influencing the basic marketing problem.

Survey Memorandum

Upon completion of the preliminary survey, a "survey memorandum" should be prepared which will record the results of the preliminary probe into each operating area. The survey memorandum is an internal reporting device and is not transmitted to clients. Incorporated in it, on an exception basis, will be the operational control deficiencies, if any, found in each functional area with an evaluation of the significance and effect of the absence of effective policies and operating controls in particular functional areas. The preparation of the survey memo is in itself a management control or discipline forcing appraisal of the preliminary survey findings by the staff auditor.

On the basis of the relative magnitude of the findings in each functional area, preliminary decisions can be made about the operating areas to be audited in depth.

At this point, the "budgeted" hours to be allotted to the audit in depth of a particular functional area (or areas) should be provisionally established.

Because of the limited scope of the preliminary survey, the conclusions derived from it are necessarily tentative. Subsequent testing in depth could conceivably modify or change the preliminary survey findings. For this reason, the operational control deficiencies highlighted by the preliminary survey should not be discussed by the auditor with the client until completion of the depth audit and preliminary findings are confirmed with substantial documentation. Occasionally, a depth audit will reverse or modify preliminary indications.

The Depth Audit

The scope of the depth audit should be adequate to substantiate the preliminary survey findings in the indicated problem area or areas. Ideally, just that amount of additional audit work should be programed to support, document or complement the preliminary survey findings. The staff auditor performing the operational audit requires a considerable amount of

self-discipline to keep his focus on the target areas and to develop comprehensive data in the problem areas in the shortest possible time. Experience has shown that the temptation to pursue other trails in operational auditing is great. The seasoned operational auditor learns early in his career to differentiate the substantial from the minutiae and develops skill and judgment in recognizing the relative significance or insignificance of a particular "symptom" and whether or not it relates to the fundamental problem.

Since the findings in the depth operational audit will ultimately appear in a formal written operational audit report issued to a client, adequate documentation to support the formal report is essential and is a basic element in maintaining a "quality control" over reporting mechanisms.

The final operational audit report should be highly organized, the comments and/or recommendations should be pertinent and the language, to the extent possible, should be nontechnical so that the report itself may be an effective communication vehicle to various levels of management.

Three Basic Approaches to Operational Control

Since the nature and function of operational controls vary, the auditor should direct his review and assessment to three basic approaches: policy, control and evaluation.

For example, assume that an auditor has made a preliminary survey of a purchasing department. While there are many operational control elements needed to effectively control the operations of a modern purchasing department, we will assume that the auditor found deficiencies in three of these control elements-- the department:

Audit Finding
1. Did not obtain competitive bids.

Significance
    The company thus did not avail itself of the opportunities to achieve "price" economy by a vigorous and continuous shopping of the market for the lowest prices obtainable consistent with quality, delivery and financial reliability requirements.

Audit Finding
2. Did not purchase each productive inventory material from more than one vendor.

Significance
    The company, therefore, was not protected against partial or complete stoppages of production in the event of the inability of a single vendor to deliver in case of strikes, transportation failures, acts of God or other failure beyond his control.

Audit Finding
3. Did not receive reports from the inspection department as to the quality reliability of vendors based on inspections of incoming productive inventory.

Significance
    The purchasing department thus was in no position to determine the quality reliability of vendors, an important consideration in future purchase order placements to avoid production interruptions arising from poor quality products or failure on the part of vendors to meet specifications.

Having uncovered these deficiencies in the first stage, his preliminary survey, the auditor would concern himself with the *policy, control* and *evaluation* aspects of these three control deficiencies in the second stage, his depth audit.

The Policy Approach

This is the determination of the existence and extent of policy directives.

The auditor's first step should be to determine whether policy directives had been issued by the company relative to each area of deficiency and whether they were adequate from a business standpoint.

Assume for the sake of illustration that policy directives did not exist in two of the three control elements selected for testing; however, a company policy directive did exist requiring the solicitation of competitive bids.

In his initial approach, the auditor can focus management's attention on the control deficiencies and their significance to the overall operation. In his final report, he might recommend that management consider the issuance of formal policy directives covering the two control elements for which policy directives did not exist.

The Control Approach

This is the determination of the means or methods employed to carry out policy directives. In the subject case, although a policy directive existed requiring the obtaining of competitive bids, assume that the auditor found that there were no implementing operational controls to carry out such policy directive.

A possible supporting operational control that the company might have initiated would have required the purchasing agents or buyers to obtain written competitive bids from a minimum number of vendors and to record these vendor quotes on bid summary sheets for review and evaluation by purchasing management to ensure that the orders for productive materials would go to the lowest bidding vendor consistent with quality, delivery and financial reliability requirements of the company.

Such a system would have provided management with a control routine to monitor compliance with the policy statement. The auditor would have subjected the system, had it existed, to procedural and other testing in a depth audit to determine its adequacy in supporting the policy statement. His final report, in this instance, would cite the effect of the absence of such an operational control; in other situations, his report might include an appraisal of the strength or weakness of existing controls, where appropriate.

The Evaluation Approach

The auditor's next step is to concern himself with whether or not management has established control reports or other management controls as a means of evaluating compliance with policy directives.

In the evaluation approach to a policy statement requiring competitive bid solicitation, the auditor might find that management had instituted procedural routines requiring the periodic preparation and circulation of reports. They might show the actual savings achieved through competitive bidding routines and through an aggressive pursuit by the purchasing

department of new sources of supply capable of performing within the company's requirements and standards.

If the auditor is not satisfied with the adequacy of these procedural routines, his report might cite the possibility of a breakdown of the entire control mechanism.

These examples illustrate how the auditor would use the same policy, control and evaluation approaches in a depth audit with respect to each deficiency found in his preliminary survey of a purchasing department.

Frequently, operational control deficiencies found in one functional area of a company have an impact on deficiencies or problem areas in other functional departments. The interrelationships would have been explored during the depth audit, and the final report issued to a client would cite the interrelationships and their effects.

The formal operational audit report issued to a client might contain recommendations suggesting the establishment or modification of policy directives and supporting operational controls or procedural routines or reports to permit management to evaluate the effect of compliance with policy and operational control directives. On the other hand, the auditor, if satisfied in his testing, might assure management of the adequacy of its directives, the compliance with them and the techniques employed to evaluate the overall effectiveness of operational controls.

A Diagnostic Approach

In the operational auditing approach, the role of the auditor is that of a fact finder. His approach is diagnostic and the end product of his work is the preparation of a formal operational audit report to management bringing to management's attention important problem factors or areas that may be inhibiting the maximization of overall profit objectives.

The first step in the solution of operating problems is for management to be aware of the location, nature and dimensions of problem areas. The analytical and diagnostic skills of the auditor in zeroing in on major problem areas and making enough of a penetration in depth to recognize the size and dimensions of major problem areas provides an extremely valuable service. It focuses management's attention on these problem areas and frequently includes specific recommendations for their correction. The formal operational audit report, therefore, is *diagnostic*.

Implementing Corrective Action

Often the conditions described in formal operational audit reports to clients may be corrected or improved by the initiation or modification of policy directives or operational controls in particular functional areas. Sometimes such corrective action can be effected by a reassignment of duties. In other situations, the complexity of a problem might impel the auditor to recommend the hiring by the client of additional staff or of a specialist in a particular field. For those public accounting firms with management services arms, corrective action can be effected if desired by the client through the application of such services as the accounting firm provides.

Typical Findings in Marketing

Here are some typical inquiries, findings and conclusions an auditor might develop in performing a pilot operational audit of a marketing function:

Inquiry
Does the company procedurally prepare sales forecasts broken down into realistic scheduling elements; that is, the specific number of each item in the line to be sold within definitive time periods or cycles?

Findings
Many companies in pilot audit groups never prepared sales forecasts. In others, forecasts consisted only of aggregate estimated *dollar* sales by major product groups or for all product groups.

Significance
(a) The absence of sales forecasts automatically prevents the development of a forward production schedule.
(b) Sales forecasts expressed only in dollar amounts were inadequate because they did not specify quantities, products and particular time relationships. They were, therefore, of no value in developing an operating program or, more specifically, a forward production schedule.

Without a forward production schedule, it is impossible for the company to plan productive inventory requirements in terms of quantities or time relationships, determine present and future manpower requirements, or plan, within the capacity of facilities, the fabrication of a given volume of product in a specific time cycle.

Inquiry
Are the sales-volume targets incorporated in the overall sales forecast based on specific marketing criteria for each territory or other unit?

Findings
In several operational audits, client companies

had no knowledge of marketing criteria. Mechanical sales forecasts were made which added a growth factor to the previous year's actual sales volume. The current year's sales forecasts, for example, represented last year's volume plus 10 percent.

Significance

Because these mechanical sales forecasts were not predicted on any marketing criteria, they did not necessarily represent the potential of the market. The fixing of individual sales quotas for salesmen within such an estimated sales approach respects a meaningless management control, since there is no way of knowing whether the quotas assigned represent an adequate market penetration.

In fact, such a sales forecast approach obscures the possibility that the market as a whole, or certain territories, may not have been fully exploited in previous years, a condition that would continue undetected under this system.

Inquiry

Does the company monitor current sales orders so that if there is a substantial impact on the original sales forecast that fact may be brought to management's attention immediately for corrective action?

Findings

Most client companies subjected to operational audit reviews did not monitor current sales orders. Even in those companies where the sales forecasts were relatively sophisticated (i.e., were based on marketing criteria and were definitive as to quantities and products in a time relationship) frequently there was no procedure to monitor current orders.

Significance

If significant trends or current order patterns varied substantially from the sales pattern included in the original sales forecast, the impact of such changes on future sales and production planning would remain undetected and, among other things, the opportunity to communicate to the purchasing department the necessity for immediate acceleration or deceleration of procurement would be lost.

In approaching this phase of the operational audit of a marketing area, the auditor would have developed certain background information on the respective clients, utilized operational audit inquiries to develop certain key control data and also examined physical facilities, documentation and made some procedural testing in order to focus his findings.

It should be emphasized that these are fairly obvious, if typical, examples of findings in a preliminary survey, each of which may be a candidate for a depth audit. They serve to illustrate, however, the basic approach and audit techniques which can be applied to any potential problem area within the company.

Using the same approach to other potential problem areas in which similar audit techniques were applied, the following information was developed with respect to production control, including the labor control aspect of production control.

In each of the cases mentioned below, the specific operational audit inquiries have not been enumerated for the sake of brevity. However, the audit findings are spelled out as is the significance of the audit findings.

Production Control: Audit Findings

1. Either production control did not exist; or its functions had been diluted by other departments; or its personnel were inadequate to develop and utilize modern control concepts, including inventory management concepts.

2. The basic function of production control of correlating material, manpower and machines was poor. Substantial audit tests showed that at different times during the year:
The man was there, the machine was there, but no material was available.
The material was there, the machine was there, but no manpower had been scheduled.
The man was there, the material was there, but no machine was available for his use.

3. In general, there was a lack of "sophisticated" process and operational sheets to define how to make the product and in what operational-step order; what special tools or facilities were needed; and there were no reasonable time relationships established for each step.

4. Machine feeds and speeds had not been formally established by industrial engineers. In some situations, although machine feeds and speeds had been set, the work force ignored them and operated at their own respective paces.

5. The department had no knowledge of the capacity of individual facilities and had no knowledge of the overall capacity of the plant to produce any indicated volume of products.

6. Generally, formal machine loading and scheduling systems did not exist. Informal ones did but, by and large, these were inadequate to "monitor" production orders to ensue finishing on originally scheduled dates.
Tests of production orders in process indicated that a substantial number had to be rescheduled because the majority of original production target dates were not regularly met. Rescheduling of production orders to new dates was the rule rather than the exception. A corollary result was the later "bumping" of small orders in the plant to fabricate the larger orders (with more profit potential);

delivery delays to customers were frequent, as was customer dissatisfaction.

7. Random tests indicated that overall machine idleness in the plant amounted to about 40 percent at a time when the company's marketing department was forecasting a modest 3 percent sales gain in the next year. Obviously, this produced a significant amount of unused capacity, a severe burden on overall costs and raised a question as to the adequacy of the sales forecast.

8. The production control department did not keep records and reports on idle facility time and the related causative factors.

9. Although the overall sales cycle was seasonal, the companies gave no recognition to this fact by attempting to level-load production. They thus had expensive production; heavy hirings and firings of labor force, an expensive indulgence; and poor quality production.

10. Salesmen were accepting orders for large and complex products in amounts far greater than were normally carried in inventory, and unrealistic delivery date promises were made to customers (without prior production control concurrence) that bore no relation to normal production lead time.

11. The production inventories were far removed geographically from the first step in the production process, causing excessive and unnecessary material handling costs. As a matter of fact, the overall plant layout was exceedingly poor and inefficient. This resulted in many interruptions in the work flow, excessive material handling costs and general inefficiency.
Additionally, the plant had no formal preventive maintenance program. Consequently there were periodic breakdowns of the facilities, causing partial or complete production stoppages. Remedial maintenance after a production stoppage is costly.

Production Control:
Significance of Audit Findings

Each of these findings demonstrated the need for the hiring by the clients of a sophisticated production control specialist to develop a modern production control system. Only in this way could reliance be placed on the plant to produce, in a given time relationship, a given quantity of the product which would be programed to the sales forecasts.

Such basic improvements would enable the development of adequate and reliable production lead times which, in turn, could be utilized in production and sales planning.

The continuance of the present system results in an inordinate amount of excess production costs and waste and continuous customer dissatisfaction because of delivery delays arising from the constant rescheduling of production orders within the plant.

The development of a sophisticated production control system will establish realistic production and delivery date times that can be co-ordinated with customer needs, inventory levels and the sales forecast requirements.

Labor Control:
Audit Findings

1. Although production levels varied substantially from month to month, no variations in direct labor levels throughout the year were noted.

2. Indirect labor had become frozen at a relatively high level.

3. There were no time and motion study standards, incentive standards, work quotas, or "bogey" standards with which to measure the productivity of the labor force.

4. Operational audits of many plants showed that the entire plant labor force, direct and indirect, were day workers, and there were, therefore, no established productivity measurement standards. These men were paid for *time* rather than *production*. Industrial engineers are agreed that as a bench mark such workers operate at not more than 70 percent of standard efficiency.

5. Physical observation of conditions in the plant revealed large groups of employees milling about, waiting for material, machines, operation sheets, specifications, special tooling, etc. There were excessively long coffee breaks. Most of the plant direct-labor employees stopped their machines about an hour before shift-change time to wash up and stand in line for relatively long periods to be the first to leave the plant. In view of the number of employees involved, this was a significant and costly condition.

6. Where work measurement standards did exist, the labor-time accountability reporting did not distinguish between set-up time, production time, fatigue time, idle time and day work. There were thus no means to measure the actual labor productivity versus the standard. In other situations, no work tickets or travelers or other ways of recording production time existed.

7. Where it was possible to make comparisons of actual versus scheduled production in some plants, it was found that such measurements should have been made on an individual-worker basis. Comparisons of groups of employees' actual versus scheduled production, as was being done, are not especially meaningful.

8. In some plants, it was noted that for practically all direct-labor employees some "day work" was scheduled at the end of each day to "fill in" the employees' work day. This was an expensive policy that some companies could ill afford.

Labor Control: Significance of Audit Findings

The lack of effective labor productivity standards has resulted in excessive labor costs and waste. Under the present system, there is no means of determining direct- and indirect-labor hour requirements or staff.

The excessive amounts of the direct-labor employees' day work and idle time that cannot be controlled under the present system and the lack of work quotas or labor productivity measurement standards all severely inhibit the overall production planning.

The client companies also have no way of knowing whether a given volume of production can be accomplished within a specific time cycle because of the general uncontrolled labor productivity conditions.

As part of the development of a modern production control system already recommended, the client companies should begin the development of labor productivity measurement standards by industrial engineers.

Conclusion

Under the operational auditing approach to a client's problems as part of an "integrated" audit, the audit staff should be trained, on an evolutionary basis, to recognize immediately the kind of surface symptoms that will "ring bells and light lights." In this way, the auditor can put his findings into some logically organized thought pattern and become expert in assessing the probable causative factors. The focusing and evaluation of his findings put him in a position to make significant recommendations to his client for operating improvements, cost reductions and increased profitability.

In the future the accountant will no doubt have undergraduate courses in industrial engineering, production scheduling, marketing and many other functional areas that will be part of his body of knowledge and training for an integrated approach to auditing. It may well be that such courses will be mandatory for candidates for a CPA certificate. The operational audit approach must come to the profession on an evolutionary rather than a revolutionary basis because of the cost of retraining and refocusing the auditor's traditional objectives to include the expansion of the audit work into the areas of operational control and authority.

At the same time, it behooves present professionals to recognize the great potential and opportunity offered the profession in operational auditing in meeting the critical need of business management for more comprehensive and reliable information on how its plans, policies and programs are being carried out.

The Danbury
Steel Corporation

Case

The Danbury Steel Corporation was incorporated in Connecticut in 1945 as a producer of "wire mesh for reinforced concrete, chain link fence, washers, and other fabricated steel products." Control of the corporation is in the hands of members of the same family. There are approximately 200 minority stockholders. Members of the controlling family hold all of the executive positions.

The company produces and sells annually approximately one million short tons of wire road mesh to 200 contractors through the country. Wire fencing and washers are sold nationally through one hundred distributors. The company's gross sales this year amounted to $4,000,000 of which $3,000,000 represented road mesh, $750,000 resulted from sales of fencing, and $250,000 resulted from sales of washers. The factory, located in central Connecticut, employs 100 production workers. The company's offices, adjacent to the factory are staffed by thirty-five employees.

The rapid expansion of operations in the past five years had resulted in an appreciable expansion of the office staff with little consideration of the necessity of an adequate system of internal control. New job functions are assigned to departments on the basis of the skills of the department head with little consideration given to a logical organizational structure. Any segregation of accounting functions that does exist is primarily the result of business requirements with slight incidental control benefits.

The president of the corporation recognizes the inadequacy of the internal control procedures. In recognition of the need to establish an adequate system which can be the basis of a continued orderly expansion of the firm's operations, he has asked our firm to evaluate the adequacy of the system of internal control.

An initial survey of the accounting procedures together with an organizational chart of the company are summarized in the following report prepared by us.

The senior has asked you to read the report, analyze the company's system of control and review the job functions as shown in the attached organization chart in the following manner:

1. List the deficiencies in the client's system of control. Enumerate job functions which are incompatible with one another when performed by the same employee.

Figure 1. Danbury Steel Corporation organization chart: report on survey of accounting procedures.

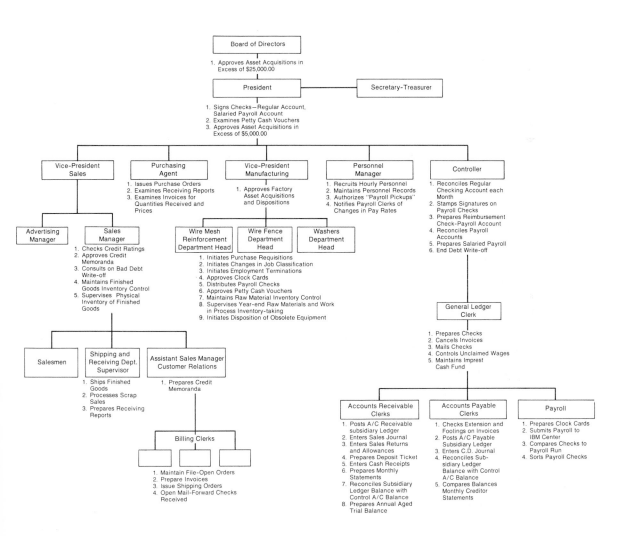

2. Suggest changes in the client's accounting procedures and distribution of work among employees which will improve the client's internal control system and operating efficiency.

Report of Survey of Accounting Procedures

Sales. Sales originate through salesmen who canvass customers in their respective sales territories. Customers' orders are reviewed by the sales manager who: (1) determines that the ordered items are in stock; (2) examines the customers' credit ratings; and (3) forwards the approved orders to the billing clerks.

The billing clerk prepares a prenumbered manifold invoice on which she enters the quantities and description of items which are ordered by the customer. The last two copies are forwarded to the shipping department to authorize shipment of the product. After shipment is made, the shipping clerk returns a signed copy of the shipping order to the billing department. The billing clerk prices and extends the amounts on the invoice for those items actually shipped. A new manifold invoice is prepared for the quantities not shipped. The new invoice is filed with the open orders.

The original copy of the priced invoice is mailed to the customer. A duplicate copy is forwarded to the accounts-receivable clerk in the accounting department. A third copy of the invoice is retained in the billing department.

The accounts-receivable clerk enters the information from the duplicate copy of the invoice to the customer's account in the subsidiary ledger. After posting the invoices to the subsidiary ledger, the clerk runs a tape of the invoices and enters the total sales for the day in the sales journal.

Claims received from customer for defective and returned goods are forwarded to the assistant sales manager in charge of customer services. He evaluates the claim, and if it is proper, he prepares a credit memorandum. The credit memorandum is forwarded to the sales manager for approval. An approved copy is forwarded to the accounts-receivable clerk for entry to the subsidiary ledger and in the sales returns and allowances journal.

Scrap Sales. Large quantities of scrap wire, cuttings, and turnings are generated in the production process. Each day, scrap is delivered from the production departments to a special area in the shipping department. Twice a month, a scrap dealer, personally known to and trusted by the shipping clerk, weighs the scrap in the presence of the shipping clerk. The shipping clerk gives the scrap dealer a receipt (marked paid and initialed by the shipping clerk) and the shipping clerk receives a check in payment for the scrap. The shipping clerk forwards the receipt to the billing clerk and the check to the accounts-receivable clerk. A sales invoice is prepared to record the sale on the books. The original of the invoice is stamped paid before it is mailed to the customer.

Cash Receipts. All incoming first class mail is opened by a billing clerk. Checks received from customers are segregated from customers' orders and other correspondence. A billing clerk forwards the checks to the accounts-receivable clerk.

The accounts-receivable clerk compares the amount on each of the checks to the amount shown in the customer's ledger account and determines the discount taken and the invoices paid. The name of the customer and the amount of the remittance are entered on a manifold deposit slip.

The third copy of the deposit slip includes provision for entering the discount taken and the credit to accounts receivable. The copy is used as a daily record of cash receipts.

After all of the day's receipts are recorded, the clerk asks the bank to send a messenger to pick up the deposit. A stamped duplicate deposit slip is returned to the bank.

The accounts-receivable clerk posts the credits to accounts receivable from the daily record of cash receipts. The total of the receipts for the day is entered in the cash receipts journal.

There are no cash collections other than mail receipts and the checks received from the scrap dealer.

Purchases. All requisitions for outside purchases are initiated in the various departments, approved by department heads, and forwarded to the purchasing agent. The purchasing agent buys the requisitioned goods in the best available market by issuing a prenumbered purchasing order.

A copy of the receiving report, prepared in the receiving department, is forwarded to the purchasing agent. The purchase order, if filled, is transferred to an inactive file. A notation of the goods received is made on the "open purchase order" if the receipt represents a partial shipment against the goods ordered.

Cash Disbursements. Creditor's invoices are forwarded to the purchasing agent by the billing clerk who opens the mail. The purchasing agent examines the invoice, and if the quantities received and prices are correct, he forwards the invoice to the accounts payable ledger clerk in the accounting department.

The ledger clerk verifies the extensions and footings and enters the invoices in the purchase journal. The verified invoice is placed in a "tickler" file according to date of payment.

The general ledger clerk prepares a check in payment of the invoice. A check protector is used to enter the amount on the check. The invoice is stamped "paid" and submitted with the check to the president. The president compares the check to the invoice, and if no irregularities are found, he signs the check. The check is mailed to the creditor by the general ledger clerk. The accounts-payable clerk enters the check in the cash-disbursements journal (from the duplicate copy) and posts the disbursements to the subsidiary ledger.

The controller reconciles the cash account monthly.

Payroll. The personnel manager recruits all hourly personnel. After an initial screening by the personnel manager, the job applicant is interviewed by the appropriate department head. If hired, the applicant reports back to the personnel department to complete the necessary forms. The personnel manager authorizes the addition of new employees to the payroll by forwarding a "payroll pickup" slip to the payroll clerk.

The personnel manager is responsible also for authorization of changes in rates of pay and the maintenance of personnel records.

Pay-rate changes result from changes in job classification, length of employment, and changes in the union contract. The department heads notify the personnel manager of all changes in job classification. The personnel manager is responsible for initiating pay increases based on length of service and changes in the union contract. The personnel manager notifies the payroll clerk of pay-rate changes in written memoranda.

The department heads notify the personnel manager of all employment terminations. A copy of the notification is sent to the payroll clerk by the personnel manager and authorizes the removal of the employee's name from the payroll.

Clock cards are prepared by the payroll clerk, who types employees' names and numbers thereon. At the end of the two-week pay period, the department head collects the punched-clock cards, approves the hours worked, and forwards the cards to the payroll clerk. She submits the cards together with a list of changes in pay rates and payroll deductions on an IBM service center. A payroll register and payroll checks are prepared at the service center. The payroll clerk verifies the checks to the payroll run. The payroll checks (drawn on a special payroll bank account) are imprinted with "NOT GOOD FOR OVER $125.00" and "NOT GOOD 30 DAYS AFTER DATE." The verified checks and the payroll register are given to the controller who runs the checks through a payroll-signing machine. The signatures of the controller and the treasurer are stamped on the checks.

The checks are sent to department heads for distribution. Unclaimed checks are returned to the general ledger clerk for safe-keeping. Checks which are not claimed within thirty days are deposited in the regular bank account.

The payroll account is reimbursed twice a month in the amount of the net pay. A reimbursement check is prepared by the controller and signed by the president.

The payroll clerk receives the bank statement for the payroll account and sorts the checks. The sorted checks are given to the controller, who prepares a monthly reconciliation.

The salaried payroll is prepared monthly by the controller. The salaried payroll checks, drawn against a separate payroll bank account, are signed by the president and distributed by the controller. Salary changes are authorized by the president.

Petty Cash. A petty cash fund of $1,000 is maintained by the general ledger clerk on the imprest basis to meet immediate cash requirements for miscellaneous expenses, advances to employees, and cashing employee checks.

Cash payments are made against properly approved petty cash vouchers. All department heads are authorized to approve petty cash vouchers.

The imprest cash fund is reimbursed periodically. A check is drawn to the order of cash and endorsed with the corporate name. The reimbursement check together with the cancelled voucher is submitted to the president. The president examines the vouchers, and if they are correct, he signs the reimbursement check. The bank is instructed by the general ledger book-keeper to send the required cash by messenger. The reimbursement check is given to the messenger in exchange for the required cash.

Accounts Receivable. Monthly customer statements are prepared by the ledger clerk after she reconciles the subsidiary ledger balance with the amount in the control account. The subsidiary ledger trial balance together with a list of past-due accounts are verified by the controller.

An aged trial balance is prepared by the subsidiary ledger bookkeeper at year-end. Bad debts are written off once a year at year-end by the controller after consultation with the sales manager. Collections from customers whose accounts had been written off are credited to miscellaneous income.

Inventories.

No formal perpetual inventory records are maintained. Production department heads maintain a record of raw materials on hand for production control purposes. The sales department maintains records of finished goods on hand.

A physical inventory of finished goods is taken every two months under supervision of the sales manager. A physical inventory of raw materials and work in process is taken each year under supervision of the production department heads.

Property, Plant, and Equipment.

The vice-president in charge of manufacturing is responsible for capital budgeting. He approves all capital asset acquisitions of $5,000 or less.

The president approves all capital asset acquisitions in excess of $5,000. The board of directors approves all capital asset acquisitions in excess of $25,000. Assets with an expected life of two or more years which cost $500 or more are charged to the plant account in the general ledger. A subsidiary plant ledger is not maintained.

The company's policy is to scrap or sell all obsolete machinery. A special sales order is prepared by the production department head for sales of machinery. The order is approved by the vice-president in charge of manufacturing. An invoice is prepared in the billing department from the sales order. The invoice is processed with the sales invoices issued to customers.

The production department head secures approval of the vice-president in charge of manufacturing to scrap obsolete machinery which cannot be sold. The machinery is dismantled by the regular production crew and is sold together with the scrap generated in the regular production process.

Accounts Payable.

A monthly trial balance of the accounts-payable subsidiary ledger is prepared by the accounts-payable clerk. Creditors' balances are verified to submitted monthly statements by the clerk. The total of the balances in the subsidiary ledger is reconciled to the control account balance in the general ledger every month.

John C. Clark

Disintegration, Inc.   Case

To illustrate the problems of information inadequacy, their development and possible means of solution, let us consider the following case—a hypothetical one, perhaps, but only so in the aggregate and in the sequence of events. The detail occurs too often in industry to be imaginary.

A company's development will be traced briefly through various stages of growth and each stage will be related to the information system employed to satisfy its evolving needs. Although these stages might span a period of several years, their characteristics can be seen in varying degrees and in different combinations in industries today.

Stage 1

Accounting Meets All Internal Information Needs. A small business enterprise made and sold its products in a comparatively captive market. The owner-manager supervised

the production force directly, and sold through local merchants.

Its information system, adapted to support the company's expansion borrowing, was maintained by one bookkeeper and consisted only of basic books of account, monthly and annual financial statements (for treasury and tax purposes), and an informal system based on the owner's direct supervision and intimate knowledge of the current production and marketing cycles. It was basic. Minimum manufacturing and sales information was supplied by the formal accounting system, and the need for further detail was obviated by the owner's informal information feedback.

Stage 2

Accounting Is Expanded To Meet External Demands. Faced with increased product demand, the company required further expansion capital. The owner-manager floated a stock issue, although continuing to run a "one-man show."

Adapted from "The Disintegration of an Information System," by Neil Milroy. Reproduced by permission from the *Canadian Chartered Accountant*, May 1963.

Since information was required by the company's new shareholders, the investing public, legislation, and external auditors, and since (at this stage) the internal requirements were few, the satisfaction of external demands received greater emphasis in the accounting system (Figure 1).

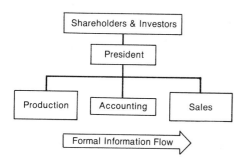

Figure 1. Accounting meets all formal needs.

These demands, though basic, were not easily satisfied. The company hired a qualified accountant to discharge the responsibilities created by the increased external demands.

At this stage in the company's development, financial accounting constituted a corporate information system, to the extent that formal data and reports were required. No matter how complex the operations, under the existing organizational and personnel circumstances, the financial accounting system was considered quite adequate by all concerned.

The owner-manager-president, however, began to feel the strain of pressures imposed by his booming enterprise. He therefore delegated the responsibility for the two main functions of production and sales to two senior executives, and he himself retained control of product research and public relations.

His directives were quite specific. He charged the production vice president with the achievement of two basic objectives: increased production efficiency, and effective use of production facilities.

The sales vice president was charged with: improving sales volume, and improving the percentage return on sales.

These over-all responsibilities dictated the provision of specific information for each vice president, without which neither the scope of their undertakings nor the channelling of effort could be defined. This information was basic, not specialized or requiring outside sources. It did require, however, detailed analysis of sales performance and costs, modification of the data-accumulating procedures and considerable clerical effort. Their information needs also included the establishment of valid standards and the subsequent comparison of actual performance against these.

The accountant's training might have suggested the adoption of a standard cost accounting system and use of high speed data processing equipment, as well as a radical revision of the existing accounting system. However, circumstances conspired against him. A reluctance to accept standards in the valuation of inventories, the apparent high cost of data processing equipment, and the inertia of an accounting system that had proved satisfactory for years, all prevented—or at least seriously delayed—the necessary action.

The needs for information relentlessly continued. They were even desperate. The accountant was faced with mounting daily routine demands and countless technicalities raised by accounting theorists. The achievements of the system became further inadequate despite his increased efforts. Whatever the reasons, the transformation into stage 3 had now begun.

Stage 3

Separate Information Systems Created To Fill the Vacuum. Attempts by the vice presidents to obtain the statistics vital to the fulfillment of their duties were politely but firmly given second priority to financial requirements.

The production vice president could not fathom why the system was unable to use his valid standards for both assessment of operating efficiencies and valuation of inventories. Finally he developed his own system to improve performance. It assigned attainable efficiency standards and measured performance against them.

The sales vice president was forced to take a similar expedient course, creating his own sales statistics and analysis department. Even if the statistics had been produced originally, they would have contained marketing inaccuracies caused by untimely raising of invoices, lack of indication of sales territories, and so on.

The creation of separate information systems, though not serious at this point, was rationalized by all concerned as providing essential specialized information service. It was argued that there was no duplication and that each one was designed according to particular functional needs. This information system might be illustrated as in Figure 2. Again, only total production and sales information is incorporated into the official accounting system.

Despite arguments in favor of information specialization, however, it should be noted that all departments were deriving their basic historical data from the same source and, further, that all these data were finding ultimate expression in financial statement terms.

The president began asking searching questions arising, ironically, out of the information supplied by the separate systems.

"Which products are yielding highest returns?"

"Why are we still in that unprofitable market?"

"Why is our gross profit down despite increased sales?"

"Why are our profits down in spite of supposedly lower unit production costs?"

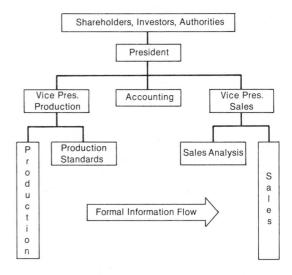

Figure 2. Separate systems fill information vacuum.

The answers could not be readily supplied. No single information system was equipped to do so. The systems were incomplete and contained arbitrary allocations of overhead costs that clouded the pertinent information required to provide answers to specific questions.

While modern accounting techniques using a marginal or direct costing approach could have readily provided greater insight into the nature and behavior of costs, such improvements had not been made due to many technicalities of an accounting nature. The accounting system, though accurately reporting results for financial purposes, fell more and more into operating disuse. More detailed and time-consuming analyses were developed by all information systems to provide answers to the president's questions. As this process continued, the metamorphosis into Stage 4 was accelerated.

Stage 4

Duplication and Confusion Result in Disintegration. In this atmosphere of narrow information systems (which were, in effect, designed to satisfy specific requirements to the exclusion of others), the disintegration process became serious because the company experienced the following wastes, over and above the increase in clerical costs:

1. Duplication in information coverage as each system used and interpreted the same data to suit its own needs.
2. Breakdown in corporate communications as fundamentally identical information was distorted by different interpretations.
3. Executive and management confusion as the decision-making process was complicated by the need to evaluate conflicting information supplied by different sources.
4. Waste of specialized talents as some (whose aims in corporate life were the development, manufacture, or sale of products) were dissipating these skills by the need to administer what amounted to accounting routines.
5. Inefficient data processing as no one system was large enough to justify the best equipment.

These costly results of the inefficient information system were overlooked while the various functions expanded to provide for their evolving information needs. The production division, requiring more accurate estimates of sales demands, organized a planning department over and above its standards and scheduling or "control" departments. The sales division, charged with the responsibility of moving the inventories, organized an inventory control section. And since the division was also responsible for improving the return on sales, a product control department was organized to support selective selling decisions with detailed product-cost studies.

Disintegration of the information system (see Figure 3) had, of course, been developing for some time but it became a confirmed reality when the president never accepted information without a nagging doubt.

Belated Salvaging Attempt. The president then made, in effect, a belated attempt to salvage what was left of the information system. He authorized the appointment of an analyst in the accounting department whose primary function was to restore some order to the information chaos. Our analyst, however, became another member of the accounting department which, under the circumstances, was of little help to either production or sales vice presidents. The financial accounting system merely became more refined and the degree of "accuracy" increased but still within the same framework.

The production vice president still maintained his own standards. Admittedly they were not accurate, as variances always existed, but how much more accurate were the "actual"

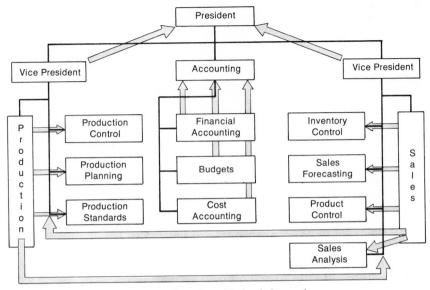

Figure 3. Duplication and confusion of conflicting information.

costs which contained prorations, allocations, deferments, accruals and certain "adjustments for tax purposes"?

The sales vice president continued to rearrange figures (instead of developing new business) because he had to prove to the president that market "X" was providing some return, in spite of indications to the contrary by the company's absorption costing system.

Again the president tried. A controller was hired and the accountant was made treasurer to handle the task of providing shareholders and income tax authorities with "consistent" accounts.

The controller assessed the situation as chaotic and hired a systems man and a data processing expert with all the necessary tools. These were all justified to the president on the basis of accounting needs and were intended to improve the accounting function even further.

The systems man devoted much time to streamlining accounting routines, forms and reports. Improved reports appeared containing an even greater degree of accuracy than before. Available time on the data processing equipment was used "productively" to analyze items of cost of relatively little consequence (such as postage and telephone costs) and even to calculate the cost of each mechanized application.

Some attempts were made to provide for the company's need to plan its activities and to subsequently assess its actual performance against those plans. Corporate budgeting and basic control accounting were developed, but these potentially valuable control tools were weakened by their adherence to financial accounting principles.

The ultimate in specialized information refinement was being reached, but the fundamental problem had remained unchanged in nature and had greatly expanded in degree and cost. The situation was now ready for the development of Stage 5.

Stage 5

Elaborate Structure Built on Shattered Foundation. Our president, aging rapidly, then employed an administrative assistant whose primary function was to assist him in analyzing past trends for purposes of short- and long-range planning. The historical analysis was so time-consuming that formal planning became a hopeless task. A planning director was therefore employed who was later to be assisted by an operations research specialist. Both spent many long hours developing ways and means of using available information to discharge their responsibilities.

By then there was a wealth of information. There were five or six information systems operating at full capacity. Deciding on the relative accuracy of each and separating the wheat from the chaff took most of the time. Obtaining valuable information for decision-making and planning could receive very little attention.

Our information system can perhaps be illustrated, again schematically, as in Figure 4.

The interaction of all these new information requirements resulted in the progressive refinement of each system. The whole process could have been written off to the pains of evolution and the strong features of each system could have been salvaged. The situation could have been salvaged, in fact, at any of the

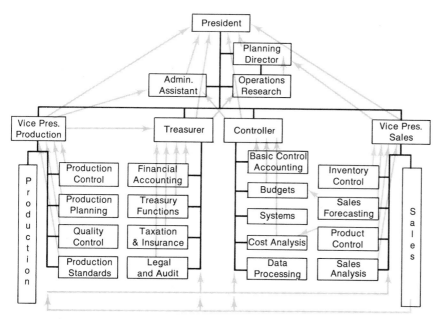

Figure 4. Fundamental error compounded into chaos.

previous stages, although at successively increased cost. Unfortunately, our company selected another approach.

Stage 6

The Final Bitter Irony. Having allowed the information "system" to develop haphazardly into such a time-consuming, confusing and costly monster, the president was advised that confusion would be minimized by the use of written instructions.

Accordingly, a paralyzing blow was struck. The chaos was reduced to standard procedures (which had to be observed and could not be changed except after careful consideration and approval by a procedures committee). The laudable purpose was to ensure that current procedures were not amended unless all those affected approved of, or made due allowances for, the change. The effect, however, was to introduce an inflexibility that defied any attempts to centralize the information system. The creeping paralysis continued as more current procedures were reduced to writing and as more proposed changes were added to the

agenda for the procedures committee. Nevertheless, the company earned some profits, not because of the system but in spite of it.

The company took many actions that were, in themselves, worthwhile. They were well intentioned and, in theory (as often in practice), desirable. To draw a contrary conclusion is not the intention. Neither should it be concluded that the personnel employed were unnecessary, that their potential value was not significant, nor that they acted irrationally. All the positions created and the departments organized could have provided the company with extremely valuable service had they been supported by an adequate information system. In this situation, however, their efforts were, to a greater or lesser extent, wasted and unproductive.

Discussion Questions

1. Why did the disintegration take place?
2. What program would you recommend to restore order to the system?
3. What service could an auditor render in this situation?

Great Western
Rice Company

Case

Background

Great Western Rice Company originated shortly after the turn of the century out of a decision of a group of rice growers in the Sacramento Valley of California to form a corporation to process, package, and market their production and carry on such related operations as would be in the general corporate interest. Accordingly, the Company built a plant in San Francisco for the processing and packaging of both polished and brown rice, and, in conjunction with the factory, provided office space to house marketing operations and administrative activities. As the growers who originally formed the Company became older they sold their rice-growing acreages to the Company, so that eventually the Company owned all original acreages of the founders, plus additional acreages purchased whenever advantageous opportunities to acquire them occurred. As outlets for its products expanded, Great Western also bought production from private growers, whose operations were interspersed among its own holdings, until it became the major processor and marketer of rice in the West.

A container division was ultimately established to round out the San Francisco operation. This factory bought fiberboard from paper manufacturers and made cartons and cases for packaging its products.

As the Company's sales expanded beyond available productive capacity of California growers, Great Western directed its attention to Arkansas as a source of much needed production. Its initial move into Arkansas was to acquire and plant considerable but somewhat scattered acreage in the vicinity of Glencoe, a small city in the rice growing area.

There followed a decision to build both a processing and packaging as well as a container plant in Glencoe, a town of about 6,000 population. Decentralization was presumed to be more efficient than to expand the facilities in San Francisco, which could only be done at a high cost, including that involved in the acquisition of additional land at a premium price.

Reprinted with permission from Nielsen, *Cases in Auditing* (Homewood, Ill.: Richard D. Irwin, Inc.) pp. 183–201.

This establishment of operations in Glencoe was accomplished by sending out from San Francisco a cereal chemist to set up the processing and packaging plant and to serve as its manager. Comparable duties were assumed by the man who had served as the assistant manager of the container division of San Francisco. A horticulturist, graduated from the department of agriculture of the University of California at Davis, was sent out to manage the farming operations. The rice plant and farm managers reported directly to the executive vice-president in San Francisco. The manager of the container division reported to the manager of the container plant in San Francisco.

Each of these three managers dealt with different people in the community, but all agreed that good public relations in the town of Glencoe would be beneficial to Great Western. The processing plant employed about 700 workers and the container plant employed about 400 factory workers. Additional office and sales personnel amounted to about 100 and 10, respectively. The farm employees consisted of about 90 men, who operated the efficient machinery (and hauled rice to the factory from Great Western's own acreage as well as from the acreage of private growers.) Most of these approximately 1,300 workers belonged to the local union. All were recruited in the local community.

Despite the size of the Arkansas operation, top management in San Francisco felt that it was not as profitable as it ought to be and that the basic defect in the operation had been an infiltration of the labor union into management so that the plant and farm managers were unable to operate effectively. The details of the weaknesses, however, were not specifically known in San Francisco, nor was it possible to get specifically useful information from any one of the three managers in the Arkansas operation.

This disturbing situation in Arkansas, together with the distressing lack of means to detect and eliminate causes of inefficiency prompted top management to approach their auditors to see what could be done about the difficulties. The result was that the auditors were retained to send men to examine the Arkansas operation until the specific weaknesses had been discovered, with the added assignment that they were to make specific recommendations of a set of controls that would assure efficient operation in Arkansas.

Three men from the San Francisco office of the auditing firm went to Arkansas, made their observations, and prepared a set of recommendations for top management. A summary of their observations follows. The student should prepare a set of recommendations with respect to the internal controls for Arkansas that will restore the prerogative of management to Great Western and that will assure efficient operations.

Finding—Rice Processing and Packaging Plant

Purchasing. The purchasing department buys all materials used by the rice plant except direct materials such as rice, containers, etc. During the past year this department purchased and issued materials and supplies amounting to approximately $2.7 million of which $1.8 million consisted of stock items. The balance was special materials, major capital repair parts, and property and equipment. There were 33 employees in this department, consisting of:

Purchasing agents	2
Buyers, also serving as storekeepers	2
Secretary	1
Clerks	28
Total	33

In addition to purchasing, this department also controls the inventory as well as the receipt, storage, and issuance of maintenance and operating supplies used in rice processing and packaging. This department also approves invoices received from suppliers and forwards them to the accounting department for payment. The purchasing department's work involves negotiations with suppliers to determine the price and availability of materials. They issue all official purchase orders. Observations disclosed that:

1. *Many items are not being purchased at the lowest possible prices.* Instead they are obtained locally, in small quantities and at the local merchants' retail prices. Thus the company is failing to take advantage of its purchasing power by going directly to factory sources of supply and, by such means, to obtain prices comparable to those being paid by the local merchants.

2. *Personnel in purchasing have outside interests and relationships which can conflict with proper discharge of their duties.* We realise that frequently people working for a large company and residing in a small community actively participate in community affairs and we believe this to be beneficial to both Company and community in the majority of cases. However, we seriously question the desirability of people actively engaged in purchasing doing so. Election to a local office or appointment to some civic board or commission might cause the employee to become indebted to people from whom he would be purchasing, thereby making it extremely difficult to discharge Company responsibilities satisfactorily. Although we cannot say definitely that such outside interests as practiced by purchasing personnel at Glencoe have influenced the purchasing practices, we do believe that they do indicate a lack of prudence on the part of those involved.

Moreover, the practice of making purchases from suppliers who are relatives of purchasing department people in itself poses no problem. However, when purchases are made from such suppliers at retail prices higher than those one might expect a large company to pay in the normal course of business, one is justified in raising questions concerning possible "conflict of interest."

In 1963, the purchasing department acquired supplies for the maintenance crew, such as rain suits, rubber boots, mill brooms and padlocks, amounting to approximately $9,000 from a supplier related to the purchasing agent. All of those items were purchased at retail prices.

3. *Inadequate control is exercised over local purchases.* Many of the purchases from local suppliers are accomplished without the use of purchase orders and, frequently, without any foreknowledge of what prices are involved. Even when purchase orders are prepared they are not always signed by the buyer but, instead, are initialed either by storeroom or inventory clerks.

For example, review of purchases from one local hardware store indicated that for the first four months of 1963, 396 separate purchases were made. These orders involved a range of from 3 to 9 items and usually involved a number of separate trips each day. Many items purchased, such as padlocks, rain suits, and flashlights were in such large quantities that they were even questioned by the rice plant manager himself.

4. *The scope of authority of the purchasing agent is too broad.* It extends to receiving, stores, inventory control, and approval of invoices. Thus he directs all activities that permit making payment to a vendor and even to fictitious vendors.

5. *Purchasing methods are inefficient.* The purchasing department has failed to utilize recent improvements in purchasing techniques. For example, instead of filing copies of purchase orders it copies, by hand, all purchases into a "purchase book" and otherwise fails to use mechanized procedures on traveling requisitions which are pre-run in quantity with much of the repetitive information. There is opportunity for reduction of personnel here.

6. *The purchasing activity is overstaffed.* Outside of the purchasing agents and the buyers six clerks are allocated full time to purchasing.

Inventory Control. This is one of those sections operating as part of the purchasing department. The following items subject to improvement were disclosed:

1. *Inventory levels are higher than necessary.* Currently the Company carries stockroom supplies at approximately $1,100,000. This is exclusive of items considered "too small for inventory control." Generally, the Company turns this inventory over about three times a year. Although this might be adequate for the stock as a whole, our review of selected items in stock indicated purchases even when adequate supply was on hand.

2. *The system of reordering is inadequate.* Currently established reorder points reflect no consideration of changes in trend of usage of many items carried. Reorder points are adjusted so infrequently that a significant percentage of items are carried in quantities well above current needs.

3. *No regular review is made to eliminate obsolete or overstocked items.* Consequently capital is tied up unnecessarily and increased carrying costs are incurred.

4. *The inventory section appears to be overstaffed.* A review of the workload of this section as well as observation of the general pace of work in this section and the amount of time people are idle convinced us that there were more people here than would be needed under a more effective system of management. There are four employees in this section.

5. *Inadequate use is made of machines for record-keeping purposes.* All records were being kept manually. Any one of a number of machines on the market would permit mechanical recording at a labor saving cost in excess of the machine cost entailed. The Company is currently studying the record keeping system in the inventory section and should be encouraged to pursue this work to an early completion.

Stores Section. This is the third section in the purchasing department. It has responsibility for receiving, stocking, and issuing materials and supplies. There are eight clerks in this section. Supervisory work is done by the buyer and the assistant buyer. Although the physical area for stores appears well kept and arranged, certain procedural defects were observed. The more important of these are:

1. *Receiving reports are not prepared properly.* Instead of being prepared by making independent counts of goods received, the quantities frequently are obtained from the file copies of the purchase orders. In some cases the notation on the receiving notice was simply, "as per invoice." Sometimes receiving reports failed to bear the initials of the person presumably responsible for the count.

2. *Merchandise is issued without properly authorized requisitions.* The existing regulation

that all disbursements of merchandise must be on the authority of requisitions appropriately signed by department heads is not always followed. Instead, workmen frequently appear at the stores window and write out a requisition from a blank pad at the window, without signature. Occasionally, if the worker's hands are very dirty, the stores clerk makes out the requisition for him in order to avoid soiling the form. In either case signature or department to which issued or both are omitted.

3. *Inadequate security exists in the storeroom.* The storeroom was readily accessible to anyone. If the attendant happened to be absent from the window, all one had to do was to reach in and press the buzzer to unlock the adjacent door. Frequently, workers were seen roaming about in the storeroom, finding what they wanted, and presumably making out a requisition for it on the way out.

4. *Storekeepers have access to inventory records.* Stores clerks make physical counts of inventory on a continuous basis. Upon making a count, the stores clerk compares it with the balance on the inventory record, regardless of whether the posting of it is current or not, and if the book balance varies from the physical count the storekeeper corrects the book inventory to his count. All items in stock are counted at least once a year. Storekeepers' counts are never spot checked for accuracy of either enumeration or identification of items.

5. *Storekeepers issue local purchase orders.* Being employed in a section of the purchasing departments, stores clerks may issue purchase orders directly without going through either the purchasing or inventory control section. Such orders are placed with the usual, local sources of supply, without bringing up any questions as to prices.

6. *Storekeepers issue gate passes.* With the storekeepers having authority to issue gate passes, it is possible for employees to make unauthorized removals of materials, supplies, and small tools from the premises.

7. *The stores section appears to be overstaffed.* The ten people in this section frequently are engaged in idle conversation, administering betting pools on athletic contests, and engaging in such activities with people who came from other areas for materials. It appears that staff reduction should in no way hamper the rendering of services.

Summary with Respect to the Purchasing Department. Our appraisal did indicate that the purchasing department has been effective in nearly always having available the materials needed to keep the plant in operation. The major shortcoming of the department has been its inability to do this at a minimum level of cost. Extra costs have been or are likely to occur because of the following conditions which require attention:

1. Inadequate attention to purchase prices and quantities, a condition resulting partly from overemphasis of community relations and perhaps partly from some apparent conflicts of interest of Company employees.

2. Over-extension of the scope of the purchasing agent's authority.

3. Inefficient and ineffective procedures in almost all areas.

4. Failure to follow established routines.

5. Poor employee work habits.

6. General overstaffing.

Persistence of these conditions will prove to be constraints against providing needed operating materials and supplies at a minimum cost to the company.

Findings—Industrial and Community Relations Department

This department carries on the following wide range of activities:

Community relations
Relations with unions
Personnel
Timekeeping
Cashiering
Plant security
Operation of company houses
Safety
Operation of car wash facilities

These activities are carried on by the following employees:

Department head	1
Assistants	4
Secretary	1
Stenographers	2
Timekeepers	4
Labor checkers	4
Assistant supervisor of safety	1
Switchboard operators	3
Cashier	1
House maintenance employees	5
Total	26

One significant observation with respect to these activities is that they are carried on independently for the container plant and the farms, whereas many of these activities could more properly be combined for all three operating divisions in the Glencoe area.

In general the activities of this department were characterized by:

1. Overemphasis on community relations.
2. Lack of consistent policy in administration of union agreements with a consequent lack of protection with respect to the Company's managerial prerogatives.
3. Absence of, or inadequate attention to, proper functions of a personnel department.
4. Failure to properly direct and control other activities entrusted to the department.
5. Inclusions within the department of activities not proper for it.

These conditions will be borne out by the following statements relative to our findings.

Community Relations. There has been strong emphasis on community relations at Glencoe. Although we believe in the importance of a regard for the community, we feel that such relations have been mishandled in two important respects and that certain changes should be inaugurated with respect to this activity.

1. *Community relations are handled as a separate activity for each division of the Company at Glencoe.* According to our view, the basic purpose of community relations is to establish a favorable corporate image in the minds of residents of the community. In this respect, an individual resident looks upon the Company as a whole and usually is unable to distinguish the separate activities of the several divisions. Unified community relations activities in Arkansas should simplify the creation of an acceptable Company image, at a reduced cost under an administration of maximum effectiveness.

2. *Community relations have been overemphasized and misdirected.*

    a. The Company buys operating materials and supplies from local merchants without any apparent attempt to seek lower factory or warehouse prices. Apparently this procedure is costly out of proportion to the benefits it yields.

    b. To further community relations, the Company maintains sizeable bank balances at the First State Bank of Glencoe in both a general commercial account and also a payroll account. In addition, the Company also, by means of payroll deductions, collects for the bank installments due on loans that employees have made at the Bank at 8 percent interest. The reason for instituting this practice was the supposed benefit to community relations that would accrue. It is doubtful that this simplification of payment procedures, with its inducement toward indebtedness and consequent reduction in take home pay is as beneficial to the Company's community relations as might be assumed. About 60 percent of the hourly employees have weekly deductions with the bank ranging from $5 to $80 per week for total deductions in 1961 of about $1,300,-000.

    c. Further payroll deductions are made to repay employee loans made with the Company employees' credit union.

    d. Another aspect of community relations has been the renting of Company owned houses to persons not presently employed by Great Western. Monthly rentals range from $14 to $20, insufficient amounts to cover the costs of operating the houses.

Relations with Unions. In dealing with unions at Glencoe, there is lacking any consistent policy to protect the prerogatives of the Company's management.

1. *Union contracts have been supplemented by numerous side agreements.* It has become almost standard practice at Glencoe to grant any request made by the Union at grievance meetings, with the result that many problems of the grievance committee have become the subject of side agreements. Moreover, there is no complete company file of these available, although the plant manager has a non-indexed file of 134 of them, some going as far back as 20 years. Frequently, supervisors call the business office of the Union to determine what side agreement is in effect relative to a specific problem. With the existence of this situation, the manager of the rice plant handles negotiations with the Union rather than relying upon the industrial relations personnel to do so.

2. *Fringe benefits are improperly administered.* In addition to the usual benefits of holiday and vacation pay, employees receive funeral leaves, and meal and tool allowances. Funeral allowances are given without any apparent check on their validity. Meal and tool allowances likewise are given without proper authorization.

Personnel. Existing practices hamper the Company's efforts to secure the best qualified employees and restrict its ability to direct and appraise performance after they are hired. Although our study was not all-inclusive, the following deficiencies which we noted are worthy of mention:

1. *Employees are selected improperly.* There is no adequate screening at time of selection by

aptitude, intelligence, or other tests. Contrarily, there is a claim of conscious attempts to avoid hiring intelligent people. Friends and relatives, rather than properly qualified persons, have been hired in many cases. During the course of our examination the son of a union leader was hired instead of the qualified man the office manager had selected.

2. *Organization charts and position descriptions were nonexistent or inadequate.* This condition has been recognized at Glencoe and organization charts and job descriptions are being prepared by a task force from the manager's office.

3. *No procedure exists for orderly and effective promotion of employees or granting salary increases.* Promotions have been made largely on the basis of seniority, even in the cases of non-union employees where there is no compulsion to do so. The result has been to stifle initiative.

4. *Salaried employees are paid in excess of their maximum classification rates each year.* Monthly payments in excess of existing classification rates run from one dollar to 200 dollars, with the greatest excess payments going to the oldest employees. Total excess payments amount to about $45,000 annually.

5. *Supervision is inadequate.* Due to lack of policy direction and failure to give proper training, first line supervision has not been an effective arm of management. Thus, these supervisors go to the Union rather than to their superiors for interpretation of union contracts or side agreements. These supervisors also hesitate to take disciplinary action against employees, with the result that equipment is used without regard for protecting its usefulness and serviceability. They do not feel responsible for cost levels. They are not required to approve job tickets in their departments nor to validate payments in excess of basic hourly rates. Some supervisors

cannot write and many read only with difficulty, thus rendering written communication to them very difficult, almost to the extent of precluding any training program.

6. *Existing personnel procedures are not properly administered.* Apart from the deficiencies in terms of Union negotiations and formulation on effective personnel policies those policies which are in effect are frequently not properly administered.

Sometimes employees are given meal tickets, authorizing the purchase of meals at privately operated restaurants located on Company property. The Company is billed for all meals served on these tickets. No record could be found of the number of tickets issued but meal allowances increased from $8,000 in 1959, to $9,000 in 1960, to $3,300 in the first four months of 1961.

Foremen may allow a worker a meal allowance if he works late but decides to go home for his supper after completion of the day's work. This is done by issuing a prenumbered meal ticket, which is posted to his earnings record as authorization for an extra half hour of pay in lieu of a meal. The cost of these allowances, granted at the discretion of foremen, cannot be determined since the pay appears as if it were for time worked.

Meal tickets are attached to invoices received from the restaurant for meals served during the month but no attempt is made to reconcile the tickets to the invoice on the grounds that the meals consumed by various employees differed according to their appetites and eating habits. The invoice is merely approved and sent to the accounting department for payment and the returned meal tickets are discarded.

No attempt is made to reduce unauthorized absences. Absentees are replaced by persons from the "reserve pool," a group of workers held in readiness for this purpose. These replacements frequently carry higher wage rates than those whom they replace, with the result that effective average hourly rates increase due to absenteeism.

7. *Termination procedures are inadequate.* Until recently there was no termination procedure, not even to the extent of assuring that company property, such as small tools, was returned. Although a procedure has been formulated recently, the Company still relies on the employee's word that he has returned all Company property.

8. *An excessive number of payroll deductions are allowed.* Currently the Company provides for as many as 16 different payroll deductions, several more than most manufacturers allow. We understand that the Company plans to discontinue deductions to cover installments due at the bank.

Another practice is that of making deductions for voluntary contributions made by one employee to another. This is a practice that developed in helping out employees in such bad straits that they could not make loans. These deductions would run from 50 cents to one dollar per employee.

Timekeeping. Although in general timekeeping appears to be handled satisfactorily, there are several aspects subject to improvement.

1. *Timekeeping should not be a function of the industrial and community relations department.* The hiring and participation in determination of wage rates should not be combined, through timekeeping, with determination of hours worked. The result is excessive control over the functions relative to payment of employees. Since such practice even could make fraud possible through addition of fictitious names to the payroll, we believe in the separation of timekeeping from personnel activities.

2. *Inadequate control is exercised over the determination of hours worked.* Timekeepers currently match hours on job cards with hours on attendance cards, which would make it possible for the timekeeper in collusion with the employee to overstate hours worked.

3. *Timekeepers have excessive authority in determining the amount to be paid an employee.* Timekeepers have authority to grant an "Interim Pay Authorization," which accomplishes a special change in an employee's rate of pay. If the foreman fails to inform the timekeeper, the basis upon which he usually raises pay rates, the employee may do so. In such a case the timekeeper makes a note on the employee's record. Adjustment is then made on the basis of the foreman's memory of the situation and becomes the basis for supplemental payment to the employee.

4. *Labor checkers are used to determine that employees have reported to the job assigned them.* Employees who are assigned to a work center from the "reserve pool" have their presence on the assignment verified by a labor checker, a procedure that would be redundant if the foreman approved the job cards.

During the course of our examination, we also learned of studies being made to develop a new timekeeping procedure that would put this function under the office manager.

Cashiering. Receipts of cash are limited to miscellaneous receipts from sale of scrap, sales to employees, collection of rentals for housing, etc. No evidence was found of defalcation but the controls surrounding these receipts were so faulty that it is doubtful that fraudulent practices would be disclosed. The two major faults are:

1. *Cashiering is improperly located in the community and industrial relations department.*

2. *Existing procedures to control cash collections are inadequate.* Prenumbered sales invoices are lacking for cash sales to customers. No specific procedure exists with respect to depositing collected amounts to the Company's bank account. The cashier, however, is required to use a prenumbered cash receipt book that provides for the retention of a duplicate.

Plant Security. Deficiencies noted include:

1. *Vehicles can move in and out of the gate without having a gate pass.* This condition invites the possibility of unauthorized removal of Company property.

2. *No permanent record is made of gate passes issued.* Thus there is no tie-in with collections for "will call" sales or for sales to employees or for charging employees for removal of company equipment.

Operation of Company Houses. Forty per cent of the loss incurred by this activity is for the benefit of persons not employed by the Company. This is true since houses are rented at a loss to persons not connected with the Company.

Operation of Car Wash. In addition to the availability of free facilities for employees to wash their own cars, the company provides for the washing of supervisors' cars, both arrangements claiming as justification the preserving of appearance of supervisors' cars, often becoming dusty or muddy from drives out to rice farms. Supervisors are supposed to pay $2.50 per month for their participation in this service, which is performed by one full-time employee and two Company chauffeurs when they are not otherwise employed. We observed that:

1. *Revenue received was insufficient to cover labor cost of this service.* During 1962, the Company received $300 for this service and, by allocating a portion of chauffeur time to this operation, must have incurred at least $7,000 of labor cost.

2. *Not all supervisors are paying for this service.* For example, six supervisors whose cars we found washed were not being billed.

3. *Record keeping was inadequate.* Only recently was a record established for cars washed, by ownership.

4. *Some cars were washed more frequently than appeared necessary.* We learned that in one month 107 car washings and 7 waxings were performed for 16 supervisors. One supervisor had 15 car washings done for him. During this observed month, Company owned cars accounted for 66 washings and no waxings. We find it difficult to justify the existence of this service unless supervisors are willing to pay for it.

The Office of the Rice Plant. Except for preparation of payrolls by use of tabulating equipment in the rice plant, each of the three operating divisions at Glencoe has separate and distinct accounting and administrative departments. The rice plant office at Glencoe is staffed by 50 employees under Mr. Walter McGuire, the office manager. He is assisted by an assistant office manager, a chief accountant, and a production records supervisor. The office manager is located a block down the street from the main office, resulting in his making frequent trips between offices to carry out his duties. The main office, located in a building that formerly housed a small experimental laboratory, is not conducive to conducting effective operations. The following specific deficiencies merit special mention:

1. *Payroll preparation is not adequately controlled.* Foremen do not assume responsibility for determining that each man in the crew is present and working. Usually he does not approve job time tickets. The only attendance record is the time card at the entrance to the plant. This lack of control allows for errors in classification of work paid for, incorrect reporting of hours, and even unreported absences.

   Upon distribution of payroll checks, employees report complaints on shorted time, rate errors, and shift differentials to the timekeepers, who relay them to the payroll clerk, who prepares an adjustment sheet for each man's complaint. This form is undated and does not describe the nature of the adjustment; nor is an approval indicated on it. The number of adjustments each pay period ranged from 10 to 40. About one-half of them were paid immediately and the remainder the next week.

   Documents related to special or supplementary payments are neither dated nor canceled after use. Such absence of identification would enable their re-use.

   Since the payroll clerk does much of his work under the direction of the tabulating department, he has no control over the work there. Since no one else checks this work, there is no assurance that tabulating is performed accurately.

   The payroll department exercises the entire control over the blank checks which it uses. Its major control is the monthly bank reconciliation, which it performs with the use of payroll personnel. Thus the control advantages of independent checking are lacking.

   The files of the payroll department are not kept current and are poorly and unsystematically organized.

2. *Control over the accounts payable function is weak.* As indicated previously, invoices received from suppliers are routed directly to the purchasing department for processing. Invoices for local purchases lack support by copies of purchase orders. Receipt of goods was not always indicated clearly or correctly. Instead, approval was indicated by initialing a copy of the invoice by the purchasing agent or one of his assistants.

   Some paid vouchers are filed alphabetically by vendors, while others are grouped according to account classification, without cross-reference to suppliers.

   Paid vouchers are not canceled to prevent duplication of payment.

3. *Cost accounting does not facilitate cost control.* There are no standard costs or budgets with which to compare performance. Consequently, the computing and analysis of variance also is lacking.

   Special reports are incomplete. For example, one report on the cost of such items as flashlights and rain coats is a listing of the usage of these items by employees. The report, however, is entirely unrelated to inventory or purchase of these items and, consequently, fails to show that all items are accounted for. Similarly, by way of further example, a report on trips made by chauffeurs contains neither indication of time consumed in this manner nor of percentage utilization of chauffeurs.

Maintenance records show labor and material, both separately and in total, monthly for each piece of equipment. Records are only cumulative for one year and contain no explanation of large charges.

Cost reports prepared at Glencoe are not made available to foremen or superintendents in charge of the various phases of operations.

4. *The preparation of records of raw material usage and of quantities of production and inventories is an improper function of the office manager's department.* A group of seven employees—a supervisor, four clerks, and two typists—are assigned to this function. They record production by type and machine for use in the production planning and scheduling department for comparison with previously formulated schedules and for assistance in further scheduling. At the end of the month this group supplies the accounting department with material usage, production, and inventory figures for statement purposes.

5. *The office is overstaffed.* Our observation disclosed a slow work pace applied to carrying out cumbersome and outmoded procedures. An accelerated work pace and improved procedures could effect a considerable reduction in the office manager's staff.

Plant Maintenance. The cost of this department approximates $4,200,000 a year. About two-thirds of this cost is for labor.

A detailed examination of this department was omitted because Beltz and Botz, management consultants, have been studying this phase of the business at length. This firm now is installing an entirely new system of administration and control for plant maintenance. Therefore, we confine our remarks about this activity to impressions gained from our observations of other departmental activities and during visits to various areas of the plant.

1. *Labor productivity is low.* Our impression of low labor productivity in this department is confirmed by the studies of Beltz and Botz, who found labor to be about 50 per cent productive and then idle about one-fourth of the time.

2. *Maintenance programs are improperly planned.* Programs for orderly services of equipment are lacking. There is insufficient attention to preventive maintenance. This results in premature breakdown or excessive servicing time or both.

For some items of equipment repair costs are considerably larger than original cost. For example, one fork-lift truck, which was purchased for $4,300, had repair costs of $17,796. One yard truck, originally costing $2,300 in 1957, had total repair costs of $6,400.

Expected repair costs are not estimated accurately, often running far in excess of what was planned. Conversely, a black-topping job estimated at $7,000 actually cost $4,250. Such looseness in estimating inhibits the making of sound decisions on maintenance and repair. Moreover, after work orders are completed, they are not reviewed for nature or cost of performance.

3. *Spare parts are inadequately controlled.* Here we merely cite an example of the looseness of control. Batteries were purchased with what we consider to be excess frequency. Gas Welder No. 3 had five batteries purchased for it during the period from January, 1962, to May, 1963. Air compressor No. 7 and truck No. 36 each had three batteries purchased for them during the same period. These batteries have a 48-month guarantee. There was no record of the replaced batteries having been returned for (1) recharge or for (2) replacement or other claim against the guarantee. The garage foreman suggested the possibility that employees acquired these batteries for personal use.

4. *Improper use of equipment has increased maintenance cost.* Lift trucks were driven too fast and forks were not raised high enough to clear obstructions. Other evidences of abuse of equipment, such as improper handling of motor trucks, were evident. In all of these cases the incurring of extra repair costs resulted.

Findings—Container Plant

The container plant makes corrugated cartons for rice packages and also fabricates the cardboard packages for rice. Excess plant capacity is absorbed by making containers for other manufacturers within a radius of 500 miles. The plant has about 400 employees,

most of whom are paid on a direct labor incentive basis. The manager reports back to the manager of the container plant in San Francisco. The office of the San Francisco container plant handles the collection on sales invoices and does most of the accounting for the Glencoe container plant.

Our critical comments about this plant should not be construed to indicate that all phases of its operations are substandard. Discussion of the many favorable features would only lengthen this report unduly.

Deficiencies occurring at the Container Plant as well as at the Rice Processing and Packaging Plant and Farm Operations result primarily from poor management. We discovered no evidence of deliberate misappropriation of funds. Our comments relate to inventory management, duplication of functions performed by other divisions, payroll procedures, and other (miscellaneous) activities.

Inventory Management. Control and handling of inventories of paper stock and maintenance supplies are substandard. Much of the difficulty stems from lack of coordination between the container plant and the other activities at Glencoe.

1. *Storage is poorly arranged.* Raw paper (such as large rolls of corrugated paper and cardboard) is stored uneconomically. Inside storage is crowded and poorly arranged. Rolls stored outside are on end and, consequently, are subject to deterioration through rain seepage. In San Francisco, rolls stored outside are on their sides and covered with some water-shedding material.

No record of inventory is kept by age since all roll lists are destroyed after recording. We saw evidence of a number of rolls that were aged and weathered sufficiently to make unattractive containers. We were told that some rolls were at least 15 years old and that about 18 per cent of the stock had not moved in more than six months.

2. *Inventories are larger than required.* Our studies indicated that inventory turnover was decreasing and that current production could be covered by concurrent purchases.

3. *The container plant inventory of operating and maintenance supplies is largely controlled by one man.* The inventory is controlled by a container plant storekeeper. He and his assistants list, price, and check the physical inventory to the perpetual records. The storekeeper adjusts unit prices for price changes and acts as purchasing agent and receiving clerk for the Glencoe container plant. Paper stock and adhesives are ordered through the San Francisco container plant. Supplies, including inks, are purchased from retail outlets in Glencoe.

4. *Work in process inventories are incorrect.* Because local personnel fails to recognize proper month-end cutoff procedures, erroneous quantities are reported to San Francisco. However, we understand that whenever these reported figures vary from those on the records kept in San Francisco then the latter are used.

Duplication of Functions Carried on by Other Divisions. Many container plant functions duplicate those carried on by the rice plant and the farming operations. More than because of their duplication, other functions warrant more serious consideration because of their inefficiency. Yet, we mention them here because machinery to perform them exists elsewhere.

1. *Gasoline is obtained from a local service station instead of from pumps operated by the plant.* The container plant operates a long-haul truckline of GMC tractors and a full complement of trailers. All local purchases of gasoline for these vehicles are made from one dealer in Glencoe at current retail prices. The same dealer also sells and services the trucks. The rice plant buys the same type of gasoline in tank truck lots for eight cents per gallon below retail price. On the road the container plant trucks use credit cards and buy gasoline at discounts ranging from two to five cents per gallon.

   Gasoline bought locally at retail price was as follows:

1960	$32,600
1961	29,900
1962	28,900
1963 (first four months)	10,400

   In addition to these purchases at retail price the container plant bought gasoline for its local equipment (station wagon, sedan etc.) delivered to its own pumps at five cents below retail price. The long haul trucks never use this pump. Because of the long-standing practice of buying trucks from and servicing them at the local dealer's, no consideration has been given to using diesel powered tractors to take advantage of their cheaper fuel rates.

2. *Purchasing, stores, and maintenance functions largely duplicate those at the rice plant.* The result is duplicate carrying of maintenance and repair supplies and equipment.

Payroll Procedures. The container plant maintains its own payroll department, consisting of seven clerks and a supervisor. This group is responsible for paying about 400 hourly employees, many of whom work on an incentive basis, with the resultant added complexity of wage computation. As indicated by the following observations, a number of situations exist where improvements are possible.

1. *Payrolls are prepared almost entirely by manual methods.* While manual methods are used here the tab department in the rice plant office is used only to transcribe information and to prepare pay checks.

   The incentive payroll is computed by assigning a different clerk to each department. One desk handles all deductions. After gross pay and deductions are prepared, the rice plant tab department computes income and social security tax withholdings, posts all payroll data to earnings records, and prepares a payroll journal as a carbon copy of all payroll checks.

   Checks are signed by machine and a separate deduction slip plus a "safety rule" are stapled to the check stub before distribution.

   Deductions include those resulting from payroll advances, credit union payments, hospital insurance, union dues, and payments to Citizens National Bank. (The same system for making deductions exists at the rice plant.) Amounts deducted for payments due Citizens National Bank are listed on 3 x 5 cards, which contain no signature from the employee authorizing the making of these deductions.

2. *The distribution of checks is improperly controlled.* Although we distributed the pay checks for one pay period by being present from 5:00 a.m. to 4:30 p.m. on Friday and from 10:00 a.m. to 3:00 p.m. on Saturday, we found that a number of employees were unable to get their checks at the accustomed time. The payroll department ordinarily begins issuing checks on Thursday evening. Many checks are called for by persons other than the payee.

3. *Incentive pay computations are not adequately controlled.* Work cards, which contain the volume of production by worker and other information needed to compute incentive pay, are not approved by the foreman. The next shift foreman turns them in to the time office.

Other Activities.

1. *Adequate control is lacking with respect to data and documents sent to San Francisco and over checks issued locally.* There is no assurance that invoices sent to San Francisco are in order for payment. Receiving reports and purchase orders are not matched up with them. Checks prepared in Glencoe for local purchases are returned to the voucher clerk after they are signed. He then mails them. This is a situation that would enable diversion of funds to the voucher clerk's own benefit.

2. *Efficiency of preparation of sales invoices can be improved.* Sales invoices are prepared entirely from production orders without reference to customers' sales orders. This eliminates an important means of detecting errors.

   No use is made of equipment that can pick up data from the sales order and make it a common source of preparation of production orders and sales invoices.

3. *Trucks, maintenance, and operating supplies are obtained principally from one supplier without obtaining quantity discounts.* As mentioned previously, the container plant's truck fleet is bought from, maintained and serviced by a single dealer located in Glencoe. Purchases from this dealer, including gasoline but excluding the original cost of equipment, were:

1960	$114,700
1961	99,300
1962	93,900
1963 (first four months)	34,300

In spite of this volume the dealer charged full retail price for gasoline.

Findings—The Arkansas Rice Farms

The major activities of the Arkansas Rice Farms is to grow rice on the Company's own acreage and to procure rice from other growers. Although we found no indications of fraud, we found a number of evidences of mismanagement.

The Glencoe farm manager has already taken a number of steps to centralize his control over operations, particularly with respect to purchases. He now personally, or under his close supervision, approves all invoices for purchases except those for rice from local producers. There still are a number of weaknesses that merit attention.

Farm Land Management. The Company operates a twin-engine airplane for spraying fungicides and insecticides over the growing crops. Passengers are also carried, although this use has decreased considerably in recent years.

During the first three months of 1963 approximately 40 hours of flying time were logged on the airplane. Total fixed and variable operating costs amounted to $140 per hour, exclusive of the pilot's time. We determined that a suitable spraying and dusting service could be obtained for about $25 per hour.

Community Relations. On the premise that good community relations are desirable, the Company has maintained a picnic ground on one suitable location on its land holdings.

Gradually the practice has developed of chartering bus service for groups reserving the picnic area for use. In addition, the Company has now found itself providing free picnic box lunches, as well as ice cold soft drinks and beer for picnickers.

The performance of these services has spread to other than local groups. The State organization of Future Farmers of America was accommodated at a splendid picnic, with transportation, and lunch, including soft drinks and milk.

The Arkansas Rice Growers Association had a fine picnic at Company expense, including bus transportation, Southern fried chicken luncheon, beer, coffee, and soft drinks. In return, the Company received a fine letter of appreciation and the farm manager was presented with a desk set, appropriately engraved to commemorate the occasion.

Similar entertainments were provided for several chambers of commerce.

Without disparaging the policy of maintaining good public relations, we seriously question whether these elaborate overtures to the public justify the expense incurred.

Rice Procurement.

It was especially disturbing to us to learn of the loose practices in transporting harvested grain to the rice plant. In many cases the truck drivers did not remember or were not sure whether loads of rice came from the Company's own farms or from the lands of private producers. The uncertainty entails the danger of private growers being paid for production from the Company's own farms.

Furthermore, despite the fact that expert production forecasts of crop conditions are made, there is no attempt to reconcile delivered rice with the forecasts of crop prospects.

Other Purchases.

Many items are not purchased at the lowest possible prices.

1. *Many items are bought locally at retail.* As in the case of the container plant, gasoline and truck servicing is bought in this manner. This is also done for many supplies and repair parts for farm machinery.

2. *No advance approval is required for purchases made.* For example, truck drivers or operators of farm machinery arrange to buy repair parts and incur other repair costs without any administrative approval of the economy of continued repair work.

Disbursements.

Tabulations of rice deliveries and payments for them are made manually.

The farm office supervisor, under whose charge vouchers are prepared, also serves as co-signer for checks.

Checks are issued on the basis of monthly statements, thus lessening effective control over payments.

Checks are mailed by persons who either prepare or request them.

Chapter 10

Auditing the
Procurement System

The procurement data cycle begins with a need for the purchase of materials or equipment as determined by operating requirements; it continues with the issue of purchase orders, the receipt of the material or equipment ordered, and concludes with the conversion of cash into an inventory cost or expense, or an asset required. Figure 1 is an overall flow chart of the procurement cycle.

To audit this data cycle, the auditor must understand the procurement process and its primary data output. Then he must evaluate the adequacy of information generated by the process, as to both its reliability and its relevance to the decision-making process. In so doing, he will certainly review the system's primary outputs, including inventory files, vendor-history files, open-purchase files, accounts-payable files.

Normally, the procurement cycle begins with requisitions from departments such as the Production Control Department for production materials, and from foremen and other operating management personnel for supplies and maintenance items. Such requisitions may also be received from inventory clerks or others whose responsibilities include the "monitoring" of current inventory levels of supply and maintenance items against a fixed reorder point or possibly a fixed minimum amount.

Understanding the Procurement Function

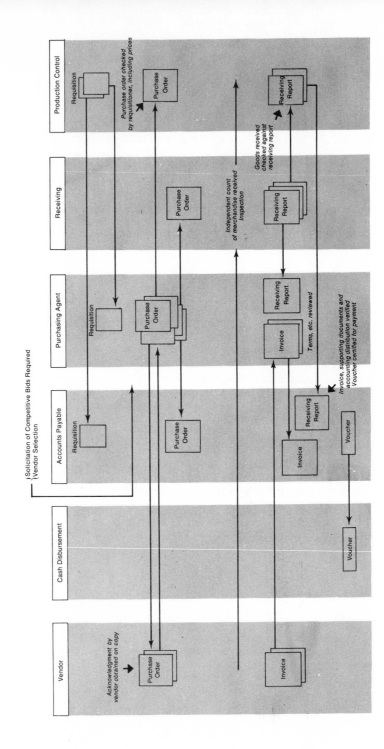

Figure 1. Flow chart of the procurement system. Adapted from AICPA's flow chart found in *Internal Control: Elements of a Coordinated System and Its Importance to Management and the Independent Public Accountant* (Special Report by the Committee on Auditing Procedure—Copyright 1949 by the American Institute of Accountants)

Instead of requiring the preparation of a detailed requisition for each supply and maintenance item as needed, many companies utilize a "traveling" requisition form—a document recording the various sources of supply, the exact material specifications, historical price data, past and current reorder history, historical usage information, etc. The value of a traveling requisition form to the reorder of supplies and maintenance items is that substantially all of the necessary information, including the specifications, already appears on the traveling requisitions and a minimum amount of current information—for example, the current quantity needs—has to be inscribed on the requisition. After the Purchasing Department fulfills the traveling requisition requirements, the form is again routed to the requisitioner for future reuse.

Quantity Determination

Those preparing requisitions must determine the quantity of each item of material to be ordered. Such a determination has been the subject of considerable attention in recent years and has led to the development of the "scientific inventory management" concept. "Economic Order Quantities" (EOQ) should be developed after considering procurement and administrative (purchase-order processing) lead times and forward production-schedule needs. Theoretically, the EOQ should be just that quantity that will avoid a stock-out situation and hence a plant production interruption, but simultaneously will not unnecessarily build up inventory levels to an excess-stock position, thereby tying up the company's resources, reducing return on investment, and adding to inventory holding costs.

Economic order quantity buying represents a "balancing" of the "acquisition cost savings" achieved from larger quantity buying with the increased "inventory holding costs" automatically incurred on the larger inventory levels maintained. Under modern inventory-management concepts, then, companies should order from suppliers productive materials (and significant supplies and maintenance items) in *economic order quantities*, as determined by the anticipated volume of business and the anticipated inventory levels needed to service the forward sales forecast.

One output of the procurement system should be the inventory master file containing information on each inventory item. In many companies, the inventory records are maintained on computer-readable files such as magnetic tapes or disks. A typical raw-material inventory record for a tape-oriented inventory system is shown in Table 1. Note the integration of operating data (e.g., order point and monthly usage on order quantity, vendor quantity, forecast order quantity) with accounting data (e.g., unit of issue, unit cost, stock on hand). This integration provides data useful to the auditor in evaluating obsolete and slow-moving items and in evaluating the company's procedures for determining how much inventory should be on hand.

Vendor Selection

Another very significant aspect of the procurement cycle is the selection of the vendor. Knowledge of the vendor's reliability in meeting order specifications (quantity, quality, delivery date) is an important information output required by most companies.

Where *quality reliability* requirements are vital, incoming materials from vendors should be *immediately* inspected by the Inspection Department in order to make sure that the quality tolerances, etc., are met. The results of such inspection should be formally recorded in inspection reports, and copies of such inspection reports should be routed to the Purchasing Department so that it may maintain its records as to the *quality* reliability of each vendor furnishing significant production or other material.

In timing its production inventory requisitions for any particular materials, components, parts, or subassemblies to the Purchasing Department, the Production Control Department must consider the *procurement lead time* for each vendor if a requisition is to be *timely*. Ordinarily, the procurement lead time of a vendor for an item must be dependable so as to avoid "stock-out" inventory positions. Hence, key factors in the relationships between the buying company and the vendor are delivery reliability and the success with which the forward production schedule can be coordinated and implemented.

Table 1. Inventory Record

Field Description	Number of Characters
Part number	4
Part description	31
Unit of issue	2
Vendor number	3
Last actual cost	10
Average unit cost	10
Order point	6
Stock on hand	6
Month to date usage	6
Average monthly usage	6
Lead time (days)	4
Last date of issue	6
On order quantity	6
Previous vendor	6
Minimum vendor quantity	6
Maximum issue quantity	6
Forecast order quantity	6
Vendor's standard package quantity	6
Perpetual Inventory quantity difference	6

In addition to the vendor file recording past relationships, the procurement data system may include the systematic gathering of data regarding potential suppliers not presently being used. Such a file may be based on many sources. Salesmen who call on a company frequently leave data about their firm's product and service capability. Advertisements in trade publications, observation of exhibits at trade shows, and referrals from customers and other suppliers may also be sources of potential vendors.

In many firms, the selection of vendors may also be the concern of the marketing department. There is considerable debate in both legal and ethical terms in today's business environment as to the desirability of practicing "reciprocity" in purchasing by favoring the customers of the firm in selecting vendors. It is apparent that a large purchase order may be an effective marketing tool, and most companies therefore feel that as well as making data on the firm's vendors systematically available to the marketing group, the firm's information system should inform purchasing agents of potential marketing considerations in the buying process. The usefulness of this information will vary from being of prime importance in vendor selection to being a modest plus factor that favors one vendor over another in an "other things equal" situation. In considering information outputs in this area, the firm and the auditor must be highly sensitive to the implications and use of these data. They must be certain that a carefully considered policy in this respect has been developed after consultation with legal counsel and that the information system reflects this policy.

Purchase Orders

Following the receipt of a purchase requisition in accordance with company policy, a purchase order is issued which provides information such as quantity ordered, description of material ordered, unit price (unless purchased on the basis of price on the date of delivery, as is the practice in buying steel or other metals), F.O.B. points, discounts (trade and cash), routing instructions, and date on which material is expected to be received.

Usually, the original and a second copy of a purchase order are forwarded to the vendor with whom it is placed so that the second copy may be signed and returned by the vendor as evidence of his acceptance of the transaction. Not only is this procedure valid of a means of providing confirmation that the vendor reviewed and accepts the terms of the purchase, but it is an assurance that the order has been received and that in due course the material ordered will be shipped.

Additional copies of purchase orders are sometimes routed to the Production Control Department or to expediters (for filing in a date-ahead file—perhaps a week before the anticipated delivery date of the material) so that the expediters may "chase" the material by communicating with vendors in advance of the indicated delivery date to make certain that the delivery will be timely as originally indicated. If a company maintains a commitment register, copies of the executed purchase orders might be processed to that function for "cash-flow" planning purposes.

Another important output from the procurement cycle is the open purchase-order file. Information from this file is necessary in maintaining inventory levels and cash flow control and in meeting production schedules.

An additional copy of the purchase order is usually routed to the receiving room, but this copy of the purchase order usually does *not* disclose the quantity ordered. This purchase-order copy alerts the receiving room that a shipment is due and serves as an authorization to receive designated materials from a particular vendor. Since the quantity is not disclosed, however, the receiving clerk is forced to count carefully and validate the quantity of merchandise received, which he records on his copy of the purchase order that he formally signs as confirmation of the receipt. This copy will be ultimately transmitted to the Accounts Payable Department, which has already received its own copy of the purchase order that is to be subsequently matched with receiving reports and vendor invoices.

Receiving and
Accounts Payable

Incoming materials should be inspected for quality and condition and should be counted, weighed, or measured in accordance with company policy and directives in order to verify the incoming shipment. The results of the receiving procedures should be reported on the receiving copy of the purchase order that is routed, as mentioned above, to Accounts Payable and any requesting departments.

The Accounts Payable Department is concerned with (1) vouching or verifying the papers that support the propriety and amount of a liability and the terms and conditions of subsequent payment; (2) recording the accounts payable and charging the proper account(s) for the purchase; and (3) disbursing the cash in payment of the liability created by the purchase.

The receiving reports and vendor's invoices should be compared, and those that match should be forwarded for further processing. Unmatched invoices and receiving reports should be held in separate files until the matching documents arrive. The Accounts Payable Department should audit the matched invoice and receiving reports with their copy of the purchase order to determine approval for payment. The auditing steps should include verification that the quantity received agrees with the quantity ordered and invoiced, that the price and terms on the invoice agree with those specified by the purchase order and that extensions and footings on the invoice are correct. Discounts should also be calculated, and the invoice should be coded to indicate the general ledger account or accounts to which it is to be charged. A copy of the invoice should be forwarded to the inventory-control clerk for entry in the detailed perpetual-inventory records.

The invoice is then recorded in the general accounting records to reflect the liability and make the corresponding charge to an asset or an expense. At this point in the process, a voucher-check form is usually prepared together with a voucher register with expense distribution columns. The invoices and voucher-check forms are then filed by due date and on the due date are released to the cash disbursements unit for payment.

Normally, the cash-disbursements unit, under the treasurer's jurisdiction, reviews the supporting documents submitted with the check in order to ascertain that the disbursement is for goods or services rendered to the company and that the check is drawn for the correct amount and to the order of the person or firm indicated by the supporting documents. The check is then signed, either in handwriting or by a check-signing machine; supporting documents are cancelled; a check register is prepared as a record of all disbursements and a source of general ledger posting for disbursements. The checks are then mailed to the payees. This function will be further discussed in the chapter on auditing the cash-management system.

The first step in the auditor's evaluation of the procurement cycle requires him to define the system in existence and then to test the system to confirm his understanding of its operation. He must then exercise his professional judgment to determine whether the system is performing its business purpose effectively, and must undertake any additional tests he deems necessary to satisfy himself that the information outputs are reliable.

In defining the system, the auditor should begin by reviewing the client's documentation and records to determine the types of purchase transactions that may occur and the categories of materials, equipment, supplies, and services that are procured. The auditor should flowchart the procedures supposed to be in existence by reviewing the organization of the procurement function: the purchase requisition procedures; the buying sequence, including determination of economic order quantities, selection of vendors, and distribution of purchase orders; the maintenance of catalogues, price lists, etc., records; the receiving room procedures; and the accounts-payable function.

After defining the system supposed to be in existence, the auditor should select representative purchases and trace them through the procurement cycle. Before selecting these transactions, the auditor should first ascertain what categories of materials, equipment, supplies, expenses, and services (other than payroll) are procured. He should also develop an estimate of the frequency and dollar importance of each category and select several transactions in general proportion to the frequency of occurrence. An audit program for this transaction analysis is found in the appendix on page 526.

Once the auditor has defined and tested the system, he should have sufficient evidence to evaluate its strengths and weaknesses. As part of his evaluation, he should determine the effectiveness of the client's procedures to protect against:

1. unauthorized persons making purchases;
2. purchasing from other than the best source of supply;
3. purchasing items not constituting the best means of serving the function (value analysis);
4. purchasing various specifications which could be consolidated for larger volume and therefore more advantageous price or discounts;
5. paying excessive prices;
6. purchasing material currently needed in other than economic ordering quantities;
7. paying for merchandise or services not actually ordered.

The auditor should also evaluate the efficiency of the procurement procedures and give consideration to the ways by which paperwork and clerical effort can be reduced.

The auditor should evaluate the organization of the procurement function and the segregation of duties among people involved in the authorization of the purchase, those involved in the custody of the assets acquired, and those involved in the records which maintain accountability of the assets acquired. Some examples of duties assumed by some purchasing departments that are not sound because they do not assure adequate internal control are:

1. The Purchasing Department receives invoices directly from vendors. —The routing of vendors' invoices initially to the Purchasing Department would put that department in a position to substitute, amend, or otherwise dispose of vendors' invoices to cover up an unauthorized purchase or a defalcation or some other unauthorized transaction.

2. The Purchasing Department actually prepares receiving reports for incoming material.—Sound internal control would require an "independent" validation of the receipt of material—i.e., by individuals other than those responsible for the procurement in the first instance. Again, the opportunity to issue receiving reports puts the Purchasing Department in a position to cover up unauthorized transactions by the issuance of fictitious receiving reports.

3. The Purchasing Department is functionally in charge of the receiving room and/or the receiving clerks or both.—If the Purchasing Department is in administrative control of the receiving room it can cause a receiving report to be prepared by exercise of its administrative authority over the receiving room, thus creating fictitious receiving reports to be used to validate an unauthorized payment to some vendor.

4. The Purchasing Department validates vendors' invoices for payments by matching the receiving report with vendors' invoices and the original purchase order (or some combination of these responsibilities) and verifying prices, quantities, materials, discounts, f.o.b., etc.—In summary then, it is performing the entire validation function which properly should be performed by an Accounts Payable Department independent of all other aspects or ramifications of purchasing transactions. This condition is found fairly commonly in smaller companies that allow the Purchasing Department to partially or totally process vendors' invoices for payment. This is a significant exposure, since such a procedure does not provide the independence of assigned responsibilities that constitutes good internal control.

5. The Purchasing Department keeps the records relating to inventories, posts the additions and issuances to such inventory records, and computes

Table 2

Procedures in the Evaluation of Output (Balances) from Procurement System	External Confirmation of Balances	Search for Quality Attributes	Comparison of Balances with Transactions as Key to Remainder	Inferences Based on Logical Relationships	Determination of Appropriate Generally Accepted Accounting Principles
Inventories					
Participate in planning of inventory-taking	X				
Observe the taking of inventory	X				
Make test counts and compare counts with final summaries of inventory	X				
Compare the completed physical inventory to perpetual inventory records	X				
Verify existence of goods held by public warehouses and goods out on consignment	X				
Review inventory files for slow-moving, obsolete items		X			
Review purchases and sales commitments		X			
Determine whether any inventories have been pledged		X			
Obtain a letter of representation on inventories from client		X			
Review cutoff of purchases by examination of records of receiving and purchasing			X		
Review cutoff of sales by examination of records of shipments and sales			X		
Test the reasonableness of inventories by comparison with prior years by application of the gross profits percentage method, by computing rate of turnover, etc.				X	
Review the bases and methods of inventory pricing					X
Test pricing of raw materials or purchased merchandise					X
Determine clerical accuracy of inventories by verification of extensions, footings, and summaries					X
Determine proper balance sheet presentation					X

Accounts Payable

Obtain a trial balance of accounts payable and reconcile total to general ledger account X

Reconcile liabilities with monthly statements from creditors X

Consider confirming accounts by direct correspondence if statements are not available X

Vouch balances payable to selected creditors to supporting documents X

Trace balances owing to affiliated companies to books of respective companies, or confirm by correspondence if books are not available X

Investigate debit balances for collectibility, and reclassify if substantial in amount X

Search for unrecorded accounts payable X

Obtain a representation from the client regarding the inclusion of all liabilities X

Compare cash disbursements subsequent to the balance sheet date with the accounts payable trial balance X

Determine proper balance-sheet presentation X

inventory balances.—The Purchasing Department is thus in a position to cause the disbursement of corporate funds (by issuance of purchase orders), and if a disbursement is fictitious or invalid, it can compensate for such embezzlement or defalcation by adjusting the entries and balances in the inventory records. Many studies of embezzlements from companies in the United States show this to be one of the classical routes of the embezzler.

6. The Purchasing Department, as mentioned previously, validates the "quality" of the commodity or materials that it purchased.—In effect, then, the Purchasing Department acts as its own Inspection Department. Since the element of quality has a direct relationship and bearing to the price paid, the appraisal of the quality of the material or products received should ideally be independent of the Purchasing Department. It should be the responsibility of the Inspection Department.

Based on his evaluation of the procurement system, the auditor should then determine:

1. Additional audit procedures required in areas where weaknesses exist. These procedures may take the form of additional transaction analyses or the evaluation of the output produced by the system.
2. Recommendations for improving the procurement system in light of information requirements of the client.

Evaluation of Output

The primary accounting and financial outputs resulting from the procurement system are records and reports on inventories, accounts payable, and property, plant, and equipment acquisitions. In evaluating these financial outputs, the auditor performs certain fundamental tasks using selected audit procedures. For example, Table 2 presents selected audit procedures for inventory and accounts payable in relation to the fundamental audit tasks discussed in Chapter 5. The selected audit procedures are those found in traditional auditing texts or in audit programs used by CPA firms.[1] These procedures illustrate the additional audit steps that may be used to evaluate outputs from the procurement system once the system has been analyzed.

---

[1] For example, we have used audit procedures found in Meigs and Larsen, *Principles of Auditing*, pages 363 and 516.

Chapter 11

Auditing the
Production System

In most manufacturing and merchandising concerns, the production system, including work-in-process inventory and finished-goods inventory, presents major problems in accounting and information processing. The number of transactions and the amount of money involved, and the many types of production systems that may be encountered all require the auditor to have a good understanding of this important data cycle.

The production data cycle begins with the development of production requirements and proceeds through production scheduling, material requisition, fabrication, and inventory control. Although the production process is best characterized by physical properties and activities, the auditor should be primarily concerned with the flow of data about these physical activities and the information available to management for planning and controlling production operations and inventories.

Although most often associated with manufacturing and merchandising concerns, production systems do not always involve physical production. In a broad sense, the production system creates a commodity or service and thus includes some kind of transformation process. In manufacturing, the process is a physical transformation of raw materials, inputs, to create a desired output, the product. In the distribution of that product, the production process transforms its availability in one place to availability in another place in time. In other kinds of production systems, we may find that the transformation is of information on a piece of paper or on a computer, as is true in banks and in administrative offices of schools and government institutions. In consulting and public-accounting firms, we find that resources are combined to create a desired service or report, the product, for a particular client.

Understanding the Production System

Since any system to be evaluated must first be understood, evaluation of a production system requires that the auditor understand its production operation. Because of the many different production processes that can be found in American business, information or data flow related to production is likely to differ from one company to another.

There are two major classifications of production systems: continuous systems and intermittent systems. In *continuous* systems, the producing activity is dictated by the nature of the forecasted demand. In such systems, typified by the automotive industry, we find carefully designed production lines to produce a relatively large volume of standardized items for stock. In *intermittent* systems, the demand is normally for customized items, such as machined parts or custom furniture. On a small scale, such systems are commonly called job shops, while in an industry created by recent technological advances, such as the aerospace industry, the intermittent system is on a large scale: a large production capacity producing a small quantity of each item. This requires the production system to be a flexible one, which can be set up for a wide variety of styles, sizes, or item designs as is the case, for example, in jet aircraft production. Other examples of intermittent systems are found in the construction industry, defense industry, and space program; among these are large-scale, one-time projects such as the SST program and the Apollo program.

In continuous systems, production design and operation are geared to the basic requirement of producing for inventory and of holding levels of inventory to supply varying demand as it occurs at the consumer, distribution, production, or raw-material supply levels. For example, one type of continuous system is the almost pure inventory system—that is, no physical production but the holding and distribution of goods—in retailing and wholesaling operations and in many military-supply situations. In the type of continuous system where standardized inventory is produced in high volume to meet anticipated demand, we find more complexities than in the pure inventory systems found in retailing or other merchandising activities.

Within the production cycle, in addition to consumer demand and the determination of inventory levels, must be considered the problems of long-range planning of production facilities, of production facility design, and of production planning and scheduling. Designers of information and decision models for production planning and scheduling in production-inventory systems must consider not only inventory costs but a host of other costs, such as labor-turnover costs, overtime, excess-capacity materials, and plant fixed costs.

In the intermittent systems, production is geared to the basic requirement that facilities and manpower be held "in inventory" to supply a demand that varies in design, style, and technology. In such systems, the problems are those of design and layout of the system to minimize total handling costs; of forecasting demand; of planning for use of facilities; of scheduling orders to meet promised delivery dates and scheduling labor and equipment to minimize total costs of machine set-up, machine downtime, labor overtime, and in-process inventories; of scheduling equipment to utilize the most efficient process; of procuring materials in economical quantities to mesh with production schedule; and of obtaining orders at margins that will achieve a balance between the use of labor and facilities and the desire for profit.

The increased complexities of the job-order system arise from the custom nature of the fabrication process: Each order or job will require individual planning and scheduling and will follow a unique processing sequence.

The Inventory Problem

Inventories are part of all systems mentioned above and indeed are a crucial part of all production systems. Accordingly, the auditor should be familiar with the nature of inventory and information necessary for inventory management and control. The management of inventory is for most businessmen as important as the management of cash and often more difficult: Cash can be used for a variety of purposes; inventory, and more particularly each item in inventory, is an asset with a much more limited use.

There are many factors in a need for inventories, some of which are:

1. variations in demand for products;
2. variations in production lead times;
3. variations in delivery lead times of raw materials;
4. variations in production rates;
5. costs associated with variations in the labor force;
6. costs associated with shortages or delayed deliveries.

The proper management of inventories requires much information—

usually factual knowledge combined with estimates and projections. To develop a good inventory-management system, it is usually necessary to:

1. Estimate the future demand for products—this requires a forecast of future sales and inventories and an analysis of orders on hand.
2. Write up the specifications of the materials and parts going into the final product.
3. Prepare production schedules based on the forecast of customer-inventory requirements and product specifications and efficient manufacturing practices.
4. Create a reporting system giving the status of production inventories to backlog.
5. Analyze the financial cost of carrying inventories.

The auditor has traditionally been somewhat concerned with the inventory management process in order to determine the physical existence of inventories and the valuation of the assets represented by inventory. In his more current role as an evaluator of the firm's information system, however, he has a much broader responsibility. He must be familiar with inventory-control systems and procedures, and in addition to satisfying himself that inventory figures on the financial statements are reliable, he must determine whether the information outputs about inventory are sufficient to enable management to make appropriate economic decisions.

The objective of inventory-control procedures is to minimize the total costs of inventories, including the opportunity costs described above, while at the same time keeping the cost of control at a low level. Basically, this objective is carried out by classifying items of inventory according to some criteria such as usage, dollar value, and type of item, and by establishing different control procedures relevant to each classification of inventory, so that expenditures for control are concentrated on those items that, because of the nature and the magnitude of the inventory, produce the highest return on dollars invested in control.

Evaluation of the Production System

In developing his procedures for auditing the production system, the auditor must first consider the nature of the client's production system.

[1] Arthur B. Toan, *Using Information to Manage*, page 69.

The approach to evaluating the production data cycle for each previously described production system will differ. For example, scheduling in a job shop would deal with specific orders, while scheduling in a continuous-process plant would deal with total scheduled utilization of the productive facilities based upon general sales plans. Scheduling in a plant with proprietary lines would most likely deal with a review of finished inventory levels converted into production requests.

In addition to the consideration of different production systems, the review of the production data cycle should be concerned with the physical aspects of production in addition to the data flow and information processing. Trips to the plant should be made to determine the physical nature of the processing operation: the nature of its various products, the physical layout of the plant, the nature of the equipment being used, and the nature and extent of labor involved in the production system.

In selecting production orders for tracing through the cycle, the auditor should include both normal production orders of all major classifications of products made, and abnormal production orders, including rush orders, late orders, orders that occur very rarely, etc. The purpose of such selection is to enable the auditor to learn about the methods and controls of the entire production activity. Most often, production flows are upset by the exceptions. Rework orders, small customer orders, delayed orders, orders with special features are all potential troublemakers. Accordingly, if the auditor is to understand and evaluate the functioning of the production cycle, he must select representative troublemaking orders as well as orders which constitute normal production flow.

In his review the auditor should evaluate the client's internal control and accounting procedures to give assurance against:

1. production of items in a job-shop system that have not been ordered, or, in a continuous system, for which there is no satisfactory evidence of demand;
2. holding of inferior-quality items in stock;
3. unusual delays in work-in-process orders;
4. costs-to-date plus cost-to-complete all work in process exceeding realizable values;
5. theft, spoilage, and unauthorized withdrawals by employees.

He should evaluate the procedures used to develop production requirements to ensure that:

1. updated bills of material, product, and process specifications are complete and current at the time production orders are issued;
2. work cannot be done without proper authorization;
3. requirements are coordinated with anticipated forecasts;
4. styles, colors, sizes are developed by people having knowledge of production requirements;
5. the time between the receipt of the customer's order and instructions to the factory is a reasonable interval.

He should evaluate the client's production-planning procedures to determine that:

1. the productive capacity and the methods of using them have been geared to adequately support the sales policy of the company as to delivery time, quality, etc.;
2. capacity has been related at least annually to sales plans;
3. standards used for determining shop loads are evaluated for accuracy by use of statistics, and the loading policy and delivery promises are based on shop-load standards.

The auditor should evaluate the client's production-scheduling and control procedures to determine that:

1. delivery promises are made in the light of past performance;
2. the scheduling process recognizes the use of priority techniques in order to change the rate of flow and to improve utilization of equipment;
3. appropriate techniques, such as linear programming, are used when a processing operation involves several facilities with different individual productive capacities that may be used to work alternately on different orders;
4. queueing techniques (waiting-line models) have been used to determine the number of facilities or processes performing similar functions;
5. the control reports provide information on actual work completed, stock-outs and obsolete and slow-moving items, availability of critical material, slipped schedules, comparisons between planned and actual monthly production and reasons for significant variations;
6. reliable standards are used for computing shop load, and these same standards are used for cost control and estimating;
7. production quantities are issued in economic order quantities.

The auditor should evaluate the client's material-control procedures to determine that there are satisfactory assurances that:

1. parts are available at assembly point;
2. material in excess of that authorized by production control cannot be withdrawn for work;
3. measurements and/or counts are made at points in the material flow at which losses occur;
4. adequate documentation is available to communicate the nature of the work to be done and the manner in which it is to be performed. Such documentation includes routing sheets, drawings, process instructions, and methods instructions, including speeds and feeds and the tools to be used.

The auditor should evaluate the client's cost-control procedures to ascertain that they provide information on:

1. costs of using different materials and ingredients for production production processes that utilize ingredients with a fluctuating market price;
2. costs of material with exception reports to highlight slow-moving and excess quantities, and significant variations in actual material used as compared to standards for material;
3. wage and salary costs;
4. indirect costs and the activity factors for setting standards on indirect costs;
5. significant variations between perpetual inventory amounts and physical inventory amounts.

The auditor should also evaluate the techniques used to develop performance standards, work efforts, and develop better work methods. He should also determine if there is any evidence that production facilities are not being properly utilized because of bottlenecks and work-scheduling procedures. He should evaluate the procedures used to ensure the quality of work, and, in this regard, he should determine if there is independence of the production personnel from the quality-control or inspection group; he should review warranty costs; he should review inspection methods and statistical quality-control techniques.

**Testing the
System**

To confirm his understanding of the production system and to determine the existence and effectiveness of production-system procedures, the auditor should select a sample of production orders and trace them through the cycle. The sample selection will normally be stratified—a series of samples, each drawn from a specified part of the universe of orders—so that the auditor can be certain that the various types of orders will be sampled. Since production systems tend to be more complex than other data cycles, the sampling process must be carefully structured. In addition to sampling representative orders, the auditor may also test exceptions to the normal system, since the ability of the system to deal with abnormal events may be the greatest test of its adequacy.

The sampling process should be stratified to include orders within each of the company's product lines and effort should be made to select a variety of orders to ensure coverage of all production facilities. Where classes of facilities exist, such as a machine shop and an assembly plant, orders should be selected that utilize all the classes of facilities. A production plant with a single product that releases production schedules for specific periods of time may appear to have no separate production orders. In such cases, the time period used for planning should generally be considered as an order.

By his testing, the auditor must determine whether the level of exceptions in information processing and output is within the predetermined limits he established after review of the system. If this is not the case, the auditor must consider what additional audit procedures are necessary including increasing the size of the sample to determine a more accurate estimate of the level of exceptions.

A typical audit program for the analysis of transactions and the testing of a production system is reproduced in the appendix to this chapter.

**Observation of
Physical
Inventory**

One test of the production control system that auditors are required to make is the physical observation of inventories. This test became a required auditing procedure after a major inventory fraud in the 1930s, at McKesson and Robbins, a pharmaceutical manufacturer. The specific pronouncement of the Committee on Auditing Procedure of the AICPA on the subject is as follows:

> . . . where the independent certified public accountant intends to report over his signature on the financial statements of a concern in which inven-

tories are a material factor, it should be generally accepted auditing procedure that, in addition to making auditing tests and checks of the inventory accounts and records, he shall, wherever practicable and reasonable, be present, either in person or by his representatives, at the inventory-taking and by suitable observation and inquiry satisfy himself as to the effectiveness of the methods of inventory-taking and as to the measure of reliance which may be placed upon the client's representations as to inventories and upon the records thereof . . . .[2]

The original objective of this auditing procedure was the verification of the inventory balance at a point in time, and the reconciliation of that balance to the balance-sheet figure. As auditing objectives have evolved, however, this procedure has increasingly come to be part of the test of controls rather than a verification of a specific balance. The auditor is reviewing the system by which the company methodically compares actual physical goods on hand with inventory balances shown on the books. In addition, since it requires the auditor to physically perceive and understand the production operations of the business, this procedure is an important part of the review of the production data cycle.

The auditor's first step in the physical observation procedure is to obtain data as to the nature and location of the company's inventories. This can be done in part by inquiry and in part by walking through the production facilities of the firm. Then the company's description of its own inventory-taking procedures should be obtained.

In some cases, physical-inventory counting is done on a 100 percent basis on a single date, while in others counts are performed periodically throughout the year, sometimes on a random basis and often at a particular point in the ordering cycle, such as the point of reorder when physical stocks are low. On many items, physical counts are performed only on a statistical-sampling basis.

The auditor must evaluate the controls over the counting process to satisfy himself that adequate division of authority exists. It would be inappropriate, for example, were the storekeeper responsible for keeping an item in stock to also be the sole counter of inventory quantities. Additionally, the auditor must review specific procedures for counting to assure himself that adequate protection exists against omitting some items from the inventory or counting some items twice. To this end, various techniques such as inventory tags, team counting, and double counting are used.

---

[2]AICPA, *Statements in Auditing Procedure, Number 36*, pp. 33–34.

Another important step that must be taken before comparing counts with book figures is to determine that adequate cut-off procedures exist. These are procedures designed to assure that between substantial receipts or shipments of inventory no significant time lapse occurs that, during inventory, could result in a disparity between the inventory count and the actual physical inventory. Such procedures normally include checking the last receiving and shipping report numbers recorded on the books prior to inventory taking and then being certain that the next numbered report forms are on hand when the count is made.

Once he has evaluated controls over the inventory taking, the auditor must determine the extent to which he will be present during the actual counting process. If controls are unsatisfactory, he may feel it necessary to have a representative on every count team, but normally he will observe the counting itself on a sample basis while paying particular attention to the actual existence of the controls specified in company procedures. In addition, he will participate in the planning process that precedes the actual physical inventory and will be particularly alert for production problems, obsolete goods, storage deficiencies, inadequate receiving and issuing controls, and other problems which may arise related to inventories.

If inventory counts are made on a cyclical basis rather than all at one time, the auditor still has the same basic responsibility to observe some of the counts, though in this case he normally emphasizes procedures to an even greater extent. Cyclical counts are only an acceptable substitute for a periodic count when good controls exist. Occasional checking of physical quantities by a stock clerk responsible for those quantities would not be considered a satisfactory control system.

One of the greatest benefits to the auditor in observing physical inventories is that it puts him in touch with production and other operating personnel whom he might not otherwise contact. This opportunity should be used to ask questions and gain understanding of the production process and any production problems which exist. The insights gained may be very valuable in the total appraisal of the production system and the information requirements of the system on an operating level.

Evaluating Output

Cost-accounting records and inventory reports are the major accounting and financial outputs of the production system. Cost-accounting records are necessary to account for the usage of raw materials, to determine the content and value of work-in-process inventories, and to compute the finished-goods inventory. These records serve to accumulate labor costs and indirect costs such as depreciation on assets used in the production of goods that contribute to the work-in-process and finished-goods inventories.

As part of the evaluation of the system, the cost-accounting system and records should be tested for reliability and relevance. The work-in-process inventory and finished-goods inventory should be evaluated for reasonableness, and various mechanical checks of cost accumulation should be undertaken. Where inventories have special accounting problems, such as when percentage-of-completion accounting is used on construction projects, additional auditing procedures must be undertaken so that the auditor can satisfy himself as to the adequacy of estimates used.

In addition to financial outputs, a production information system requires many outputs relating to physical quantities, time spent, idle time, and other items. The auditor must review these outputs as well to satisfy himself that the information needed by operating managers is being supplied and is reliable.

Production Cycle
Transaction Analysis

Appendix

---

1. Trace orders to the development of production requirements.

a. In the case of orders for end products, obtain the paper evidence that shows how the requirements for the order came about. This could be a customer order, production plan, or record of an inventory stock level. Identify the orders being traced with the requirement developed. How and by whom

were colors, styles, sizes, and other specifications developed?

b. In the case of direct orders for components and component orders flowing automatically from the orders issued for the end product, obtain the document reflecting the development of the requirement for the component. In the event that components for end products are not ordered to be built along with the end product, trace the demand for the component that the end product has generated into the records for developing component requirements.

c. Obtain the parts lists and ascertain how they are updated, and how effectively they are controlled. Trace information back to the engineering-department record.

2. Trace orders to scheduling and work-load records.

a. Obtain the summary loading schedule and trace the following items back to their source.
   i. Computations of capacity.
   ii. Time factors used to determine work load. (Are these the same factors used for cost control and cost estimating?)
b. Obtain the sales production plan and locate the classification in which the orders being traced were planned.
c. Obtain the documents which established the priority given to the order. It would be particularly true that priorities would be given to rush orders, late orders, rework, and so forth.

3. Trace orders to records used for withdrawal of materials, supplies and tools.

a. Obtain the material requisition, shop order, or production schedule used for moving materials, supplies, and tools from stores to the production area.
   i. Ascertain where the authority was initiated.
   ii. Review the computations of quantities issued and the basis for including or excluding allowances for anticipated spoilage.
   iii. Obtain the document for material issues subsequent to the initial issue. Such issues would occur to cover spoilage,

initial short deliveries, and so forth.
   iv. Ascertain the authority required and the evidence left by the recipient for the issuance of material from stores.

4. Trace orders to records for controlling the time and materials during fabrication or processing.

a. Obtain time records used for recording direct labor.
b. Obtain the document on which time standards for the work were communicated to the foremen.
c. Obtain the record communicating the standard for setup time.
d. Obtain the methods sheets, as well as the routing sheets and engineering drawings.
e. Obtain the record of counting or measuring at all of the points at which losses have been measured.
f. Obtain travelers, move tickets, and so forth and determine what accountability is set up as quantities move from point to point. Are counts made against documents at the next stage of production or at storerooms?
g. Obtain the document with which components moved to assembly areas.
   i. Are components maintained at control stations?
   ii. Are components maintained in open bins adjacent to the work?
   iii. Are components returned to and issued from raw-material stores?
h. Obtain shortage reports, scrap reports, and other trouble reports, and determine whether the orders being traced appear on such reports.
i. Obtain quality-control reports, such as inspection reports and minutes of action committees and review reasons for rejects and actions taken.

j. Obtain standards used by inspectors and review how inspectors are instructed as to manner of counting, selecting, etc., and how quality characteristics such as dimensions, weights, color, etc., are established.

k. Obtain budget reports for departments in which orders were processed and:
   i. determine the nature and source of variances, and trace back to their source the variances reported.
   ii. determine whether the original budgets are engineered, scattergraphed, or estimated.
   iii. review variance reports given to departmental management and ascertain what action was taken.

5. Trace to the inventory record of manufactured items.

a. Identify the quantities completed in the selected orders with the receipts shown on the storeroom inventory records.

b. On component items, examine the perpetual records to determine to what extent they have been used in the past and determine the need for having issued the order being traced.

c. On finished stock items, also examine activity and relate to the need for having issued the order being traced.

d. Trace items to stock-out reports rendered by the storeroom indicating they have not been able to fill either (i) production orders or (ii) sales orders.

6. Trace to records indicating computations of unit costs and variances.

a. Ascertain whether variances are reported by man, job, or cost center.

b. Ascertain whether indirect costs are brought together in centers responsible for the expenditures and determine if there is a distinction made between standards for product costs and performance measurement.

c. Trace piece-work rates to time studies and determine how incentives are included in standards.

d. Compare pay rates with union contracts, personnel files, and so forth.

e. Determine techniques used for computing product costs, including the bases used for deciding which costs are to be included as product costs.

1. The Moss Company manufactures household appliances that are sold through independent franchised retail dealers. The electric motors in the appliances are guaranteed for five years from the date of sale of the appliances to the consumer. Under the guaranty defective motors are replaced by the dealers without charge.

Inventories of replacement motors are kept in the dealers' stores and are carried at cost in The Moss Company's records. When the dealer replaces a defective motor, he notifies the factory and returns the defective motor to the factory for reconditioning. After the defective motor is received by the factory, the dealer's account is credited with an agreed fee for the replacement service.

When the appliance is brought to the dealer after the guaranty period has elapsed, the dealer charges the owner for installing the new motor. The dealer notifies the factory of the installation and returns the replaced motor for reconditioning. The motor installed is then charged to the dealer's account at a price in excess of its inventory value. In this instance,

to encourage the return of replaced motors, the dealer's account is credited with a nominal value for the returned motor.

Dealers submit quarterly inventory reports of the motors on hand. The reports are later verified by factory salesmen. Dealers are billed for inventory shortages determined by comparison of the dealers' inventory reports and the factory's perpetual records of the dealer's inventories. The dealers order additional motors as they need them. One motor is used for all appliances in a given year, but the motors are changed in basic design each model year.

The Moss Company has established an account, Estimated Liability for Product Guaranties. An amount representing the estimated guaranty cost prorated per sales unit is credited to the Estimated Liability account for each appliance sold and the debit is charged to a Provision account. The Estimated Liability account is debited for the service fees credited to the dealers' accounts and for the inventory cost of the motors installed under the guaranties.

The engineering department keeps statistical records of the number of units of each model sold in each year and the replacements that

From Uniform CPA Examinations.

were made. The effect of improvements in design and construction is under continuous study by the engineering department, and the estimated guaranty cost per unit is adjusted annually on the basis of experience and improvements in design. Experience shows that, for a given motor model, the number of guaranties made good varies widely from year to year during the guaranty period, but the total number of guaranties to be made good can be reliably predicted.

Required:

a. Prepare an audit program to satisfy yourself as to the propriety of the transactions recorded in the Estimated Liability for Product Guaranties account for the year ended December 31, 1963.

b. Prepare the worksheet format that would be used to test the adequacy of the balance in the Estimated Liability for Product Guaranties account. The worksheet column headings should describe clearly the data to be inserted in the columns.

2. On January 11, 1964 at the beginning of your annual audit of The Grover Manufacturing Company's financial statements for the year ended December 31, 1963, the Company president confides in you that an employee is living on a scale in excess of that which his salary would support.

The employee has been a buyer in the purchasing department for six years and has charge of purchasing all general materials and supplies. He is authorized to sign purchase orders for amounts up to $200. Purchase orders in excess of $200 require the countersignature of the general purchasing agent.

The president understands that the usual examination of financial statements is not de-signed, and cannot be relied upon, to disclose fraud or conflicts of interest, although their discovery may result. The president authorizes you, however, to expand your regular audit procedures and to apply additional audit procedures to determine whether there is any evidence that the buyer has been misappropriating Company funds or has been engaged in activities that were a conflict of interests.

Required:

a. List the audit procedures that you would apply to the Company records and documents in an attempt to:
   1. Discover evidence within the purchasing department of defalcations being committed by the buyer. Give the purpose of each audit procedure.
   2. Provide leads as to possible collusion between the buyer and suppliers. Give the purpose of each audit procedure.

b. Assume that your investigation disclosed that some suppliers have been charging The Grover Manufacturing Company in excess of their usual prices and apparently have been making "kick-backs" to the buyer. The excess charges are material in amount. What effect, if any, would the defalcation have upon (1) the financial statements that were prepared before the defalcation was uncovered and (2) your auditor's report? Discuss.

3. Often an important aspect of a CPA's examination of financial statements is his observation of the taking of the physical inventory.

Required:

a. What are the general objectives or purposes of the CPA's observation of the taking of the physical inventory? (Do not discuss procedures or techniques involved in making the observation.)

b. For what purposes does the CPA make and record test counts of inventory quantities during his observation of the taking of the physical inventory? Discuss.

4. The client's cost system is often the focal point in the CPA's examination of the financial statements of a manufacturing company.

Required:

a. For what purposes does the CPA review the cost system?

b. The Summerfield Manufacturing Company employs standard costs in its cost accounting system. List the audit procedures that you would apply to satisfy yourself that Summerfield's cost standards and related variance amounts are acceptable and have not distorted the financial statements. (Confine your audit procedures to those applicable to *materials*.)

5. During your examination of the financial statements of the Gary Manufacturing Company for the year ended December 31, 1965, you find that at January 1, 1965 the Company had installed the following punched-card processing system for recording raw material purchases:

1. Vendors' invoices are sent directly to the accounts payable department by the mail department.

2. All supporting documents to the invoices are accumulated in the accounts payable department and attached to the invoices.

After being checked and cash discounts computed, the invoices are accumulated in batches and adding machine tapes prepared of the net invoice amounts to provide predetermined totals. Then the batches of invoices and tapes are sent to the tabulating department.

3. In the tabulating department key punch operators prepare for each invoice an accounts payable punched card and one or more punched cards for the related debit distribution to several departmental inventories.

4. The invoice register is prepared by tab runs of the distribution cards and accounts payable cards. In this run totals of distribution cards are compared by the tabulating machine with the amounts punched for the related accounts payable cards. Tab run subtotals by invoice batches are taken for checking to the predetermined totals.

5. The general ledger control account is posted monthly from the totals shown in the invoice register and all other journals.

6. By sorting, the distribution and accounts payable cards are separated. The distribution cards are filed for further processing. The accounts payable cards are sorted by due dates and tab runs prepared to determine cash requirements.

7. On the due dates the accounts payable cards are processed to prepare combined check and remittance statements.

8. At the end of the month the accounts payable cards in the unpaid file are tabulated for comparison with the general ledger control account.

Required:

a. List the audit procedures that you would employ in the examination of raw material purchases. In this part limit your discussion to procedures up to and including the preparation of the punched cards.

b. What audit procedures would you employ to satisfy yourself as to the reasonable-ness of the accounts payable balance at December 31, 1965?

Taylor
Manufacturing
Company

Case

The Taylor Manufacturing Company, a subsidiary of a diversified corporation, is one of the country's major manufacturers and distributors of high-quality kitchen utensils and appliances with annual sales of approximately $25,000,000. The company does not engage in retail sales but sells exclusively to selected retail outlets. Furthermore, the company has approximately 1,700 items in its product line.

The company's manufacturing plant is centrally located in Ohio and the plant employs about 1,000 people. In addition to the main warehouse that is located near the manufacturing plant in Cleveland, Ohio, the company also maintains twenty branch warehouses plus a sales force of 70 men throughout the country.

Recently, company management decided to install an IBM 1410 system for inventory control and sales analysis, even though this would probably increase their current operating costs. Company management felt that the increases

Reprinted with permission from Thomas Prince, *Information Systems for Management Planning and Control* (Homewood, Ill.: Richard D. Irwin, Inc.), pp. 164–166.

in reporting effectiveness in both the sales and inventory functions, plus the anticipated benefits from future applications, justified the added expense. These future applications included production control and payroll accounting.

Each of the 20 branches does its own billing; however, the accounts receivable and inventory functions are centralized in Ohio. Branch inventories are replenished automatically from the Cleveland warehouse stocks based upon computer-generated orders.

Former System

Prior to conversion, inventory replenishment was handled on a manual decentralized basis. Monthly, each branch manager would take a physical inventory and would then place orders equal to 30-day usage (the branch's reorder quantity) for any item in inventory falling below a predetermined level. This predetermined level or order point was based upon each branch manager's own estimate of his sales for the next 90-day period. With this 90-day base figure for each item, the branch manager would place a new order if *quantity on hand plus quantity on order but not received is less than the next 90-day sales*. Under this procedure, the Taylor Manufacturing Company was consistently carrying a 45– to 60–day inventory of finished goods.

New System

Under the new system, the inventory control function has been centralized at the main office and converted to computer processing. All branch inventory transactions are analyzed weekly by the computer system. Any items requiring replenishment as well as the quantities needed are determined automatically by the computer system.

The formula used by the computer program for inventory replenishment is basically the same method used by the branch managers under the previous system. However, because the inventory levels are being reviewed weekly instead of monthly, the reorder point has been lowered to 75-day usage (from the original 90-day level), and the reorder quantity has been reduced to a 15-day supply for many of the items in the product line (from the original 30-day level). Using this new system, company management feels that inventory levels have been reduced from 15 to 20 percent.

Management decided against adopting any of the "sophisticated" inventory control formulas for determining reorder points and for forecasting future sales initially because (1) there was a lack of sales history data upon which to base such forecasts and (2) manage-

ment felt that a new purchasing concept would aggravate any centralization problems which might arise during the conversion of the branch inventory functions. A master file, however, has been established in the computer system to record the high month's sales and the low month's sales quantity in addition to total sales and number of months included in total sales. These statistics can be used in the future to determine average sales and deviations. With these latter data plus seasonal trends, management plans on developing more sophisticated formulas in the near future.

With the conversion to automatic data processing, management now obtains more effective and timely sales analysis reports as well as increasing the number of stockout conditions. Now that the sales analysis and branch inventory functions have been converted to electronic equipment, management is proceeding into the production control application. Following this, the plans are to program the complete payroll function and to integrate this system with the other computer programming systems.

Required:

1. Evaluate the centralized inventory control and sales analysis system.

2. Your brief study of the Taylor Manufacturing Company's operations indicates that the company is extremely profitable. From your review of the new centralized inventory control and sales analysis system, what would you expect to be the general nature of the company's environment? What type of cost-selling price relation would you expect to exist?

3. Do you agree with company management's movement toward a "total computer system"

(integrated inventory control and sales analysis system; next, integrated inventory control, production control and sales analysis system; then, mechanized payroll operations with integrated inventory control . . .)? Be specific and include illustrations and examples in support of your comments.

4. Assume that company management is reconsidering the question of maintaining the reorder point at 75 days and the reorder quantity at 15 days. Indicate the format of a report that you might prepare for management which would provide guidelines for making a decision on this question. Even though the format of the report may be sketchy, please be specific as to *where* and *how* the information on the report would be *obtained* and *processed.*

The Thurber Division

Case

The Parent Company

In the last decade, the International Gothic Company went through a planned transition from what was basically an automotive supply business to a broadly diversified company serving many industries and markets. This intensive and somewhat successful effort to

Taken from Frank Greenwood's *Casebook for Management and Business Policy* (International Textbook Company).

This case was prepared by Professor Thomas Burns of Ohio State University as a basis for class discussion. It is not designed to illustrate either effective or ineffective handling of administrative problems.

broaden the base of Gothic's markets and to find new product lines was necessary to replace diminishing markets and outmoded product lines. New products added in this period included pneumatic controls and actuators, aircraft landing gear, metal alloys, and instruments. By developing new products and purchasing other companies with different product lines, diversification was accomplished (see Table 1).

Under each product group, Gothic had a number of divisions which totaled 19 (composed almost equally of foreign and domestic companies) in 1964. The largest product group in number of divisions was Aircraft Products with 8

Table 1. Total Sales Percentage

Product Group	1956	1963	Increase (Decrease)
Castings and forgings	44%	38%	(6%)
Automotive products	44	25	(19)
Aircraft products	3	22	19
Machine tools	9	15	6

divisions consisting entirely of companies purchased since 1956.[1] Foreign Aircraft Products companies were located in West Germany (2), France, England, Italy and Japan.

The Division

The Thurber Company was a manufacturer of electro-mechanical devices and sensitive instruments which are used in measuring the performance of missiles and in controlling automated industrial equipment. Since its founding in 1954 by an Ohio State University engineering professor, the company had developed rapidly. In December 1959, the company was purchased by Gothic and grouped with the Aircraft Products division.

Prior to its purchase by Gothic, only limited records were kept by Thurber. The reports prepared had been for tax, credit, or loan purposes. Even these apparently had been incomplete since Gothic found upon purchase that some Ohio taxes had not been paid for many years. Most of the accounts receivable purchased turned out to be worthless since they represented returned instruments for which no credit memos had been issued. There were so many discrepancies in the inventory records that they had little value. Plant records were practically nonexistent. In order to stay solvent, the founder and inventor had not been able to pay himself salary, royalties, or dividends. In its pre-Gothic period, the corporation had been barely able to meet a payroll which normally consisted of from 5 to 10 persons. The wife of an employee had been hired to do the record-keeping. A factory employee informally kept track of production.

Once Gothic took over in 1959 it attempted to improve Thurber's accounting by installing Gothic's system which was used in Aircraft Products divisions (see Figure 1). Due to the unavailability of any present Thurber or Gothic employee who could account adequately, the Gothic controller decided to hire a competent accountant for this purpose. Since Thurber had never been profitable for Gothic, it was anticipated that such an action (coupled with the starting IBM accounting services for Thurber in 1962) might provide better controls which would result in substantial cost reductions, increased manufacturing efficiencies, and eventual profits.

In February 1963, an accountant, Mr. Christopher Fry, age 27, had been hired in Cleveland to become controller of the Thurber division. Gothic officials regarded themselves as fortunate in securing his services due to his college record, his excellent experience as a Navy auditor and supply officer, and especially because the labor market for accountants was very tight.

---

[1]The function of this group is to create controlled pneumatic power to handle jobs in defense and other industries. Pneumatic means gas in motion—it is the process of transmitting power, pressure or motion by means of gaseous force. In modern industrial and defense systems, pneumatic power is created by a pump or compressor much as a generator creates electric power and is transmitted through tubing or hoses. The medium used is compressed air under pressure as high as 3,000 pounds per square inch. If rotary motion is needed the gas is forced through a pneumatic turbine or motor. If linear motion or force is needed, the gas acts as a ram or pneumatic cylinder.

In September 1963, the university professor (who continued to be Thurber's chief executive) hired Thurber's first production manager. Mr. Charles Brown, formerly employed at the Dayton factory of Thurber's chief competitor, to improve the manufacturing operation.

Meanwhile Gothic sales had increased from $110.7 million in 1956 to $158.2 million, the highest in history, in 1963. But net earnings in 1963 equaled $3 per share which was $.35 to $.50 less per share than it had been for many years.

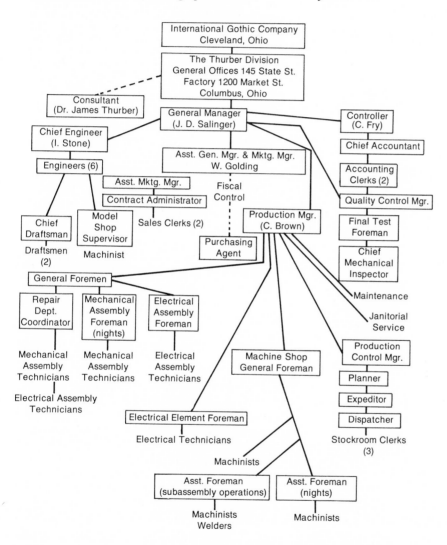

Figure 1. Thurber Division, International Gothic Co. Organizational Chart

As a result of this and several major management changes, Thurber found itself under increasing pressures to improve its operating situation. The long-time chairman of Gothic retired in 1963 after 37 years of company service. In addition to a new chairman, a new Gothic president and a new Gothic vice president for the Aircraft Products group of divisions were also appointed. At Thurber, the founder voluntarily relinquished his post as line executive in January, 1964.

Since Gothic had taken over, many new instrument models had been introduced and well accepted. For instance, in 1963 a very promising model for use in ground-testing rocket engine components was developed. Prices of Thurber products currently range for $200 to $700, with a few as high as $2,000. Due to a major change in production to manufacture parts previously purchased, the number of Thurber employees had increased from 79 in March 1963, to 144 in July, 1964. Of those 106 were nonsalaried and 11 were salaried. Up until six months ago, all activities had been carried out in a separate building, production personnel did not run off the stencils, handle the mail, and furnish an employee part-time for accounting as they had done previously.

The Immediate Situation

On August 6, 1964, after having been in the hospital for eight weeks Thurber's general manager, Mr. J. D. Salinger,[2] returned to his office. Immediately he called in the assistant general manager (and marketing manager) Mr. William Golding, to consider the current state of company affairs. During this discussion, Mr. Golding said:

Our really acute problem is our production department. Information should flow out from production to sales to customers regarding the status of the jobs. It is our normal selling practice to quote the customer a price whereupon he may place an order immediately or within the next 60-90 days. In the sales-engineering-planning stages the order is under complete control but once it gets into the factory, control is nonexistent. If anything happens to the order in the factory, there is no feedback of such information to the sales force. For instance, if jobs run into production difficulties which might necessitate more engineering, literally nothing is done to keep the sales force informed. There have been numerous situations where jobs have been stopped for over two months; the only way the sales force finds out is when the customer complains.

Even then we can't always pacify the customer because we may not be able to track down the job in the factory for three or four days. Besides taking an inordinate amount of the time of a small sales force to find the job, even when found there is still the problem of trying to establish when delivery will be made. If we want to stay in business, we must at least take our key orders and expedite them.[3] Even so, we continue to run the grave risk of permanently alienating our other customers.

We must keep in mind [Mr. Golding continued] our tremendous growth in the face of the increasing competitiveness of our industry. In the almost five years since Gothic came in and you and I started here, Thurber has grown over five times in annual sales going from $.4 million to $2 million despite increasing severe price competition. It used to be that only one instrument specification would be offered by a particular company; now some six or seven companies do.

___

[2]Before becoming the first general manager in 1962, Mr. Salinger had been chief engineer.

[3]The maximum delivery time on a government order is 120 days.

We face direct price competition on every job today. Consequently, our pricing must be based upon:

1. What has the instrument cost us in the past?
2. What economics can we make in the future?

Nowadays we use the *slide rule*[4] to pare off costs in the hope that we can come in with a price that will secure the order. It used to be that if you were 10% to 20% off on a bid it wasn't so important since you could adjust on the following order. This is not so today; instead every cent counts. There is presently a great need for more accurate cost information. Formerly the cost information that was available often really wasn't utilized.

I reiterate, we simply must be competitive costwise these days. Four years ago there were two or three firms sharing a $10 million sales market. Nowadays there are fifteen companies cutting up a $20 million sales market. And of these companies, two out of three are extremely capable.

It used to be that a customer had to stick with you. Now if he doesn't get the price and service he wants, there are any number of competent firms waiting in line to take the business. McNamara's cost cutting influence is felt all the way down the line. Another thing is that we must now bid to a much more precise set of specifications. All of these things influence our cost consciousness.

Our accounting department is working very hard. I am confident we will be getting better information from them but production must help them out.

We have helped out production by giving them many more large orders. The stuff they are making this summer is all this way. To make 800 of the same thing has been a rarity around here; last summer we had only 400 of this order. Sales have been very successful in increasing the size of orders from Republic and Douglas and others.

For example, last year we got an order for 50 instruments. This year we got an order for 300. All of this makes for many economies but it all hinges on how production is handled.

As a company, our competitive advantage is engineering. In engineering, we are rated tops in the industry. In sales, we are considered as good as we ought to be perhaps.[5] It is commonplace for the industry to describe us as the firm that can make wonderful instruments if you can wait long enough for them. The word is that you can order with two months' quote but it will run a year or more before you get delivery.

We brought Brown in last fall to solve our production problems and I am still hopeful that he can solve them, given time.

After lunching with Mr. Golding, Mr. Salinger called a haggard-looking Mr. Brown into his office and asked him to report on Thurber production. Charlie Brown said:

In order to stay in business nowadays, J. D., you must "chop away at price" and take marginal orders since "pickings are slim." Salesmen "clutch at every straw" and pick up "garbage" in the way of orders. Meantime overhead keeps going up. . . .

Mr. Salinger interrupted to point out that that was "the nature of their beast."

Well, anyway production is caught in a squeeze to produce more economically and standardize products more while the product is perpetually in the state of being improved. Last month, by actual count, we were producing some 42 models (out of a possible 55 models) each with some four to eight variations.

---

[4]Mr. Golding is an MIT graduate.

[5]The company sells through: 1) manufacturers' agents and 2) telephone calls to customers. Manufacturers' agents are reasonably loyal to company if company is competitive in price and delivery.

Another aspect of this is the size of the order. It is damn difficult trying to schedule production when the typical order has been two or three pieces. Ten pieces in an order is unusual and an 800-piece order like we have now is a rarity. And to complicate all of this now we face a shorter delivery schedule. Nowadays, if it takes more than 60 days' delivery time the customers go elsewhere.

When I came here we had a backlog of over a million dollars in orders while we were shipping orders out at the rate of $100,000 per month. On June 1, (1954) we had $450,000 of back orders—a sharp reduction from last September (1963)—but some $300,000 of this couldn't be scheduled until late August or September. Some of the latter will be canceled before they can be produced while the one-third which can be scheduled is insufficient production for our current quarter. The major sales effort is on government-oriented companies such as Martin, Fairchild, and Republic. The little customers, such as the universities, are neglected and go elsewhere. But the government-oriented company contracts usually turn out to be long-range jobs which leaves a lack of immediate jobs to earn current profits.[6]

We still operate on two nominal eight-hour shifts, which really comes down to a shift-and-a-half since only the first shift is a full shop. We still have our problems with the night shift too. I was called to the phone at 3:30 this morning (after having put in a 15-hour day here yesterday) by the night foreman needing papers so he could ship out production to meet our closing deadline. Naturally nobody in accounting was available at that time.[7]

One must also keep in mind the complete reformation that production has undergone since my arrival. When I came in September, production purchased 70% of the parts; nowadays, we purchase about 7%. In short, we have converted an assembly shop into a truly producing one.

We still have to cope with our special inventory problem. We may not have any need for a certain item for an entire year, yet suddenly in a single day the engineers want a dozen. There are the 55 models with up to 10 variations apiece—I know I'm biased from the production point of view—but it's a real painful situation. . . .

I have worked out rather carefully that it takes 70 days on the average to produce an instrument with 60 days the absolute rock bottom minimum. Yet in order to get the order the salesman will say, "I'll write it for 60 days, but I promise verbally to get it to you within 45 days." So, at the end of 45 days the customer will start inquiring and there never was any possibility that the cycle would be less than 60 days. This makes for very poor customer relationships. But you know instruments are not the type of product one can "crash" out. No clear-cut policy about this sort of thing has been worked out here as is true of so many of our arrangements. They should be in writing.

As Mr. Salinger started to speak, Brown hurried on:

Yes, I can shave this 60-day figure on some jobs if I want to have a hand-carry job, but how many hand-carry jobs can I have at once out of the 1,000 jobs on the floor?

And to top it all off, there is absolutely no cost control. The accounting situation around here has often caused me to seriously think of giving up in despair. Presently an average markup is applied

---

[6]In a year, the total number of Thurber customers is about 200 but 15 customers account for 70% of sales, 8 for 60%, and currently 2 for 40%.

[7]Each accounting month ends on the 20th so that accounting can prepare reports to be sent to Cleveland by the end of the month. The following reports are sent monthly: Comparative Balance Sheet (21 items), Details of Property, Plant & Equipment and Intangible Assets (25 items), Comparative Summary of Operations (24 items), Comparative

Summary of Operating Results (30 items), Cost of Production and Burden Details. The applied burden normally is about 40% of the actual burden.

to a job whether it costs $45 or $450. I can't understand why we don't get a standard cost system in here. But of course, I am leery about using such information to quote jobs since we have gone from buy decisions to make decisions so recently.

All the pricing is still being done by hand by production. We do use the IBM reports and we don't have the situation we had when I came. But still there may be a two-or-three-week lag with sometimes as many as 1,000 documents waiting to be priced.

Under our accounting system, if we ship out 10 pieces from a 20-piece order accounting will hold out costs until the entire order is completed, which plays havoc with both the inventories and the cost of goods sold. The Work-in-Process account is also off because if the quantity added hasn't been priced it is listed regardless, so you have a situation where total quantities are compared to total partial prices. This results in only one correct balance, which is one of quantities not of dollars.

The biggest problem around here is "people who don't know they don't know." Accounting around here is a headquarters function. The controller got his mandate from Cleveland and reports and budgets his time accordingly.

I have gotten into a number of heated discussions with them. If you ask for how many items on an order are left on the floor, where a partial shipment has been made, their answer is: "Look at the packing slips." Their attitude is "This is accounting; you are production." If we are two screws off in the inventory, it is up to us to find them despite the fact that the accountants were the people who set up the system and made the counting errors in the first place.

The accounting department never has time to meet to discuss our mutual problems. I can understand that accounting is hard pressed at the end of the month but the controller surely could arrange to spend a few days with us in the middle of the month. Fry is not a factory accountant, but instead is an auditor. His approach too often

is that the Navy way is the right way. He rejects our criticisms yet he never gets over to see how we do things. A few trips to the factory would help him (as much as us) by providing him with some on-the-job training regarding our stockroom and production scheduling.

Late in the afternoon, Mr. Salinger went over to talk to Mr. Fry whom he found out with his staff completing a payroll. While waiting, Mr. Salinger idly observed on a table in back of Fry's desk a number of Navy souvenirs, and three accounting books, a Montgomery and two Finney and Millers.

When Fry came in, Salinger asked how the controller compared his present position to being a supply officer on a ship.

Really quite similar [Fry replied] except here you don't have to consider the personal life of the men as much as you did in the Navy, but the general dealing with people is the same.

The controller mentioned he sometimes felt rather isolated in his job—that he "had nobody to talk to" and that the Gothic controller had only been able to manage two visits totaling a day and a half in the year and a half since Fry had come to Thurber.

Our problems have continued while you were away. We still depend upon production to furnish us our information for about everything we do. For example, if production doesn't send over the information when they start a job, we can't open a job card to accumulate costs. If we don't receive information to open a job card, it is possible to pick up the discrepancy from the daily labor time cards but this is extremely awkward.

There was a problem with partial shipments also. If we ship out units (where overruns had been made), all the costs would continue in Work-in-Process most likely. I am now planning to minimize this in two ways: by taking a monthly check on the large inventory items, some 25 or 30 items, and also hereafter we will divide jobs into sublots according to the anticipated shipping dates.

Fry reminded Salinger that the practice of overruns (units produced for a job above sale order units) to provide for a high rejection rate had resulted in inflating inventory. Consequently this practice was being discontinued and this would eliminate much of the partial shipments problem since all the units produced would be shipped.

When Mr. Salinger asked why jobs weren't closed promptly in the first place, Fry gave two explanations:

1. Accounting has never mentioned sales and cost of sales as there is no pressure from Gothic to do so.
2. Production is responsible for sending over job close-out information. Such information is usually not sent promptly and sometimes not at all.

The controller reported that he was continuing to work with the IBM Service Bureau Corporation in order to have all reports furnished promptly.[8] He mentioned that he had to deny Brown's request for a Work-in-Process report on a weekly basis because the cost would be prohibitive. In considering the possibility of a standard cost system some day, he had established cost centers. He concluded by mentioning that with the division's increase in business, his accounting staff was handicapped since production was doing less than they had done previously for accounting despite the increase in production employees.

Requirements

1. Diagram the historical development of accounting controls for Thurber indicating how specific needs were satisfied by specific controls.

2. Giving particular attention as how these recommendations should be implemented what should Mr. Salinger recommend, if anything, to:
   - Mr. Fry
   - Mr. Brown
   - Mr. Golding
   - International Gothic Company

3. Is Mr. Fry's role the same as that of the executive in charge of any staff function, ignoring technical differences?

---

[8]The following are made weekly: Payroll register, deduction register and year-to-date earnings totals; monthly: Work-in-Process detail and summary, closed jobs, closed work and inventory reports, purchase balance listings, and direct-indirect labor report; and quarterly, the model analysis.

Wallace Tool Industries

Case

James Brock recently became the controller of Wallace Tool Industries, Inc., following the unexpected death of the former controller. Brock has been employed by a certified public accounting firm for the past five years, and he terminated his employment with this firm last month to accept the controller position. The president of Wallace Tool Industries, Inc., stated that Brock's diversified background and experience should bring needed, increased competence for coping with the firm's problems.

The president of the firm discussed with Brock the findings of the recent annual audit. Specifically, the audit manager of the certified public accounting firm performing the audit expressed concern over the increase in size of finished goods inventory. The president said that he had discussed this problem with the previous controller, and he (the former controller) had worked a few days in analyzing the inventory position based on a sample. The president said that he was sure Brock's secretary (who was also employed by the former

Reprinted with permission from Thomas Prince, *Information Systems for Management Planning and Control* (Homewood, Ill.: Richard D. Irwin, Inc.), pp. 187–196.

controller) knew where the working papers were for the inventory study.

The president asked Brock to complete the inventory study and to take into consideration the question: "Would a reduction in inventory result in a reduction in customer services and extend delivery dates?"

The Company

Brock was already familiar with the history of the Wallace Tool Industries, Inc.—how the firm had grown from its small two-man shop to its present size of almost $3 million of sales in a period of less than fifteen years. It seemed to be the consensus of opinion by top management that Wallace Tool Industries, Inc., had almost reached its "fair share of the market" in terms of new customers, and some of the key officers stated that emphasis should be shifted from the new customer area to trying to expand the volume of services to existing customers. Furthermore, recent changes in the financial market necessitated that accounts receivable and inventory levels be reduced to a minimum.

Wallace Tool Industries, Inc., designs, develops, manufactures, and sells industrial tools. Currently, there are 2,647 different stock items which on December 31, 1963 had a cost of $1,042,137. About 80 percent of the inventory is stored at the home office warehouse in Chicago, with the remainder of the inventory located in five regional warehouses: Boston, Cincinnati, Dallas, Denver, and San Francisco. Annual sales are $2,850,000.

Perpetual inventory records are maintained on a manual basis for each item of finished goods inventory including the identification of place of storage. Another set of records is manually maintained in production and control for the purpose of providing the appropriate information for manufacturing operations including the scheduling of production.

Previous Study

Brock's secretary located the former controller's working papers for the inventory study. These papers contained:

1. An analysis of finished goods inventory turnover for stocked tools (Table 1).

2. An analysis of finished goods inventory for stocked tools based on the working papers for the December 31, 1963, physical inventory count with cost extensions (Table 2).

3. A random sample of finished goods inventory with an identification of the number of units on hand at each of the six warehouses

---

Table 1. Wallace Tool Industries, Inc.

Finished Goods Inventory Turnover
for Stocked Tools for 1963

Annual sales for stocked tools	$2,850,000
Cost of sales (40 percent)	X .40
	$1,140,000
Average finished goods inventory	
Beginning	$ 826,715
Ending	1,042,137
	$1,868,852
Average	$ 934,426

$$\frac{\text{Cost of Sales}}{\text{Average Inventory}} = \frac{\$1,140,000}{\$934,426} = 1.22$$

Note: The tool industry surveys indicate that the finished goods inventory turnover ranges from 2.0 to 5.0, with 3.4 being an average of these surveys.

Table 2. Wallace Tool Industries, Inc.

An Analysis of Finished Goods Inventory for Stocked Tools for 1963

Number of Items	Percent of Total	Percent of Total Inventory Value
662	25%	76%
397	15	15
1,588	60	9
2,647	100%	100%

Number of Items	Percent of Total	Unit Cost
318	12%	Over $.50
873	33	$.50–$.25
1,456	55	Under $.25
2,647	100%	

Table 2 is based on the working papers for the December 31, 1963 physical inventory count with cost extensions.

as of December 31, 1963, and an identification of the number of units sold from each warehouse during the past six months (Table 3).

4. An analysis of the above random sample including the cost, sales, gross profit, and carrying cost for finished goods inventory (Table 4).

5. An analysis of 697 orders shipped from the home office directly to customers for the period November 1-10, 1963. This exhibit compares the cumulative percent of the number of items promised for delivery within varying number of days with the cumulative percent of deliveries of time (Table 5).

6. An analysis of the above orders indicating the number of days elapsing between the promised delivery date and the actual delivery date (Table 6).

7. An indication of the lead time on the above orders, in other words, the actual number of days from order day to delivery date (Table 7).

Table 3. Wallace Tool Industries, Inc.

Inventory and Sales Information for a Random Sample of Units

		Chicago		Cincinnati		Denver		San Francisco		Dallas		Boston	
Number	Cost	Inventory 12/31/63	Sales for 6 Months	Inventory 12/31/63	Sales for 6 Months	Inventory 12/31/63	Sales for 6 Months	Inventory 12/31/63	Sales for 6 Months	Inventory 12/31/63	Sales for 6 Months	Inventory 12/31/63	Sales for 6 Months
WTI–													
421610........24¢		120	65	140	—	210	—	—	—	—	—	—	—
622612........72		704	71	—	—	—	—	11	3	70	28	47	—
532621........38		320	460	198	—	40	—	65	—	43	—	54	—
422636........10		1,450	225	114	—	102	—	—	—	—	—	—	—
621621........24		6,520	12	510	62	230	—	104	—	65	—	100	—
846614........46		4,210	1,236	—	—	—	—	—	—	—	—	—	—
231617........46		2,620	4,172	450	310	250	—	120	—	96	23	47	—
423632........ 8		3,605	—	140	24	52	—	89	—	—	—	75	—
474612........98		1,850	1,630	350	278	131	—	100	—	75	—	—	—
842624........20		2,210	265	503	—	140	545	25	—	48	—	—	—
622642........16		93	62	110	—	195	—	—	—	—	—	—	—
533512........26		578	—	50	—	—	—	800	600	—	—	650	—
422721........30		1,742	78	259	—	—	—	52	—	25	—	55	—
544721........24		1,247	122	30	—	300	110	25	—	75	15	—	—
832738........20		806	218	—	—	—	—	74	25	—	—	—	—

Table 4. Wallace Tool Industries, Inc.
Analysis of Inventory and Sales Information for a Random Sample of Units

Number	Cost	Chicago Inventory 12/31/63	Chicago Sales for 6 Months	Cincinnati Inventory 12/31/63	Cincinnati Sales for 6 Months	Denver Inventory 12/31/63	Denver Sales for 6 Months	San Francisco Inventory 12/31/63	San Francisco Sales for 6 Months	Dallas Inventory 12/31/63	Dallas Sales for 6 Months	Boston Inventory 12/31/63	Boston Sales for 6 Months
WTI													
421610	24¢	120	65	140	—	210	—	—	—	—	—	—	—
		a 28.80	d 39.00	a 33.60	—	a 50.40	—	—	—	—	—	—	—
		b 1.44	e 23.40	b 1.68	—	b 2.52	—	—	—	—	—	—	—
		c 2.88		c 3.36		c 5.04		—					
622612	72¢	704	71	—	—	—	—	11	3	70	28	47	—
		a 506.88	d 127.80	—	—	—	—	a 7.92	d 5.40	a 50.40	d 50.40	a 33.84	—
		b 25.34	e 76.68	—	—	—	—	b .40	e 3.24	b 2.52	e 30.24	b 1.69	—
		c 50.69		—		—		c .79		c 5.04		c 3.38	
532621	38¢	320	460	198	—	40	—	65	—	48	—	54	—
		a 121.60	d 437.00	a 75.24	—	a 15.20	—	a 24.70	—	a 18.24	—	a 20.52	—
		b 6.08	e 262.20	b 3.76	—	b .76	—	b 1.24	—	b .91	—	b 1.03	—
		c 12.16		c 7.52		c 1.52		c 2.47		c 1.82		c 2.05	
422636	10¢	1,450	225	114	—	102	—	—	—	—	—	—	—
		a 145.00	d 56.25	a 11.40	—	a 10.20	—	—	—	—	—	—	—
		b 7.25	e 33.75	b .57	—	b .51	—	—	—	—		—	
		c 14.50		c 1.14		c 1.02		—					
621621	24¢	6,520	12	510	62	230	—	104	—	65	—	100	—
		a 1,556.80	d 7.20	a 122.40	d 37.20	a 55.20	—	a 24.96	—	a 15.60	—	a 24.00	—
		b 78.24	e 4.32	b 6.12	e 22.32	b 2.76	—	b 1.25	—	b .78	—	b 1.20	—
		c 156.48		c 12.24		c 5.52		c 2.50		c 1.56		c 2.40	
846614	46¢	4.210	1.236	—	—	—	—	—	—	—	—	—	—
		a 1,936.60	d 1,421.40	—		—	—	—	—	—	—	—	—
		b 96.83	e 852.84	—		—	—	—		—		—	
		c 193.66		—		—		—		—		—	
231617	46¢	2,620	4,172	450	310	250	—	120	—	96	23	47	—
		a 1,205.20	d 4,797.80	a 207.00	d 356.50	a 115.00	d —	a 55.20	—	a 44.16	d 26.45	a 21.62	—
		b 60.26	e 2,878.68	b 10.35	e 213.90	b 5.75	e —	b 2.76	—	b 2.21	e 15.87	b 1.08	—
		c 120.52		c 20.70		c 11.50		c 5.52		c 4.42		c 2.16	
423632	8¢	3,605	—	140	24	52	—	89	—	—	—	75	—
		a 288.40	—	a 11.20	d 4.80	a 4.16	—	a 7.12	—	—	—	a 6.00	—
		b 14.42	—	b .56	e 2.88	b .21	—	b .36	—	—	—	b .30	—
		c 28.84		c 1.12		c .42		c .71		—		c .60	
174612	98¢	1,850	1,630	350	278	131	—	100	—	75	—	—	—
		a 1,813.00	d 3,993.50	a 343.00	d 681.10	a 128.38	—	a 98.00	—	a 73.50	—	—	—
		b 90.65	e 2,396.10	b 17.15	e 408.66	b 6.42	—	b 4.90	—	b 3.68	—	—	—
		c 181.30		c 34.30		c 12.84		c 9.80		c 7.35		—	
842624	20¢	2,210	265	503	—	140	545	25	—	48	—	—	—
		a 442.00	d 132.50	a 100.00	—	a 28.00	d 272.50	a 5.00	—	a 9.60	—	—	—
		b 22.10	e 79.50	b 5.03	—	b 1.40	e 163.50	b .25	—	b .48	—	—	—
		c 44.20		c 10.06		c 2.80		c .50		c .96		—	
622642	16¢	93	62	110	—	195	—	—	—	—	—	—	—
		a 14.88	d 24.80	a 17.60	—	a 31.20	—	—	—	—	—	—	—
		b .74	e 14.88	b .88	—	b 1.56	—	—	—	—	—	—	—
		c 1.49		c 1.76		c 3.12		—		—		—	
533512	26¢	578	—	50	—	—	—	800	600	—	—	650	—

Table 4. Continued

Number	Cost	Chicago Inventory 12/31/63	Chicago Sales for 6 Months	Cincinnati Inventory 12/31/63	Cincinnati Sales for 6 Months	Denver Inventory 12/31/63	Denver Sales for 6 Months	San Francisco Inventory 12/31/63	San Francisco Sales for 6 Months	Dallas Inventory 12/31/63	Dallas Sales for 6 Months	Boston Inventory 12/31/63	Boston Sales for 6 Months
		a 150.28	—	a 13.00	—	—	—	a 208.00	d 390.00	—	—	a 169.00	—
		b 7.51	—	b .65	—	—	—	b 10.40	e 234.00	—	—	b 8.45	
		c 15.03		c 1.30		—		c 20.80		—		c 16.90	
422721........30¢		1,742	78	259	—	—	—	52	—	25	—	55	—
		a 522.60	d 58.50	a 77.70	—	—	—	a 15.60	—	a 7.50	—	a 16.50	—
		b 26.13	e 35.10	b 3.89	—	—	—	b .78	—	b .38	—	b .83	—
		c 52.26		c 7.77		—		c 1.56		c .75		c 1.65	
544721........24¢		1,247	122	30	—	300	110	25	—	75	15	—	—
		a 299.28	d 73.20	a 7.20	—	a 72.00	d 66.00	a 6.00	—	a 18.00	d 9.00	—	—
		b 14.96	e 43.92	b .36	—	b 3.60	e 39.60	b .30	—	b .90	e 5.40	—	—
		c 29.93		c .72		c 7.20		c .60		c 1.80		—	
832738........20¢		806	218	—	—	—	—	74	25	—	—	—	—
		a 161.20	d 109.00	—	—	—	—	a 14.80	d 12.50	—	—	—	—
		b 8.06	e 65.40	—	—	—	—	b .74	e 7.50	—	—	—	—
		c 16.12		—		—		c 1.48		—		—	

Symbol a represents the cost of inventory (unit cost X number of units on hand).
Symbol b is an estimate of the carrying cost of inventory based on an estimated annual cost of 10 percent of cost (since this information is for six months, 5 percent of cost is used).
Symbol c is also an estimate of the carrying cost of inventory based on an estimated annual cost of 20 percent.
Symbol d represents sales (sales price X number of units sold) which was based on the assumption that cost of stocked tools was 40 percent of selling price.
Symbol e is the gross profit on sales.

Recap of Table 4

	Total Inventory Cost of Sample	Total Sales of Sample for 6 Months	Gross Profit on Sales of Sample for 6 Months	6-Month Carrying Cost of Inventory Based on Annual Estimate of Cost 10 Percent	20 Percent
Chicago	$ 9,200.52	$11,277.95	$6,766.77	$460.01	$ 920.06
Cincinnati	1,019.94	1,079.60	647.76	51.00	101.99
Denver	509.74	338.50	203.10	25.49	50.98
San Francisco	467.30	407.90	244.74	23.38	46.73
Dallas	237.00	85.85	51.51	11.85	23.70
Boston	291.48	—	—	14.58	29.14
Total	$11,725.98	$13,189.80	$7,913.88	$586.32	$1,172.60

Table 5. Wallace Tool Industries, Inc.

Customer Service—Promise Dates

Number of Days from Order Day That Shipping Date Is Promised	Cumulative Percent of Orders Promised for Shipment within Specified Days	Cumulative Percent of Orders Shipped on Time
1	30	19
2	36	24
3	55	36
4	60	40
5	62	41
6	64	42
7	69	46
8	72	48
9	74	49
10	80	54
11	82	55
12	84	56
13	86	57
14	100	69

Table 5 is based on an analysis of 697 orders shipped from the home office directly to customers for the period November 1–10, 1963.

Table 6. Wallace Tool Industries, Inc.

Customer Service—Lateness of Orders

Number of Days after Promised Shipping Time	Cumulative Percent of Orders Shipped within Specified Days from Promised Time
0	69
1	90
2	82
3	85
4	88
5	90
6	92
7	94
8	95
9	96
10	97
11	98
12	99
Over 12	100

Table 6 is based on an analysis of 697 orders shipped from the home office directly to customers for the period November 1–10, 1963.

Table 7. Wallace Tool Industries, Inc.

Customer Service—Lead-Time Analysis

Lead Time—Days from Order Date to Shipment Date	Cumulative Percent of Total Orders That Were Shipped within Specified days from Order Day
1	28
2	33
3	51
4	58
5	60
6	62
7	67
8	70
9	73
10	78
11	80
12	83
13	85
14	95
Over 14	100

Table 7 is based on an analysis of 697 orders shipped from the home office directly to customers for the period November 1–10, 1963.

Chapter 12

Auditing the
Marketing System

In most businesses, the marketing system is the most critical management system in determining the success or failure of the firm. No matter how effective the production system, if its output cannot be sold at an adequate price and cash collected from that sale, the firm will not be able to survive.

In order to fulfill its function, marketing management must undertake a variety of responsibilities. First, it must be deeply involved in the strategic planning of the firm. Decisions as to what lines of business to enter, what products to develop or drop, and the extent of resource commitment to various classes of goods produced and services rendered all are predicated on estimates of demand and market structure, which are the primary responsibility of marketing executives.

Additionally, within the framework of the firm's strategic plans marketing managers must develop and implement operating plans for selling goods. This requires a determination of the policies to be followed in promoting goods, in the techniques of pricing, in the organization of the marketing force, in the selection of adequate channels of distribution, and in the means by which products can be serviced after sale. The implementation of these plans must then be monitored and variations from plan reported and acted upon. Sometimes this will require an updating of the plan while in other cases specific corrective steps may be taken.

Finally, the marketer's job is not complete when he has customers ready to buy. He must also recognize that the firm will only benefit from a sale if cash is ultimately collected from the customer, and accordingly the credit function must be performed. This includes the setting of payment terms (which are really part of price), the evaluation of the debt-paying capacity of customers and potential customers who wish to buy on credit, and the follow-up with customers through appropriate procedures until cash is received. While some of these credit functions are conventionally performed by personnel outside the sales department, they remain an integral part of the marketing cycle of the business.

The Marketing-Information System

The marketing-information system must provide information to assist management in performing its various functions and in monitoring the results of its activities. In order to achieve this result, a considerable variety of data must be gathered, from sources both inside and outside the firm. The kinds of data required will depend very significantly upon the nature of the firm and its markets; it is therefore impossible to describe the "typical" information system, but some generalizations can be suggested.

In the first place, the needed information can be classified both by purpose and by source of data. Information is required for strategic planning, operational planning, monitoring results, and for performing the credit and collection function in the business. Such data may come from external sources or from within the firm, and in the latter case they may be generated by the conventional financial-information system of the firm or may represent nonfinancial data gathered directly for marketing purposes.

Strategic Planning

The information needed for strategic planning largely originates outside the firm. Top management, which is primarily responsible for the strategic plan, requires data on the economy, forecasts of population and income trends, and long-range supply-and-demand forecasts for the products or services which the firm produces and may produce. Such information will enable management to estimate the impact of new products and external competitive forces on the firm's success and to identify areas where new markets offer the potential for future profitable growth. None of these data is readily available from the conventional financial-information system; yet they must be developed if strategic planning is to be accomplished in the most productive fashion.

Valuable data for strategic marketing planning also arise in the accounting records of the firm, particularly when the strategic plan envisages some continuation of past activities. Data on historical sales and price trends are useful in this respect, as are cost data that may be essential in forecasting future costs relevant to the strategic plan. Finally, the non-financial-information systems of the firm may include data on productive capacity and capability as well as on human resources available for future activities; these are essential inputs for a strategic plan.

Most of the data required for strategic planning will be accumulated on an *ad hoc* basis at the various points in time that a strategic plan is developed. In the average company, too many of these data are developed only when a plan is being prepared. There is much to be said for the continuing accumulation of strategically relevant economic data and the preparation of up-to-date forecasts by company economists. Additional regular data, interpretation, and forecasts may be obtained from economic-consulting firms. The economics departments of many large companies do perform such a service, but their ability to communicate it effectively varies widely.

Operational planning is the function that develops specific plans for the fulfillment of the strategic objectives that are set forth in the strategic-planning process. Such plans are developed frequently and are generally revised on a continuing basis.

Operational Planning

In the marketing area these plans are of many types. A forecast of sales by product line and geographic area in units and dollars is usually a major end product of the operational planning process. The development of such a forecast requires planning the sales effort within the framework of the expected economic environment. Plans must be made for advertising and direct-selling techniques, the forms of customer and sales incentives to be used, distribution channels for the product, the organization of the sales effort within the firm, and pricing policies to be followed, including warranties and terms of sale.

In the large company, many different managers will be involved with this planning process as well as with its implementation; accordingly, the various plans must be coordinated to produce certainty that they are internally consistent within the marketing area, within the firm's operational planning in the areas of production, financing, personnel, and procurement, and at each of the many interfaces of these areas.

Since operational plans are updated frequently as circumstances change, continuing data accumulation and information outputs are required for the adequate performance of this planning function. Many of these data will be developed from sources external to the firm. One group of data will be related to the routine monitoring of economic indicators for signals of economic changes in the economy and, more specifically, in the markets served. If the firm has an economics department, it may be assigned the responsibility for obtaining and interpreting such economic data, and developing revised short-term forecasts of economic activity. Included in these forecasts will normally be data on general consumer demand for the kinds of products the company sells. In addition, in certain areas of the economy, data which may be valuable regarding consumer buying intentions are gathered by external groups.

In addition to economic data developed by monitoring outside the firm, important information may be obtained from an intelligence system specifically designed to monitor the actions of customers and competitors in the marketplace. Normally, such a system is the essence of the firm's marketing-research activity, which may be established as a separate department or included in the normal product organization of the firm.

The market intelligence system will include such routine activities as subscribing to trade journals and systematically observing advertising efforts of competitors. It may also include the accumulation of data on pricing and other marketing activities of competitors, and consumer response to the activities of both the competitors and the investigating firm itself. These kinds of data may be developed by the field sales force of the firm, by a special market-research group doing interviews and comparative shopping, or by both.

In many firms, marketing research is still done primarily on an individual-project basis, but increasingly a continuing data-accumulation system is being established in recognition of the continuing information requirements relating to the marketplace.

Many consumer-oriented enterprises may employ, in addition to the firm's own intelligence system, the services of an outside market-research organization to gather from consumers data about brand acceptance, consumer desires, and advertising impact. Such data may be obtained, on either an *ad hoc* or continuing basis, solely for the particular company, or they may be obtained on a broader scale and made available by subscription to many customers. Examples of the latter are the data developed by A. C. Neilsen and Company about the activities of 12,000 retail establishments, and the national consumer study performed by Audits and Surveys which summarizes the results of many thousands of continual interviews performed annually.

Operational planning also requires a large amount of data that are generated from within the firm. Many of these are available from the conventional financial-information system, although detail varies greatly from firm to firm. Virtually all systems provide sales-analysis data that break sales down by district, product, salesman, or other responsibility unit. Information about direct-marketing costs such as advertising and selling expense is also routinely developed. Adequate information on the costs of physical distribution and customer service is less frequently found, but does exist in some present accounting systems. In general, the adequacy of accounting data in the marketing area is proportional to the communication that exists between marketing and financial executives.

Beyond data directly related to the sales activity, the accounting system provides much cost information required in the pricing process and in determining the areas of sales which are most profitable and should be emphasized. While there is considerable disagreement about the role of cost in pricing decisions, it is generally agreed that data about costs and cost-and-profit behavior under various volume conditions are a valuable input to the pricing process. Where price justification is required, accounting data play a vital role—whether to mute public criticism or to meet legal requirements such as the Robinson Patman Act, which forbids discriminatory pricing not justified by cost differentials.

In addition to accounting data, various forms of nonfinancial marketing data from within the firm will also be required in the operational-planning process. Information on the physical volume of goods sold, the time between order and delivery, the degree of capacity utilized, and other similar data would be important elements in planning. Additionally, information about the demographic characteristics of customer groupings such as age, family status, and income levels may be important to the marketing effort. While this discussion has not been exhaustive, it does indicate some of the classes of data that will be required in effectively planning the marketing operations of the firm.

In addition to planning, the firm's information system must provide a means by which operating results are monitored. External data can primarily be monitored by comparing the actual level of various economic indicators with those that had been forecast in developing the strategic and

Monitoring Results

operational plans. Variations can then be interpreted and plans changed where appropriate; for certain industries there may be particular economic danger signals which indicate the need for particular actions on the part of management.

The financial-information system conventionally develops a large amount of information useful to the monitoring function. Conventional reports should compare actual sales and marketing costs with those that had been anticipated, broken down by product and responsibility unit. These data are normally developed on both price and 'volume bases, so that an analysis of the reasons for variations from plan is possible, and are conventionally summarized in various forms of exception reports to management, highlighting areas where attention is required. In addition to such general reports there may be a number of pieces of information developed to monitor results of specific marketing activities or programs. For example, there may be data developed to measure the effectiveness of a particular advertising campaign or of a special offer.

Finally, various forms of nonfinancial information are required to monitor the marketing system. Probably the most important of these are customer-service data: complaints and other customer responses that are accumulated and reported. In this connection it is important that the information system reflect the extent to which the firm is meeting the promises of its salesmen, as to both time and quality, and the way in which customer complaints are handled when they occur. In addition, data on product quality, number of sales personnel, adequacy of sales training, and other nonfinancial data may be developed as part of the monitoring process.

Credit and Collection

An additional set of data required for the marketing process is that associated with the credit and collection function of the firm. This may not be thought of as marketing data in the conventional sense, but it certainly relates to the basic selling-data cycle and must be considered within the marketing section of the business.

Those responsible for credit and collection must have economic data relevant to their function. Such data may include information as to economic trends affecting various industrial and geographic sectors of the economy. For example, credit granted to employees or firms in the construction industry may be in large part determined by expectations as to employment trends in that sector. Similarly, if economic indicators show potential weak spots, collection activities may be intensified in the expectation of more delinquencies.

In addition to macroeconomic data, credit granters must also obtain data on the individual customer who requests credit. These data may arise from specific questions asked the customer on a credit application, from data collected by salesmen from the customer, and from other credit-information channels such as banking institutions and credit-investigating firms.

Much information relevant to the credit function also arises from data generated within the firm. Past collection experience with customers is usually an important determinant of credit worthiness. Data on former customers who are not presently buying but who have good credit records may be a valuable promotional tool, as will data on current customers with additional credit capacity available.

In addition to data relevant to a specific customer's ability to pay, granters of credit need information on the cost structure of the firm and the marketing potential of various customers who are proposed. Credit worthiness is not an absolute characteristic but rather a probabilistic one, and the extent of risk that should be absorbed is a function of future sales potential and variable profit margin. Where variable cost is a small percentage of sales, for example, a high probability of loss can be profitably absorbed.

The firm's financial-information system must also produce such data necessary to effect collection as accurate accounts-receivable records and adequate documentation, as well as summary reports on the way in which the function is being performed. Such reports may include aging analyses of receivables, records of delinquencies and delinquencies restored to current status, accounts written off, dollars collected compared with plan, costs of collection, credit granting, and many others, depending upon the structure of the firm.

Organization of the Marketing-Information System

The above discussion of the various outputs of marketing-information systems indicates that the nature of the firm and its markets is the principal determinant of the kind of information needed. Certain reports and market data mentioned are primarily relevant to the firm dealing with a consumer market while others may be most appropriate for enterprises marketing industrial goods. The description above of "typical" information needs must have the same deficiencies as any general statement. Regardless of the marketing-information system's specific outputs, however, some generalizations can be made about its organization. In the first place, the marketing-information system is a part of the management system of the firm. Without an effective management organization, the marketing and other information generated cannot be used efficiently. Much of the structure of the marketing-information system is directly related to the structure of marketing organization. The marketing-management system includes a definition of organizational responsibilities and planning and control procedures that are established as the basic means of conducting its activities. The information needed by each of the many decision-making managers will depend upon his responsibilities; if the responsibilities are not well defined, neither can his information needs be.

Once a company has decided to hold its product managers responsible for sales, market share, and profit contribution, it has in fact specified the kind of information which they need and which higher levels of management need to control their operation. Without this definition, a good control system could not be set up regardless of the data-processing technology that is brought to bear. There is a tendency for corporate managers to associate a good information system with a computer on a cause-and-effect basis, rather than to see the computer solely as a sometimes-efficient tool within the framework of a logically defined system for information accumulation, processing, and presentation. If information quality is raised before systems and managerial quality is developed, the payoff from better information may not be obtained.

A second factor which must be recognized in observing and evaluating a marketing-information system is the requirement for information of many different types. This generally necessitates integrating functions that have traditionally been performed independently. Marketing-research, accounting, and economics departments have traditionally been independent "information fiefdoms," and they may not relish integration. Failure to integrate, however, makes it much more difficult for any logical and unified information system to be developed. A good information system integrates data of all types and does not separate responsibility for data according to whether they have a dollar sign in front or whether they originate within the firm.

Auditing the Marketing-Information System

The auditor of the marketing-information system must meet two objectives. First, he must determine whether or not the system is producing adequate relevant information to enable marketing managers to make the decisions necessary to run the business. Second, he must determine that the information being produced is reliable and that controls over the system are adequate to keep it that way.

In considering the adequacy and relevance of information, the auditor should first appraise the marketing function's plan of organization to see that responsibilities are defined and serve as a sound basis for the marketing-information system. He can then turn to a review of the information produced by the system.

An initial step in review of information is to obtain or examine copies of all statements and other information outputs which are regularly used in the marketing function; many of these data can be obtained from the accounting department, but other sources of information must also be explored. The auditor may then sit down with various representatives of the marketing group to determine how the system's information output is used. He should become certain of the reasons why information is presented in various forms and whether or not sufficient information is communicated for action on the part of the managers. In these interviews, he should also determine what information marketing managers think they need to perform their function adequately. If other forms of information are sought but not prepared, he should ascertain that in fact the data is not prepared and determine why this is the case.

On the basis of these interviews and considerable thought about the nature of the business and the marketing function, the auditor should draw some conclusions about whether or not the information generated is adequate for the purposes it purports to serve. In reviewing any information system the auditor must always bear in mind that as well as benefits, information has a cost, in terms of both the out-of-pocket outlays to accumulate it and the opportunity costs of the time involved in its use. The right amount of relevant information is therefore what is sought rather than the maximum amount. It may be that in some systems too much information is being presented or the wrong kind of information is being developed. Statements which are not being used or other outputs which do not seem related to management action may be clues to this situation. It may be also that some additional information would be useful but not of sufficient benefit to warrant the cost of accumulating it. It is unlikely, however, that the auditor will be able to mathematically demonstrate that in any system the optimum is being produced. He therefore must use his judgment in his evaluation of the adequacy and relevance of the information presented.

The second objective of the audit of the marketing-information system is to judge the reliability of its outputs. The first step is to determine the way in which the system's information is developed. The usual technique is to flowchart the system from the point where data first enter the firm to the information output that is received by the various managers. This is normally easier when the data inputs and outputs are related to the financial-information system of the firm, but other information-accumulation systems as well can be checked by this approach.

The basic financial-data cycle associated with the marketing function is shown in the three flow charts below, Figures 1 to 3, covering a transaction from the point where an order is received through the point where cash is paid to the firm. The cycle consists of the following major aspects:

1. order origination and processing, including credit authorization, pricing, discounts, delivery schedules, commissions;
2. order analysis;
3. coordination of order-entry process with information about inventory availability or production scheduling;
4. order editing to assure accuracy of order data and propriety of order-recording procedures;
5. order fulfillment, including the assembly, packing, and shipping of the order and the preparation of appropriate documents for invoice preparation;
6. sales-invoice preparation and recording of sale in sales journal, summary, or listing;
7. accounts-receivable posting and preparation of customer statements;
8. accounts-receivable aging and credit-collection and control procedures;
9. handling, recording, balancing, depositing, and summarizing of cash receipts;
10. sales analysis;
11. procedures for handling returned goods, price adjustments, invoice errors, write-offs, etc.

Techniques of Auditing

Once the system has been initially understood and flowcharted, tests must be undertaken to ascertain that it is operating as advertised, and efficiently so. To do this the auditor will select a number of documents which he will walk through the system to determine that company personnel are in fact processing the input and preparing the output according to the instructions provided by the company and the statements of company officials.

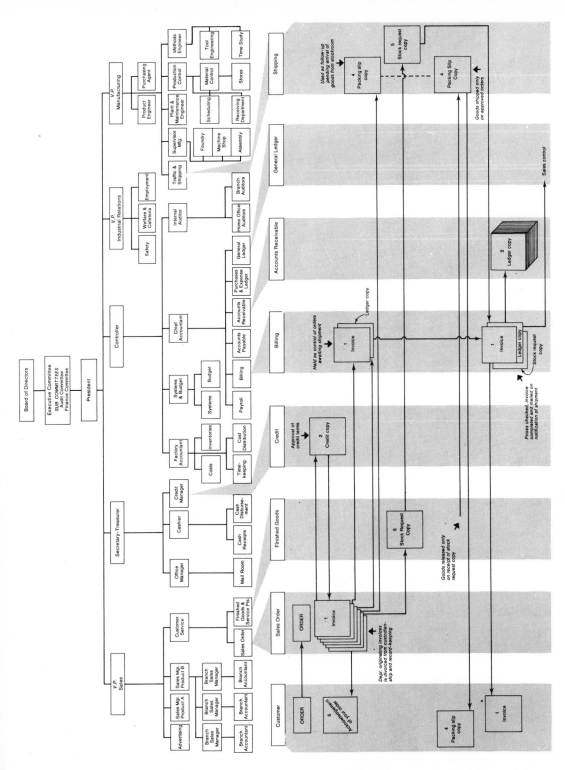

Figure 1. Sales. Procedural flow chart shown in relation to organization chart to portray the control obtained through segregation of functional responsibility

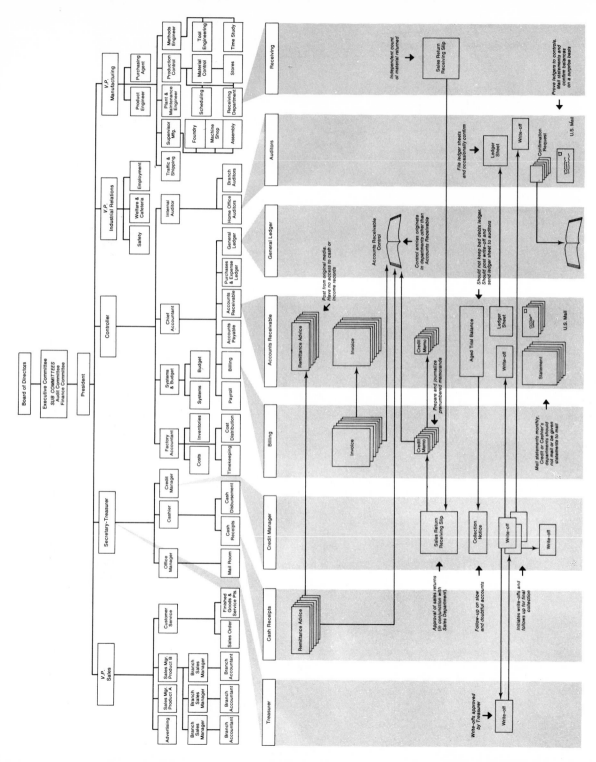

Figure 2. Accounts Receivable. Procedural flow chart shown in relation to organization chart to portray the control obtained through segregation of functional responsibility

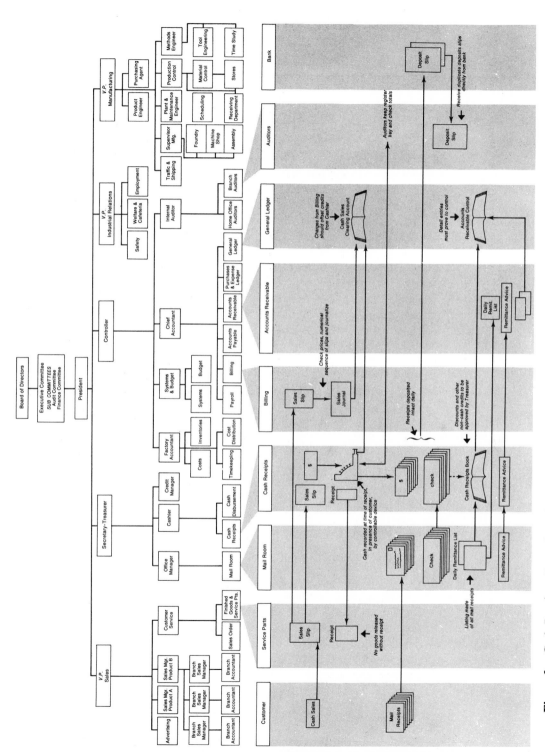

Figure 3. Cash Receipts. Procedural flow chart shown in relation to organization chart to portray the control obtained through segregation of functional responsibility

In selecting transactions on which to perform this test, the auditor should attempt to choose items which cover most of the typical kinds of transactions that occur. Since the primary purpose of this procedure is to be certain that the auditor understands the system as it exists, there need be no effort made to select a sample large enough to draw statistical inferences about processing accuracy.

At this point the auditor must exercise his professional judgment to determine the adequacy of the system of internal control. This means that he must determine the extent to which there are adequate checks and balance to guard against errors of various sorts and, to a lesser extent, against fraud. If he is satisfied that the system is one which makes error improbable he may limit his additional tests significantly, while if the system is not well designed, he may feel that substantial additional testing will be required.

On the basis of his judgments he will establish a series of tests that will be performed to determine whether or not the company employees are accurately processing data and whether or not errors which should be caught by the system are in fact being picked up. These tests will normally be based upon various statistical sampling techniques using predetermined criteria, as discussed in Chapter 7 above. Frequently, acceptance sampling will be used: Documentation will be examined and any errors or exceptions to prescribed procedures noted. If within a predetermined sample there are fewer than a predetermined number of exceptions, the auditor will accept the adequacy of the system and the accuracy of the data presented thereby. If the number of exceptions is greater than the prescribed limit, his sampling will be extended. In the event of continued unsatisfactory results with larger samples, sampling procedures may ultimately be extended far enough to allow the auditor to develop a reliable estimate of the figures presented in the information output being audited.

The technique of estimation sampling can also be used to estimate the number of exceptions that will appear in the processing of documents. Under this system, a random sample is selected and the number of exceptions in the population is estimated by the number of exceptions found in the sample. The auditor must exercise his judgment to decide whether the level of exceptions satisfies his desired degree of reliability.

A problem for the auditor in the use of statistical sampling techniques is his definition of an exception. For example, should any deviation from prescribed procedures—such as the absence of an approving signature on an order received, or the failure to invoice on the day of shipment—be considered an exception, or should only items that represent actual errors in outputs be so defined? It is also possible to design different tests with different sampling levels for various classes of exceptions.

In the appendix to this chapter, a typical audit program for the review of the order-shipment accounts-receivable data cycle is reproduced. This program does not indicate the statistical techniques to be used, such as the details of the sampling plan to be followed or the levels of acceptability of error which must be established by the auditor, but it does demonstrate the kinds of checking that may be done once a sample has been selected.

The Techniques of Confirmation

Testing transactions for error is one technique for testing the adequacy of corporate marketing activities; another is confirmation. Confirmation is normally applied to accounts-receivable balances but its principal objective usually is not, as it originally was, to estimate the balance due, but rather to test the validity of the claims reported by the company's system and to find any possible weaknesses in product quality, customer service, or record keeping which result in the sending of incorrect billing statements to customers. It is well known that customers who think they have been mistreated in any way will complain with enthusiasm, and accordingly the auditor's contact with customers gives him a valuable indication of the adequacy of the corporation's marketing-data cycle.

In confirming accounts, the auditor must first solve the problem how to select accounts to be confirmed. This normally is done on a stratified basis—stratified as to account balance—so as to reach a more representative sample of the customers of the firm than would a pure random sample. Within the strata, the accounts to be confirmed are selected on a random basis.

The second problem to be considered is whether the confirmation requests shall be positive or negative. The positive confirmation request is for a specific reply confirming the amount due to the corporation; the negative asks for a reply only in the event that the amount being confirmed is incorrect. Positive confirmation gives a more certain verification of the validity of a claim but also requires more audit time to process for each confirmation sent. Where the objective is to find weaknesses rather than to verify balances, there is much to be said for negative confirmation of a larger number of accounts. At the present time positive confirmations are generally used for large account balances, while negative requests are generally made in the case of a voluminous number of small-consumer accounts.

For tests in the process of confirmation to be meaningful, the auditor must control selection of accounts; the confirmations should be controlled by the auditor from the time they are prepared until the time they are mailed to the customer, and all replies should be controlled. The replies should be made directly to the auditor, not to the client; the original envelopes should have been sent with the accountant's return address rather than the corporation's. These steps assure that the confirmation process does obtain independent external verification of the data being presented.

In certain cases auditors are required to confirm accounts in a specific way. In the audit of members of the New York Stock Exchange for example, auditors are required to count 100 percent of the securities and confirm 100 percent of the receivables in a positive fashion. This is very time consuming and still is not certain to summarize relevant action for the stockholder, but it is required by law and hence must be performed.

Market Cycle
Transaction Analysis

Appendix

---

1. Select representative orders for testing using an appropriate sampling technique which reflects the various types of sales transactions weighted for their frequency and dollar importance.

2. Locate original orders for the sales to be examined.

a. Compare the data on the original order with the details on the client's order form to determine accuracy and completeness;

b. Determine that the order has been specifically processed for:

1. credit authorization;
2. prices—including necessary cost estimates;
3. discounts to be allowed (volume discounts, trade discounts, etc.);
4. promised delivery dates;
5. commission to be allowed.

3. Trace order to incoming order analyses.

a. Examine the following analyses for inclusion (or provision for inclusion) of the selected order:

1. analysis by source (salesman, house order, promotion, etc.);
2. product analysis (by line, by item);
3. salesman analysis;
4. territory analysis;
5. sales-quota fulfillment records;
6. repeat business versus new business;
7. products sold in conjunction with related products, or sold alone;
8. record of stock outs;
9. comparison with industry statistics;
10. comparison of market penetration with Buying Power Index.

4. Trace order to customer-history record.

a. Examine the customer-history record for entry of this transaction.
b. Determine the uses of the customer-history record, and arrive at an evaluation of its adequacy for these purposes.

5. Trace order to the inventory-availability record.

a. Examine the record for evidence that this transaction has been cleared (set up as a requirement) through the availability record and that it has been posted to the record.
b. Ascertain the procedures for adjusting this record to the physical merchandise available, when and if discrepancies arise.
c. Scan the availability records, observing the manner and frequency of adjusting and correcting entries.

6. Trace order through other steps in order-editing routine.

a. Verify that procedures have been followed to assure the correctness and propriety of all pertinent order data, including salesman code, customer code, product codes, terms of agreement to sell, etc.
b. Verify that the procedures in existence are adequate to insure that the client's announced policies are enforced.

7. Trace customer's order to client's rewrite of order.

a. Ascertain whether the original customer's order was rewritten onto client's own order form, whether a single sheet, a multiple copy form, or a duplicating machine master. Compare the data shown on the original order after editing with the information on the rewrite.
b. Ascertain distribution of copies to customer, salesman, shipping, order fulfillment, inventory control, purchasing, and other functions or individuals.

8. Trace order through back-order routine.

a. Examine back-order records for evidence that back-ordered items were properly recorded and ultimately shipped.
b. Evaluate adequacy of control that back-ordered merchandise is shipped when it becomes available, and the priority of release of such merchandise is in accordance with client's established policies.
c. Consider whether excessive back orders may arise from inadequate inventory-control

techniques, poor scheduling, poor product mix, etc.

9. Trace order through fulfillment routine.

a. Observe the picking, assembling, packing, and shipping of order, including, where possible, tracing to picking tickets, packing instructions, etc.
b. Trace the selected orders to the bind records.
c. Trace the selected orders to the perpetual inventory records.
d. Evaluate the controls against the possibility that merchandise may be shipped without proper authorization (either deliberately or in error).
e. Determine reasonableness of freight, parcel-post, and insurance charges on the selected orders. Trace these charges through to ultimate billing to the customer.

10. Trace order through invoice preparation.

a. Compare invoice with source data.
b. Check any new factors occurring on invoice, such as extensions, prices (including discounts), coding, etc., and determine why new data is necessary.

11. Trace order to sales journal.

a. Compare copy of invoice with entry in sales journal.
b. Verify correctness of distribution of the sale.
c. Trace postings of sales totals to the general ledger.

12. Trace the sale into the sales analysis.

(Note: In companies having a sizable backlog of orders, there may be analysis of incoming orders and, after shipment, analysis of sales. Because of cancellations, substitutions, partial shipments, etc., there may be material discrepancies between the two analyses. In such situations, evaluate the adequacy for management control purposes of the analyses available.)

a. Examine the following analyses for inclusion (or provision for inclusion) of information on the selected sale:
   1. source of business;
   2. product analysis (line, item, etc.);
   3. sales of substitute merchandise;
   4. sales volume in quantitive measure (dozens, tons, cubic feet, etc.);
   5. salesman analysis;
   6. territory analysis;
   7. geographic analysis (may or may not correlate with territory analysis);
   8. sales-quota fulfillment records;
   9. record of cancelled orders;
   10. comparison with capacity statistics (e.g., sales per square foot of display space, sales as a percentage of production capacity, etc.)
   11. comparison with industry statistics.

13. Trace posting of sale to accounts-receivable ledger.

a. Compare the selected invoices with the postings to the accounts-receivable detail ledger.
b. Compare totals shown in sales journal with debit posting to accounts-receivable control ledger.

c. Evaluate the adequacy of the control and proof methods used in the system. Consider the protection against:
   1. failure to post the sale at all;
   2. posting to the wrong account;
   3. posting the incorrect amount;
   4. picking up the incorrect old balance;
   5. misfiling the ledger card.
d. Determine the procedures used when there is a discrepancy between a trial balance of the detail ledger and the control records.

14. Test the accuracy and completeness of the aging by tracing selected past-due items to the aging.

15. Trace the selected sales transactions to customer statement.

16. Trace the ultimate receipt of payment for the sale.

a. From the customer's ledger card, note the references to the cash journal where payment of the selected transactions has been recorded.
b. Locate entries in cash journal and compare the entries with the amounts posted to accounts receivable.
c. Trace the item in the cash journal to the receipted duplicate bank deposit ticket.

Problem in Auditing the Marketing Data Cycle

The customer billing and collection functions of the Robinson Company, a small paint manufacturer, are attended to by a receptionist, an accounts receivable clerk and a cashier who also serves as a secretary. The Company's paint products are sold to wholesalers and retail stores.

From the Uniform CPA Examination.

The following describes all of the procedures performed by the employees of the Robinson Company pertaining to customer billings and collections:

1. The mail is opened by the receptionist who gives the customers' purchase orders to the accounts receivable clerk. Fifteen to twenty

orders are received each day. Under instructions to expedite the shipment of orders, the accounts receivable clerk at once prepares a five-copy sales invoice form which is distributed as follows:

a. Copy #1 is the customer billing copy and is held by the accounts receivable clerk until notice of shipment is received.

b. Copy #2 is the accounts receivable department copy and is held for ultimate posting of the accounts receivable records.

c. Copies #3 and #4 are sent to the shipping department.

d. Copy #5 is sent to the storeroom as authority for release of the goods to the shipping department.

2. After the paint ordered has been moved from the storeroom to the shipping department, the shipping department prepares the bills of lading and labels the cartons. Sales invoice copy #4 is inserted in a carton as a packing slip. After the trucker has picked up the shipment the customer's copy of the bill of lading and copy #3, on which are noted any undershipments, are returned to the accounts receivable clerk. The Company does not "back order" in the event of undershipments; customers are expected to reorder the merchandise. The Robinson Company's copy of the bill of lading is filed by the shipping department.

3. When copy #3 and the customer's copy of the bill of lading are received by the accounts receivable clerk, copies #1 and #2 are completed by numbering them and inserting quantities shipped, unit prices, extensions, discounts and totals. The accounts receivable clerk then mails copy #1 and the copy of the bill of lading to the customer. Copies #2 and #3 are stapled together.

4. The individual accounts receivable ledger cards are posted by the accounts receivable clerk by a bookkeeping machine procedure whereby the sales register is prepared as a carbon copy of the postings. Postings are made from copy #2 which is then filed, along with staple-attached copy #3, in numerical order. Monthly the general ledger clerk summarizes the sales register for posting to the general ledger accounts.

5. Since the Robinson Company is short of cash, the deposit of receipts is also expedited. The receptionist turns over all mail receipts and related correspondence to the accounts receivable clerk who examines the checks and determines that the accompanying vouchers or correspondence contain enough detail to permit posting of the accounts. The accounts receivable clerk then endorses the checks and gives them to the cashier who prepares the daily deposit. No currency is received in the mail and no paint is sold over the counter at the factory.

6. The accounts receivable clerk uses the vouchers or correspondence that accompanied the checks to post the accounts receivable ledger cards. The bookkeeping machine prepares a cash receipts register as a carbon copy of the postings. Monthly the general ledger clerk summarizes the cash receipts register for posting to the general ledger accounts. The accounts receivable clerk also corresponds with customers about unauthorized deductions for discounts, freight or advertising allowances, returns, etc. and prepares the appropriate credit memos. Disputed items of large amount are turned over to the sales manager for settlement. Each month the accounts receivable clerk prepares a trial balance of the open accounts receivable and compares the resultant total with the general ledger control account for accounts receivable.

Required:

Discuss the internal control weaknesses in the Robinson Company's procedures related to customer billings and remittances and the accounting for these transactions. In your discussion, in addition to identifying the weaknesses, explain what could happen as a result of each weakness.

The Wheelox Corporation: Part C

Case

In The Wheelox Corporation: Part A, you are asked to prepare a flow chart of the company system.

Requirement:

Based on your understanding of the system:

1. Prepare a list of strengths and weaknesses in the system and recommendations to improve the system.
2. Indicate how you would test the effectiveness of the controls described in the system.

Lusterbrite Paint Company

Case

During your audit of the Lusterbrite Paint Company, you determine that the present marketing information system has some weaknesses. After discussion of its weaknesses with management, you conduct a more detailed analysis of their marketing system and determine the following.

The primary data for this case were developed by two MBA students of the Graduate School of Business Administration of the University of Washington, Scott Thompson, and Dennis McCarter.

The Company

The company is a regional manufacturer and distributor of paints, finishes, and accessories. Their marketing region encompasses all of Washington, northern Oregon, Alaska, and parts of Idaho. There are about 60 full-time employees; in the marketing division, there are 12 to 15 employees. The company has four of its own factory stores, all in the Seattle area, as well as dealers throughout the marketing region.

The company owners have not been happy with the profitability of their firm and have felt that much of the trouble might be found in the marketing division. The most recent annual financial statements are shown in Tables 1 and 2. Analysis of recent financial statements shows that the company's earnings and growth have lagged in the past few years, while competitors have been growing in a rapidly expanding market.

Figure 1 indicates the major organizational groupings of the company. Figures 2 and 3 indicate the data flow for credit and cash sales.

Marketing Activities

The company classifies sales monthly and yearly by major customer classes—factory stores, General Services Administration (government sales), and all other sales. There is no breakdown, however, by type of ultimate customer; i.e., when a sale is made in a store, there is no code made to determine whether the customer is a business, a painter, or a housewife. The salesman's monthly statements do break down products for which they are responsible according to different commission rates. For example, these monthly statements indicate 1 percent commission for sales to the General Services Administration, 3 percent for dealer sales, and 6 percent for sales to painters. This lack of breakdown by the type of customer purchasing the product makes it difficult to note historical trends and leaves unanswered questions such as: Who really buys the product? What products are they buying? and, Where are the sales gains and losses? Also, it is very difficult to make any analysis of the profitability by type of customer.

The products are currently sold through three basic channels: factory stores, shipments to resellers (dealers and distributors), and direct shipment to large users. There is no current breakdown of sales by type of distribution. Accordingly, it is difficult to make analyses of distribution costs, and to determine the profitability of the various methods of distribution.

In development of prices for the various products, a standard price book is maintained, and marketing personnel have access to this book for pricing purposes. Whoever writes an invoice is responsible for initial pricing. The office manager or his assistant then checks the prices and extensions of all invoices later in the data-flow cycle (see Figure 2).

Pricing schedules for new customers are usually determined by the salesmen in the fields or the store manager, subject to change by the sales manager or president if either feels it is necessary. There is no set policy on this, although there is a general price schedule for painters, one for dealers, etc. There are six basic potential price schedules available. New prices are determined by the president, sales manager, and office manager working together.

Usually the policy has been to adjust prices to competitive levels for quality lines. For example, in November, 1967, Lusterbrite raised all prices of all products 5 percent following an industry move.

A standard raw-material cost book is maintained by the office manager for all products, both manufactured and jobbed items, at latest market cost. The office manager costs all invoices of store deliveries, i.e., for shipment of products to stores; he enters the cost from the comprehensive raw-material price book. Twenty percent of variable cost is added as a fixed cost in determining each factory store's cost of goods sold. He costs invoices approximately every two months. A profit and loss statement is developed annually.

Some bidding is done, particularly on governmental business, usually by the sales manager or office manager and one industrial salesman. The objective is to maintain a margin over variable costs at about 15 to 20 percent, although this may drop some during the slow season or in accordance with what competitors are bidding.

In promoting the products, all decisions and expenditures are made by the president in conjunction with an advertising agency. Usually, campaigns are explained to marketing personnel directly in meetings prior to the launching of the promotional campaign. There is no written memorandum to appropriate personnel relating to approaching advertising programs. Store managers and dealers are requested to send in all coupons they receive from customers when coupons are used. Otherwise, the effectiveness of advertising is generally determined by word of mouth from customers and store's management. There is no formal mechanism for determining the allocation of expenditures for advertising, although the budget for direct advertising is around 2 percent of sales annually. There is no information about competitors' allocations. All direct advertising is pointed at the home-owning consumer. Meetings and dinners are held annually for dealers.

There is no direction from top management to the store managers about point of purchase displays or window displays. In addition, there is little communication among store managers concerning such displays, although the sales manager and president will on occasion give verbal suggestions to store managers. Allocation of funds for display purposes is left to the discretion of the store manager within some predetermined limits.

Figure 4 is a copy of a standard call-report form filled out by salesmen in the field daily. It includes expense vouchers on the back of the form. These forms are given to the sales manager and president and then filed. Although no explicit sales quotas are defined, usually the sales manager and president informally expect each salesman to match or improve his performance over quota sales of the year before.

The sales manager distributes weekly information about building-permits applications in the area surrounding the metropolitan area for salesmen to follow up. There is no procedure for determining what follow-up was made on these leads. Each salesman and store manager has his own account book in which are listed all company accounts, the price schedules, tax schedules, and addresses. If there are changes in the account information, they are made by the credit manager, often with direct discussion with relevant managers or salesmen; and notices of changes are distributed whenever necessary. The sales manager and president receive monthly statements of each salesman's sales and commissions for the preceding month (see Table 3). Because no quotas or forecasts are currently used, the evaluation is somewhat informal.

Credit is decided upon according to the following procedure. The potential customer fills out a credit application form (see Figure 5). This form is then sent to the credit manager by either the store manager or salesman. The credit manager checks the application and decides whether or not the credit is to be granted. In many cases this is done over the phone if speed is required. Once the account is open, notification of the new account is sent to all holders of account books. In granting credit, the credit manager checks with any of three credit bureaus and on occasion will check with personal references or suppliers. There is no set rule for allowing credit, and the credit manager uses his discretion in many cases. The bad-debt

expense has been very good, the range being from 0.5 to 1.5 percent.

The credit manager makes a monthly accounts-receivable review.

Required:

1. Evaluate the current marketing information system of Lusterbrite and determine the specific weaknesses in the current system.
2. Make recommendations as to improving the system and include specific recommendations as to:
   a. Coding patterns.
   b. Report formats.
   c. Information flows.

Table 1. Balance Sheet

Assets		
Current assets:		
Cash		$ 33,072
Accounts receivable, less allowance		
for doubtful accounts of $5,000		123,158
Due from officers and employees		2,334
Inventories, at lower of cost or market:		
Manufactured products	$106,494	
Raw materials	67,849	
Other merchandise	57,960	
Containers and cartons	7,871	240,174
Prepaid expense		4,336
Total current assets		$403,074
Equipment and fixtures, at cost:		
Machinery and equipment	119,960	
Automobiles	16,437	
Leasehold improvements	10,562	
Furniture and equipment	10,268	
Signs	3,278	
	160,505	
Less accumulated depreciation	101,706	58,799
Other assets		
Cash surrender value of life ins.	12,846	
Corporate securities, at cost	575	
Lease deposits	350	
Trademarks	289	14,060
Total assets		$475,933

Liabilities and stockholders investment		
Current liabilities		
Accounts payable		$ 50,115
Notes payable to stockholders		21,000
Taxes, other than on income and amt.		
w/held from employee's earnings		2,084
Accrued salaries and commissions payable		50,290
Accrued interest payable		1,260
Employee benefits payable		564
Federal taxes on income		4,355
Contract payable		672
Total current liabilities		$130,340
Stockholders' investment		
Capital stock, par value $100 per share		
Authorized, 3,000 shares		
Issued and outstanding, 2,664 shares	266,400	
Retained earnings	79,193	
		345,593
		$475,933

Table 2. Statement of Earnings

Sales — net		$1,416,382
Cost of sales		1,011,532
		404,850
Selling expenses:		
Salaries and commissions	138,786	
Advertising	49,448	
Freight out	26,620	
Automobile and travel	16,105	
Taxes, other than on income	11,157	
Rent	9,943	
Entertainment	5,486	
Depreciations	2,596	
Insurance	2,384	
Machine rental	1,393	
Telephone and telegraph	1,286	
Heat, light, and water	1,168	
Dues and subscriptions	1,030	
Repairs and maintenance	781	
Supplies and expense	778	
Laundry and cleaning	775	
Miscellaneous	5,578	
	275,314	
Administrative expenses	112,477	387,791
		17,059
Other income		4,637
Earnings before provision for federal taxes on income		21,696
Provision for federal taxes on income		4,355
Net earnings		$ 17,341

Figure 1. Major organizational groupings of the company.

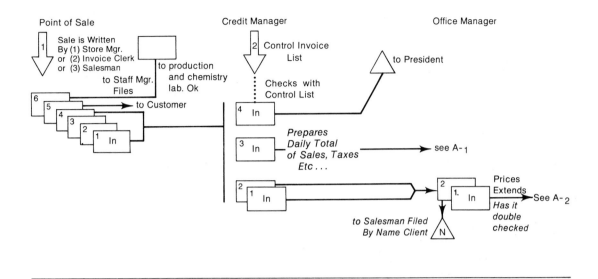

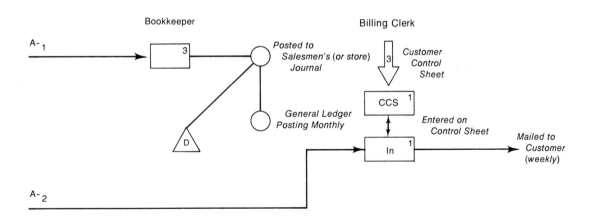

Figure 2. Credit sales data flow.

Point of Sale   Credit Manager   Bookkeeper

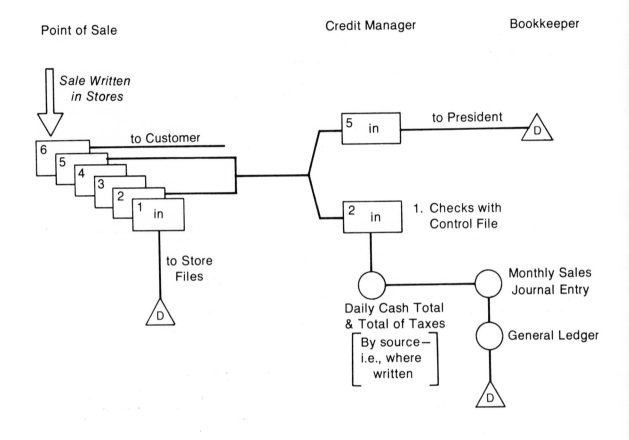

Figure 3. Cash sales data flow.

Salesman _____ Date _____

Date	Customer—Name and Address	New or Old	Result of Interview and Remarks	Date To See Again

Figure 4. Salesman's weekly report.

Table 3. Monthly Statement of Salesman's Sales and Commissions

Lusterbrite Paint Company

Statement of Commissions

R. W. Berg .... 4 ...... February 1968
....

Salesman   No.   Month

	Months	Accumulated Sales	Percentage of Sales		Earned Commission	Received: Salary, Car Allow., Exp.	Salary, etc., in Excess of Earned Comm.	Earned Comm. in Excess of Salary, etc.
Balances of Previous Month	2	20,707.80			1,214.25	1,307.80	93.55	
			12 % of	246.47	29.58	S. 500.00		
			10 % of	1,798.75	179.87	C. A. 125.00		
			8 % of	2,083.68	166.69			
			6 %	582.33	34.94			
			3 % of	4,068.66	122.06			
			1 % of					
			0 % of					
Monthly Totals:	1	8,779.89		8,779.89	533.14	625.00	91.86	
Accumulated Totals:	3	29,487.69			1,747.39	1,932.80	185.41	

Figure 5. Sample credit application form

Lusterbrite Paint Co.

Credit Application

Name of Company _____ Date _____

Street _____ City _____ State _____

Phone No. _____

If an Individual Proprietorship — Owner _____

If a Partnership — Members _____

_____

If a Corporation — Pres. _____
Vice Pres. _____
Sec.-Treas. _____
In what State incorporated? _____

Type of business _____ How long in business as above? _____

Previous business experience _____

What amount of credit will cover your average monthly needs? _____

Our regular terms are 1% 10th prox. — Will discounts be taken? _____

Banks with _____

Suppliers and references _____

_____

_____

_____

_____

_____

Remarks _____

_____

_____

_____

_____

_____

Sign here _____

Chapter 13

Auditing the
Cash-Management System

One of the principal management systems in any enterprise is the cash-management system. In this area, management is essentially responsible for four major functions:

1. the planning of cash inflows and outflows with the objective of being certain that business needs for cash are adequately met;
2. the direction of cash receiving and disbursement;
3. the maintenance of adequate bank balances and bank relationships; and
4. the investment of short-term cash excesses in appropriate income-earning instruments.

In a large corporation, these functions most frequently come under the control of the treasurer, although practice is not uniform in this respect. Some aspects of the cash-management function relate to the broad strategic plans of the firm and hence are generally the concern of top management, while others fall into both the management and operational-control classifications.

The most significant function of the cash-management system is planning cash inflows and outflows. In fulfilling this function, management must consider several different levels of decision and varying projected time spans for planning.

Planning Cash Inflow and Outflows

At the most general level, the entire planning system of the firm can be converted into cash inflows and outflows. For the purpose of ultimate analysis, some financial and economic theorists view a firm as simply a series of cash flows, and the basic decisions of how cash will be obtained and how it will be allocated are the principal strategic decisions which top management must make. At this level, it could be suggested that the audit of the cash-management system is the audit of the entire firm.

For the purposes of this book, however, such a catholic concept of the cash-management system is not contemplated. We have discussed the need for the auditor to understand the strategic planning system of the firm and its implementation through the development of managerial controls. We have also emphasized that the auditor must be aware of the information requirements for strategic planning, and the need to evaluate the adequacy of the information system in meeting these requirements.

In this chapter, therefore, the cash-management system will be discussed at the level of management and operational control, and the system's information needs will be considered at that level.

Cash-flow planning requires a projection of the cash implications of management's strategic policies. These projections are generally prepared for different time spans. The cash manager must be able to obtain information from various operating forecasts that will enable him to project the probable effects of operations on cash inflows and outflows. Such forecasts are normally associated with a long-range plan (perhaps of five years' duration), with the annual profit plan (usually for four quarters in advance), and with the detailed operating plan for the next quarter or month.

The five-year cash-management plan is a general guideline which assists top management in recognizing the implications that strategic plans have for the corporation's cash position and its need for funds. This plan will serve as the basis for major financing decisions by top management. The auditor has a responsibility to determine that such a plan exists and that the conversion of real strategic plans into cash terms is being realistically performed.

In addition, the auditor must ascertain that the cash manager is using the information provided by the five-year plan to prepare for the responsibilities which he will have in implementing its financing aspects. Where the plan contemplates new financing, is adequate capital market information being produced by the firm's information system? Are contacts with underwriters, bankers, and institutional investors being maintained so that the financing strategy called for by the plan can be carried out in the most efficient way?

The cash forecast derived from the annual profit plan is the vehicle by which the cash manager must bring the broad guidelines of the long-term forecasts into specific terms. The profit plan normally includes projected results on a month by month (or at least a quarter by quarter) basis. These results must be converted into cash terms so that the effectiveness of cash-deficit and surplus timing can later be ascertained. By this conversion, the manager has the data necessary to develop plans for financing deficits and investing surpluses. In this fashion, he can make the necessary arrangements to be sure that no out-of-stock cash position arises, since out-of-stock costs in this area are normally extremely high.

In addition to a monthly forecast, most cash managers also prepare a daily forecast of cash inflows, outflows, and balances for one to three months in advance. This forecast is used to exercise control over disbursements, bank balances, and short-term investments. The cash manager's information system must produce virtually real-time data in order to verify the accuracy of his forecasts so that he can act in a timely and efficient way in transferring and investing funds. Much of this function can be converted into an operational control system where cash transfers and short-term cash investments are programmed to take place automatically, subject to certain constraints built into the system.

The auditor must satisfy himself that an adequate system exists for the control of cash inflows, outflows, and balances. He must determine that cash planning takes place in the intermediate term to avoid crisis conditions, that variations from plan are reported by the information system to the cash manager in a timely fashion, and that the system protects the firm against overdraft and cash-excess conditions.

The specific steps for auditing this aspect of the cash-management system would include, first, to develop an understanding of the information available in the area and the way in which it is used. This understanding would be obtained through interviews with responsible corporate officers and the study of the various reports and other sources of information that they use in performing their functions. Copies of periodic reports should be obtained for the working papers if possible. Tests should then be undertaken to determine the extent to which the system described is in fact the one being used. Files should be examined to see whether the information which is said to be prepared is in fact available on a timely basis. The auditor must also determine whether any of the extreme conditions that the system is designed to protect against did in fact take place. Externally developed evidence may be a part of these procedures; the company's principal bank may be asked to confirm whether an overdraft condition or a balance over a certain limit did occur during the year, and if so, how often. This could be included in the bank confirmation request that is part of the audit of cash-receipts and disbursements procedures described below.

The basic objective of auditing the cash-flow planning part of the cash-management cycle is to satisfy the auditor that sufficient information is being developed to assure a smooth flow of the cash resources of the business without the high costs of stock-out or the opportunity cost of excess cash funds.

Cash Receiving and Disbursement

The second major responsibility of the cash manager is the efficient handling of cash receipts and disbursements. There are several dimensions to this responsibility. First, procedures must be established to assure that cash receipts are converted into useable form at the earliest possible time and that cash disbursements are not paid prior to their due date, while at the same time assuring that they are paid at an early enough time to qualify for cash discounts when applicable. Second, cash transfers must be made and received in accordance with the approved needs and commitments of the corporation. Finally, since cash is a readily spendable asset, there must be sufficient controls established to protect the firm against fraud as well as error.

There are many techniques for getting cash receipts rapidly into useable form in the banking channels of the corporation. These include multiple cash-receiving points, lock-box systems, self-dumping bank accounts with automatic wire transfers, daily deposit policies, and others. These may be simple or complex depending upon the cash-receipts pattern of the corporation. In addition, the cash receiving system must assure the proper recording of cash inflows, the rejection of inappropriate payments, such as a partial payment of a receivable marked "payment in full," and the avoidance of the danger that corporate cash will be converted into employee's use.

The first step the auditor must undertake in the audit of cash receipts is a flow chart of the entire system from customer to bank and the preparation of appropriate reports and posting media for other systems within the corporation. The system is generally determined by inquiry and examination of procedures manuals, and a few selected transactions of each type are then "walked through" the system to see that all steps described are in fact being carried out. A sample flow chart of a cash-receipts system is included in Chapter 12, above (page 446).

The cash-disbursements system must be similarly reviewed from the point where documentation for payments enters the cash-management system to the bank withdrawal and the creation of reports and posting media for other systems (See Figure 1).

Effective cash disbursing includes payment at scheduled dates with a capability for both significantly delayed and extremely rapid disbursement when necessary. Additionally, adequate controls are needed to be certain that cash is disbursed only for approved corporate purposes and that appropriate records of disbursements are generated to inform responsible corporate personnel of the amounts being disbursed. Such information must be combined with cash-receipts data and will enter into the cash-flow information system outlined above. To be useful such data must be timely, and one of the criteria of adequacy of information must therefore be the speed with which it is produced.

Finally, effectiveness in both cash receiving and disbursement can be related to the cost of performing the functions. A system might be excellent in every other respect, but could be totally unsatisfactory overall because of the high costs of making it operate. In this aspect of the cash-management system, where a high volume of repetitive tasks are performed, it is normally possible, if the functions are appropriately organized, to establish cost controls on a volume-of-production basis. Standards for clerical work output can be established by time study or other techniques, and information can be developed comparing performance to standard.

It must be recognized that in cash-management cost-reduction objectives often may conflict with the objectives of maximum protection of assets, control, and the rapid development of data. In any management system there are conflicting costs to be balanced and in this area the cost-control specialist and the auditor may differ on the relative utility to be accorded to various objectives. Decisions in such matters are the responsibility of management, and once the auditor has communicated to management the control problem, if one exists, and his estimate of the possible costs of reduced control and improved control, he must be willing to accept management's judgment on whether the improved control is worth the cost. Naturally, if the potential error is significant in amount, audit procedures may have to be adjusted to reflect the system's greater vulnerability to error.

Once a cash-receiving and disbursing system has been described and appropriate flow charts, sample reports, and relevant cost data are included in the work papers, the system must be evaluated. This evaluation will require the auditor to answer three interrelated questions:

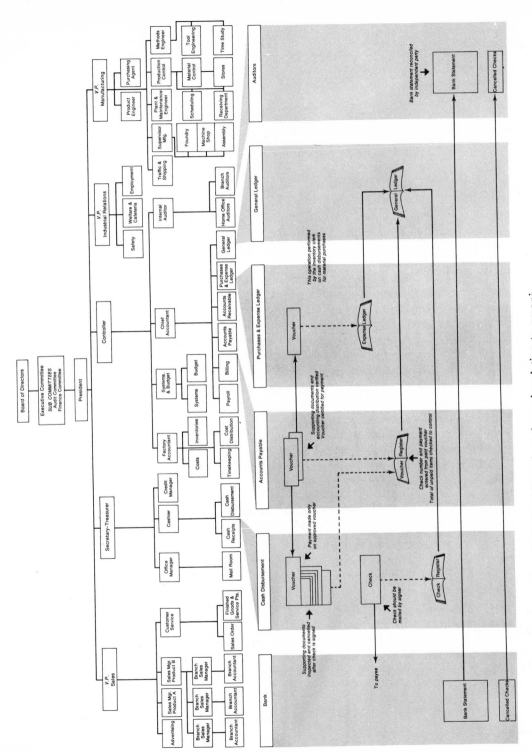

Figure 1. Cash Disbursements. Procedural flow chart shown in relation to organization chart to portray the control obtained through segregation of functional responsibility.

1. Does the system achieve its business purpose?
2. Does it produce adequate, timely, and reliable information about its functioning?
3. Does it do so efficiently and at least possible cost?

These are not easy questions to answer, but if business objectives and the system used have been adequately analyzed, the intelligent auditor should be able to develop satisfactory answers. The answers, however, will seldom be yes or no in the traditional fashion of the internal-control questionnaire. Rather they will represent a summary of the analytical process undertaken by the auditor, prepared in the form of a memorandum for the workpapers.

On the basis of the auditor's evaluation of the cash-receipts and disbursements system, specific audit steps can be designed to verify data on cash-receipts and disbursements and the resulting balances; the auditor must decide what type of tests are required to satisfy himself that cash receipts and disbursements are properly reported.

If the company's system is adequate it may be that very limited testing is necessary. Traditionally, the audit of cash has resulted in the largely unproductive use of substantial amounts of junior accountants' time and talent. Cash has been overaudited for two reasons. First, cash figures are precise, and as a result this audit gives the auditor the satisfaction of precision in his results; cash can then be attested to with virtual certainty and this of course is satisfying to the temperament of many auditors. Second, and more important, the overaudit of cash dates back to the day when the auditor's principal function was the detection of fraud. Since virtually every fraud must ultimately result in the transfer of cash out of the corporation, the auditor was led to a particularly intensive review of this area. The auditor who spends a great deal of time verifying endorsements on checks and reconciling bank accounts is still operating with this approach in mind.

Given the objective of the auditor today, there is no reason why the detailed work in the audit of cash need exceed that required in any other phase of the auditor's task. Cash data is merely one other aspect of the financial information needed to operate the firm successfully.

In the audit of the cash-receipts and disbursements system, therefore, the auditor will design sampling procedures to test for various attributes of a satisfactory system. On the cash-receipts side, he may test for such input controls as prompt deposit of receipts, accurate and timely development of posting media from data entering the system, and coordination of shipments and invoices. In connection with cash disbursements, sampling can be made of such attributes as approval of invoices and vouchers, adequate supporting documentation for payments, and properly dated payments.

In addition to these tests of the accuracy of receipts and disbursements data, certain tests in regard to cash balances may also be carried out—not necessarily of the balances that appear on the balance sheet, but rather of the balance data which is a significant part of the cash-management information system. Such balance checks can be made by examining bank statements and bank reconciliations prepared by the client or the bank and testing for situations where book balances varied significantly from those reported by the bank.

One part of the test of balance data is the bank confirmation that has traditionally been associated with the verification of cash balances. Actually, such a confirmation has the principal purpose of obtaining corroborative evidence from an outside party about many items of which the cash balance is only one. The conventional bank confirmation serves as a test for unrecorded liabilities and corporate commitments through guarantees and other similar arrangements which would not routinely appear in the financial records of the firm. Additionally, the bank confirmation can be designed to elicit information about abnormal conditions in the bank account if the bank is asked to report unusual fluctuations in the balance during a period of time.

The total audit of cash receipts and disbursements, therefore, encompasses primarily a review of the system followed by a test of the data produced by the system, including information on both the flows of cash within the firm and the balances at various points in time.

Bank Relationships

Another important role of the corporate cash manager is the maintenance of adequate relationships with the company's various banks. This task requires that the officer satisfies himself that the various services offered by the company's banks are known and where appropriate are being used. He must also determine that banks are being adequately compensated for the services they are performing while at the same time trying to prevent overcompensation.

The payment for bank services is traditionally the maintenance of bank balances with the firm's principal banking institutions, and accordingly it is a difficult cost to account for. The conventional accounting system, for example, would attribute no costs to the maintenance of substantial balances, and therefore carelessness in developing an adequate system of control over this area might result in substantial overcompensation to banks involved.

The company's cash-management information system must first accumulate data on the bank services being performed for the corporation in both the major money-market centers and various other geographical locations.

It is surprising to find that in many corporations no regular accumulation is made of data on the company's use of bank services; in some companies different divisions call upon the various banks that serve the company, but no attempt is made to gather such information. Similarly, international operations frequently make extensive use of banking relationships without accumulating data on this use.

Certainly an adequate information system for this area will require at a minimum a list of banking services supplied and a measure of the costs in terms of some appropriate return on average balances. Only then will the management be able to weigh the costs and benefits in a systematic fashion.

The principal task of the auditor evaluating this system is to assure himself that appropriate data for this aspect of the cash-management decision is being accumulated and that the various implicit costs associated with the development of bank relationships are recorded in some fashion. Additionally, the auditor should satisfy himself that the company does have an adequate system of compensation to its banks for services rendered and a control system to prevent substantial deviations in compensation. Such a system primarily requires a means by which each bank balance is manually or automatically controlled to not exceed a predetermined limit measured by the level of services that bank supplies.

In accumulating data on services, the firm must be careful to include not only the concrete and readily measurable services such as processing checks, deposits, and so forth, but also the intangible benefits of bank counsel in various areas. These are difficult services to cost out on a dollar and cents basis, but, at a minimum, certain implicit values can be assigned by evaluating the balances being maintained in the accounts.

As time passes it seems likely that major banks will increasingly depend upon service charges for their revenues, and the role of demand deposits will shrink. There is already some evidence of this effect: Demand deposits in the economy have not grown at nearly as fast a rate as time deposits, as corporate treasurers increasingly attempt to obtain additional return from their liquid funds.

In dealing with bank relationships, the auditor must also be aware of those items that are of greatest concern to the banking community. He must be certain that covenants and other less formal arrangements are being honored and that no hidden liabilities are being accumulated as a result of bank reliance upon corporate representations other than those intended as guarantees.

The Investment in Short-Term Liquid Instruments

The final aspect of the cash-management system in an enterprise is the investment of short-term cash excesses in appropriate income-earning instruments. The importance of this function will vary dramatically from corporation to corporation depending upon the proportion of resources which are maintained in liquid form. In some companies the investment of such balances represents merely a limited seasonal function, while in others it is apparent that the liquid assets on hand will be available for a much longer time.

The information system of the firm must first develop data as to the availability of cash and the length of that availability. These data should arise from the system of cash-inflow and outflow planning described above, and from the determination of appropriate balances to maintain bank relationships. Second, the short-term investment-information system must develop data about external investment opportunities. Such data may not be tied in with the financial accounting system of the firm but must nonetheless be available if this investment function is to be adequately performed.

Many corporations have adopted the philosophy that the investment of excess cash funds is merely a peripheral part of the business, but a careful analysis of the potential returns in this area leads to the conclusion that many corporations with substantial liquid-asset portfolios cannot avoid being in the investment business. Accordingly, the company's system must develop data about appropriate instruments and yields, and about the success of the investment policy being followed by the executive responsible.

While there is no simple means of evaluating the performance of a liquid-asset portfolio manager, it is certainly possible to compare investment performance with a variety of commonly used investment indicators such as the Treasury bill rate, the Dow Jones average, and the performance of certain appropriate mutual funds. If desired, more sophisticated measurements can be developed that compare the yields obtained to the investment opportunities that are derivable from the cash-flow patterns of the corporation and the instruments available to the portfolio manager. The traditional view that short-term investment is a stepchild in the cash-management function is gradually disappearing, and if liquid-asset balances are significant the auditor must be certain that adequate information about investment opportunities and investment performance is being developed.

It is quite conventional for top management to apply a utility function to the risk-return choice that must be made in the selection of securities. If this is the case, the information system of the firm must provide adequate data to advise management that its guidelines are being followed. In this connection it is important that the system produce data other than period-end balances since many of the more dramatic violations of corporate policy may occur within a period and not be carried over its end. While the auditor need not scan all investment transactions, he should be certain that the reporting system will automatically disclose variations in the investment mix for the perusal of the management.

In addition to reviewing the short-term investment system, the auditor must satisfy himself that there do exist adequate physical safeguards over securities held. This is normally not a problem since most large corporations keep investments of this sort in custody accounts at financial institutions and therefore the possibility of loss or theft is small.

Summary

Cash has traditionally been one of the most extensively audited areas of corporate existence. This dates back to the time when fraud prevention was a major audit objective. Given today's audit objectives, however, there is no reason why the audit of the cash-management system should require any more detailed work than any other part of the audit.

In reviewing this system, the auditor must establish that adequate and timely information is being developed about each of the principal cash-management functions: planning cash flows, receiving and disbursing cash, managing bank balances and bank relationships, and investing excess liquid assets. He does this by determining and flowcharting the company's procedures by inquiry; evaluating the adequacy of these procedures; and then testing the procedures by a sampling plan designed on the basis of the evaluation. While limited checks of balances may be a part of this audit plan, the traditional verification of year-end balance-sheet balances will not be required if the company's system is satisfactory.

Chapter 14

Auditing the
Personnel System

The personnel system is concerned with data about people. It is per-haps the most misunderstood and least defined system—misunderstood because the management of people presents an infinite number of problems including those which are psychological, philosophical, moral, political, and biosocial in nature; ill-defined because all managers and supervisors in various functions throughout the organization are deeply involved in per-sonnel management. The personnel-management function is concerned with the recruitment, selection, utilization, and development of human resources by and within the enterprise.

Traditionally, the auditor's involvement in the personnel system has been only with evaluating the compensation process. Obviously a major part of the personnel system, the compensation process involves compensa-ting people for services performed and motivating them to attain desired levels of performance; this includes both financial and nonfinancial re-wards and may consist of such activities as wage surveys, job evaluation and establishment of job rates, the recognition and stimulation of individ-ual and/or group productivity through merit increases, incentive systems, profit-sharing, etc. Other components of the process may include the awarding of vacations, holidays, relief time, sick leave, and provision of

Understanding the Personnel System

essentially noncost rewards such as recognition, privileges, and symbols of status.

In the auditing of this portion of the system, the auditor reviews activities such as:

1. hiring of employees and the development of personnel records with data relevant for personnel decisions and payroll processing;
2. termination of employees;
3. time recording and reporting;
4. payroll processing including:
    a. preparation of gross and net payroll;
    b. preparation of payroll checks or cash pay envelopes and methods of distribution;
    c. preparation of employees' earnings records;
    d. calculation of incentives, bonuses, commissions, overtime, etc.
5. accounting distribution of payroll costs, including the determination of overhead labor rates and methods of distributing wages and salaries to inventory and expense accounts.

Figure 1 is a flowchart of the payroll process.

Employment

Hiring of employees is the initial part of the personnel process and consists of screening and engaging new employees. Usually the screening process involves interviews and aptitude tests to determine the applicant's competence and suitability for employment. Applicants who satisfy the initial hiring tests are normally referred for final acceptance to the line manager or supervisor under whom they will be expected to work. For example, in the recruiting of professional staff for a public accounting firm, applicants are first interviewed on a university campus or in the office that may have advertised the position through a classified advertisement in a business publication such as the *Wall Street Journal.* As a result of the initial interview, applicants may be interviewed by additional partners and members of the staff to determine suitability for employment. This process involves a review of the applicant's resume and personal discussions to allow the applicant to amplify his previous experience and education, and to present his career objectives and job values. Hiring procedures for nonprofessional people may be less extensive and time-consuming but should be effective enough to gain sufficient information from the applicant for a proper decision to be made about his employment.

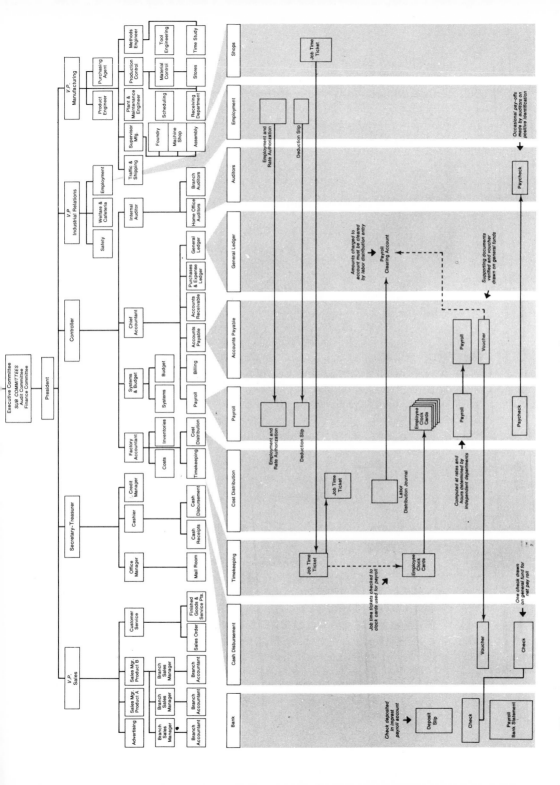

Figure 1. Payroll. Procedural flow chart shown in relation to organization chart to portray the control obtained through segregation of functional responsibility

Once an applicant is employed, he should complete the necessary personnel forms to provide information for withholding-tax purposes and for authorizing amounts to be deducted for insurance, savings, union dues, etc. This information, together with the employee's pay rate, must be recorded in the employee's master record for personnel and payroll-processing purposes. Such master records or data files contain data used in a variety of personnel-processing purposes. Analysis must be made to determine those data elements common to most personnel applications, and to so structure the personnel data files as to avoid duplication of data in the files and to provide compatability between files.[1]

Termination

In addition to the hiring of employees, the employment department should be actively involved in the termination process. Information should be obtained from the employee in an "exit" interview about his reasons for quitting, since he can be an important source of information about working conditions, job motivation, compensations, etc. The exit interview also affords an opportunity for explaining to an employee temporarily or permanently dismissed the reasons for such dismissal. To satisfy internal control need, the exit interview should be required before giving the terminated employee his final check. There also must be a system to remove the employee from the personnel-payroll file at the time of termination to provide protection against payment to a person who does not actually perform any work.

Timekeeping

Timekeeping involves procedures that record and report data related to attendance-time at work, to jobs, and to time spent on specific jobs or orders. The timekeeping department, or function, is responsible for the collection of attendance and job time for each employee covered under the timekeeping system.

Attendance of each employee is kept on time cards, time sheets, or other records appropriate to the conditions of work. The most familiar process for collecting data on attendance is the time card that is inserted in a time clock to print times of arrival and departure from place of

---

[1]For a detailed discussion of data-file design, see "The Corporate Data File," *EDP Analyzer*, November 1966.

work. Time recording should be supervised by security personnel to ensure accurate and reliable time records.

In jobs and factories where labor costs must be charged to jobs, orders, products, processes, etc., job time must be kept on a record that shows time spent by each employee on each job, order, etc. This process allows the collection of data which may be used to charge production for time worked. Normally, indirect labor time is also charged to production, but is charged to production-overhead accounts on the basis of attendance-time cards only. Such indirect labor time is usually for those supervisory employees or other employees where it is very difficult to directly relate time spent on a job to a particular product or process. A great variety of forms is used to keep track of time spent on specific jobs or orders. There is a trend toward automating the labor-recording process in many companies today and below is a description of a case study involving the automated system for recording labor transactions in a major plant for a large manufacturer.

Automatic time-recording devices are located throughout the shop areas. For the 11,600 employees covered by this system, these devices have completely replaced the human timekeepers and manually prepared time cards. Data from the system flows through to the company's payroll and job-order cost-accounting and control records. Basic timekeeping tools are (1) the plastic employee badge, prepunched with identifying information, and (2) the job card, prepunched with the charge number and other information about a particular job.

Automated Timekeeping: Case Study

The badge is permanently assigned to each employee. The job cards follow the parts or assemblies to be worked on. Exceptions are indirect labor and other special cards, which are located in racks adjacent to the time records. Clock-in on reporting for work requires only insertion of the badge into the time recorder, and depression of certain keys. Check-in on a job requires insertion of the badge and one or more job cards, and depression of other keys.

All time recorders are linked electrically to a central control box, a master clock, and an in-line key punch that creates a punched card for each entry. The cards are converted to magnetic tape for passing through computer processes. The first of these, a match against an employee-identification master tape, begins one-half hour after the beginning of each shift.

Within an hour after shift start, an exception report has been prepared for distribution to shop foremen. This report indicates absences, tardy clock-in, preshift overtime, and failure to check in on a job. Each exception must be approved by the shop foreman. Transactions accepted in this first processing routine plus transactions accepted for the remainder of the shift are "posted" to a random-access file arranged by employee. Transactions rejected must be analyzed and corrected for reentry into the processing cycle.

All labor transactions for the day are read out onto another magnetic tape that goes through a series of further computer processes:

1. Preparation of final report to shop foremen. Again prepared for exceptions only, this shows overtime, early clock-out, and other items for approval by foremen.

2. Daily report that balances job time by employee with time between clock-in and clock-out.

3. Daily labor tape prepared after step 2.

4. Matching of job transactions against a random-access file of job numbers. This processing involves application of labor standards on certain jobs, accumulation of time by classification, and preparation of output tapes for numerous reports. These reports include daily reports of actual and budgeted time to certain shops, summary management reports by type of labor, and job-status reports.

5. Entry of the daily labor tape from step 3 above into another computer for the payroll process.

Payroll Processing

Basically, payroll processing consists of three phases: calculation of gross pay, deductions, and net pay; preparation of payroll forms, reports, and documents associated with payroll; distribution of labor costs to appropriate chargeable inventory and expense accounts.

Although there are many methods of processing payroll, all involve an approval of time records and then using authorized rates, the calculation of gross pay, deductions, and net pay. The records normally maintained include:

1. Payroll register listing all employees for the payroll period and showing for each employee information such as hours worked, gross earnings, various deductions from his pay, and his net pay.

2. Check and earning statements for each employee. The earning statement is usually in the form of a stub attached to the check and contains information for review by the employee indicating the gross pay and various deductions that go into calculating the net pay.

3. Earning record for each employee. For various reporting purposes, including external reports to taxing authorities, there is a need for an up-to-date record showing earnings and deductions for each pay period throughout the year. Such a record is used to prepare for FICA, unemployment tax, and quarterly reports on earnings, and to prepare the annual W-2 form showing total earnings and income taxes withheld.

From totals developed in preparing the payroll register, payroll disbursements are normally made through a special payroll account maintained on an imprest basis. A payroll voucher is prepared which becomes the basis for drawing a transfer check resulting in a transfer of cash from the regular cash account into the payroll account equal to the total net pay for the period. Checks are then drawn on this payroll account. Normally the checks are signed by the Treasurer or by a check-signing machine under the treasurer's control. Signed checks are then distributed to the employees. The distribution of checks must be done in such a fashion as to prevent any payroll padding. The identity of each employee who receives a check should be verified and no person should receive more than one check. Control over unclaimed checks should be maintained by preparing a list of these checks and submitting the checks to the cashier or another person in the organization designated to handle unclaimed checks. Under the escheat laws of many states, unclaimed wages ultimately must be turned over to the state, and records adequate for this purpose must be maintained.

In addition to calculating various payroll amounts and preparing and distributing payroll checks and maintaining appropriate payroll records, the payroll department must allocate payroll amounts to various expense accounts affected. In simple situations where employees always work within the same department, the amounts for distribution can be readily obtained by grouping the employees by departments on various payroll registers and obtaining expense totals for each department. However, in cases where employees shift from one department to another or from one job to another, job-time records (after being balanced with attendance-time records) usually form the basis for the payroll distribution. These records, of course, are sorted and grouped according to the appropriate account number and the proper expense account is then charged.

Since the payroll in many companies is the most significant operating cost and involves the disbursement of significant amounts of cash, the **Segregation of Duties** establishment of strong internal control is important to prevent misappropriation of payroll funds and to prepare the payroll and the necessary payroll reports on a timely basis. To establish strong internal control the functions of employment, timekeeping, payroll preparation and record keeping, and distribution of pay to employees should be separated. The advent of computer processing of payrolls, particularly by outside computer service centers, may assist in the segregation of these functions.

Other Aspects of the Personnel System

In his review of the personnel system, the auditor should also be concerned with the staffing process, the appraisal process, and the training and development process.

The *staffing process* is, in a sense, the flow of human resources into, within, and out of the enterprise. The process includes manpower planning and authorization for staffing, recruitment, transfers, demotions, promotions, and separations. The most important aspect of this process is manpower planning, the development of short- and long-range plans for the continuous and proper staffing of the organization. Such planning involves an analysis of skill levels in the organization and analyses of current and expected variances, and requirements. From these analyses, plans are developed to include activities such as internal shifting of manpower, cutbacks in recruiting, expanded recruiting efforts for certain types of manpower, training and development of present employees, promotions, etc. Such planning requires a manpower-information system for collecting relevant data on employees, outlining their current abilities, shortcomings, career interests, job assignments, and previous training and education. The system should be able to provide information on employees eligible for promotion to vacant positions; provide information for designing career ladders for individual employees; and provide information for designing appropriate training and supply data about labor turnover. Obviously the development of such a system requires an analysis of manpower decisions and information required to make such decisions.

For a manpower-information system one of the major sources of data about an employee's abilities, shortcomings, and interests is the *appraisal process*, which involves the systematic evaluation of individuals within the organization. Such evaluations are necessary for providing data for managerial decision-making with respect to selection, correction, training, pay increase, promotion, transfer, etc. Appraisals are designed to provide data about past, present, and expected performance and may vary from highly subjective, almost subconscious, evaluations to highly systematized appraisals focusing on specific behavior.

The *training and development* process consists of many techniques for increasing the individual's capability to contribute to the attainment of personal and organizational goals. The training and management development process includes much more than specific formal training courses. It includes the determination of training and development needs, orientation sessions, skill training, appraisal interviews, counseling, and job rotation, in addition to specific courses conducted by the company and/or by other institutions such as universities and colleges, and professional and trade associations. In short, training and development is an array of activities to improve current or future performance by imparting information, conditioning attitudes, or increasing skills.

The information required for adequate performance of the personnel function is not limited to that generated within the firm. External data relating to the availability of manpower of various skill classes is a necessary part of the planning process. In addition, information about the competitive situation in various labor markets must be gathered. This may include such items as salaries and wage rates paid by others, fringe benefits and work practices, potential availability of workers due to layoff, and competitive recruitment and training practices. The information system of the firm must include an intelligence system to obtain such information, although it may be qualitative in character and not considered part of the standard financial-information system.

In evaluating the aspects of the personnel system related to staffing, appraisal, and training and development, the auditor should determine:

Evaluating the Personnel System

1. The company's policies and procedures for developing manpower requirements and forecasts. These forecasts need to be integrated with the firm's long-range plans and need to specify requirements by classes of personnel.
2. The nature and extent of the company's inventory of manpower. The functioning of the personnel system requires the interchange, storage, and retrieval of data about people. The manpower-inventory file ought to consist of a uniform set of data concerning people that could be easily accessible for manpower decisions.
3. The company's policies and procedures for reviewing performance and for developing a program to improve performance. Such procedures should include evaluation techniques, counseling, on-the-job training, and management-development programs.
4. The company's compensation program and payroll process.

In evaluating the payroll process, the auditor should select some representative payroll transactions and trace them through the system. For example, in auditing the automated labor-recording and payroll process described earlier in this chapter the auditor tested the labor-recording and payroll system by use of simulated, but realistic, transactions designed to test not only the routine processing performed by the computerized process but also the various exception procedures. Examples of such transactions might include:

1. Employee clocks in on time, works normally for full shift.
2. Employee checks in on job without clocking in.
3. Employee clocks in but fails to record a job transaction.
4. Employee leaves before shift ends.
5. Night shift employee clocks in on day shift.
6. Employee works overtime into next shift.
7. Employee charges jobs improperly (for example, direct as indirect time).
8. Employee has rate change greater than programmed limit.
9. Employee charges labor hours while on vacation.
10. Employee requests vacation hours exceeding vacation-hours balance in master record.
11. Employee charges labor hours exceeding the programmed limit.
12. Terminated employee charges labor hours.
13. Employee has accumulated year-to-date earnings and FICA tax is taxable limit prior to processing of valid labor hours.
14. Employee requests tax exemptions exceeding programmed limit.
15. Valid employee charges normal labor hours.[2]

In his evaluation of the payroll process the auditor may also wish to work with outputs of the system—namely, payroll records. For example, from the payroll records of one or more pay periods, he may wish to trace to records maintained in the personnel department such information as names, pay rates, and deductions. He may wish to trace hours worked to production reports and other labor reports developed for management purposes.

In his evaluation of the output, the auditor should evaluate the nature of management reports used to control people and labor costs. Such reports

---

[2]For a detailed description of this system and the evaluation of the system, see Porter, *Auditing Electronic Systems*, pp. 61–66.

should provide information and statistics on such matters as labor turnover, absenteeism, lost time from illness or accident, overtime, idle time, and number of employees hired or terminated and reasons for termination. Management reports should also show labor-cost variances for various departments, jobs, and projects.

Problem in
Personnel Auditing

The Kowal Manufacturing Company employs about fifty production workers and has the following payroll procedures.

The factory foreman interviews applicants and on the basis of the interview either hires or rejects the applicants. When the applicant is hired he prepares a W-4 form (Employee's Withholding Exemption Certificate) and gives it to the foreman. The foreman writes the hourly rate of pay for the new employee in the corner of the W-4 form and then gives the form to a payroll clerk as notice that the worker has been employed. The foreman verbally advises the payroll department of rate adjustments.

A supply of blank time cards is kept in a box near the entrance to the factory. Each worker takes a time card on Monday morning, fills in his name, and notes in pencil on the

time card his daily arrival and departure times. At the end of the week the workers drop the time cards in a box near the door to the factory.

The completed time cards are taken from the box on Monday morning by a payroll clerk. Two payroll clerks divide the cards alphabetically between them, one taking the A to L section of the payroll and the other taking the M to Z section. Each clerk is fully responsible for her section of the payroll. She computes the gross pay, deductions and net pay, posts the details to the employee's earnings records, and prepares and numbers the payroll checks. Employees are automatically removed from the payroll when they fail to turn in a time card.

The payroll checks are manually signed by the chief accountant and given to the foreman. The foreman distributes the checks to the workers in the factory and arranges for the delivery of the checks to the workers who

From the Uniform CPA Examination.

are absent. The payroll bank account is reconciled by the chief accountant who also prepares the various quarterly and annual payroll tax reports.

Required:

List your suggestions for improving the Kowal Manufacturing Company's system of internal control for the factory hiring practices and payroll procedures.

4

Chapter 15

The Reporting
Function Today

The auditor's function has essentially two parts. First is the systems-review and verification function which has been previously discussed. It is in this area that an overwhelming majority of time is spent. The end product of the audit, however, is not the work done but the report issued—the second part of the auditor's function. A magnificent audit with no report is of little benefit to anyone since the audit results would be locked in the mind and heart of the auditor. In order to be effective, therefore, the complete auditor must have a communications skill to match his skills in information-systems review. The auditor's reports are normally intended for two audiences and the reports will differ according to the intended recipient. One group of reports are made to the management and are intended primarily or exclusively for use within the firm. The second group of reports are those rendered with the intent that they be used by outside parties to increase the reliability of data supplied by the corporation and in a very few cases to make additional data available to outside parties.

In the ideal audit engagement, where an effective working relationship has been established between the auditor and his client over a period of time, a large part of the communication that takes place is of an informal

Reporting to Management

nature and occurs at many levels. The alert audit-staff senior when completing an engagement at a plant or a branch will frequently talk with the client's local financial executive and offer his reactions to the engagement and various suggestions for possible improvements in the systems of the organization. At a higher level, the partner in charge of the engagement is normally in contact with the chief financial officer of his client at frequent intervals throughout the year and during the actual audit itself. In these conferences, the partner can communicate any problems that are arising during the course of the audit. Such problems can be of either a managerial or an accounting nature. He will discuss the availability of improved controls, possible improvements in the firm's information system, and various methods of dealing with accounting problems as they arise. Not infrequently, the outside auditor is aware of problems at a division level before they become apparent to the chief financial officer.

In one case, for example, a divisional audit turned up a practice used by the local management of making extensive use of reserve, suspense, and other accrued liabilities accounts to obscure or at least postpone the day of reckoning due to an unfavorable budget variance. The audit partner mentioned this to the financial vice president and an internal auditor was dispatched to get additional details and bring the division's reporting back into line with reality. In such a situation, the financial-statement manipulation would have been corrected by year-end but management might have received an unpleasant surprise in the fourth-quarter results of that division.

To cite another example, one division of a large manufacturing corporation had a very large cost-plus contract with another industrial firm. At an interim audit date the audit team, led by a senior accountant, discovered that the cost being incurred on this contract were 60 percent above the original estimates of costs made before the contract was undertaken. The senior accountant also discovered that the customer had not been notified of the full extent of the overrun. The amounts involved in this situation were very large and the senior accountant, receiving no satisfaction from divisional management, brought the matter to the attention of the partner in charge of the job, who raised the issue at the home office. The investigation that began resulted in the discovery not only of a substantial set of possibly uncollectible billings but of a number of other control weaknesses that led to a complete restructuring of the corporate control system.

While one cannot conclude from a few examples, it is clear that informal communication is a highly effective means of communication between people, for it lacks the constraints which sometimes exist when a written report is rendered. There is often a defensive behavioral reaction to a written criticism or comment that is not provoked when the same point is presented orally.

Some care must be taken, however, to control informal communication in order to protect the auditors involved. Guidelines must be laid down as to who talks to whom. Staff accountants should be careful about making sweeping recommendations, even informally, without a total picture of the company and the experience that an audit partner normally brings to an engagement. While some guidelines may be established, these are largely problems of judgment, and no hard-and-fast rules can be suggested. All significant communications with a client should be recorded in the working papers so that the partner in charge of the engagement will have a record of what was said to whom under what circumstances.

While informal communication is of great importance, formal written communication to the management is also an important part of the audit process. It puts the auditor on record and permits distribution of his comments. In many cases informal communications and comments are tested in verbal discussions with the client and then formalized into written recommendations "for the record" at conclusion of the audit.

The principal report that today is regularly issued specifically to clients is the management letter that virtually all accounting firms require be issued at the conclusion of an audit. This letter, sometimes called the "internal control letter," summarizes for the management the various recommendations of the auditor for improvements in controls and information flows that the auditor has developed as a result of his engagement.

While some letter of this sort is issued on virtually all engagements, its form and content vary significantly. In some cases it is primarily compendium of relatively modest problems in accounting control ("the petty-cash fund at the Columbia plant is not balanced regularly"). In other cases the letter will emphasize the broadest problems of the firm's information system. It may indicate the absence of adequate budgetary control, problems in the long-range planning process, or other subjects with major policy implications. Perhaps most frequently the letter deals with problems somewhere in between these two orders of magnitude. It will deal with inadequacies in a cost-accounting system in a division or plant, the need for standard-cost system to control various types of manufacturing or clerical operations, the absence of adequate documentation to support various types of corporate activities and similar problems.

The management letter is conventionally issued annually at the conclusion of an engagement. It is not primarily intended as a public statement but as a private communication between auditor and client. Nevertheless, in writing the letter, the auditor must be aware that a number of outside parties have become aware of its existence and have been requesting copies of it from the client. Bankers and other credit grantors have been particularly active in this regard and accordingly, in drafting the letter, the auditor must consider the implications of his words to an outside party as well as specifically to the client. An example of such a "management letter" follows this chapter as Appendix 1.

In addition to the management letter, the auditor will frequently render special reports to management either in connection with his regular audit or in connection with a specific engagement undertaken for a purpose. Clearly, virtually all management-services reports fall into this category, although some consulting-type recommendations may arise from an audit and be reported on in that connection.

One characteristic of special reports is that they seldom include a formal opinion of the public accounting firm involved. Management-services reports will normally result in recommendations and may include detailed statements of findings, but the formal opinion of the CPA is normally reserved for his attest function and not used in consulting reports to management.

These special reports to management are of such wide variety that a complete cataloguing would encompass the entire scope of a public accountant's consulting practice. The reports may cover control reviews, the results of executive-search activities, recommendations that result from clerical-work measurement studies, the results of an acquisition investigation, and many others.

In addition to extra-audit activities, the management of a company may request certain specific information in report form at the conclusion of an audit engagement. Such requests may be for detailed financial information in the form of a consolidating report, a complex aging analysis of receivables, or other details. Today such reports are relatively unusual, since managements have generally found that their own accounting group can prepare them more economically and just as correctly as outside accountants. When a client is small, however, and the accounting staff is overburdened, the auditor still may be asked to prepare reports of this sort. Sometimes when such reports are being submitted to outside parties such as creditors, the additional reliability associated with the auditor's name may be sought.

In addition, the auditor is occasionally asked to prepare detailed financial information on sensitive areas such as expense-account reporting, executive-payroll data, and others.

Reporting to the Public: The Attest Function

While reports to management are an important part of the CPA's reporting function, the most significant audit reports are still those in which the auditor communicates the results of his activities for the use of parties outside the corporation.

In such reporting, in an overwhelming majority of cases the auditor is not supplying the basic source information in his report. Rather, his report is one which adds to the reliability of representations generated by others. In performing his attest function, the auditor, therefore, gives his opinion on the financial statements or in some cases other statements of his client. Except for explaining the scope of what he has done, he does not make any representations on his own.

Since the audit function is performed primarily on reports issued by corporations, it is necessary to identify these reports and discuss the extent to which audit reports are included in them.

The most important single vehicle of communication between the corporation and its stockholders and the general public is its annual report. In this report, management describes the operations of the business, its achievements in many operating areas, and to some extent its plans for the future. It also includes financial statements of the previous year.

Public Reports by Corporations

The form and content of annual reports vary greatly. Some corporations simply send a set of financial statements to their stockholders with a mimeographed covering letter. Others print elaborate hundred-page documents with copious illustrations. In addition to differences in bulk, there are significant differences in information content. Some corporations set forth in their annual report a great deal of information very useful to analysts in understanding the corporation. Details of the operations and operating results of different parts of the corporation may be disclosed. In other cases, the annual report is used as an advertising tool to extol the products of the corporation rather than to report seriously on the operations of the year past and plans for the future.

The financial statements also differ in form and content, although there is a greater uniformity here than elsewhere in reports. Virtually all reports include a balance sheet and income statement and an auditor's report covering them. Most corporations today also include a statement of source and application of funds, although this is sometimes included in the managerial text rather than in the formal financial statements. Some companies go on to show additional statements relating to the history of the corporation, details of capital changes, details as to the operations of subsidiaries, foreign operations, etc. In addition to supplying additional statements and information, some corporations are much more inclined to give detail in their basic financial statements than others.

The auditor's report that is included in the annual report normally refers only to the financial statements. It will not cover historical summaries, other operating data, or representations of management in the body of the annual report itself. Even though the report does not specifically cover these items, the auditor will normally read the part of the report for which management is responsible with considerable care while it is in draft or proof form to be certain that any financial information given therein is not inconsistent with the financial statements. The auditor will also routinely check the figures where it is possible to do so from his audit work papers to be certain that no mechanical error has occurred. Frequently, the auditor will also offer suggestions about the content of annual reports, and he will be particularly articulate when he feels that the financial statements are not being described in appropriate terms in the president's letter.

In the final analysis, however, the auditor does not consider that he has any responsibility for the sections of the annual report outside of the financial statements. He may suggest changes, but he does not have the authority to require them. The auditor's report would not be qualified in respect to statements made in the president's letter.

In the case of financial statements, the auditors do have an important responsibility, but the primary responsibility remains with management. The basic representations are being made by the management of the corporation, and the auditor is merely expressing his opinion that they are a fair presentation of results within the framework of generally accepted accounting principles.

There are a few persons today who are protesting this refusal of auditors to accept at least joint responsibility with management for the form and content of financial statements. Representatives of some user groups have suggested that the professional accountant should consider himself to be a professional reporter with at least joint and perhaps prime responsibility for presenting financial data in the most meaningful fashion. Such recommendations have dealt with both the problem of selecting among alternative accounting principles and the extent of detail that is to be supplied. It seems highly unlikely, however, that such suggestions will become a part of the reporting firmament in the near future, if ever. Management feels that its reports to its shareholders are part of its responsibility, and the legal environment strongly supports this suggestion. Auditors in their turn are certainly not anxious to place themselves in the position of reporters with the liabilities which this might entail. While auditors are and should be heard when decisions on financial reporting are made, it seems unlikely that primary decision-making authority will ever rest with them in this area. They are content to be auditors rather than fiscal reporters.

In addition to the annual reports of corporations, quarterly reports are generally issued with a brief statement by management disclosing operating results and an abbreviated set of financial information. The financial information in these quarterly reports is normally limited to income-statement data, although a few firms will also present balance sheets; in these statements virtually no firms will supply supplemental information beyond this. Such quarterly statements are required by the New York Stock Exchange for listed companies. While auditors normally receive copies of these reports, they do not conventionally receive them prior to release and their name is not associated with them in any way. For though corporate financial management will normally consult its auditors when significant accounting problems arise in the preparation of quarterly reports, this is done on a purely voluntary basis.

There have been some questions raised in recent years about whether or not the auditors have any responsibility for quarterly financial statements when in the course of an audit in progress or in any other way it comes to their attention that the reports are misleading. It seems clear that there is no legal responsibility in this area, but some ethical problems do arise. Some individual auditors have suggested that in such a situation they would be certain that the board of directors was informed about the situation, and a few have said that if the board took no action, they would withdraw from an audit engagement, but no formal communication would be undertaken with any outside party.

A more serious problem confronts the auditor when he discovers subsequent to issuing a report that facts existed at that time which would have affected his report had he been aware of them. While such a situation is unusual, it can occur due to either inadvertance or an intentional effort by management to withhold information. Examples might include a significant unrecorded liability, an undisclosed contract with material impact, errors in the determination of percentage of completion, and many others. A distinction must be made, however, between the case in which post-report happenings demonstrate than an estimate included in the financial statements was in error, and the case in which the auditor discovers that facts existed at the time the report was issued that made it misleading. The former will inevitably occur in any system that includes estimates of the future, while the latter should be very exceptional.

When material facts existing at the time of the report are subsequently discovered, the auditor must consider whether there are parties currently relying on the financial statements who would be affected by the facts that have come to his attention. If he concludes that there are such parties, "he should advise his client to make appropriate disclosure of the newly discovered facts and their impact on the financial statements to persons who are known to be currently relying or who are likely to rely on the financial statements and the related auditor's report."[1] This disclosure normally takes the form of revised financial statements.

If the client refuses to make the necessary disclosure, the auditor's problem is even more acute. Under such circumstances, the Committee on Auditing Procedure recommends that the auditor first notify each member of the board of directors of his findings; if no satisfactory resolution is reached, he should then notify the client that his report is no longer to be associated with the financial statements; regulatory agencies and known users of the financial statements should be notified that his report should no longer be relied upon.

In addition to annual reports and quarterly statements issued to the public, the corporate community must also make a series of reports which are filed with the Securities Exchange Commission and are available for public inspection. The principal reports in this connection are the registration statement that must be filed whenever securities are offered to the public (Form S-1), the annual report (Form 10-K) that must be filed annually, and proxy material that must be filed and submitted to shareholders prior to any meeting of the stockholder group.

An audit report covers the financial statements in the registration statement, and the auditor must separately give his consent to the inclusion of his report because of the increased liabilities associated with its inclusion. As in the case of the annual report, in the registration statement the auditor's report covers the financial statements but not the text. Again, however, the auditor conventionally reads the text in draft form with great care to check for inconsistencies and to guard against error, to the extent that it is possible for him to do so. The Form 10-K is accompanied also by an auditor's report but the auditor is not required to report on the data included in proxy material and in the periodic reports (Form 8-K) which are filed by the corporation with the SEC.

The Form of Attestation

In reporting for public consumption on the performance of the attest function, the auditor has a number of standards which he must consider. These standards exist both in generally accepted auditing standards and in the code of ethics in the AICPA. The code of ethics indicates that the auditor "may be held guilty of an act discreditable to the profession if he fails to report any material misstatement known to him to appear in the finan-

---

[1]AICPA, *Statement on Auditing Procedure 41*; this statement discusses the problem of subsequent discovery of facts thoroughly.

cial statement or he fails to direct attention to any material departure from generally accepted accounting principles." The code also provides that a member shall not permit his name to be associated with statements purporting to show financial position or results of operations in such a manner as to imply that he is acting as an independent public accountant, unless he expresses an opinion of some sort or disclaims an opinion or prominently identifies the fact that the financial statements have not been audited.

Generally accepted auditing standards include four standards of reporting as follows:

1. The report shall state whether the financial statements are presented in accordance with generally accepted principles of accounting.
2. The report shall state whether such principles have been consistently observed in the current period in relation to the preceding period.
3. Informative disclosures in the financial statements are to be regarded as reasonably adequate unless otherwise stated in the report.
4. The report shall either contain an expression of opinion regarding the financial statements, taken as a whole, or an assertion to the effect that an opinion cannot be expressed. When an over-all opinion cannot be expressed, the reasons therefor should be stated. In all cases where an auditor's name is associated with financial statements the report should contain a clear-cut indication of the character of the auditor's examination, if any, and the degree of responsibility he is taking.[2]

All of these standards and rules are of a fairly general nature and do not tell the auditor specifically what he should say. In order to provide some uniformity for investors and to avoid the need for an auditing firm to create a separate report each time it renders an opinion on financial statements, the Committee on Auditing Procedures of the AICPA has developed a standard "short form" report:[3]

To The Board of Directors and Stockholders
X Company

We have examined the balance sheet of X Company as of June 30, 19x1 and the related statement(s) of income and retained earnings for the year then

[2] AICPA, Auditing Standards and Procedures.
[3] *Ibid.*

ended. Our examination was made in accordance with generally accepted auditing standards, and accordingly included such tests of the accounting records and such other auditing procedures as we considered necessary in the circumstances.

In our opinion, the accompanying balance sheet and statement(s) of income and retained earnings present fairly the financial position of X Company at June 30, 19x1, and the results of its operations for the year then ended, in conformity with generally accepted accounting principles applied on a basis consistent with that of the preceding year.

Young, Ross & Co., CPAs

August 14, 19x1

This is the most conventional report found with financial statements. The Committee on Auditing Procedures is now working on a revision of this report in an attempt to make it reveal more of what an auditor is actually doing and what responsibility he actually takes. At the present time a large majority of reports issued on financial statements are in this form, although one of the national accounting firms, Price Waterhouse and Company, has revised the arrangement of the words somewhat.

The first paragraph of the report is called the "scope" paragraph since it indicates the extent of the audit performed and the compliance with generally accepted auditing standards. The second paragraph is labeled the opinion paragraph. In it the auditor gives his opinion on the statements and reports on the consistency of application of accounting principles.

Subsequent Events

The date on the auditor's report also has significance; it indicates when the auditor completed his audit field work, and therefore measures the period during which he takes some responsibility for events subsequent to the balance-sheet date that have an impact on the financial statements. While an auditor is not expected to perform an audit of transactions occuring after the balance-sheet date, part of his examination is necessarily performed subsequent to that date. It is most appropriate that in satisfying himself as to the accuracy of estimates made at year-end, the auditor examine transactions in such a period.

In addition to examining post-balance-sheet-date events and transactions that he feels may be relevant to specific year-end figures, the auditor must also undertake a general review of available data relating to the subsequent period to see that nothing has occurred so noteworthy as to require disclosure or adjustment in the financial statements. This review generally encompasses reading minutes of all directors' and executive-committee meetings held up to the date on which field work is completed, a careful reading of interim financial statements to see if unusual items exist that require consideration and understanding prior to issuing a report, and a discussion of company affairs with a top officer of the client.

In the case of audit reports on statements included in registration statements filed with the SEC, the auditor's responsibility for subsequent events extends to the date the registration statement becomes effective. This requires the auditor to make an additional investigation (called an S-1 review) before he consents to the use of his report in such a statement. Such an investigation is not an audit, but includes a careful review of the registration statement, a reading of corporate minutes, a review of interim financial information and comparison with like statements for the previous year, inquiry of officers and other executives as to whether all necessary adjustments have been made both to audited and unaudited interim statements, whether any unusual transactions or material adverse changes in financial position have occurred since the audit period and what the current status is of items accounted for on an estimated basis at the audit date. In addition, a letter of representation will be obtained from a corporate officer indicating the extent to which transactions had occurred after the balance-sheet date that might have a material effect upon the financial statements.

Recent court cases have indicated that the auditor's responsibility for a registration-statement review goes beyond casual conversation with the client. In the BarChris case, the court held that the S-1 review performed was inadequate, both in the time devoted to it and in that the auditor "was too easily satisfied with glib answers to his inquiries." The court went on to say:

> This is not to say that he should have made a complete audit. But there were enough danger signals in the materials which he did examine to require some further investigation on his part. Generally accepted accounting standards required such further investigation under these circumstances. It is not always sufficient merely to ask questions.[4]

In the light of this decision, some extensions of the S-1 review have been instituted by auditors and the Committee on Auditing Procedure of the AICPA has a new statement on this subject under consideration.

---

[4] *Escott* v. *BarChris*, et al., U. S. District Court, Southern District, N. Y., 62 Civ. 3539.

The Qualified Opinion

While most audits are concluded in such a way as to permit the issuance of a standard unqualified short-form report, there are circumstances when this is not possible. When this is the case, the auditor must render a qualified opinion, or, in extreme cases, an adverse opinion or a disclaimer of any opinion. Any time an auditor's name is associated with financial statements, he must take one of these alternatives, since he must disclose his relationship to the financial statements under the fourth standard of reporting indicated above.

Reports can be qualified for four different reasons: scope of audit, material and defined uncertainty as to the future, disagreement in regard to certain accounting principles, or lack of consistency in the application of accounting principles from year to year.

A report that is qualified as to the scope of the audit will normally include this qualification in its first paragraph, where the auditor describes himself and his work after the expression that says "our audit was performed in accordance with generally accepted auditing standards and accordingly included such tests of the accounting records as we considered necessary in the circumstances." The auditor will add the words "except that" and then outline the limitation on the scope of the audit engagement. The nature of this limitation may vary widely. In some cases, it may simply represent a standard auditing procedure, such as the confirmation of accounts receivable, that was not feasible because the customer was unwilling to confirm balances. The United States Government, for example, will frequently not confirm account balances. In this case, if the auditor is able to satisfy himself by other means, he so reports, and the qualification as to scope is not carried on into the opinion paragraph.

On other occasions the scope of auditing procedures to be followed may be limited by the terms of the engagement or by the time at which the auditor was engaged. For example, the client may have requested that the auditor not confirm receivable balances, or the auditor may have been engaged at a time when it was impossible for him to observe physical inventories at the beginning of the year. Under these circumstances, other procedures may not be sufficient to enable the auditor to fully satisfy himself and if so the qualification in the scope of the audit may be carried down to be included in the opinion paragraph of the report as well.

Not infrequently, some part of an entity being reported on in consolidated statements will be audited by another public accounting firm than the one signing the report on the consolidated statements. In such a case, if the subsidiary is material, the report on the consolidated statements will include a qualification as to scope. This will normally state that certain subsidiaries were audited by other public accountants. In most situations of this sort, the qualification will be carried down to the opinion paragraph as well, which will then read:

> In our opinion, based upon our examination and upon the reports of other independent public accountants referred to above, . . .

There are significant differences in the extent of reliance placed on the report of other public accounting firms. In some cases, the parent-company auditor will simply accept the report of another firm. In others, the parent auditor will review audit working papers and programs, and occasionally will supply a comprehensive audit program for the other auditor to follow. In recent years, after a few unfortunate experiences,[5] auditors are generally increasing their surveillance over the work of other auditors on whose reports they rely.

In some situations the scope of the audit is so limited that the auditor cannot express an opinion on the financial statements taken as a whole. If, for example, a significant part of operations could not be audited, or if a material inventory could not be verified to the auditor's satisfaction, it might be impossible for him to express an opinion on the financial statements taken as a whole. The auditor should not issue a report in which he gives an opinion subject to scope restrictions so great as to indicate he could not perform an adequate audit. The extent to which a limitation on audit scope would forbid the expression of any opinion or require the use of a qualified opinion is a subject for the individual auditor's judgment in the light of the facts of a particular case.

The second form of qualified report that an auditor can issue is a report qualified by some major future uncertainty. While all financial statements are subject to some uncertainty because estimates of future performance do exist in many accounts, there will sometimes be situations where a single major uncertainty exists and its resolution might create a material change in the financial statements of the corporation. If, for example, a corporation is subject to the possibility of a material renegotiation refund, or the imposition of a tax on undistributed earnings, or an adverse finding in a law suit, the auditor may feel that his opinion on the financial statements should be qualified by the existence of this uncertainty. The same might be the case if there were a very major account receivable which might not be collected or if substantial costs had been incurred on behalf of a project whose success was subject to doubt.

---

[5]See for example the case of Atlantic Acceptance Corp.

In these cases the auditor conventionally uses what is called a "subject to" opinion, in which he describes the uncertainty or refers to footnotes describing it and then gives his report. The "subject to" qualification will normally appear following the words "in our opinion" in the opinion paragraph of the report.

In such cases, the auditor frequently writes an additional paragraph when he feels that the item is of such significance that it should be specifically described in his report. Three "subject to" qualified opinions are presented below. In one example, the scope paragraph is also reproduced since it includes a frequently seen scope qualification, while in the other two, the standard scope paragraph is omitted.

Example 1: Fotomat Corporation

On February 12, 1969 Eastman Kodak Company brought an action against the Company alleging unfair competition and infringement of trademarks and trade dress and requesting injunctive relief. The existence of their litigation has had and may continue to have an adverse effect on the Company's ability to sell franchises, see Note L.

In our opinion, subject to the effect on the financial statements of uncertainties resulting from the Eastman Kodak Company litigation referred to above, the statements referred to above present fairly the consolidated financial position of Fotomat Corporation and consolidated subsidiaries at January 31, 1969, and the consolidated results of their operations for the two years then ended, in conformity with generally accepted accounting principles consistently applied.

Touche, Ross, Bailey & Smart
Certified Public Accountants

San Diego, California,
February 24, 1969.
(April 17, 1969 as to Note L)

Example 2: Graphic Sciences, Inc.

In our opinion, subject to the successful development of a commercial market for the products referred to in Note C and to the obtaining of adequate financing, the financial statements mentioned above present fairly the financial position of Graphic Sciences, Inc. and the consolidated financial position of the Company and subsidiary company at November 30, 1967, and the results of their respective operations and their respective cash receipts and disbursements for the period from March 6, 1967 (date of incorporation of the Company) to November 30, 1967, in conformity with generally accepted accounting principles.

S. D. Leidesdorf & Co.

New York, N.Y.
December 8, 1967

Example 3: Maust Coal and Coke Corp.

Haskins & Sells
Certified Public Accountants

Two Broadway
New York 10004

The Board of Directors and Stockholders
of Maust Coal and Coke Corp.:

We have examined the consolidated balance sheet of Maust Coal and Coke Corp. and its subsidiaries as of March 31, 1968 and the related consolidated statement of income and retained earnings (deficit) for the year then ended. Our examination was made in accordance with generally accepted auditing standards, and accordingly included such tests of the accounting records and such other auditing procedures as we considered necessary in the circumstances; we did not observe the physical inventories taken at March 31, 1967 as we were not the Company's auditors at that date, but we carried out other auditing procedures with respect to such inventories.

Subsequent to March 31, 1968, the Company has failed to make principal payments due on the 5% promissory notes; accordingly, the holders of such debt could have demanded payment (and in the event of such demand, the holders—other than the principal stockholder—of all other debt of the Company could have also demanded payment) of all debt outstanding. Pursuant to an agreement dated June 4, 1968, referred to in Note 1(a) to the consolidated financial statements, among certain institutional holders, such demand has not been made to this date. As shown by the accompanying consolidated balance sheet which has been prepared on a going concern basis, current liabilities (including long-term debt currently due by its original terms) are substantially in excess of current assets.

In our opinion, subject to the continued forbearance of the holders of debt in making demand for the payment of all applicable debt, the accompanying consolidated balance sheet and consolidated statement of income and retained earnings (deficit) present fairly on a going concern basis the financial position of Maust Coal and Coke Corp. and its subsidiaries at March 31, 1968 and the results of their operations for the year then ended, in conformity with generally accepted accounting principles applied on a basis consistent with that of the preceding year.

Haskins & Sells

June 10, 1968

A third form of qualification exists when the auditor and the client disagree on some matter of accounting principle. If, for example, a stock dividend were issued and accounted for as a transfer from retained earnings to paid-in capital at the par value rather than the market value of the shares involved, the auditor would have to call attention to this fact in his report since generally accepted accounting principles require that the market value be transferred. Many other items might also give rise to such a situation. Under these circumstances, the auditor will conventionally insert a phrase "except for" immediately following the words "in our opinion" in his report spelling out the source of the disagreement and generally expressing its amount in monetary terms.

An example of such a report is the Ernst and Ernst report on the accounts of O. M. Scott & Sons for the year ended September 30, 1968. In this year, Scott provided a revenue reserve which was charged against income in the amount of $443,000, approximately 12 percent of net income. The Company described this provision as an adjustment to earnings to take into account the inventory carried by its dealers which was felt to be at a level such that it might reduce sales in fiscal 1969. Their auditors concluded that such a provision represented an arbitrary shifting of income, and their opinion therefore was as follows:

In our opinion, except for the revenue reserve which is at variance with generally accepted accounting principles, and the effect of which was to reduce net income as explained in note (d), the accompanying balance sheet, statements of income and retained earnings, and source and application of funds present fairly the consolidated results of their operations and consolidated source and application of funds for the year then ended, in conformity with generally accepted accounting principles applied on a basis consistent, except for the aforementioned change, with that of the preceding year.

The last phrases of this report also illustrate the fourth form of qualification found in audit reports. This is the qualification as to consistency in application of accounting principles from year to year. When a company changes accounting principles followed, the auditor is required to disclose this fact by qualifying his report where he expresses his opinion that the financial statements are presented in accordance with generally accepted accounting principles applied on a basis consistent with that of the preceding year. In this section the auditor will include a sentence with the words "except for" and spell out the area in which there has been an accounting change, its significance in the financial statements, and in some cases his approval of the change. The disclosure either in the report or in the notes to the financial statement should include the effect upon income of the accounting change and should indicate what income would have been had the change not been made.

A dramatic example of such a qualification appeared in the report of Peat, Marwick, Mitchell & Co. on the 1965 statements of Control Data Corporation. In this case, the auditors considered the changes to be so significant that they wrote a separate paragraph, as well as qualifying the consistency section of the opinion paragraph. The relevant sections of their report were as follows:

> As explained in note 2 to the consolidated financial statements, certain development and application costs and marketing expenses, heretofore charged off as incurred, have been deferred and are being amortized over a period of three years. Also, as of January 1, 1965, the Company changed from an accelerated method of recording depreciation of computing systems and related equipment to the straight-line method with no change in estimated lives. The effect of these changes was to increase net earnings for the year ended June 30, 1965 by approximately $3,390,000.
>
> In our opinion, such financial statements present fairly the consolidated financial position of Control Data Corporation and subsidiaries at June 30, 1965 and the results of their operations for the year then ended, in conformity with generally accepted accounting principles which, except for the changes which significantly increased net earnings as described in the preceding paragraph, have been applied on a basis consistent with that of the preceding year.

It should be pointed out that consistency qualifications arise only when the method of accounting for similar economic conditions is changed between periods. When the accounting change reflects a change in economic reality, such as the discovery that particular capitalized research and development expenditures will not give rise to a salable product, to reflect this reality by writing off capitalized costs would not constitute a change in accounting principles.

Disclaimers and Adverse Opinions

There will be times when some of the items mentioned above become of such overwhelming importance in interpreting the financial results of operations or the financial position that the auditor cannot adequately qualify his opinion in their regard. This was discussed briefly in connection with audit scope, and the same situation exists in connection with uncertainties and disagreements as to principles. In such circumstances it may be necessary to give a disclaimer of an opinion or an adverse opinion.

If, for example, the uncertainty affecting the company is of such a magnitude that an adverse determination would terminate the company as a viable economic entity, it does not make sense to express an opinion that except for the uncertainty the financial statements fairly present the company's financial position, since the contingency is so overwhelming that the rest of the statements are basically insignificant. A recent sample of this situation is the case of Hazeltine Corporation, which got into an antitrust law suit with Zenith Radio Corporation. In 1965, no decision had been reached in the case, and accordingly due to this uncertainty the auditor's opinion was qualified. By the time the 1966 report was issued, however, Hazeltine had lost the lawsuit in the first court and a judgment had been entered against it in an amount substantially in excess of the company's net worth. At this point, the very existence of the corporation was called into question and the auditors were required to disclaim an opinion, which they did in the following words:

> Because of the possible material effect of the litigation referred to in Notes 1 and 2 to the consolidated financial statements, the outcome of which is uncertain, we do not express any opinion on the consolidated financial statements taken as a whole. Were it not for the referenced litigation, in our opinion, the accompanying consolidated balance sheet and consolidated statement of income and earned surplus would present fairly the financial position of Hazeltine Corporation and its wholly-owned subsidiaries at December 31, 1965, and the results of their operations for the year then ended, in conformity with generally accepted accounting principles applied on a basis consistent with that of the preceding year.

This approach had to be taken due to the magnitude of the contingency. In other words, when he renders an opinion on financial statements, the auditor cannot be in the position of answering the question, "Aside from that, Mrs. Lincoln, how did you enjoy the show?"

If the qualification is the result of a dispute over principle and is of enormous materiality, the auditor is once again forced to consider whether a qualified opinion adequately expresses his reservations. If the disagreement about principle is over a matter of significant importance, such as the recording of depreciation or the inclusion of overheads in inventory, the auditor may be forced to conclude as a result of this violation of principle that the financial statements as presented by the company do not fairly present the results of operations. In such circumstances, an adverse report must be rendered. Such reports are extremely rare, since the auditor usually will have resigned the engagement or been dismissed at the point where such a report would be issued.

The Long-Form Report

The short-form report in its many variations is by far the most common issued by auditors today. Historically, auditors were the principal source of financial information about a company, and in earlier times it was conventional for the auditor to present substantial additional information over and above the financial statements in the report he rendered to the client. This resulted in what was called a "long-form report," which included breakdowns of individual accounts and various forms of analytical presentations that supplemented the basic data presented. The long-form report included the words of the short-form report on financial statements but presented far more detail. The additional information was covered by the auditor's opinion as being a fair presentation "in all respects material to the financial statements taken as a whole." As the financial-information systems of corporations improved, the corporation seldom felt the need of having the auditor prepare detailed schedules when its own accounting department could do so very satisfactorily and at much less cost. Accordingly, the use of the long-form report has so decreased in frequency as to be seldom found.

As will be discussed in the next chapter, however, some users of accounting information have suggested that the practice of rendering a long-form report be revived, but that the content of the report represent a marked change from what was traditionally included.

Reports to Special Parties

In addition to reports on financial statements, from time to time the auditor is asked to make reports on the results of his audit investigations to various special parties with particular interests. For example, long-term creditors frequently ask an auditor's opinion that the provisions of debt covenants have been complied with. Bonus committees of boards of directors may seek an audited determination of the amount of profit available for profit sharing under an agreement. In such cases, the auditor must design his report to the given specific purpose, and an opinion will be given on the more limited subject being covered.

Another report that is regularly requested of auditors is the "cold comfort" letter supplied to underwriters in connection with the registration and public sale of securities. Such letters are generally requested by underwriters as an aid in discharging their responsibilities under the Securities Act of 1933. The letter normally deals with the accountant's independence, formal compliance of the financial statements with the requirements of the Securities Act, the unaudited interim financial statements appearing in the prospectus, the findings of the S-1 review undertaken by the auditor and any other matters specified in the underwriting agreement. In such a letter, where the auditor is commenting on certain aspects of an enterprise when he has not performed a complete audit, he may frequently use the negative assurance format where he describes procedures and states that in performing them nothing came to his attention which caused him to believe that interim or other statements were misleading. An example of a "cold comfort" letter, taken from AICPA Statement on Auditing Procedure 35, is included as Appendix 2 to this chapter.

As will be discussed in the next chapter, it seems likely that the demand for an expansion of various nonstandard reports will grow in the years to come and the auditor will increasingly have to think about leaving his standard reporting format as he is asked to expand the function he performs.

June 1, 19x1

Mr. Jones, President
XYZ Company
Jackass Flats, Arizona

Dear Mr. Jones:

In connection with our examination of the financial statements of the XYZ Company for the year ended December 31, 19x0, we reviewed the system of internal control and accounting procedures. Our observations and recommendations are submitted herein for your consideration.

Formal Long-Range Business Planning

As an aid in planning and effectively controlling future growth and expansion of the company, we suggest that you consider adopting a formal approach to strategic business planning. Alternative strategies should be developed and evaluated within the framework of defined corporate objectives. Resource gaps in facilities, finances, organization, systems and products should be identified. The selected strategy should then be converted into action plans which are assigned to specific individuals.

Data Processing

We believe the company's data processing systems and operations are not functioning effectively, and the standards and controls in use are not adequate to provide a reasonable degree of reliability and accuracy.

Our survey of user departments indicated the following conditions exist with respect to the material obtained from the Systems and Data Processing Department:

1. An excessive number of errors and reruns.
2. A lack of timeliness in the processing of files and reports.
3. An inadequate program for testing new applications and changes.
4. A lack of adequate controls available to the user department to determine the accuracy of reports and documents produced by the Systems and Data Processing Department.

Our review of the computer applications disclosed a significant number of major deficiencies which in our opinion largely contribute to the above problems. The major areas of deficiency are:

1. Documentation
2. File Protection
3. Systems Design
4. Scheduling
5. Testing and Changes

Published standards covering proper practices in these areas of deficiency are essentially non-existent; it follows that employees cannot be effectively directed and supervised unless such standards are made known to them. These deficiencies are described and commented upon in detail in a separate report which we have furnished to you. In our opinion, these deficiencies are the primary contributing factors to the lack of reliability and accuracy of the work performed by the Systems and Data Processing Department.

Further, in our opinion, these deficiencies result from a basic lack of technical management in the systems and data processing organization. A basic responsibility of technical management within such an organization is to establish, promulgate, and enforce adequate technical standards.

We recommend that you take steps to remedy these deficiencies by upgrading technical management, establishing adequate technical standards, instituting a training program for personnel in the application of these standards and establishing procedures to enforce compliance with the standards.

Cash

There is no independent review of the computer-prepared checks from the time of their preparation to their issuance. To improve internal control, we suggest that a review of these checks be made by a person independent of their preparation. We also suggest that a person in authority approve all new vendors to be coded into the computer.

Commission and rent checks should be supported by a check request signed by the treasurer or some other responsible officer as an indication of approval for payment. We recommend also that a formal check request be signed by the person initiating the request and approved by the treasurer to cover all disbursements on which no invoice is received.

Inventories

Two complete sets of records are presently maintained to allow for the preparation of financial statements on a full cost basis for inventories. We believe that the only records required for this purpose, in addition to your general ledger, would be a memo record, posted monthly, reflecting labor and overhead in inventories and the related deferred taxes. Use of such a record would eliminate the present duplication of work by the accounting department.

Purchasing Department

The files of open order cards and open raw material requirement cards are presently being maintained by a clerk in the purchasing department. We recommend that the file of open raw material requirement cards be maintained in the production control department along with the remainder of the open requirement cards.

We recommend that open order cards be maintained at the receiving and inspection area, so that reports of receipt of merchandise can be transmitted directly to the computer immediately after inspection.

In order to avoid possible conflicts of interest, we suggest that the company establish a formal policy with regard to the following practices:

1. Direct or indirect ownership or association by officers and employees with suppliers.
2. Provision for several quotations or bids on major purchases.
3. Gifts from vendors, vacation trips or entertainment paid for by vendors, and similar matters.
4. Independent review of purchasing effectiveness.

Internal Audit

To control subsidiary and branch operations more effectively, and to provide management with a means of improving company procedures and monitoring compliance with company policies, we recommend that you consider establishing an internal audit department. Reports prepared by this department would be submitted directly to top management so that necessary action could be initiated.

In this connection, administrative and accounting manuals should be prepared so that company policies and procedures would be clearly defined for all employees. We believe that such manuals would also be useful in training new personnel.

Records Retention

We suggest that record retention schedules be prepared on a formal basis to meet the specific requirements of various operating locations. These schedules should include a program covering the micro filming and subsequent destruction of the original document. At a minimum, the original documents should be retained at least one year.

Property, Plant, and Equipment

In order to improve control over property, plant, and equipment we suggest that a physical count of equipment be made and agreed to the detail records. Further, the cost and accumu-lated depreciation of items no longer present should be written off.

We again recommend that a minimum dollar limit be set for capital items and that all items less than $100 be charged to expenses.

The cost of your new building and the cost of remodeling for the training center both exceeded the amounts authorized by the Board of Directors. We suggest that a policy be established whereby formal authorizations are prepared for all projects in excess of a set dollar amount. Total costs, accumulated by project, should be compared to the authorizations. Additional authorizations should be required for projects where expenditures exceed the original authorization by a set dollar amount or a set percentage.

As an aid in determining the desirability of making major capital expenditures, we suggest that you consider the return on investment approach.

Production

Conceptually, the XYZ Company has an advanced and sophisticated manufacturing system, particularly for a company of its size. In recent periods, however, we have observed a number of things leading us to feel that the system is not functioning effectively. For example:

1. Inventories of work in process and raw materials have increased substantially during the past year;
2. Subcontractors have been used increasingly to perform subassembly work; this is typically more expensive than the same work performed in the company's plant;
3. A heavy preponderance of shop orders is being completed significantly behind the original schedule date (This observation holds true even when actual completion dates are compared with rescheduled completion dates);

4. The dollar cost of inventory supporting certain specific shipments is almost double the minimum required level.

We believe that a comprehensive review of the manufacturing system should be conducted, including both computer and manual portions. This would enable management to establish specific priorities and authorize the sequence of events necessary to rectify the difficulties.

Cost of Products Sold

Costs of products sold are now determined for interim financial statement purposes on a basis which does not provide explanation and analysis of the type most useful for management decisions. As a result, management places greater reliance (in decision making) on other data than on the company's financial statements. We suggest that action be taken to revise the flow of information so that specific reasons can be pinpointed for:

1. Changes in gross margin percentages compared to plan.
2. Variances from standard cost of sales.
3. Differences between physical and book inventories.

We suggest that a monthly report for management be prepared showing as precisely as possible all of the variances between actual gross margin and plan.

The failure to analyze variances from standard costs used in computing cost of products sold results from two principal causes:

1. The variances developed are too general to provide the type of information which would be useful. As an example, the labor variance includes both a wage rate variance factor and an efficiency factor. We believe these two factors should be segregated so management can determine where the most significant variations occurred from planned results.

2. The variances are not properly analyzed to determine the factors causing the variance; thus not enough useful information is provided for management to formulate decisions. As an example, the material usage variance was affected by a sizeable increase in the amount of production work subcontracted. The effect of subcontracting was not analyzed, with the result that the variance had little effective information content for management purposes.

We recognize that precise and complete analysis of all periodic variances may not be practical or even desirable. We feel confident, however, that valuable information can be developed with little effort in this area.

Analysis should be made each year of the reasons for the differences between actual variable burden and standard variable burden. Such an analysis could provide management with important information for planning future operations and assessing the effectiveness of past operations.

The items mentioned in this letter have been previously discussed with you and other operating personnel and in some cases steps have already been taken to improve deficiencies noted.

This letter summarizes the areas of internal control weakness and potential systems improvement which came to our attention in the review of internal control undertaken in connection with our examination of the financial statements of XYZ Company for the year ended December 31, 19x0. Since our annual audit is not intended to be a detailed review of all systems and procedures, this report should not be considered to be all inclusive of the areas where improvements might be achieved.

Very truly yours,

2: Sample Letter for Underwriters

Appendix

Dear Sirs:

We have made an examination of the balance sheet of Blank Company (the "Company") as of December 31, 1964, the related statement of income for the five years then ended, and the related statement of earned surplus, and schedules, for the three years then ended, and our opinions (qualified as set forth therein) with respect to the foregoing are included in the registration statement (No. 2–00000) filed by the Company under the Securities Act of 1933 (the "Act"). Such registration statement and the related prospectus, as amended at the time such registration statement became effective, are herein referred to respectively as the "Registration Statement" and the "Prospectus."

We are independent public accountants as required by the Act and the applicable published rules and regulations thereunder.

In our opinion, the financial statements and schedules examined by us and included or incorporated by reference in the Prospectus or elsewhere in the Registration Statement comply as to form in all material respects with the applicable accounting requirements of the Act and the published rules and regulations thereunder, with respect to Registration Statements on Form S–1.

We have not made an examination of any financial statements of the Company as of any date or for any period subsequent to December 31, 1964; and although we have made an examination for the year ended December 31, 1964, the purpose (and therefore the scope) of such examination was to enable us to express our opinion as to the financial statements as of December 31, 1964 and for the year then ended but not as to the financial statements for any interim period within each year. Therefore, we are unable to and do not express any opinion on the unaudited balance sheet as of March 31, 1965, interim statement of surplus for the three months then ended, and interim statements of income for the three-month periods ended March 31, 1965 and 1964 and related schedules contained in the Prospectus or included elsewhere in the Registration Statement or on the financial position or results of operations as of any date or for any period subsequent to December 31, 1964.

However, we have at the Company's request carried out procedures and made inquiries:

with respect to the three-month periods ended March 31, 1964 and 1965, as follows:

1. read the unaudited statements of income for these periods included in the Prospectus;
2. read the unaudited balance sheet as of March 31, 1965, and unaudited statement of surplus for the three months then ended included in the Prospectus and the related unaudited schedules included elsewhere in the Registration Statement;
3. read the 1965 minutes of the meetings of the stockholders, the Board of Directors, and the executive and finance committees of the Company as set forth in the minute books at June 25, 1965 (having previously read the 1964 minutes as a part of our examination of the financial statements for that year), officials of the Company having advised us that the minutes of all such meetings through that date were set forth therein; and
4. made inquiries of certain officials of the Company who have responsibility for financial and accounting matters as to whether the unaudited financial statements and schedules referred to above are fair presentations of the financial information they purport to show and have been prepared on a basis sub-

stantially consistent with the audited financial statements and schedules included in the Prospectus or elsewhere in the Registration Statement; and

with respect to the period from March 31, 1965 to June 25, 1965, as follows:

5. read the interim unaudited financial statements of the Company for the months of April and May 1965, officials of the Company having advised us that no such financial statements as of any date or for any period subsequent to May 31, 1965 were available;
6. read the 1965 minutes of meetings as set forth in (3) above; and
7. made inquiries of certain officials of the Company who have responsibility for financial and accounting matters, as to whether since March 31, 1965 there had been any change in the capital stock or funded debt of the Company or any material adverse change in its financial position or results of operations.

The foregoing procedures and inquiries do not constitute an examination made in accordance with generally accepted auditing standards; also they would not necessarily reveal material adverse changes in the financial position or results of operations or inconsistencies in the application of generally accepted accounting principles.

We may state, however, that the foregoing procedures and inquiries did not cause us to believe that:

a. The unaudited financial statements and schedules, described above, included in the Prospectus or elsewhere in the Registration Statement are not fair presentations of the information they purport to show (but the subject matter of the qualification expressed in our opinion included in the Registration Statement and Prospectus is pertinent also to the unaudited financial statements), have not been prepared on a basis substantially consistent with the audited financial statements and schedules included therein, or fail to comply as to form in any material respect with the applicable accounting requirements of the Act and the published rules and regulations thereunder with respect to Registration Statements on Form S–1, or

b. during the period from March 31, 1965 to June 25, 1965 there was any change in the capital stock or funded debt of the Company, or any material adverse change in the financial position or results of operations, in each case from that set forth by the latest financial statements in the Prospectus, except in all instances as set forth in or contemplated by the Registration Statement and Prospectus

or as occasioned by the declaration or payment of dividends.

The terms "financial position" and "results of operations" are used in this letter in their conventional accounting sense; accordingly, they relate to the financial statements of the business as a whole and have the same meaning when used in this letter as in our opinion contained in the Registration Statement and Prospectus.

This letter is solely for the information of the Company and the Underwriters and is not to be referred to in whole or in part in the Registration Statement or Prospectus or quoted by excerpt or reference outside the underwriting group in connection with the registration under the Act or the sale of securities, except for any reference to it in an underwriting agreement or in any list of closing documents.

Problems in Reporting by Auditors

1. The auditor's client is a manufacturing corporation with annual sales of $20 million and total assets of $18 million. Net income is $2 million. The auditor was unable to observe physical inventory at the beginning of the year since he was not engaged at that time. No other auditor observed the inventory. The client uses a perpetual inventory system and controls over inventory are very good. Inventory balance at year end was $4 million while at the beginning

of the year it was $5 million. Observation of year end physical inventory resulted in no audit adjustments.

a. What kind of report should the auditor give? Make any explicit assumptions you desire.

b. Would your answer be different if a periodic inventory system was used?

2. The client is a retail store which has always sold on a cash basis. In the fall of 1969, the credit terms were changed to "nothing down, 24 months to pay." At year end, an analysis of the accounts indicates past due payments of less than 1% of the $18 million receivable balance. The client believes that a 2% allowance for uncollectibles will be adequate.

a. What evidence should the auditor obtain in regard to this account?

b. What kind of disclosure should be given in the auditor's report?

3. The following footnote appeared in the 1961 accounts of Tenax, Inc., relating to installment contracts receivable of $4 million (out of total assets of $8.5 million).

Note 2 Installment Contracts Receivable

In accordance with trade practice, installment contracts receivable and reserves held by financial institutions due after one year are included in current assets. Subsequent to September 30, 1961 all installment contracts receivable have been pledged to secure notes payable and contingent liabilities with certain financial institutions with whom installment contracts receivable have been discounted. A substantial portion of installment contracts is delinquent and in various stages of collection. In the opinion of management, the reserve is a reasonable amount to provide for losses, including liquidation and collection costs, but the ultimate amount of such losses is not readily ascertainable.

Assuming that all other accounts were in good order, what form of auditor's report should be presented?

4. Comment upon the following auditor's report:

We have examined the accompanying consolidated balance sheet of Tastee Freez Industries, Inc. and subsidiaries as of January 31, 1963 and the related statements of income and stockholders equity for the year then ended. Our examination was made in accordance with generally accepted auditing standards, and accordingly included such tests of the accounting records and such other auditing procedures as we considered necessary in the circumstances.

As explained more fully in Note 4 to the financial statements, substantial sales of mobile units have been made during the past two years under contracts generally providing for payment over a five year period. The mobile unit and Port-a-Store program is relatively new; insufficient time has elapsed to establish experience upon which estimates of unknown losses, if any, can be based, and the ultimate collectibility of the contracts depends upon the future success of the program.

As explained in Notes 2 and 4, Carrols, Inc. is a franchise holder which began operations in 1962 and in which the Company holds a 14% stock interest. The ultimate collectibility of the aggregate indebtedness of Carrols, Inc. of $14,794,150 arising from the sale of mobile units and drive-in store locations during the current fiscal year depends upon the success of Carrols' future operations which consist of Carrols' drive-in locations and the mobile unit and Port-a-Store programs. Carrols Inc. had limited operations during the fiscal year ended January 31, 1963 and incurred substantial losses during this initial period of operations.

In our opinion the financial statements referred to above present fairly the consolidated financial position of Tastee Freez Industries, Inc. and subsidiaries at January 31, 1963 and the consolidated results of their operations for the year then ended in conformity with generally accepted accounting principles applied on a basis consistent with that of the preceding year.

Touche, Ross, Bailey and Smart

Chicago, Illinois
4/26/63

The total assets of Tastee Freez amounted to $21.5 million, while the company had income of $1.2 million on revenues of $15.8 million.

Chapter 16

Expansion of the
Reporting Function
by Auditors

In the previous chapter we have discussed the reporting function of the auditor as it has been traditionally performed. This is related primarily to the report on the financial statements of an enterprise. As the audit objective changes and develops, however, it seems clear that this traditional reporting function will be expanded to include a variety of other reports. This expansion will be a natural one, since to perform an audit of the entire information system and produce a report on only one of its aspects is an under-utilization of the professional skills employed.

More importantly, this expansion will occur because of the increasing disclosure which will be required of corporations. At the present time there is substantial pressure being brought to bear for additional information about relevant economic facts. This pressure arises from government agencies and from the various users of financial information today who feel that in its current form financial reporting has many inadequacies.

The basic functions of public financial reporting by corporations are generally agreed to be a scorekeeping function and an investment-decision-oriented function. The first relates to the historical success of the corporate management in performing its stewardship of the assets of the corporation, and the second relates to the needs of investors who are making decisions to commit resources to an enterprise or to withdraw resources therefrom. It is the latter purpose—to inform investors—that provides the rationale for the disclosure sections of the securities laws. The underlying hypothesis is that through disclosure, investors will be able to make better decisions which will result in both a more efficient allocation of the resources of the economy and reduced unexpected speculative losses by individual investors.

There are doubts today about whether the conventional financial report adequately performs either the scorekeeping or the investment-decision-making function. In connection with scorekeeping, there has been considerable criticism of financial statements because of the availability of a diversity of generally accepted accounting principles that could be used to describe the same economic reality. Thus, one corporation's "score" revealed by the financial statements is not comparable with another's. While the trend for a single corporation may be meaningful, even this is subject to doubts, since corporations do on occasion change the principles they use. Even though the effect of the change must be disclosed, there are questions whether its impact is fully comprehended by users of the statements. Since management has the primary responsibility for preparing a report, the auditor is not in a position to insist upon what is in his judgment the best possible form of reporting, as long as the principles selected by management fall within the scope of generally accepted accounting principles.

In addition to such problems in the implementation of conventional accounting principles there are also problems which arise from the very nature of accounting methodology. Accounting principles are based on matching appropriate costs with revenues as they are earned. Revenues are considered to be earned when the task of the corporation is essentially complete in regard to the product or service being provided. As the time span of management decision-making extends, it is clear that the financial statements do not reflect the appropriate scorekeeping measurement of the decisions which management has made in a particular period. The chief executive of one large corporation observed recently that he finished managing 1969 before the end of 1968. Thus, it is clear that a significant lag exists between the point at which management is making decisions and the point at which the scorekeeping function is performed. This lag is variable and depends upon the decisions involved, and accordingly there is no systematic way in which the decisions of management can be evaluated by the financial statements at any time close to the decision-making point. In general, it can be said that there are major difficulties inherent in the accounting model for associating actions and results; therefore, the generally accepted accounting "score" may not appropriately reflect the economic implications of the corporation's activities during the particular period being reported on.

In addition, the arbitrary time period for which an accountant must report clearly accentuates the problem of associating actions and results. A year represents the length of time it takes the earth to circle the sun. There is no apparent connection between this length of time and the appropriate time cycle for success-measurement within a business enterprise.

Finally, the accountant's scorekeeping does not reflect the uncertainty that is characteristic of the end result reported. Within the framework of generally accepted accounting principles numerous estimates of the future must be made in preparing financial statements: the ultimate amount of cash to be collected in connection with sales that have been made, the salability of inventories, and the economic life of productive assets are three of the most significant forecasts generally required. Since forecasts are involved, financial statements are by their very nature probabilistic. Yet, in their presentation, single-valued figures continue to be used to represent probabilistic estimates. The uncertainty of many figures in today's financial statements is, therefore, not appropriately indicated.

In addition to scorekeeping, financial statements purport to be useful in helping investors to make decisions about the commitments of assets to the corporation. Since the effectiveness of investment decisions depends upon the ability of the analyst to forecast the future effectively, the assumption implicit in this use of financial statements is that the past is a useful tool in forecasting the future. The same difficulties associated with the scorekeeping function are of course part of the problem of using financial statements to forecast effectively. If management's decisions about the future do not represent a continuation of the actions of the past, forecasts arrived at from projections of conventional accounting data may be misleading. In addition, major economic events may occur which are not reflected in financial statements as conventionally presented until some later point in time. Accordingly, while financial statements do represent an input that may be useful in the forecasting process, they are far from comprehensive in this regard.

Given these inadequacies in the current disclosure required of corporations, serious questions have arisen whether financial statements are sufficient for analysts who are charged with investment responsibility. Whenever possible, analysts naturally seek to go beyond financial statements through such vehicles as company interviews, industry surveys, etc. In recent years, however, the SEC has evidenced a tendency to suggest the elimination of these forms of additional preferred disclosure to certain parts of the investment community without making equivalent disclosure to all potential investors. Accordingly, the analyst is being increasingly restricted to the gathering of publicly available data of which the financial statements are perhaps the most significant part.

It seems likely, therefore, that analysts and other users of financial information will begin aggressively seeking substantial additional public data as the basis for investment decisions. Evidence of this trend has recently been seen in the successful pressures for business-segment data from conglomerate companies. Demands for both more comprehensive historical data and additional future-oriented information will soon be heard as well. There are many different forms which this demand may take, some of which will be discussed below.

As more data is presented, it seems likely that the auditor's attest function will expand as well, since data made available to the public may frequently require the increased reliability that can be given to it by an auditor's attestation. In addition, it seems very likely that the auditor's reporting function will expand to include reports on many other aspects of his examination than simply the financial statements prepared in accordance with generally accepted accounting principles.

Methods of Expansion

As it develops, the auditor's reporting function can expand in several directions; the most common expansion will be in reporting to management. The auditor who has reviewed the adequacy of the information system of the business and found it lacking in any way will undoubtedly report thereon to the management—either informally or formally. This is simply an extension of current reporting practices, but it does represent a considerable addition to the standard management letter that is issued at the present time.

Since to audit the information system the auditor will be operating continuously, it is clear that he will not examine each of the systems of the business in the same detail in every year. In some years the procurement cycle will receive more attention, in others the marketing cycle or the production cycle. Similarly, differences in geographical emphasis will occur. Therefore, in reporting to management on the results of his activities, the auditor will continue to have some general observations on the adequacy of information within the firm as a whole, and he will have recommendations in more detail about the systems he has studied with most care in the particular year being reported on, or on the geographical locations in which he has spent the most audit time.

It is likely that reporting to management in this area will cease to be an annual proposition, but will occur periodically as particular parts of the firm's information-system review are completed. This would be consistent with the concept of the continuing audit that seems to be developing today, as opposed to the periodic audit of the year's financial statements.

These reports to management will be a natural outgrowth of auditing procedures, although the diagnostic skills required are today generally thought of as associated with consulting activity. The auditor of the future will require these skills in order to achieve the audit objective we have defined. Special engagements will continue to be undertaken and reported on by the consulting group at the public accounting firms.

While the increase in reporting volume that results from the developing audit approach will be found chiefly in reports to management, perhaps its most significant form will be found in reports to other parties as the public role of the auditor is increasingly recognized. Such outside reporting will fall into two categories: reports to specific parties for particular uses, and external reports, available generally to the public.

There are various specific parties outside of management that may wish reports; one of the most obvious, still within the total environment of the corporation, is the board of directors. Traditionally, the board has received from the auditors the report on the standard financial statements, but beyond this, practice varies widely. In some cases there is an audit committee of the board of directors which meets regularly with the auditors and questions them as well as receiving their comments resulting from the audit, while in other cases, the board may receive a long-form report from the auditors.

In recent years, legal cases and an increasing sense of business professionalism have combined to increase the directors' sense of responsibility. As this trend continues, it seems probable that directors, and particularly outside directors, will turn to the auditors for more information about the operations of the firm. There are now several boards of directors that ask that, both informally at regular meetings and formally in a written presentation, their auditors supply them with an opinion on the adequacy of the firm's internal control. Such an opinion is different from the auditor's traditional opinion, which is associated with figures, but more and more accounting firms are being asked to write and are writing such opinions. Additionally, the directors may ask the auditors for certain forms of financial analyses and a review of procedures in particular areas such as forecasting, profit planning, purchasing, and others; professional advice on the form and content of public financial reporting will also be sought. Presumably, the development of these reports will be in addition to the expansion of the consulting function and reports of the results of those activities.

It is interesting to note that in many European countries the auditor's report form includes a recommendation that the management of the firm be discharged from the liability for the year just completed, and in some countries, such as Sweden, an opinion on the effectiveness of administration is offered. The report of the auditors of AB Volvo for 1968, for example, included the following:

> During our audit nothing has given rise to any criticism concerning the Annual Report, the Company accounting procedures, the inventory of its assets or otherwise in regard to the administration of the Company.
>
> The proposal of the Board and Managing Director for the disposition of earnings does not conflict with the provisions of Company Law concerning transfers to legal reserves, or with good business practice.
>
> We recommend:
>
> *that* the Balance Sheet as at December 31, 1968, which is included in the Annual Report and signed by us, be approved;
>
> *that* the Members of the Board and the Managing Director be discharged from liability for their administration during the period covered by the Annual Report; and
>
> *that* the proposed disposition of earnings be approved.

An investigation of Swedish auditing procedures indicates that the audit of company administration and good business practice referred to in the report are not as extensive as might be hoped from the report issued, but nonetheless, the report indicates a direction in which the accounting profession might move. As directors became increasingly aware of their responsibilities, they may push the American auditor toward this kind of an audit in substance as well as in form.

In addition to directors of the firm, there are various specific parties outside the firm that may desire particular reports. The creditor group is the most active in this respect; at the present time auditors do report to creditors in a variety of ways. In addition to reporting on financial statements that are supplied to creditors, the auditors may express opinions on compliance with debt covenants and on other specific information, such as aging analyses of receivables that are presented by the management.

As creditors become more sophisticated, it seems likely that they will begin to seek more information; for it is clear that creditors are interested in the adequacy of the corporation's control system. Even today, many lenders are asking for copies of the management letter that the auditor usually submits to the company after each audit. Moreover, there are a few creditors who are now asking for routine permission to talk to auditors, either with or without management's being present. Some are going even further and seeking a system whereby the auditor will be asked by the client to contact the creditor whenever he becomes aware of any material adverse financial event affecting the corporation. Requirements of this sort may be more easily fulfilled with a continuing systems-oriented audit, and it seems likely that more of such reports will be demanded even though auditors are not enthusiastic about assuming such obligations and in some cases have resisted them strenuously. There is a significant risk which must be recognized in advocating increased communications between the auditor and third parties such as creditors. In the first place, management may be bypassed; and yet it is management who is the primary factor in determining the course of the firm's development. In addition, the desire of creditors and others to interview and talk in depth with auditors about their report and to seek supplemental disclosure from them may lead toward a variety of behavioral reactions, from both auditor and management, that could have an adverse effect upon the success of the audit. The chief result of increased communication between auditor and banker may be decreased communication between auditor and client, which would be a high price to pay.

Perhaps a more productive approach is the development of reports prepared specifically for creditors in which accounting data is expanded and restructured on a basis appropriate for their use and to which reliability can be added by an auditor's attestation. At the present time, generally accepted accounting principles are directed toward stockholders, and the development of these principles seems to be pushing more and more away from the cash basis of accounting that perhaps is most significant for creditor purposes. Accordingly, it may well be that one of the information requirements of creditors as a condition for loans will be special-purpose and cash-basis statements on which auditors will be asked to express an opinion as well as on conventional financial reports.

One example of this that is already common is the questionnaire which has been designed by the bank-credit grantors' association, Robert Morris Associates, for finance companies. As a result of a few credit disasters in the finance industry, this trade group developed a questionnaire which banks now require virtually all finance companies to submit. This report includes substantial additional details not available in conventional financial statements and the auditor is often asked to include the questionnaire in his report, although this is not invariably the case.

At the present time, a top-level group established by leaders of the accounting and banking professions, the National Conference of Bankers and CPAs, is working to improve understanding and communication between lenders and auditors. One of the outputs of this cooperation may well be a new kind of long-form report which will become a standard part of the data required in any lending agreement.

The format of such a report would emphasize those kinds of information most relevant to creditors' needs. The following kinds of items are typical of what might be sought by creditors in a new long-form report:

1. balance sheet, income statement, working capital, and cash-receipts and disbursements data by division and subsidiary;
2. schedule of working capital defined on a liquidity rather than an operating-cycle basis;
3. forecasts of future operations with ranges of possible results and assumptions specified;
4. loan liquidation schedules on the basis of company forecasts;
5. list of major accounting principles followed including an indication of alternative acceptable principles and their effect on results;
6. opinion by auditor that principles followed were the most appropriate in his professional judgment under the factual circumstances that existed;
7. opinion by auditor as to the adequacy of the company's internal control and financial information system;
8. list of all lending and other covenants entered into by corporation and auditor's opinion on compliance therewith;
9. aging analysis of accounts receivable;
10. concentration analysis of accounts receivable and sales showing proportions relating to major customers;
11. turnover analysis of inventory by category;
12. concentration analysis of inventory;
13. schedule of current replacement cost of inventory;
14. list of all lenders utilized by company during the year;
15. schedules of activity levels and maximum balance levels in inventories, receivables, payables, marketable securities, and cash balances during period.

While such a list is not exhaustive, and on the other hand includes some items which companies might resist disclosing, it does indicate the direction which creditors might take in seeking additional audited information.

In addition to the directors and creditors of the firm, it may well be that the auditor's attest function is expanded in the area of reports to Government agencies. Many agencies require that financial information of various sorts be presented to them, and in some cases this must have been already audited. In other cases, government auditors themselves verify data. As the audit function moves toward the inclusion of the entire information system of the firm, it may well be that the government will accept the CPA's attestation of information produced by that system without requiring a supplemental government audit.

The most dramatic case, of course, could arise in the area of taxation where tax returns might be attested to by CPAs. In such situations IRS audit work might be reduced to a minimum and the figures essentially accepted as filed.

Similarly, many of the other data requirements of the government, such as in connection with Robinson-Patman price-justification hearings, utility-rate hearings, and redeterminable contracts, may be subject to audit and report by the independent CPA. While such reporting would require some expansion of the audit work done, the expansion would not be very significant since all of these requirements would have to be considered in the determination of the adequacy of the firm's own information system.

Besides these three principal nonmanagement groups that might logically require reports from the CPA, many others may conceivably do so in the future as their needs develop. Employee groups and unions, for example, often have a desire for information with increased reliability in regard to the operations of some facets of the firm. Customers may need data as to the reliability of goods and services supplied.

Finally, the auditor's reporting function may expand as a result of increased demand for reports by the general public. These reports might fall into two general categories: attestation to increased corporate reports, and reports of the CPA of his own opinions and representations based upon his examination.

Expansion of Public Reporting Function

In the first case, corporations are putting out many forms of data and may put out many more that would be subject to audit. Nonfinancial operating data today is included in the annual reports of corporations, but it is not audited by the public accounting firms. Certainly such data is auditable and might be reported on.

Perhaps more significantly, it appears that some demands may be made upon the auditor to associate his name with forecasts and other future-oriented rather than strictly historical data. This will represent a major innovation in the audit field if it comes to pass, since at the present time the auditor is excluded by the AICPA Code of Ethics from associating his name with forecasts in any fashion, where it might be construed as approval of the forecast.

As was discussed above, past-oriented data may not give the analyst the kind of information that he needs to evaluate a firm. Since the group most likely to be able to estimate the future path of the firm is the management, it is not inconceivable that disclosure of management budgets and forecasts to the public will be required. Although there are many problems involved in the development of acceptable means of reporting this data and of auditing it, it is certainly not beyond the realm of the feasible. There are many analysts who feel that corporate-management reporting would be far more effective and useful if it followed the same pattern that managers require of their own subordinates, i.e., the preparation of a plan or budget and the explanation of deviations from that plan. Many problems exist in publishing forecasts. Management may present conservative forecasts so as to be able to exceed them or optimistic forecasts with the aim of improving the investment stature of the company. In addition, there may be a tendency to adjust subsequently reported historical data to make it agree with previous forecasts. Despite these behavioral problems, such forecasts may well be part of the reporting firmament of the future.

The auditor therefore would have the problem of determining what form of audit could be performed on a forecast. Clearly, he could not attest to its truth since this will not become known until the time being forecast comes to pass. Nevertheless, a number of procedures can be undertaken that would add reliability to the forecast. In the first place, in understanding the corporate information system the auditor needs to have some notion of the forecasting techniques used by the management. Forecasting can represent a systematic analysis of the probabilities of the future or simply a collection of numbers based on random thoughts about what may occur. Some principles of budgeting would have to be developed, but given this requirement, it should be possible to produce an audit report that increases the reliability of forecast data. This subject is discussed in greater length by Yuji Ijiri in the article which follows this chapter.

In developing techniques of presenting future-oriented data, some form of probabilistic statements will clearly be needed to make explicit the uncertainties involved. This may take the form of reporting ranges in forecasts, or a more rigorous form of probabilistic presentation may be developed. Ultimately, the auditor may be able to express an opinion on a probability-distribution as well as on a single-valued figure.

Even beyond attestation to expanded corporate reports, tomorrow's auditor may also find the areas expanding in which his own representations based upon his professional judgment are required. In such cases, the auditor will not simply report on the statements of management, but he will be offering his own observations on matters which have come to his attention during an examination of the information system of the firm.

Some evidence of this trend is already apparent. A few auditors are now expressing an opinion on the adequacy of a corporation's internal control system. Price Waterhouse & Co., for example, rendered the following opinion to the public in a registration statement in connection with its audit of the Chemical Bank New York Trust Company:

> Our examinations included an evaluation of the effectiveness of the bank's internal accounting controls, including the internal auditing. In our opinion, the procedures in effect, together with the examinations conducted by the bank's internal audit staff, constitute an effective system of internal accounting control.

As the auditor's objective expands, similar but more comprehensive reports on the adequacy of a corporation's information system for decision-making may be presented. Ultimately, data on the effectiveness of management may be compiled and reported on by auditors as well. Such reporting might take the form of a new long-form report made available to the public, a questionnaire answered and filed with the SEC or a stock exchange, or many other possible formats. This subject is explored in more depth in the author's articles on the management audit which follows Chapter 4 above.

In addition to expanded reporting on corporate activities, there are many exciting opportunities for reporting by auditors in the nonprofit and governmental sectors of the economy. The principles of program budgeting and cost/benefit analysis have been developing in these areas, and the need seems great for external and independent appraisals of many of the estimates made. While auditors could never solve the guns-versus-butter problem of the political scientist and economist, they could appraise public estimates of costs and benefits associated with various public plans and programs, and lend assurance at least that estimating had been done systematically and in good faith.

In all of these areas, expansion of the auditor's reporting function will bring problems and increased potential liabilities. Examination and reporting techniques will have to be devised and tested, and the accountant's traditional desires for quantitative objectivity will have to be amended in many ways. Nevertheless, it is the authors' belief that this expansion must and will occur. If the profession opts otherwise out of fear of increased liability and uncertainty, a major opportunity for service will be lost and the future of the profession will be curtailed due both to decreased demand for its limited services and to its inevitable inability to attract the innovative and creative minds needed for growth.

Introduction to
the Readings

This chapter presents a vision of the future that spells a dramatic expansion for the reporting function of auditors. Most of the ideas expressed are still simply ideas without any substantial practical experience or theoretical development to support them. In the article accompanying this chapter, Yuji Ijiri attempts to develop a more comprehensive theoretical framework for one form of expanded auditing and audit reporting envisaged in the chapter—the audit of budgets and forecasts. While the problems of implementation and the development of standards remain, Professor Ijiri has started along a productive road. Perhaps future editions of this book will be able to include additional examples of both theory and implementation relating to an expanded reporting function by auditors.

Yuji Ijiri

Proposals for Budget Disclosure

As one way of providing more useful information to stockholders and investors of a firm, there have been growing attentions on budget disclosure. According to Cooper, Dopuch, and Keller [4], a proposal for budget disclosure was first introduced in accounting literature in 1947 by Stuart A. Rice at the Sixtieth Annual Meeting of the American Institute of (Certified Public) Accountants [7]. More than a decade later, a number of articles followed this proposal.

For example, Nielsen stated:

The predictive quality of budgetary information is one of its most important characteristics. The very problem of integrating the components of projections tends to disclose what is necessary in order to achieve harmony in an operation so that the maximum benefits to the firm may result. The disclosure achieved by such projections tends to show what is necessary in order to maximize benefits accruing from the total operation of the firm. [6, p. 586].

Similarly, Bevis considered certification of business planning (prospective accounting) as being one of the important areas where the CPAs' attest function would be valuable and stated:

Since budgetary control already is oriented to the prospective view, it is suggested that this would be as excellent an avenue as any to commence auditing's new future in this field of business planning. [2, p. 34].

Birnberg and Dopuch, in discussing the need for a new framework of disclosure, expressed their opinion as follows:

In order to inform the external parties of what they anticipate the future to hold for the entity, management must provide the investor with the information on three types of expectations. 1. Prospects for the economy. 2. Prospects for the industry and the enterprise as a member of that subset. 3. The specific expectations which underlie the *major* investments made in resources and the projects undertaken in attempting to achieve the enterprise's goals. [3, p. 58].

Reprinted with permission from *The Accounting Review*, vol. XLIII, no. 4, October 1968, 662–667. Copyrighted 1968 by *The Accounting Review*.

Lazarsfeld, an eminent sociologist, emphasized at a meeting of the Long-Range Objective Committee of the AICPA the budget function as an important future area of possible accounting practice and as an example he stated:

An article in the *Public Opinion Quarterly* titled "Dollars and Sense" has pointed out that budgeting and auditing of scientific research projects is a completely new problem in our society. This is true for both physical and social science research. At the present time governments and foundations do not know how to budget research projects and they do not know how to audit research budgets submitted to them. [1, p. 5].

Similarly, Solomon pointed out forecasting as one of the major scopes of the accounting function and "hence the scope of his education and his thinking." [8, p. 24].

Wilkinson and Doney [9] followed Bevis in advocating that auditing and reporting boundaries be extended to include budget auditing, and analyzed the effects of budget disclosure and budget auditing on management, stockholders and investors, creditors, competitors, the government, and independent auditors.

Cooper, Dopuch, and Keller [4] have gone farther to analyze "how a budgetary framework of disclosure brings into a new perspective several of the recent proposals for altering the historical cost basis of accounting reports."

From an analytical viewpoint, Ijiri, Kinard, and Putney [5] explored budget incentive systems which will stimulate reasonable forecasts on goal levels in profit, sales, etc., that management expects to attain and, at the same time, will stimulate better performance over and beyond estimated goal levels whenever

possible. The attempt was to solve the problem that the discrepancy between estimated and actual goal levels cannot be the only basis of reward or penalty if efforts to attain better goal levels should always be stimulated irrespective of the estimates.

Following these efforts for budget disclosure and budget auditing, this present paper tries to move a step toward its implementation. In particular, the author will attempt to analyze the nature of budget audits and outline some essential factors in the generally accepted budgeting principles and procedures as well as the generally accepted budget-auditing standards and procedures. (For simplicity the term "generally accepted" will be omitted throughout this paper.) It will also discuss the contents of budget-audit reports as well as the responsibility of auditors concerning budget auditing.

Although budgets may be prepared and reported in various forms, it will be assumed for purposes of this discussion that firms publish financial statements in the following form and auditors are asked to express their opinions on such statements.

Comparative Financial Statements
XYZ Corporation
as of December 31, 1968

Account Names	1967 Actual	1968 Estimate	1968 Actual	1969 Estimate
xxx	xxx	xxx	xxx	xxx
xxx	xxx	xxx	xxx	xxx

For example, financial statements as of December 31, 1968 include actual figures for 1968 and estimated figures for 1969 where estimates are made based on the data available at the time the financial statements are prepared. For comparative purposes, they also include actual figures for 1967 and estimated figures for 1968 which have been reported in the previous financial report.

This method of reporting budgets has an advantage over other methods in that budgets are directly tied in with the financial statements for the past periods. This allows a direct comparison between estimates and actual in order to determine the reliability of past estimates.

The Nature of Budget Audits

Budget audits are similar to audits on audits in the sense that the central task of both types of audits is to check whether reasonable inferences were made in preparing budgets or in preparing audit reports, and not to make inferences by the auditors themselves.

In ordinary financial-statement audits, auditors gather evidence to infer the existence or non-existence of certain factors in the operations or in the financial state of the firm as well as in their accounting records in the period under examination. For example, auditors examine purchase orders, material-receiving slips, invoices, cancelled checks, etc., to infer material purchases and the procedures taken to record them. Cash count and reconciliations are means to infer the balance of cash at the end of the period examined as well as the effectiveness of the surveillance on cash.

However, no matter how painstakingly auditors gather and examine the evidence they cannot be 100 percent certain that they have made correct inferences, since there always exist possibilities, however small, that the evidence auditors examined may have been falsely produced. Therefore, in evaluating auditors' work, what is significant is whether the auditors' inferences are "reasonable" or not. This is exactly the point that partners of a CPA

firm check when they review audit working papers prepared by field auditors. That is, the auditors' task in reviewing audits made by others (namely, audits on audits) is to see whether original auditors' inferences are "reasonable"; patently their task is not to make such inferences by themselves.

Similarly, in preparing budgets the management must make inferences on various factors in the future based on clues that are available at the time of the prediction. Therefore, the essential of budget audits lies in checking whether the inferences that the management made in preparing the budgets are reasonable or not.

This is analogous to the so-called "beyond-reasonable-doubt" notion in legal processes. A cautious juror may not be able to reach a conviction without any doubts whatsoever, but he is nonetheless supposed to avoid "unreasonable doubts." However, there are no natural and absolute standards to be used in distinguishing between reasonable and unreasonable doubts; the distinction is a social one, hence it depends upon time and place.

Therefore, in such situations, it is important to provide explicitly a set of standards by which members of the society understand what are considered to be "reasonable" doubts or "reasonable" inferences. In this sense, the most requisite step toward the implementation of budget disclosure and budget auditing is to develop a set of budgeting principles and procedures as well as a set of budget-auditing standards and procedures.

Budgeting Principles and Procedures

First, a set of budgeting principles and procedures must be prepared after a thorough investigation of what are involved in actual budgeting processes in various types of industries. It is hardly possible to elaborate on the components of the principles and procedures in detail here. The following discussion is intended to be only an outline of what are essential to the formulation of the budgeting principles and procedures.

The budgeting principles and procedures can be divided into two parts, one concerning the predictions of events and the other the recording of predicted events. The latter deals with the ordinary accounting procedures after certain events are predicted according to the former. Therefore, if the budgets are to be reported in the form of projected financial statements, we may simply quote the generally accepted accounting principles and procedures and state that the predicted events must be recorded according to them. Thus, the cost principle, the realization principle, the matching principle of revenue and costs, etc., will all be observed. Of course, it is possible to set up a different set of accounting principles and procedures for the recording of predicted events, allowing, for example, the firm to evaluate assets by factors other than their acquisition costs. However, unless they are also accepted in the preparation of ordinary financial statements, such dual principles and procedures would simply result in confusion and lack of comparability between budget and actual.

Two basic principles will govern the prediction of events. One is to make the inference process explicit. Just as auditors are required to prepare audit working papers as supporting documents of their inference processes, the management is asked to prepare "budget working papers" so that the processes of preparing the projected financial statements are made clear and explicit. This is essential since if the budgets are made by somewhat mysterious implicit hunches of management, there is no way to make an independent investigation on the budgets.

A second principle which will govern the prediction of events is consistency. The consistency principle covers a broad area of prediction. It may be divided into internal consistency and external consistency. Internal consistency deals with the data internal to the firm that are used in budgeting. It has two aspects: historical consistency, i.e., consistency between current estimates and estimates made in the past, and current consistency, i.e., consistency among current estimates. If a firm estimated the production capacity as 40,000 units a year in preparing a budget for 1968, the same number of units should be used in preparing a budget for 1969, unless there have been explainable changes in the factors related to the production capacity. This is historical consistency. Furthermore, estimates for 1969 should be mutually consistent. If the sales figure is estimated based on the production capacity of 50,000 units, and the production cost is estimated based on the production capacity of 30,000 units, the estimates lack current consistency. Similarly, if the cost of Product A is estimated based on the assumption that the plant will be expanded by the end of June 1969 whereas the cost of Product B that is produced by the same plant is estimated based on the assumption that the plant will not be expanded by the end of June 1969, the estimates lack current consistency.

Contrary to internal consistency, external consistency deals with consistency of budget estimates with estimates on industry and general economic factors. For example, if it is clear that the demand for the industry is going to be cut in half for the coming year because of the defense cut-back, it is inconsistent with external factors if the firm does not take into account this effect in preparing budget estimates. It is also inconsistent with external factors to make budget estimates based on the assumption that the price of the products will be doubled when industry economic forecasts see only moderate increases in prices. Of course, the firm's estimates may turn out to be correct, but the point is that in such cases the firm must explain why their estimates are more reliable than others.

Budget-Auditing Standards and Procedures

In addition to budgeting principles and procedures, a set of budget-auditing standards and procedures must be prepared in order to define methods of examining budget working papers and related evidence which support the inferences as well as the extent of examination. They must also provide reporting standards for budget audits.

The main purpose of budget audits is to make sure that the budgeting processes are carried out as specified by the budgeting principles and procedures.

In particular, budget-auditing standards and procedures must specify the extent to which auditors are asked to check internal and external consistency of budget estimates. For example, it may be required that auditors seek some external evidence in trade journals, government and other reputable sources of economic indicators, etc., to satisfy themselves as to external consistency of budget estimates.

The budget-auditing standards and procedures must also specify the types of budget-

audit reports that auditors are supposed to provide. Since such a budget-audit report will be published together with the firm's financial statements (actual and projected), care should be taken not to mislead the readers as to the nature of budget audits and budget-audit reports. Auditors' responsibility should be clearly spelled out in the budget-auditing standards and procedures so that there will not be any misunderstanding by the readers. Since this topic of budget-audit reports and auditors' responsibilities is important, it will be elaborated in more detail below.

Budget-Audit Reports and Auditors' Responsibilities

As in audits on ordinary financial statements, auditors should be required to state in their budget-audit reports whether their budget audits are done in accordance with the budget-auditing standards and procedures. If not, they should state the reason why adherence to them was not possible, and what alternative procedures they have adopted to supplement the procedures not followed.

Auditors should in addition be required to state whether or not, in their opinion, the firm's budgets have been prepared under the budgeting principles and procedures. They should also be asked to disclose any significant deviation from them in the firm's budget preparation. Especially, any inconsistency in prediction, external or internal, current or historical, should be reported together with their effects upon the budgets. Any significant deviation from the accounting principles and procedures in recording the predicted events, including inconsistent treatment of predicted events, should also be reported, together with their effects upon the budgets.

In the budget-auditing standards and procedures, it may be appropriate to require auditors to express their opinion if they feel that the budget estimates are extremely optimistic or extremely pessimistic, although within the boundary of being consistent estimates, and approximately by how much they deviate from what the auditors consider to be reasonable. Auditors should also be allowed to remind the readers of the financial statements as to how deviations existed between estimated and actual figures during the last few periods. These are necessary safeguards against the possibilities of misleading the readers due to the fact that there may be a wide range of estimates which are consistent.

In addition, the budgeting principles and procedures as well as the budget-auditing standards and procedures should state specifically the condition under which the firm and/or the auditors are required or allowed to report any major uncertain factors upon which the budget estimates critically depend. Examples of such factors are major government contracts which the firm may or may not get, major expansion plans which may be delayed because of financial arrangements with banks, major investment in oil well drilling, etc. Of course, the interest of the firm in keeping managerial secrets must be preserved. However, since these are important factors which materially affect the projected financial statements, the readers should be informed as to how these uncertain factors are treated (e.g., optimistically or pessimistically) and how the financial statements should be modified in the event that they do not turn out as expected.

The four types of audit reports in the case of audits on ordinary financial statements can also be applied to budget-audit reports, namely reports with unqualified, qualified, and adverse opinions as well as opinion-disclaimed reports. In addition, a long-form and a short-form budget-audit report may be prepared as in audits on ordinary financial statements.

Auditors' responsibility should be judged primarily based upon whether they have followed the budget-auditing standards and procedures and have done the budget audit with "due professional care." The firm is the one who is primarily responsible for the budgets and the auditors' responsibility is secondary as in the case of ordinary financial statements. It is possible that the firm may be held responsible for improper budgets if they neglect or conceal major factors which had become certain "beyond reasonable doubt" by the time the budgets were prepared and if they would materially affect the projected financial statements. Similarly, it is possible that the auditors may be held responsible for the negligent failure to detect an obvious and serious inconsistency in the projected financial statements. Contrary to the penalty on estimated income tax that is underestimated beyond a given percentage limit, it would be unreasonable to state admissible error ranges quantitatively until the system of budget auditing is developed substantially. However, any major deviation from actual figures would require the firm's and, in some cases, the auditors' explanation.

Conclusions

Although, as pointed out by the articles cited earlier, the usefulness of budget disclosure to stockholders and other investors is unquestionable, the implementation of budget disclosure must be supported by effective budget auditing in order to insure the reliability of the budgets. For this purpose, it becomes crucial to develop a set of generally accepted budgeting principles and procedures and a set of generally accepted budget-auditing standards and procedures so that firms and auditors have some frameworks to rely upon in developing budgets and in performing budget audits.

Coordinated research efforts by accounting institutions and associations to develop such principles, standards, and procedures will be the most needed and fruitful step toward expanding the traditional boundaries of accounting and auditing.

References

[1] American Institute of Certified Public Accountants—Long-Range Objective Committee, *Profile of the Profession: 1975.* "From the Viewpoint of a Sociologist," prepared by N. M. Bedford in consultation with Paul F. Lazarsfeld of Columbia University.

[2] Bevis, Herman W., "The CPA's Attest Function in Modern Society," *The Journal of Accountancy,* (February 1962), pp. 28–35.

[3] Birnberg, J. G. and N. Dopuch. "A Conceptual Approach to the Framework for Disclosure," *The Journal of Accountancy,* (February 1963), pp. 56–63.

[4] Cooper, W. W., N. Dopuch, and T. F. Keller, "Budgetary Disclosure and Other Suggestions for Improving Accounting Reports," *The Accounting Review,* (October 1968), pp. 640–648.

[5] Ijiri, Y., J. C. Kinard, and F. B. Putney, "An Integrated Evaluation System for Budget Forecasting and Operating Performance—With a Classified Budgeting Bibliography," *Journal of Accounting Research,* (Spring 1968). pp. 1–28.

[6] Nielsen, Oswald, "New Challenges in Accounting," *The Accounting Review,* (October 1960), pp. 583–89.

[7] Rice, S. A. "Uses of Accounting Data in Economics and Statistics," in *Challenges to the Accounting Profession, 1947.* (American Institute of Accountants 1947).

[8] Solomon, Ezra, "Accounting in the Next Decade," *The Journal of Accountancy,* (January 1965), pp. 22–26.

[9] Wilkinson, J. R. and L. D. Doney, "Extending Audit and Reporting Boundaries," *The Accounting Review,* (October 1965), pp. 753–56.

1. *Select representative purchases.* Review client's records to learn the types of purchase transactions that may occur. Ascertain what categories of materials, equipment, supplies, expenses, and services (other than payroll) are procured. Also develop an estimate of the frequency and dollar importance of each category of purchase. Select several transactions to vouch, in general proportion to the frequency of occurrence. To accomplish this, do the following:

a. Ascertain the client's method of recording the account distribution of purchases. This may be:
   i. Columnar analysis in a voucher register.
   ii. Distribution ledger cards (usually posted by bookkeeping machine).
   iii. Analysis runs, prepared on punched card equipment or computers.
b. Read the distribution analysis for one month, mentally noting names of vendors associated with each amount and quick-scan it for the year, exhausting each account charged before proceeding to the next account. This permits learning what vendors are classified under various accounts and whether or not the same vendors appear for several account classifications.
c. Select transactions to be vouched by listing the vendors' names and references numbers of the items representative of the charges to the account. Particularly, select at least one item

of a vendor from each of the account classifications for these vendors with charges distributed to more than one account.

2. *Trace purchase to the vendor invoices.*

a. Obtain the invoice or voucher for the transactions to be traced.
b. Compare the distribution indicated on the media with that shown in the distribution analysis.
c. Compare the individual invoices to the voucher, checking the distribution.
d. Check that each invoice has been approved for:
   i. receipt of merchandise or service.
   ii. prices.
   iii. extensions and footings.
   iv. discount or anticipation.
e. Compare the quantities, prices, and other pertinent data on the invoice with:
   i. the receiving slips or other receiving records.
   ii. purchase order.
   iii. purchase request, comparing these requests with the client's announced policy for authorization to purchase.

3. *Trace purchase to the original procurement authorization.* Trace the transactions to the following and compare the related data:

a. Purchase requisition. Examine approvals for purchase and compare with authorization manual or announced policy on authorization.
b. Source record establishing need to purchase and to record of specifications.
c. Source record establishing the need to purchase (stock cards, bill of materials, etc.), and to the record of specifications (e.g., book of standards).
    i. Compare specifications.
    ii. Compare order quantity.
    iii. Ascertain, record, and recompute the basis for arriving at (a) the order quantity, and (b) the time to order.

4. *Trace purchase to purchase department records.*

a. Trace purchase order to the approved vendor card or other record.
b. Trace purchase order to price history record or to bid data, as appropriate.

5. *Trace through flow of material.*

a. Trace receiving slip (or invoice) to record of receipt in receiving department (also to notice to expect shipment):
    i. Note records of counts and inspections.
    ii. Compare with vendor's bill of lading.
b. Trace receiving slip to record of receipt in the Inspection Department. On a partial or complete rejection, trace to shipping records, debit memos, and entry in voucher register.
c. Trace the entry for receipt to the bin records in the storeroom.
d. Trace the entry for receipt to the perpetual inventory record.

6. *Trace payment.*

a. Trace the voucher to the check. Ascertain payment procedures, verifying that there is:
    i. Provision for timely payment to obtain discounts.
    ii. Provision for audit.
    iii. Multilation of the payment voucher to protect against duplication of payment.

7. *Trace equipment purchases.*

a. Trace the purchase of an equipment item to (1) the Plant Property Record and (2) the record where it is classified for depreciation purposes.
b. Determine the capitalization policy. Does the equipment record reflect the same items that are summarized in the fixed-asset account in the general ledger?
c. Determine the depreciation policy used by the client.

8. *Select a capital item sold or retired during the year.*

a. Trace to the general ledger the gain or loss on the sale or retirement.
b. Trace to the Plant Property Record, noting its removal from this record.
c. Trace to the depreciation classification records, noting its removal from these records.

9. *Trace material and supply items to inventory lists.* For each item in the sample that is a purchase of production material or a supply (either production or general), trace to the category of inventory listing where it should be included. Based upon this review:

a. List the kinds of items inventoried and those not inventoried.

b. Ascertain the basic of cost valuation.

c. Ascertain how "market" value is determined.

d. Ascertain the flow of costs (LIFO, FIFO, etc.).

10. *Trace to general ledger accounts (journal entries, where necessary).* For year-end and monthly statements, separately, determine by tracing the appropriate transactions, the accounting policies (What is expensed? What is deferred? What is set up as a liability? How much is so treated?) for each of the classes of items included in the sample.

a. Trace all service items consumable over a period of time to prepaid and deferred accounts (prepaid advertising, rent, etc.).

b. Ascertain at what point of the transaction purchases are reflected as a liability with particular reference to treatment of in-transit items.

c. Trace all acquisitions where the usage is over a period of time to accrued liability accounts (rent, etc.).

11. *Select transactions representing vendor charge-backs.* Examine the numerical file of receipt and inspection reports to uncover situations where merchandise has failed to pass inspection.

a. Trace to preparation of debit memo
  i. Compare the explanation shown on the debit memo with that shown on the receiving report.
  ii. Recompute the dollar value of the debit memo.

b. Trace debit memo to ultimate settlement verifying that the manner of filing charge-backs to vendors permits offsetting the charge against the next invoice, if prepared after the current invoice has been paid.

Selected Bibliography

Publications: American Institute of Certified Public Accountants (New York)

Accounting and Auditing Approaches to Inventories in Three Nations (Accountants International Study No. 1), 1968.

Accounting Trends & Techniques (published annually since 1946).

Auditing and EDP, by Gordon B. Davis, 1968.

An Auditor's Approach to Statistical Sampling, 1967–1969.
Vol. 1, An Introduction to Statistical Concepts and Estimation of Dollar Values.
Vol. 2, Sampling for Attributes.
Vol. 3, Stratified Random Sampling.
Vol. 4, Discovery Sampling.

The Auditor's Report—Its Meaning and Significance, 1967.

Audits of Banks, 1968.

Audits of Brokers or Dealers in Securities, 1956.

Audits of Construction Contractors, 1965.

Audits of Fire and Casualty Insurance Companies, 1966.

Audits of Personal Financial Statements, 1968.

Audits of Savings and Loan Associations, 1962.

Audits of Voluntary Health and Welfare Organizations, 1967.

Case Study on Audit of a Union–Industry Welfare Fund, 1959.

Case Studies in Auditing Procedure
No. 1: A Loading and Hauling Equipment Manufacturer, 1947.
No. 2: A Newspaper Publisher, 1947.
No. 3: A Department Store, 1947.
No. 4: A Public Utility, 1947.
No. 5: A Corn Processing Company, 1947.
No. 6: A Management Investment Company of the Open-end Type, 1947.
No. 7: A Grain Company, 1949.
No. 8: A Steel Fabricating Company; A Small Restaurant, 1950.
No. 9: A Wholesale Distributor of Newspapers and Magazines, 1950.

No. 10: A Smaller Commercial Finance Company, 1956.

No. 11: A Hospital, 1956.

No. 12: A Medium-Sized "Small Loan" Company; An Electronic Equipment Manufacturer, 1958.

No. 13: An Industrial Machine Company; A Small Loan (Consumer Finance) Company, 1962.

No. 14: A Medium-Sized Dairy, 1962.

Case Studies in Internal Control

No. 1: The Textile Company, 1950.

No. 2: The Machine Manufacturing Company, 1950.

Case Studies in the Observation of Inventory, 1959.

Computer Research Studies, 1966–1968

No. 1: Survey Results—Voluntary Comments.

No. 2: Current Basic Sources of ADP Information.

No. 3: Computer Applications to Accounting Operations.

No. 4: Relationships among CPAs, Banks and Service Bureaus.

No. 5: Software Trends—Hardware Characteristics.

No. 6: An Approach to the Use of EDP in an Accounting Practice.

CPA Handbook (two vols.), 1956.

Departures from Generally Accepted Auditing Standards and Accounting Principles
Practice Review Bulletin No. 1, 1966.
Practice Review Bulletin No. 2, 1968.

The Independent Auditor's Reporting Standards in Three Nations (Accountants International Study No. 2), 1969.

Internal Control, 1949.

Practical Accounting and Auditing Problems by Edmond F. Ingalls (three vols.), 1966.

Professional Accounting in 25 Countries, 1965.

Special Reports, 1960.

Statements on Auditing Procedure

No. 33: Auditing Standards and Procedures (incorporates statements Nos. 1–32), 1963.

No. 34: Long Term Investments, 1965.

No. 35: Letters for Underwriters, 1965.

No. 36: Revision of "Extensions of Auditing Procedures" Relating to Inventories, 1966.

No. 37: Special Report: Public Warehouses—Controls and Audit Procedures, 1966.

No. 38: Unaudited Financial Statements, 1967.

No. 39: Working Papers, 1967.

No. 40: Pooling of Interests, 1968.

No. 41: Subsequent Discovery of Facts Existing at the Date of the Auditor's Report, 1969.

Basic Auditing Textbooks

Cadmus, Bradford, *Operational Auditing Handbook*, The Institute of Internal Auditors, Inc., 1964.

Cashin, James and Garland C. Owens, *Auditing* (second edition), New York: The Ronald Press Company, 1963.

Holmes, Arthur W., *Auditing Principles and Procedure* (sixth edition), Homewood, Ill.: Richard D. Irwin, Inc., 1964.

Johnson, James T., and J. Herman Brasseaux (eds.), *Readings in Auditing* (second edition), Cincinnati: South-Western Publishing Co., 1965.

Lenhart, Norman J., and Philip L. Defliese, *Montgomery's Auditing* (eighth edition), New York: The Ronald Press Company, 1957.

Mautz, Robert K., *Fundamentals of Auditing* (second edition), New York: John Wiley & Sons, Inc., 1964.

Ray, J. C. (ed.), *Independent Auditing Standards—A Book of Readings*, New York: Holt, Rinehart and Winston, Inc., 1964.

Stettler, Howard F., *Systems Based Independent Audits*, Englewood Cliffs, N. J.: Prentice-Hall, Inc., 1967.

Chapter 1

Bevis, Herman W., "The Accounting Function in Economic Progress," *The Journal of Accountancy*, August 1958.

Carey, John L., *The CPA Plans for the Future*, New York: American Institute of Certified Public Accountants, 1965.

Chapter 2

Carey, John L., "What Is the Professional Practice of Accounting?" *The Accounting Review*, January 1968.

Carey, John L., and William O. Doherty, *Ethical Standards of the Accounting Profession*, New York: American Institute of Certified Public Accountants, 1966.

Levy, Saul, *Accountants' Legal Liability*, New York: American Institute of Certified Public Accounts, 1954.

Roy, Robert H., and James H. MacNeill, *Horizons for a Profession*, New York: American Institute of Certified Public Accountants, 1967.

Chapter 3

Brown, R. Gene, "Changing Audit Objectives and Techniques," *The Accounting Review*, October 1962.

Campfield, William L., "Trends in Auditing Management Plans and Operations," *The Journal of Accountancy*, July 1967.

Edwards, James Don, *History of Public Accounting in the United States*, East Lansing: Michigan State University Bureau of Business and Economic Research, 1960.

Chapter 4

Kaufman, Felix, "Professional Consulting by CPA's," *The Accounting Review*, October 1967.

Trueblood, Robert M., "The Management Service Function in Public Accounting," *The Journal of Accountancy*, July 1961.

Chapter 5

Mautz, R. K., and H. A. Sharaf, *The Philosophy of Auditing*, Evanston, Ill.: American Accounting Association, 1961.

Skinner, R. M., and R. J. Anderson, *Analytical Auditing*, London: Sir Isaac Pitman & Sons, 1966.

Chapter 6

Barden, Horace G., "The Meaning of Auditing Standards," *The Journal of Accountancy*, April 1958.

Levy, Saul, "Audit Working Papers and Legal Responsibility," *The Journal of Accountancy*, May 1956.

Mautz, R. K., *Fundamentals of Auditing* (second edition), New York: John Wiley & Sons, Inc., 1967, pages 54–128.

Chapter 7

Arkin, Herbert, *Handbook of Sampling for Auditing and Accounting*, New York: The McGraw-Hill Book Company, Inc., 1963.

Cyert, Richard H., and Justin Davidson, *Statistical Sampling for Accounting Information*, Englewood Cliffs, N. J.: Prentice-Hall, Inc., 1962.

Skinner, R. M., and R. J. Anderson, *Analytical Auditing*, London: Sir Isaac Pitman & Sons, 1966.

Vanasse, Robert W., *Statistical Sampling for Auditing and Accounting Decisions*, New York: McGraw-Hill Book Company, Inc.

Chapter 8

Davis, Gordon B., *Auditing and EDP*, New York: American Institute of Certified Public Accountants, 1968.

Haskins and Sells, *Haskins and Sells Auditape Manual*, Haskins and Sells, 1967.

Moore, Michael R., "EDP Audits: A Systems Approach," *The Arthur Young Journal*, Winter 1968.

Porter, W. Thomas, Jr., *Auditing Electronic Systems*, Belmont, Calif.: Wadsworth, 1966.

Chapter 9

Anthony, Robert N., John Dearden, and Richard F. Vancil, *Management Control Systems*, Homewood, Ill.: Richard D. Irwin, Inc., 1965.

Dearden, John, and F. Warren McFarland, *Management Information Systems: Text and Cases*, Homewood, Ill.: Richard D. Irwin, Inc., 1966.

Hare, Van Court, *Systems Analysis: A Diagnostic Approach*, New York: John Wiley & Sons, Inc., 1967.

Heckert, J. Brooks, and Harry D. Kerrigan, *Accounting Systems* (third edition), New York: The Ronald Press Company, 1967.

Johnson, Richard A., Fremont E. Kast, and James E. Rosensweig, *The Theory and Management of Systems* (second edition), New York: McGraw-Hill Book Company, Inc., 1966.

Prince, Thomas R., *Information Systems for Management Planning and Control*, Homewood, Ill.: Richard D. Irwin, Inc., 1966.

Chapter 10

American Institute of Certified Public Accountants, *Practical Techniques and Policies for Inventory Control* (Management Services Technical Study No. 6), New York: American Institute of Certified Public Accountants, 1968.

Cadmus, Bradford, *Operational Auditing Handbook*, The Institute of Internal Auditors, 1964, Sections 2 and 5.

Lee, Lamar, Jr., and Donald W. Dobler, *Purchasing and Materials Management*, New York: McGraw-Hill Book Company, Inc., 1965.

Starr, Martin K., and David W. Miller, *Inventory Control: Theory and Practice*, Englewood Cliffs, N. J.: Prentice-Hall, Inc., 1962.

Chapter 11

Beyer, Robert, *Profitability Accounting for Planning and Control*, New York: The Ronald Press Company, 1963.

Magee, John F., and David M. Boodman, *Production Planning and Inventory Control* (second edition), New York: McGraw-Hill Book Company, Inc., 1967.

Chapter 12

American Management Association, Inc., *Analyzing and Improving Marketing Performance—"Marketing Audits" in Theory and Practice* (AMA Management Report No. 32), American Management Association Inc., 1959.

Kotler, Philip, *Marketing Management: Analysis, Planning, and Control*, Englewood Cliffs, N. J.: Prentice-Hall, Inc., 1967.

Schad, T. G., and W. Erskine, "The Marketing Audit," *Management Controls*, April 1969.

Chapter 13

Colman, Robert F., *Linear Programming and Cash Management/CASH ALPHA*, Cambridge, Mass.: Massachusetts Institute of Technology, 1968.

Emery, John M., "Managing Cash for Profit," *Financial Executive*, April 1968.

National Association of Accountants, *Cash Flow Analysis for Managerial Control* (N.A.A. Research Report 38), National Association of Accountants, 1961.

Chapter 14

American Management Association, "Case Study II: Payrolls," *EDP and the Auditor* (Management Bulletin 81), American Management Association, 1966.

The Institute of Internal Auditors, *Internal Audit and Control of Payroll and Accounts Payable* (Research Committee Report No. 4), The Institute of Internal Auditors, 1957.

Chapter 15

Burton, John C. (ed.), *Corporate Financial Reporting: Conflicts and Challenges— A Symposium*, New York: American Institute of Certified Public Accountants, 1969.

Rappaport, Louis H., *SEC Accounting Practice and Procedure* (second edition, revised printing), New York: The Ronald Press Company, 1966.

United States Securities and Exchange Commission, *Regulation S-X: Form and Content of Financial Statements*, Washington, D. C.: United States Government Printing Office, 1968.

Chapter 16

Clarke, Robert W., "Extension of the CPA's Attest Function in Corporate Annual Reports," *The Accounting Review*, October 1968.

Stettler, Howard F., "CPA/Auditing/2000±, *The Journal of Accountancy*, May 1968.

Index

A